FRANCE, THE COLD WAR AND THE WESTERN ALLIANCE, 1944–49: French foreign policy and post-war Europe

John W. Young

St. Martin's Press, New York

First published in the United States of America in 1990

Printed in Great Britain

ISBN 0-312-04193-4

Library of Congress Cataloging-in-Publication Data

Young, John W., 1957
    France, the Cold War, and the Western alliance, 1844–49 : French
foreign policy and post-war Europe / John W. Young,
        p.   cm.
    Includes bibliographical references.
    ISBN 0-312-04193-4
    1. France—Foreign relations—1945–   2. France—Foreign relations-
-Europe.   3. Europe—Foreign relations—France.   4. Cold War.
I. Title
DC404.Y68   1990
327.44—dc20   89-29481
                                                                                    CIP

To my Mother.

Contents

Illustrations

Preface

This study of French foreign policy in post-war Europe was stimulated by one particular question: how did France come to sign the Atlantic pact in April 1949 after having signed an alliance with the Soviet Union less than five years earlier? Strictly speaking the two commitments were not incompatible and the 1944 Franco-Soviet Treaty was not denounced by the Soviet Union until the mid-1950s. But NATO was always chiefly intended as a safeguard against Russian attack whereas in December 1944 Charles de Gaulle saw the Treaty of Moscow as the foundation stone of his European security policy. The focus of the book is therefore very much on the beginnings of the Cold War and the birth of the Western alliance, and is the first work which fully surveys French foreign policy in this period using archival evidence which has become available during the 1980s.

Various articles have been produced on certain aspects of post-war French foreign policy in recent years, especially on the themes of European unity and Franco-German relations, and Raymond Poidevin has written an excellent biography of Robert Schuman. The theme of the origins of the Cold War has however been dominated by US and British historians, using Anglo-American sources which too often view France unsympathetically. She is usually mentioned in Cold War histories only as an aside, and where she does make an appearance is often treated as a weak and vacillating power, obsessed with outdated ideas of a German 'menace'.

In contrast to previous eras, certainly, France did not have a decisive role in shaping the new order after 1945. Yet France was not without significance. She was the fourth occupation power in Germany and Austria, with a seat on the 'Council of Foreign Ministers' (CFM) responsible for writing the post-war peace treaties. On the world stage she was the second largest colonial empire with a permanent seat on the UN Security Council. Paris was an important diplomatic centre, the venue for meetings of the CFM, UN and the last European peace conference, in 1946. Furthermore, even in decline, France had influence. Economic and military weakness and political division did not reduce her strategic importance in Europe, Africa and South-East Asia. European economic recovery and Western defences depended on her and she had a major impact on the exact shape of post-war Europe, not least in laying the basis for European political and economic co-operation.

There are many people and institutions without whose kind help and support this book could not have appeared. My greatest thanks go to the British

Academy, which provided a generous grant to finance research in Paris over three years, 1986–89. Without such support work on the book would have been impossible. I would like to thank the various archives at which I have worked in France and Britain, including the *Archives Economiques et Financières*, *Archives Nationales*, the archive services of the *Assemblée Nationale*, the *Fondation Nationale des Sciences Politiques* and the *Ministère des Affaires Etrangères*, the *Service Historique, Armée de Terre*, the departmental archives of *Aveyron* (at Rodez) and the *Moselle* (at Metz), the Public Record Office at Kew, Churchill College Archive Centre in Cambridge, the British Library, and the libraries of Leeds University and the London School of Economics. I am especially grateful to Madame Irigoin of the *Section Contemporaine* at the *Archives Nationales* for her helpful advice on post-war historical sources in Paris and for arranging access to the private papers of Georges Bidault, an extremely valuable collection of documents. Access to the Bidault papers was by kind permission of Madame Bidault, and I would also like to thank the following for providing me with permission to consult certain documents: Président René Pleven for access to his papers; Madame Jacques Lucius for the Raoul Dautry papers; Madame Claude Papeloux for the André Marie papers; Madame Oudin, of the Quai d'Orsay, for the René Massigli papers; and the *Directeur-Général des Archives de France* for the series F60 and F60 Ter at the *Archives Nationales*.

Numerous academic colleagues discussed various aspects of French policy with me and encouraged the work as it progressed, but I would particularly like to thank 1. Christopher Andrew, Mike Dockrill, 2. Bob Frazier, John Kent, David Stevenson, Phil Taylor, Geoffrey Warner and Donald Watt. The text was typed up promptly and accurately by Janet Smith, Rebecca Glyn Jones and Jackie Stanley despite a frequently untidy manuscript. Alec McAulay, his predecessor Peter Boulton, and their staff at Leicester University Press helped bring the book to fruition. Finally, thanks to Brigette for her support and tolerance, as well as for reading over the manuscript.

John W. Young
3 July 1989

Abbreviations

For abbreviations used in the notes see the select bibliography.

ACC	Allied Control Council, Berlin
CEEC	Committee of European Economic Co-operation
CFLN	Comité Français de Libération Nationale (French Committee of National Liberation
CFM	Council of Foreign Ministers
CGT	Confédération Générale du Travail (French Confederation of Trades Unions)
CNR	Conseil National de la Résistance (National Council of the Resistance)
EAC	European Advisory Commission
ECO	European Coal Organisation
EMDN	Etat-Major Général de la Défense Nationale (French General Staff)
FFI	Forces Françaises de l'Intérieur (French Interior Resistance Forces)
EXIMBANK	US Import-Export Bank
IAR	International Authority for the Ruhr
IMF	International Monetary Fund
MAP	Military Assistance Programme
MRP	Mouvement Républicain Populaire (Christian Democratic Party)
MSB	Military Security Board in West Germany
NAT(O)	North Atlantic Treaty (Organisation)
OEEC	Organisation for European Economic Co-operation
PCF	Parti Communiste Français (Communist Party)
RPF	Rassemblement du Peuple Français (Gaullist Party)
SDECE	Section de Documentation Extérieure et de Contre Espionniage (French External Intelligence)
SFIO	Section Française de l'Internationale Ouvrière (Socialist party)
UN	United Nations
ZOF	Zone D'Occupation Française (French occupation zone)

Free France, the Big Three and Post-War Planning. 1940–44

Free France, and Free France alone, represents the will of the French people. It should be treated as if it were France.
– René Cassin, writing in *Foreign Affairs*, October 1941, 112.

On 26 August 1944, surrounded by crowds of cheering onlookers, a group of French dignitaries began a triumphal march from the Arc de Triomphe to celebrate the liberation of Paris. The previous day German forces in the city had surrendered and over four years of occupation had ended. Suddenly the *tricolore* seemed to hang from every building. As the procession descended down the Champs Elysées it was led by the towering figure of General Charles de Gaulle, leader of the Free French, who in the dark days of 1940 had maintained the war effort on the Allied side and who was now greeted as the leader of all France. And with de Gaulle walked his own followers, Free French generals like Alphonse Juin and Leclerc de Hautecloque, and leaders of the Resistance from within France, including the small figure of Georges Bidault, President of the *Conseil National de la Résistance*. At one point Bidault began to walk beside de Gaulle, but the General would tolerate no rival and commanded, 'Sir, a little further back if you please!'. Bidault duly obeyed.[1] Within a few weeks the two men were leading members of the new French government: de Gaulle as President, Bidault as his Foreign Minister. The foreign policy they pursued was influenced heavily by the French experience of defeat, occupation and liberation since 1940 – and by the fact that the fate of the world was now largely in the hands not of France but of three other powers: Great Britain, the United States and the Soviet Union.

* * *

It was on 22 June 1940 that France had signed a humiliating armistice with Nazi Germany, in the same railway carriage, parked in the same woodland clearing, where Germany itself had conceded defeat in 1918. France's rapid military collapse in 1940, after the third German invasion in seventy years, was to haunt the French policy-makers thereafter. Marshal Philippe Pétain, hero of the 1914–18 war, blamed the defeat not on the Army's failings but on the unstable governments of the Third Republic, the social reforms of Léon Blum's 'Popular Front' coalition, and the 'defeatism' of the French Communists, whose Soviet

1

mentors had entered into an alliance with Adolf Hitler in 1939. Pétain it was who, as Prime Minister in June 1940 rejected the idea of a government-in-exile, agreed to an armistice and became the head of a new corporatist state based in the spa-town of Vichy. Here he maintained an uneasy 'independence' of the Third Reich with the allegiance of most of France's people and colonies. The future of France, however, lay not with Pétain but his one-time protegé, Charles de Gaulle. De Gaulle too was a critic of the *régime des parties* which, as he saw it, had divided France under the Third Republic. A military man, and politically a conservative, de Gaulle sought a powerful presidency after 1944. But he differed from Pétain fundamentally in his belief in a truly strong and independent France, a France possessing *grandeur*.

Charles de Gaulle had a 'certain idea' of France:

> All my life I have thought of France in a certain way. This is inspired by sentiment as much as by reason . . . I have a feeling that Providence has created her either for complete success or exemplary misfortunes. If . . . mediocrity shows in her it strikes me as an absurd anomaly.[2]

Many outside observers saw de Gaulle's behaviour as based on selfish ambition, but his attitudes reflected a complex interpretation of French history and French destiny. Born into a Catholic, nationalist family, he had joined the Army as the most noble and worthy profession possible, and was one of the leading military thinkers in France in the 1930s, becoming Under-Secretary for Defence in 1940. He had already criticised the defensive mentality of the Third Republic, with its reliance on the Maginot line and the British alliance for protection.[3] Vichy, with its unnecessary admission of defeat and share in Hitler's 'New Order' was simply unworthy of France. For de Gaulle greatness was part of France's inner self, and her security and Great Power status could be guaranteed only by a strong Army and an independent foreign policy: international organisations and treaties were worth nothing unless backed by national armed forces and eternal vigilance. To regain its status, independence and self-respect after the débâcle of 1940, France had to rely on other Allies, especially America and Britain, to liberate French soil. But the General was determined, even in war, to demonstrate his independence of these whenever possible. Like Joan of Arc and Georges Clemenceau before him, he would represent the true 'spirit' of France. He insisted on being recognised as the true representative of France despite the existence of Vichy, he sought a full role in the defeat of Germany, Italy and Japan, he believed that France was a nation deserving Great Power status and a full share in the peace settlement, and he posed as the defender of the French Empire from all encroachments. His character – austere, proud, superior – certainly did not make him a likeable figure, but he soon proved able (especially in his radio speeches) to inspire popular support and to be politically adept – if ruthless – in overcoming any rivals for his position. He even made a virtue of his distant, arrogant manner: by making himself difficult he made himself heard.

Throughout the war de Gaulle had a complex love-hate relationship with his first and closest ally, Britain, and particularly its Prime Minister Winston Churchill. Churchill, a francophile whose faith in the 'army of Napoleon' was undimmed by the events of 1940, understood de Gaulle's stand for the French 'spirit' and the two men, each fighting for their country's survival, often co-operated well. But the gregarious Prime Minister could find the General's aloofness an irritation; and Churchill also had many more concerns than those of France. On one occasion, when told 'De Gaulle believes he is Joan of Arc', Churchill is said to have replied, 'I know, but I cannot get my bishops to burn him!'[4] When de Gaulle fled to London the British, desperate for allies, gave him radio facilities for appeals to France, financial aid and recognition as the 'leader of all Free Frenchmen', and throughout the war Britain was committed to the restoration of France and the French Empire. The British Foreign Office looked forward to close co-operation with France after the war as a fellow west European, liberal-democratic and colonial state, with whom a community of interest naturally seemed to exist, and consistently saw de Gaulle as the only possible French leader. But the simple fact was that de Gaulle's followers numbered a paltry 30,000 in August 1941, the month that an Anglo-Free French expedition failed to capture the key African port of Dakar from Vichy. Equatorial Africa and the Cameroons joined de Gaulle, as did such formidable individuals as Georges Catroux, the former Governor of Indochina, but the bulk of the French Empire, including North and West Africa and Indochina remained loyal to Pétain and the British could not afford to alienate the ageing Marshal completely. De Gaulle relied on the British for his survival in 1940–42 therefore, but he came to resent their moderation towards Vichy, their refusal to share military plans with him and the fact that London would not recognise his 'Council for the defence of the French Empire', inaugurated in October 1940, as the successor to the Third Republic.[5]

In mid-1941 de Gaulle had his first major clash with the British over the fate of France's two mandated territories in the Middle East, Syria and Lebanon. The Levant mandates were seized from Vichy control by an Anglo-Free French force in a short campaign which saw Frenchman fighting against Frenchman. The British then associated themselves with a promise made by de Gaulle's representative, Catroux, to give the Arabs in Syria and Lebanon independence. To de Gaulle, however, this smacked of interference in French colonial affairs and it was only after difficult negotiations that he agreed to confirm the independence promise in return for British approval of French 'predominance' in the Levant. Despite this agreement, the Levant problem rumbled on, not helped by the behaviour of Churchill's personal envoy in the area, Sir Edward Spears, who fuelled suspicions that the British wanted the Levant for themselves. Meanwhile, de Gaulle remained determined to secure military, economic and cultural rights in the Levant. In November 1943 he arrested, then – under British and American pressure – released, members of the recently-elected Lebanese government. The Levant problem remained unresolved in August, 1944.[6]

Increasingly after 1941 de Gaulle's behaviour also affected the country which soon became the most powerful Allied nation, the United States. In September 1941 the General's authoritarian attitude had seemed to improve in Anglo-Saxon eyes when he created an eight-man 'French National Committee' in answer to calls for a more democratic Free French movement. But in December, the month America entered the war, de Gaulle bitterly offended the US government (though not the American press) when Admiral Emile Muselier

3

forcibly seized the islands of St Pierre and Miquelon, off the North American coast, from Vichy. Then in early 1942 the General showed his undemocratic side by throwing Admiral Muselier off the Free French leadership because he was emerging as a rival. When in May 1942 the British invaded the French colony of Madagascar without forewarning de Gaulle, the General even talked of breaking with both Britain and America, a move which Catroux and others violently opposed. None of this helped to sway American President Franklin Roosevelt from his belief, encouraged by such advisers as Admiral William Leahy, Ambassador to Vichy, that de Gaulle was a vain upstart, unrepresentative of France, and that for practical reasons America would do better to maintain close relations with Vichy in the hope of weaning Pétain from the Nazis. In November 1942 de Gaulle's relations with the Anglo-Saxons reached a nadir when they failed to forewarn him of the invasion of French North Africa, and then entered into a much-criticised agreement with the Vichyite Admiral François Darlan so as to put an end to fighting between Allied and Vichy troops. When Darlan was assassinated, the Americans still refused to treat de Gaulle as French leader and instead backed General Henri Giraud, a brave but undynamic conservative, who had recently escaped from France, and who could hardly be considered a democratically 'representative' figure. In January 1943 a reluctant de Gaulle had to journey to Casablanca where Churchill and Roosevelt, by now close friends, forced him to agree to form a joint leadership with Giraud. The two generals also had to give a stiff handshake for the benefit of press cameras.[7]

The agreement at Casablanca was a bitter pill to swallow, but de Gaulle's acceptance of it reflected his own political good sense and his continued reliance on Britain and American. To bring de Gaulle to heel, Churchill had threatened to cut off all support to him. And de Gaulle's material reliance on the Americans was growing all the time. Over the course of the war French armed forces eventually received over two billion dollars in American 'lend-lease' supplies – 8 per cent of all the US War Department's lend-lease aid, and a greater share than that given to China. The US eventually built up the French Army to over half-a-million men by summer 1944 and equipped sixteen French Air Force squadrons.[8] The Americans also increasingly helped to shape British policy: Britain too relied on American lend-lease, Britain and America established a 'Combined Chiefs of Staff' (from which de Gaulle was excluded) and Churchill was deeply committed to the American alliance, despite the desire of the Foreign Office and Foreign Secretary, Anthony Eden, to be more positive about de Gaulle and independent of Washington. De Gaulle had to be cautious with Roosevelt because despite the failure of the President's 'Vichy gamble'[9] – in November 1942 Vichy forces had *not* gone over to the Allies – FDR remained contemptuous of the General, and refused to recognise anyone as the constitutional leader of France until free elections were held after the liberation. He also privately talked of ending French rule in certain parts of her empire, such as Indochina. 'Anything', Roosevelt believed, 'must be better than to live under French colonial rule.'[10]

* * *

4

What especially helped de Gaulle to resist American pressure in 1943–44, and to reassert his independence was, first, growing evidence of support for his his movement in Metropolitan France, and secondly the political failure of Giraud. The Resistance was always a minority of the French population and was divided amongst various groups, including Communists, Socialists and Christian Democrats. But the German occupation of Vichy France in November 1942 and the clear bankruptcy of Pétain's government brought greater support to the Resistance movements, who increasingly co-operated together, shared the anti-Nazi and anti-Vichy outlook of the Free French and, like de Gaulle's followers, looked forward to the post-war renewal of France, the restoration of democracy, the punishment of Vichyites and an active international role. This did not mean that de Gaulle shared all the ideas of the Metropolitan Resistance precisely: his political conservatism and desire for a strong post-war presidency rested uneasily alongside Resistance plans for far-reaching social reforms and a powerful National Assembly; and his belief in French *grandeur* and the restoration of the empire was very different to calls for a 'moral' foreign policy and the recognition of colonial rights. He was particularly concerned at the strength of the Communists, whose good organisation and determination had helped them revive from the days of the Hitler-Stalin Pact. Though unable to dominate other groups completely, the Communists created an impression of vigour, patriotism and a desire for reform. It was in order to establish control of the Resistance in general, and the Communists in particular, that de Gaulle created the *Conseil National de la Résistance* (National Council of the Resistance, or CNR) in May 1943 under Jean Moulin. It was when Moulin was killed in 1944 that his place was taken by a Christian Democrat (whom de Gaulle did not know), Georges Bidault. In March 1944 de Gaulle also formed a military organisation to direct and control Resistance activity during the forthcoming liberation. The *Forces Françaises de l'Intérieur* (French Forces of the Interior, FFI) were commanded by a Free French General, Pierre Koenig.[11]

In order to impress the Resistance, de Gaulle after April 1942 talked of a 'revolution' in post-war France. In return all the major Resistance groups backed the General as the only possible leader who could unite France, and who was certainly preferable to Giraud. In late February 1943 Jean Monnet, a French businessman and international civil servant (he had been Deputy Secretary-General of the League of Nations in 1919–23), who had been working in Washington to secure economic supplies for Britain since 1940, arrived in North Africa. He came partly to assist with French rearmament but also to bring about a Giraud-de Gaulle agreement, and soon saw that de Gaulle was more politically able than Giraud. Only in May, the month of the CNR's formation and thus of a major boost in *Gaulliste* support, did de Gaulle finally agree with Giraud on the future control of French administration. They became joint heads of the *Comité Français de Libération Nationale* (French Committee of National Liberation CFLN), based in Algiers, in June. Against de Gaulle's Free French movement, Resistance support and clear political programme, Giraud however could only muster an interest in military matters, American sympathy (though even the US press criticised FDR's support for him) and political notions akin to Pétain's. After the Americans had set him up as commander of the new French Army, Giraud took little interest in political affairs, and no part

5

in de Gaulle's dramatic establishment of a consultative Assembly in Algiers in September, and resigned from the CFLN in November. In April 1944 he even ceased to be Army commander and, on the eve of D-day, de Gaulle stood as the unrivalled leader of all fighting Frenchmen.[12]

In retrospect the US could only be grateful that the Darlan and Giraud experiments had failed: neither would have been welcomed in France in 1944, and neither could have controlled the Communists as de Gaulle did. The Communists accepted the establishment of the CNR and FFI because of the need to prosecute the war as vigorously as possible, not least in order to ease the burdens of the Soviet Red Army, which was fighting the bulk of the German *Wehrmacht* in the East. For the moment an alliance with the 'patriotic' wing of the *bourgeoisie* had precedence over any class war for the Communists. But the loyalty of such a powerful group to an external power – the Soviet Union – created problems for French policy, internally and externally, in the long term, not least because the Soviet Union was rapidly emerging as the second most powerful state in the world, with enormous military might in Eastern Europe. Largely due to geographical separation, de Gaulle's relations with Moscow lacked the intensity of relations with the Anglo-Saxons, but the two sides, amidst a great deal of suspicion, developed a reasonable working relationship during the war, largely based on the usefulness each had for the other. De Gaulle, the defender of French civilisation and the Rights of Man, could have little liking for Joseph Stalin's totalitarianism; Stalin, contemptuous of France's fall in 1940 and seeking to extend Soviet influence in Europe, could have little use for a strong France, especially a France which was the traditional defender of Polish independence, the architect of the inter-war *cordon sanitaire* and ruler of an extensive colonial empire. But in September 1941, three months after entering the war, Moscow recognised de Gaulle as Free French leader and the two sides exchanged diplomatic representatives. The Soviet representative to the Free French in London, and later Algiers, had a particularly important role in maintaining good relations over the following years. A former philosophy professor, educated before the 1917 Revolution, heavily built, with a taste for expensive food and a healthy fear of his superiors in Moscow, Alexander Bogomolov was the ideal representative to France. Hard-working and well-informed (he freely admitted to a British representative that Russia was intercepting all Free French correspondence!), as well as genuinely likeable, 'Bogo', according to one observer, 'Lavished upon de Gaulle the formalities customarily accorded to a chief of state. These courtesies cost nothing and paid handsomely'. Whenever relations with the Anglo-Saxons were strained Bogomolov would press de Gaulle on the benefits of Soviet co-operation – though this did not prevent the Russian from telling Harold Macmillan, the British Minister-Resident in Algiers, that the French were inept and duplicitous.[13]

Sometimes de Gaulle was all too ready to play the 'Russian card' offered by Bogomolov. At one point he worried the British by proposing to send two Free French divisions from North Africa, where they were vital for the Libyan campaign, to the Eastern front. He actually did send the *Normandie-Niémen* squadron of aircraft to Russia, and on a later occasion considered Bogomolov's suggestion that the seat of the CFLN should be moved to Moscow. The Soviets, furthermore, did provide de Gaulle with some real concessions, not least by giving the CFLN fuller legal recognition than did Britain and America. But de Gaulle never did carry out his threats to abandon the Anglo-Saxons in Russia's favour, and the Soviets proved no more willing than Britain and America to treat France as an equal. At the Tehran conference of 'Big Three' leaders in 1943 indeed, Stalin was as contemptuous as FDR about France. For Stalin, de Gaulle had his uses: he was preferable to Pétain or Giraud, and proved willing to co-operate with the French Communists, bringing two of them onto the CFLN. Also, of course, he could not be considered a British or US puppet. De Gaulle, for his part, hoped that good relations with Moscow would help moderate Communist behaviour inside France and pave the way to post-war co-operation against Germany through a revival of the 1894 Franco-Russian alliance. But in 1944 the relationship between the two was strained on various issues: Moscow resented the General's links with the Polish government-in-exile in London who were themselves suspicious of Soviet aims in Eastern Europe; whilst de Gaulle demanded from Bogomolov more concrete evidence of Soviet support, and especially a French role in the decision-making of the Great Powers.[14]

* * *

Aside from the day-to-day problems of relations with the Allies, de Gaulle and his diplomats had also given consideration to questions of post-war political planning by mid-1944. Since 1940 the General had had an embryonic 'diplomatic service' attached to his movement. In June 1941 it still numbered only thirty-four people, a reflection of the General's lack of attraction to career diplomats before November 1942, but in 1943 a more formidable foreign policy machine was created under the veteran diplomat, René Massigli, a former Ambassador to Ankara and *Directeur* of the French Foreign Ministry, who had represented France at numerous inter-war conference.[15] Meanwhile in December 1941 de Gaulle had set up four commissions to study French post-war problems, including economic and social issues, foreign policy, defence and legal and intellectual concerns.[16] Many studies were drawn up over the next few years and in 1944 work began to fuse them into a coherent whole. On the foreign policy side the main concerns were to prepare a position on the peace settlement, to maximise French standing in the world, and to gear international activity to the needs of France's economic recovery.[17] It was automatically assumed that France would have a major role in the post-war world, despite the events of 1940. International economic problems, the preserve of a young, energetic and intelligent *Inspecteur des Finances* named Hervé Alphand, were to prove an abiding concern for post-war foreign policy-makers. And economic questions were closely linked to the two most important areas of post-war foreign policy planning: Germany, and Western European co-operation.

French concern with the German problem after three invasions across the Rhine in living memory - 1870, 1914 and 1940 – was easy to understand, and French thinking about Germany and European security after 1944 is impossible to comprehend without an appreciation of the failure of France's German policy after 1918. Charles de Gaulle himself had been raised amidst stories of the humiliations of 1870–71 at Prussian hands. In 1918, however, after four bitter years of war which left millions of Frenchmen dead or maimed, the German enemy appeared to be destroyed. Despite the collapse of Russia's war effort in 1918, after the seizure of power by the Bolsheviks, France, the backbone of the Allied cause in the Great War, had seen the Kaiser's army defeated. The Treaty of Versailles in 1919 seemed to ensure both the destruction of German military might, through such measures as the limitation on armed forces and the occupation of the Rhineland, and the safeguarding of French economic security, via the ownership of German mines in the Saarland and the payment of large reparations. The French government failed to secure the political separation of the Rhineland, the traditional invasion route into France, from Germany, but she had the promise of American and British support in the event of a German revival, and she was also able to forge alliances with newly-emergent nations of Eastern Europe, especially Poland and Czechoslovakia. But in the years following Versailles, France's apparently strong position disintegrated. A firm American security guarantee failed to emerge: instead the Americans, disaffected with the peace settlement, slipped back into isolationism. The East European states failed to grow into model democracies; Poland and Czechoslovakia bickered with each other in border disputes. Britain remained an ally but refused to commit itself closely to French security or to make the new League of Nations into an effective peace-keeping body, and instead became an advocate of Germany's rehabilitation. Italy, another wartime ally, went fascist. In 1923 France's inability to enforce the 1919 settlement, and particularly her reparations demands, were amply demonstrated in the ill-fated occupation of the Ruhr.[18]

The later 1920s had seen France shift her ground, to try to control Germany by conciliation and co-operation. This policy reached its zenith in 1929–30 when Aristide Briand began to advocate a European federation, partly as a way to match American economic might in the post-1918 world economy, but also in response to ideas, emanating from the French foreign and finance ministries for some time, that Germany could be controlled by embracing her in a web of far-reaching European co-operation. As will be seen this shift in policy, from the draconian approach of Clemenceau and Poincaré, to the pan-Europeanism of Briand, was a significant lesson for policy-makers after 1944. But in the 1920s it came too late to succeed. In 1929 the 'slump' hit the United States and spread throughout the capitalist world, bringing unemployment, declining trade and political nationalism in its wake. In the 1930s France became politically divided, economically and demographically stagnant and increasingly defensive in its military and foreign policy. In contrast Germany fell under the control of Adolf Hitler, began to revive economically after 1933 and adopted a dynamic international policy, culminating in the *blitzkrieg* of 1940. Once again Germany became the author of France's humiliation, a humiliation even greater than 1870. France in 1918, the predominant power in continental Europe, had in 1940 lost its Great Power status. The exact reasons for this decline would continue to be debated, but Charles de Gaulle at least hoped that France's leading role in world affairs could be regained – the land of Louis XIV and Napolean could not easily accept a descent to secondary status – and in planning for the post-war world the French were determined to put an end to the German menace at last, largely by rehabilitating the policies of 1918–19 in a revised form.

The general lines of a German peace settlement were studied both by the French themselves and in co-operation with the many Allied governments-in-exile in London, where an Inter-Allied Committee for the study of an armistice was formed in November 1943 with French, Belgian, Dutch, Polish and other representatives. This body helped to create a unity of view among the exiled groups vis-à-vis the Big Three, who dominated the effective preparations for a post-war settlement. The Committee studied a military occupation, demilitarisation measures, a reparations policy and far-reaching economic disarmament of Germany, with controls on certain German industries and the prohibition of others. By August 1944 it had drafted its own armistice agreement.[19] The internal French studies took a similar line, and a memorandum of 19 February 1944 by de Gaulle's officials revealed a far-reaching approach to the German problem. Germany's surrender, its withdrawal from occupied territories, were obvious moves. The destruction of the *Wehrmacht*, and Allied occupation of Germany, the punishment of war criminals, a programme of denazification, the restitution of goods seized by Germany, and a large-scale reparations programme, all eventually became part of Allied post-war policy. Other French documents, significantly, emphasised the need for economic controls on Germany, both to reduce its war-making capacity *and* to use its resources (of coke and coal for example) to contribute to the post-war reconstruction of France. In French planning the control of the Rhineland invasion route and of German coal and steel production in the Ruhr were particularly vital. Although the exact method of control in the Ruhr and Rhineland remained to be defined, the French were determined, as in 1919, to guarantee both their military security and their economic well-being via the peace settlement. Work on this area was still under way when Paris was liberated, but on 12 August 1944, before leaving Algiers for Europe, de Gaulle told the Free French *Comité de Défense National*, which drew together military and civilian figures for consultation on defence matters, that the Rhineland must be occupied indefinitely, that the Ruhr must be placed under a form of international control and that there must be no return to a centralised Reich in Germany.[20]

The German problem also had a significant influence on French thinking about West European co-operation in general. Although on one hand de Gaulle was a nationalist who believed in the strength of nation states in the world, and although on the other he had a 'total' vision of of European civilisation – a belief that ultimately all the continent 'from the Atlantic to the Urals' shared a common identity[21] – he was willing to consider particularly close co-operation with France's smaller European neighbours. Given the position of Britain and Russia as members of the Big Three, de Gaulle often argued that France was the ideal power to defend 'European' interests in the councils of the Great Powers. (Another, similar aspect of post-war French diplomacy would be France as the defender of all 'small' powers against the Great.) Discussion of the particular theme of Western European co-operation began in earnest in September 1943, with ideas from Hervé Alphand and the CFLN's Commissioner for Communications, René Mayer. On 17 September, a memorandum by Alphand suggested that customs barriers could be temporarily suspended after the war, in a Europe where pre-war tariffs were likely to have little relevance and where, in any case, most trade was likely to be controlled by quantitive restrictions.

Alphand wanted to use the early post-war years, before new vested economic interests were established, to create a healthier trading environment and perhaps to set up European customs unions. He was particularly interested in a French customs union with Belgium, Holland and Luxembourg. The maintenance of the current Anglo-American system of 'Combined Boards' after the war would help to share out vital commodities like food, coal and steel. It could also foster closer European economic co-operation, with expanded markets. There were, however, numerous potential problems with such a course. Radical changes would be needed in French industry and agriculture to cope with increased competition, a 'transitional' phase would be needed for adjustments, and political approval of the idea could only come after the liberation, when all the French people could express their view. There was also the need to sound out American and British reactions, given their vital economic importance.

America, the most powerful economy in the world, would clearly remain essential in fulfilling French supply needs for years after the war and this fundamental truth was important for shaping French thinking about her wider economic policy. The US government was known to espouse a freer, more equal and expansionist trading system after the war – 'multilateralism' – designed to prevent a return to the depression, unemployment and political extremism of the 1930s. The 1944 Bretton Woods conference laid the foundation for such an economic system, making the dollar the basis of the world currency system, proposing an International Monetary Fund to manage exchange problems and looking forward to an International Bank for the finance of reconstruction work. In this programme there was a danger of American hegemony in the post-war world, especially for a weakened country like France with her expected need to import food, coal and industrial equipment from America in future. But France hardly had a choice. Alphand had recognised by 1943 the France *must* accept the 'open' world economy, and many planners welcomed this: France could share in the increased world prosperity so long as the new multilateral system was introduced gradually and she was able to expand her own production. America – the champion of liberty, opponent of colonialism and propagator of the Atlantic Charter – was not expected to use its economic predominance to fulfil any 'imperialist' designs of her own. The problem about a West European customs union, however, was that it could appear as a closed, selective group, the very opposite of 'multilateralism'.

René Mayer's schemes were put in a memorandum of 30 September 1943 which argued that, the time having come to think of Europe's future, France should seek an 'economic federation' (apparently more extensive than a customs union) not only with Belgium and Holland, but also 'Rhenania' – that is the western parts of Germany, including the Rhineland and Ruhr – and maybe even Italy and Spain. He proposed detailed studies of the economic and political results of such a course, including the effect on Germany as a whole and neighbouring states like Britain. Mayer's ideas were thus wider in geographical area, and in the extent of economic co-operation, than Alphand's.[22] Another Frenchman in Algiers who gave consideration to European co-operation at this time was Jean Monnet, who had advocated an Anglo-French Union in 1940 and who wrote on 5 August 1943: 'There will be no peace in Europe if States re-establish themselves on the basis of national sovereignty ... To enjoy . . . prosperity and social progress . . . the States of Europe must form . . . a "European entity", which will make them a single economic unit.'[23]

Monnet was thus prepared to see a loss of French sovereignty for the sake of economic expansion. When the Alphand and Mayer memoranda were discussed by de Gaulle and his advisers in meetings during October, Monnet became more specific and raised the possibility of forming Europe into a single free trade area, with Germany split into several states within this system and German economic resources, especially those of the Ruhr, used for the benefit of all Europe. Monnet's plans were thus even more dramatic than Mayer's, and like Mayer drew on the idea of tying Germany into post-war economic arrangements. But de Gaulle found the idea of embracing the *whole* of Germany in French plans too ambitious: he feared that such a course could merely strengthen the German economy and eventually increase the influence of the Germans in Western Europe. Like Alphand and Mayer, de Gaulle wished to concentrate on Belgium and Holland at first, perhaps later drawing in 'Rhenania' (which would be cut off from Germany), Italy and Switzerland. There was general agreement in these discussions that France should take advantage of the liberation period to establish a new political and economic system in Western Europe, to provide for security and prosperity, with France as the leading state, and with the economic future of the Ruhr and Rhineland linked to the whole project. René Massigli, as Commissioner for Foreign Affairs, was anxious to keep these discussions on a 'realistic' level, pointing out the need to consider the views of the Big Three, the difficulty in predicting post-war conditions and the need to consider the impact of a customs union very carefully. He was criticised as being negative, but the advocates of dramatic action themselves seemed confused over many points, for example, whether to seek French predominance, a particular set of alliances or a more far-reaching 'supranational' entity in Western Europe.

De Gaulle himself decided in October that France must not be seen to want a French-led autarchy in Europe and he recognised the need to satisfy the Big Three on this point. He especially recognised the likely post-war strength of America and Russia. Russia, he expected, would expand westwards during the war, but so long as she respected French independence he was ready to make a treaty with her against Germany, and perhaps to create a 'triangular' security system in Europe with both Moscow and London. American friendship must be maintained too. But in Western Europe security against Germany required particular co-operation with Belgium, Holland and Luxembourg, and perhaps Britain. The General was ready to study a political and economic 'federation' in the area. Massigli, who preferred the term 'confederation' (to emphasise a European entity made up of separate states rather than a single body under common institutions) and who had grave doubts about the possibilities of separating 'Rhenania' from the rest of Germany, had a note drawn up on 30 October which set out de Gaulle's strategic thinking vis-à-vis the Big Three. The note stated that France must operate in future in an 'open' international market, and proposed that a study be made of a federation with Belgium, Holland and Luxembourg, possibly extended to other areas. Since Algiers lacked the necessary statistical material for such work, it was decided to set up a commission for technical studies in London. This commission was put under the chairmanship of the Inspector-General of Mines, Laurent

Blum-Picard, because of his knowledge of pre-war intra-European trade. The Free French political representatives in London, Pierre Viénot (representative to the British Government) and Maurice Dejean (who had been head of the Free French policy machine before Massigli, and who was now representative to the Allied governments-in-exile) were asked to carry out the studies discreetly. The Alphand and Mayer memoranda were sent as bases for study and the commission was asked to look at a wide range of issues regarding an economic union, including: the effect on Europe's colonies, demography, agriculture and industry; the effect on key areas of French production; the transitional arrangements and institutions which would be needed; controls on Germany; and the impact on the Big Three and Eastern Europe. The commission also had to consider several hypotheses about geographical extent, including the basic union with Belgium, Holland and Luxembourg, and possible extensions to 'Rhenania', then to Italy and Switzerland, and finally Britain.[24]

Meanwhile, on 21 October, Belgium, Holland and Luxembourg, the countries central to Free French hopes for economic co-operation had signed a financial accord to foster their own post-war trade, which, as de Gaulle's officials' knew, was seen by the Belgian Foreign Minister, Paul-Henri Spaak as the first step towards a far-reaching economic union.[25] In July 1943 Spaak had told Massigli of his desire for close links with France as well.[26] There thus seemed real hope for West European economic co-operation in future.

Among those who supported the idea of closer West European co-operation were officials of the Consultative Council for Alsace-Lorraine, who in August 1943 had argued that the Rhineland was a natural area for the development of French trade and who especially hoped that the Saarland (with its coal deposits) could again be tied into a customs union with Alsace-Lorraine, as it had been from 1871 to 1935, first under the German Empire, then under the terms of Versailles. Saar coal was a vital counterpart to the Lorraine iron ore deposits in providing the basis for France's iron and steel industry.[27] In December the Consultative Council's Economic Commission expressed its interest in a customs union to Alphand, and noted that by including France, Holland, Belgium, their colonial empires, and the Ruhr industrial basin, it would be 'a powerful economic bloc, disposing of considerable resources'.[28] Other Free French elements continued to share this enthusiasm. Thus a note of 3 December, summarising opinion on West European co-operation, argued that after the war the only continental state in Europe capable of maintaining the 'engines of modern war' would be Russia. What was needed in the West was a federation which was neither too extensive (the Soviets and, in this paper, the British should be excluded) nor German-dominated. A customs union with Belgium, Holland and Luxembourg, which included colonial and defence co-operation, and controls on the Ruhr, Rhineland and Saar, would be able to match Germany in terms of population and – of vital significance – be able *to take over the German role of heavy industrial production in Europe*. The three smaller states, by acting together, need not fear French domination.[29]

By early 1944 some problems had emerged in the work of the Blum-Picard commission. Even though it had been asked only to settle issues far enough to allow a decision on an economic federation 'in principle', the tasks it had been given in October were far-reaching and demanding. Practical difficulties soon developed over the scale of the work, and the studies that were done revealed complex problems surrounding the surrender of sovereignty to central institutions, the ability of agricultural interests to adjust to a customs union, and the practicality of separating the Ruhr from the rest of Germany, to which it was economically vital.[30] But there were also positive signs: French industry would undoubtedly prosper in a wide customs union.[31] In late February, eager to settle French policy on Germany, de Gaulle pressed Massigli for a report on armistice terms, reparations, the economic and strategic effects of the separation of 'Rhenania' from Germany, and the possibilities of tying 'Rhenania' to 'a strategic and economic federation between France, Belgium, Luxembourg and Holland', to which perhaps Britain could be attached.[32] The Belgian Spaak at this time, concerned that Europe's future lay entirely in the hands of the Big Three – he was particularly concerned at Soviet power in Eastern Europe – still seemed eager to cooperate with France. But the Dutch were cautious about upsetting the British and Americans, and on the French side René Massigli remained a sceptic: he convinced the CFLN on 14 March that the full strategic and political effects of a union in Western Europe must be studied, as well as its economic impact; and he told the Dutch minister Paul van Zeeland that there were great practical problems with a customs union and that no decision on it was yet possible.[33] Dutch doubts and the need to settle Britain's position (on which the French seem to have been very unclear) were pointed out in a memorandum of 18 March, which was also noteworthy for the way it drew together the future of Western Europe and the future of Germany. The German question, it was said, 'has to be subordinated to a reorganisation of western Europe, which responds to the needs of our security and of our economic reconstruction'. Put simply: Western European co-operation was vital for the effective control of Germany, and German economic resources were vital for the reconstruction of Europe.[34]

It was at this point that de Gaulle took the European issue dramatically into the public arena with a speech to the Consultative Assembly in Algiers, in which he talked of the need for France to defend the European case in world affairs after the trials of war, and declared, in rather grandiose terms:

> . . . we think that a kind of western group . . . principally formed on an economic base . . . could offer great advantages. Such a group, extended to Africa, in close relations with the Orient, and notably the Arab states of the Near East . . . – and to which the English Channel, the Rhine, and the Mediterranean would be as arteries – would seem to constitute a central pillar in a world organisation of production, trade and security.

France was, he said, ready to enter talks on such a scheme with other interested states.[35]

Hardly had the issue become public, however, than the idea of a French-led West European bloc ran into a series of serious problems, not least because of the reaction of the Big Three. First, on 20 March, only two days after de Gaulle's speech, Bogomolov complained in Algiers that Russia had not been previously consulted about a West European group. He was told that the proposal was still in the study stage, and was reminded that Russia seldom consulted the Free French on its foreign policy decisions, but he left in a sour mood. In Moscow Deputy Foreign Minister Vladimir Dekasanov took a different line with the Gaullist representative Roger Garreau, arguing that the 'Western bloc' was designed to isolate Russia and must be influenced by 'anti-Soviet' elements. This was an early indication to de Gaulle of Soviet suspicions regarding Western co-operation. These suspicions continued after the war despite Western European protests of their good intent, and despite Russia's own organisation of a series of Eastern European alliances.[36]

Soviet doubts alone might easily have forestalled further moves on a customs union, but the British and Americans, whilst not declaring against French plans, also seemed reserved in their reaction, being suspicious of 'exclusive' economic arrangements in Western Europe.[37] Furthermore, practical problems with the Blum-Picard commission only intensified in the spring, as it became clear that a customs union was technically complex, that sufficient statistics for planning did not exist even in London, and that it was more profitable in the short term to concentrate on the daunting economic problems relating to the end of the war.[38] When the Belgian representative in Algiers, Romrée de Vichenet, put forward a memorandum on possible future co-operation on 25 April, he was met with a reserved attitude and did not receive a formal response until 18 May, when the French proposed to negotiate only on such short-term, practical issues as the expansion of trade and a monetary agreement with each of the Low Countries. Contacts with the Belgians were maintained in the summer but with no major new initiatives,[39] and though studies continued on an economic union in London (producing memoranda on such issues as West European demography, trade patterns and cereal production) it was conceded that the statistical base for these was too flimsy to provide for important decisions.[40] Meanwhile Belgian and Dutch moves towards the 'Benelux' customs union also went slowly and both Spaak and the Dutch now seemed to prefer co-operation with Britain rather than France. René Massigli too hoped that Britain would take the leadership of a 'Western bloc'.[41] In fact British Foreign Office officials did favour the idea of a 'Western bloc' in 1944, including France, the Low Countries and Scandinavia. This would provide security in Europe, help control Germany and strengthen Britain's world influence. But they too were wary of upsetting the Soviets and Americans, and Winston Churchill disliked the 'Western bloc': he did not feel that Britain could bear the financial burden of acting as 'paymaster' to such a group.[42]

The studies of a Western European customs union in Algiers cannot, in the end, be said to have achieved much in providing a basis for post-war policy. But during the course of discussions a number of problems and possible lines for future investigation had been drawn out. The concentration on Western Europe (especially the Low Countries), the unclear position of Britain in French schemes, the interest in colonial co-operation alongside a customs union, and above all the whole debate over the place of Germany in West European co-operation – and the place of West European co-operation in controlling Germany – were vital pointers to the shape of the post-war foreign policy debate. De Gaulle's planners shared with the Metropolitan Resistance (albeit in a more 'realistic' form) the ideal of a West European group united by cultural and social values, where national independence could give way to far-reaching co-operation. So far as Germany was concerned the need, as seen in the studies on both Western Europe and a German armistice, was not only to destroy Nazism and prevent another German military revival, but also to use German industry to contribute to the reconstruction of France and Europe. The studies confirmed the obvious importance of the Big Three in future, and particularly the pre-eminence of the Soviet Union and the United States, neither of which de Gaulle could afford to alienate.

De Gaulle in 1944 was wary of Soviet ambitions in Eastern Europe, offended by Russia's refusal to treat him as an equal and upset by her suspicions of the 'Western bloc' but he recognised her significance as the strongest continental state, needed her co-operation to placate the powerful French Communists, and hoped that she would help control Germany in future. In March–July the General sent Pierre Cot, a former minister in Blum's 'Popular Front' and a Communist sympathiser, to Russia to sound out Soviet views on the post-war world. Cot received full Soviet co-operation during his visit and wrote a long report on his return which was extremely positive. On foreign policy Cot conceded that Russia was guided by Marxist doctrine, suspicious of 'bourgeois' states, opposed to colonialism and critical both of the 'Western bloc' and French links to the Polish government-in-exile. But he also believed that the Soviets wanted Big Three co-operation, the development of a new United Nations to replace the old League of Nations, and the destruction of Nazism and militarism in Germany. Cot importantly found little enthusiasm for a separate 'Rhenania' in Moscow, but he argued that the Soviets had an affinity with France due to the 1789 Revolution and, after seeing Foreign Minister Vyacheslav Molotov, believed that Russia wanted a strong, independent, democratic France with a major role in Europe.[43] Unfortunately Cot's political views seem to have clouded his judgement and events surrounding the Liberation of Paris confirmed the negative side of Soviet policy: the Soviets were slow to report the liberation, no Russian official attended French celebrations of the event in Moscow, and the Moscow press – ominously – emphasised the importance of the domestic Resistance over de Gaulle.[44]

De Gaulle's relations with the United States also remained strained at this time. American assistance was much more vital to the General than that of the Soviets. He needed America – and to a lesser extent now, Britain – for finance and arms, he realised the need to join in an American-led 'multilateral' trade system and its political counterpart, the United Nations (which was yet to be established), and after 6 June 1944 he relied on US, British and Canadian armies for the liberation of French soil. Yet, once again, he was not fully informed of Anglo-American plans for the invasion of Normandy, a visit he made to Washington in July failed to alter FDR's suspicious view of him, and even clear demonstrations of French popular support – beginning with the General's visit to Bayeux on 14 June – could not induce Washington and London to give official recognition to his 'Provisional Government', declared on 26 May. It was only thanks to the American Supreme Commander in Europe, Dwight D. Eisenhower that, as Allied forces broke out of Normandy and sped eastwards, the Second Free French Armoured Division, under General Leclerc was given the honour of liberating Paris, whose people had already risen against the Germans. And it was thanks to Eisenhower too – as the soldier on the scene forced to face up to practical needs – that, with Paris liberated, *de facto* recognition was given to de Gaulle's regime in the form of a 'civil affairs agreement' by which it could govern areas behind the fighting front.

On 25 August de Gaulle was able to enter the capital in the wake of Leclerc and give clear indications of his determination to take control there. Thus he visited the Prefecture of Police, (which had long co-operated with German occupation) to thank the police for their contribution to the liberation of Paris, before he visited the Hôtel de Ville, where Bidault and the Resistance leaders were gathered. Then he pointedly rejected any declaration of a new Republic, saying that the Republic had never ceased to exist. The refusal to allow Bidault to share the place of honour in the triumphal parade down the Champs Elysées the following day merely confirmed the message of these earlier gestures: Charles de Gaulle was in full control of the French government, and would do most to shape France's post-war foreign policy.

Chapter 1

The Rebirth of Foreign Policy, August – December 1944.

An alliance with the West? Yes. How could we do otherwise. But an alliance with the East as well.
– Georges Bidault speaking to the French Consultative Assembly on 21 November 1944 (from the Assembly's *Journal Officiel*).

Charles de Gaulle's triumphant return to Paris marked both the end and the beginning of an era. The capital was liberated; Vichy was destroyed; Free France was vindicated. But the Gaulle's 'government' was not recognised by her three major allies, much of France remained under German rule, and the daunting work of reconstructing the economy, rebuilding political life and achieving international respect had now to begin. In the closing months of 1944 the General began to forge French foreign policy anew, against the background of continuing war and deep internal problems.

The liberation of the bulk of French territory actually occurred with remarkable speed. The pace of the Allied advance in northern France after the break-out from Normandy was maintained and by mid-September Eisenhower's forces had swept across Belgium into Luxembourg. In mid-August furthermore, General Jean de Lattre de Tassigny's First French Army had landed with the Americans in Provence, in 'Operation Anvil', and drove northwards so rapidly that they joined with the Normandy forces near Dijon on 11 September. At the end of the month the only areas of France outside Allied control were various enclaves on the Atlantic coast, the Italian border and Alsace. But, as the *Wehrmacht* dug in along the Vosges mountains and as Eisenhower consolidated his supply lines the pace of the advance slowed. Metz was not taken until 20 November, Strasbourg three days later, and in December the Germans still held the region around Colmar. Though the failure to take the Colmar 'pocket' could be blamed on de Lattre's forces, the French were proud of their contribution to the liberation. French regulars may have had a minor role in the Normandy invasion but they formed the bulk of the troops in 'Operation Anvil'. Just as important, as the Germans retreated, large areas of south-western France were liberated by the 'French Forces of the Interior' (FFI), the Resistance fighters under General Koenig, who numbered over 300,000 men.

De Gaulle was gravely disappointed not to received more Americans supplies and finance to train and equip further French units at this time. There were obviously enough volunteers to form several divisions. But the United States was unwilling to use its resources to train French forces, a process which could take months, at a time when the war in Europe seemed likely to end quickly. Americans rightly predicted serious problems in disciplining the irregular *maquisards* and fusing them with de Lattre's army. France itself lacked the transport, fuel and arms to carry out the task of rearmament and in late 1944 there was no factory in the country capable of manufacturing heavy armaments. The army had other problems: discipline was undermined by the triumph of the de Gaulle's Free French over the majority who had remained loyal to Pétain; the French people still identified the Army with the defeat of 1940; and de Lattre's forces were mainly formed of colonial troops who were exhausted by earlier campaigns and unused to European weather. De Gaulle believed that limiting the French role was a deliberate American policy: a major military role in war would, after all, lead to a major diplomatic role at the peace table. But there was little de Gaulle could do about the situation. Like it or not, he depended on Washington for what forces he had and day-to-day command over French forces in the field lay with Eisenhower.[1]

Behind the Allied lines another struggle was taking place, to re-establish unity, order and a stable economy in France. De Gaulle always knew that national unity was as vital to *grandeur* as was a strong army, and his success in maintaining order and gaining popular support helped to win Allied recognition of his government. The scale of problems facing liberated France was daunting.[2] Fatalities during the Second World War were much less than in the First, but nonetheless totalled over half-a-million. In 1946 the French population was less than it had been ten years earlier. Material losses, on the other hand, were often greater than in 1914–18, simply because a larger area of the country was fought over. The transport system was devastated: in September it was impossible to reach Lille, Marseilles, Toulouse or Bordeaux by rail from Paris. Food stocks had been depleted by the Germans and food production was hindered by a lack of labour, fertilisers and farm machinery. With a very cold winter in 1944–45, rations had to remain low whilst the black market thrived. Malnutrition and disease were widespread. A particular problem for the country was the supply of coal. The ill-fed workers in the coal mines could produce only 67,000 tons per day in 1944, compared to more than twice that amount before the war. In 1938 France, the world's largest coal importer, had absorbed 23 million tons of coal from abroad, but even in 1946 she would receive only 10 million tons from America, Germany, Britain, Poland and elsewhere. The coal shortage led to lower production throughout the economy, a problem compounded by low rations, a shortage of suitable labour, German seizures of machinery and raw materials during the war and the collapse of foreign trade. The Lorraine steel mills in 1944 only reached about an eighth of their pre-war output; industry as a whole found its production cut by nearly two-thirds. Furthermore, what production there was usually contributed to de Gaulle's rearmament effort. Inflation, an enormous trade deficit, a weak currency and large-scale government borrowing would dog the French economy for years to come and have a major impact on the country's international policy, which became heavily influenced by the need to ensure loans, wheat, coal and other items from abroad. At the same time industrial and financial weakness would make it impossible to maintain large armed forces, or to play the part of a Great Power which de Gaulle always wanted.

Economic problems inevitably brought popular discontent. Strikes and the looting of bakeries followed a new bread ration in December. Discontent was often vented on former collaborators, several thousand of whom faced summary execution in late 1944, a process which did little to enhance France's reputation in America and Britain.[3] Ill-feeling grew too against the liberation forces, particularly the Americans, because of the requisitioning of supplies, the inevitable civilian deaths at Allied hands, or the feeling that captured Germans were too well-fed.[4] And ironically, problems were heightened by the very success of the Liberation. As de Gaulle himself recalled, 'many Frenchmen tended to identify the Liberation with the end of the war': the psychological sense of release in August and September ended in disappointment with the continuing conflict.[5] And yet, amidst all the difficulties, there emerged no challenge to de Gaulle's authority. On the Right, Vichy simply melted away. On the Left there were attempts by some Communists to foment discontent over the economic situation, calls for a *levée en masse* and 'democratic' reform in the Army, and even attempts to keep control of local government where this had been seized by *maquisards*. But in general the PCF leadership still saw their most vital aim as being to contribute to the war effort, indirectly helping the Soviet Union in its 'Great Patriotic War'. To this end Communists joined de Gaulle and other political parties in government, agreed to the absorption of the FFI into the regular Army, and – reluctantly – even accepted the abolition of armed resistance groups on 28 October.

At national level, on 30 August 1944 the 'Provisional Government' was formally moved from Algiers to Paris, and on 9 September de Gaulle formed a new government of 'national unanimity' in which several Metropolitan resistance leaders joined men from Algiers, including two Communists. De Gaulle dominated the new Cabinet as he had the CFLN. 'This man is extraordinary', wrote Henri Teitgen, on a note to his fellow-Christian Democrat Georges Bidault, during the first Cabinet meeting; Bidault passed it back, having written, 'Was not Lucifer the most beautiful of the Angels?'.[6] It was another month before the General agreed to reconstitute the Consultative Assembly and it did not meet for the first time until 9 November. De Gaulle could not deny that its creation helped to win respect abroad, but he considered 'that Assemblies, despite their fine speeches, are ruled by fear of action' and had no liking for political parties, or for the leaders of the Metropolitan Resistance.[7] 'The General was disappointed ... by the rarity of men of valour raised by the Resistance ...' recalled Michel Debré later, whilst one of de Gaulle's personal *cabinet* added more bluntly that the two things the General found most insufferable were 'the Allies and the Resistance.'[8] In fact the Resistance failed to form a single political force after the Liberation, despite attempts to do so. The truth was that most Frenchmen had *not* been in the Resistance and that those who were were disunited politically. Many shared a desire for social and economic reform to bring a more just and equal society but within this general viewpoint there emerged three powerful groups: Communists, loyal to Soviet policies and methods; Socialists, hoping to create the strongest post-war political force with the promise of social democracy; and Christian Democrats –

who in November formed the *Mouvement Républicain Populaire* (MRP) – willing to ally with the Left but standing for the protection of individual freedom in society. De Gaulle refused to associate with any of these groups.

As part of the establishment of a new government came the recreation of the diplomatic service. On 29 August René Massigli, accompanied by Hervé Alphand and others, arrived to take charge at the Quai d'Orsay.[9] Massigli however, was soon to be made Ambassador to London. In his place as foreign minister de Gaulle might have been expected to appoint someone amenable to his views. Instead, after considering the loyal René Pleven (the CFLN's Commissioner for Colonies), de Gaulle chose Georges Bidault, whom he did not know but who was young, intelligent and ambitious and whose appointment confirmed that de Gaulle and the Metropolitan Resistance were united. As a Catholic, a conservative, a student of history and a critic of Munich, whose personal bravery could not be doubted, Bidault could be expected to share a common outlook with the General. Both were firmly nationalist in their outlook on the world, both were lonely, rather secretive figures personally. But Bidault, a former academic and journalist, and a leader of the new MRP, was in many ways the opposite of the General; more given to compromise, lacking in stamina and confidence, frequently unwell and often nervous.[10] The two men co-operated badly and de Gaulle later declared about Bidault, 'I ask forgiveness from God and man every day for having installed him at the Quai d'Orsay'.[11] In fact Bidault, who had been cut off from the international scene for four years, and had expected to become Minister of Justice, was at first shocked to be told of his appointment to the Quai.[12] For the next sixteen months he spent an hour with de Gaulle every few days discussing foreign affairs.[13] De Gaulle did most of the talking and also took many major foreign policy decisions without any reference to his Foreign Minister. Often the Chief of Staff, Alphonse Juin, was a closer collaborator of the General's than was Bidault.

Bidault soon felt like 'some strange animal, lost in the huge, antiquated, deserted palace of the Quai d'Orsay'. He was without adequate archives (much had been destroyed in the war; many documents were in Vichy; Free French material took time to arrive from Algiers), without sufficient experienced diplomats, and without personal knowledge of the international scene. All that Massigli left, complained Bidault, 'was some dispiriting advice, his [*directeur de cabinet*] and one chauffeur'.[14] It took some time to restructure the foreign policy machine to cope with the post-war world, and the Communists considered that rather too many 'collaborators' were retained in Bidault's ministry,[15] but in 1945 the government established the Quai on a rational new basis.[16] The political head was Bidault, assisted by his personal *cabinet*, whose *directeur* was, first Guy de Charbonnière, a young career diplomat favoured by Massigli, and then Pierre-Louis Falaize who, as a fellow journalist (from *L'Aube*) and resistance fighter, was personally loyal to Bidault. As Deputy Director Bidault appointed another resistance member, Suzanne Borel, whom he later married. His commitments to the MRP meant that Bidault also had to give much attention to domestic politics, but for day-by-day running of the foreign ministry he could rely on its official head, the Secretary-General. Initially this post was filled by Raymond Brugère who had had an illustrious diplomatic career stretching back before 1914, but who other officials felt lacked the energy to restore the Ministry's fortunes.[17] He was soon sent to Brussels as Ambassador. The new Secretary-General in January 1945 was Jean Chauvel, an anglophile, close to Massigli, who had been pre-war head of the section of the Quai concerned with Asia-Oceania. Chauvel developed very good relations with Bidault and for four years successfully bore the burden of running the Quai.

Under Chauvel, in addition to various technical services (protocol, communications and the like) were grouped four *Directions Générales*: political affairs; economic and financial affairs (a new department reflecting the importance of international economics and headed by the formidable Alphand); administrative and social affairs; and cultural relations. The key *Direction Générale des Affaires Politiques* was headed by Maurice Dejean until September 1945, when Maurice Couve de Murville – destined in the 1960s to become the longest serving French Foreign Minister since the *Ancien Régime* – took it over. A Giraudist who had been eliminated from the CFLN in November 1943, Couve had later become a loyal Gaullist and French representative in Italy. Like Alphand he was an outstanding young official, an *Inspecteur des Finances* who had specialised in international economics in the 1930s. Couve was viewed as the perfect civil servant – coldly efficient, hard-working and thorough. Under his authority were the four geographical *directions* at the Quai for Europe, America, Asia-Oceania and Africa-Levant, which did much to shape French foreign policy towards individual states.

Despite the successful recreation of the diplomatic machine however, until 1946 much of French policy was decided by de Gaulle. 'We were lucky when we were given some hint, though certainly not an explanation, of de Gaulle's decisions . . .', Bidault later complained, whilst Chauvel too bitterly criticised the General for his contempt of his advisers, and for his over-ambitious policies: 'The man had declared France free and great. It was necessary that she was effectively free with regard to her allies as well as her enemies, and that her greatness was manifested at every occasion'.[18] De Gaulle's policy required, first, recognition by the Allies of his government's sovereignty in France; secondly, recognition of France's Great Power status through her inclusion in the councils of the Big Three; and finally a full French role in peace-making with Germany, where lasting security guarantees had to be secured. As in London and Algiers the General's policy meant a pricklish attitude to any remotely demeaning treatment, an unwillingness to compromise French independence, and a series of diplomatic incidents with his allies. France would be part of the the anti-Nazi alliance, but this did not mean that her aims were coterminus with those of her allies (any more than, say, American aims were the same as the Soviet Union's). Despite the complaints of Bidault and Chauvel over the methods he used, de Gaulle's aims were understandable: France had been a great power for centuries, she still possessed the second largest colonial empire in the world and she was of essential importance to the future political shape of Europe. But there were obvious problems with de Gaulle's policy. For, whatever the General's faith in *grandeur*, France was psychologically drained, economically weak, militarily second-rate; she relied on America and Britain even to stay alive; and so she could not possibly command genuine 'equality' in economic and military terms with Britain, America and Russia, the three states who would do most to shape post-war world politics.

* * *

The liberation of Paris, the return of French officials and deputies from Algiers, and above all the clear support for the 'provisional government' helped de Gaulle achieve some of his aims before the end of 1944, including full recognition by the Allies and a share in official discussions on Germany. On 25 August, in his speech at the Hôtel de Ville de Gaulle had made clear that France wanted a full share in the defeat of Germany, and the following day Massigli told the Americans that France wished to share in all Big Three decision-making.[19] The French were particularly keen to join the London-based 'European Advisory Commission' (EAC) of officials, established by the Big Three in 1943 as a consultative body to discuss the surrender and post-war treatment of Germany. But in September the key question was that of securing legal recognition of de Gaulle's regime.

Britain's representative Duff Cooper, a former professional diplomat, leading Conservative, opponent of appeasement and lover of all things French, arrived in Paris from Algiers on 12 September and two days later Bidault pressed him for recognition of France and a role in the German settlement. In London the Foreign Office certainly wanted to recognise de Gaulle's government and the French press service reported that Winston Churchill was likely to argue for this course with President Roosevelt. Many American officials, including the acting 'representative' in Paris, Selden Chapin, felt non-recognition was indefensible and even destructive: if America alone was seen to oppose recognition it could alienate the French people at a time when American standing with them, thanks to the Liberation, stood high; if maintained it could undermine de Gaulle's authority and lead to disorder, or perhaps a left-wing takeover. Secretary of State Cordell Hull, though no admirer of de Gaulle, was impressed by these arguments and on 21 September Washington took the important step of appointing a full representative to Paris. Jefferson Caffery, a career diplomat with previous experience in Berlin, Tokyo and (in 1918) Paris itself, was serious-minded and diligent, enjoyed reading Aristotle for relaxation, and was considered 'the best reporting officer in the Foreign Service' because of his succinct but informative despatches.[20]

In mid-September Franklin Roosevelt however was still not ready to recognise de Gaulle. He apparently hoped that an alternative non-communist leader could yet emerge.[21] For a time Winston Churchill stood by Roosevelt's position, but on the 28th, under Foreign Office pressure, the British leader told the House of Commons that recognition might not be far off. Churchill conceded to Eden that de Gaulle was at least preferable to a Communist France. Massigli and the Quai continued to see Roosevelt's attitude as the real stumbling block.[22] On 14 October Churchill went further and wrote to the President privately that 'we can now safely recognise General de Gaulle's administration',[23] and other pressures were growing on Roosevelt. The US presidential election was imminent and recognition could win votes.[24] Even Admiral Leahy, the leading architect of the Vichy gamble felt de Gaulle *must* be recognised now.[25] And from Paris on 20 October Caffery reported Eisenhower's view that recognition was vital for two reasons. In the short term, a stable French government was essential for the prosecution of the campaign against Germany. In the long term 'Eisenhower ... believes that if France falls into the orbit of any other country the other countries of Western Europe will do the same ... He does not believe that it would be in our interest to have the continent ... dominated by any single power'. It was not stated which power was likely to dominate. But Eisenhower did not think it would be Britain or France.[26]

By 21 October Roosevelt had given way and the State Department suddenly asked Britain and Russia to agree to recognition in two days time. Churchill, on his way back from visiting Stalin in Moscow, was shocked by the pace of Roosevelt's sudden turnabout, which seemed like an American attempt to 'steal a march' on the British and Russians, both of whom would willingly have recognised de Gaulle earlier.[27] At 5 p.m. on 23 October however, all the Big Three representatives went to see Bidault to extend legal recognition. The French were singularly unimpressed. Bidault merely accepted the change in status of the Allied 'representatives' to the position of 'ambassadors' verbally, and de Gaulle told a press conference a few days later, when asked about recognition, 'the Government is satisfied to be called by its correct name'. At the same conference the General complained about the inadequacy of US military supplies to France, made the bold claim that at the end of the war French troops 'will occupy the German territories that they have taken from the German armies' (though there had been no talks with the Big Three on this), and outlined some of France's plans for post-war Germany, including special controls on the Rhineland and Ruhr.[28] By delaying recognition of de Gaulle's government so long, the Allies had only driven home the point that the General had made *himself* leader of France. He did not need to rely on the goodwill of others. His next major aim, it was clear, was to achieve a full say in the future of the old enemy, Germany, beginning with a French place on the European Advisory Commission.

French representatives had consistently pressed for a place on the EAC for months and again it was the Americans who seemed to have done most to thwart them. On 7 August a Soviet official told Roger Garreau in Moscow, with some exaggeration, that Russia had wanted French participation in the EAC since the body was set up in 1943. This was to counter British claims that Russia opposed French membership.[29] The Americans showed no such desire to compete for French favours. In mid-August the State Department made it plain to the French, and to the British, that the most de Gaulle could expect in the way of consultation on German policy were informal talks with the EAC.[30] It was in the light of this that, on 22 August, Jacques Camille-Paris, French *chargé* in London, wrote to the then-chairman of the EAC, US Ambassador John Winant, that 'the surrender of Germany is of fundamental interest to France ... and France could certainly not consider herself bound ...' by decisions she had not been involved in making.[31] At the same time Massigli pressured Anthony Eden on the need for a French place on the EAC. The British Foreign Office, desiring to build up France as a loyal ally in Western Europe, so as to bolster Britain's diplomatic influence and hold down Germany, approved the French aim.[32] But still the most the US would agree to was *consultation* between the French and EAC, not actual French membership of the body.[33] Eventually in mid-September the French formally wrote to the Big Three requesting 'a seat on the Commission . . . to ensure that France may take her part in the task of reconstructing and reorganising Europe.'[34] This followed de Gaulle's speech at the Hôtel de Ville on 25 August and another on 12 September, stating France's determination to share in decisions about Germany's, and Europe's, future.[35] But privately at this time the General feared being excluded from Germany by Roosevelt, telling his aides that France was 'entirely on her own': only strong armed forces could ensure her independence and a role in the European peace settlement.[36]

Although Anthony Eden told Massigli on 27 September, rather ambiguously, that Britain and America both supported a French 'part' in the EAC's work,[37] America's John Winant still felt that France's inclusion would unnecessarily complicate matters and was 'certain' the Soviets also opposed the idea: in early October it was a lack of instructions to Russia's EAC delegate, Fedor Gousev, which prevented an early invitation to France to consult with the EAC on German surrender terms.[38] In conversation with Garreau in Moscow however, Deputy Foreign Minister Vladimir Dekasanov still claimed to favour a French role in the EAC and, at the end of October, with de Gaulle's government recognised, and continued complaints from the General about his exclusion from peace-making,[39] the Russians began to adopt a far more positive policy towards France, in acts as well as words. This change was possibly inspired by the rapid American turnabout on the recognition issue. In Moscow there was now greater press interest in French affairs,[40] and in the EAC not only did Gousev agree to consult Paris about German surrender terms, he also supported full French *membership* of the EAC. Gousev told Massigli of Russia's new position, Bogomolov informed Bidault of it, and this placed the British and Americans in an embarrassing position. Faced by the new-found Soviet enthusiasm for de Gaulle, the Western powers had little option but to agree to invite France onto the EAC.[41]

On 7 November Massigli as a first step was invited 'to take part in the consideration of German affairs',[42] and a British *aide-mémoire* to the Americans that same day argued in favour of France's full EAC membership: the British considered that 'the present time is a critical one in the formation of future French foreign policy and it would be dangerous to risk inclining France away from [the] western democracies'.[43] With this FDR finally agreed. The decision to invite France onto the EAC was announced on 11 November and Bidault accepted six days later. In the end, however, the Soviets would not be outdone by the Western powers, both Molotov and Dekasanov insisting in conversations with Garreau that they had led the way in securing France's EAC place.[44] Yet again, as over the recognition issue, the Big Three had proved divided among themselves, ultimately falling over each other in bids to impress the French. In particular Eisenhower's arguments regarding recognition, and the British arguments of 7 November regarding the EAC, showed the desire of many in the Western camp to prevent any shift by de Gaulle towards Moscow. Events had shown that the General could hope to play the Big Three off against each other and that, though his country was still weak in material terms, her potential future importance was important enough to win major concessions.

French potential had been further confirmed in October by a decision of the Big Three and China, meeting at Dumbarton Oaks in America during

August–October to lay the basis for a new 'collective security' system via a United Nations Organisation. In these talks, largely at British insistence, and despite de Gaulle's absence, a permanent seat had been reserved for France alongside the other four powers on the new UN Security Council.[45] In the wake of recognition by the Big Three furthermore, French representatives abroad resumed their traditional titles and a host of ambassadors were accredited to Paris from minor states. The Vatican was inept enough to reappoint Monsignor Valerio Valeri, previously accredited to Vichy. But de Gaulle would tolerate no disrespect even from the Papacy and refused to accept him. The Vatican turned to a new appointee, Monsignor A.G. Roncalli, the future Pope John XXIII.[46]

* * *

Whilst a place on the EAC was being secured, the French had continued to define their policy towards Germany. As de Gaulle made clear on 25 October, France would wish to share in the military occupation of German territories. In April Massigli's predecessor in London, Pierre Viénot, had told the British that France would want to occupy the Rhineland to the north of Alsace, including the Saar, and in August, before leaving Algiers, de Gaulle apparently envisaged a zone including the Saar, the western bank of the Rhine up to Cologne, and several West-German provinces – the Palatinate, the Hesses and Baden.[47] The British Foreign Office, in late August, decided to support a French share in the occupation of Germany to help London's security policy in Western Europe, possibly by giving France a part of Britain's zone. But the Big Three themselves had not yet defined their occupation zones in Germany,[48] and Eisenhower informed de Gaulle that whilst France could 'initially' administer areas it conquered, final zones of occupation must be decided at government level.[49] Discussions on a French zone did not finally take place until early 1945. For the moment the French had to define their German policy without the promise of an occupation zone.

In his memoirs, de Gaulle's aims in Germany were set out in clear, precise terms with several main elements, including the abolition of a centralised Reich, 'international control' of the Ruhr, a permanent occupation of the Rhineland, and economic ties between France and the Saar. These measures would not only prevent further German aggression, they would also stop French confidence being sapped, as in the 1930s, by German revival. The General also noted that his 'conception of tomorrow's Germany was closely related to my image of Europe' and his outline of French policy in the press conference of 25 October 1944 showed this 'European' dimension when he described the Rhine as 'a road uniting the countries to its west with the countries to its East', and of the Ruhr as 'an economic arsenal for the benefit of man'. All European nations should join in controlling Germany, and all could share in the use of her industrial resources.[50]

In fact, of course, much of the policy which de Gaulle outlined had already been discussed in Algiers. Indeed a memorandum dated 21 August, entitled 'The German Problem', was passed from Massigli to Bidault which outlined diplomatic, military, economic and political measures to control the 'permanent danger' from Germany and use her resources to rebuild France. The first, diplomatic section spoke of the 'absolute necessity of a military alliance with the USSR in view of our continental defence, and of a military alliance with England [sic] for the protection of our colonial Empire', but felt that, as after 1919, the US would not wish to involve itself closely in European affairs. The Franco-Soviet-British alliance would be backed by British ties to the Commonwealth, French association with the three Benelux states and Soviet links to the 'Slav states' of Eastern Europe, making German expansion impossible. Other measures would include a long military occupation, complete German disarmament and Allied control of the three 'bastions' of Posnania, Bohemia and the Ruhr-Rhineland; limits on German industrial output and international control of Rhineland-Westphalia; and the destruction of Germany's central government, with lands east of the River Oder being annexed by Russia and Poland. The memorandum also wanted to discuss the 'connection' of France and the Saar and the *encouragement* of 'particularist tendencies' in the German provinces. Importantly it was feared that *enforced* dismemberment of Germany would lead to a strong irredentist movement and so this was ruled out. In a highly significant, positive point the memorandum also advocated the long-term return of Germany to the community of nations by the development of European co-operation.[51] Other documents inherited from Algiers included detailed studies of ways to secure German economic disarmament.[52]

Despite the work in Algiers, however, and the clear exposé in de Gaulle's memoirs, many details about French policy remained to be decided, not least the precise status of the Saar, the form of international control over the Ruhr and Rhineland, and the geographical definition of these areas. A special study group on these questions was set up under Chauvel's overall control, with members from the Quai, the Army, economic ministries, and de Gaulle's office. It finally reported in 1945, but a memorandum of 9 November set out the basis of thinking in the Quai on economic controls. The essential point was the belief that Germany would break free of obligations placed on it from outside in a peace treaty in the style of Versailles. What was needed to ensure peace was a radical *transformation* of the German situation. One possible way to achieve this was the 'Morghenthau Plan', the draconian scheme, conceived by the US Treasury in 1943 to 'pastoralise' the German economy, turning an economic giant into a helpless agricultural state, but – despite later accusations of being draconian in their own schemes – the French rejected this because it would create economic chaos in Germany and, more important, deprive France and Europe of the use of German industrial resources. Wholesale dismemberment of Germany (such as the Big Three considered at this time) was also, again, rejected as likely to provoke a renewal of German nationalism. It is important to underline the fact that France *did not* want a *general* policy of dismemberment. Instead what France advocated was the political detachment of only one or two key areas on the periphery of Germany: Silesia in the East, to be placed under Polish control, and Rhineland-Westphalia in the West. To prevent Soviet and American opposition to the detachment of the Ruhr both these powers should share in the international supervision of the area with France, Britain and the Benelux states. Military occupation would be used to counter any irredentist ambitions by the local German population (a transfer of the 15 million-or-so people from the area was considered, but ruled out as too grandiose). The same day that this memorandum was written, Alphand, who had a leading role in defining the German policy, met with a group of experts and agreed that the Saar should be tied to France in a 'special regime' short of annexation. Already, however, a separate note of 8 November had raised an important question: what would be the effect of the separation of the Ruhr, Germany's industrial heart, on the remainder of the German economy?[53] Using the resources of the Ruhr to help the recovery of Germany's victims was all very well, but the effect of its removal on what remained of Germany would not just be military weakness – it could be economic catastrophe. For the moment this question went unanswered.

De Gaulle's aims vis-à-vis Germany in late 1944 went beyond even what Clemenceau, in a much stronger diplomatic position, had achieved twenty-five years before. The General believed no doubt that the experience of the Second World War vindicated such a comprehensive, hard-line approach to Germany. He also hoped that the rebuilding of French military power, and the withdrawal of US and British forces from Europe after the war, would strengthen his hand. But he had no guarantees that this would be so, and some problems with his policy became evident even before the end of the year in two important personal meetings, first with Winston Churchill, then with Josef Stalin.

* * *

De Gaulle had invited Churchill to Paris in a message of 30 October. An invitation was also sent to Roosevelt. The President eventually declined it, due to the pressure of other commitments, but Churchill accepted the idea enthusiastically, suggesting Armistice Day as a suitable date.[54] 'He wants to steal my 11 November!', complained de Gaulle, but Massigli recognised the date as providing an opportunity to impress the Prime Minister in the most effective way, with moving speeches and historic ceremonies.[55] On the public level this first major visit by a foreign leader to Paris since the Liberation went perfectly. Churchill arrived on 10 November and was delighted to be accommodated at the Quai d'Orsay in a suite originally decorated for George VI's state visit in 1938, and more lately occupied by Hermann Goering, complete with gold bathroom fittings. The Armistice Day celebrations, despite fears for Churchill's safety, included a ceremony at the grave of the unknown soldier, a motorcade through Paris, and a visit to Marshal Foch's tomb at Les Invalides. The reception given by the Parisians was ecstatic and the two leaders seemed extraordinarily friendly. When the band played 'Le Père de la Victoire' the General told Churchill it was 'For You'; stopping in Les Invalides to look at Napoleon's tomb, Churchill declared, 'In all the world there is nothing greater'. On 12 November the Prime Minister was made a citizen of Paris at the Hotel de Ville, and on the 13th went with de Gaulle to review de Lattre's army.[56]

For Charles de Gaulle, however, just as important as the public show was what Churchill and Eden said in private. Before the visit the British had accepted a French agenda which included an exchange of views on general issues (including Soviet policy and the future of Eastern Europe) and important specific questions such as EAC membership, Germany, the Levant and France's role in the Japanese war.[57] It was in conversation on 11 November that Churchill and Eden revealed the invitation for France to join the EAC for the first time and expressed support for French revival, but as always de Gaulle wanted more than tokens and words: he demanded a full share in military victory over Germany and in Big Three decision-making. On these points he later professed to having found his guests 'reserved' and 'vague' because 'they considered themselves players at a game to which we were not admitted . . .'. The British tried repeatedly to impress de Gaulle, but at each step the General was disappointed. Thus Churchill promised to discuss France's rearmament needs with Roosevelt and undertook to provide some surplus military equipment from Britain, but this did not amount to much in concrete terms. As Bidault said, if the French Army did not play a full role in the war 'Germans will not look on them as conquerors' and a point of great psychological significance would thus be lost. Actually only the Americans could really help France on the armaments issue: Britain herself now relied on US equipment supplies. Regarding Germany Eden declared that the French could share in the occupation of the British zone and Churchill stated that the Ruhr and Saar 'can no longer be permitted to serve as an arsenal for Germany'. De Gaulle however was upset that firm decisions on Germany could only be taken by the Big Three and that he could not be told precisely which areas France would occupy. The two sides agreed – unsurprisingly – on the need to preserve colonial rule in each of their empires, but on detailed questions there were problems. In particular the British, concerned for their own position in the Middle East, felt that France would 'provoke trouble' by seeking to preserve military and political rights in Syria–Lebanon, as de Gaulle still hoped to do. On wider issues there was less division. Both sides agreed that a global security system under the UN was preferable to a return to 'bloc' politics after the war. De Gaulle himself was still cautious regarding Soviet fears of a 'Western bloc'. On the Soviet theme Churchill gave an account of his recent meetings with Stalin in Moscow. He seemed remarkably confident that Moscow would respect the independence of East European states, and de Gaulle said that this must certainly be the case regarding France's historic ally, Poland.[58]

On 13 November de Gaulle continued to press Churchill on the need for full French equality with the Big Three and, according to his (frequently unreliable) memoirs, raised the possibility of Anglo-French co-operation to prevent a future division of the world between America and Russia. But the British, though increasingly aware of their relative decline vis-à-vis their two partners, were still committed to Big Three co-operation and the Prime Minister replied that France must be patient about the pace of her revival. Once more de Gaulle felt disappointment.[59] Despite EAC membership France was excluded from 'the club of the Great Powers' where effective decisions were taken and on 17 November the General told a group of Socialist leaders that, 'appearances and symbolic gestures' being worthless, France must dedicate all her efforts to rebuilding her own strength.[60] The British were the Great Power most willing to revive France's role in world affairs it seemed, but only in so far as this suited British interests, and de Gaulle was certainly not interested in returning to the unequal alliance of the inter-war years when French needs were always subservient to those of Britain.

In fact, in the wake of his Paris visit, Churchill *did* try to have France included in Big Three talks in future. He suggested this in letters to both Roosevelt and

Stalin in mid-November, but Roosevelt predictably scotched the idea when he replied that de Gaulle's presence could only confuse matters. Despite pressure from his own military chiefs and Churchill – who was increasingly fearful of America's withdrawal from post-war Europe and the military vacuum it would create – Roosevelt also refused to increase military supplies to France. Stalin, however, following the EAC episode, was now more positive and evidently hoped to win influence over de Gaulle for himself. On 20 November Stalin not only told Churchill that he was ready for a 'meeting between us three and the French' he also announced that de Gaulle was about to visit Moscow.[61] The latter piece of news came as an unpleasant surprise to the British, who were given no warning of such a visit from the French side.

Despite the General's later claim that Ambassador Bogomolov had urged him to visit Moscow, Stalin was quite clear that *de Gaulle* had been the first to express an interest in such a journey, and the terms of the formal Soviet invitation to de Gaulle of 14 November confirmed this point.[62] The General had evidently raised the idea with Bogomolov even *before* Churchill's visit, and the outcome of the Franco-British talks can only have strengthened the desire to meet Stalin. If Churchill was unable or, as de Gaulle saw it, unwilling, to grant France equality and a share in the German settlement, perhaps the Soviets could provide these things. Already, of course, the General wanted to forge an alliance with Russia to control Germany in future. Despite ideological differences with Moscow the French believed such an alliance was 'natural'.[63] Also, just by visiting Stalin, de Gaulle could demonstrate his independence of the two Anglo-Saxon powers on the world stage and impress the French Communists. Since returning to Paris de Gaulle had been careful not to antagonise Russia. In his press conference of 25 October indeed, whilst speaking of co-operation with other West European states, he had tried to placate the Soviets by criticising the idea of an exclusive 'Western bloc',[64] and on 11 November, in a newspaper interview to coincide with Churchill's visit, Bidault had talked of France as a 'bridge' between East and West. The 'bridge' idea was attractive for a number of reasons: it suggested that France could play a significant role in the world; it would allow links to both America and Britain (vital for military and economic supplies) and Russia (vital to hold down Germany in future); and it would help to unite the three major political parties at home.[65]

On 21 November, during the Consultative Assembly's first foreign policy debate, Bidault announced the forthcoming Moscow visit and declared that France must have alliances with both East and West. The following day, in a much fuller speech, de Gaulle spoke of France's diplomatic resuscitation over recent weeks, called for her to be given a place alongside the Big Three in all major discussions and outlined some general aims regarding Germany, 'for France, a question of life or death'. There were some elements too of his 1943 Algiers speech on European co-operation. He wanted France, Britain, Belgium and Holland to ensure the security of the Rhine and favoured a 'frank reconciliation' with Italy. But again there was no call for exclusive Western co-operation: instead de Gaulle talked of European co-operation being built around the 'three pillars' of Paris, London and Moscow. Thus the General now sought improved relations in Western Europe only insofar as this was compatible with co-operation between France and the Big Three.[66]

Despite the hopes placed upon it, arrangements for the Moscow visit were hasty and improvised. Only on 24 November, the day of their delegation's departure, did the Quai, having heard nothing from the Soviets about organisational matters, notify the Moscow Embassy to expect de Gaulle on the 28th; he would stay for three or four days and wished to discuss general issues such as 'collective security' and Eastern Europe, bilateral issues (such as the position of French churches in Russia) and also, of course, the German problem. The Quai hoped amongst other things, to reassure Moscow about French hopes for economic links to the Benelux states and at Bidault's request, Chauvel asked his officials to prepare for possible talks on a treaty with Russia. The Quai correctly guessed that if Stalin did want a treaty it would be on the lines of the Anglo-Soviet Pact of 1942, a twenty-year treaty which promised co-operation against German aggression.[67] De Gaulle, Bidault, Maurice Dejean, General Juin and others in the party, accompanied by Bogomolov and equipped with plenty of fur clothing, left Paris on 24 November and spent two days flying to Baku in the Caucasus. But poor weather, and Soviet reluctance to let a French pilot overfly Russian territory, then caused delays and de Gaulle only reached Moscow, after a slow train journey from Baku, on 2 December.[68] He was upset by the late arrival and immediately offended his hosts by refusing to stay in the accommodation they had provided. According to his memoirs he stayed at the French Embassy so as to 'remain apart from the comings and goings' of the negotiations. Actually the Embassy, which had suffered from German shelling, was cold and uncomfortable, and the General seemed more concerned that a Soviet hotel would be 'laced with microphones'.[69]

Over the next eight days de Gaulle had fifteen hours of talks with Stalin, whom he later described as 'a Communist disguised as a Marshal, a dictator preferring the tactics of guile, a conqueror with an affable smile . . .'.[70] In contrast to Churchill's Parisian visit there was little public warmth. Russian crowds were largely indifferent to de Gaulle's presence, and the General was frequently bored by the entertainments provided by the Soviets.[71] What mattered most was said in private meetings. But for de Gaulle the first Kremlin meeting with Stalin, on the evening of 2 December, began badly. The Soviet leader, perhaps because of the Frenchman's snub over accommodation, was cold and aloof; he drew geometrical figures with his red pencil throughout the meeting and let his visitor do most of the talking. When de Gaulle began to discuss post-war economic problems, making no secret of France's enormous reconstruction needs, Stalin pretended that the USSR had few such difficulties. When de Gaulle declared that a strong France was vital for European security, and dismissed 1940 as an 'accident', Stalin cryptically remarked that France should have the diplomatic position she deserved. And although, the Marshal declared 'it is right that France should be on the borders of the Rhine', he also said, like Churchill, that such issues could only be settled by the Big Three. The real positive point in this meeting was that Stalin *was* interested in the idea of a Franco-Soviet pact against Germany: indeed, according to the French version of the talks he was the first to propose that one should be made. The following day the French presented a possible treaty text to the Russians and discussions proceeded on the basis of this draft.[72]

Over the next few days problems with the Russians continued. First, Molotov questioned France's ability to ratify a treaty given the 'provisional' nature of her government. The French, feeling insulted, were adamant that there was no problem on this point.[73] Then, at a dinner, Stalin raised the position of the French Communist leader Maurice Thorez, condemned as a deserter during the era of the Hitler-Stalin pact, who had recently been the subject of an amnesty by de Gaulle. (He had arrived back in Paris, from Moscow, on 27 November.) 'I know Thorez . . .', Stalin remarked, 'if I were in your place I would not put him in prison. At least not right away!' De Gaulle was annoyed at this attempt at meddling in French internal politics and simply replied, 'The French government treats the French according to the services it expects of them'.[74]

Most worrying of all, however, was Soviet pressure on the French to enter official relations with the Polish 'National Liberation Council', a group of Moscow-trained Communists who had been installed by the advancing Red Army in Lublin in Galicia, and who declared themselves as the 'provisional government' of Poland in December. The 'Lublin Poles' were being maintained by Stalin despite the existence of the Polish government-in-exile in London, successor to the right-wing pre-war regime which Stalin and Hitler had united to destroy in 1939.[75] On 5 December Molotov told Bidault that the Russians did not necessarily want France to break off relations with the 'London Poles', but they *did* want an exchange of officials with Lublin. Even before the Moscow visit in fact, Paris had wanted to send a 'representative', Captain Christian Fouchet, to Lublin for the practical purpose of protecting French interests in Poland as it was liberated.[76] But there were problems with giving the Lublin Poles too much by way of official recognition. Not only was France the traditional defender of Polish independence – Hitler's attack on Poland was of course the reason France went to war in 1939 – but also Poland was seen as a 'test case' for Soviet behaviour in Eastern Europe in future. In Britain and America there was great concern at this time over possible Soviet ambitions in Eastern Europe, an area which was about to be 'liberated' by the Red Army.

Already, in mid-November, the Quai had determined to keep in step with the Anglo-Saxons on the issue of recognising Lublin and Averell Harriman, America's Ambassador to Moscow warned de Gaulle on 5 December that he could expect strong US criticism if he recognised Lublin.[77] When the General met Stalin for their second formal meeting on 6 December the fate of Poland was a key concern. The conversation this time began well. Stalin assured the Frenchman that any Franco-Russian alliance would be unconditional; its value, for example, would not be undermined by any 'collective' arrangements under the new United Nations, as de Gaulle seemed to fear, and he promised to respect the independence of Eastern European states; the General for his part agreed to the idea of a westward shift in both the Soviet-Polish and Polish-German borders (moves which would extend Soviet territory and reduce Germany's size, whilst preserving a strong Poland). But de Gaulle also insisted that 'Poland must remain an independent state' and his determination on this point began to annoy Stalin, who became increasingly agitated, snapping that the 'London Poles' were like supporters of Vichy, arguing that agrarian reforms by Lublin were similar to what happened in France after 1789, and finally trying to change the subject by attacking the idea of a 'Western bloc' – at which the General declared that some

West European links were understandable and need not divide the continent. All in all, this meeting marked a much superior performance by de Gaulle to that of 2 December, and he later assured Harriman that France would not recognise Lublin without Anglo-American approval. 'Soviet policy [will] make for great fear among the small nations of Europe', de Gaulle told the Ambassador and added that France could use such fears to make herself the leader of Europe's 'small nations'.[78] When Molotov again raised the Polish problem with Bidault on 7 December the Frenchman once more insisted on the need for Polish independence.[79]

On 7 December yet another problem emerged for a Franco-Soviet treaty when Molotov raised the idea of a *tripartite* pact between Russia, France and Britain. Stalin, in marked contrast to de Gaulle, had kept London and Washington informed of the Moscow talks and had asked for their views both on a Franco-Soviet alliance and the Rhineland question. On the Rhineland both Roosevelt and Churchill confirmed that decisions could only be made by all the major powers meeting together. Regarding the alliance issue the British hastily considered the question and it was they who had suggested a tripartite arrangement to the Russians.[80] De Gaulle however saw the idea of a tripartite pact as representing British interference in matters which did not concern them. The General wanted an alliance with Britain at some time in future but he did not believe that Britain shared the same urgent interest in controlling Germany as did France and Russia, and he also told Bogomolov that differences with Britain over the Levant issue prevented a British treaty.[81] When de Gaulle and Stalin met on 8 December, to clarify issues regarding an alliance, the General explained his thinking on Germany and the primary need for a Franco-Soviet pact; a British alliance was of secondary importance. Stalin made only a half-hearted attempt to defend the tripartite proposal, but he was not so ready to drop the Polish problem. Indeed the Marshal was willing to put his negotiating position on Poland quite bluntly, telling de Gaulle, 'If you make an arrangement with the Lublin Committee . . . we will make a pact with you'. After this undisguised offer of a quite cynical arrangement the meeting drew to a rapid close, however. De Gaulle would not be intimidated: the most he would give Stalin was an exchange of 'representatives' with Lublin without diplomatic status.[82] He repeated this to Lublin representatives the following day.[83] Even given the undoubted exaggerations in his own account de Gaulle was proving a tough opponent for Stalin on Poland by now.

On the evening of 9 December came the grand finale of de Gaulle's visit, a banquet in the Kremlin hosted by Stalin. But the Polish issue was unresolved, and a Franco-Soviet treaty hung in the balance. De Gaulle looked decidedly glum, and Harriman was told by Stalin that he found his guest 'an awkward and stubborn man'. Stalin tried to impress the French delegation with some remarkably exaggerated behaviour. He insisted on announcing thirty toasts at the end of the meal with such remarks, when toasting Soviet officials, as 'He'd better do his best. Otherwise he'll be hanged for it'. After dinner, when the guests retired to a *salon* and Bidault continued to discuss a treaty with Molotov, the Marshal called out, 'Someone go and get me a machine gun. Let's kill these diplomats!'. Not to be outdone, de Gaulle turned to another guest and remarked in a loud voice that he did not think it would be possible for Western nations to co-operate with Russia after the war. Stalin then insisted that de Gaulle watch a 1938 Soviet propaganda film, 'If War Comes Tomorrow', in which the Russians easily routed the Germans and established lasting peace on the basis of Communism. 'I'm afraid Monsieur de Gaulle was not pleased by the end of the story', commented Stalin, to which the General caustically replied, 'At the beginning of the actual war, relations between you and the Germans were not as we saw them in this film'. It was then midnight and – to the astonishment of Stalin and Molotov – the General stood up, thanked the Marshal for his hospitality, and left. Bidault was soon ordered to follow, and it was then apparent that de Gaulle was willing to leave Moscow without a treaty rather than recognise the regime of the 'Lublin Poles'.

In the end de Gaulle's forcefulness won through and Stalin showed that a French treaty was more valuable to him than the recognition of Lublin. By 2 a.m. Dejean and Ambassador Garreau had agreed a text with the Russians which appointed Captain Fouchet as France's 'representative' in Lublin, simply for the protection of his country's interests. A Franco-Soviet Pact was finalised on the lines of the 1942 Anglo-Soviet agreement, with commitments to pursue the war to final victory and to co-operate in future 'to eliminate any new German menace'. It also included a general promise of economic co-operation and a commitment not to enter any alliances against each other. De Gaulle returned to the Kremlin in the early morning for the signature and was told by Stalin 'You played your hand well!'. The Marshal then insisted on drinking a final toast to 'a strong, independent and democratic Poland' and as a final act of black comedy turned to his interpreter, Boris Podzerov (who had attended all the meetings with de Gaulle) and told him, 'You know too much! I'd better send you to Siberia'. The French left Moscow later that morning, arriving back in Paris on 16 December.[84] Meanwhile, at the Quai, Jean Chauvel had been kept poorly informed about the Moscow talks and learnt of the treaty signature on the radio.[85]

The Moscow alliance seemed to promise close co-operation with Russia on Germany in future and Hervé Alphand hoped that it could be followed by a British treaty, financial help from America, and economic and military co-operation with Belgium and Holland.[86] The press were positive and the public seemed enthusiastic about the pact.[87] Even Roosevelt told the French Ambassador, Henri Hoppenot, that a Franco-Russian alliance would be an important pillar of future world security.[88] De Gaulle could consider his negotiations in Moscow ultimately successful: he had secured an important element in his long-term security policy vis-à-vis Germany, had asserted his independence of America and Britain, had strengthened his position at home, stood up well in the 'test of will' with Stalin,[89] and had resisted the pressure to recognise Lublin. (France only finally recognised a Polish government alongside Britain and America in mid-1945).[90] On 22 December both Bidault and de Gaulle spoke to the Consultative Assembly about the treaty, which was well-received – though the Socialist André Philip, for one, hoped that it could quickly lead to a tripartite arrangement with Britain. Bidault, in a nervous, repetitive performance which invited insulting comments from de Gaulle, again spoke of the need for links to both East and West and made clear France's interest in a truly independent Poland. De Gaulle's speech concentrated on the German menace as a reason for the Soviet treaty but agreed on the need for a British alliance, a security link to America through a new United Nations organisation, and for co-operation with the smaller countries of Europe like Belgium, Holland, Poland and Czechoslovakia. Yet again the General made it clear that France would not tie herself exclusively to any one of the Big Three and that he would use co-operation with small powers to balance the power of the Great.[91]

Much later, however, de Gaulle noted that the Moscow meetings revealed 'disturbing probabilities' about Russian policy, whilst Bidault considered 'our conversations with Stalin were not very encouraging'.[92] Stalin had confirmed that his first loyalty in the international field was to Russia's own security needs (particularly in Eastern Europe) and that his second was to the Big Three alliance. The Marshal may have made a treaty with France, but it was no more than he had given Britain and was couched in general terms. There was no Soviet support for the details of France's German policy – a separate Ruhr and Rhineland for example – nor any commitment to revive France's Great Power status. Bogomolov indeed told a Quai official at Christmas that, though Russia wanted close co-operation, Paris must respect the primacy of the Big Three in world affairs.[93] And if Stalin had given away little, he had also succeeded in making some gains. For one thing, Fouchet's arrival in Lublin *did* upset the London Poles,[94] and de Gaulle had shown that (like America and Britain) he could do nothing to limit Soviet power in Eastern Europe. For another, the Moscow events were a boost for the French Communists: when the Lublin representative arrived in Paris he was fêted by Communist representatives.[95] Neither can the point have been lost on Stalin that whilst he had a formal alliance with France, Britain did not. Both Chauvel and Massigli were dismayed by de Gaulle's insistence that the British must agree to French aims on the Rhine and in the Levant before he would make a treaty with them.[96] These twin conditions for a treaty would harm Anglo-French relations for the next two years. The British for their part were deeply offended by de Gaulle's visit to Moscow and his rejection of the tripartite pact with them.[97] As for de Gaulle's stubbornness in Moscow, the evidence from 1945 is that this only made Stalin less eager to work closely with France in future. It was quite clear that the General would not be amenable to Soviet ambitions in Eastern Europe, and in early 1945 the Russians turned back to a more reserved attitude towards France. The Quai meanwhile was under no illusion about the nature of the Stalinist regime. Duff Cooper noted that most of the French delegation returned from Moscow with anti-Soviet attitudes (though de Gaulle's *chef de cabinet*, Gaston Palewski, insisted to Cooper that the General himself had got on well with Stalin).[98] Early in 1945 the Quai became concerned about the dangers of Soviet expansionism in Eastern Europe, perhaps even into Germany itself.[99] Such concerns would grow in 1945.

'During the autumn of 1944', Bidault later recalled, 'we were not really on good terms with anyone.'[100] De Gaulle had won recognition as French leader from his allies, he had gained a share in talks at official level on Germany, he had asserted French independence at every possible point, and his Moscow visit marked a dramatic return for France to the diplomatic stage. But the

General was the leader of an exhausted nation and a demoralised people, his ambitious foreign policy aims were backed by limited resources, and in mid-December his relations with the three greatest Allied powers were at best mixed. It was then that the Germans launched their last offensive against Western forces, in the Ardennes. There would be no early end to the war.

Chapter 2

Victory in Europe. January – June 1945

A waiting game is . . . the best solution for us at the moment. Weak as we are, it is
obviously a delicate matter to take issue with the strong.
– Charles de Gaulle, writing to Georges Bidault before the San Francisco conference,
17 April 1945 (from the General's *War Memoirs*, the third volume of documents, 237).

The initial success of the German offensive in the Ardennes brought a military
crisis for France at New Year 1945. On 28 December the American General
Jacob Devers, whose Sixth Army Group included de Lattre's forces, gave orders
for a withdrawal from Alsace to the Vosges, to prevent units being cut off by
the Germans. But such a withdrawal meant abandoning the city of Strasbourg
which, as de Lattre explained to Devers, was a 'symbol of the resistance and
grandeur of France'. On New Year's Day de Gaulle wrote to Eisenhower,
asking that Strasbourg be defended, and to de Lattre ordering him to defend
the city in any event. When de Lattre expressed concern over the dangerous
position he would face without American support, de Gaulle insisted that the
French First Army was ultimately under French government authority and must
defend Strasbourg alone.[1] Fortunately independent military action by de Lattre
proved unnecessary because, with the containment of the German advance in
early January, Eisenhower agreed – after meeting de Gaulle and Chief of Staff
Alphonse Juin on 3 January – that a withdrawal to the Vosges was no longer
needed.[2] By early February the Allied advance had resumed and all Alsace
was soon liberated. But de Gaulle had demonstrated in the 'Strasbourg affair'
that he was willing to challenge orders from the Supreme Commander, that he
would defend French interests above all else and that he was prepared to pursue
a military policy independent of his allies.

De Gaulle's argument with Eisenhower was only one example of the
possible strains in Franco-American relations as 1945 began. Whilst de
Gaulle concentrated his attention on the meetings with Churchill and Stalin
late in 1944, France's war effort still relied heavily on American support. De
Gaulle himself stated that America's friendship was vital for the future, even
if the US was not expected to remain closely involved in European affairs
after the war,[3] and French diplomats believed that an American return to
isolationism in future would harm France's economic and security interests.
Henri Hoppenot, in his last report as French Ambassador to Washington,
underlined the need for 'solidarity' with America for reasons of collective
security and economic reconstruction, alongside 'solidarity' with the Soviet
Union for European security and with Britain for the defence of imperial

interests.[4] At New Year a new Ambassador, Henri Bonnet, presented his credentials to Franklin Roosevelt and felt him to be well-disposed to France.[5] But when, on 1 January, de Gaulle pleaded with the President for more military supplies to France he got a lukewarm response.[6] Despite real concern over the Ardennes offensive the Americans still refused to give de Gaulle all the arms he wanted. Bidault was once told by Ambassador Caffery that the latter was tired of attending French military parades to 'see *my* tanks passing with *my* petrol in them'.[7] Another request from de Gaulle for arms was turned down in March,[8] and the French continued to play only a secondary military role in the war in the West. None of this helped to impress foreign opinion: in late March the Moscow embassy reported Russian disappointment with France's role in the invasion of Germany, and the Quai d'Orsay drew up a list of French military actions in an attempt to impress the Soviets.[9] As de Gaulle always feared, a weak role in the war led to a lack of international standing in general. The campaigns of 1944–45 would not expunge the memories of 1940.

France's need for US aid in the economic sphere was as great as that in the military field. In September 1944 Bidault asked Jean Monnet to head the French Supply Council in Washington and it was Monnet who handled the complex but vital business of securing shipments of US goods to France.[10] Monnet had done similar work for France and Britain in the First World War and in 1939–40, and was well-known and respected in Washington. He hoped not only to meet the basic needs of French survival with US supplies but also to improve France's war effort and to begin the work of long-term reconstruction. But these ambitious aims were difficult to achieve. Americans were well aware of France's enormous needs in the Liberation period and knew that French external trade would take time to revive to the point where she could pay for imports. A supply effort named 'Plan A' was launched by the Allies after D-day designed to forestall 'disease and unrest' with supplies of food, clothing and medicines. But the Americans did not want to be made responsible for financing French reconstruction in the long term as this would be a massive and costly exercise. By January 1945 French dissatisfaction with US policy was coming to a head. It was clear that the war would not end quickly, and the French felt that the time for 'emergency' aid was past.[11] In January France complained to America and Britain over both the failure to fulfil supply promises and procurement of much-needed coal by the Allied armies. The Americans and British promised to moderate their coal demands but cited a shortage of shipping as the reason for limited imports into France.[12]

Paris was encouraged in early February by a speech in which Joseph Grew, America's Under-Secretary of State, promised greater military and economic aid.[13] And later in the month France and America signed a 'Master Agreement' governing lend-lease arrangements. For months the French had been pressing for a lend-lease programme valued at over $2 billion, to include some materials and industrial machinery which could be used *after* the war. The principle of supplying such 'long-utility' goods in a programme that was intended for war purposes provoked great debate in Washington, but a deal was finally hammered out on the lines which Paris had hoped for and Monnet later judged that 'France had never concluded a foreign agreement on such a scale'. The Master Agreement included $900,000 worth of 'long-utility' supplies. But

Monnet's memoirs omitted to mention the concessions made by the French in return. For example, France now committed herself in writing to joining an international economic system based on the liberal trading principles which the US advocated. More troublesome were the reduction of quantities of certain goods below what was originally hoped, the extent of US control in carrying out the programme, the knowledge that most supplies would still be for the purpose of prosecuting the war and the fact that 'reciprocal aid' (or 'reverse lend-lease') to be provided by France to the US was made retroactive to D-day. Alphand was even driven to comment, 'We are getting nothing for nothing', but Monnet assured de Gaulle that the agreement would help build up French military power, allow more rapid economic recovery and give France financial independence, and the Interministerial Economic Committee in Paris approved the deal on 19 February.[14] In the US too there was criticism of the Master Agreement. Despite government insistence that this was the way to mobilise France's war effort, Congress saw little need to supply such items as locomotives, fishing boats and mining machinery. As the war drew towards a close US opinion became more critical of the behaviour of its allies – of Soviet ambitions in Eastern Europe and Britain's colonial policies, as well as de Gaulle's independent behaviour and petty insults – and less willing to spend American dollars, however abundant they were, on post-war schemes. Against this background, it was highly unlikely that Washington would be able to continue any 'lend-lease'-type programme after the war.[15] This made it vital for France to resolve her own economic problems.

In early 1945, however, France had barely begun her efforts to reconstruct her financial and economic base. Despite its fundamental importance to France's international strength, opinions differ as to how far de Gaulle interested himself in economic policy,[16] but the General has been much-criticised for his failure to adopt the radical programme put forward by Pierre Mendès-France, his Minister of National Economy. Mendès, one of the few dynamic figures in French post-war politics, advocated a bold policy of sacrifices by the French people (with price controls, higher taxes and controls on government finance) and the development of a long-term recovery programme under the control of his own ministry. The French situation in 1945 certainly seemed to demand radical measures. Aside from the need for structural changes in the economy to create a stronger industrial base, build-up exports and compete in world markets, the budgetary situation was terrible; normal receipts barely covered the demands of the military, and less than half of total government spending; the fiscal system was archaic and inflationary pressures left by the war were a constant menace. But other ministries, especially the Ministry of Finance under René Pleven, opposed Mendès's schemes, and in April he resigned from the government. Pleven argued, and de Gaulle became convinced, that France was too weak in psychological and in material resources to bear the rigours of the radical course. The Finance Minister agreed on the need to stabilise the economy, tackle inflation and reform France's taxation system, but explained to Mendès that 'It is on means, on possibilities . . . that we differ'. For Pleven the natural post-war revival of production and trade would steadily (if slowly) improve France's economic situation in any case, and the government could use specific limited measures to control inflation and improve government finances.[17] Unfortunately, however, such actions did *not* succeed in controlling inflation, which began to run out of control by the end of the year. Problems in the economic sphere would continue to dog France's international policies.

There was an inevitable inter-play too between international policy and the political debate in France. All the main political parties in 1945 saw that France must restore the losses of war and address the causes of long-term weakness in order to play a leading international role. There were certainly differences on France's future foreign policy: whilst de Gaulle advocated the pursuit of Great Power status, Communists were most anxious to maintain Soviet co-operation, and liberal elements were likely to press for a more 'internationalist' role. There were also some criticisms by mid-1945 of de Gaulle's concentration on foreign affairs to the detriment of domestic problems.[18] But for the moment a consensus in government was possible whilst France began the task of rebuilding[19] and, having returned to Paris from Moscow, the Communist leader Maurice Thorez ended any uncertainty in the party by confirming the policy of maximum support for the war effort and for de Gaulle.[20] This policy of moderation brought great dividends over the next few years, when the PCF made a strong showing in elections and won a major role in government. It could be read as a cynical attempt to end the suspicions of the middle class and peasantry about Communist aims. But there was no doubt that Communist good behaviour was vital for re-establishing order and starting reconstruction.[21]

Communist strength and links to Moscow were of concern to the Western Allies however, and not least to the US Ambassador, Jefferson Caffery, who as early as 27 October 1944 had told Washington that, 'As France goes, the Continent of Europe will probably go and it is not in our interest to have the continent ... dominated by any single power – friend or enemy'. This was a similar view to that held by Eisenhower[22] and the need to forestall Soviet influence in France had of course affected both Britain and America in their decisions to recognise de Gaulle and bring him onto the EAC. Whilst insisting on the Provisional Government's ability to maintain order, French representatives themselves also used the spectre of a Communist take-over as a lever to win concessions from the Americans and British.[23] Caffery went on to warn that the PCF was an 'aggressive and militant' group, whose triumph would mean that 'the entire continent ... might fall into the Russian orbit', and he agreed that there was no alternative for America but to support the 'sour puss' de Gaulle. Some weeks later Caffery warned that US economic supplies to France must be maintained, partly to preserve a market for US goods, but also to prevent France falling under foreign domination. Caffery, like Britain's Duff Cooper, was impressed by the Provisional Government's assertion of authority in France and recognised the lack of militancy in Thorez's PCF, but the Ambassador's fear of Communism was strong and lasting. By early 1945 opinion in the State Department was also moving towards the position that de Gaulle must be supported and France's European role strengthened. In part this was simply because de Gaulle was now well placed in power; in part no doubt it was affected by British arguments; but also, with the defeat of Nazi Germany drawing closer, decisions about the shape of post-war Europe had to be made and there was no doubt about the strategic importance of France, if only because of her geographical position at the centre of Western Europe, with an area greater than any European country save Russia.[24]

In late December René Massigli had circulated a note to the EAC in London pressing for a French part in signing Germany's surrender and, more important, a share in both the occupation and post-war control of Germany.[25] This amounted to a French request for equality in German affairs with the Big Three and it was unsurprising that the British representative, William Strang (an old acquaintance of Massigli[26]) expressed support for it.[27] The new US Secretary of State, Edward Stettinius, however also recommended approval of the French *desiderata*. Stettinius even told President Roosevelt that in future America should treat France 'on the basis of her potential power and influence' rather than her actual strength.[28] Nonetheless, action on Massigli's requests was delayed by FDR. A new Big Three conference was now planned, at Yalta, and the President wanted to discuss the French issue personally with Stalin and Churchill.[29]

Paris learnt in mid-January that a Big Three meeting was to be held and the Quai d'Orsay presented a memorandum on the matter to the Big Three, asserting France's importance in war and peace and asking for a share in all Great Power decisions.[30] But, although Anthony Eden told Massigli on 20 January that Britain wanted de Gaulle to attend,[31] Churchill told Eden, 'I cannot think of anything more unpleasant than having this menacing and hostile man in our midst . . .'[32]; and though the Soviets told the French, unofficially, that Moscow favoured de Gaulle's attendance, Stalin's behaviour at Yalta soon demonstrated that he had returned to his contemptuous view of France, seen earlier in the war. Even so, de Gaulle knew 'that the explicit refusal' to let France attend 'came from Roosevelt'[33] and certainly even the pro-French Stettinius shrank from recommending de Gaulle's attendance at Yalta to the President.[34] In a press conference on 25 January the General was oddly subdued about the whole affair: he made it plain that he wanted a share in Allied decisions, but insisted that relations with the Big Three were good.[35] Yet there can be no doubt that he was furious about Yalta.

The Americans did try to placate de Gaulle at this time. At the end of January Roosevelt's special adviser, Harry Hopkins, a master of personal diplomacy who had established warm relations with Stalin, visited Paris *en route* to Yalta. It was Hopkins who had ensured that Roosevelt's 'State on the Union' address on 6 January included positive remarks about France and Henri Bonnet felt that the visit could prove important for gaining a French place in future Allied talks.[36] With Bidault, Hopkins discussed French plans in Germany, US plans for the future United Nations and a new idea for an 'emergency high commission' of the Big Three *and* France to oversee the liberation of Europe, maintaining order, reviving the continent's economy and promoting free elections. Bidault correctly saw the last proposal as a way to resolve arguments amongst the Big Three over the future of Poland, which had become the most divisive issue faced by the Allies. The Paris meetings were friendly enough, but de Gaulle knew that Hopkins' visit 'was supposed to "sugar-coat" the pill' of exclusion from Yalta. On 27 January, with Hopkins and de Gaulle about to meet, Bidault warned the American, 'General de Gaulle believes that Frenchmen always try to please the man to whom they are talking. He . . . adopts a different attitude. He makes no effort to please'. In the meeting, after hearing of Hopkins' desire for closer Franco-American co-operation the General duly launched into an attack on US isolationism before 1941 and insisted that, if America really wished to help France, she must give her more arms and immediate Great Power status. Later, at a luncheon with leading ministers Hopkins raised the idea of a meeting between Roosevelt and de Gaulle after Yalta. Those present felt this would have little good effect, but Bidault put the idea to the General a few days later and he did not seem opposed to the suggestion.[37]

At the time of the Yalta conference it was clear in fact, despite the periodic upsets in Franco-American relations, that the two countries already recognised their reliance on one another in important areas and that, though the US was hugely more powerful than France, Washington could not treat Paris with disdain. Roosevelt may have disliked de Gaulle, but the General's independent behaviour at least showed that France was no US puppet and gave France pride in itself. France may have fared badly in 1940, but she remained vital to the strategic balance in Europe by simple virtue of her size and geographical position. Jefferson Caffery might have been fearful of PCF strength, but this very fact made it essential to support de Gaulle's regime politically and economically. As to the French, they might be disappointed with the scale of US military and economic aid, but they recognised America's importance to world security and to the world economy for the foreseeable future.

Yet, in early 1945, Roosevelt's insensitivity and de Gaulle's pride continued to undermine the desire of the professional diplomats on both sides to improve relations. In early January, FDR was still talking privately of disposing of areas of the French Empire. His latest idea was to give Djibouti, in East Africa, to Ethiopia.[38] That same month he agreed that, to help in the Pacific war, the US Navy should set up a weather station on Clipperton, a small, uninhabited, island, 800 miles off Mexico – which happened to be French. De Gaulle, informed only *after* the Americans landed, was furious and the French military attaché in Mexico City was ordered to go to Clipperton. His chartered fishing boat was not allowed to land but, on 3 February, after a protest from Bidault, Caffery agreed that a French officer should visit the island. The Americans still refused to let France take over the running of the weather station, which remained there until the defeat of Japan. Nonetheless, de Gaulle let the matter rest after February, having once again shown that he would bear insults from no one.[39]

* * *

Despite his disappointment in Paris over the exclusion from Yalta, the conference actually proved quite beneficial for de Gaulle. Though Roosevelt and Stalin competed to insult France in a meeting on 4 February,[40] the British 'fought like tigers for France',[41] and Hopkins, Harriman and others successfully prevailed on Roosevelt to give de Gaulle a share in the occupation and control of Germany. The fact that FDR announced his intention to withdraw all US troops from Europe within two years strengthened Churchill's argument that France was vital for the future military control of Germany in the West. And after the President's change of heart on an occupation zone, Stalin too seemed ready to agree. The French zone would be taken from the areas designated as

British and US zones, however, not from that of Russia.[42] On 12 February Caffery, on behalf of the Big Three, delivered three communications to the French government. First, there was the invitation to share in the occupation and Allied administration of Germany. Secondly, 'in the interests of Europe' France was invited to adhere to a 'Declaration on Liberated Europe', which stated Allied hopes for the restoration of independent states, the introduction of democracy and the creation of economic stability across the continent. Finally, on the global level, France was asked to become co-sponsor of a conference of all Allied states at San Francisco to settle the details of a new United Nations Organisation (UNO). Henri Bonnet, however, had already warned Joseph Grew that France would not 'automatically' accept the Yalta decisions.[43]

De Gaulle in fact was in no mood to be friendly towards the Big Three over Yalta. On 5 February he again declared in a radio address that 'France will . . . be committed to absolutely nothing she has not been in a position to discuss'.[44] He felt that the three communications of 12 February gave 'important satisfactions', but when Caffery returned later in the day to deliver a further, personal message from Roosevelt, the General became incensed. In the new message the President took up Hopkins's idea of a face-to-face meeting with de Gaulle, but the proposal was put in a quite inept way: FDR asked the General to come to meet him on French territory, in Algiers. 'But how could I agree to be summoned to a point of national territory by a foreign chief of state?', asked de Gaulle later. The next day, after consulting his ministers, he called Caffery back, told him it was quite impossible to go to Algiers, and added that Roosevelt was still welcome, as he had been in November, to visit Paris. Accounts differ as to how the President reacted to this message,[45] but the American press, so often pro-de Gaulle during the war, was outraged by the 'snub', which also upset international and some French opinion. Once again FDR's insensitivity and de Gaulle's pride forestalled a possible improvement in Franco-US relations.[46]

Meanwhile the Quai d'Orsay had gathered what information it could on Yalta[47] and concluded, like de Gaulle, that 'the results of the conference . . . are favourable to our interests'. The main need was to clarify some of the Yalta decisions, including the nature of the Declaration on Liberated Europe – Hopkins had earlier led Bidault to expect an inter-allied *institution* rather than a declaration – and the basis on which France would sponsor the San Francisco gathering.[48] Within a few days the Americans, anxious to proceed with the invitations to San Francisco, replied to the French points and made clear that there would be no special Allied institution in liberated Europe: the Yalta Declaration, in itself little more than a high-sounding propaganda-piece, was the best that America and Britain could obtain from Stalin in their attempts to limit Soviet domination of Eastern Europe. The French were disappointed by this, but eventually adhered to the Declaration. Much more divisive were issues surrounding the UNO conference, where Paris not only wanted to reserve her position on the Dumbarton Oak Proposals (drawn up by the Big Three and China in October 1944 to serve as a basis for talks on the UNO) but also wished to put her own proposals forward to serve, on an *equal* footing, as a basis for talks. This new demonstration of France's desire for full equality with her Allies succeeded in upsetting each of the Big Three over the next few weeks.[49]

On 25 February Bidault visited Anthony Eden at the latter's invitation. Eden hoped to improve relations with France by giving a personal account of the Yalta conference. But omens for the meeting at Binderton, Eden's country home, were not good. The British were upset by de Gaulle's recent snub to FDR over the proposed Algiers meeting whilst Bidault, after numerous arguments with de Gaulle, was very emotional, even talking of resignation from his post. He complained to the British that de Gaulle's temper was worse than ever at present because of toothache. Yet Bidault still loyally executed de Gaulle's foreign policy. Despite Eden's insistence that Britain wanted co-operation with France, Bidault argued that an alliance still required agreements on the future of Germany and the Levant, and complained about France's absence from Big Three meetings. He also expressed fears that the UNO proposals would undermine the value of the Franco-Soviet treaty in Europe and affect France's colonial rights in her empire. Eden promised to consult the Americans on French doubts about Dumbarton Oaks, but this, the first visit by a French foreign minister to Britain since 1940, ended with a sense of disappointment.[50]

By late February the Americans were deeply concerned at France's position on the UNO. Stettinius, by the Yalta agreement, was supposed to issue invitations to San Francisco on 1 March. But his officials felt it was impossible for French proposals to serve as an *equal* 'basis for discussion' on the UN with those drawn up at Dumbarton Oaks, because discussions could hardly proceed on the basis of two separate documents. At best France could put *amendments* to the Dumbarton Oaks proposals. The British supported an attempt at compromise and in early March, after a delay in sending invitations, the French and Americans were both ready to accept textual changes in the invitation which would make plain France's right to put amendments to the Dumbarton Oaks decisions. It was the Russians however, who, on 2 March, rejected this idea as 'equivalent to a change in the [Yalta] decision . . .'. Bidault was shocked: he had believed that American and British attempts at compromise already had Soviet approval. The whole affair, though apparently rooted in diplomatic minutiae, ended with bitter recriminations. The Americans, thoroughly exasperated and arguing that the affair had become a Franco-Soviet problem, sent out invitations to San Francisco on 5 March. The French, unable now to act as an inviting power for the conference, issued a public criticism of American behaviour.[51] In mid-March Stettinius bluntly asked Bonnet if France would attend San Francisco with the intention of provoking trouble. And on the 23rd Washington was further upset when Paris published proposed amendments to Dumbarton Oaks. These were notable for asserting France's Great Power status, her sovereignty in the empire, and her right to make bilateral treaties (such as that with Russia) despite the creation of a 'collective security' system. The amendments also proposed to extend the rights of minor powers in the UN, in a bid to strengthen France's standing by making her the 'protector' of small nations. The Quai traced this last policy back, somewhat fancifully, to the ideals of the Holy Roman Empire.[52]

In light of Yalta, public doubts about the US hardened. In September 1944 a Gallup Poll showed that 69 per cent of Frenchmen felt America would be the power which would do most to help France's war recovery. In February, despite the massive scale of actual American assistance, only 24 per cent took this view whilst faith in Soviet aid had risen from only 6 per cent to 25 per cent.[53] And yet it was the Soviets who had finally prevented France from acting as an inviting power at San Francisco, and the Soviets too who kept France from membership of a new body established at Yalta, a Commission to discuss reparation payments by Germany and its allies. The French, with their deep interest in seeing Germany pay for the destruction it had caused during the war, bitterly resented exclusion from the Reparations Commission and raised the matter with the Big Three on a number of occasions. Britain and America were sympathetic, but the Soviets repeatedly argued that France's contribution to the war was no greater than that of Poland or Yugoslavia and that, if France joined the Reparations Commission so should they. With this approach the British and Americans, willing now to treat France on the basis of her *potential* power, and quite unwilling to give a special role to two of Stalin's East European allies, would not agree. The Soviet dictator was perhaps merely trying to ensure that Russia was not outvoted three-to-one on the Commission. But his attitude also showed his low view of France and his appreciation of one particular source of diplomatic influence: the possession of military force. The French warned that they would not be committed to decisions on reparations taken in their absence, but by June, when the work of the Commission began, they had failed to move the Soviets.[54]

The Frenchman who dealt most closely with the Soviet Union during 1945–48 was General George Catroux, who presented himself as Ambassador to President Mikhail Kalinin on 27 February in succession to Roger Garreau. The ex-Governor of Indochina had originally been offered the Moscow embassy in October 1944, but took time to accept it because he had little knowledge of Russia and still hoped for a return to colonial service. De Gaulle told Catroux that his mission was to build confidence with the Soviets whilst protecting French standing and to make the Moscow Treaty the foundation of a common policy between the two states, especially towards Germany. With the Quai's archives still in a poor state, Catroux was forced to glean what information he could about Russia from a pre-war Ambassador, Robert Coulandre, and more recent, pro-Soviet visitors there, Pierre Cot and Maurice Thorez. He left Paris in early February and met Molotov for the first time on the 23rd. The Foreign Minister was reassuring about the need for Franco-Soviet friendship, but Catroux soon found himself being harassed on what would become familiar topics. During an *entr'acte* at the Moscow Opera he was pressured by Andrei Vyshinsky, the Deputy Commissar for Foreign Affairs, to make an alliance with Poland.

Catroux's first meeting with Stalin on 20 March had strong echoes of de Gaulle's encounters in December. The Marshal greeted Catroux quietly in a stark room at the Kremlin, omitted all compliments and drew geometrical figures on a sheet of paper. Stalin insisted that he would stand by the Moscow Treaty despite the creation of the UNO, but he would give no promises about France's future inclusion in Big Three meetings nor offer support for specific French plans in Germany, and he made clear that France could not join the Reparations Commission unless membership was also extended to Poland and Yugoslavia. Catroux soon discovered that even Stalin's commitment to the Franco-Soviet alliance probably said less about his view of France than it did about his attitude towards the UNO. In late March it was announced that the Soviet delegation to the San Francisco conference would be led not by Molotov, but by the young Ambassador to Washington, Andrei Gromyko. Even given Gromyko's ability and later illustrious career, this was a calculated insult to Roosevelt's great project to guarantee future world peace. It was a depressing start to a new diplomatic appointment, especially given de Gaulle's high hopes for Catroux's success, and the Ambassador soon felt doubly discouraged by the failure of the Quai, as he saw it, to keep him fully informed of French foreign policy. A diplomatic bag from Paris, the main source of all sensitive information, arrived only a few times each month and the Soviet Foreign Ministry often seemed better informed than Catroux about events in France.[55] Other ambassadors complained too about the effect of spending cuts and communications weaknesses on the Quai's conduct of post-war diplomacy,[56] but the sense of isolation in a totalitarian state was particularly intense.

Difficulties in Franco-Soviet relations in early 1945 were not enough to bring an improvement in relations with Britain. In January 1945, the British Foreign Office, though eager to rebuild France as a major power and to pursue West European co-operation in the long term, remained upset by de Gaulle's Moscow visit and were not prepared to agree to French policies in Germany and the Levant as the price of an alliance. So far as an Anglo-French treaty was concerned Churchill believed that 'it is for [de Gaulle] to make the proposal, not us.'[57] At New Year the Quai seemed to accept the impossibility of making a treaty, arguing in a circular telegram to its embassies that it would be hard to achieve a detailed agreement on all aspects of relations with Britain and that, in any case, an unwritten *entente* already existed between the two. Ambassador Massigli was not satisfied with this, however, and for long afterwards argued that in early 1945 a great opportunity was lost for establishing a firm Anglo-French alliance. To Massigli it seemed unrealistic to expect Britain, a member of the Big Three, to give approval to de Gaulle's aims in Germany without consulting America and Russia. Stalin too had refused to commit himself to French plans because of Big Three solidarity. But Massigli believed it *would* be possible to resolve the German and Levant problems far enough to allow a formal treaty with Britain. In a letter to Bidault on 9 January the Ambassador argued that the existence of a Franco-Soviet treaty without a British treaty risked both alienating the British and undermining France's independence, by making her reliant on the USSR, a state which was rapidly emerging as the dominant power on the continent 'up to the Oder, Vienna and Fiume'. But Massigli had another worry. Unlike many other observers he did *not* believe that the United States would retreat from European affairs after the war. And once the British realised this he felt they would look to America, not France, for protection. By the end of January Massigli decided it was useless to keep pressing his opinions on Paris,[58] but he told Eden on 22 January of the personal view that agreements on Germany and the Levant should not be made 'preconditions' of a treaty.[59]

Significantly there was some support in the Quai for Massigli's views, especially from Secretary-General Jean Chauvel. Although, in a review of work by the ministry's European section in February, there was reasonable satisfaction with the state of bilateral Anglo-French relations, a note to Bidault of 1 February argued that a British treaty should have been made in December when, alongside the Moscow treaty, it could have boosted French prestige enormously. As it was the Soviet treaty was of limited value in that Russia refused to treat France as an equal.[60] But de Gaulle's radio address of 5 February still put agreements on Germany and the Levant as preconditions for a British pact, and Churchill held to the view that Britain must await a French initiative for a treaty.[61] In February the Quai drafted a British alliance on the same terms as that with Russia[62] (Britain of course already had its own anti-German pact with Moscow) for the Eden-Bidault talks at Binderton, but those talks only confirmed the impossibility of an early treaty.

Many on the British side shared Massigli's concern at the drift in Anglo-French relations. Ambassador Duff Cooper continually hoped for a treaty and the Foreign Office remained concerned about the need to balance Soviet power in Europe if, as Roosevelt had stated, American troops were withdrawn in 1947.[63] The emergence of Soviet power in the East was a major concern in a converstation between Eden and Massigli in mid-March, when Eden told Massigli that it would be valuable to have an Anglo-French pact before the great international gathering in San Francisco. Massigli then recommended negotiations on a treaty to Bidault, pointing to the disappointments over the Franco-Soviet alliance and underlining the need for strength vis-à-vis Russia.[64] In the wake of this Bidault, influenced by Jean Chauvel, invited the Ambassador to Paris, where Massigli discussed a possible treaty with the Quai, then Duff Cooper and, on 3 April, de Gaulle. The General seemed for once to be favourable to the idea, which he discussed with Duff Cooper on the 5th. Importantly de Gaulle seemed to want such a treaty for the same reason that affected Massigli and Eden: he was concerned at increasing Soviet strength. And, although de Gaulle gave no *formal* agreement to the proposal, Chauvel now began to prepare for negotiations with the British in London. It seemed Massigli's efforts would at last be rewarded.

But the hopes for an alliance were dissipated as quickly as they had risen. De Gaulle, whose fear of the Soviets was, for the moment, fitful and who was still determined to be treated by the British as an equal, soon had second thoughts on the question. On 11 April he told Bidault that he still wanted Britain to agree to French policies in Germany and the Middle East before an alliance was made. Chauvel had been too hasty in his preparations, and once again the British were let down. Churchill's doubts about 'running after' the French were confirmed once again.[65] Indeed, in conversation with Duff Cooper late in April, de Gaulle said he agreed with Churchill's cautious approach.[66] Despite the popularity of a British treaty in France[67] there was no Anglo-French alliance in time for San Francisco.[68]

* * *

The great gain at the Yalta conference for France was her inclusion in the occupation and control of Germany. In early 1945 France was defining her aims in Germany more closely. The special studies set up in 1944 to look at policies in Germany were now completed. Officials in the Quai d'Orsay favoured the political detachment of areas from Western Germany see Map 1 based on a Quai memorandum p.47) with three distinct entities: the Saar, in customs union

Map 1.   French Plans for Western Germany, 1945.

The Delimitation of the French Zone

———— International and zonal borders, after July 1945
- - - - Original French claim to a zone, February 1945
—·—·— Länder boundaries within the French zone
NB France obtained parts of Hessen-Nassau, Baden, Württemburg
and Lindau from the U.S.: other areas from Britain.

Map 2.   The Delimitation of the French Zone.

with France; the west bank of the Rhine, under predominantly French military occupation; and the Ruhr area with its concentration of coal and heavy industry, under military occupation and international control. This threefold division became the basis of France's policy towards Western Germany in future, but other possible measures were considered which showed the continuing fluidity in planning. The Ruhr and Rhineland could form a single customs union; the Rhineland might be subdivided into smaller states; British forces might occupy an area north of the Ruhr; and (following a decision by the National Defence Committee in August) certain bridgeheads over the Rhine should, as after 1919, be occupied by the Allies.[69] One note raised a problem with such plans. French occupation forces in Germany would number 165,000 at a time when all available, workers would be required in French fields and factories. To this there was an obvious solution, however – a transfer of German population to France. A transfer of human as well as material resources could be used, to strengthen France at the same time as weakening the German economy.[70] At one point indeed de Gaulle talked of absorbing two million Germans into France.[71] And he evidently did not simply think of using them as labourers. According to Bidault he once joked during a parade by the Foreign Legion, 'There goes the future of German youth!'.[72]

A memorandum of 30 March made clear that the political detachment of Western Germany and the destruction of war industries must be accompanied by the integration of German production into an international economic system, where these resources would be used for the good of all.[73] In April and May the French began to make their detailed views known abroad.[74] But not everyone in Paris was happy about the German policy. Throughout the first half of 1945 the Assembly's Foreign Affairs Commission discussed policies to adopt in Germany and agreed on such aims as the destruction of German war industries, the removal of large reparations and special controls on the Ruhr, Rhineland and Saar. But, as seen in a discussion on 3 May, there were disagreements over whether the Rhineland should form a separate state or be annexed to France and, more importantly, doubts about the practicality of creating an independent Ruhr. Such doubts were echoed in the Quai. When, during a meeting with Alphand and others, Chauvel first saw the detailed proposals for the detachment of Western Germany he claims to have been 'stupefied'. All too aware of France's limited resources, Chauvel asked whether the Big Three would really accept such an 'extraordinary' scheme and whether the plan would not bring a nationalist resurgence in Germany. To this Maurice Couve de Murville had a simple answer: 'If we do not obtain this, we have lost the war'.[75]

Meanwhile negotiations began on bringing France into the German occupation. According to Robert Murphy, Eisenhower's political adviser, a French zone was hastily defined in 1945, with the Americans inclined to give concessions to France to avoid quarrelling with de Gaulle.[76] This is nonsense. Armand Berard, the Counsellor at the Washington embassy, found many Americans such as Eisenhower's deputy, General Lucius Clay, obstructive on the zonal issue[77] which took many months to resolve. Although Massigli had told the EAC in December that France might accept a small zone at first, with later additions,[78] the French Cabinet decided on 5 February to ask for an extensive zone in Germany, as well as an area of Berlin and a portion of Austria[79] (both of which were to be occupied by the Allies on a separate basis from their occupation of Germany). From the British zone in north-western Germany the French hoped to obtain the whole of the west bank of the Rhine, including Cologne. Control of such an area would help in carrying through France's security policy in the Rhineland. (French military planners hoped to establish a defence 'glacis' well within Germany). From the American zone in the south-west, French hoped to obtain the provinces of Baden and the Hesses (see Map 2). These areas lay outside the Ruhr-Rhine-Saar region, and so were not intended for political separation from Germany, but the French hoped to encourage 'particularist' tendencies in them and so weaken any future central authority in Germany. In late November 1944 French military planners had been shocked to discover that the Soviet occupation zone in Germany would lie as close as 140 miles to the French border. Significantly the proposed zonal boundary was partly drawn in order to touch this Soviet zone. This decision may have been designed to help France forestall the spread of Russian influence, or it could have been a step towards greater Franco-Soviet co-operation. It is also important to note that, even before Yalta, France only intended to carve its zone out of areas originally given to the US and Britain. Even de Gaulle feared that France might be asking for too much with its claim, however, and Massigli, who put the proposal to the EAC, shared this fear.[80] These doubts soon proved justified.

Both Britain and America were slow to answer French claims for a zone, which led to long consideration in London and Washington. The British were ready to give de Gaulle much of what he wanted, but *not* Cologne, which was vital for the defence of the Ruhr and commanded the Belgian border: the British would be the occupation power in the Ruhr, and they hoped to use Belgian troops to assist in occupation duties. Eden explained this to Massigli in mid-March,[81] and the British assured the French that zonal borders would not prejudice the possible future separation of the Ruhr and Rhineland from Germany. But de Gaulle continued to demand the control of Cologne, which he called 'the key to our security', until June.[82] As to the Americans, it was clear that they would wish to amend the French claims, mainly because of the need to secure US communication lines from southern Germany to the North Sea ports (the source of supplies from outside Germany) which America controlled in agreement with Britain. If the French zone reached over to the Soviet zone it would straddle the American supply routes.[83] The French appreciated this and in April Chief of Staff Juin made clear that a smaller zone would be acceptable, so long as it included all of Baden.[84] Eisenhower, however – who was told by Winston Churchill to beware of a Franco-Soviet 'combination' in future – wanted to offer a small zone to France and his staff, particularly Robert Murphy, wanted to give de Gaulle radically different areas to those he originally wanted.[85]

It was largely through frustration over the painfully slow process of delimiting a zone that, on 25 April, de Gaulle ordered General de Lattre to hold onto the major town of Stuttgart, which had been liberated by the First French Army, but which de Lattre had been ordered to leave by his superior, the American General Devers, who needed it as a supply centre. The 'Stuttgart Incident' seemed more serious than the Strasbourg incident of January. Eisenhower was appalled that de Lattre, for political purposes, should disobey a military superior in the midst of war and threatened a complete cut in US military supplies to France, but de Gaulle was unapologetic and insisted that de Lattre would stay where he was until French occupation areas were decided; the problem need not have occurred if America had defined France's occupation zone more quickly. Fortunately both sides proved willing to moderate their behaviour. De Gaulle expressed a willingness to let Stuttgart be used by Devers as a supply centre; the Americans, despite later claims in certain memoirs to have forced de Lattre out, allowed the town to remain in French hands until zonal borders were defined.[86] But this new difference with America apparently left de Gaulle pessimistic about the future. Just a matter of days before the end of the war in Europe, in conversation with Jefferson Caffery about Stuttgart, the General not only raised old complaints – about the lack of US supplies and exclusion from Yalta – but also expressed fears of Soviet intentions and commented, 'The British Empire will not be strong enough after this war to count for much. If I cannot work with you I must work with the Soviets . . . even if in the long run they gobble us up'.[87] Such worries over Russia had been growing in de Gaulle's mind for some weeks. The General had *first* raised the danger of Soviet domination with Caffery on 11 April, and had added that US aid might be needed to maintain French independence.[88] This, of course, was at the same time as his flirtation with the British treaty proposal, and of Stalin's decision to send Gromyko to San Francisco. Possible Soviet ambitions were evidently of grave concern to de Gaulle as the war ended.

Whatever de Gaulle's success in holding onto the city itself, the Stuttgart incident did nothing to help France's claim for a large slice of the US zone. In early May the Americans offered to hand over only the southern portions of two provinces, Baden and Württemberg, even though the French had shown no interest in controlling the latter. This proposal answered American concerns over communication links to the north, but it certainly did not provide a basis for the French policy of encouraging particularism in Germany: two half provinces would be quite useless for this purpose, especially since the Americans intended to hold on to the administrative capitals of both Baden and Württemberg. The zone offered by the US did not even adjoin that being offered by the British! Despite French arguments over the following weeks, however, the Americans would make few additions to their original offer, and meanwhile events become pressing.[89] On 30 April, as the Allied armies drove deep into Germany, Adolf Hitler committed suicide; on 8 May came the end of the war in Europe; and on 5 June the four occupying powers formally assumed authority over Germany.

On 20 June de Gaulle reluctantly instructed Bidault to accept what the Americans and the British had offered France,[90] and even then it took until 26 July to define the final area of French control. This delay was largely due to a Soviet refusal to hand territory in Berlin to the French. As on the zonal question, the French sector in the city had to be drawn exclusively from areas previously designated as British and American.[91] The final zonal division was accompanied by certain additional agreements, including an American and British promise 'at a later stage to review . . . the assignment of areas of occupation . . .',[92] but over the following years the French pressed in vain to be given more areas of Baden and Württemberg by America.[93] In view of the difficulties in defining a French zone it is extraordinary that de Gaulle should have written later that 'I myself had determined the areas we would control'. Chauvel considered the shape of the French zone to be 'absurd'.[94] France had gained control of the Saar but the zone as a whole was small and lacking in resources, a hotch-potch of areas known (from its shape) as the 'brassière'. It was not a strong basis for French policy in Germany.

* * *

During the final collapse of the Third Reich French troops had swept across Bavaria into Austria, and de Lattre immediately set out to underline to the Germans that the French had come as conquerors. His men treated the Germans with contempt and his own behaviour soon earned him the nickname of 'the uncrowned king'.[95] De Gaulle himself visited 'The Army of the Rhine and Danube' in late May and was able to see the destruction wrought on Germany. An opinion poll taken at the time showed that 80 per cent of Frenchmen believed France in this moment of victory to be a Great Power.[96] But amongst the elation de Gaulle told the Assembly that 'the end of the war is not an end in itself . . . it is but a start'.[97]

A major boost for France's diplomatic recovery seemed to come with the much-heralded San Francisco conference which opened on 25 April. The conference opened in the wake of a stunning blow to the Allied cause – the sudden death on 12 April of Franklin Roosevelt. Despite their earlier differences de Gaulle received the news with regret[98] and the Quai feared that the wartime Grand Alliance was now threatened. With Churchill past his prime and the Soviets strong in Eastern Europe, the Quai supposed that Anglo-Saxon co-operation with Moscow would be strained; a major force for unity was gone. Importantly the Quai believed France must play a conciliatory role at San Francisco to help the situation. They also hoped for good relations with the new President, Harry Truman.[99] Truman was a little-known quantity in April 1945 but in time the Quai came to see him as a sincere, open man who bore the burden of the presidency well.[100] Unfamiliar with many foreign policy issues, his reliance on State Department advice undoubtedly helped the French: one of the first documents to arrive on his desk was an appraisal of world affairs which advocated the rebuilding of French power.[101] He had also served in France during the First World War and when called upon by Bidault, who was *en route* to San Francisco, on 19 April, the new President spoke of America's 'high esteem' for France.[102]

In their instructions for the conference, Bidault and his delegation were told to assert France's Great Power status, to bid for the support of smaller powers and to protect 'European' interests. De Gaulle hoped to use the UN to associate Washington with European security issues, but as a *realpolitiker* he had limited faith in a reborn League of Nations. Thus he was determined to preserve the validity of bilateral treaties like the Franco-Soviet Pact in any framework of 'collective security', and he insisted that France must maintain her sovereignty in the Empire.[103] The delegation was well aware of the need to maximise the French impact on events,[104] but de Gaulle told Bidault that, with France's strength growing all the time 'a waiting game is the best solution for us';

Bidault need not rush into agreements and must maintain French negotiating positions 'even if an outcry is raised' since 'our most successful moves have been those which have raised the most violent storms' – a revealing comment upon the General's diplomatic style.[105]

Even if he did not share the widespread enthusiasm for the UNO, de Gaulle considered that France 'achieved all that we were most eager to obtain' at San Francisco.[106] France's right to make bilateral treaties (like the Franco-Soviet Pact) was protected; fears that the new conference would interfere with imperial rights and provoke US arguments with France[107] proved unfounded; French was adopted as an official language; various French amendments to the Dumbarton Oaks proposals were accepted (though many were not); and, most important of all, France was included as one of the five members of the permanent 'Security Council' with the power to veto UN decisions. Despite France's refusal to be a sponsor of the conference, Bidault joined the Big Three and China in their private meetings, after 7 May.[108]

The San Francisco conference was also significant for showing further signs of Franco-Soviet differences. After the death of Roosevelt, Stalin had repented of his earlier decision to send a low-level delegation to San Francisco, and instead sent Molotov. But US-Soviet relations remained strained and on 23 April Molotov had been forced to hear a harsh condemnation of Soviet policy in Poland from President Truman.[109] Truman, like Roosevelt before him, still hoped for co-operation with Russia, but strains in US-Soviet relations were quite evident at this time. On 30 April Bidault met Andrei Gromyko, Russia's Ambassador in Washington, who suggested that their two countries could act in concert at San Francisco, and Bidault, keen to act as a conciliator between America and Russia where possible, expressed interest in this idea. But when the two men turned to specific issues there were clear differences between them. Thus, France favoured Argentinian membership of the UN even though Russia condemned the regime there as 'Fascist', whilst Gromyko wanted Poland to join the UN even though France had still refused to recognise the Communist government in Warsaw.[110] A disgruntled Molotov showed his displeasure the following day by asking Bidault whether France still supported the Soviet alliance.[111] On 10 May Bidault informed de Gaulle that Russia seemed 'isolated' at the conference and that her relations with America were 'getting worse'.[112]

In contrast to the difficulties with Molotov and Gromyko, relations with America seemed to improve at this time. In early May President Truman expressed the wish to meet Bidault on his way back from San Francisco and told René Pleven, who was on a visit to Washington, that America wanted a strong France and would do all possible to help her with food and coal supplies.[113] Secretary of State Stettinius told the President that Bidault had been 'fully co-operative' at San Francisco. The Quai too felt that the conference had greatly helped relations with America.[114] Bidault met Truman on 18 May and the President was so positive that he even promised to consider a French part in future Big Three meetings. This was due to the influence of Under-Secretary Joseph Grew, who was determined 'to eliminate the impression that it is the US which is preventing [the French] return to a status of full equality'.[115] In other talks in Washington Bidault requested a French share in the Far Eastern war, won an assurance that French rule would be restored in Indochina after Japan's defeat, and outlined French plans for the Ruhr, Rhineland and Saar. Both Truman and Grew were interested in these plans. Grew even raised the possibility of moving thousands of Polish refugees into the proposed new states in Western Germany.[116] Unfortunately, however, Bidault's closing meeting with Truman on 22 May was soured by a new problem in Franco-Soviet relations: the occupation, by French troops, of the Val d'Aosta in northern Italy.

* * *

Whatever the success Bidault had had at San Francisco it was quickly overshadowed by two international crises which had developed in his absence: one over the Val d'Aosta, which upset the Americans; the other a new Anglo-French clash in the Levant. In both cases de Gaulle tried to use military power to strengthen France's position as the war ended. In both cases France suffered humiliation, and her relations with her Western allies were harmed.

The Val d'Aosta incident arose because of French territorial claims on the Italian border. De Gaulle was always determined to punish Italy for joining in the Nazi invasion of France in 1940, and was particularly interested in annexing areas like the region of Tende and Brigue on the French side of the Alps. The Val d'Aosta was on the Italian side of the Alps, but the French had a possible ethnic claim to it, and there was a local separatist movement there. In September 1944 reports that Valdotians wished to be united with France led the Quai d'Orsay to hope for a post-war plebiscite in the valley, but officials took the view that France could not be seen to pre-judge the peace settlement by annexing such areas.[117] In January, however, the Quai learnt that de Gaulle was studying a possible occupation of the valley,[118] and at the end of the war he ordered that it should be occupied by General Doyen's 'Alpine Army Detachment'.[119] De Gaulle did not, he declared, want to annex the Val d'Aosta but he did want the Italian government to grant special rights to the region. In 1943 France had been excluded from talks on the Italian armistice but the General was determined to be heard regarding the future Franco-Italian border, and his action was intended in part to underline this point. However, the American government feared the French would detach the Val d'Aosta from Italy,[120] and the local American commander ordered Doyen to withdraw.

A situation similar to the Stuttgart incident quickly arose. The French insisted on the limited nature of their aims, argued that the Valdotians' future should be settled by talks between France and Italy, and took the view that troop movements should be decided 'on the diplomatic plane' given that the war was now ended. The Americans (backed by Britain) accused Doyen of disobeying orders from a superior, felt that France was again using military force for political ends and feared that such behaviour would be followed by others – such as the Yugoslavians who had just unilaterally occupied the region of Venezia Giulia in north-eastern Italy.[121]

The situation rapidly deteriorated. By early June diplomatic pressure had failed to move the French and Doyen warned the Americans locally that any attempt by them to set up a military government in the Val d'Aosta 'could have grave consequences' and would be resisted 'by all necessary means . . .'.

Even de Gaulle, in his memoirs, conceded that this was inept on Doyen's part; Couve de Murville, the Ambassador to Rome, found it quite laughable.[122] The US reaction was even worse. A furious Truman wrote to de Gaulle of 'the almost unbelievable threat that French soldiers ... will combat American ... soldiers whose efforts .... contributed to the liberation of France ...', and made the threat that Washington had shrunk from making in earlier crises: all US military supplies to France would be cut off if Doyen did not withdraw from the Val d'Aosta. Some of Truman's advisers, including Leahy, wanted to make this threat public. The Secretary of War, Henry Stimson, felt de Gaulle had become 'psychopathic' and Winston Churchill believed that, if released, Truman's message 'would have led to the overthrow of de Gaulle ...'. But Ambassador Caffery begged Washington not to publish the message, and as it transpired this was unnecessary.[123] Bonnet and Massigli both appealed to de Gaulle for moderation and, writing to Truman on 8 June, the General stated 'there has never been any intention ... to oppose by force the presence of American troops ...'. He offered to send Juin to the Allied headquarters in Italy to settle the affair.[124] On arrival Juin admitted that de Gaulle had mishandled matters and told American and British officers that 'only the Russians will profit if we are ... divided.'[125] In conversations with Caffery and Duff Cooper, Bidault too blamed de Gaulle for the problems and declared that the Val d'Aosta was not worth 'the skin of a cat'.[126] After more military talks French troops were withdrawn from the area which was put under an allied military government.[127] The incident had done nothing for de Gaulle's standing in Washington. Chauvel believed that it had ruined all Bidault's careful work at San Francisco.[128] It had certainly shown America's ability, in the last analysis, to force de Gaulle down in a crisis.

In contrast to the 'serious incident' over the Val d'Aosta, de Gaulle considered events in the Levant a month after VE-day to be 'a major crisis'.[129] The General, in early 1945, still hoped to obtain guarantees for France's 'special position' in Syria and Lebanon with military, economic and cultural rights analogous to British treaties with the Arab governments in Egypt and Iraq. Beside such guarantees he was prepared to fulfil the 1941 promise to grant independence to the Levant states. He hoped to create a better atmosphere for talks by allowing Syria and Lebanon to attend the San Francisco conference.[130] The British too, as the predominant power in the Middle East, claimed to want both independence for the Levant states and respect for France's 'special position'.[131] But they and the Arabs complained when the French Cabinet, at the request of General Beynet, the local French commander, decided to send reinforcements to the area. On 19 May the Syrian and Lebanese governments, feeling intimidated and unwilling to make concessions, broke off talks with the French. On 29 May serious fighting between Beynet's soldiers and the Syrians culminated with a French artillery bombardment of Damascus. By 31 May hundreds of people had been killed and it was at this point that British forces intervened in Syria in force to separate the two sides.[132]

A message to de Gaulle from Churchill on 31 May stated that Britain had acted 'with profound regret' and 'in the interests of the security of the whole Middle East'. Actually the British were concerned to avoid trouble for their own position with the Arabs. But a delay in sending Churchill's message meant that de Gaulle did not receive it until *after* Anthony Eden read a copy to the House of Commons. To the humiliation of seeing British troops march into Damascus, was added the snub of having a personal message read out prematurely in public. De Gaulle, who still suspected the British of wanting the Levant for themselves, believed the snub was deliberate. Outnumbered, the French in Syria had no choice but to withdraw to their barracks, but de Gaulle claimed that the French had already effectively restored order themselves,[133] and he was not inclined to be moderate in the face of humiliation. 'We are not, I admit, in a position to open hostilities against you', he told Duff Cooper on 4 June – in a frank admission of French weakness – 'but you have insulted France and betrayed the west. This cannot be forgotten'.[134]

The General subsequently annoyed Churchill by refusing to decorate British officers, or to see French troops receive British medals[135] and, more worrying for London, he threw 'a pebble in [the] diplomatic pond' on 2 June by suggesting that Russia, alongside the other permanent members of the UN Security Council, should join in a conference to discuss *all* Middle Eastern matters, including British-ruled areas.[136] He maintained this idea for weeks afterwards, in preference to Britain's desire for talks between themselves, France and the Arabs, but the Russians were not willing to upset Britain and America by backing de Gaulle on the issue.[137] Both de Gaulle and Bidault also warned Caffery that the Levant crisis could strengthen Russia's hand in France, but Caffery refused to be intimidated and the Americans, who had supported Britain's intervention and opposed the idea of a French 'special position' in the Levant, felt the best solution to be a mutual Anglo-French withdrawal from the area.[138] More galling for the General, most Frenchmen also took a moderate line. Chauvel and his diplomats felt the whole crisis to be distressing and unnecessary, and de Gaulle was furious at the lack of sympathy he found from the Quai, the press and the politicians.[139] The 'peculiar Jacobins' in the Assembly debated the problem and, though critical of Britain's behaviour, called for talks with the Arabs and for an Anglo-French alliance to be made.[140] On 8 July de Gaulle, having agreed to talks with the Arabs, surrendered control of locally-raised 'special troops' to Beirut and Damascus, and so removed a major source of argument with them. But he still refused to talk to the British.

Far more dramatic and divisive than the Strasbourg and Stuttgart incidents, the crises over the Levant and Val d'Aosta soured relations with Britain and America at an important point, the end of the war in Europe, and after the apparent improvement in French standing at San Francisco. France's diplomatic position had undoubtedly improved in the first half of 1945 with the victory over Nazism, a share in the occupation of Germany and a place among the 'Big Five' at the UN. But relations with the Americans and the British were particularly sensitive if only because they were powers on whom France relied for its very existence at a time when she sought to reassert her independence and greatness in the world. America and Britain might genuinely want French revival, but this did *not* mean that their interests were coterminous with de Gaulle's. They each wished to 'grant' France a major role for their *own* purposes: for the British as a loyal lieutenant, able to bolster London's imperial and European position against Washington and Moscow; for the Americans, already, as a barrier to Soviet Communism in Europe and a vital constituent of both the UNO and multilateral world trading system. But for de Gaulle, the personification of French *grandeur*, a Great Power role was not something to 'earn': it was France's due. He wanted to co-operate with all the Big Three but only on his own terms. For France had her own interests to defend and her own view of future world security, chiefly the maintenance of the French Empire, the creation of an anti-German alliance system and a comprehensive policy to tap German resources for French security and recovery.

De Gaulle was concerned, especially in April and May, over Soviet strength in Europe and, with the British in decline, he apparently appreciated the possible need for US support against Russia. But, despite strains in their bilateral relations, Russia remained geographically separate from France, Thorez's Communists were quiescent and it was the Anglo-Saxon powers whose strength seemed most overbearing. De Gaulle hoped that France herself would soon prove strong enough to resist economic and military pressures from abroad but there were few signs that this would occur quickly. Deep economic problems continued within France. The constitution of the new Fourth Republic had yet to be written. Bidault and the Quai d'Orsay had demonstrated, time and again, their preference for diplomatic manoeuvre over de Gaulle's refusal to compromise and his liking for military force. Against this background it was perhaps not surprising that the General had already considered the possibility of resignation.[141]

Chapter 3

An Uncertain Peace.
July – October 1945.

The provisional Government . . . have at various times publicly stressed the paramount importance they attach to preventing the Rhineland and Westphalia ever again becoming an arsenal, corridor or base for an attack by Germany on her western neighbours. They feel that the final separation of this region, including the Ruhr is . . . an essential condition for the security of Europe and the world.
– French memorandum to the Council of Foreign Ministers, meeting in London, 14 September 1945.

During July 1945 Allied troops in Germany moved to their respective zones of occupation[1] and the Allied Control Council (ACC), through which the four powers would govern the country, held its first session in Berlin on the 30th.[2] The French military had been planning the practical side of the occupation for several months[3] and in Paris the aims of occupation were now clearly defined. Memoranda issued during July hoped for a united Allied front and the enforcement of a 'severe but just' occupation. In the French zone vigorous policies of denazification, political re-education and the punishment of war criminals were to be carried out, and financial costs to France were to be minimised, whilst maintaining a bearable standard of living for the population. In the long term Paris hoped to encourage provincial loyalties in Germany, to decentralise the government, and, of course, to detach the Ruhr, Rhineland and Saar. But it was acknowledged that the French zone itself made little administrative, political or economic sense. It included areas which France was ready to leave within Germany, and excluded those she wished to cut off. In order to achieve their aims in Germany the French would have to work with the other occupation powers, especially Britain which controlled the Ruhr.[4] Economic policies were laid down in an important note by Hervé Alphand's officials on 7 July which set out two principal aims. First, the economic and military disarmament of Germany, and secondly, a transfer of resources, to reduce German potential whilst simultaneously building French strength. The policies needed to fulfil these aims were by now well-developed in Paris and included the prohibition of certain types of industrial production (especially arms industries), the payment of reparations, the use of German labourers by France, the reduction of German living standards below those of her wartime victims and, again, the detachment of the Ruhr, Rhineland and Saar. Importantly the paper also further underlined the necessity of maintaining

Allied unity, for a number of reasons. First, because a long occupation was vital for enforcing French policies. Secondly, because the French did not wish to repeat events after 1919, when Allied unity had broken down and the Germans had exploited the divisions. And finally because of the practical point that the French zone, except for the Saar with its coal mines, simply could not survive as an independent economic entity.[5]

Already, however, French representatives had some doubts as to whether four-power co-operation *would* be effective. As early as 2 June Bidault was concerned at reports of Soviet behaviour in Eastern Germany. The Soviets seemed determined to act unilaterally in their zone, seizing large amounts of goods and material without accounting for them to the other Allies and carrying through such social and economic reforms as the destruction of Junker estates and the redistribution of land. Bidault was concerned that if such actions continued the agriculturally-rich Soviet zone would become cut off from the rest of Germany, creating problems for the more industrialised Western zones.[6] Following more reports on Russian behaviour, a Quai note for Bidault underscored France's need for Allied unity but raised the question of what to do if unity broke down. One possible solution, autarchy in the small French zone, would be difficult for the reason given above: the zone was not economically viable in itself, nor was it a major industrial region. There was thus really only one solution. In the event of four-power disunion, France must seek economic stability in *Western* Germany alone, in co-operation with America and Britain.[7] This was an important consideration for the future. Meanwhile American and British officials in Germany were also concerned at Soviet behaviour. Field Marshal Bernard Montgomery, the British commander, warned London in July that 'there is a complete "wall" between the Russian zone and the zones of the Western Allies . . .'.[8] And Robert Murphy, now political adviser to the US zonal commander, told his French opposite-number Jacques Tarbé de St Hardouin that the omens for Soviet co-operation were not good.[9]

On 27 July General de Lattre's brief 'reign' as French Governor in Germany came to an end, when he returned to Paris to become Army Chief of Staff. His successor, General Pierre Koenig, was a career officer, intensely loyal to de Gaulle and determined to carry through a tough policy in Germany. He had a major impact on France's German policy until 1949. Koenig reported directly to de Gaulle at first, and dominated the administration of the *Zone d'Occupation Française* (French Occupation Zone, ZOF), despite the emergence of potential rivals. A young Civilian-Administrator, Emile Laffon, was sent out from Paris in July and clashed with Koenig many times. Laffon, formerly a lawyer and engineer, co-operated badly with the military and, though he shared their aims of demilitarising Germany and tapping its resources, he also hoped for a reconciliation between the French and the Germans. The result was confusion between military and civilian bodies in Germany until Koenig finally managed to remove his rival in November 1947.[10] In Paris an inter-ministerial committee was set up in July to supervise the German and Austrian occupation,[11] and in December 1945 René Mayer was made head of a *Commissariat-Général aux Affaires Allemandes et Autrichiennes* (Commissariat-General for German and Austrian Affairs) to prepare studies on occupation policy, provide instructions for the zonal administrations and act as an intermediary between Koenig,

General Emile Béthouart (the French commander in Austria) and the various ministries in Paris who were concerned with German policy.[12] But these government bodies failed to prevent a high degree of independence in Baden-Baden, the administrative centre of the zone, and throughout the ZOF Koenig's lieutenants carved out 'fiefdoms' for themselves.

Koenig and his deputy in Berlin, Louis-Marie Koeltz, were both intensely disliked by the Communist Party, who attacked the 'men of Little Vichy' (Baden-Baden, like Vichy, was a spa-town) and the 'capitalists' who accompanied them in the exploitation of Germany. Many others joined in the criticism of the zonal administration which was accused of inefficiency, high living and overstaffing. In December 1945 the National Assembly set up a Commission of Enquiry, against government wishes, into the way Koenig and Béthouart ran their zones. Some of the criticism was justified; much was doubtless unfair. The Army was an easy target for jibes of 'Vichyism', its numbers in Germany were actually cut back from over a million in May 1945 to 75,000 two years later, and there were efficiency and discipline drives. Also the Army did succeed in exploiting German resources as Paris wanted, through a range of activities: by the 'restitution' of goods which had been removed from France under the Nazi occupation; by requisitions of agricultural produce and the enforcement of cash payments to cover occupation costs; by the removal to France of timber, coal, machine tools and even electricity; and by a commercial policy deliberately shaped to benefit the occupying power (over 80 per cent of ZOF exports in 1947 were to France). In 1945–47 in contrast to the Americans and the British, the French found their zone quite profitable, with an $8 million surplus in 1947. The Germans were subjected to heavy taxes, strict rations, a wage freeze, and a general attitude of contempt from the French Army. There was a positive side to the policy, however, particularly with the introduction of a free press, democratic elections to local bodies and a re-education policy which emphasised French and European cultural achievements.[13] Interestingly, like the other occupation powers, the French made use of German scientists and technicians after the war, who were taken to work in France. Some were experts in rocketry, and would help to lay the basis for later French developments in this field.[14]

Whatever policies were pursued in its own zone, however, France's wider German policy relied on co-operation with her Allies. Measures such as the political detachment of the Ruhr, Rhineland and Saar could only be carried out by agreement with the Big Three. In mid-June the French had learnt, however, that the latter powers were to meet again without France, on the lines of Yalta.[15] De Gaulle felt 'renewed irritation' and later criticised the Potsdam conference as marking a major advance for Soviet interests; if France had been there she 'would have defended the equilibrium of Europe while there was still some point in doing so'. But exactly how France could have fared better than Truman and Churchill in controlling Soviet ambitions – short of beginning another war – the General did not say, and the fact was that Yalta had already revealed the likely domination of Moscow over Eastern Europe.[16] At the time the French complained about their exclusion, but after the Val d'Aosta and Levant crises could not realistically expect an invitation to attend. Henri Bonnet raised the issue of exclusion with Joseph Grew on 25 June, taking the opportunity to outline other points of complaint, including France's desire to share in the

Japanese war and her resentment at America's attitude to the Levant crisis.[17] Following this, on 5 July, just before leaving for Europe, Truman made a point of seeing Bonnet to reassure him that French interests would not be harmed at Potsdam, and that France might attend later Big Three meetings.[18] In London Massigli too sought reassurances that French interests would be protected at the conference. But whatever reassurances were given, the main subject at Potsdam was one of essential importance to France – the future of Germany – and that made France's absence doubly regrettable.[19]

Significantly, American briefs for Potsdam dismissed the Val d'Aosta and Levant crises as 'unfortunate incidents', argued that 'our policy of treating [France] on the basis of her potential power rather than her present strength ... should continue'[20] and felt that French plans for Germany 'should be given extremely careful consideration', especially since she would pursue them 'with the utmost tenacity'.[21] Bonnet had believed for some time that the US might be sympathetic to French plans for the Ruhr-Rhineland,[22] and the British too gave the appearance of protecting French interests in Germany. Thus on 30 July, (after a Labour government succeeded Churchill's Conservatives in the British election) the new Foreign Secretary, Ernest Bevin, refused to discuss a Soviet memorandum on the Ruhr, ostensibly because this issue was vital to France. Actually, however, the British had another weighty reason for opposing such discussion: they did not want the Soviets to share control of the industrially-vital Ruhr. Any 'joint administration' in the area would mark a major advance for Soviet interests in Western Europe. This point was to prove of essential importance to international discussion of the Ruhr in future. Members of the US delegation shared Britain's concern over Russian penetration into Germany's industrial heartland and some also questioned the economic and political feasibility of detaching the Ruhr-Rhineland from Germany, on the grounds that it would create economic havoc and lead to a nationalist backlash.[23] Potsdam furthermore saw the Big Three rule out a general policy of 'dismemberment' of Germany into several states. Thus, although French plans for the Ruhr-Rhineland – which did *not* amount to a *general* policy of dismemberment – were yet to be fully discussed, there were already many signs of difficulty for them.

On 31 July, two days before the conference ended, the French were presented with a series of three-power decisions which, as at Yalta, were actually quite beneficial to them. Most important perhaps was an invitation to sit on a 'Council of Foreign Ministers' (CFM) alongside the Big Three and China, 'to prepare treaties of peace with the European enemy states, for submission to the United Nations'. Members of the CFM could only 'prepare' treaties with states against whom they had fought, a point which restricted France to treaties with Germany and Italy; she would not be able to draft treaties with Hitler's Eastern European allies. But to be invited onto the new body was a major step, especially given France's interest in drafting a German treaty. The French were also invited, at last, onto the Reparations Commission and were notified of other Big Three decisions, including a westward shift in the German-Polish border, and a statement of principles on the future political and economic treatment of Germany.[24] In explaining the results of the conference to French diplomats, the British and Americans were at pains to point out that they had defended French interests in the Ruhr by refusing the Soviet desire for discussions. But Bonnet later discovered that Soviet policy on this question had frightened both Anglo-Saxon powers, and Molotov told Catroux that the real problem for French policy in Germany was that the Anglo-Saxon powers opposed dismemberment in principle. There were other differences in the explanations given by the Big Three to the French about Potsdam. Thus an American representative blamed Russia for France's exclusion from the Eastern European treaties, but Molotov told Catroux that he wanted France to take part in discussions on *all* the peace treaties: the important point was that final *decisions* on individual peace treaties should be restricted to those countries which had fought against particular states.[25]

Some of the Potsdam decisions, such as the political principles of denazification and the punishment of war criminals, were easy to accept, whilst others, such as the Polish border changes, were practically impossible to challenge. But two issues did cause debate in Paris. The first was France's exclusion from the East European treaties. On this René Massigli and the Quai's legal department took a similar line: rather than challenge the decision, and risk exclusion from the CFM, France should attend the CFM and raise the issue of the Eastern peace treaties there. The legal department suggested that Bidault had 'a task analogous to that of Talleyrand . . . . at the Congress of Vienna', in that he must bring France back into the ranks of the Great Powers after a major defeat. This interesting parallel revealed a remarkable faith in France's ability to match the Big Three. Then again, if de Gaulle could be Clemenceau, why should Georges Bidault not be Talleyrand?[26]

The second problem, as underlined in a note from the Quai d'Orsay to de Gaulle on 2 August was that, in their principles for the future running of Germany, the Big Three hoped to establish 'central administrations' (soon known, less grandly, as 'central agencies') staffed by Germans and based in Berlin. These bodies would preserve a semblance of German unity, with single transport and financial systems across the country for example, whilst the Allies decided on its future. It was *not* intended that zonal divisions should become the basis for entirely separate Allied administrations in Germany. The trouble for France was that, however limited the role of such 'central agencies', their very existence seemed to suggest that a central government would be recreated in Germany in future. And the recreation of anything like the old German Reich was something which the French had no wish to see. 'There is thus a German state', de Gaulle noted, on seeing the Potsdam plans, 'Inadmissible'.[27] Bidault told Jefferson Caffery of French fears on this point, and added that central agencies could hold another danger: since they were based in Berlin, which lay deep within the Soviet zone, they might become vehicles for Russian influence throughout Germany.[28] De Gaulle and the Quai had of course been growing steadily more concerned at Soviet influence in Europe and Germany, and Bidault's argument could be expected to have an impact on Washington, where fear of communism was strong.

On 7 August Bidault delivered full French replies on Potsdam to the ambassadors of the Big Three. The French accepted all the major decisions but, to emphasise their independence, on every point they made 'observations' or 'reservations'. Thus, on the Polish border it was noted 'that the problem of the frontiers of Germany forms a whole', a clear reference to France's desire to discuss the western borders. On the CFM France pointed out its 'interest' in the Eastern European treaties and, on the principles for governing Germany, France's opposition to any central German government was stated, as was her objection to central agencies which covered 'the whole of German territory, which is not yet defined' – another reference to the Western borders. There was also a general request to know 'if the information which has been furnished ... covers the whole of the results of the conference' and there was a statement that France's policy on reparations might differ from that of the Big Three.[29] Bogomolov complained about the host of French reservations,[30] but the Big Three tried to placate Paris in mid-August by informing her of certain secret agreements made at Potsdam, including a decision not to take reparations from Austria.[31] That the Allies continued to hold back information was discovered by Bidault soon afterwards, however, when he learnt of plans to dispose of the German fleet and merchant marine. In early September the French demanded to be included in talks on this subject.[32]

* * *

Less than a fortnight after Potsdam the Second World War came to a sudden end, with the dropping of two atomic bombs by the US Air Force on Japan. The atom bomb emphasised America's strength on the world stage and at the same time underlined the relative weakness of states, like France, which had been largely cut off from technological advances during the war. Particularly after VE-day in May the French had pressed for an active role in the Far Eastern War.[33] De Gaulle had always been determined to play a full part in the defeat of Japan as well as of Germany, and despite a lack of enthusiasm from the US military, Truman had agreed in principle that two French divisions should be formed to help fight the Japanese. This, however, would not be until Spring, 1946.[34] Now, with the war ended early all France could do was join in signing Japan's surrender and watch the Americans take over the administration of Japan.[35]

Victory in the Far East did open the way for France's return to the colony of Indochina, however. In 1940 Indochina had remained loyal to Vichy and was occupied by Japanese troops with Vichy compliance. In 1943–44 Roosevelt, the great critic of France and of colonial empires, had considered that after the war Indochina should be taken from the French. But British support for their fellow-colonial power, vague French promises of reform, and the move in the State Department towards support for French revival in 1945 put an end to Roosevelt's schemes.[36] When the Japanese took over full control of the Indochinese government on 9 March 1945, being met by unsuccessful local French resistance, de Gaulle claimed to have an active role in the Far Eastern War and warned Roosevelt that a failure to help France in Indochina could drive her into the hands of the Soviets.[37] France's inability, for logistical reasons, to move troops to the Far East by August 1945 meant that Indochina was initially liberated during September by the British in the south of the colony, and the Chinese in the north. De Gaulle feared the ambitions of both these powers,[38] but co-operation with the British General, Douglas Gracey, was good: amongst other actions he helped restore order after anti-European riots broke out in Saigon in late September.[39] General Leclerc, the French military commander, and Admiral Thierry d'Argenlieu, the Governor-General, were able to establish themselves in Saigon and take over responsibility for security in the south by early 1946. The Chinese General Lou Han, who arrived in the north with thousands of troops, dismantled French fortifications and introduced Chinese currency, proved more difficult to dislodge. De Gaulle's agent Jean Sainteny could not negotiate their departure until February 1946 and Leclerc's forces did not enter Hanoi until 18 March. By then, however, it was clear that French rule was threatened not by British, Chinese or American ambitions, but by the nationalist aspirations of the local 'Viet Minh', who had fought the Japanese since 1941 and whose leader, the Communist Ho Chi Minh, had proclaimed Vietnam's independence on 2 September 1945, apparently hoping for American sympathy.[40] Initially de Gaulle, as anxious as ever to see France respected, approved Leclerc's policy of asserting authority over Vietnam by force *before* negotiating with the nationalists,[41] but by the end of the year Leclerc and d'Argerlieu were impressed enough by the Viet Minh's armed resistance to feel that talks with Ho might be necessary.[42]

* * *

The defeat of Japan made a fitting backcloth to de Gaulle's second major overseas journey since the Liberation of Paris, his visit to North America beginning on 22 August. The proposal for such a visit had actually been made by Truman to Bidault in May, and it was indicative of the improvement in Franco-US relations since Yalta that, despite delays, even the Val d'Aosta incident and the Potsdam conference did not prevent the visit from finally going ahead.[43] In preparing for the conference the Quai gave careful consideration to such issues as the need for US economic support, and the dangers of Soviet-American tension in future. Thus a Quai memorandum of 20 July noted both 'a marked incomprehension' between France and America and a growing rift between Russia and America, but pointed out that the Soviets were 'industrially incapable of furnishing us with the equipment necessary to rebuild our industry' and that France *must* therefore co-operate with America. Two weeks later another memorandum suggested that, whilst avoiding an overtly 'anti-Soviet' line, France would do well to portray herself in Washington as an important barrier to Russian expansion in Europe. Already the French were learning how to play the 'communist card' in Washington.[44] It was felt that Truman remained well-disposed to France despite the Stuttgart and Val d'Aosta incidents,[45] and on 10 August Bidault told Caffery of France's 'desire to wipe the slate clean of the past . . . and work with the US as closely as we possibly can . . .'.[46] But one worrying development was that on 21 August, with the war at an end, the US also ended the 'lend-lease' scheme. France, along with other Allied states, would no longer be able to rely on American government 'gifts', but instead would have to deal with US economic agencies and suppliers on a commercial basis.[47]

A large number of briefs were prepared for the Washington visit, reflecting the desire of the Quai to discuss all possible topics with the Americans, from

French desiderata in Germany and the Italian peace treaty, to events in the Near East and Indochina.[48] The German problem was clearly the most vital to the French but in many documents the dangers of Soviet power, and concern over US-Soviet rivalry were apparent. Thus, in the Near East it was vital, the Quai believed, to make clear to Americans that French policy would *not* bring Russia into the region, and that France would co-operate with Britain and the Arabs. A paper on European borders argued that the extent of Soviet power was one of the main issues to resolve in Europe over the coming years, but the Quai hoped for joint action with Britain and America to oppose the liquidation of Western economic interests in Eastern Europe, and it was intended to maintain French cultural links with the area.[49] In an analysis of 21 August, based on America's recent opposition to Yugoslav ambitions in Trieste, Bidault's officials told him that: 'The experience of events in central Europe has shown to Americans that wherever a vacuum is left in Europe the Soviets will exploit it – but that when they meet with resistance they give up their pressure.' This was a remarkably succinct and clear outline of the policy of 'containment' which the Americans adopted against the Soviets after the war – though it was only formally initiated in 1947.[50] The Washington embassy, however, was concerned with the impact of Soviet–American suspicion on French policy in Germany. With the passing of the initial shock of the concentration camp discoveries, Nazism's complete defeat and US possession of the atom bomb, Bonnet felt America was becoming less fearful of Germany, whilst at the same time concern with Soviet policy was growing. The impact of these trends together could prove detrimental to France. Bonnet feared that Washington would not only object to joint four-power control of the Ruhr in future on anti-Soviet grounds, but also that Americans would support a revived economy as a way to undermine the appeal of German Communism, and would support a centralised Germany in order to squeeze out Soviet influence. He therefore argued that France must press forward quickly with its aims in Germany before US policy developed further on anti-Soviet lines.[51] This too was a remarkably insightful paper. A Quai analysis, written a few days earlier, also recognised the danger of a relaxation in American views on Germany and of Soviet-American competition on the subject, but felt that there were still good grounds for French co-operation with Washington. America nominally stood for decentralisation and disarmament in Germany and had shown an interest in the detachment of the Ruhr-Rhineland.[52]

In contrast to Moscow in December, de Gaulle and Bidault were given a lively reception by the Washington crowds. The General later went on to visit New York, Chicago and Canada and everywhere got an excellent press reception. 'I have seen de Gaulle frequently', wrote one reporter during the visit, 'but for the first time yesterday he seemed happy ...'. The British Embassy was equally surprised: 'He not only kissed babies ... but Mayor La Guardia [of New York] ... and the American Chiefs of Staff as well ...'.[53] Sometimes the American reception was over enthusiastic, even vulgar. At a dinner in Chicago (where Alphand found himself on the seating plan as 'Heurv Al'pen') even the waiters seemed drunk and the General, besieged by pressmen and photographers, had to be dissuaded from walking out.[54] But everywhere de Gaulle, Bidault and their party were struck by the prosperity, vitality and self-confidence of the US, a confidence bolstered by the atom bomb, and in marked constrast to the pessimism, poverty and exhaustion of Europe.[55]

A statement at the end of the Washington talks spoke of 'the fundamental harmony between French and American aims in the construction of the post-war world',[56] and much attention was paid in the conversations to post-war reconstruction. At Truman's request the first talk with de Gaulle was dedicated to French economic problems, especially the need for greater coal supplies. This was a promising start, showing the American interest in French recovery and a stable European economy. The second meeting, on the evening of 22 August, saw de Gaulle outline France's German policy in full, including the need to detach the Ruhr and Rhineland, and to avoid a centralised Reich. Truman and his new Secretary of State, James F. Byrnes, were not convinced that the central agencies envisaged at Potsdam marked a step towards a new Reich, however, and in many respects their attitude seemed to fulfil the fears raised earlier about US policy in Germany by Bonnet. For Truman and Byrnes the physical destruction wrought on Germany and America's possession of the atom bomb would prevent any new German menace. They were most concerned that Soviet influence should be kept out of the Ruhr.[57]

These important points of difference were seen again when Bidault and Byrnes discussed Germany and other issues on 23 August. Bidault raised the spectre of central agencies being a vehicle for Soviet influence in Germany, and argued that the agencies must not have authority over the Ruhr-Rhineland if this area was to be politically detached from Germany. But Byrnes again insisted that Germany was in no position to threaten the peace and repeated the danger of allowing Russia into an internationalised Ruhr. Byrnes also raised an idea, originally suggested by Senator Arthur Vandenberg for the four occupation powers to join in a twenty-five-year German demilitarization treaty, but Bidault was not convinced that this promised France security either. There were also signs of difference between the two men on the issue of German reparations. Bidault pointed out that France had received over 50 per cent of German reparations after 1919. She could not expect a similar amount now, but she did want to remove machinery, coal and labour, and she particularly wanted the 'restitution' of the huge amount of goods seized from France during the war. Byrnes was sympathetic about restitution, but spoke of the need for a 'balanced' German economy in terms of imports and exports, *before* reparations were removed. This was the so-called 'first charge' principle. Americans had learnt different lessons from France from the inter-war years and in particular did not want to subsidise German reparation payments to European powers, as they had done in the 1920s when the German economy was kept afloat by US loans. If reparations were removed it should only be from a stable German economy whose trade was balanced.[58] Economists in Paris, however, feared that the 'first charge' principle which was written (albeit ambiguously) into the Potsdam agreements, would seriously reduce the amounts available for reparations.[59]

De Gaulle took the opportunity to repeat French views about Germany to Truman on 24 August, but also raised other points. He talked of respecting 'popular' wishes in Indochina, complained about US support for Britain in the Levant and outlined a mild approach to the Italian peace treaty, which would

66

be the first item for the new CFM to discuss, and on which the Americans also took a moderate line. Despite the Val d'Aosta incident the General said he wanted only minor border readjustments with Italy, supported the Italian claim to Trieste over that of Yugoslavia and, as part of his policy of friendship with Italy, advocated its retention of its largest African colony, Libya.[60] After de Gaulle had left Washington, Alphand remained to discuss economic issues, including increased US coal exports to France, French economic plans for Germany and possible US loans to France in succession to lend-lease. The Americans were ready to increase coal exports but raised a number of difficult, technical problems with the political separation of the Ruhr, including the likely effect of such dramatic action on the economy of the rump German state.[61] Regarding the financial situation they proved willing to negotiate a $550 million loan through their Export-Import Bank (EXIMBANK), in order to wind down lend-lease deliveries gradually and so reduce the impact on France. But it was clear that France would remain in need of further loans in future. Jean Monnet, still head of the French Supply Council, negotiated most of the details of the EXIMBANK loan in September and October. He had told de Gaulle, whilst the latter was in Washington, that France needed a convincing plan for reconstruction and modernisation to put to the Americans in order to win their confidence and so obtain more funds. France could promise Washington that, once on her feet, she would be able to play a full role in a 'multilateral' trading system, to which she made a renewed commitment in the EXIMBANK agreement. But the Americans would also expect other concessions in return for a loan, including perhaps access to French colonial markets. For Monnet reliance on the Americans in future for financial reasons remained inevitable, whatever the differences between Paris and Washington on other issues.[62]

* * *

In September world attention centred on the first meeting of the new CFM, held in London.[63] Bidault left Paris for the British capital on the 8th well aware of the challenge he faced, as the successor to Talleyrand, in seeking a secure place for France amongst the great powers but well aware too, as he told Caffery, that France still lacked economic and military strength.[64] Hardly had Bidault arrived in London, however, than he was faced, with little warning, by a personal initiative from de Gaulle, who had a major interview published in *The Times* on 10 September on Anglo-French relations.

For weeks the new British Foreign Secretary, Ernest Bevin, had made clear his desire for better relations with Paris. Bevin, like the Labour premier Clement Attlee, had been a Gaullist supporter during the war and, in contrast to Churchill, fully shared Foreign Office enthusiasm for West European co-operation as a way to bolster British influence in the world.[65] On returning from Potsdam Bevin told Massigli of his belief in a 'community of interests' with France on the political, economic and colonial levels, and his determination to resolve problems like the Levant.[66] On 13 August the Foreign Secretary, at a meeting with his officials and the Ambassador to France, Duff Cooper, spoke of building up West European co-operation around a French alliance. He stated his readiness to study French plans in the Ruhr-Rhineland and he wanted to discuss a mutual Anglo-French withdrawal from Syria. Importantly, however, Bevin, like de Gaulle in 1944, saw the need to ease Russian fears of an 'anti-Soviet' bloc in Europe before proceeding with Western European co-operation.[67] Massigli, informed of the new policy by Bevin, was much encouraged,[68] and Bidault was told by Duff Cooper that an alliance might soon be possible.[69] But in Paris, de Gaulle remained suspicious of Britain and deeply wounded by the Levant affair. He had told General Beynet, in Beirut, that France's diplomatic recovery and the likely weakening of Britain following Churchill's election defeat, made it unneccessary to negotiate on the issue.[70] In late August de Gaulle rejected Bevin's idea of a mutual withdrawal[71] and, on 7 September, accused Massigli and the Quai of 'muddled' thinking, since withdrawal would both extinguish French influence in the Middle East and justify Britain's intervention there.[72] *The Times* interview outwardly marked a friendlier view of Britain from de Gaulle, perhaps intended to impress opinion in France where a British alliance was still a popular idea. The General, like Bevin, talked of common Anglo-French interests as West European liberal-democracies with colonial empires, each allied to Moscow and seeking co-operation with Washington. But the fundamental point was that de Gaulle still wanted to establish joint policies on Germany and the Levant *before* making an alliance with Britain,[73] and the British were not impressed by the interview.[74] Bidault met Bevin and Attlee at the French Embassy on 10 September and when the Frenchman spoke of de Gaulle's desire for co-operation Bevin bluntly declared 'I'm like Stalin, I want an advance payment'. The Foreign Secretary also warned Bidault on the Italian treaty, 'Don't ask for territories', and told him that as regards Germany, 'I am not against you, but we must advance carefully to prevent a Russian intrusion'.

Bidault found Bevin, the bulky, strong-minded, ex-trade union leader to be 'very different' to Eden, the upper class Oxford-educated professional politician, but the French delegation saw that, unlike Eden, Bevin appreciated the impossibility of proceeding with a treaty before resolving the Levant and German problems,[75] and relations between the two delegations soon improved. Behind the scenes in London Bevin wanted to resolve Anglo-French difficulties[76] and, away from the overwhelming presence of de Gaulle (as at San Francisco) Bidault proved ready to develop a moderate line, at least on the Levant. On 15 September at Chequers, the British premier's country residence, Bidault offered to withdraw French troops from the Levant in return for the recognition of France's 'special position', the possession of a military base, and a general agreement on the 'spheres of influence' of each side in the Middle East. The last point was particularly important, Bidault and Chauvel believed, in order to win de Gaulle over to any settlement: the General must convinced that Britain would not take the Levant when French forces left.[77] Meanwhile Bidault reported the talks on the Levant to de Gaulle only in the vaguest terms.[78] Bidault's general proposal served as the basis for talks between officials over the following weeks which resulted, in early November, in a draft agreement for mutual withdrawal by Anglo-French forces.[79] An improvement in Anglo-French relations, on the level of the foreign ministers at least, could be counted one of the successes of London.[80]

The London conference as a whole, however, was a grave disappointment for France and for world hopes of Great Power co-operation. The CFM opened on 11 September with mixed blessings. On the positive side, without any Talleyrand-like display from Bidault, it was agreed that 'all members of the Council should have the right to attend all meetings and take part in all discussions', though they could only vote on treaties with states whom they had fought against. This meant, despite the terms of Potsdam, that Bidault and the Chinese representative would be allowed to *discuss* all the peace treaties, including those with East European states, though France could only take part in decisive *votes* on the Italian and German treaties. (It was the position which Molotov had set out for Catroux in August.) But on the negative side, when the CFM set its agenda, the French were very upset to find that whilst Italy, as had been expected, was the first item, Germany – the essential subject for France – was placed near the end, even beneath such subjects as inland waterways and the future of the Black Sea straits.[81] In mid-August Bidault had asked Bevin, as host of the London session, to place Germany first on the agenda, and the Quai had later sent London a full statement of French plans for Germany, their worries regarding central agencies and their wish to resolve the issue of Germany's western borders. The British were willing to listen to French views, but the Big Three as a whole had only just discussed German issues at Potsdam and wanted to dispose of the 'minor' treaties, with Italy and Eastern Europe, before returning to the daunting and complex problems of Germany. Bevin had no wish to provide a new opportunity for Russia to intrude into Western German affairs, and Molotov himself was adamant that the Potsdam decisions, agreed to by Stalin, could not be challenged.[82] It was decided to give French views a hearing only with reluctance. Bidault was asked to set out his views precisely, which he did in two memoranda.

The first French memorandum, of 14 September, put the French case for the political separation of the Ruhr-Rhineland for the sake of European security, expressed the fear that central agencies 'would look like the first sign of a rebirth of the Reich', raised the point that such agencies would not have authority east of the Oder-Neisse (in the areas put 'under Polish administration' at Potsdam) and argued that 'if central administrations are to be set up . . . their authority should not extend to the Rhineland and Westphalia'. Thus the French did not oppose central agencies outright, but they certainly did not want their authority to run to the Ruhr-Rhineland since this would create the impression (in contrast to the fate of areas under Polish control) that the region would remain part of Germany. The strength of French feeling on this matter was underlined in the memorandum by the closing warning that their representatives on the Allied Control Council in Germany would veto any decisions which affected the Ruhr-Rhineland until the CFM settled its future. Since the ACC worked by unanimity this was a threat to undermine the Potsdam decisions on the unity of Germany.[83] Even so de Gaulle, who did not see the memorandum before its submission, considered its tone 'feeble'.[84] Bidault was not able to discuss the memorandum until 26 September,[85] when he pointedly read out its closing threat *verbatim* and said he was ready to discuss the Ruhr-Rhineland issue by any means the Council might suggest. Bevin and Byrnes were prepared to let the foreign ministers' Deputies (the officials who handled detailed topics of discussion) take up the problem during the CFM, a course which Bidault favoured. But Molotov, presumably to prevent any serious change in the Potsdam agreements, suggested pursuing the matter through diplomatic channels between the four occupation powers. Significantly there was an interchange between Molotov and Bevin during the discussion in which the former asked to discuss the issue of four-power control in the Ruhr but Bevin refused.[86] It was partly because of British and American fears over Soviet plans for the Ruhr and the arguments this could cause among the Deputies, that Bidault, on reflection, decided that the issue should be pursued by diplomatic channels. He told the CFM on 28 September that he wanted this to be done quickly.[87] Yet again, however, Bidault had displeased de Gaulle who criticised his failure to get a full discussion on Germany in London and argued that, instead of diplomatic contacts with each of the Big Three, France should have insisted on discussing the Ruhr at a special meeting in Paris: separate discussions with each of the Big Three were likely to generate a range of different problems.[88]

The second French memorandum, of 20 September, dealt with German reparations, a problem which the Russians too wished to discuss. In mid-1945 France developed a clear policy on reparations to help weaken Germany and contribute to European reconstruction, as well as for reasons of 'justice'. The French hoped, without causing chaos in Germany, to take coal, capital equipment (such as industrial machinery and locomotives), consumer goods, services (including manpower), German legal rights overseas and shares in German industry as reparations and to remove them quickly so as to prevent a repetition of the delays and resentments of the 1920s. They also wanted investigations to start quickly into the 'restitution' of a wide range of goods – from machinery to works of art – taken from France to Germany during the war. The restitution of 'stolen' goods had been promised by a 1943 Allied declaration and in the French view should include *all* removals, not just those seized by force. 'Equivalent' objects should be taken where items could not be replaced.[89] The memorandum of 20 September was notable for concentrating on restitution rather than reparations and for highlighting French fears that goods that ought to fall under the category of 'restitution' – such as a piece of machinery from a French factory – would find their way into the reparation pool, and be sent to a country other than France. The French interest in adopting this approach was clear. Given her secondary role in the war she could not expect a large share of reparations from Germany. But, if she could get a favourable definition of goods for restitution, this would represent a large volume of material which would be *guaranteed* to France. This point had been emphasised during August when a French delegation, led by the financial expert Jacques Rueff, took its place on the Reparations Commission in Moscow and found that the Soviets proposed to take half of all German reparations, giving Britain and America one fifth each, and leaving France to fight over the remaining 10 per cent for 'other' countries. Although the Reparations Commission proved unable to reach agreement on the complex problems facing it, and broke up in disagreement in early September, the debates there revealed a major difference between France and Russia on reparations and restitution. For, in contrast to France, the Soviets had every interest in obtaining large reparations but little interest in restitution, partly because their 'scorched earth' policy during the war meant the Germans gained relatively little from seizures of Russian goods.[90]

The reparations memorandum, like that on the Ruhr, ended with a warning: if France was not reassured on restitution she would oppose the removal of reparations from the three Western zones of occupation to Russia.[91] This again was a clear attempt to upset the Potsdam agreement, on which the French had 'reserved' their position. At Potsdam, in a complex agreement which reflected the distrust between East and West, it had been decided that whilst Russia would remove reparations from its own zone for itself and Poland, and whilst the Western powers would remove reparations from their zones for themselves and all other Allied powers, Russia should also receive a quarter of all reparations from the three Western zones. In part this was to ensure that the Soviets received due reward for their leading role in destroying the *Wehrmacht*, but in part too it was to ensure shipments of desperately needed agricultural produce to the Western zones from east Germany. Agricultural goods from the East would be 'exchanged', in effect, as the reparations deliveries were made. 'Advance deliveries' of reparations under this system were supposed to begin immediately, although the final amount available for reparations would not be set by the ACC until early 1946. The final amount would not be set as a fixed amount. Instead the ACC would define a 'level of industry' needed in Germany to allow its people an average European living standard. Any industrial capacity in excess of this 'level of industry' would be available for reparations in the form of factories and industrial machinery, which would literally be dismantled and shipped out of Germany.[92] The French threat to ruin this delicate scheme by disrupting the removal of reparations to Russia was little more than bluff, however, since only one factory in the French zone (compared to 16 in the American and 13 in the British zone) had been earmarked for 'advance delivery' to the Russians at this time.[93] Yet again the small size of, and paucity of resources in, the French zone proved a weak lever with which to extract concessions. And in London the French got little satisfaction on their requests. It was thanks to Soviet pressure that the CFM agreed on the need to quicken the pace of preparing a reparations plan and moved the work of the Reparations Commission to Berlin. The ACC was 'instructed to examine urgently the question of restitution' but beyond this the French got no concrete concessions. Both Molotov and Byrnes pointed out the enormous practical difficulties in identifying 'stolen' goods and, although some consideration was given to setting a time limit for the definition of restitution, it finally proved impossible to do this because Molotov insisted on the time-consuming course of consulting economic experts in Moscow.[94]

Apart from Germany the other important issue for France in London was the Italian peace treaty, on which de Gaulle had outlined a moderate position to Truman in August.[95] The main French demand was for border amendments, partly to ensure a more secure border, partly to demonstrate (as de Gaulle also sought to do with Germany and Japan) that France was a victor power and Italy a defeated one. There was disagreement, however, between the Quai and military planners in Juin's *Etat-Major Général de Défense National* (the General Staff of National Defence, EMDN) as to how much territory to demand from Italy. Whereas the EMDN wanted to secure certain military aims, based on the experience of fighting the Italian invasion of 1940, the Quai wished to keep

71

claims to a minimum (principally to Tende and Brigue) to avoid upsetting Italy, America and Britain. De Gaulle had favoured the Quai line in August but in September he seemed to favour Juin, and the French did not finally define a set of claims until early 1946.[96] Nonetheless the CFM agreed in principle, on 14 September, to consider French claims.[97]

Other aspects of the Italian treaty provoked much greater controversy. On the fate of Trieste in particular there were differences between the Soviets, who supported Yugoslavia's claim to the city, and the British, American and French who supported the Italians. The French position on this matter displeased Molotov.[98] More worrying for France, however, was the fate of Italy's colonies, particularly Libya, which General Leclerc's forces had helped to conquer during the war, where France wanted certain border readjustments and whose future was of great significance for France's colonial position in North Africa. De Gaulle feared that America and Britain would favour Libyan independence, a course which could undermine respect for French rule in her colonies and he insisted 'Lybia *must* remain Italian'.[99] This was the position which Bidault adopted in London, but he soon found himself isolated on the issue. Byrnes and Bevin criticised Italian colonial rule and favoured a 'trusteeship' of Libya under the UN. The Americans felt independence could be given after ten years; the British wanted to act as 'trustees' for Cyrenaica, the Libyan region adjacent to Egypt. All three Western powers were terrified, however, when Molotov suggested that Russia should also have a trusteeship over part of Libya.[100] The prospect of Soviet rule in Africa shocked the British, Americans and de Gaulle, who told Bidault that such a course would be as 'disastrous' as Libyan independence.[101] Bidault, however, successfully asked that the issue of Italian colonies be put to the Deputies for study, a course which, given the scale of differences, suited everyone.[102] During the conference the Italian Foreign Minister, Alcide de Gasperi, met de Gaulle in Paris and thanked him for French support over Trieste and Libya. He also expressed hopes for greater Franco-Italian co-operation in future. But he was not pleased by France's border claims in Tende and Brigue.[103]

The ultimate blow to the French in London was that, in early October, the conference broke down over the very issue which had boosted Bidault's position at the start, France's right to discuss all the European peace treaties. By 22 September[104] Molotov had become concerned at the trend in the talks towards division with the British and the Americans, especially over the future of Eastern Europe, and specifically the constitution of the Bulgarian and Rumanian governments. Clashes between Molotov and Bevin were particularly bitter.[105] The French had tried to avoid becoming embroiled in the Bulgarian-Rumanian problem,[106] but Molotov was evidently upset about Bidault's tendency to follow the Anglo-Saxons on other issues, such as the Italian treaty. Bidault's hopes of forming a 'bridge' between East and West had, in practice, been difficult to carry out. On 22 September the Russian told Byrnes and Bevin in a private meeting that it had been a 'mistake' to let France and China into all the treaty talks at the conference. He now wanted to return to a narrow interpretation of the Potsdam agreement and restrict France to discussions on the German and Italian treaties. China's role would also be restricted. Molotov was probably, by this tactic, seeking to divide the Western powers, to extract concessions from them or, failing that, to bring the conference to an end. But Byrnes and Bevin were unwilling to humiliate France and insisted on an appeal to the Heads of Government.[107] This served little purpose, however, since Stalin backed his Foreign Minister.[108] Meanwhile Bidault was informed by Byrnes and Bevin of Molotov's position and was furious. Bidault had dined with Molotov on 21 September and had been given no indication of any problem, though the Russian had criticised France's failure to act as 'a friend' at the London conference. Byrnes believed that attack on France's position hid Molotov's real worries, which concerned Eastern Europe,[109] and Bevin felt the same.[110] The nervous Bidault, however, sensed that France's whole position as a major power was at stake.

On the evening of 23 September Bidault and Molotov had a sharp twenty-minute meeting but the Frenchman was quite outclassed by the veteran Soviet performer, who claimed merely to be acting in fulfilment of Potsdam and made the shrewd step of pointing out that France had not, in her response to the Potsdam decisions, made any 'reservations' about her exclusion from the East European treaties. This was quite correct. After Potsdam the French had only 'observed' that they were interested in the Eastern treaties. But now Bidault made the clumsy error of stating that France *had* made 'reservations'. He even offered to produce a text to prove it. When the two men met again on 25 September the Russian made Bidault eat his words, insisted that 'Molotov cannot modify that which Stalin has decided', and went on to assault French foreign policy, claiming that Bidault supported Soviet policies no more than 'five per cent', referring to recent Paris press reports of a 'Western bloc' and then asking why France kept a representative in Madrid with the right-wing dictatorship of General Franco. Bidault, overwhelmed, insisted that there was no French tendency to support the Americans and British, and that he wanted Soviet co-operation. Afterwards he wrote a selective account of the meeting to de Gaulle, minimising Molotov's insults.[111]

An internal French memorandum at the time actually conceded that Bidault *had* tended to support the Anglo-Saxon case, even on Eastern Europe,[112] but on 25 September the Cabinet supported Bidault's stand against Molotov. It now seemed that the conference could end in deadlock,[113] with René Massigli telling the British politician, Harold Nicolson, to 'imagine the most difficult and suspicious characters you have ever known, multiply the first and treble the second, and you have some idea what this conference is like'. Bidault told Nicolson that the Russians 'hate us'[114] and by 28 September the French felt that the conference was doomed.[115] Numerous meetings between Molotov, Byrnes and Bevin, from which Bidault was annoyed to be excluded,[116] failed to shift the Soviet position, despite a tendency from Byrnes in particular to offer compromises. A number of five-power meetings also failed to make any headway, with Bidault repeating time after time that he could not accept France's exclusion from any discussions.[117] De Gaulle fully backed his Foreign Minister's stance on Eastern Europe but remarked that, since Bidault seemed excluded from any meaningful discussions, he might as well return to Paris.[118]

On 2 October the CFM drew to its close with no agreed protocols, not even a communiqué.[119] World opinion was shocked to find, so soon after the war, that the major Allies could so readily fall out with each other. A disappointed

Bidault, who seemed to one of his officials to 'be at the end of his tether,'[120] returned to Paris wondering how to account for Soviet behaviour but pleased that Byrnes and Bevin had not abandoned him.[121] Most observers agreed that France's right to discuss the East European treaties was the occasion, rather than the fundamental cause, of the London breakdown. More important to Molotov was the need to defend the Soviet case, especially on Bulgaria and Rumania, from the Americans and British.[122] During October, the French felt that Soviet-American tension grew worse. Massigli believed that the Russians were fearful both of the atom bomb and of the global network of military bases retained by America after the war.[123] And, in his annual Navy Day address of 27 October, Truman seemed uncompromising in his commitment to US military strength, the democratic ideals of the Atlantic Charter and the liberal-economic principles of 'multilateralism'.[124] But whatever the reasons for Molotov's behaviour, Soviet contempt for France was worrying. The Russians seemed to want to treat France as a pawn in their rivalry with the Anglo-Saxons. On 7 October *Pravda* criticised France's performance during the war and argued that she had less right to discuss Eastern Europe matters than had Yugoslavia, Poland or Czechoslovakia.[125] This was the culmination of a gradual deterioration in Franco-Soviet relations since the Moscow treaty. Catroux had been disappointed that there was no mention of the Franco-Soviet pact in the Soviet May Day declaration, that France got only a lowly mention in Russia's VE-day announcements and that at the Moscow victory parade in June France received no mention at all. There were also mounting day-to-day problems. The Soviets would not allow French representatives into Eastern Europe (they even delayed a visa to the new French air attaché to Moscow), they complained about France's failure to repatriate Russian POWs, and they seemed indifferent to pressure to get French POWs returned home. The last was a particularly disturbing and distressing problem, since tens of thousands of men from Alsace-Lorraine, which was incorporated into Hitler's Reich in 1940, had been drafted into the *Wehrmacht* and sent to fight in Russia, where many presumably had been captured. But whenever the French press raised the issue Bogomolov would complain to the Quai about 'anti-Soviet' propaganda.[126]

Ambassador Catroux remained most sympathetic to the Soviet case at this time. He felt Molotov's behaviour in London was affected by continuing fears of a 'Western bloc' which had probably been increased by de Gaulle's *Times* interview. Certainly Soviet press criticism of a Western bloc had intensified during the CFM.[127] Catroux, who felt there was a genuine Russian fear of isolation, discussed the state of Franco-Soviet relations with Bogomolov after the CFM and both men agreed that the picture was disappointing. Bogomolov insisted that Russia would help France to control Germany in future, said that the only thing Moscow wanted in Eastern Europe was a system of 'friendly' governments and even tried to play down ideological factors in Soviet policy by claiming that there was a higher percentage of Communists in France than Russia! But Catroux could not tell if this was more than Bogomolov's personal opinion[128] and the general Western reaction to the CFM's breakdown was one of concern, disappointment and confusion. The war had been won, but the peace would evidently have its own difficulties and dangers. For France the achievement of Great Power status – a seat on the ACC in Germany, on the Reparations Commission and on the CFM – had not been matched by a parallel improvement in material power. She remained, by far, the poorest of the 'Big Four', she still needed US economic aid and was unable to have her case on Germany, the key element in her foreign policy, properly heard. Worse still, with the emergence of East-West division came the prospect of unpleasant choices. France wanted US material aid, but Henri Bonnet could foresee American opposition to France's German policy. France wanted good relations with Russia, but the Soviets treated France with contempt and were critical of any 'Western' orientation in her policies. For the moment France shared the hope that the Big Three would resolve their differences and secure a lasting peace. Ideally she wished to maintain her independence in an alliance structure which bound together all the Big Three against Germany. But the London conference showed that the choice between East and West might not easily be escaped.

Chapter 4

The Departure of Charles de Gaulle.
October 1945 – January 1946.

Do you not think that we are once again 'between two wars'?
– de Gaulle, writing to Joseph Paul-Boncour, 7 November 1945 (from the General's *Lettres, Notes et Carnets, 1943–5*, 111.)

In the aftermath of the London CFM the political focus in France was on the first post-war general election set for 21 October 1945. Early in the month, with a view to attracting popular attention before the vote, de Gaulle visited the French zone of Germany and made a series of speeches urging the restoration of ordinary life there, the reconstruction of the economy and the need for the Germans and French to work together 'because we are Europeans and Westerners', though he also urged the separation of the Ruhr and Rhineland.[1] On returning to Strasbourg on 5 October he maintained the theme of co-operation, saying the Rhine must become a force for unity rather than division.[2] He then went on a visit to Belgium where, at Brussels University, he advocated 'a western grouping having the Rhine, Channel and Mediterranean as its arteries',[3] and he told the French press that he hoped for a customs union with Belgium in the future.[4] All this was strikingly similar to the General's Algiers speech of March 1944, and he was disappointed that the French people did not warmly embrace his proposals.[5]

The fact was that French co-operation with Belgium, Holland and Luxembourg had progressed little since 1944. The Belgian Foreign Minister, Paul-Henri Spaak wanted to work with France,[6] the Belgian press were interested in West European co-operation,[7] and the Quai d'Orsay had hoped that the September 1944 declaration-of-intent to form a Benelux customs union would make the Belgians more confident about dealing with France on an equal basis. But Europe's daunting economic problems made a customs union difficult to negotiate,[8] and Belgian officials (most of whom had remained in Brussels during the war) were sceptical even about the Benelux proposal, which made only slow progress.[9] There were advances on the technical side of restoring Franco-Belgian trade, but Spaak was interested in co-operation with Britain as much as with France. There were problems too with the Dutch, who were economically reliant on trade with Germany and thus, in contrast to France, favoured the revival of a healthy German economy. The Quai feared, as early as November 1944, that Dutch influence on Belgium would cause the latter to oppose French aims in the Ruhr.[10] In November 1944 Spaak had visited Paris but the French themselves were then cautious about co-operation with Belgium because of de Gaulle's forthcoming Moscow visit. There was no wish to upset Stalin at that time, of course, on the question of a possible 'Western bloc'.[11]

After the Moscow visit there seemed a chance of improvement. Bidault told the Interministerial Economic Committee that, with a customs union the ultimate goal, a Franco-Benelux 'mixed council' should be formed to develop economic co-operation. A memorandum drawn up by the Quai and the economic ministries argued that a customs union would pay economic and political dividends, though it would need a reasonable 'transition' period and changes in France's protectionist policies, and it could damage certain industries. It was not felt that Britain would join a customs union because of its imperial interests, yet the Quai believed a union would fit in with US views on expanded trade.[12] De Gaulle's radio address of 5 February expressed hopes for co-operation with the Benelux,[13] and later in the month Spaak visited Paris once more. He signed a commercial accord and discussed a possible Franco-Benelux 'mixed council'.[14] A visit by the Dutch Foreign Minister Eelco van Kleffens followed in March,[15] and on 20 March a Franco-Benelux 'Council of Economic Co-operation' was formed. Apart from talks on trade, it promised to provide a forum for discussions on Germany's economic future.[16]

Franco-Benelux economic links caused some concern in London in 1945. Duff Cooper feared the French might concentrate on this area to the detriment of Franco-British co-operation.[17] But the Belgians and Dutch seemed reluctant to move too far towards reliance on France without British approval[18] and the Council of Co-operation actually made only modest progress. Five sessions took place in 1945 and various studies were prepared, notably on coal and steel, with a view to building up Franco-Benelux co-operation, exploiting German resources and making the Council members 'the major furnishers of steel in Europe in . . . place of Germany . . .'. But it was also recognised that Britain and America would have the greatest say in west Germany's economic future and there were clear differences on Germany between the French and Belgians on one side, with their concerns over Germany as a *security* threat, and the Dutch on the other, who saw Germany as an important *commercial* market.[19] On the Franco-Belgian level the Quai was disappointed that Belgium refused to take more French luxury imports.[20] The Benelux states continued to concentrate on the technical problems of their own customs union, the Dutch feared French domination and hoped for greater co-operation with Britain, and Spaak remained reticent about any categorical commitment to support either a customs union with France or detailed French plans for Germany.[21]

A major additional problem for Franco-Benelux co-operation remained the fear of offending Russia. When de Gaulle made his visit to Belgium in October 1945 the Quai recognised that too much pressure for a Western bloc 'would run the risk of offending the Soviets, who distrust any manifestation of occidentalism'.[22] In fact the Moscow press had little to say about the General's German and Belgian visits,[23] but continued to be critical of a Western bloc in general, arguing that it would undermine Big Three co-operation.[24] The Quai remained concerned at Soviet touchiness regarding France's Western links.[25] Late in November *Pravda* even criticised a recommendation from *Le Monde* for a 'policy of equilibrium' as a 'variation' of the Western bloc.[26]

The British too remained cautious about annoying the Soviets[27] even though during the London CFM Molotov had told Bevin that he would *not* object to a Franco-British treaty.[28] Paul-Henri Spaak was disappointed with the lack of British leadership in Western Europe,[29] but other wartime enthusiasts for a Western security system, such as Norway's Foreign Minister, Trygve Lie, who had advocated an 'Atlantic bloc' in 1940–41, also now preferred to play down such notions in favour of the continuation of the Big Three alliance.[30] So it was that, as in Algiers in 1943–44, progress towards radical Franco-Benelux co-operation was hindered by technical problems, bureaucratic doubts and fear of the Soviet reaction.

The failure of schemes for closer Franco-Benelux co-operation was only one example of a general failure to forge strong links to the smaller nations of post-war Europe after the war. In December 1944 an alternative policy for the restoration of French power had been suggested to the Quai, in the form of a 'Latin union' of France, Italy, Spain and maybe Portugal, together perhaps with their African colonies. This was similar to fascist proposals for union in the 1930s, however, and was given short shrift by officials. The interests of the proposed member states were too diverse (Portugal for example was a non-Mediterranean power), their agriculturally-based economies were competitive not complementary, and co-operation with Spain was impossible too on political grounds.[31] The last argument alone would have killed off the Latin union proposal after the war when relations with Spain became a major problem for French foreign policy. Bitter memories of the Spanish Civil War, feelings of guilt over its outcome and frustration at General Franco's survival led to public demands for the *Caudillo's* overthrow and for support for his opponents, many of whom had fled to France. Socialists and Communists were sympathetic to José Giral's 'government-in-exile'. Then again Franco had not joined Hitler and Mussolini in the war, no Spanish army had invaded France, and the regime in Madrid seemed secure. To revive the civil war could prove no more than a destructive gesture, and the Americans and the British (who knew that, if nothing else, Franco was anti-communist) would give no support to such a policy. There was also the practical point that Spain, having escaped the destruction of the Second World War, was a valuable source of raw materials for France and a provider of merchant shipping. De Gaulle tried to steer a middle course in relations with Spain, making a commercial accord with it in September 1945 but insisting that 'it is only on the democratic road that France and Spain can . . . march together'. He told the Cabinet that France should take a 'moral position' on Spain but must hope for a peaceful transition to democracy.[32] But this was not enough for the left-wing parties who increasingly called for a break in relations with Madrid and who treated this issue, at the end of 1945, almost as *the* most vital question in foreign affairs (as can be seen in the discussions of the Assembly's Foreign Affairs Commission.)[33] Eventually, in 1946, this pressure forced the closure of the Franco-Spanish border, making co-operation between the two countries even less likely.[34]

French policy seemed to have a greater chance of fruitful co-operation in the case of Italy, where there were also grandiose ideas for a 'Latin union' in 1945.[35] Despite Mussolini's role in the war many Italians in 1944 hoped for co-operation with France, and de Gaulle seemed ready to take up this idea, with encouraging remarks about Italy in his speech of 28 November 1944 to the Assembly.[36] Yet numerous problems prevented a rapid improvement in Franco-Italian relations. Despite Italy's change of sides in 1943, memories of 1940 lingered. The French were determined in the peace settlement to pursue demands for reparations and restitution from Italy, to demilitarise the Italian side of the border and to make border claims in the Alps (especially around Tende and Brigue) and in Fezzan (in North Africa). The French also wanted to end Italian rights in Tunisia which had existed since the 1896 Tunis convention.

After America and Britain reopened formal diplomatic relations with Rome in October 1944 the Italians hoped for a similar move from France and were ready to give concessions to de Gaulle, such as the renunciation of the Tunis convention and the annulment of the 1940 armistice. But the Italians also wanted concessions in return, including France's abandonment of reparations claims, and these de Gaulle was not prepared to give. The General was ready to co-operate with a democratic Italy and saw the value of Italian aid in countering US and British strength. But he was also determined that France should be recognised as a 'victor' power and that Italy should be punished for its 'enemy' status during the war.[37] Faced by de Gaulle's intransigent approach and fearing the effect of poor relations with France in future, the Italians agreed to change the Tunis conventions without gaining any concessions in return. This paved the way for the appointment of Couve de Murville as Ambassador to Rome in February 1945[38] and the Italians again felt that a turning point in relations had been reached. Premier Ivanoe Bonomi hoped for 'an entirely new relationship' with France and Foreign Minister Alcide de Gasperi believed that co-operation with France was 'the fundamental condition' of Italy's post-war renaissance.[39] But the Val d'Aosta affair marred relations within a few months and even the moderate Bidault supported French territorial claims against Italy in Tende and Brigue.[40]

De Gaulle's desire for some form of Italian co-operation was strengthened in 1945 by strategic considerations, especially by traditional rivalry with Britain and by the growth of 'Slav' influence in the Adriatic, via Tito's Yugoslavia. In July he told the Italian Ambassador, that Italy should play a strong European and colonial role, and act with France as a balancing force to British and Soviet power in the Mediterranean.[41] He particularly saw Italy's position in Libya as a barrier to British power in North Africa. But at every step de Gaulle also wanted to keep Italy in a subservient role. He was determined that France, with its North African colonies, should be *the* dominant power in the western Mediterranean and in all his conversations with Italian representatives he maintained the claim to Tende and Brigue, largely as a 'moral' point following Italy's behaviour in 1940.[42]

By late 1945, therefore, the French recognised that they and Italy had shared values and common interests in the Mediterranean and Africa, that together they should forestall 'the Slav push towards the West', and that they could help each other's demographic problems in that France could absorb Italy's excess population as labourers. But the wartime experience meant that Italy's power must be restored only gradually and that France must be given certain security guarantees.[43] It became clear at the London CFM in fact that, whatever support France gave to Rome on issues like Libya and Trieste, her desire to extract concessions in other areas would antagonise the Italians. Until an Italian peace treaty was completed, relations between Paris and Rome continued to be upset by French demands for such concessions.

Attempts to maintain links with the smaller states of Eastern Europe, notably Poland and Czechoslovakia, also failed to progress far in 1945. In the wake of the First World War, Poland and Czechoslovakia had been vital elements in France's *cordon sanitaire*, designed to hold back Bolshevik influence from Europe. But the Munich conference and the defeat of Poland in 1939 shattered France's reputation and influence in Eastern Europe, and in December 1944 de Gaulle had made the Franco-Soviet treaty as a more effective means to control Germany in future. With the Red Army the predominant military force in Eastern Europe in 1944–45, with Poland and Czechoslovakia (as well as Rumania, Bulgaria, Hungary and, apparently, Yugoslavia) under the Soviet shadow and with the memories of the Munich 'betrayal' still fresh in everyone's mind, de Gaulle seemed to have little choice in his selection of East European allies: if he wished to prevent a further revival of German militarism he must align himself with the Soviet superpower. But the Free French had already entered into agreements with both the Polish and Czech governments in exile in London during the war. The Poles and Czechs had given strong diplomatic support to the *Gaulliste* cause in London, and the Quai d'Orsay had high hopes of recovering influence in Warsaw and Prague when the war was won, as well as of regaining economic and cultural rights in Eastern Europe in general.[44]

French interest in developing co-operation with Poland and Czechoslovakia was clear at the end of the war. On 4 August 1945, the day after Roger Garreau (formerly Ambassador to Moscow) presented his papers as France's new Ambassador to Warsaw, a Quai d'Orsay memorandum reviewed relations with Poland. At the Potsdam conference, which closed two days earlier, the Big Three, after their previous arguments on the issue, had expressed satisfaction with the remodelling of the Polish government, so that pro-Western representatives of the London government-in-exile joined the Communist regime which had been set up under Soviet tutelage. The Big Three had also confirmed a major westward shift in Poland's borders with losses to Russia east of the 'Curzon line' and (in principle) gains from Germany up to the Oder-Neisse river. The French, who now established full relations with the Warsaw regime, were well aware that these changes in Polish government and geography meant the end of Soviet–Polish rivalry and the onset of Soviet domination. The Quai, however, recommended that France should strengthen its representation in Poland, rebuild intellectual and cultural links, and try to defend Warsaw from Soviet pressure, by the use of France's 'good relations' with Moscow. This ambitious hope was tempered, however, by a realisation that Polish policy, under Soviet influence, already had a very unattractive side. In particular Warsaw had asked for the forcible repatriation of Poles in France. A later memorandum, on 29 October, also pointed out the harm being caused to French economic interests by Poland's radical nationalisation policy and the tendency of the Polish press to repeat any Soviet criticism of French policy (for example, stories that France advocated an anti-Soviet 'bloc' of Western powers).[45] Repatriation, nationalisation and press attitudes would continue to blight France's relations with Eastern Europe throughout the period 1945–48.[46]

On 29 October 1945 a memorandum was also drawn up discussing the improvement in relations with Czechoslovakia since September 1942, when de Gaulle had formally denounced the Munich agreement. On 22 August 1944, after considerable pressure from the Czech leader, Eduard Benes, a Franco-Czech declaration had stated the two countries' determination to revive their former alliance. A French diplomatic mission had been sent to Prague soon after its liberation. There had been various visits by French notables, including General Leclerc in July 1945, a commercial treaty had been signed and cultural links were reviving. In contrast to 1938, France now supported the expulsion of Germans from the Sudetenland and the new Ambassador to Prague, Maurice Dejean (previously the Political Director at the Quai) who arrived on 4 December, was a keen advocate of close Franco-Czech co-operation, and argued from the moment of his arrival that the Czechs were well-disposed to France despite Munich. Certainly among Czech leaders, President Benes, Foreign Minister Jan Masaryk, and even the Communist Deputy Foreign Minister, V. Clementis, all declared themselves in favour of co-operation with France, not least over Germany where both countries wanted firm controls on, and reparations from, their former enemy. But, as with Poland, there were problems with Czechoslovakia due to nationalisation policies and Soviet influence in the press.[47] It was significant that, despite the joint declaration of August 1944, de Gaulle had as yet been unwilling to discuss a formal treaty with Czechoslovakia. The French wished instead to see how events unfolded in Eastern Europe with regard, first to Soviet ambitions, and secondly to co-operation among the Slav countries. France had no desire to become embroiled in Czech wrangles with the Slovaks, nor, as had occurred after 1918, in Czechoslovakian arguments with the Poles on such border issues as the fate of Teschen. Neither was there any desire to repeat the Third Republic's mistake of becoming deeply involved in a region where France lacked effective, tangible power – the mistake which had led to the Munich humiliation in the first place.[48]

In the light of these considerations it was unsurprising that most pressure for a treaty in late 1945 came not from the French government but from Eastern Europe, and specifically from Poland. The initial inspiration, however, came from one of the French Communist leaders, Jacques Duclos. It was on 24 August 1945, a year after the Franco-Czech declaration and the liberation of Paris, that the Polish newspaper *Glos Ludu* published an interview with Duclos in which he advocated a Franco-Polish treaty. Duclos's motivations can only be guessed at, but solidarity with a Communist-dominated government was clearly appealing to him, and subsequent events showed that Moscow might have an interest in such a scheme. Rumours that the French wanted a Polish treaty continued to circulate during September and de Gaulle was quizzed about the idea at a press conference in October. He made a vague declaration of amity towards Poland and talked of co-operation against Germany, but he still refused to commit himself to a formal alliance and the Quai d'Orsay certainly had no desire to negotiate a treaty. In any case, if treaties with Eastern Europe were to be pursued, the Quai wanted the first treaty to be with *Czechoslovakia*, not

Poland, because of the August 1944 undertaking to Benes. This was a significant condition because it was the Poles alone, not the Czechs, who continued to press for a treaty at this time.

Early in November the Poles presented a draft twenty-year alliance to the Quai. This alliance was designed to 'amend' that of 1921, in particular by including anti-German, rather than anti-Soviet, clauses. Consideration of such a treaty by Paris was delayed by the French general election, but Polish enthusiasm for a pact continued unabated. On 30 November a clearly government-inspired article appeared in *Zycie Warszawy* in support of a treaty. Officials at the Quai d'Orsay, however, were utterly unenthusiastic about the treaty text with which they had been presented. The text was much more radical than the Franco-Soviet treaty of December 1944. The Poles wanted extensive co-operation on foreign policy issues, their text had hardly any mention of the new United Nations (a reflection perhaps of lack of faith in the new body) and it embodied a guarantee of the Polish borders as defined at Potsdam, even though these were only 'provisional' – so far as the Polish-German border was concerned – until a German peace treaty was formally negotiated and signed. The Quai believed that the Polish initiative was Soviet-inspired; by it the Russians hoped to divide France from America and Britain and, as Stalin had hoped to do in the December 1944 talks, to win French approval for the new order in Eastern Europe. But the French had no wish to become tied to Soviet schemes for hegemony in the East, nor to antagonise the Anglo-Saxons through such a policy. An entirely negative response to the Polish initiative was ruled out, since the Quai *did* want co-operation with Warsaw on the German question, but in the New Year Garreau told Poland's Deputy Foreign Minister, Zygmunt Modzelewski, that a treaty ought to be delayed until the future of Germany, and of its borders, was clearer.[49]

Thus, as in the case of Franco-Benelux co-operation, the emergence of East-West differences hindered French co-operation with the small countries of Eastern Europe. Paris wanted to restore its traditional influence in the East, to regain economic rights there, to establish joint policies vis-à-vis Germany and to limit Soviet predominance in the area, but Soviet power was simply too great, shaping the foreign and domestic policies of the East European states in ways detrimental to France and effectively destroying their independence.

* * *

Despite de Gaulle's visit to Germany in early October, and his emphasis on German co-operation with Western Europe, French diplomatic efforts on Germany in the wake of the London CFM remained centred on the three issues raised by Bidault at the conference – central agencies, the Ruhr and reparations.

Whilst French diplomats began to explain their views on the Ruhr-Rhineland to the Big Three governments, French representatives on the Allied Control Council (ACC) in Berlin carried out Bidault's threat made in London, and vetoed the creation of any central administrations in Germany. Indeed the first veto, of a central agency for transport, had been made on 22 September whilst the CFM was still under way. On 1 October General Koenig explained to his Big

Three colleagues in Berlin that, since France rejected the Potsdam decisions to create central agencies and since talks on the future of the Ruhr-Rhineland were under way between the foreign ministers, support for a central transport system was out of the question.[50] France went on in late 1945 to veto all other attempts at centralisation, including formation of national trades unions.[51] American, Soviet and British representatives in Berlin all criticised the French action, which put at risk the Potsdam principle of maintaining German economic unity under the occupation. Koenig's greatest critic was the American Deputy Governor, General Lucius D. Clay who hoped to establish a stable situation in Germany swiftly, allowing US troops to return home. (As yet, of course, there was no expectation that GIs would stay in Europe beyond 1947.)

Clay took a determined line, arguing that America should form central agencies with Britain and Russia alone, but such an approach did not appeal to Secretary of State Byrnes, or to Britain's Ernest Bevin, who in late September were trying to protect France's position from Molotov at the London CFM. Byrnes and Bevin could hardly defend France in London whilst attacking her in Berlin. There were other considerations. First, French policy was legal. France was not committed to the Potsdam decisions on central agencies, and she had the right to veto ACC decisions. Secondly, America and Britain already saw Soviet actions as undermining German unity, and the Russian zone was effectively sealed off from the others. The British, of course, were also hoping to improve relations with France at this time, and had no wish to introduce new problems to add to differences on the Levant and Ruhr-Rhine. So, both Byrnes and Bevin instructed their representatives in Germany to take a moderate line with the French for the moment, and assured Bidault that they would not press him hard to agree to central agencies yet. The British hoped that French policy would change once discussions on the future of Western Germany began,[52] and Byrnes still hoped to reassure Bidault about a resurgent German menace by discussing the idea of a twenty-five year treaty for German demilitarisation by the four occupation powers.[53] To their worries about centralisation and the future of the Ruhr-Rhineland, however, the French continued to put another worry to American and British representatives: the danger that the Soviets would use central agencies as a vehicle for asserting their influence throughout Germany, thus raising the forbidding spectre of a Russo-German combination.[54] Over the coming years London and Washington would continually underestimate the impact of this spectre on French policies in Germany.

Despite their instructions, neither the American nor the British staff in Berlin were pleased at the moderate policy towards France. On 5 October both Clay and his British opposite number, Lieutenant-General Brian Robertson, appealed to their governments for strong action against the French and warned that, without central agencies, there would be economic chaos in Germany and, in effect, the existence of four separate zonal administrations. But significantly, both Clay and Robertson were also concerned at difficulties with the Russians. Clay even began to consider privately whether it would not be better for America to form central agencies with Britain and *France* – omitting the Soviets.[55] As to the Soviets, they too put diplomatic pressure on France to change her policies. For example, in mid-October Bogomolov warned Catroux that French policy would cause 'chaos' and could even divide Germany 'into two parts'.[56] But

Soviet representatives on the ACC rejected the idea of establishing agencies without France.[57] Like the Foreign Office and the State Department, the Soviets evidently concluded that a moderate approach to the French was best at present.

In the Quai d'Orsay officials *were* concerned that agencies might be formed without them, on an Anglo-US-Soviet basis, and that this might even exclude France from having a say in the future of the Ruhr.[58] But they were prepared to accept this course rather than give way,[59] as Couve de Murville made quite plain to the British Foreign Office late in October.[60] For his part, de Gaulle remained unapologetic about French policy. In a press conference on 12 October he reiterated French aims in the Ruhr-Rhine and, when quizzed about central agencies remarked, 'Consider this: that we are neighbours of Germany, that we have been invaded three times by Germany in a single lifetime, and you will conclude that we want no more of the Reich.'[61] At the end of the month the General told Koenig that, in view of the problems on central agencies and the failure to get a settlement of the Ruhr-Rhineland, France must press on with her policies in her own zone, including the exploitation of such resources as manpower and Saar coal, the revival of local administrations and the development of 'particularism' in the German provinces under French rule.[62] Not all French officials supported a policy of isolation, however. One of Koenig's deputies, Henri Navarre, felt that France's concentration on the Ruhr-Rhineland region left a long-term danger of Soviet predominance over the rest of Germany, and advocated co-operation with the Anglo-Saxons to ensure the triumph of 'Roman' over 'Barbarian' influences in Western Germany.[63]

In mid-October the British, after some half-hearted diplomatic pressures on the French, tried to bring a compromise solution to the central agencies problem, by suggesting a process whereby the German-staffed agencies would operate under close Allied supervision and would be set up 'without prejudice' to the future west German border. Massigli, who was closely involved in drawing up this compromise and who was concerned about alienating the Anglo-Saxon powers, urged Bidault to accept the compromise. Massigli pointed out that French vetoes on central agencies were justifying Russia's independent policies in its zone. But in November, though grateful for British attempts at conciliation, Bidault rejected the compromise proposal as failing to give enough guarantees either about a future central government in Germany or the Ruhr-Rhineland. In Paris it was felt that Russian policy was at least as much to blame for Germany's division as was French policy. The Americans and Soviets had not, in any case, shown much enthusiasm for the British plan and the Quai remained of the view that central agencies carried the danger of spreading Soviet influence over all Germany. De Gaulle put French fears on the latter point dramatically to Jefferson Caffery: 'You are far away and your soldiers will not stay long in Europe ... The British ... are worn out. We can expect nothing from them in the way of facing the Russo-German combination.'[64]

In November it seemed that France had nothing to fear in the way of Anglo-US-Soviet co-operation anyway. Although Clay continued his hard line and now even suggested (to Field Marshal Montgomery) that if necessary central agencies should be formed only between the Americans and the British, London and Washington continued their moderate policy. The fact that French elections were held at this point, and were followed by an uncertain period for the French government, with the danger of growing Communist influence on policy, strengthened the view that threats against France should be avoided. Bevin particularly took this view and ruled out Clay's idea of forming central agencies on an Anglo-American basis.[65] On 24 November, in the ACC, the Russian Marshal Zhukov again ruled out the idea of forming central agencies without France. The French position meanwhile held firm. In late November the Quai dismissed a suggestion that central agencies could be formed and staffed by Allied (rather than German) officials.[66] The French did *not* object in principle to inter-zonal links in trade and communications systems, but they did not believe that central agencies were needed to bring this into effect: co-operation among the Allies individually could achieve it.[67] As far as Paris was concerned, French security was at stake in this matter, France had made her views on both centralisation and the Ruhr-Rhine clear for months, and she was not single-handedly to blame for Allied divisions in Germany.[68] In the New Year de Gaulle told the Interministerial Committee on German and Austrian Affairs that Germany must be re-formed as a confederation, not a Reich. Such institutions as an all-German financial system could only be created after strong *Länder* (provincial) administrations had been formed, each of which could send representatives to a central committee.[69] Meanwhile only US military representatives in Germany seemed ready to put real pressure on France or to form central agencies without her. At a dinner party in mid-December, in the presence of French guests, Clay embarrassed his own staff by launching into an attack on de Gaulle's policy regarding central agencies and explaining how the war had been won by American money.[70]

Although de Gaulle's memoirs oddly have no mention of the issue, it can be argued that by vetoing central agencies France had a major role in dividing Germany after the war, since in the absence of any central agencies the country broke up on zonal lines. The Americans and the British have been accused of sharing the responsibility for this in that – in contrast to, say, the Val d'Aosta episode – they failed to press the French, in any meaningful way, to change the policy of veto.[71] Fear of the French Communists, the feeling that Russia was dividing Germany on zonal lines already, and Britain's desire for a French alliance help to account for the weak Western response. Then again, the Soviets too avoided pressuring the French. This may seem ironic in view of de Gaulle's fear that the Soviets would use central agencies to extend their own influence in Germany. The Soviets, however, could equally gain from the failure to set up central bodies, in that this justified the free hand taken in their own zone. From the French perspective, of course, there were other arguments to justify their policy. The basic point was that France was not committed to Potsdam and wielded her veto in Berlin quite legally. The second was that the French wanted an administrative policy in Germany based on strong *Länder*, without any strong central institutions. But the final factor dictating opposition to central agencies, of course, was the desire to separate the Ruhr-Rhineland from Germany. The French would do nothing to suggest that the Ruhr-Rhine would remain politically part of Germany in future and used the threat of vetoes to goad the Big Three into discussions on the future west German border. And this raises an important question. If the Big Three really wanted to set up central agencies, why did they not quicken their consideration of French plans?

Talks on the Ruhr-Rhine, as agreed in London, were held with all the Big Three in turn late in 1945. Since these were preliminary discussions, in which the French outlined their plans, serious arguments were avoided but it was clear that none of the three powers was fully sympathetic with French aims of creating an independent Ruhr state, whose resources could be used by the Allies. The French were already aware of the argument that political separation of the Ruhr would create economic chaos in the rest of Germany, but believed that Germany could develop such exports as electricity and send its excess population abroad.[72] De Gaulle remained determined in his pursuit of such policies, telling the Quai on 8 October that France could never rely (as she had in 1919) on an Anglo-Saxon military guarantee, that Britain must approve an international regime in the Ruhr and that France must detach and occupy the Rhineland. He warned Bidault to carry out the first round of Ruhr talks, with Britain, 'with great prudence' and to leave 'effective negotiations' for a final conference in Paris.[73]

Talks with the British, vital as the occupation power in the Ruhr, were held by Couve de Murville, Alphand and other officials in London for two weeks after 12 October. There were discussions about a possible political statute for the Ruhr, a separate customs system and the make-up of an international control body, the separation of the Rhineland and Saar, and an occupation of all these areas. But British officials were concerned that French plans could provoke an irredentist movement in Germany and lead to a collapse of the German economy. They were not convinced that the problems of the German rump could easily be overcome, even if, as the French suggested, the presumably huge trade surplus of the Ruhr was used to offset the predicted deficit of the rest of Germany. Instead Britain might be forced to inject millions of pounds into the country to create stability.[74] Massigli felt these doubts were shared by Labour party politicians.[75] Ernest Bevin *did* seem interested in using the Ruhr as a powerhouse for European recovery, but he remained opposed to any Soviet role in controlling the area.[76] As Massigli and the British Foreign Office recognised, Bevin's policy would inevitably upset the Russians.[77] Probably because it was such a controversial point, the French were uncertain themselves about Russia's role in the Ruhr, saying that *all* Allied states should share in the general control of the area but that a narrower group would control the region's administration. It was not clear which group Russia would be in.

Informed of the British doubts, de Gaulle was quite unimpressed, and repeated the need to separate the Ruhr-Rhine. But when Couve de Murville and his officials went to visit Washington, from 9 to 20 November, they faced similar arguments. The Americans had been kept fully informed, by both France and Britain, about the London talks, and shared British concern over the Soviet role in the Ruhr, a possible German movement to regain any separated areas, and the economic stability of the remainder of Germany. The Americans were particularly concerned that the French were determined to remove reparations from Germany and the Ruhr, on the lines of the Potsdam agreement, regardless of the economic impact of the Ruhr's separation on Germany's economic position. Thus, once again, economic doubts, backed by fear of Russia, served to undermine the French case.[78]

In December it was Alphand who journeyed to Moscow for the third series of talks. He arrived amidst continued Soviet fears of a 'Western bloc', a bloc which might utilise the arsenal of the Ruhr for its own purposes. Molotov remained unconvinced by Catroux's insistence that a Western bloc did not exist.[79] In contrast to London and Washington, where Couve had held several long and detailed talks with large groups of British and American officials, Alphand, accompanied by Georges Catroux and an interpreter, held only two meetings, and these were face-to-face with Molotov. In the first, on 12 December, Alphand outlined the French plans and admitted that Britain and America had been non-committal on them, but Molotov only really seemed interested in the question of Russia's share in the 'control' of the Ruhr. Alphand tried to play down the notion of 'control', saying that the area, though occupied, would be an independent state, governed by an international agreement of which Russia, along with France, America, Britain and perhaps the Benelux states, would be a 'guarantor'. Molotov merely promised to study this. In the second meeting, on 22 December, the French put two memoranda forward and tried to instil a sense of urgency into the proceedings, with Catroux declaring 'If the Ruhr is not detached, France will have lost the war, and the United Nations too. The situation of 1918 will repeat itself'. But Molotov still seemed doubtful about the French plans, and pointed out that 'the Ruhr is now in English hands and . . . it is necessary to have their view before anything else'. Alphand was able to discuss the 'English' view with Bevin, who was also in Moscow, at this time, but the Foreign Secretary remained suspicious of Soviet aims and ruled out any idea of the Red Army sharing in the Ruhr's military occupation. There therefore seemed little chance of agreement with both Britain and Russia.[80]

The French hoped in early December that, after Alphand's mission, it might be possible to hold four-power talks on Germany[81] but had to consider the lukewarm response to French plans from all their allies. The Americans and British could evidently accept economic controls on the Ruhr, but not its political detachment; the British were especially fearful of a Soviet share in the region's administration but the Russians were interested in obtaining such a share before anything else.[82] In January Massigli delivered a new memorandum to the British which attempted to answer their doubts on political separation by showing how a trade surplus from the Ruhr could compensate for a deficit in the rest of Germany. Massigli also asked for an early international meeting on the question, but the British were still carrying out their own studies on the Ruhr and the Americans felt the issue was best discussed by the Council of Foreign Ministers.[83]

In France support for the government's policy on the Ruhr was very strong. A Gallup poll in December showed 63 per cent support for the international control of the region. (In January 1945 only about a quarter of people had favoured this course and annexation by France had been the most popular alternative.)[84] But, despite such support and despite de Gaulle's determination to adhere to his bold aims,[85] difficulties with French plans for the Ruhr were quite clear. Following a visit to the French zone in mid-January furthermore, René Mayer sent a letter to de Gaulle which highlighted numerous other problems for French policy in Germany: French policy as a whole was made uncertain by the lack of Allied decisions on such key questions as central

87

agencies and the future Western border; French policy on the Rhineland (as opposed to the Ruhr) was not yet defined in detail and many suspected France of seeking the region's annexation; the future of the Saar was just as unclear; the French still needed to win a transfer of territory from the American zone of north Baden, to help make sense of their policy of 'particularism' in the *Länder*; ideas for encouraging emigration from Germany had not been transformed into policy; and there were serious problems with the organisation of the French zone and the quality of its staff.[86]

There were also difficulties for the French in late 1945 in the field of reparations and restitution. In the wake of the London CFM France urgently needed a definition of 'restitution', of goods removed from France to Germany under the occupation. But it took months to achieve this. In October America and Britain agreed to receive small missions from France and other states into their zones to look for goods taken during the war. But the French had to give advance notice of what they hoped to find and allow for verification once stolen goods were discovered, and the scheme was no more than an 'interim' solution.[87] Talks on the subject were held in the ACC's Reparations-Restitution Directorate in Berlin. Here the French rejected the argument that reparations should be shipped out of Germany speedily, without adequate checks as to whether they included 'stolen' goods. The French, for reasons of 'justice', as well as reconstruction needs, wanted first of all to verify who owned any property to see if it should be treated as 'reparations' or as 'restitution'. For France, who had suffered so much from wartime seizures, restitution should come before reparations. But such arguments led to a clash with the Soviets who wanted a narrow definition of restitution and rapid shipments of reparations, the bulk of which they had been promised. General Clay too disagreed with the French.[88] The State Department and the British adopted a more sympathetic line to the French in November, but only in mid-January was a decision on restitution reached in Berlin, and even then it was quite vague. It allowed for the replacement of goods which had been removed to Germany 'by force', but much relied on the interpretation of the word 'force'.[89] (Meanwhile in November and December a conference of eighteen Allied states, who were to receive reparations from the Western zones, met in Paris to discuss the shares that each should receive, and the French received the third largest share, after Britain and America.[90])

An even greater disappointment than the failure to define 'restitution' swiftly was the failure to define a policy on coal reparations. The problem of coal supplies had been seen as the key to French recovery from the first days of the de Gaulle government. At home the revival of coal production was hindered by transport problems, a shortage of wood for pit props and poor motivation amongst the workforce.[91] The needs of the Allied armies in 1944–45 also increased demands for coal.[92] But even if these problems were resolved France, the world's largest pre-war importer of coal, would need to obtain supplies from abroad, with Germany the most obvious source. The need for German coal was the reason why the Quai d'Orsay considered 'that the mines of the Saar are a necessary complement to the French economy'.[93] Fortunately the Saar lay within the French zone and its resources could easily be tapped. The Ruhr, however, did not. Yet the Ruhr was even more vital as a source of coal than the Saar because of France's particular need for coke-oven coke, vital in the production of steel, which was itself the backbone of the whole economy. In 1929 France had fulfilled less than two-thirds of its coke-oven coke needs from its own mines, and two-thirds of its imports in this essential commodity had come from the Ruhr.[94]

France's urgent wish to resolve the issue of German coal supplies was seen in April 1945 when, a few weeks before VE-day, Bidault threatened to cut off coal supplies to American and British armies unless France was guaranteed both coal from Germany and the creation of an inter-Allied coal supply body. The threat was not carried out because, on 25 April, America and Britain promised to remedy France's coal shortage and to supply coal from Germany.[95] The French were at least able to establish the principle that coal should be taken from Germany as reparations, and importantly coal was removed despite the Potsdam principle that the 'first charge' on Germany should be a balance between imports and exports. Before the war Britain, Poland and Germany had been Europe's largest coal exporters, but the British and Poles now had their own reconstruction problems, making the need for German coal even greater. The Potter-Hyndley Report of June 1945, by two US experts who visited Europe at this time, argued that West German coal exports must be increased 'irrespective of the consequences to Germany' in order to avoid a 'coal famine' in Europe. (This was despite massive shipments of US coal to Europe.) As a result of this Report, on 24 June President Truman sent to de Gaulle and Churchill the text of a proposed directive for the Western commanders in Germany 'to assign the highest priority' to coal exports from Germany.[96] De Gaulle promptly wrote back that the proposal was 'in entire agreement with the views of the French government'[97] and Churchill also agreed to issue such a directive. But, at Montgomery's insistence, the British also introduced an amendment to the directive allowing commanders to keep coal in Germany 'to prevent . . . unrest and disorder'.[98]

A lack of miners, of adequate rations, of pit props and of transport all helped to hinder exports from the Ruhr. True, in early June production stood at less than 30,000 tons per day and this increased to 3.5 million tons per month in November. But in January 1946 production had still only reached 12 per cent of 1943 levels and after that, thanks to ration cuts on the miners, it fell back. Most coal actually continued to be used for military and civilian uses inside German. The French were represented on the European Coal Organisation (ECO), provisionally set up under American pressure in May to improve and distribute coal supplies. But it did not formally come into being until January 1946, was largely made up of Western states (the Soviets refused to join) and was an advisory rather than an executive body. It fell far short of French hopes for close regulation of the coal situation in Europe by a powerful organisation.[99] The US remained ready to help the French. Truman, of course, made this clear to de Gaulle in their meetings in August,[100] and in November Monnet and the Americans agreed to ask the British for higher production in the Ruhr. Three-power (French-American-British) talks were held and the British made promises of improvements. But January's export allocation represented a cut on December's, Koenig remained frustrated at British attitudes to the problem, and by New Year it was clear that French hopes of substantial coal imports from the Ruhr were not being fulfilled.[101]

* * *

The French election of 21 October confirmed the strength of three main political groups. The Communists were strongest with 26 per cent of the vote) but the MRP (25.5 per cent) and Socialists (24.5 per cent) were not far behind.[102] The result made a 'tripartite' government with these three parties almost inevitable. In a referendum accompanying the election the electors also decided, first, that the Assembly should draw up a new constitution to replace the Third Republic, and secondly, that the Assembly should meet for only seven months after which the new constitution would be subject to a referendum. The second vote was a victory for de Gaulle over the Communists, who had not wanted any restrictions on the new Assembly, which they hoped could become a vehicle for unfettered reform. But de Gaulle's difficulties with the Communists continued after the election. The Constituent Assembly met on 6 November but only a week later, after considerable party debate, was the General confirmed as President. On the 15th he began to form a government but Maurice Thorez insisted on taking one of the three main ministries, the Interior, Foreign Affairs or Defence. The General, however, was not about to give the Communists control of the police, army or foreign policy, and he therefore announced he could not form a government.

The crisis was short-lived, because de Gaulle was immediately re-elected as President by the Assembly, with only the Communists in opposition, and it was the PCF, sensing isolation, who gave way and entered the new Cabinet on 21 November, with none of the three main ministries.[103] Though the largest party, the Communists had not outstripped their nearest rivals enough in the elections to dictate their own terms, and clearly could be checked by popular opinion (as in the referendum) or a strong president. Nevertheless the election increased British and US concern at PCF strength. In July Jefferson Caffery had told Secretary Byrnes that the Communists were a Soviet 'trojan horse' (a term he would use again and again) and de Gaulle told the Ambassador on 7 December that 'There are only two real forces in France today: the Communists and I. If the Communists win, France will be a Soviet Republic . . .'. In order for him to win, the General made clear, he would need international successes and economic supplies from abroad.[104]

Over the following six weeks, however, neither international nor domestic success was forthcoming for de Gaulle. Instead, on 7 December, the French received a major blow when their new-found 'equality' with the Big Three was put into question. In Washington Henri Bonnet was called to see Byrnes and told that the Big Three foreign ministers would meet in Moscow, on the 15th, without France. Catroux had warned for some time that the Soviets were not likely to attend another CFM without first obtaining some US concessions[105] and the Moscow meeting was Byrnes' idea to resolve the divisions seen at the London CFM in September. Despite wariness over Soviet intentions in Eastern Europe, the American public still hoped to base world peace on Big Three co-operation and the UN, and had been shocked by the CFM's failure.

Given the importance of France's position to the breakdown in London, Byrnes decided to leave her out of the new talks. The American even made it plain that, if necessary, he would go to Moscow without Britain's Ernest Bevin, who had grave doubts about such a meeting.[106] Byrnes told Bonnet that a three-power conference was provided for in the Potsdam agreements, that it would concentrate on subjects like the Far East and atomic energy and that, at Bevin's insistence, issues of importance to France (such as Germany) would not be covered. But it was clear that future procedure on peace treaties, the issue on which the London talks had broken down and which *was* vital to France, would be discussed. Bonnet told Byrnes that Paris would not be pleased.[107] Meanwhile Britain's Ambassador Duff Cooper saw Bidault to explain the situation to him, and repeated the assurance that Germany would not be discussed at Moscow. Bevin told Massigli that Byrnes had taken the 'road to Canossa'. Bidault was shocked at US behaviour[108] and de Gaulle sensed 'a return to the systematic exclusion of France' from Great Power decisions.[109]

At the Moscow CFM of 16–26 December, Byrnes did succeed in re-establishing personal relations with Molotov, at the cost of giving way somewhat on such issues as the Bulgarian and Rumanian governments. One of the compromises reached was a return to a strict interpretation of the Potsdam agreement on the preparation of peace treaties, so that only those who had fought against a particular enemy state could prepare a peace treaty with it. This again restricted France to preparing the German and Italian treaties. It was planned, however, that all the peace treaties should be discussed by *all* UN states at a peace conference, to be held after 1 May. And, in order to tempt France to accept this process, the Big Three offered to hold the peace conference in Paris, which would thereby have its status as a major diplomatic capital confirmed. The British, though not as pleased with the conference results as Byrnes, felt that France was given the best possible deal.[110]

Byrnes and Bevin sent a copy of the Moscow agreement to Bidault before the conference ended but the Christmas holiday, and a devaluation of the franc, at this point meant that a Cabinet discussion on the issue was not held until 28 December. Bidault told Caffery that, though resentful, de Gaulle would 'go along' and the Big Three decisions.[111] 28 December however, happened to be the day that Bidault married the deputy head of his *cabinet*, Suzanne Borel. The Foreign Minister indeed rushed straight from the wedding ceremony to the Cabinet meeting, but still annoyed de Gaulle by arriving late. (Mme. Bidault returned to her office at the Quai!) Nervously Bidault explained the Moscow decisions to ministers, expressed disappointment with them, but recommended that France accept them under protest. De Gaulle, however, was furious, arguing that France could not be treated like 'Ethiopia' and must have a role in preparing all European peace treaties since 'Europe is essentially Russia and France'; Bidault's approach, he said, showed the weak-mindedness of the Quai. Unless the Allies gave reassurances to France on the future role of a *five*-power CFM (with France and China), and promised effective powers for the proposed peace conference, de Gaulle wanted to reject the Moscow decisions. Despite support for Bidault from Thorez (who stood by the Soviet position on this, as on other issues) it was agreed to draw up a reply to the Big Three on de Gaulle's lines.

Bidault then left Paris for a week in Lugano, after giving Jean Chauvel an extremely vague account of the Cabinet meeting. It took some time for the Quai to clarify what had been decided there.[112] Only on 3 January, after further vain protests in the Cabinet from Thorez,[113] did Francisque Gay, the acting Foreign Minister in Bidault's absence, send a message to the Big Three enquiring about the future of the five-power CFM and the powers of the peace conference. The Big Three replied in mid-January that the CFM would continue to meet on a five-power basis in future, that France could put memoranda forward even on treaties she would not sign, and that the peace conference would allow genuine discussions on all the treaties. On 17 January the French accepted these assurances and the next day Couve de Murville went to London to help the foreign ministers' Deputies begin work on drafting treaties for the next CFM, which would meet in Paris in April.[114]

Even if France had ultimately accepted the Moscow decisions, however, at the start of 1945 relations with each of the Big Three seemed as mixed as ever. Byrnes' behaviour over the Moscow conference had been especially distressing and relations with Russia in December 1945 seemed much worse than a year before. Although Catroux felt that, by reassuring the Soviets about a 'Western bloc', by seeking links to Eastern Europe and by offering co-operation on Germany, France could work towards co-operation with Russia, *Pravda* bore no mention of the first anniversary of the Franco-Soviet alliance. Instead it included an article by Pierre Cot, critical of French policy.[115] Relations with the British for a time seemed rather better. On 20 November Massigli had optimistically told Bidault that a settlement of differences on the Levant and a general agreement on the Ruhr–Rhine could pave the way to a British treaty quite quickly.[116] And in the wake of Britain's defence of French interests at the Moscow conference, opinion in the Quai felt there was an opportunity to work closely with Bevin, who seemed to want to turn 'towards the old countries of Western Europe, towards those who represent a tradition of Christianity and humanism, those for whom the word liberty still keeps its meaning'.[117] On 13 December, furthermore, the two countries signed an agreement for mutual withdrawal from the Levant states, together with a vaguely-worded general agreement on areas of interest in the Middle East, such as had been discussed by Bidault in London in September.

The spirit of Anglo-French co-operation did not last long, however. In January even relations with Britain were soured, when the Levant agreement rapidly broke down, criticised by the Arabs, who saw it as a European attempt to foist a settlement on them, and by de Gaulle. The agreement had an important contradiction which only became clear once Anglo-French military talks on putting it into effect began (in Beirut). To de Gaulle, whose easy acceptance of the agreement had surprised Bidault and the British, the agreement had seemed to mean that *all* British forces would leave Syria and Lebanon, whilst a token French force remained until, as was hoped, a French military base was established there under UN auspices. (A military base, probably in Beirut, was one of the concessions de Gaulle had always wanted in the Levant from the Arabs.) But the British, insisting fully on the principle of mutual withdrawal, now said that a token British force must also remain in Lebanon alongside the French. De Gaulle, convinced that Bidault, Chauvel and Massigli had been fooled, broke off the agreement on 7 January[118] and attacked British policy in the Cabinet as representing 'their old policy of rivalry with us'.[119]

In Paris a lengthy Assembly debate on international policy on 15–17 January highlighted the fact that de Gaulle's problems in foreign affairs were not only with the Big Three. Speeches showed significant differences between the main political parties about the international scene. For the Socialists, Daniel Mayer spoke of the need to base France's reputation on democracy and morality as well as on such traditional indices as armed forces and size of population. He wanted France to oppose bloc politics, to support disarmament in the UN and, in co-operation with America and Russia, to build 'a federation of free peoples' across Europe, beginning with the West European democracies. The Socialists also showed a desire to reduce French armed forces and to seek reconciliation with Germany. Florimond Bonte, however, for the Communists, condemned those 'perfectionnistes' who believed that the UN alone could guarantee peace, criticised those who wished to revive Germany and divide Russia from Britain and America, and called for the maintenance of the Big Three alliance and a harsh policy towards Germany, as the true basis of peace. Amidst much barracking he even accused the French people of showing 'jealousy' over their recent exclusion from the Moscow conference. Bidault, about to leave for the first regular session of the UN in London, gave a lengthy explanation of government policies on such issues as Germany and Spain and, amongst other points, denied that the Ruhr would be used to arm a 'Western bloc.' He did not reject the idea of a 'moral' role for France, nor deny the desirability of Big Three co-operation, but he took a *Gaulliste* line on the need for French economic and military strength and her inclusion in all major decision-making.[120]

There were many other problems for de Gaulle at this point. On 26 December the franc had been devalued, a reflection of France's continued financial weakness. A threatened strike by civil servants at the same time was avoided, partly thanks to the efforts of Thorez, but at New Year the General was deeply upset over an attempt by the Socialists and Communists to cut back defence spending in the budget debate. And there was the growing realisation, as work on a new constitution began, that de Gaulle might not be able to enforce his desire for a strong presidency in future. It was against this background that, in January, whilst on several days holiday in the Antibes – his first holiday for many years – de Gaulle decided that he would resign.[121] After returning to Paris on the 14th he warned some individuals of his intentions, but swore them to secrecy.[122] On the 20th he called all available ministers to his offices at the defence ministry in the Rue St Dominique, entered the room in uniform, and in a short statement announced that, the distasteful *régime des parties* having returned, he was departing. The ministers were stunned and said nothing before the General left to join his family at Neuilly, where he refused to be contacted.[123]

Rumours of de Gaulle's likely departure were not new. In mid-1945 especially there were many who expected that, tired and disappointed at the trend in domestic and foreign affairs, he might quit office.[124] And in November, of course, he had used the threat of resignation to keep the PCF in order. But when the resignation actually came it took most observers by surprise. Jefferson Caffery was warned what might occur by Gaston Palewski, the head of de

Gaulle's *cabinet*, but Duff Cooper completely failed to predict the event.[125] As to the justification for the action, the argument used in de Gaulle's formal letter of resignation to the Assembly President, Félix Gouin, was that the General, his historic mission completed during the war, always intended to retire once 'the political parties were in a position to take up their responsibilities' and 'France, after immense trials, [was] no longer in danger'.[126] Even some close to de Gaulle knew that this view reflected 'artificial optimism' by him, however, and feared that, putting his own ambition before France, he had abandoned her in time of crisis.[127] A more convincing explanation of the resignation is that de Gaulle, his myth tarnished by the failure to overcome France's economic, political and international weakness, had decided to retire in order to reinforce the idea of his indispensability: once the political parties had failed to deal with France's problems he would be recalled to power by popular acclaim.

If de Gaulle did expect this, his hopes proved ill-founded. Ministers like Georges Bidault had little desire to see the General return. 'If only you knew how he treats us; us, his ministers!',[128] Bidault had complained to one of de Gaulle's *cabinet* a few weeks earlier, whilst de Gaulle remarked before the resignation, 'In any event, I do not want Bidault for a successor'.[129] The Foreign Minister was at the UN Assembly in London in January, he was not forewarned of the resignation by de Gaulle, but discovered what was afoot via Francisque Gay and Chauvel. Bidault tried to get back to Paris to see de Gaulle but suffered a series of mishaps. His new wife had just been knocked down by a car, his attempt to fly back to Paris was delayed by fog, and when he did get back de Gaulle had already left the capital. But, as he explained to Duff Cooper on 26 January, Bidault felt de Gaulle's action – though hurtful – would make the job of foreign minister much easier. The problem in future, Bidault added, would be the strength of the Communists.[130]

In Bidault's own party, the MRP, which liked to portray itself as *Gaulliste* for electoral reasons, there was some pressure to leave the government alongside the General, and for a time it seemed that Thorez would attempt to become premier, in a Socialist-Communist coalition. But neither the Socialists nor the MRP wanted to see the Communists dominant, especially when a new Constitution was about to be framed. As a result all three parties decided to stay in government with a compromise candidate as premier, the Socialist Félix Gouin, a gruff, modest and good-natured man who viewed his new position with horror. Behind the scenes, importantly, the army was also opposed to a Communist government. General Revers, commander of the Paris region, was concerned on the point and so (with Alphonse Juin absent in London) was the acting head of the EMDN, General Pierre Billotte. Billotte told the MRP's Maurice Schumann, that a Communist-dominated government might lead the Sultan of Morocco to declare independence, the Americans and British to occupy the French zone in Germany, and France itself to slip into civil war! It would be unjust to see this as threatening a coup by the Army, which remained loyal to de Gaulle's successors. But Billotte was soon sounding out Duff Cooper about possible British support for a new, moderate (and mythical) political party. In February furthermore (according to one source) Billotte was sent by the Army minister, the MRP's Edmond Michelet, to America to explore a US military commitment to Europe. Bidault knew of this mission, but Gouin only found out thanks to a warning from Henri Bonnet, and Billotte was then recalled.

From the start therefore it was clear that the system of *tripartisme* – coalition government by the PCF, Socialists and MRP – would see each of the parties try to outbid each other for support.[131] On the other hand *tripartisme* did survive de Gaulle's departure and there would be no rapid, triumphant return to power for the General, who told his nephew years later, 'I have made at least one political error in my life: my departure of January 1946 . . . I thought that the French would call me back quickly . . .'.[132]

* * *

To the last de Gaulle, concerned above all with France's stature in the world, had maintained his policy of *grandeur*. He had sometimes seemed willing to embrace other roles as well, as the defender of small nations at the UN, the economic partner of the Benelux states or a 'bridge' between the Soviets and Anglo-Saxons. Soon after his resignation he also privately insisted that he had wanted to join with Britain in leading a strong, West European group, independent of America and Russia.[133] But all such policies had remained subsidiary to the restoration of national independence, sovereignty in the empire and the achievement of Great Power status, and the search for *grandeur* itself undermined the other policies. De Gaulle the *realpolitiker* never had much faith in a revamped League of Nations and, once a permanent place was gained on the UN Security Council, France took less interest in supporting the 'small' powers. De Gaulle's insistence on being recognised as an equal by Britain, and particularly his desire for Anglo-French agreement on the Ruhr and Levant, helped to forestall an alliance with London. Hopes for close co-operation with Russia were also undermined, in part, because de Gaulle insisted on being treated by Stalin as an equal.

With a French role in the UN Security Council, the German ACC and CFM, France had the outward trappings of a Great Power in 1945, but the Yalta, Potsdam and Moscow conferences showed how uncertain such status was, and in the all-important talks on Germany's future French plans won little sympathy. The basic fact remained that France lacked a strong enough economy and army to underpin Great Power rank. De Gaulle had contained the Communists, restored the empire in Africa and Indochina and begun the work of reconstruction, but even his immense energy could not compensate for the physical and psychological costs of the war. He had been unable to prevent the return to party government, nationalist movements were already stirring in the Empire and a bold economic course had not been pursued. Despite the General's insistence on portraying France as a victor power over Germany, Japan and Italy, it could be argued that Britain's diplomatic support, American money and France's geographical position did more than de Gaulle to win her resuscitation as a major power. Then again, though his obsession with the past sometimes blinded him to new realities – his desire to avenge the humiliations of 1940, for example, prevented an early improvement in relations with Italy – he was always open to new ideas, including the possibility of Western European economic co-operation and the need to embrace post-war Germany within a greater whole. He clearly recognised too, in 1945, that there were only two 'very great powers'[134] and that some day France might have to choose between Washington and Moscow. His anti-communism and reliance on US financial aid suggest that he favoured the former over the latter.

Perhaps de Gaulle's greatest achievement between 1940 and 1946 was that, whilst he never matched the power of America, Russia or Britain, he maintained the image of independence from them. In 1940–41 he relied almost entirely on Britain for support; after 1943 he needed the Americans. But through all this, by his own inner strength, by the arrogance of his character and by his faith in the spirit of France, he had kept his charge free of alien domination. His successors, less obsessed with France's international standing and faced by the division of Europe, proved less adept at maintaining France's freedom of manoeuvre in foreign affairs. De Gaulle himself predicted that Bidault would be dominated by the officials of the Quai and be forced into concessions abroad,[135] and the sense of decline after the General's departure began immediately. To Jacques Dumaine, Head of Protocol at the Quai, the reception of the diplomatic corps on 9 February presented an appalling spectacle:

> M. Gouin, who was wearing a morning coat which reached right down to his ankles, ploughed his way through everything with the hearty shyness of a Marseillais. His entourage lacked style and distinction; as he left, he ground out his cigarette on a carpet depicting the coronation of Charles X . . .[136]

Chapter 5

Between East and West.
January – June 1946.

French internal politics are based on the principles of democracy . . . Whilst the foreign policy of France is founded on the principles of collective security and international organisation . . .
– Léon Blum, addressing the National Advisory Council in Washington, 25 March 1946 (reproduced in *L'Oeuvre de Leon Blum 1945–7*).

On 28 January 1946 it was announced that Léon Blum, the veteran Socialist leader and pre-war premier, had been made 'Ambassador Extraordinary' by the new French government, and it was soon learnt that he would visit Washington to discuss future economic needs with the US. Blum's mission reflected France's continuing reliance on American economic aid after the war and was later condemned by the Communists for fastening the country closely to an American alliance. There seemed, however, to be little alternative. The British too had to go to America for a loan at this time, and the Soviets were quite incapable of fulfilling France's supply needs.

Since December 1944 Ambassador Bogomolov had favoured economic co-operation with the French[1] and Hervé Alphand had discussed economic and financial issues with the Russians during his Moscow visit of December 1945. But French hopes of a wide-ranging commercial agreement, alongside accords on financial relations and air-sea communications, came to little. A Soviet trade representative was sent to Paris after Alphand's visit and commerce was put on a 'most-favoured nation' basis, but there were limits to the volume of goods that could be exchanged, Moscow gave trade with East European nations priority over trade with France, and Russia could not supply any loans.[2] Catroux saw the sparse results of the Alphand talks as further evidence of Soviet displeasure with France at this time and suggested that the situation might change if, say, France demonstrated its interest in co-operation with Eastern Europe by making an alliance with Poland. However in February the signs of Moscow's displeasure continued. Molotov remained reluctant to talk about French aims in the Ruhr-Rhine and remarked that, whilst the government in Paris had changed 'Monsieur Bidault has kept his place. Thus the policy which he followed previously will not be modified'. And, as far as Molotov was concerned, Bidault's policy was not agreeable to Russia.[3]

French planners like Alphand and Jean Monnet had long been ready to commit themselves to the multilateral trade system espoused by the US and recognised that American credits would be needed to build France up so that she could take part in such a system. De Gaulle's government committed itself to multilateralism as part of the February 1945 lend-lease agreement and in December, in the EXIMBANK loan deal. France had also formally committed herself to the Bretton Woods economic agreements on 31 December 1945, with the explicit understanding that she would have to modernise before she could compete in a multilateral world.[4] Thanks mainly to Monnet the need to modernise, to obtain US aid and to join in a liberal economic system were also linked to a comprehensive recovery and modernisation plan. The plan was designed not only to heal the scars of war but also to transform France's stagnant economy, with its large agricultural sector, its lack of heavy industry, its reliance on such luxury exports as perfume, wine and dried flowers, into a modern, heavy industrial economy able to provide strength and independence and to outmatch Germany. The only alternative to this course, Monnet believed, was weakness and decline. De Gaulle had been attracted to Monnet's ideas during the Washington visit of August 1945, when the General had been struck by America's technical prowess, and a few months later, with the EXIMBANK loan almost complete, Monnet returned to Paris, gathered a loyal staff around him, and began preparations for both a modernisation plan and talks with the US. The two subjects were inextricably linked: US money would finance the Plan; the Plan would convince Americans that their money would be well spent.

Economic planning under State direction was not a new idea. It had been seen in Mendès-France's economic proposals in 1944, and in the Vichy government before that. Neither was it an original idea to transform France's economic position by the use of resources from abroad. In 1943–44 Alphand wished to modernise the French economy with US finance and links to the Benelux states and to take Germany's place as the heavy industrial producer on the Continent of Western Europe. At an interdepartmental meeting on 24 October, reviewing the situation as regards American financial aid, it was Alphand who insisted on the need for a long-range French economic programme including the use of German resources.[5] In the Ministry of National Economy in October 1945 furthermore, it was felt 'legitimate that France should continue to accumulate debts for a certain number of years for the reconstruction of its economy and the modernisation of its machinery', although it was hoped, rather ambitiously, to wipe out the deficit on day-to-day imports by the end of 1946.[6]

However it was Monnet's work which drew together, in a coherent scheme, the three aspects of planning; reconstruction in the international environment and the acceptance of government-promoted industrial growth, even if, in the short term, this meant foreign indebtedness and an unbalanced budget.

On 5 December Monnet had sent de Gaulle a basic proposal for a national plan to develop productivity and trade, ensure full employment and increase living standards. It must be a genuine 'national' effort with the support of businessmen and the people including, importantly, the Communists and the Communist-influenced trades union organisation the *Confédération Générale du Travail* (CGT). The Plan would not work by Soviet-style state control but by a looser form of direction concentrating on a few key industries (such as coal, steel and electricity) with a 'Planning Council' to set production targets and monitor progress. The idea of a Plan was accepted by the Cabinet before Christmas, a *Commissariat-Général* was set up under Monnet on 3 January and the new Gouin government maintained support for it. Works on a detailed scheme began in earnest in February, but throughout the preparations Monnet had insisted on the necessity of foreign loans to finance the Plan: 'without these loans modernisation . . . would necessarily take longer and the French people would have to . . . accept greater cuts in domestic consumption'. With an enormous investment effort, the use of German resources *and* foreign loans the Planning Council, meeting on 16 March, hoped by 1950 to surpass the production levels of 1929, the best year for economic performance in the inter-war period.[7]

French economic plans in early 1946 clearly depended heavily on the willingness of the US to supply large-scale loans over a long period. In October 1945, in view of the successful EXIMBANK talks, Monnet optimistically hoped that – in contrast to the post-1918 situation – Washington would cancel Europe's war debts, remain involved in world affairs through the multilateral trade system, and provide economic aid to give countries like France stable economic foundations. Monnet hoped for US assistance over a period of five years, the time it would take to achieve a balanced trading position.[8] However such optimism proved over-inflated. True, after 1945 America did not repeat the mistakes of the 1920s concerning the repayment of war debts, and it avoided a return to isolationism. But just as it was hoped on the political plane to withdraw US forces from Europe by 1947, relying on Big Three co-operation to maintain world peace, so on the economic plane the US hoped to create a multilateral trading system whilst avoiding large-scale financial assistance to Europe. This was already evident in Congressional reactions to the 1945 lend-lease agreement with France,[9] and in March 1946 one US official with experience of European conditions 'was struck with the attitude of rather casual and easy optimism about European revival in many Washington circles'.[10]

Britain's experience with its loan request to America, which resulted in an agreement on 6 December 1945, did not augur well for France. In talks with Lord Keynes the US agreed to settle Britain's lend-lease debts and granted a credit of $3,750 million, repayable over fifty years at 2 per cent interest. This seemed generous, but as René Massigli noted, it reflected a compromise: London had hoped for a more generous loan, perhaps without interest payments, and had been forced by American 'intransigence' to accept not only the principle of multilateral trade, but also such practical measures to achieve this as the convertibility of sterling into dollars.[11] France's financial *attaché* in Washington watched the British talks carefully and warned Paris not to expect any 'gifts' from America.[12] In January 1946 Guillaume Guindey, Director of External Finances at the Finance Ministry in Paris, discussed possible tactics to use vis-à-vis America with Lord Keynes.[13] Monnet himself recognised that France was not as vital to the world economy as Britain, whose currency was still the basis of half the world's trade, but hoped that in any loan talks the Americans would appreciate the greater scale of destruction suffered in France during the war.[14]

The British loan conditions were not the only sign of possible problems for Monnet. Although Washington seemed pleased by the survival of *tripartisme* and the promise of strong economic measures after de Gaulle's resignation,[15] Jefferson Caffery was upset by the absence of Pierre Mendès-France, with his bold ideas on economic reform,[16] from the Gouin government and remained pessimistic about the state of Franco-American relations, especially over German central agencies.[17] In mid-January Monnet[18] and his staff told US embassy officials that France would need financial assistance, ideally in a lump sum to cover three years, in order to join in multilateral trade and the Americans made clear that sound statistical evidence would be needed to justify such a loan.[19]

Blum's loan mission[20] was originally set to begin on 26 February, but the Socialist leader's poor health meant that this date had to be set back by a month.[21] Meanwhile the *Wall Street Journal* felt it 'ironical to see how determinedly the descendants of Karl Marx believe in Santa Claus'.[22] Americans made it clear that French requests were likely to be presented again to the EXIMBANK, where any loan would be on strict conditions (goods would have to be purchased from America for example), and that certain reciprocal concessions might be necessary, such as a lessening in restrictions on US tourists to France, an agreement regarding tax relief on American societies and greater Hollywood film imports.

It seemed that Congressional discussion on the British loan – a loan which the American government described as 'exceptional' – would increase the wariness in Washington about large credits for France,[23] and opinion in the US administration was known to be divided on a French loan.[24] Even Caffery was unwilling to predict whether a loan would be given, and told Jean Chauvel that American dissatisfaction over central agencies would damage Blum's chances of success.[25] The head of the Quai d'Orsay's American section, Etienne Dennery, felt that while the Blum mission would be useful for an exchange of information with Washington, the US would avoid large credits at present because of France's uncertain political future and because her reconstruction plan was only embryonic.[26] In mid-February Monnet's staff foresaw numerous potential problems with the forthcoming talks, because of American doubts about France's political state, disagreements over Germany and the concessions Washington seemed likely to demand.[27] According to one source Monnet now gave up hopes of a large, long-term loan,[28] yet even in late March one of his assistants continued to argue that a loan must not only allow 'France to continue a precarious existence, but also the means to make good . . . the reconstruction and modernisation of its economy so as to put it quickly on the level of other major countries . . .'.[29]

The State Department in February 1946 did indeed rule out a British-type loan for France and expected the French to provide both concessions (on taxation matters for example) and evidence of a viable reconstruction plan, in return for a short-term loan of about $500 million. In the long term the International Bank, to be created under the terms of Bretton Woods, would provide more funds for France. Caffery gave an outline of US thinking to Bidault on 22 February and Bonnet was told that a multibillion dollar loan was out of the question.[30] A large body of statistics was amassed and Blum's delegation was authorised to explain French needs fully and frankly, with promises both to adhere to multilateral trading principles and to seek finance from all possible means in addition to a loan, such as internal spending controls and reparations from Germany. The possibility of the talks' failure was considered in Paris, however, and in this case France would take 'necessary measure' to defend her balance of payments position and refuse all economic concessions to America.[31] Significantly there were also divisions in Paris over the visit. Within the French government Bidault, who had not been consulted by Gouin about Blum's appointment,[32] was resentful of the degree of independence given to the ex-premier, disliked Blum's personal links to Caffery and saw the mission as a Socialist attempt to make political capital out of foreign affairs. In the Quai there were criticisms of Blum's 'begging visit' and even fears that he would barter 'our future security with a momentary easing of our financial difficulties' by making concessions to the US on Germany.[33] There was some basis for this fear in that, before setting out, Blum *did* ask Bidault to settle differences with Washington over German central agencies.[34]

The Communists also sensed a Socialist attempt to score political points with Blum's mission but they had their own cards to play in this situation. Thus, despite the failure of earlier economic talks with Moscow, in March the Russians suddenly gave France a large loan of wheat. French demand for wheat at this time was almost as desperate as their need for coal. Supplies from North Africa could not meet French needs, and imports from America and Canada failed make up the shortfall. In early March however, Maurice Thorez persuaded the Cabinet to request supplies from the Soviet Union and, astonishingly, wheat shipments were agreed in only two days of talks with the Russians.[35] America's Secretary of the State Byrnes saw the Russian deal as a political move designed to help the PCF in the next general election which (it was announced on 19 March) would be held on 2 June.[36] Already, on the American side, Caffery had argued that the French loan 'should be weighed in terms of its political significance' and not merely on commercial grounds. If France wanted coal, cereals and machinery from America, then America should use this desire to preserve democracy in France.[37] East-West competition in the economic sphere, with a view to influencing France's political future, was thus a significant factor as Blum's mission began.

Blum arrived in Washington on 17 March. The ever-optimistic Monnet arrived two days later, with the latest decisions and statistics from the Planning Council. According to the latter's memoirs, these amounted to a 'well documented case'[38] but actually statistics on France's economic situation remained uncertain at this time. During 1946 the trade deficit for 1946–49, for example, was variously projected at between four and seven billion dollars.[39] It was originally expected that the talks would last about two weeks; they eventually went on for eleven. Monnet later described them as 'a triumph for (the) great humanist' Leon Blum and certainly, even though he was 76 and had never visited the US before, Blum's reputation had a positive effect on Americans. However, whilst the ex-premier made major speeches before Congress and other bodies, it was Monnet who bore the behind-the-scenes role of explaining French plans to the Americans in detail, and in such a way that, it was hoped, the logic and justice of France's case would naturally become apparent. Numerous French documents were shown to the Americans and various committees were established to look at such issues as the final settlement of lend-lease debts, commercial policy and taxation issues.[40]

Blum admitted the prime importance of Monnet's work in a letter to Gouin of 4 April, and at the same time confirmed that concessions would be needed as the price of any loan.[41] In daily talks with American experts Monnet insisted that French hopes of surpassing the production levels of 1929 within five years were realistic (in mid-April he was sent a draft modernisation plan for the years 1946–50 from Paris[42]) and promised that France would do all possible for her own modernisation through rationing, price controls, public spending cuts and a shift in the workforce from agriculture to industry. American money would be well spent. The delegation also kept up pressure for improvements in coal supplies to France arguing that coal was 'the life of the French economy', insisting that at least 20 million tons of German coal should be shipped to France every year from 1947, and blaming Britain for the failure to achieve adequate coal imports into France so far.[43] By 22 April Blum felt that the French case had been discussed as fully as possible.[44]

Throughout the talks rumours persisted in Paris that the delay in reaching agreement was because of American demand for 'political' concessions and that there was an important political element in the talks. Monnet always insisted that, regarding the length of the talks, the problems were technical ones, but even he admitted that Blum used 'political' arguments in his speeches.[45] Thus Blum's first major address, to the inter-departmental National Advisory Council (NAC) in Washington on 25 March, included a reference to France's forthcoming elections.[46] Blum's son Robert told Gouin in mid-April that many Americans saw the loan in political terms and that Blum was pressing his hosts, in private, to announce an agreement, or at least its main lines, by 15 May, presumably in order to have an impact on the French elections.[47] The State Department was definitely aware of such electoral considerations. Early in the month, with the first shipment of Russia's wheat loan about to arrive at Marseilles, where it was personally greeted by Ambassador Bogomolov, Caffery reminded Washington of the PCF menace, pointed out that the Socialists were relying on Blum's success and argued that 'anything we can do in this critical pre-election period to encourage Frenchmen to believe that we are not abandoning Europe ... should work to our long-term political and economic advantage'. In reply, Byrnes promised that 'all possible steps will be taken to enable [a] billion dollar or slightly greater credit' to be announced.[48]

However, the simple fact was that the State Department alone could not dictate US government policy at this time and that not everyone in Washington was yet obsessed with anti-Communist considerations. In the NAC on 25 April Will Clayton, the Under-Secretary of State, argued for a generous loan partly on political grounds, but representatives of other departments had doubts about the scale of aid for France,[49] and these doubts held up the grant of a loan as the French elections grew nearer and nearer. The arguments continued on 6 May when the Commerce Secretary, Henry Wallace, forced Clayton to agree that 'bad' loans should not be given for political reasons. The Treasury Secretary, Fred M. Vinson, however, said there were good economic *and* political reasons to provide a loan to France and it was finally agreed to grant an amount of $650 million via the EXIMBANK.[50] Even then other agreements remained to be settled, and it was only after personal appeals by an impatient Blum to

Truman and Byrnes[51] that the NAC approved a final package of agreements with France in late May.[52]

The Blum-Byrnes Accords, as they became known, were signed on 28 May. They effectively extinguished French lend-lease debts, by reducing the residue of these from over $2 billion to only $720 million. A new EXIMBANK loan (formally agreed in July [53]) was granted for the purchase of machinery and raw materials, a $275 million loan was made to purchase US surplus goods and France received seventy-five 'Liberty Ships' worth $42 million, which sizeably increased her merchant fleet. The International Bank, once established, would consider a further $500 million loan and, unlike Britain, in re-committing herself to multilateralism France made no commitments regarding the convertibility of her currency. Monnet and Blum had no doubts about recommending the package to the French government.[54] Monnet felt that the best possible deal had been achieved and that France's modernisation plan could now proceed – indeed *must* proceed, since the US loans had been given on the basis of the Plan.[55] He later claimed that he never expected a large loan to last over several years, and he always denied that there was any political element to the deal, unless it was the agreement, as one of the French concessions in the package, to import more Hollywood films. However Blum was disappointed with the accords, complaining, 'I can't have appealed powerfully enough to their feelings',[56] and the Communist Minister of Reconstruction, François Billoux, soon feared both that Monnet had obtained too little and that France had taken 'a step towards the loss of its independence'.[57] Communist writers continued to argue long after that the Accords committed France to US economic and political policies for little reward, and rumours of 'secret' political concessions by Blum persisted.[58] The existence of 'secret' agreements is, by definition, impossible to disprove, and it would be naive to deny that such wide-ranging financial agreements had no political impact. Caffery, the American who had insisted most on the political significance of any loan, was 'delighted' with the final deal.[59] However the Soviets too had tried to use France's economic needs in early 1946 to influence the elections, with their wheat loan, and the debates in the NAC in Washington showed that political considerations did *not* dominate the decisions of the US government. However rich, America was not 'Santa Claus', and Washington's economic departments were not ready to grant endless amounts of money to a doubtful financial proposition; however interested in preserving liberal democracy, Americans did not rush to provide a loan at the ideal time – the middle of May – when it could have affected the French elections. Instead the Blum-Byrnes Accords were signed only a few days before the elections at a time when, as will be seen below, the Communists were already on the electoral defensive.

The economic, rather than political criticisms of the Accords were arguably therefore the more important ones. For the loan terms were far less than Monnet had hoped for at the New Year. Compromise in the talks was inevitable and some had not thought Blum would obtain all that he did, but France's future balance of payments deficit under the Monnet Plan was only partially covered, she would still have to make great efforts to cut imports and expand exports, and she would have to go back to the US (via the International Bank) for more money in future, thus subjecting herself to regular economic reviews and potential political pressures from Washington. The agreements of 28 May were much better as a settlement of past debts than as a long-term guarantee for Monnet's modernisation plan. However, in the last analysis the cruel truth, again, was that France had little choice in this. No other country, certainly not Russia, could supply French needs and without US aid modernisation would be painfully slow, leaving the country weak and its people discontented. Despite the criticisms of Blum, even the Communists and the CGT accepted Monnet's modernisation plan and the Blum-Byrnes Accords. It also needs to be borne in mind however that, as Monnet realised, once modernisation got under way America would find it difficult *not* to provide more aid to see the Plan through, especially since the denial of US credits in future could provoke social discontent in France and ruin hopes of a multilateral world. Political pressures in the Franco-American economic relationship need not always be one way, and although the US loan strengthened French ties to the West rather than the East, it did not necessarily, fatally undermine French independence.

*   *   *

Despite the importance of the German question, the Americans never categorically insisted that the Blum loan be conditional upon a change in French policy regarding central agencies. Vain attempts to reach a compromise over this problem continued in January 1946. On the 12th, after a long lull in discussions on the subject in the Allied Control Council (ACC), General Montgomery, backed by the American and Soviet representatives, proposed a central agency for finance with limited powers. Both General Koenig and officials in the Quai recognised the potential problem of inflation in Germany and were reluctant to reject a moderate British proposal on financial reform outright. As a result the Interministerial Committee for Germany suggested that a German 'Commission of Experts' should be founded to advise the Allies on financial policy. However the French put a number of conditions as the price of this: the 'Commission of Experts' would only have consultative powers; its writ would not run west of the Rhine; and it should be formed of individual representatives from the *Länder* *after* strong *Länder* had been organisede east of the Rhine. These conditions were so strict that the American and Soviet representatives rejected it out of hand.[60] Franco-American tensions went on: French officials believed that their most determined opponent, the American General Clay, deliberately disrupted wheat supplies from America to the French occupation zone at this time, as a means to pressure them on central agencies.

In early February Alphand was extremely concerned at Allied criticisms of French policy and urged Bidault to seek, once again, talks with the Big Three on the future of the Ruhr, Rhineland and Saar, the areas from which the French wanted central agencies to be excluded. Alphand was especially eager to settle the future of the Saar, with its valuable coal deposits, which lay entirely in the French zone.[61] The detachment of this region seemed the least that France could expect from her Allies, and an appeal was duly made to all the Big Three, pointing out the uncertainty regarding the Saar's future, and asking that it be placed under a special economic and political regime, 'without prejudice' to a final German peace treaty.[62] Meanwhile however, on 6 February, James Byrnes had written to Bidault and pressed again for the introduction of central agencies 'without prejudice' to the western borders of Germany. Both sides were talking past each other. The French wanted to settle the issue of western borders before central agencies. The US took exactly the opposite approach. On the surface it seemed that America was in the stronger position. Byrnes told Caffery to hint to the French that the disagreements over Germany might adversely affect the Blum mission,[63] and Chauvel was worried enough by the latest American pressure to prevent Byrnes' letter being seen by the Cabinet.[64]

Through February and into March US officials repeatedly asked the French to change policy.[65] Clay believed that Bidault's policy was fuelling German Communist propaganda, which was opposed to the loss of territories in the West.[66] Interestingly, Caffery specifically targeted his pressures at Socialist leaders like Gouin, Blum and Vincent Auriol. Ever since Blum's return from prison in Buchenwald the previous May the Socialists had pursued a policy that was well-tailored to the views of the US Ambassador: internally, a refusal to fuse with the PCF, whom Blum saw as Soviet puppets, and support for socialism through liberal democracy; internationally, a desire to work with Labour Britain, an interest in European co-operation and a German policy rooted not in revenge but in reconciliation. The fact that the Socialists wanted Blum's loan mission to succeed also made them amenable to pressure, of course. However, all this did *not* mean that the US could force France into line easily. Caffery realised that the SFIO could not press its differences on Germany with the MRP too far, for fear of helping the Communists.[67] The MRP, Bidault's party, continued to take a firm *Gaulliste* line on Germany. It is also significant that on 2 March Byrnes told Caffery not to press Bidault so far on central agencies that the latter resigned.[68] There were actually, therefore, strict limits on the scale of pressure that Washington was ready to use against Paris, owing to the fear of aiding the PCF.

The British too were unwilling to put real pressure on France over central agencies, but this did not mean that London had become any more sympathetic to French aims in Germany. Rather, London had come to accept the argument that central agencies could fall under Soviet control. At the UN meetings in London in February, Bevin continued to argue that the political separation of the Ruhr would cause grave economic problems, provoke German irredentism and leave the rest of Germany to be dominated by Russia. However Bidault would not alter French policy, telling Bevin that a separate Ruhr state would be safer from Soviet control than a Ruhr which was subject to central agencies in Berlin.[69] The French believed the Russians must take much of the blame for the deep divisions between Germany's four zones. On 1 March, in his formal reply to Byrnes' earlier letter on central agencies, Bidault insisted that 'the German menace will exist as long as a German government ... has at its disposal the necessary resources to reconstitute its military power' and that the Ruhr, Rhineland and Saar must therefore be severed from Germany. The French were not opposed outright to the idea of central agencies, on German external trade for example, but these must function via Allied zonal administrations not as independent organs.[70] At the same time the French redoubled their efforts to get four-power talks on Germany's western borders, especially the Saar, and complained about Clay's apparently deliberate disruption of wheat supplies to the French zone. The British and (eventually) the Americans proved willing to discuss the Ruhr-Rhine at the next meeting of the Council of Foreign Ministers (CFM),[71] but Byrnes said he was not ready to settle the future of the Saar until the 'chaotic relations between the four zones of Germany' were addressed by the French government.[72] In early April Lucius Clay was so exasperated by France's policy that he actually advocated cutting wheat supplies, not only to the ZOF, but also to France itself as a form of political pressure. He passed this view on to Washington in vain, however,[73] and it was significant by this time that American co-operation with the Soviets in Germany was also reaching a crisis.

In early 1946 the ACC's main efforts were devoted *not* to the resolution of the central agencies problem, but to establishing a 'level of industry' plan for Germany as agreed at Potsdam. The plan was intended to provide for the removal of industrial plant as reparations, whilst leaving Germany with sufficient resources to maintain itself without outside assistance. It was therefore an essential component of Allied policy in Germany. But devising such a plan proved a gargantuan task. Koenig's staff recognised that, whilst all four occupation powers agreed on such general aims as security guarantees, reparations payments and a stable German economy, there were great differences of emphasis between them. The Soviets wished to hold down German industry, the French to use Germany's resources for their own recovery, and the Anglo-Saxon powers to reduce their financial commitments in the country by allowing Germany a reasonable level of industrial activity.

Ironically Koenig's officials, in January 1946, criticised all *three* of these approaches: the Soviets' because, by ruining the German economy it could cause economic and social discontent across Europe; the Anglo-Saxon because it would mean losing effective control of Germany; and their own government's because it did not answer the problem of how to keep Germany's population of 70 million employed once its heavy industrial resources were transferred to France. The memorandum of 7 July 1945, which still guided French economic policy in Germany, did not tackle this point adequately. Koenig's officials felt the best solution was a transfer of population from Germany but, although this had been advocated in France in 1944–45, no one had yet seriously proposed to carry it out. The most France had been able to do was to employ German POWs as labourers (a policy which continued until 1948), to attract Polish refugees from Germany to work in France, and to encourage voluntary immigration by Germans into France. Koenig's officials remained frustrated in late February, having been given no indication from Paris of how to square the circle of reducing German industrial production without causing social upheaval.[74]

After much haggling, a 'level of industry' plan was finally published by the ACC on 28 March, two months later than originally hoped. Its general intention was to halve Germany's 1938 production level, to prohibit certain industries (such as armaments, synthetic oil and ball-bearings) and to restrict others (such as machine tools and chemicals). But the key limitation, which effectively governed the level of output as a whole, was the volume of steel manufacture. Steel output was set at 5.8 million tons per annum, but a potential capacity of 7 million tons was to be left in Germany in case the original level should prove insufficient. The French were quite satisfied with this volume of steel output; the British had wanted a much higher level, and the Soviets a lower one. However the plan as a whole was based on dubious assumptions, including Germany's treatment as a 'single economic unit', with exports balancing imports, and was designed to apply to all regions west of the Oder-Neisse line.[75] The French made it clear that they would wish to amend the plan once the Ruhr, Rhineland and Saar were withdrawn from Germany,[76] and in April serious problems quickly developed over it when the Russians refused to establish an import-export plan for Germany as a whole, arguing that zonal commercial policies were adequate enough. Clay, with some sympathy from French officials,[77] argued that the Soviet policy undermined the whole Potsdam agreement. If reparations were removed from Germany under the terms of the level of industry plan, but without regard to the actual balance of imports and exports, it could prove disastrous: assets would be stripped from the country even if it was trading at a loss, and it seemed that America and Britain would have to pump money into the industrial areas of Western Germany to keep them alive.[78] In May Clay responded to the growing crisis by ending all dismantlement of factories as reparations in the US zone. He made it plain in a press conference that he would only resume the reparations policy once Germany ceased to be divided into 'airtight' zones.

In justifying his decision to suspend dismantlement, Clay's remarks included criticism of French as well as Soviet policy. Some writers indeed have seen his decision as aimed *primarily* at the French: unable to get Washington to put real pressure on Paris, Clay supposedly took unilateral action of his own to bring about central agencies in Germany. There can be no doubt that Clay was angry about the French vetoes on central agencies and that his views often differed widely from those of Washington. However, in context the Russians seem to have been his main target. They would lose more than France from such an action, for although France did want reparations from Germany, her's was a far smaller volume than Russia's, and in Washington and London Clay's action was seen as a challenge to the Soviets. (Much of the concern in America and Britain over French opposition to central agencies was, of course, due to the 'excuse' the French thereby gave the Soviets for independent action in their zone.)

In the immediate term, furthermore, there was hardly any French reaction to Clay's move. The Quai took the view that they *did* support central bodies in Germany in principle, so long as these were excluded from the Ruhr-Rhine, and felt Clay's criticisms were undeserved. Officials were concerned at the cut in reparations because of France's reconstruction needs and the danger of Germany's revival, and feared that it would be difficult to restart shipments from the US zone once these were cut. However the French only explained such worries in August and September, and then (apparently) only to the British. In the short term, in mid-June, Alphand approached the Soviets to see if they would act in unison with France in trying to reach a reparations compromise with America, but Vladimir Dekasanov was extremely puzzled by the lack of public response from France to Clay's action, whilst Bogomolov seemed suspicious of French links to the Anglo-Saxons and fearful that all three Western powers would try to forge a west Germany policy independent of Russia. It seemed quite evident to the Quai in fact that the Soviets and Americans were more concerned with each other than with France. On 4 July General Clay told the French political adviser in Germany, Tarbé de St Hardouin, that France ought to agree to central agencies now, because opinion was moving in Germany's favour and the real menace to the peace was Russia.[79]

*   *   *

For a time in early April it suddenly seemed that Britain and France might resolve their differences in Germany, paving the way to an Anglo-French treaty. At the UN meeting in London in February the two sides had formally resolved their differences over the Levant issue, and so dealt with one of the two conditions set by de Gaulle for a treaty in December 1944. With the General removed from the scene, Bidault was able to pursue his moderate line on Syria-Lebanon and agreed to a mutual withdrawal of Anglo-French forces from these countries.[80]

Following this breakthrough, on 7 March a British minister told the House of Lords that an Anglo-French treaty might soon be possible[81] and, in various speeches during March, Félix Gouin seemed to suggest that differences on Germany need not prevent such a pact. At Strasbourg on the 24th, and at the Socialist Party conference four days later, Gouin, whose anglophile views were well known, said that the two essential elements in a German settlement were a long occupation and international economic controls on the Ruhr; he did *not* say that the *political* separation of the Ruhr was necessary.[82] In the light of Gouin's statements, which hinted at a major change in France's Ruhr policy, closer to Britain's policy, Ernest Bevin and his officials decided to send an emissary, Under-Secretary Oliver Harvey, to Paris to see if a treaty was indeed possible. Like the Americans and Soviets at this point, the British were looking for ways to influence the forthcoming French election and a British treaty was still known to be popular with the French people. Unlike the Americans and Soviets, the British lacked the means to give economic concessions to France and, in any case, Premier Attlee had ruled out the idea of 'political' loans to Europe. A treaty, if it were possible, could prove a cheap and easy way to strengthen the anti-Communist vote in France, at a time when PCF strength was of mounting concern.[83] Harvey's mission to Paris somewhat contradicted Massigli's view, held since de Gaulle's resignation, that the British would be extremely reticent about commitments to France, until its long-term political future was resolved, because of the power of the PCF. Massigli, who still regretted that an Anglo-French treaty had not been signed in early 1945 when he had wanted it, believed that Anglo-French differences on Germany and Britain's increasing ties to the US also made a treaty difficult.[84] His British counterpart, Duff Cooper, felt too that differences with France on Germany *would* have to be tackled before a treaty was made, whatever Gouin said, and in conversation with the latter found that he 'was neither quite sure what he had said, nor what he had meant' in his Strasbourg speech.[85]

The doubts of the two ambassadors on the chances for a treaty were soon borne out. Although Gouin and the SFIO, playing the Anglo-Saxon 'card' in electoral politics, favoured a change in the country's German policy, the Quai d'Orsay and Bidault remained firmly committed to the *Gaulliste* line in Germany, and determined to challenge Gouin. The British, by offering the French a bilateral guarantee without the political separation of the Ruhr were seen in the Quai as repeating their inter-war policies vis-à-vis Germany.[86] Oliver Harvey arrived in Paris to find opinion there divided, but in the Cabinet on 5 April the combined 'nationalist' forces of the MRP and Communists – neither of whom wished to see the Socialists make electoral capital of the international situation – brought Gouin to heel and restated de Gaulle's desiderata in Germany. 'It is essential', declared Bidault, in a speech in Lille on the 8th, 'that the Ruhr should be treated as a political entity independent of Germany'. The following day the Cabinet announced that any treaty with Britain must 'answer the wishes and the interests of both countries'. The Foreign Office, as in the talks in 1945 before San Francisco, felt 'snubbed' but Duff Cooper blamed the fiasco of the Harvey mission on the Foreign Office's haste and carelessness,[87] whilst Caffery saw the whole episode as being wrapped up in 'pre-election jockeying' in Paris. It was ironic, perhaps, to see the Communists and Christian Democrats uniting against their 'moderate' Socialist partners, but it was important for them both to pose as defenders of a 'patriotic' and popular course, and for the PCF to scotch all moves towards a British treaty.[88]

Shortly afterwards, on 17 April, the British Cabinet, as long expected, formally rejected the idea of a politically separate Ruhr state in favour of Allied economic controls on the region, which would remain part of Germany. A full account was given to the French on how such a policy could prove effective but Bidault was not impressed and talks between the officials of both sides in early May failed to move either.[89] Yet the British decision was a major blow to French ambitions. If America and Russia together had supported the French case on the Ruhr there might have been some chance of changing British policy, but the US had tended to take a similar view to London's for many months[90] and the Soviets, even if they did not like the fact, believed that Britain's view was paramount in what concerned the Ruhr.[91] In May Jean Chauvel and René Massigli were quite pessimistic about the situation. Bevin seemed on the one hand to be concerned at PCF influence in Paris and reluctant to discuss a French treaty, and on the other hand to be obsessed with the Soviet menace in Germany and reluctant to discuss the future of the Ruhr, the vital concern for France, in isolation from other German issues.[92]

* * *

On 25 April 1946 the first meeting of the Paris sessions of the CFM was opened by Bidault, as the host Foreign Minister. The Frenchman expressed the hope that the meetings would succeed in their main object of finalising draft treaties with Italy and Hitler's East European allies, for submission to a general peace conference of UN states, as agreed at Moscow in December.[93] The Quai d'Orsay's principal aims at the conference were to achieve border changes, reparations payments and disarmament measures in the Italian peace treaty, to discuss the German question, to reassert French rights in Eastern Europe and to play a major role as a host and mediator now that Paris had resumed its position as a major diplomatic centre. The Quai also hoped that, behind the scenes, Bidault could press for greater economic assistance from his allies, including coal supplies from the Ruhr, a US loan (the Blum talks were still under way) and the protection of French economic rights in Eastern

Europe. But above all came the need to maintain Big Three co-operation.[94] France had no desire to see her partners alienated from one another, since this would threaten world peace, undermine her own independence and put great strains on her coalition government.

Even before the conference began, however, the prospects for its success were dimmed by increasing tension between the Soviets on one side and the Anglo-Saxons on the other. Since the collapse of the Third Reich in May 1945 the French had felt that British policy was dominated by concern over Soviet political methods and behaviour in Eastern Europe,[95] and even during the Potsdam conference, the Moscow press criticised Britain for seeking an 'anti-Soviet' bloc in the Near East through support for the Turks (involved in border disputes with Russia) and the Greek royal government (who were involved in a civil war with Communist guerillas).[96] Massigli believed, in October 1945, that the British people saw themselves as a liberal democracy facing a police state and were unable to understand why Russia should simultaneously condemn a 'Western bloc' and create its own exclusive system in the East. Massigli wrote of pressure being put on *The Times* newspaper to change its 'appeasement' mentality regarding the Soviets, which had upset Bevin. An important by-product of Soviet policy, the Ambassador added, was to drive London towards co-operation with America.[97] The Americans too had had their differences with the Soviets, especially on the Polish issue in the wake of Yalta and over Bulgaria and Rumania as well as Far Eastern issues, at the London CFM in September 1945[98] but it was Ernest Bevin who argued most firmly with Molotov at the latter conference, whilst Byrnes had gone on to seek a compromise with the Russians at Moscow in December, and there were signs of Anglo-American division in late 1945 over, for example, the terms of America's loan to Britain.

At the UN in February 1946, the US representative, Stettinius, tried to play a mediatory role in the arguments between Bevin and the Russian Andrei Vyshinsky. Massigli had little doubt in early 1946 that, though some Britons still hoped for a settlement with Russia, a clash was taking place between 'two gigantic Empires, one continental and the other maritime', a battle which, on one level, was concerned with the balance of power, but which, on another, represented 'rivalry between the two great ideologies of the Left', Socialism and Communism. Massigli also noted that, in this struggle, some people in Britain accused America of 'desertion'.[99] Even in March 1946, when Winston Churchill spoke at Fulton in Missouri about an 'iron curtain' across Europe, the American press was generally critical of him, depicting Britain as an imperialist power and calling for Big Three co-operation. However in Washington Henri Bonnet and his deputy, Armand Berard, also noted a toughening in US policy in early 1946. American newspapers generally took Bevin's side in his arguments with Vyshinsky and feared that, by an excessive use of their veto, the Soviets were undermining the usefulness of the UN, on which US hopes for peace were based. Washington was also concerned about an ideologically-based speech by Stalin, made on 9 February, which seemed to point towards a communist-capitalist struggle in the world, and the Americans put enormous diplomatic pressure on Moscow soon afterwards to withdraw the Red Army from Iran, which they had occupied during the war. Bonnet noted that, as with the 1945 crisis over Yugoslav ambitions in Trieste, Americans saw events in Iran as 'proof that Russia renounces a dangerous initiative each time that the US shows clearly that they cannot accept it'. There were also a number of indications from Byrnes, beginning with a speech on 28 February, which showed a new-found determination to prevent further Russian expansion and force her to respect the UN.[100] Though the French themselves played little part in the arguments over Greece, Turkey and Iran, there were those in the Quai too who feared that 'the Soviet tentacles snake out in all directions . . .'.[101]

The growing East-West divide had already had its impact on the work of the CFM Deputies who had made only painfully slow progress since January in drafting peace treaties for the foreign ministers to discuss. Once the CFM met the arguments continued and it took several days to agree on an agenda. In particular Bevin insisted that any discussion on Germany must be a *general* one, not simply a debate on the Ruhr involving only the British zone.[102] There was a boost for France's position at the outset when to Bidault's astonishment but great satisfaction, Molotov announced that he was willing to let France discuss *all* the peace treaties. Byrnes rightly saw this as 'a striking withdrawal' from the Russian position at the London CFM and Bevin had no doubt that the move was designed to influence the French elections.[103] There was some debate on the French side, however, as to whether Molotov did not seek a genuine improvement in relations with them. Catroux's Embassy felt that with de Gaulle gone, the PCF strong and the CFM meeting in Paris, the Soviets might be ready for co-operation. But the Quai was still concerned at adverse Russian press coverage of France. In themselves, it was clear that such positive gestures as the recent wheat loan and a role in the East European treaties might only be intended to have an electoral impact. Catroux, who was part of France's CFM delegation, met Bogomolov on 29 April and the latter made much of the common interests between their two countries. However he also proved quite evasive when asked if Russia would now support French plans for Germany.[104]

By early May the arguments between the Anglo-Saxons and Soviets had proved quite destructive and the Quai feared that the conference was 'becalmed'. Discussions on the various treaties still proceeded slowly and it proved quite impossible to issue invitations to a peace conference on 1 May, as had been planned at Moscow.[105] Bidault told Byrnes that he saw little chance of agreement, could not understand what Molotov wanted, but feared a Soviet policy of 'security through expansion' which could mean that there would be 'Cossacks on the Place de la Concorde'. Byrnes agreed there were major problems, said he was not prepared to make concessions to Russia and was concerned enough by France's weak position to telephone Truman in Bidault's presence to discuss the Blum loan. Byrnes did agree, however, to an idea of Bidault's for small, select meetings of the four delegation leaders with their closest advisers as a way to break the conference deadlock.[106] This proposal was adopted by the CFM the next day, 2 May, and a number of informal meetings followed, which succeeded in quickening progress.[107] It was also thanks to a suggestion from Bidault that on 15 May, after numerous discussions, a settlement was reached on the procedure for future work: the CFM would recess from 16 May until 15 June, while the Deputies continued to work on the draft treaties, and then the foreign ministers would meet again in Paris to finalise preparations for the long delayed peace conference.[108] Bidault's policy of mediation was having its successes.

Amongst the tedious discussions on procedure some headway was made on individual treaties. For France the main concerns, as in London in September, were Italy and Germany. In January, after haggling between the Quai and Juin's EMDN, France defined its territorial claims vis-à-vis Italy, a total of only 720 square miles, principally in the area around Tende and Brigue and submitted these to the CFM deputies on 4 February.[109] The Americans, increasingly keen to strengthen Italian democracy, had little enthusiasm for France's demands, but Armand Berard insisted in talks with the State Department that border changes were needed, both to forestall the danger of a 'German-dominated' Italy re-emerging as a threat to France, and to strengthen Bidault against the PCF.[110] At the Paris CFM a commission was set up to investigate the French claim around Tende and Brigue.[111] According to its report, of 11 May, whilst visiting Brigue the commission 'selected at random from the market square two pro-French witnesses ... and two pro-Italian witnesses ...' to ask their view on the region's future. Unsurprisingly it came to the conclusion that opinion in the area on French annexation was divided.[112] At the CFM Bidault successfully insisted on limiting the size of the Italian navy[113] and asked for reparations payments from Italy.[114] In the debates over the fate of Italy's colonies he continued to take the line followed in London: absolute opposition to Libyan independence, criticism of ideas for an 'international trusteeship' system or of a Soviet trusteeship in Tripolitania, and preference for continued Italian rule, even if under UN auspices.[115] Bidault was delighted when Molotov, evidently to impress Italian opinion, shifted ground and supported the French argument, but the British were adamantly against Italy's return to Libya, and so the discussions stalled.[116] The CFM also failed to make any progress on another highly contentious issue, the fate of Trieste, which France (like America and Britain) felt should remain in Italian hands,[117] and most Italian issues were put to the Deputies for further study.

So far as Germany was concerned, Bidault submitted a memorandum at the first meeting which recalled France's position at the London CFM and restated her desiderata: a decentralised state, with most powers residing in the *Länder*; a politically separate Ruhr under an international regime, whose exact form, including Russia's role, was left vague; a politically separate Rhineland, possibly divided into smaller states, and occupied by France, Britain and the Benelux powers; and the inclusion of the Saar in a monetary and economic union with France, without annexation but with French ownership of the coal mines.[118] Bevin, as seen above, refused to discuss the Ruhr in isolation from other issues at the full CFM,[119] (though fruitless exchanges on the Ruhr were carried on behind the scenes at a bilateral Anglo-French level.)[120] Only on 15 May was Bidault finally able to present France's case verbally to the other foreign ministers. He hoped at least to resolve the future of the Saar, but he had hardly finished his speech before Bevin and Molotov began to bicker over the Ruhr. The Russian wanted to discuss British policy there, but Bevin stuck to his case that it was wrong to deal with the Ruhr in isolation from other German topics. The arguments continued the next day and no advance was made.[121]

There was little progress either on a proposal from Byrnes, first raised in 1945[122] but only formally put to the other occupation powers in February 1946, for a treaty between them to guarantee the complete disarmament and demilitarisation of Germany for twenty-five years.[123] Jean Chauvel saw the 'Byrnes Treaty', as it became known, as most significant for implying a long-term US security commitment to Europe, something which had never been achieved in the inter-war period, and he hoped for a favourable response to it. In itself however, neither Bidault nor the EMDN saw the treaty as a significant answer to French preoccupations. Disarmament and demilitarisation were already promised under the Potsdam accords, and the French were of course determined to enforce many other political and economic controls on Germany's war-making ability.[124] Bidault put these points to Caffery in mid-April, and recalled how Germany had broken free of military limits after 1919, though he added that France was ready to discuss the US idea.[125] Byrnes presented his treaty to the CFM on 29 April as offering a US guarantee to Europe which should reassure France and Russia about the German problem. However whilst Bidault and Bevin were prepared to study it, progress was prevented by Molotov who argued that what was necessary was not a future guarantee but an investigation into the current state of disarmament in the four zones.[126]

The first session of the Paris CFM thus ended with little progress, and little relief in the arguments between the Soviets and Anglo-Saxons which had grown particularly strong since February. The arguments in Paris had lacked the vitriol and passion seen in Bevin's earlier arguments with Molotov in September and with Vyshinsky in February, but Massigli felt that Britain remained distrustful of Russia, militarily vulnerable because of the advent of the atom bomb and long-range missiles, and eager to develop links to America.[127] The American press were firmly behind Byrnes' new, uncompromising policy, according to Bonnet.[128] Also the Soviet press accused the Americans and the British of 'ganging-up' on them. Catroux left the conference despondent and feared that Byrnes' tough policy would only harden Soviet suspicions.[129] As to France herself, it seemed doubtful whether she could long remain the mistress of her own destiny, given her relative lack of strength vis-à-vis America and Russia, and the fact that both these countries – as seen with the Blum talks and wheat loan – were intensely interested in the country's future. However French independence was precious, she had foreign policy aims quite distinct from the Big Three and she would find it extremely painful to choose between East and West for a number of reasons. Bidault might be fearful of 'Cossacks on the Place de la Concorde' and Monnet might base French recovery on US financial aid, but the French government could not easily antagonise the Soviets when one of its major constituents was the PCF, nor was there much ground for an alliance with the Anglo-Saxons on the key foreign policy problem, Germany. For the moment Bidault still chose, therefore, the role of a 'bridge' between East and West, as he had first advocated in November 1944. It gave him some successes at Paris, where he did much to break the log-jam on procedure and it meant that bilateral Franco-Soviet relations improved markedly during the first half of 1946.

* * *

On 5 May 1946, whilst the CFM was still meeting and before the general election could be held, the French people had to vote in a referendum on their new Constitution. As expected, given the Communist-Socialist predominance in the Constituent Assembly, the draft Constitution was suited to 'Marxist' ideas on the political process, with a very powerful National Assembly and a weak President.[130] The MRP and Radicals disliked the draft document and launched a determined campaign against it. As the referendum approached there was speculation that a 'No' vote might provoke the PCF into launching a coup. Caffery discounted such rumours: even if they lost the referendum, the Communists could still hope to do well in the elections which followed. However the US War Department took a different line and drafted instructions to the American Governor in Germany, General Joseph McNarney,[131] authorising him to move forces into France in the event of a 'serious disturbance' there. He was to use a minimum of personnel, to act only 'to protect US lives and property' and to 'take no part in French internal conflict'. The State Department felt nevertheless that McNarney was being given far too much discretion, and that any move by him would allow the PCF to appeal for Soviet aid. Also, there was little US property in France to be put at risk anyway. But Truman confirmed the General's instructions after a high-level White House meeting.[132] As it was, such extreme precautions were quite unnecessary. The French people rejected the draft constitution by 53 per cent but there was no Communist coup. US representatives at the CFM 'made no attempt to hide their satisfaction'[133] and Caffery saw it as a major fillip to non-Communist politicians, though he, along with professional diplomats in the State Department and the British Foreign Office, felt that the PCF vote would still hold firm in the general election.[134] That election would now elect a new Constituent Assembly to draw up a new draft Constitution. After the referendum supporters of General de Gaulle urged him to attempt a return to office, but the General himself believed that he would return to government only through some grave crisis, such as another war.[135] Thus there was no attempt to seize power by either the extreme Left or the Right, and the general election, which had inspired so many fears since its date was announced, went forward on 2 June without any serious disturbance. It saw a slight decline in the Communist vote (26.5 per cent), with the MRP (28 per cent) emerging as the predominant force and the Socialists (21 per cent) falling back.[136] On 19 June the new Assembly approved Georges Bidault as the new Premier, and he also remained Foreign Minister. This was despite the forthcoming CFM and peace conference, which would place an enormous burden on the host minister, and despite the fact that (in the absence of a figurehead president), he was also expected to fulfil the ceremonial duties of a Head of State. 'It is really a case of *reductio ad absurdum*', complained Jacques Dumaine.[137] It was quite evident that political uncertainty in France would continue for many months. Meanwhile international attention shifted back to the reconvening CFM.[138]

Chapter 6

Crying in the Wilderness.
June 1946 – January 1947.

I have the impression that when France talks of Germany it is the voice of one crying in the wilderness, and until now the wilderness has made no echo.
– Georges Bidault, speaking to the American Press Club in Paris, 26 September 1946 (copy in the archives of the Quai d'Orsay, Series Y, *Internationale* 1944–9, volume 288).

On 15 June 1946 Georges Bidault welcomed the Soviet, American and British foreign ministers to the Palais du Luxembourg, for the second session of the Paris Council of Foreign Ministers. He was able to report good progress among the Deputies during the recess and an agenda was immediately agreed.[1] In early July sufficient advance was made for the date of the long-awaited peace conference to be set for 29 July.[2] Throughout the procedural discussions Bidault continued to play the role of 'honest broker' and progress seemed better than during the first session. But behind the scenes the signs of tension between East and West continued. Both Bevin and Byrnes were determined to refuse concessions to Russia.[3] From Washington, Armand Berard reported that 'It appears today that the Fulton Speech has borne its fruits' and that most US people supported Byrnes' toughness with Molotov. Importantly, however, Berard also believed that Americans would avoid war with Russia, partly because of their dislike of large military forces in peacetime and partly because US opposition to Russia was based on ideological factors rather than any fundamental clash of interests.[4] The Quai feared that the Soviets would prove intransigent at the conference, particularly when attention turned to Germany, as it soon must.[5] Significantly Chauvel told Caffery that if four-power co-operation in Germany broke down most French officials would favour co-operation with America and Britain. Because of the Communists' position in government and the MRP's commitment to the separation of the Ruhr, Rhineland and Saar, France would not be able to co-operate openly with the Anglo-Saxons, but specific problems could be settled with them 'and eventually when a definitive French government is established there will be a possibility . . . [of] some real agreement'.[6]

By early July France had gained much of what it hoped for in talks on the Italian treaty. Her border claims in the Alps were approved[7] and the principle of reparations payments from Italy was agreed.[8] But other issues proved more divisive. It was impossible to settle the fate of the Italian colonies[9] and Trieste proved as divisive as ever. Chauvel told Caffery on 22 June, indeed, that Trieste was the key to the success of the whole conference: if progress was possible there then there could be breakthroughs elsewhere.[10] And Bidault made a special point of seeking a mediatory role on the question. He had an early success at a select meeting of the four foreign ministers on 21 June, when America and Britain agreed to accept the Italo-Yugoslav border as defined by France, as the fairest line of division. It gave more of the Trieste hinterland to Yugoslavia than they had previously been willing to offer. But Molotov still wanted Trieste as well to be given to Tito's Yugoslavia. Eventually, on 29 June, after earlier attempts at compromise had failed, Bidault put forward a detailed scheme for Trieste to become an international port, similar to the inter-war status of Danzig, and on 1 July Molotov accepted this proposal. There were some suspicions on the US side over the sudden breakthrough, and fears that Bidault had secretly 'colluded' with Molotov on the issue, perhaps to obtain concessions on other areas of the Italian treaty. But within a few days it was formally agreed to make Trieste a 'free territory' under UN supervision.[11] Though he involved himself little in settling the final details, Bidault could be pleased at the outcome. It was significant that, as Chauvel had predicted, once the fate of Trieste was settled, agreement was quickly reached on other issues.

Less satisfying was the reaction of the Italians to French policy. The Italian government under Alcide de Gasperi, struggling against daunting internal problems, had kept up its efforts to emphasise Italy's 'co-belligerency' in the war, to re-establish a European and Mediterranean role for Rome, and to minimise losses in the peace treaty. But de Gasperi felt betrayed by his fellow-Christian Democrat, Bidault, on the treaty issues.[12] The French talked of Franco-Italian friendship, supported Italy's retention of her colonies and took a pro-Italian line on the question of the Austrian border, but in many other issues seemed determined to humiliate Italy, to underline her ex-enemy status and to assert France's primary role in the western Mediterranean. At Paris Bidault's Trieste compromise helped the CFM to progress but it also meant a retreat from the US, British and French position of favouring the port's return to Italy. In May and June the Italians directed several appeals for moderation in the peace treaty at the Americans and condemned French border claims as being 'based on brutal strategic reasons' adding that 'it is not on such terms that . . . Europe can be constructed'.[13]

With the Italian, and the East European treaties resolved so far as possible, the CFM turned its attentions to Germany. In July Bidault had an article published in the influential American journal, *Foreign Affairs*, defending the French case in Germany and asking: 'Is it harsh to deprive an inveterate aggressor of the means of repeating his offense?'[14] It was presumably intended to provide a fitting backcloth to the detailed four-power discussion on Germany which France had long sought. French representatives, not least Koenig in Baden-Baden, were still determined to sever the Ruhr–Rhineland from Germany and make the remainder into a weak, confederated state.[15] Perhaps inevitably, however, when the grand, four-power debate got under way it was dominated not by discussion of French desiderata, but by the divisions between the Soviets and Anglo-Saxons. Germany was indeed the 'key to world peace', but not in the way Bidault intended this phrase in his article.

On 9 July Molotov criticised the Byrnes Treaty as inadequate to control the German menace. The speech upset the Anglo-Americans but was seen, in part, as a way to satisfy French opinion about Russia's commitment to control Germany, and also as a way to soften the blow in Paris of what was to come.[16] The following day all four ministers made statements of their respective approaches to the German problem, and clearly revealed their lack of common ground. Bidault began, with a call to resolve Germany's future in three stages: first – predictably – the settlement of territorial issues, including the severance of the Ruhr, Rhine and Saar; secondly the establishment of strong *Länder*, agreement on a reparations programme and the fulfilment of the principles of disarmament and denazification; and finally resolution of Germany's long-term status as a demilitarised, democratic country. He also expressed support for the Byrnes Treaty and a desire to resolve the problem of German coal supplies. Bevin and Byrnes then made speeches which criticised the Soviets for failing to carry out the economic agreements made at Potsdam, and made clear the Anglo-Saxon interest in minimising occupation costs in Germany.

The most dramatic statement, however, was that of Molotov, whose speech was seen by many as nothing less than an appeal for German popular support for Soviet policies. The Russian condemned proposals for a federalist German government, the separation of the Ruhr and the 'agrarianisation' of the country (the last a reference to America's Morghenthau Plan of 1943) because these were rooted 'in the same policy of destruction . . .'. Instead of breeding a spirit of revenge in Germany, Molotov suggested ways to create 'a democratic and peace-loving state'. War industries must be prohibited, reparations taken and 'the Ruhr should be placed under inter-allied control', but otherwise German industry could be developed and a centralised government should be created. Thus, simultaneously, he restated Soviet aims of a share in the Ruhr and large reparations, criticised the US over the Morghenthau Plan and France over the Ruhr, and appealed to the Germans with the offer of a strong government and economic expansion.[17]

Bitter clashes continued for two days after the speech, before the CFM adjourned, with both the Soviets and Anglo-Saxons accusing the other of breaking the Potsdam agreement. Byrnes insisted that America 'has never sought to impose a peace of vengeance upon Germany' and, in a highly important step, offered to 'fuse' the US zone immediately with any other zone which truly wanted to preserve German unity. Bidault, pushed into the background for most of the time, complained that the conference had become a series of soliloquies, but made his own final bid to keep Germany united by saying that France was now ready to accept 'Allied offices' in such areas as finance and foreign trade, to provide economic unity, so long as these were under ACC control and excluded from the Saar.[18] But the time when a compromise solution on central agencies could have made a real difference in Germany was past and General Clay was unimpressed by Bidault's latest suggestion, because agencies which operated separately in each zone would do nothing to break down Germany's 'airtight' divisions.[19]

Bidault's personal copy of the Molotov speech contains numerous pencilled underlinings, which suggest a particular concern with Soviet policies on the Ruhr, a central government and German industrial revival, none of which could appeal to France.[20] The Quai saw the speech as one of major importance.[21] It seemed designed to help the German Communist Party (KPD), with promises of political and economic revival, whereas the 9 July statement had seemed designed to please the French Communists, with promises of German demilitarisation. The Kremlin was evidently quite prepared to let the KPD and PCF make entirely different 'nationalist' points in order to impress their respective peoples.[22] The *chargé d'affaires* in Moscow, Pierre Charpentier pointed out, in a long analysis which did not arrive in Paris until September, that in fact much of what Molotov had said, such as his desire for a centralised government and large reparations, was established Russian policy. Charpentier felt that the speech was directed at America and Britain rather than France, and was designed to win concessions from them. The *chargé* optimistically argued that, so long as France took an anti-German line and remained independent of the Anglo-Saxons, she might yet win concessions from the Soviets on the western borders.[23]

Others, however, were less confident. In Germany Emile Laffon, the civilian-administrator, saw the events at the CFM as vindicating a belief he had held for some months, that France's 'thesis' on Germany would be rejected by all the other powers. René Massigli went further and argued that, with a clear East-West breakdown, France must choose to co-operate with the Americans and the British in Germany, drawing in Belgium and Holland too. These countries were all opposed to Soviet ideas of a centralised Germany, and it was the British and Americans who controlled the bulk of *Western* Germany (especially the Ruhr) which was vital to French aims.[24] But Massigli's arguments were countered by those of Hervé Alphand. In a memorandum of 18 July, Alphand noted that all the Big Three powers were opposed to French aims in the Ruhr–Rhine and interested in increasing Germany's industrial production. He agreed that the American and British policies, their willingness to integrate the Saar into France for example, were more attractive than Molotov's schemes. Nevertheless, in contrast to Massigli, Alphand concluded that France should *not* yet modify its policies, mainly because such a course did not seem necessary. The CFM had yet to turn its full attention to Germany, the Paris talks had been a mere preliminary exchange, and any major concessions on the Ruhr or central agencies could wait for the negotiations proper. France must continue to seek security guarantees from Germany, and an assurance that its own steel industry would be expanded whilst its neighbour's was controlled.[25]

Neither did Byrnes' proposal on zonal 'fusion' lead the French to veer from their independent line. On 20 July, the US formally repeated the proposal at the ACC and the British, faced with a mounting financial burden in Germany, and having much in common with American policy already, accepted it. Discussions on the formation of a 'Bizone', fusing the US and British zones, began soon after. The British insisted that this was a move towards keeping Germany together, but in Berlin St Hardouin feared it merely hardened divisions and, if anything, increased the popular appeal of Molotov's call for German reunification. Both sides, Soviet and Anglo-Saxon, were bidding for German support with promises of political and economic revival, and so undermining hopes of firm controls on the old enemy.[26] In deciding their own reaction to the Bizone proposal the French had various factors to consider. On one side they differed with the Anglo-Saxons on the Ruhr–Rhine, had pro-Soviet PCF ministers in the Cabinet, and did not wish to share the large financial deficit of the Anglo-American zones. On the other they disliked much in Molotov's speech, relied on coal supplies from the British zone, and for practical reasons (trade and communications for example) would have to work on a daily basis with the Bizone. Chauvel warned the British not to make France choose sides in this debate yet[27] and as its general policy the Quai decided to reject the proposal of fusion whilst establishing technical links to the Bizone. They also decided to continue policies in the French zone aimed at political decentralisation and the severance of the Saar and, at a four-power level, to call for a decentralised German government whilst restating their own ideas for a compromise on central agencies.[28] For the moment, therefore, France would join neither the Soviets, nor the Anglo-Saxons, in their visions of Germany, but rather continue to assert her own policy.

* * *

On 27 and 28 July a formidable array of prime ministers, deputy premiers and foreign ministers from twenty-one countries arrived in Paris to attend the Paris peace conference. Hundreds of joiners, electricians and engineers had laboured for weeks in the Palais du Luxembourg, to install a broadcasting studio, forty telephone booths and a restaurant, but *The Times* of London still considered the Senate Chamber, with its grey pillars and ageing wood panelling to be 'slightly soporific' as the venue for plenary meetings.[29] 'Peace conference' was a grandiose title for a gathering which was very different to that of 1919. Treaties with the two principal defeated powers, Germany and Japan, were not ready for discussion, nor was that with Austria. Detailed draft treaties for Italy and Eastern Europe had, furthermore, already been drawn up by the CFM and the conference, to the dismay of the smaller powers, could only 'recommend' changes to these. Bidault was quite apologetic about the last point in his opening speech as host on the 29th, but he also made references to the 1919 settlement and hoped that this time the conferences could successfully banish 'the plague of war' from the world.[30] The conference absorbed most of the energies of all the major foreign ministries until 15 October, made numerous recommendations on the peace treaties and included several private meetings of the CFM powers. But all in all it was an uninspiring affair. The talks fell broadly into three phases: a general statement of each country's view in 'gloomy sittings, devoid of human spark',[31] a detailed study of each peace treaty by a number of commissions, and finally a consideration of these studies in plenary meetings. There were many unpleasant clashes between Western and Eastern representatives.[32] The French regularly tried to work for compromises and were dismayed by the divisions. 'During these three months ...', complained Jacques Dumaine, 'the delegations have contented themselves with airing their respective, irreconcilable differences ...'.[33] The work went slowly, some delegations seemed ill-prepared and at the end, in protest at the fate of Trieste, the Yugoslav delegation did not even sit to hear Bidault's closing speech.

The French were generally held to have borne the technical burdens of the conference[34] 'with skill, grace and dignity'.[35] The worst blunder was on 25

119

August when, to celebrate the anniversary of the Liberation of Paris, the delegates were invited to the Hotel de Ville but seated in alphabetical order. Molotov, finding himself on the second row and feeling insulted, pointedly walked out of the ceremony after the Marseillaise was played.[36] So far as the actual talks were concerned, the Quai d'Orsay's main interest remained the Italian treaty. Officials hoped in vain for an improvement in Franco-Italian relations during the conference.[37] Rome remained firmly opposed to French border claims.[38] At the end of the conference Bidault expressed his pleasure that Paris had been, once more, 'the political centre of the world', but feared that a lot of work had brought little result.[39]

It was agreed, before the conference ended, that the four major powers would meet to finalise the peace treaties in New York on 4 November and that there would be a 'preliminary' discussion on Germany there, which might put preparations for drafting a peace treaty under way.[40] Whilst the peace conference was under way the chances of agreement on a German treaty had become even slimmer, however. In early September, in a speech in Stuttgart, James Byrnes made what was openly advertised by the State Department as a response to Molotov's dramatic declaration of 10 July. Byrnes' speech did not so much define a new policy as clarify and amplify what was already being done, but it nonetheless had a major impact. Byrnes offered the Germans economic revival and democratic self-government, called for the country to be treated as an 'economic unit' and said that the Ruhr–Rhineland – though not the Saar – must remain part of it. He also said that US troops would remain in Germany until the peace was secure, thereby reversing Roosevelt's policy of withdrawing troops.[41]

The press response to these declarations was predictably favourable in America and Britain, but in Eastern Europe the speech was castigated as likely to recreate a German menace, and in Western Europe the reaction was mixed. Bonnet had been assured beforehand that Byrnes' statement would have no unpleasant surprises for France, but the Paris press saw it as offering little to them, except the Saar.[42] French officials too took a poor view of Stuttgart. In Germany, St Hardouin saw it primarily as a form of pressure on Russia through an appeal to German popular opinion, but was disappointed that it proposed both industrial revival and Germany's retention of the Ruhr. Chauvel added, in a conversation with a British representative, that the speech was too centralist in conception. The *Direction d'Europe* noted that 'it is difficult to appreciate the new American position from a purely French point of view' owing to the primacy of Soviet-American rivalry in motivating the speech[43] but Armand Berard complained to the State Department about its content and about America's lack of sympathy for France. The State Department, however, believed that French worries would dissipate, and they can only have been encouraged in this belief by Chauvel's continuing reassurances to Caffery that France wanted to work with the Anglo-Americans and that, once her long-term political future was settled, her German policy could be changed.[44]

In a speech to the American Press Club in Paris on 26 September, Bidault was able to expound some French fears when he talked of the 'unchanging' nature of the German threat.[45] Byrnes addressed the same body a week later and tried to provide some succour to Bidault by dispelling certain concerns about Stuttgart. He emphasised America's desire for strong *Länder* in Germany and for economic controls on the Ruhr.[46] Meanwhile, however, preparations for a Bizone were proceeding apace, most Americans were now pronouncedly anti-Soviet, and the Stuttgart speech had made the Soviets more suspicious of US intentions than ever.[47] The sense of Soviet-American division was heightened still further by the expulsion of the liberal Commerce Secretary, Henry Wallace, from the American Cabinet after he had publicly advocated a policy of co-operation with Russia. Yet the French people felt little desire to take sides in the superpower competition. In March 1946 a poll had shown that about a quarter of French people believed the Soviets wanted to dominate the world, but a similar number thought the Americans did. And it was almost exactly the same picture a year later, in February 1947. In September 1946, in a Gallup poll, while twice as many (40 per cent) said they would sympathise with Washington rather than Moscow (21 per cent) in a conflict, the overwhelming majority (82 per cent) wanted France to avoid involvement in such a struggle.[48]

* . * . *

By Autumn 1946 it was clear that the rift between the two superpowers was having an impact on other areas of French foreign policy. Anglo-French relations, for example, remained troubled. In early July Duff Cooper personally approached Bidault to suggest an Anglo-French alliance, but the Frenchman did not take Cooper seriously.[49] A short time later, when Massigli raised the problems of Ruhr coal exports and the dangers of German industrial revival with Ernest Bevin, the Foreign Secretary lost his temper, complained that France had always resisted his attempts to work with her, and insisted that she should join the Anglo-American group in Germany in order to stand up to Russia.[50] Massigli became very concerned about the 'progressive deterioration' in relations with Britain after Bevin's rancorous remarks, and asked Bidault to address the problem.[51] Hervé Alphand too hoped for some action to improve relations and favoured an attempt to 'integrate' the economic policies of France and Britain.[52] Alphand was of course a keen advocate of co-operation with other powers to compensate for French industrial weaknesses. Economic links with Britain seemed particularly appropriate given Anglo-French proximity, their need to reduce dollar deficits with the US, and the belief, which was gaining ground late in 1946, that a 'European' voice was needed in a world increasingly dominated by Washington and Moscow. In September 1946 Winston Churchill gave great encouragement to such ideas with a speech in Zurich calling for European unity.[53] There was also the fact that, as Massigli had told the Quai in June, Bevin himself was very interested in the idea of a European customs union, as a way to create a large, thriving market for goods, which could match that of the US.[54] By late August both French and British thinking was moving, quite independently, towards the idea of a full discussion on mutual economic problems which led to talks between the two finance ministers, Robert Schuman and Hugh Dalton, in September. Debt issues were resolved, a commitment was made to reduce unnecessary, destructive competition between the two and, on Bevin's initiative, an Anglo-French Economic Committee, similar to the Franco-Benelux body, was founded to tackle bilateral problems in regular meetings.[55]

The resolution of economic issues in September 1946 fell far short of Alphand's hopes for full-scale economic 'integration' with Britain, however, and in other fields Anglo-French division continued. An exchange of views between officials on German problems confirmed their differences on the Ruhr, coal and other issues[56] and on 22 October Bevin made a speech to the Commons which, though less dramatic than Molotov's speech of 10 July or Byrnes' at Stuttgart, was a solid reaffirmation of Britain's German policy with support for the Bizone, a desire to cut occupation costs and faith in economic controls, rather than political separation, in the Ruhr.[57] Bevin also remained suspicious of pro-Soviet influence in Paris via the PCF, telling Bidault that it was impossible for Britain and France to talk 'with a third Great Power in the cupboard . . .'.[58] Massigli, aware that many in Britain (including the official head of the Foreign Office, Orme Sargent) were interested in the idea of an Anglo-French combination, and still ruing the fact that a British alliance had not been made early in 1945, feared that London was growing closer and closer to Washington as time went on, and believed that only a fundamental change in France's German policy could alter the situation. He told Chauvel: 'More than ever . . . I am convinced that we have nothing to gain from restricting ourselves to our initial policy, when we know that it is rejected by everyone else.[59] In his memoirs, Chauvel claimed to share such sentiments, but at the time he felt that an improvement in relations with Britain would only come when the French political situation was clarified.[60] Before the end of the Paris peace conference Bevin and Bidault talked about their desire for improved relations and the troubles which divided them. Bidault made much of the need to avoid the situation where France was seen as 'pro-Soviet' and Britain as 'pro-American' and, like Chauvel, hoped that things would improve after the next elections.[61]

There was also pressure on France from the Benelux states in late 1946 to change policy in Germany and work with the Anglo-Saxons. The Political Director of the Dutch Foreign Ministry told a French representative in September that if France continued to seek a conciliatory course between East and West she would fall 'between the quay and the boat'; Paris should admit the existence of the 'iron curtain' and adopt the Stuttgart speech as a programme for the future. The Dutch, needed German economic revival to help their own commercial and agricultural expansion, and in this sense were sympathetic to the Anglo-Saxons. They, and the Belgians and Luxembourgers, were also unenthusiastic about the separation of the Ruhr from Germany. But the Benelux states *were* willing to join France in pressuring America and Britain for a decentralised Germany, a long occupation of the Ruhr–Rhineland and the international use of the Ruhr's resources. (The Belgians leant rather more towards the French than the Dutch on issues of economic security.) It seemed therefore that the Benelux countries could act as a 'bridge' between French and Anglo-American policies. Nevertheless, for the moment such an idea had little appeal in Paris. The Benelux states remained excluded from the CFM discussions on Germany's future and the policies of the Big Three remained most vital for France.[62]

The French also failed to progress, during 1946, with links to the smaller East European states. It will be recalled that in 1945 the Quai had hoped to re-establish traditional friendships with countries like Czechoslovakia, with whom de Gaulle had signed a declaration of amity in 1944, and Poland, and to revive cultural and economic influence in the area. But, whilst Moscow 'froze' France out of diplomatic discussions on Eastern Europe at the London CFM, local Communist-dominated governments undermined French influence through such policies as nationalisation, and the Quai itself proved reluctant to sign a treaty with Poland. At the UN Assembly in February 1946 Bidault had discussed economic co-operation with Poland's Deputy Foreign Minister, Zygmunt Modzelewski, and the idea was raised of making a Franco-Polish declaration of amity. For the Quai the latter proposal was much better than the idea of a treaty in that it kept commitments to Poland on the same level as those with Czechoslovakia. By the end of March the Poles had drafted a declaration and amendments to it were discussed during the following month. Then, however, a series of problems began which eventually killed the proposal.

At the beginning of May Modzelewski suddenly proposed a series of changes to the draft declaration which profoundly altered its nature, differed significantly from the 1944 Franco-Czech document and raised similar problems to the treaty proposal of the previous November. Modzelewski wanted France to consult Poland on *all* important matters relating to Germany, and to affirm the need for 'just' German borders, presumably meaning the Oder-Neisse line. The Quai d'Orsay sensed in this an attempt to tie France indirectly to Soviet policy in Germany and to upset Britain and America. Modzelewski's proposal would commit France to exchange information for no reward, since Poland had no share in controlling Germany. With memories of 1939, officials also raised the problem of fulfilling commitments to Poland in future if France and Russia fell out. France, devastated by defeat in 1940 and occupation thereafter was clearly even less able to resist Soviet power in Eastern Europe than she had been to resist Hitler. Such caution was strongly reinforced by René Massigli who argued from London that France must never again be tied to weak powers on Germany's eastern border, that she must preserve her freedom of manoeuvre in talks on Germany and that alliances should only be made with the 'Big Three' or with countries, like Belgium and Holland, which were absolutely vital for French security. French officials were also concerned by continuing problems over Polish emigrés in France, increasing attacks on liberal-democratic parties in Poland and Soviet influence on Polish foreign policy. On 24 May, therefore, Modzelewski's proposals were rejected. Then, in an incredibly swift *volte-face*, Modzelewski simply accepted the French view: it was clear that he had merely been 'testing the ground' with his proposed changes to the declaration. The discussion then turned back to the original, less ambitious text.[63]

Late in June 1946, after further exchanges, a Franco-Polish declaration was finalised and it was arranged that Modzelewski should visit Paris to sign it.[64] It was then, however, that other problems began to emerge. One concerned relations with Prague. The Czechs, as in the inter-war years, were engaged in bitter arguments with Poland over the Silesian border, despite the Soviet and Communist influence in both countries, and were suspicious of any Franco-Polish links. In late April Prague was assured that the proposed Franco-Polish declaration went no further than the 1944 London declaration with Czechoslovakia, but the Czechs seemed less than happy. President Benes, Foreign Minister Masaryk and his deputy Clementis, confident that memories of Munich had faded, now wanted to make a *treaty* with France, to build on commercial and cultural accords made in October and December 1945.[65] On 9 July, the Czech Cabinet formally approved Masaryk's recommendation that a treaty with Paris should be negotiated, based on the anti-German text of the recent Czech-Yugoslav alliance (a text which was similar to a whole series of pacts negotiated between the East European nations after the war with Moscow's blessing). Russia apparently had no objection to a Franco-Czech alliance, and Ambassador Maurice Dejean hoped it could be pursued in earnest. But once again there were doubts in the Quai. In mid-July Bidault instructed Dejean to be circumspect on the Czech ideas, since one East European treaty could lead to demands for others, the Czechs might merely be overreacting to the Franco-Polish talks, and the Quai wanted to see the peace settlement in Eastern Europe completed before deciding on future policy in the region.

A Quai d'Orsay memorandum of 17 July showed, however, that officials in Paris had more doubts about a Czech treaty than those which had been revealed to Dejean. Quite bluntly it was stated here that Czechoslovakia, despite the survival of a liberal-democratic image was so dominated by Communists, who had gained 35 per cent of votes in elections in May, and who were by far the largest party in parliament and government, that the country was virtually 'part' of Russia. And a treaty with Czechoslovakia and other Soviet satellites would upset America and Britain without necessarily helping Franco-Soviet relations:

> If the Soviet Union is, in fact, the mistress of Czechoslovak destiny, our alliance with her is sufficient. If on the contrary Prague resists Moscow, the links which we form with the Czechoslovak republic would only embarrass us. Once again, we would risk shooting ourselves in the foot.

There had been no relaxation of Soviet control over Eastern Europe since the war, indeed quite the opposite, and the French were concerned about offending America and Britain with links to the Soviet puppet regimes in Eastern Europe. If the Czechs insisted on some new agreement with France, French officials wanted this to be, not a treaty, but a revamped Franco-Czech declaration. The Quai continued to face strong pressures from Prague for a treaty both from Dejean and from Czech politicians. In August, in direct contrast to the Quai's ideas, Benes pressed for a treaty on the grounds that Franco-Czech co-operation could help to keep East and West together, and so reverse the distressing trend towards Europe's division. Presumably for different reasons the Communist Premier, Klement Gottwald, raised the treaty proposal with Maurice Dejean in October. By then, however, France was engaged in its next round of elections.[66]

Meanwhile serious difficulties on the Polish side were more important in preventing the signature of a Franco-Polish declaration. In late June the Quai had been upset once again by reports that the Poles saw the declaration as implying support for the Oder-Neisse border. French officials were adamant that the declaration was one of general amity, expressing a common interest in resolving the German problem, and involving no commitments beyond those given to Czechoslovakia. Then, in mid-July, the Poles again tried to amend the declaration so that is should aim to 'stabilise the present German frontiers in the East and to fix them in an equitable manner in the West'. This could hardly be considered an 'equitable' alteration, however, from the French viewpoint: while the Oder-Neisse line was already effectively in force French hopes for amendments to the German border in the West had yet even to be discussed. But when the French rejected the new proposal the Polish Cabinet, in contrast to Modzelewski's behaviour in May, put talks on the declaration into suspense. Months of negotiation had come to nothing and, though evidence in sparse, the reason seems to have been Polish concern at the increasing East–West divide in Germany. From remarks made by Modzelewski in November it seems that, despite Soviet influence over the Warsaw government, Molotov's speech of 10 July had surprised the Poles and caused them grave concern. For Modzelewski professed to Dejean to be terrified that Soviet policy could create a new, united and centralised Reich. In such circumstances a Franco-Polish declaration was seen in Warsaw as a complicating factor vis-à-vis Russia and Germany.[67]

* * *

Faced by an increasingly divided world, the failure to forge strong alliances with the smaller states of Europe and pressures to choose between East and West, France had few sources of strength that might allow it to preserve an independent policy. Continuing economic weakness, for example, fatally undermined the strength of the armed forces, the traditional measure of a Great Power. The Army, Navy and Air Force after 1945 all had to come to terms with the memories of defeat in 1940 and internecine struggles thereafter, to meet the challenge of new military methods developed during the war, and to cope with spending cuts introduced by the Gouin Cabinet in a desperate bid to cut government spending after the end of US lend-lease. Where de Gaulle had seen the armed forces as the source of French *grandeur* and bitterly resisted budgetary reductions on them before his resignation, the Socialists and officials in the Finance Ministry argued that it was better to cut military spending so as to restore the economy. When the economy was healthy the armed forces could be strengthened once more.[68] In April, in order to cope with this 'transitional' period of financial difficulties, the number of servicemen was set at 400,000 for the Army, 50,000 for the Air Force and 45,000 for the Navy.[69]

Demobilisation, lack of equipment, poor training facilities, and the process of 'devichyisation' all led to a decline in Army morale. In May 1945 the Army had numbered about 1.3 million men. De Gaulle and General Juin hoped it could provide France with a mobile 'intervention force', to defend national interests anywhere in future at short notice. But in 1946 the idea of the 'intervention force' was dropped and the Army's role was reduced to that of occupying Germany and Austria, maintaining imperial defence, contributing to UN forces and training reservists. In October 1946, furthermore, military service was fixed at only one year, which made the task of training high-quality personnel very difficult.[70] The post-war Navy, at 400,000 tons, stood at half its pre-war size, was tiny compared to US and British forces, and could take little satisfaction from the destruction of the German, Italian and Japanese fleets. Many ships were quite outmoded, after the war shipbuilding facilities were mainly used to produce merchant vessels, research centres and the naval bases at Brest and Toulon were ruined, and commanders had to come to terms with such wartime developments as the advent of the carrier task force, the snorkel and sonar in submarine warfare, and the atom bomb. The Air Force indeed argued that the atom bomb rendered navies obsolete and, unsurprisingly, favoured concentration on air defence. In January 1946, despite assistance from the British and Americans with equipment, the Navy was forced to reduce its initial plans, and to aim at only two carrier task forces, thirty ocean-going submarines and other limited forces.[71] The Air Force, largely equipped with US and British machines, also had to address a wide range of tasks – the defence of France, bombing and reconnaissance, and air policing in the empire – in a new world of missiles and jet aircraft. Fierce debate raged, not only between the Air Force and Navy about the impact of atomic warfare, but also between the Air Force and Army over the feasibility of France 'conquering the air' and launching strategic bombing raids in future against an opponent. General Juin felt such notions were quite unrealistic and believed that the Air Force should simply support Army operations as a kind of long-range 'artillery'. Air defence should be left to France's allies – whoever they might be.[72]

The post-war decline of French armed forces was not unique. Henri Bonnet took an intense interest in American military preparedness during 1945–46, highlighting the maintenance of large armed forces, the development of a network of bases and continued technological developments,[73] but the US army was actually cut from 12 million in 1945, to 3 million in 1946, then to only 1.5 million in 1947 and remained at that size until 1950.[74] In early 1946 the British decided to cut their forces to 1.1 million by the end of the year after they had stood at 4.7 million in June 1945.[75] And Soviet forces were reduced from 11.3 million in wartime probably to 2.8 million in 1948, though contemporaries often overestimated their size.[76] In late 1945 de Gaulle had been concerned at the Red Army's slow pace of demobilisation and the EMDN considered the possibility of forming a united force in Western Europe, including US and German troops, to resist the Russians.[77] But despite such musings French defence policy in 1946 was directed, like its diplomacy, at neutralism: France would, supposedly, defend herself against anyone who attacked her.[78]

Clearly, given the poor state of all the armed forces, this placed the country in a very vulnerable position and the most dramatic evidence of France's failure to keep up with wartime military advances remained her lack of atomic technology. Although French scientists like Frédéric Joliot-Curie had been at the forefront of research into radioactivity before the war, and although several Frenchmen had worked in the Anglo-Canadian atomic programme after 1940, President Roosevelt had been reluctant to share the secrets of the 'Manhattan Project' with them.[79] De Gaulle discussed the atom bomb with the scientists in Ottawa in July 1944[80] and in October 1945 made Joliot-Curie the head of an Atomic Energy Commission (*Commissariat à l'Energie Atomique*) to research and 'promote the use of atomic energy in the . . . fields of science, industry and national defence.'[81] In 1946 attempts were made to forge links in the atomic field with Britain, Belgium (with its control of uranium in the Congo) and Norway (a source of 'heavy water' before the fall of France). These schemes did not get far, however. The British preferred co-operation with America, the Americans were suspicious of Joliot-Curie's sympathy for the PCF, and the French remained far off the ultimate prize in atomic research, the ability to produce an atom bomb.[82]

Just as France was unable to maintain its independence through military and economic strength, so it was unable to find a source of salvation in the empire. True, between 1938 and 1950 exports to the 'French Union' from the mother country increased markedly from 27 per cent to 36 per cent of total exports. The empire was used as a vital source of raw materials and could help in the defence against the power of the US dollar. But, as wartime studies showed,[83] the empire could not supply all France's raw material needs, nor all her required foodstuffs, and certainly not her requirements for coal and machinery. Increasingly, moreover, France was plagued by pressures for decolonisation, both from native peoples and from the two great anti-colonial powers, America and Russia. Despite some sympathy in the PCF by early 1947 for nationalist aspirations, most French politicians and people resisted the idea of decolonisation, hoping that the empire *could* provide the wherewithal for French independence of East and West. The fact that, between 1940 and 1944, de Gaulle had relied on the colonies for bases, troops and resources, hardened the desire to retain the empire, particularly amongst military planners. In January 1945 the National Defence Committee judged that 'war will no longer be decided at home but in the Empire': France itself might fall in war but even then salvation was possible through the colonies.[84] At the much-lauded Brazzaville Conference of colonial administrations in 1944, it had seemed that imperial peoples would gain tangible rewards for their services, but this proved to be mere illusion. In October 1946 the Constitution of the Fourth Republic established local assemblies, extended rights of citizenship to natives and transformed the empire into the 'French Union'. Yet effective power remained in Paris and with colonial governors: there was no real local government. Thus the French failed to answer the ambitions of native peoples.[85] There had already been unrest in Algeria in 1945 and a guerrilla war broke out in Madagascar in 1947. But the worst problems after 1946 were in Indochina. The Viet Minh leader, Ho Chi Minh, visited Paris in the middle of the year but found that effective independence for Vietnam was out of the question. In November violent clashes occurred in Haiphong and in December a wholesale colonial war broke out, in which the French Army, to add to all its other problems, proved quite unable to root out Viet Minh forces in the countryside. The Paris government, unwilling to negotiate with Ho under duress, vainly tried to win over local Vietnamese support and increasingly the empire – in Indochina at least – became, not a source of French strength, but a major liability. Nonetheless in April 1947 the maintenance of the French Union was laid down as the armed forces' most vital task.[86]

* * *

On 13 October 1946, despite strong criticisms from General de Gaulle about the work of the Constituent Assembly, the French people approved a text for the Constitution of the Fourth Republic. In contrast to the text voted on in May it embodied a stronger presidency and a more powerful upper house. It was hardly an enthusiastic reception for the new regime however: 9 million Frenchmen had voted 'Yes', but nearly 8 million voted 'No' and a similar number abstained.[87] A general election followed on 10 November which saw the Communists (28 per cent) overtake the MRP (26 per cent) as the dominant party, with the Socialists (18 per cent) falling even further back.[88] America's Ambassador Caffery, who felt before the election that popular morale was 'probably lower than at any time since the liberation', was disappointed with the advance of the 'Soviet Trojan horse'. His staff expected the PCF to stay within the coalition government, maintain 'their secret penetration of State institutions (and) their clandestine military preparations', and to preach co-operation with the Soviets in Germany.[89] Concern over Communist strength seemed justified when Maurice Thorez made a bid to become premier. But on 4 December he failed to win the necessary absolute majority and eventually the parties turned to an 'interim' solution, until a president of the Republic was elected. (The president, to be elected by both houses of the legislature in January, would then have the role of nominating a prime minister.) With the Communists ready to stay out of government if the MRP did, an all-Socialist government was formed under Léon Blum in mid-December.[90]

It was in the midst of the French government crisis that, from 4 November to 12 December, the CFM met at the Waldorf-Astoria hotel in New York to finalise the Italian and East European treaties. Bidault had warned the Big Three during the peace conference that he might not be able to attend the New York meetings and, as it transpired, France had to be represented only by an 'observer' in the person of Couve de Murville. It was expected that this would weaken the country's standing at the conference. There was even some exaggerated concern from Bidault and the Quai d'Orsay that the Big Three would reach an agreement on Germany behind France's back, and so the Cabinet insisted that the CFM should not discuss any substantive issues in Germany, beyond preparing for discussions on the subject at its next meeting.[91] Once in New York, Couve tried to play the role of an arbiter between East and West where possible but, after some early signs of obstructionism from Molotov, most changes to the treaties from the Paris peace conference were accepted. US-Soviet relations even seemed to improve and, by the end of November, Couve felt Russia might even prove conciliatory on Germany.[92] In early December the Italian and East European treaties were practically complete.[93] (After editing and translating, they were eventually signed in Paris, on 10 February.) As to the German and Austrian treaties, it was quickly agreed to put the foreign ministers' Deputies to work on these in London. The Deputies would hear the views of other Allied powers and both treaties would be discussed at CFM level in Moscow after 10 March. Couve pleaded in vain for the issue of German frontiers, including the Ruhr, Rhineland and Saar, to be first on the Moscow agenda.[94]

The New York meeting was also significant, however, for seeing a statement by Couve on 9 December that the Paris government might now have to introduce administrative and financial measures to sever the Saar from Germany.[95] The Saar lay completely within the French zone, of course; Bidault had hoped to resolve its future for many months and numerous studies had been completed in Paris on the technicalities of its political and economic separation from Germany.[96] During the peace conference in September Bidault had asked both Byrnes and Bevin to refrain from criticism of France if she established a separate economic regime in the Saar. Bidault had said he hoped to act on this before the November election, so as to demonstrate some tangible gain to the electorate for France's German policy. Byrnes and Bevin, however, feared that such unilateral action would provoke criticism and asked Bidault to wait until the CFM had discussed the matter. The Frenchman reluctantly agreed[97] but by mid-November Paris was determined to act.[98] Couve ascertained that both Byrnes and Bevin would now approve French action but Molotov was reluctant to agree. Instead he suggested to Couve that a deal be struck: he would support France on the Saar if she supported Russia in facing up to the Anglo-Saxons on the question of reparations.[99]

Following Couve's announcement of 9 December, and ignoring Molotov's suggestion of a *quid pro quo* on reparations, the French introduced a customs barrier around the Saar at midnight on 22 December. Stiff Soviet criticism of the action followed, in *Pravda* and in a note of protest given by Molotov to Ambassador Catroux. The French argued that Molotov had been forewarned of the action but the Russians, with good reason, replied that Couve's statement in New York had no legal force and that France's unilateral action still required international approval. The argument followed several months of reasonably good Franco-Soviet relations, however, and Catroux believed that the Soviets still favoured a deal on the lines set by Molotov, the Saar's independence in return for French action on reparations.[100] Neither were the Russians the only ones to complain over the Saar affair. Thanks to Byrnes' failure to warn General Clay about what was afoot, the latter too condemned France's action, even describing it as akin to Tito's behaviour in Trieste in 1945. Clay's comments provoked a furore in the press, Washington had to acknowledge its error in not forewarning him, and Clay, feeling humiliated, considered resignation before accepting the French action.[101] The French were now able to proceed with their policy of forging the Saar into an independent state, economically tied to France. General Koenig had ambitious plans not only to use the area's economic resources, but also to encourage Franco-Saarois marriages and to draft Saarlanders into the French Army.[102] Arguably the French had had to act in order to end uncertainty about the region's future at the end of 1946. The unilateral establishment of a customs barrier meant, however, that France could not take a high moral position when independent policies were pursued in other zones, as when the British made decisions about the future of the Ruhr.

* * *

The problem of putting the Saar customs barrier into effect had fallen to the new Blum government (as had the task of facing the Viet Minh revolt in Indochina). Despite the fact that the government only lasted a month, it also saw important decisions on Germany and on an Anglo-French alliance. Decisions on Germany were urgently needed to prepare for the Deputies' talks in London on a peace treaty, but in Paris debate on the impact of East–West division in Germany continued to rage. In mid-November St Hardouin from Baden-Baden had argued that, with the Anglo-Saxons and Soviets both bidding for German support, France must carefully consider the pros and cons, either of tapping the resources of its own zone, or of seeking co-operation with the new Bizone.

The Bizone, he pointed out, contained 78 per cent of German coal resources and 80 per cent of its steel compared to only 8 per cent and 12 per cent respectively in the ZOF.[103] Juin's EMDN in early December noted two major points about the security situation. First, that 'the peace of the world is actually based on a precarious equilibrium between the Anglo-Saxon and Russian blocs', and secondly, that 'The peace of Europe, and more particularly the security of France, depends on the solution which will be given to Franco-German relations in a European context'. This meant a dangerous situation in which, since 'the United States of Europe has not been founded, the risk of seeing Germany playing on the current instability and indecision for its own profit ... remains'. However, whereas René Massigli definitely favoured a policy of co-operation with the Anglo-Saxons in this situation, the EMDN recommended the maintenance of established French policy.[104] The memoranda prepared by the Blum government also generally maintained established policies, though with some important new definitions.

Three memoranda were submitted to the Deputies' talks in January. The first two, dated the 17th,[105] concerned the provisional political organisation of Germany under occupation, and its government after a peace treaty. Studies on these subjects had been under way in Baden-Baden and the Quai for months.[106] The French predictably wanted a decentralised Germany, with most political and economic powers residing in the *Länder*. Paris was now willing to accept central agencies staffed by Germans, but only if these were under close Allied control and made up of *Länder* representatives. In the long term there should be an Assembly of *Länder* appointees, with a president holding office for only one year and a central *Bund* with restricted powers in such areas as foreign policy, agriculture and communications, but with the *Länder* able to pursue their own policies, even in foreign affairs. All this was radically different to Molotov's policy outlined on 10 July, and went much further than American and British ideas on decentralisation, but St Hardouin for one believed that, due to provincialism and a reaction to militarism, the Germans themselves might support a federal government structure. He believed this would particularly be the case if the Germans were offered material well-being, and given a new ideal to replace that of nationalism. The new ideal should be 'the impression that they are part of a much larger community' – the ideal of European co-operation.[107] Ideas of embracing Germany in a European whole had, of course, been seen in the 1920s and amongst the Algiers planners in wartime, but were only now really coming back into consideration.

The third memorandum, dated 1 February, actually two weeks after Blum's resignation, concerned the Ruhr. It included a geographical delimitation of the Ruhr intended to embrace the smallest possible area whilst maximising the volume of coal and steel industry within it. The Ruhr was to be an international asset, with a local German administration, but also with a UN-appointed High Commissioner able to veto German decisions and, ultimately, call upon Allied troops to enforce his will. The coal and steel industries would be managed by Allied bodies formed from those countries 'directly interested' in the Ruhr, but exactly who these countries were still remained vague. The most interesting aspect of this memorandum, however, was that it concentrated on economic controls and ignored the issue of political separation. In presenting the memorandum to their Allies, French representatives tried to brush aside the last point and insisted that political separation remained the overall aim. But is was clear that Blum and the Socialists had used their brief period in office to steer the discussions on the Ruhr towards their own preferred course of economic controls rather than political independence.[108]

It is perhaps not surprising that Blum's government also saw an attempt to improve relations with Britain. Blum, who acted as his own foreign minister, and Pierre-Olivier Lapie, his Under-Secretary at the Quai, were both anglophiles,[109] and before Christmas they asked René Massigli to approach London about an extension of economic co-operation, including the 'integration' of British and French recovery programmes. This idea, it will be recalled, had been raised earlier in the year by Alphand, and the French were now in a better position to pursue it since the Monnet Plan was now on the brink of completion. Unknown to the French, furthermore, Bevin was currently trying to make a study of a European customs union in London.[110] Bevin, however, was still wary of the uncertain political situation in Paris, Britain lacked a long-term recovery plan of her own and the British told Massigli in early January that his ideas were best discussed in the Anglo-French Economic Committee. There could be no rapid progress on economic co-operation with Britain yet.[111] Meanwhile, in Paris however, Ambassador Duff Cooper had visited Blum on Boxing Day and encouraged the Prime Minister to seek an actual alliance with Britain. At first it seemed unlikely that this would be taken up. Although Lapie was interested in the idea and though Massigli was asked to sound out London's views, the French correctly guessed that Cooper's approach was a personal initiative and Chauvel was doubtful about following it, especially since Blum's government was likely to lose office very soon. More important, Blum believed a treaty would be impossible to negotiate so long as the old problem of coal supplies from the Ruhr was unresolved.[112]

Throughout 1946 France had maintained its pressure on Britain over the Ruhr coal problem, which now became of major significance. In March Koenig's deputy, Louis Koeltz, had bitterly attacked the British and Americans at the ACC for showing 'favouritism' to the Germans with coal supplies.[113] In April a formidable delegation under the Minister of Production, Marcel Paul, had discussed ways to improve Ruhr output and coal exports with the British Minister for Germany, John Hynd, but with little meaningful result.[114] Blum had asked the US (still the source of half French coal imports[115]) during the loan talks in Spring to guarantee 20 million tons of German coal over twenty years,[116] and succeeded in stiffening American criticisms of the British. Washington saw the coal 'bottleneck' as holding back European recovery in general. Nonetheless the problem was allowed to rumble on through the middle of the year,[117] and by the time Blum's government was formed the situation was reaching a new crisis. In the last quarter of 1946 coal from the British and US zones to France had been halved compared to the first quarter,[118] and the French became animated over exaggerated stories of coal trains from the Ruhr being 'pillaged' by Germans.[119] Under pressure from the Ministry of Production, Bidault pleaded with Bevin in October for an improvement. Bevin, however, declared that the German economy was weak, the physical state of the mines was poor and that the situation would get worse before it got better.[120] In November, timing his action so that it had no adverse effect on the French election, Bevin even announced a short moratorium on Ruhr coal exports, followed by shipments at a reduced level.[121] The French position then looked desperate, for although their domestic production levels and production in the Saar had reached pre-war levels, imports of coal as a whole, but especially from the Ruhr, were still well down. In 1938 France had obtained 420,000 tons of coal per month from the Ruhr; in September 1946 she received only 129,000.[122] Little wonder then that Blum was determined to rectify the situation.

It was Pierre-Olivier Lapie who, in early January, persuaded Blum to exploit his personal and political links to the British Labour Party by writing to Prime Minister Clement Attlee and suggesting that they meet together in London. Blum sent such a letter at New Year, to be personally delivered by the Minister of Public Works, Jules Moch, who was due to visit Britain. The letter made much of the current coal problems and Moch underlined the significance of this point to Attlee. René Massigli, rather offended at being by-passed by Moch was doubtful about what Blum might achieve, especially since Britain and France continued to differ so widely on Germany, the issue which had always blocked a treaty before. The Foreign Office shared his doubts but had been put in a difficult position by Blum. They could hardly snub him by saying 'No' to the visit which he had suggested. A favourable reply from Attlee was sent to Blum therefore, with Duff Cooper adding in a covering note, 'I need not say how heartily I support the Prime Minister's invitation'.[123] A conversation between Massigli and Orme Sargent, on 9 January, underscored the hopes and fears behind the visit. The Ambassador complained about British links to America but hoped that Anglo-French co-operation might dampen fears in Paris of German revival. Sargent said the French were too close to Moscow, but hoped that Britain and France together could face up to the superpowers. Later Massigli warned Blum that he would find the British suspicious of PCF strength and mild in their attitudes towards Germany.[124]

As it transpired the numerous potential difficulties did nothing to tarnish the success of Blum's visit of 13–16 January to London. Instead, in the atmosphere of Socialist brotherhood, all the old Anglo-French differences suddenly seemed unimportant. Massigli noted significant changes on both sides. Bevin overflowed with promises of meaningful co-operation with France including firm controls on Germany, greater Ruhr coal exports, and a new Anglo-French *entente* in European affairs. Blum, in response to these attractive if vague outpourings, proceeded to ignore the previous French policy of seeking hard concessions on Germany in return for a British treaty, and publicly agreed to negotiate an alliance. Then, on 16 January, his visit and the life of his government at an end, he returned to Paris to explain his decisions.[125] Exhausted, but confident that he had made the SFIO the backbone of the next government, he did not intend to remain premier.[126] Thus, after so many months of 'crying in the wilderness' France suddenly found herself publicly committed to negotiate an important new alliance with London. The Socialists, the weakest party after the November elections, had managed to seize the opportunity presented by a one-month government, to point France in the direction which Gouin had failed to take it the previous April. But even Massigli feared that Blum had brushed aside the differences with Britain in Germany too easily and the possibility remained that, with a return to *tripartisme*, the Communists and Christian Democrats would yet reject the proposal for a British alliance.

Chapter 7

Choosing Sides. January – July 1947.

... I have constantly repeated for a year that time is working against us (and) we are making, in my view, an error in refusing to enter into the the the Anglo-American system; it is the only means for us to control what is actually happening in the Ruhr ...
– René Massigli, writing to Jean Chauvel, 13 February 1947 (from the former's private papers, volume 55).

The President of the Fourth Republic, elected on 16 January 1947, was a sixty-three year-old Socialist, Vincent Auriol. A baker's son from Haut-Garonne, a close friend of Léon Blum and formerly President of the Assembly, Auriol was a highly-experienced politician, determined to maximise the importance of his new position. An ardent internationalist, he took a leading role in Cabinet discussions on foreign policy and told Jean Chauvel, soon after being elected, 'I am permanent. You are permanent', so that Chauvel should contact him in the event of serious problems.[1]

Auriol soon drew up his own '*grandes lignes*' for government policy including, in foreign affairs, loyalty to the United Nations, sound relations with the Big Three and small nations, and reparations from Germany. Such principles could be seen as a 'lowest common denominator' approach to foreign policy, highlighting Auriol's internationalism, the hopes of maintaining the unity of the Council of Foreign Ministers and the desire to tap German resources for French recovery. However the President discovered differences between the political parties on foreign affairs as he sought to find a successor to Blum as premier. For one thing, whilst Auriol himself was pleased with Blum's recent mission to Britain, the Communists were suspicious of the London talks.[2]

On 18 January, after the SFIO's Paul Ramadier had been designated as premier, a meeting also had to be arranged at the Elysée Palace, between Blum and Georges Bidault because the latter, who was about to return to office as foreign minister, was concerned over the London visit. In the presence of Auriol and Ramadier, Blum assured the Foreign Minister, 'Don't be disquieted. I have abandoned nothing, compromised nothing'. Blum insisted that he had won firm assurances about coal supplies and the control of Germany from the British and that he had merely 'clarified' policy on the Ruhr and German government in the memoranda submitted to the CFM deputies. Bidault professed to be satisfied with this.[3] There can be little doubt that the 'interim' SFIO administration had taken many decisions, on Britain, Germany and Indo-China, which Bidault might not have made, but with a Socialist as president, a Socialist as premier and nine Socialists in the new Cabinet (compared to six MRP members and five Communists), he was not in a position to overturn Blum's initiatives.[4]

The first full government of the Fourth Republic faced daunting economic, political, colonial and international problems and though *tripartisme* survived within it, strains between the three major parties were apparent from the outset. Ramadier, an experienced minister, hard-working and stubborn, caused grave concern among the MRP by appointing a Communist, François Billoux, as Minister of Defence. Billoux was able, long-serving, and the most likeable of the PCF leaders, but to many minds he was also the most dangerous. Actually Ramadier was well aware of the problems and determined to control Billoux by a cunning, if somewhat preposterous, scheme: three separate ministries were created for the Army, Navy and Air Force, the powers of the prime minister in the defence field were extended. Billoux was, quite simply, left with almost nothing to do. The MRP's Army Minister, Paul Coste-Floret, even had the audacity to occupy the Defence Ministry on the rue St Dominique as his own offices and Billoux, unwilling to provoke a crisis at the start of the government, took two days to find alternative accommodation, in an *hôtel*. Even then his private room had no telephone.[5] Yet even these antics could not paper over the clear divisions in the Cabinet. In the National Defence Committee, Coste-Floret could still accuse Billoux of abusing his position to promote Communists in the armed forces,[6] Auriol was dismayed by reports that the PCF wanted greater state direction at home and negotiations with Ho Chi Minh in Vietnam,[7] and Bidault told Jefferson Caffery on 28 January that the Communists would destroy the government before long. The Foreign Minister, who had always said that co-operation with the Anglo-Saxons might be possible when France's domestic situation was clearer, added that he was tired of working with the PCF.[8]

* * *

On 25 January Bidault informed Duff Cooper that France was ready to proceed with a British treaty and four days later René Massigli began talks on drafting such a pact with the Foreign Office's Orme Sargent. Bidault remained doubtful that the moment was auspicious for an alliance, and Chauvel and Massigli did not believe that Anglo-French differences on Germany could be disguised.[9] It was hoped, nevertheless, to sign a treaty before the CFM met in March, and since both sides planned to base the text on their respective anti-German alliances with Russia, which were themselves very similar, there seemed no reason for major difficulties. Thanks to delays on the British side, draft treaties were not exchanged until mid-February, but there was only one major problem in reaching agreement on a final text. The French, anxious to have a meaningful pact after the events of the inter-war years, wanted a commitment to eliminate 'any new menace' from Germany, but this form of words was not found in the Anglo-Soviet alliance and the British felt it was too vague and far-reaching. The Foreign Office wanted to keep the treaty quite strictly in line with British commitments to Russia, and feared that a far-reaching anti-German system between Paris, London and Moscow would lead isolationists in the US

Congress to argue that a US commitment to European security in the Byrnes Treaty was unnecessary.

The French were deeply upset that the British should pay such attention to the possible reaction of the two superpowers to an Anglo-French alliance, but agreed to safeguard the chances of a Byrnes Treaty in a covering letter to the pact, and a text was provisionally agreed on the 25th. The French Cabinet discussed it on the 28th amidst fears of PCF opposition. Maurice Thorez had said earlier in the month that an alliance ought to be conditional on guaranteed Ruhr coal supplies and in the Foreign Affairs Commission left-wing members expressed concern at French differences with Britain on Germany. At the Cabinet meeting Thorez criticised the treaty text for its poverty of content and expressed fears of a 'Western economic bloc', but in the end the pact was approved, being announced to the Assembly later in the day. The response from the Deputies, for what was still a popular proposal, was very enthusiastic. The treaty was signed on a cold, wet 4 March in Dunkirk, a venue suggested by Bidault as a fitting place to restore the *entente cordiale*.[10]

Despite the ultimate success of the negotiations, however, there were wide differences of view in Paris about the usefulness of the Treaty of Dunkirk. For some, including Auriol and Hervé Alphand, it completed the 'triangular' security system with Moscow and London which had first been suggested in December 1944, and which suited French wishes for European co-operation on an anti-German basis.[11] On an Anglo-French level Blum evidently saw it as a basis on which to build greater co-operation in future and René Massigli hoped that it would provide a fresh start for relations between the two signatories. It marked, after all, a major new departure for the British in that it was a long-term (fifty-year) commitment to the security of Europe and, after talking to officials like Sargent and Oliver Harvey, Massigli felt that 'between the American giant and the Russian colossus, England is taking notice of its European interests . . .'.[12] Charles de Gaulle, however, privately condemned the treaty as giving no real concessions to France, and as indirectly tying her to a US alliance. Certainly it did not provide what he had always wanted from Britain, a commitment to support French policy *within* Germany.[13]

The last point was of concern to the Quai as well. In February, as the Treaty of Dunkirk was being drafted, Massigli discussed the recent French memoranda on Germany with Oliver Harvey and differences between the two were clear. The British wanted a decentralised political structure in Germany but, in contrast to France, were also ready to establish a strong central parliament; they were ready to accept economic controls on the Ruhr, but remained opposed both to its political separation and to a Soviet share in its control; they felt that France's proposal of international management of industries would prove unworkable, because it would provoke arguments among the Allies; and they favoured the nationalisation of the Ruhr industries, even though the French feared that this would put a powerful weapon in the hands of a German government.[14] British plans to place the Ruhr coal mines in German hands caused grave concern in Paris in early 1947 as did Anglo-American talk of increasing German steel output.[15] Bidault was certainly not satisfied, whatever Blum had been told in January, that British policy in the Ruhr was compatible with French policy.[16] On a visit to London, Alphand gave the British a memorandum to try to convince them that other West European countries, by acting together and increasing their steel output, could make up for Germany's production in future, but this did not seem to have much impact.[17] Massigli too was concerned by British attachment to the US in the Bizone[18] and told Auriol, before the Dunkirk signature, that Britain was increasingly reliant on the Americans and differed significantly with France in Germany.[19] Clearly whatever else the new British alliance was meant to achieve, it did nothing to strengthen support for France's case at the forthcoming Moscow conference.

* * *

The Anglo-French treaty stimulated discussion about other alliances which might be made in Europe. The Belgians and the Dutch raised the possibility, once the Dunkirk talks became known, of making their own pacts with France and Britain.[20] However the British, with little time left before the Moscow CFM, felt that such talks were best left until after the four-power conference, and the French agreed.[21] More important was the revival of ideas for East European alliances in which Bidault suddenly took a real interest. In January the Czech press paid close attention to the Anglo-French treaty proposal and when the Foreign Minister, Jan Masaryk visited Paris to discuss economic issues with Bidault in mid-February, it was announced that Franco-Czech treaty would be negotiated. Exactly why Bidault should have accepted such an initiative at this time is unclear. A commitment to make an alliance with Prague was embodied in the 1944 Franco-Czech declaration, but hitherto Paris had avoided its fulfilment. Bidault may have wanted to steal the limelight from Blum, who took the credit for the Treaty of Dunkirk. However a more convincing explanation is that the Foreign Minister was concerned to maintain links to Eastern Europe at the same time as making a British alliance. This would reassure the Soviets that there was no exclusive 'Western bloc' and, equally important, could help to win over the PCF to the idea of a British treaty.

The Cabinet approved talks on a Czech pact on 14 February, and a few days later Bidault told the Assembly Commission on Foreign Affairs that a treaty might even be signed before the Moscow conference. This, together with talk of a Polish treaty, evidently impressed those left-wingers on the Commission who were suspicious of links with Britain. It is debatable, however, how seriously Bidault himself took the Czech treaty, for subsequently he made no attempt to sign the pact before travelling to Moscow. The Quai also rejected the idea that Bidault might visit Prague to sign a treaty immediately after the Moscow conference.[22] It was a similar story with the Polish alliance. The Poles too had shown an interest in the Dunkirk treaty and on 17 February, during talks on a cultural convention in Paris, Bidault and Zygmunt Modzelewski agreed to negotiate a treaty. However in March the Quai rejected proposals that Bidault might visit Warsaw in the near future to negotiate a treaty.[23]

Whilst the talk of East European treaties may have reassured some of the French Left about the direction of French foreign policy, it did little to remove Soviet suspicions about the Treaty of Dunkirk. Catroux had informed the Russians about Blum's London visit just before it went ahead in January, and simultaneously requested a meeting with Stalin to discuss the German problem.

The Blum government, in its preparations for the next CFM meeting, was ready to discuss a common approach to Germany with Russia where possible, which shows that SFIO policy was not exclusively pro-Western. Blum wanted to see if a common line was possible in particular on the Saar, international control of the Ruhr, reparations and a decentralised German government. The Russians had, of course, already proposed an understanding whereby they would support French aims in the Saar in return for a common policy on reparations. Catroux was not averse to such an arrangement and, with signs of economic expansion in the Bizone, France and Russia seemed to have a strong mutual interest in pressing for reparations from Germany.[24] Even Henri Bonnet in Washington, fearful of US policy in Germany, felt it wise to strengthen France's hand at the CFM by working with the Russians.[25]

However, the announcement of Anglo-French treaty negotiations brought a sudden resurgence of Soviet suspicions about France, not helped by the fact that Blum had told Ambassador Bogomolov beforehand that the London visit was only intended to discuss coal. French representatives vainly tried to reassure the Soviets that there would be no major change in French policy because of a British alliance but the Russians did not seem convinced.[26] When Catroux met Molotov in late January to deliver the French memoranda on the German government drawn up for the CFM deputies, Molotov said Stalin was too busy to discuss German issues with the Ambassador and made clear that Russia still wanted a centralised German government.[27] He repeated this point in a further conversation on 20 February, when he also categorically rejected any idea of a 'deal' on the issues of the Saar and reparations.[28] Catroux was so concerned that he urged Paris during February to delay the British alliance until *after* the Moscow conference, because the treaty was evidently the source of Soviet disaffection.[29] Chauvel raised the question of co-operation with Russia in a letter to Massigli at this time, but the latter believed the Russians could offer little to France in Germany in concrete terms. Massigli repeated what he had been saying for several months, that time was not on France's side, that 'it is not the Russians who occupy the Ruhr', and that the best course would be to join the Bizone as 'the only means to control what is actually happening in the Ruhr . . .'. As Massigli pointed out, the British treated the Ruhr very much as 'their' possession and not at all as an area subject to four-power control.[30]

Much later Bidault claimed that he signed the Treaty of Dunkirk partly because it 'would provide an essential basis for other agreements, if . . . we had to organise a system of defence' against the Soviets.[31] There is no contemporary evidence that he actually thought in these terms, but it *is* abundantly clear that Dunkirk upset the Russians. The Quai could only hope, in planning for the Moscow conference, that an amicable approach to the Russians would help to resolve differences with them.[32] President Auriol was given sympathetic explanations of Russia's policy in Germany from Catroux and Bogomolov at the beginning of March, but as Bidault set out for Moscow it was clear that Paris and Moscow were far apart on the Ruhr and the form of German government.[33]

The disagreements between France, Britain and Russia regarding Germany were further compounded by American views. In February Bidault, in conversation with Jefferson Caffery, was pessimistic about the chances of achieving French aims in Germany at the CFM and declared, 'I am only too well aware that France is a defeated country and our dream of restoring her power and glory at this juncture seems far from reality'. However Caffery believed that Bidault was too committed to his aims in the Ruhr-Rhineland to abandon them easily. The Ambassador rightly suspected that the French would be willing to strike a deal with Russia on Germany and warned the new Secretary of State, George Marshall, that 'while Bidault's principles are basically anti-Communist, at the Moscow conference [you] will by no means be able to count on him'.[34] General Marshall, a formidable, strong-minded and decisive character who had replaced the compromising James Byrnes in January, met Henri Bonnet for the first time in early February. The new Secretary of State had not had time to study French policy in Germany, but he reminisced about his service in France during the Great War and said he would stop off in Paris *en route* for the Moscow CFM. He made it clear, however, that whilst seeking 'collective security' he would maintain strong armed forces and said France should be more concerned with security on the Elbe than on the Rhine.[35] Bonnet was well aware that America's chief interest at Moscow would be Soviet policies,[36] but US differences with France were also quite clear. Thus although Americans wanted to increase Ruhr coal exports and create a federal German government, they were vague about controls on the Ruhr and opposed large-scale reparations.[37] Nevertheless the French recognised the need to work closely with America. Ramadier even told the *New York Times* in February that France wanted an 'alliance' with Washington. The Americans themselves treated this statement as a symbolic gesture by the Prime Minister but, in the run up to the Treaty of Dunkirk, it confirmed France's interest in having security links to all the Big Three.[38]

* * *

At every step the preparations for the Moscow conference were overshadowed by East-West tension, but the French need was still to press their *own* case,[39] the case they had adhered to since 1945, justified by three German invasions in seventy years. At the political level there must be denazification, democracy and decentralisation in Germany; to guarantee security there should be a long occupation, disarmament and the detachment of the Ruhr, Rhineland and Saar; and, on the economic level, industrial controls, reparations payments and the use of Germany's coal and manpower resources by her neighbours were needed. As ever the aim of holding down Germany was closely tied to hopes of strengthening the French economy. For Alphand's *Direction Economique* the issues of security and European reconstruction were inseparable,[40] whilst Jean Monnet sent a memorandum to Bidault in February to demonstrate that the 'level of industry' plan of March 1946 was the ideal basis for future policy. It fulfilled the requirements of security, whilst allowing Germans a reasonable living standard and providing Germany's neighbours with the means to supply Europe's steel requirements.[41] French policy at Moscow was very much bound up with the needs of the Monnet plan, especially in holding down Germany's industrial production whilst securing coal supplies for France.[42] The EMDN too wished to maintain France's established policy, so as to limit German war potential whilst providing France with a supreme position vis-à-vis her old enemy,[43] and the French intelligence service, SDECE, added some very interesting arguments of its own. In a memorandum of 1 March the service urged that France, standing as it did between capitalist America and Communist Russia, must create an economically sound but non-aggressive Germany, which should serve as a centre-piece for a *union* of European states. Specifically, in a clear throw-back to the studies made in Algiers in 1943–44, SDECE favoured a policy of co-operation between states in the Saar-Ruhr-Lorraine region which together could form a powerful industrial force. As to the chances of agreement with Russia in the near future, however, SDECE seems to have been confused, arguing alternatively that internal problems and the danger of foreign war might lead the Soviets to compromise on Germany, or that economic needs would demand the Red Army's continued presence in central Europe.[44] Meanwhile, from Baden-Baden General Koenig noted the latest disagreements between the Americans and Soviets on the Allied Control Council[45] and believed that the divisions of the Big Three would yet allow France's thesis on Germany to win through. As an absolute minimum he expected agreement in Moscow on French aims in the Saar.[46]

On 27–28 February, in a debate in the Assembly, there were general hopes for a lasting settlement of the German problem at Moscow and for guarantees of French security, tempered by fears about East–West differences. Paul Reynaud, the ex-premier, went so far as to advocate co-operation with America and Britain in order to guarantee Ruhr coal exports, but Florimond Bonte for the PCF wanted Russia to share in the control of the Ruhr and criticised the ideal of a decentralised Germany. Bidault had already assured Deputies in the Foreign Affairs Commission that he would continue to demand the territorial detachment of the Ruhr from Germany. His Assembly speech was noteworthy for emphasising the consistency of current French policy with that of Clemenceau and Poincaré after the Great War and for promising a firm defence of this policy whilst co-operating with both East and West.[47]

Yet, despite the confidence in this speech, despite all the arguments in favour of maintaining France's German policy, and despite the need to preserve East–West unity as the way to safeguard France's security and political unity, there were clear and abundant signs that Bidault's policy would not win through at Moscow. At the CFM deputies' talks in London, where Couve de Murville represented France, there were deep divisions. Eastern bloc states, asked to present their views to the deputies, lined up behind the Soviet policy of a centralised German government and high reparations, whilst Western states shared the Anglo-Saxon fears that high reparations would ruin the European economy. No other country supported France's call for a separate Ruhr state, although the Benelux countries wanted special controls on the Ruhr and a confederated German state.[48] Some officials, like Emile Laffon, shared Massigli's fear that economic needs would soon drive France into reliance on the Bizone.[49] In the Quai, furthermore, there were signs of a willingness to compromise on French aims. One memorandum suggested that, if France won satisfaction on coal supplies she could accept an increase in German industrial production; another argued that, whilst international management of Ruhr factories was the ideal way to control their production, German mines could assure deliveries of coal with mere technical controls.[50]

In early March, the American economic adviser in Germany, General William Draper, suggested to a French official that Bidault might help bring agreement in Moscow if he threatened to enter a 'trizonal' arrangement with America and Britain. The Quai was reluctant to goad Russia too blatantly but they felt Draper's idea merited attention because, if the Moscow CFM ended in disagreement, French relations with the Bizone – especially on the issue of Ruhr coal exports – would be left 'in the air'. Bidault, after signing the Treaty of Dunkirk, had quickly departed for Moscow but on 8 March the Quai cabled him suggesting that, as an indication of what was probable rather than as a 'threat', he should tell the Russians that France *must* reach an accord with the Bizone if the Moscow talks failed. This recommendation was repeated in another telegram six days later. The acting Foreign Minister, in Bidault's absence, the MRP's Henri Teitgen (who seems to have been more forthright in supporting an American alliance), said that Bidault should use the Moscow talks to gauge what France could except in return for joining a 'trizone'. Teitgen hoped for guaranteed supplies of coal, a share in the Ruhr industries, the recruitment of German manpower, the detachment of the Saar and changes in the Baden-Württemberg border.[51]

By early March 1947 it was the issue of coal supplies in particular which the Quai were most desperate to resolve with America and Britain. This issue appears time and again in official memoranda, and reflects an ever-growing concern in Paris, as the failure to resolve a vital post-war supply problem reached a crisis. André Philip, the Minister of National Economy, warned the Interministerial Economic Committee on 5 March that the coal shortage had reached such a level that serious cuts in industrial output were possible.[52] The problem was far worse than it had been in January. The winter of early 1947 had proved especially harsh and caused industrial recovery to stall across the continent. The French, of course, had already been concerned enough in late 1946 at the lack of coal supplies which were needed for France's long-term reconstruction, but heavy snowfalls and freezing temperatures had made the short-term situation even worse, disrupting coal mining and import shipments at the same time as increasing the need for supplies. Vague promises such as those Bevin had given to Blum in January were no longer sufficient. Koenig was convinced the British could increase Ruhr coal exports and the Quai pressured both US and British officials in early March to increase supplies as early as possible. The French even threatened that, unless the coal situation was resolved at Moscow, France would refuse to settle any other CFM issues.[53]

When George Marshall made his promised stop over in Paris on 6 March it was the coal issue which was predominant, in talks with Ramadier, Teitgen and Auriol. The President told Marshall quite simply 'Our problem is coal', presented figures to show how far coal imports in 1946 remained below those of 1938 and asked for supplies of one million tons per month from Germany in 1948. Unless the situation was resolved reconstruction would be jeopardised, Germany would revive more quickly than France and social and political problems would grow. Teitgen quite plainly explained that, 'If the US could find a way to meet French views on German coal exports the French would find it possible to go along with the United States on other German problems'. Marshall promised to look at the problem.[54] He had already been warned by

Jefferson Caffery that if France's economic situation did not improve 'a wave of profound disillusionment' could lead to 'some form of extremist solution'. Lacking confidence in their coalition government, many Frenchmen continued to support PCF policies, though many would prefer an alternative on the Right, such as the return of General de Gaulle.[55]

* * *

En route to Moscow the French delegation witnessed the continued devastation of Europe, less than two years after VE day. 'Germany was still in ruins ...'. Bidault later recalled, 'east Germany was ... perceptibly sadder than west Germany ... And Russia was saddest of all'. The train journey became slower at every border, reaching a snail's pace in the Soviet Union, and everyone had to don fur coats and hats for the sub-zero temperatures. The reception party in Moscow was also suitably attired, leading Bidault to quip that, 'the Russian national costume is an eiderdown and a belt'.[56] The Hotel Moskva had been entirely refitted for the conference and provisioned with caviar and Caucasian wines; cars from the Stalin works ferried guests around the city and shops had been specially stocked with furs, silverware and antiques to appeal to the guests. But even with an endless round of official entertainments Moscow could not recreate the social life seen earlier in London, Paris and New York.[57]

Bidault's arrival was followed by a number of blows. First on 10 March, the opening day of the conference, the Foreign Minister met Marshall, only to be told that if France wanted coal supplies and a share in the Ruhr, she should join the Bizone. Marshall added that German coal mines ought to be run by Germans, even if under Allied direction, a statement which led Vincent Auriol to fear the return of 'the Germany of Krupp'. Immediately Bidault's hope of steering a middle course between East and West had been threatened: Marshall would evidently use France's coal needs to force her to accept German industrial revival and trizonal fusion.[58]

Then on 12 March, President Truman, in an address to Congress in Washington, gave added impetus to US-Soviet tensions by requesting financial aid to the Greek and Turkish governments who were faced, respectively, by a Communist guerrilla campaign and Soviet diplomatic pressure. In asking Congress to make an unprecedented peace-time commitment to the security of two Near Eastern states, Truman depicted a world in which everyone had to choose between the political ideals of communism and liberal democracy, and where the US must aid the latter cause against the former. Several days earlier, on 6 March, the *chargé* in Washington, Robert Lacoste, had warned the Quai to expect 'a new definition of the external policy of the US'.[59] Lacoste felt that against the traditions of US isolationism, wealth-through-peace and universal tolerance, a new belief was growing that, with the UN a failure and the 'Slav bloc' a threat, American power should be used to enforce its desires on the world, perhaps in co-operation with Britain.[60] There was no enthusiasm for the 'Truman Doctrine' on the French side, however. Catroux felt that, yet again, the US had made a psychological error which was more likely to enrage Russia than to pacify it. Reports reaching the Quai from sources as far apart as Rio de Janeiro and Switzerland, showed worldwide concern at the Truman Doctrine.[61]

Henri Bonnet was surprised by the tone of the speech and Auriol was concerned about its likely affect on the PCF. When Thorez attacked Truman's speech in the Cabinet on 18 March, as showing a desire to divide the world and to use 'dollar diplomacy' to influence European government policies, even Teitgen did not argue. Instead, he and Auriol advocated French support for the unity of all the wartime Allies.[62]

Even as the 'Truman Doctrine' was being enunciated, the Moscow CFM was becoming, yet again, a long argument between Molotov and Ernest Bevin about who had failed to fulfil past agreements in Germany. Bidault stuck doggedly to the task of explaining France's case on demilitarisation, denazification and democratisation in Germany,[63] and even Marshall seemed surprised by the scenes of division, telling Bidault, 'Up to the present time, I was occupied with conducting war . . . To make peace seems . . . a more complicated matter'.[64] The scale of problems facing France was confirmed on 17 March, when Bidault met Stalin for the first time since December 1944. It was intended by the Russians, perhaps, as an attempt to win Bidault back to their side, after the decline in relations since January. Stalin received Bidault before seeing either Marshall or Bevin, claimed to sympathise with France's position and remarked 'It is better to be two against two than three against one'. The Soviet leader was now ready to repeat the 'deal' which Molotov had put to Couve in New York, but which had been withdrawn when the talks on an Anglo-French alliance were announced: if France would help Russia to get an agreement on reparations, Russia would not stand in France's way on the Saar. Bidault was now unimpressed by this suggestion, however, telling Stalin that France's position in the Saar was no longer in question. Since the New York CFM, the Saar could hardly be considered a valuable bargaining chip to use against France, especially if Russia wanted a major concession in return. Neither was Bidault happy with Stalin's views on other subjects, his insistence on a strong central government and a four-power Ruhr for example, or his new argument that Germany need not suffer a long occupation since it could be controlled merely be eradicating Nazism and constructing an effective international alliance system. The meeting was made even more disturbing by Stalin's apparent ignorance of events in Germany. He was surprised to be informed of France's coal supply difficulties and had to be told by Molotov that the name of Koenigsberg had been altered to Kaliningrad. Even the normally encyclopaedic knowledge of Molotov, however, seemed inadequate to describe France's current policy on the Ruhr-Rhine to the Marshal.[65]

After seeing Stalin, Bidault made vague remarks about the interview to John Foster Dulles, one of the American delegation. The Frenchman said that no agreement at Moscow looked possible and expressed a readiness to look at a fusion of the Western zones, though France could not join the Bizone just yet. In Paris, however, Teitgen was rather more informative, telling Caffery, 'Stalin told Bidault . . . "you vote with us and we will vote with you"'. Teitgen added 'that is the last thing we want to do', said that most French ministers wished to work with America and claimed that Paris might even approve trizonal union and increases in German industrial production if she could be satisfied on coal supplies and the future of the Ruhr.[66] A deal with Washington behind Stalin's back was now becoming much more enticing than a deal with Moscow behind the back of the

Anglo-Saxons. Also on 18 March the Cabinet agreed that Bidault should ask Marshall and Bevin to settle the coal issue before any other problems were resolved by the CFM. There was, evidently, concern from some ministers that the Soviets should also be included in talks on coal, but these were apparently brushed aside on the grounds that the Soviets did not control the Ruhr.[67]

In the CFM on 18–20 March Bidault explained French economic proposals for Germany on predictable lines. He wanted special regimes in the Ruhr and Saar, guaranteed coal supplies and reparations deliveries, a limited level of industrial production, economic security measures to accompany the Byrnes Treaty, and the settlement of Western border issues before central agencies could be established. However the other conferees also stuck firmly to their views, Bevin favouring an increased level of industry and a balance between imports and exports before reparations were taken, Molotov urging reparations payments at all costs and favouring four-power control in the Ruhr.[68] It was a similar story when the discussion moved to political issues. Molotov favoured a centralised government, Bidault went much further than the Anglo-Saxons in proposing that real authority in Germany must reside in the *Länder*.[69] Some observers felt that Bidault seemed strained, failing to put his case well,[70] and there was little sign of progress for anyone. 'Where are we?' asked Bevin on 26 March. 'God knows!', responded Bidault. Bevin remarked that he had not known God was at the CFM.[71] At a dinner at this time Molotov again raised the possibility of a deal with Bidault on the Saar and reparations but the Frenchman remained uninterested. His minimum aims at Moscow were to secure control of the Saar and to increase coal exports, but whereas he did *not* need Soviet approval to keep hold of the Saar, he *did* need Anglo-Soviet support to secure coal supplies. It was not worth upsetting the Anglo-Saxons by supporting the Russians over reparations, especially if the latter refused to make meaningful concessions to France.[72]

On 2 April the French Cabinet was informed of the lack of agreement in Moscow[73] and over the following weeks the situation only grew worse. There seemed to be basic agreement on the 5th that, as the French wanted, central agencies should be established under close Allied supervision, but Molotov refused to exclude their authority from the Saar.[74] Then, on 10 and 11 April, after attention turned to Germany's borders, Marshall and Bevin supported Bidault's desire for an autonomous Saar, but Molotov refused to settle the question. This came despite Bidault's support for changes to Germany's eastern border and the incident proved to be the breaking-point for Franco-Soviet relations at Moscow.[75] Molotov's behaviour was perhaps no surprise: after using the fate of the Saar as a bargaining counter against France he was hardly likely to give it to Bidault for nothing. The Soviet refusal to discuss the Saar was arguably the inevitable result of the French preference for a 'deal' with the Anglo-Saxons. Yet, at a dinner given by Marshall that evening, according to one observer, 'Bidault ate nothing, and it was obvious that he felt deeply the rebuff of the afternoon. When his time came to propose a toast . . . he said, crisply, that he drank "to those of us here who love freedom"'.[76] Franco-Soviet relations remained frosty at formal gatherings thereafter. At one banquet Molotov pointedly toasted Marshall and Bevin but not Bidault, who 'turned crimson and was furious'.[77] When Bidault paid a courtesy call on Stalin, late in the conference, the dictator would not even discuss the Saar issue.[78] François Seydoux, acting as Secretary-General of the French delegation, believed the Saar incident to be a major turning point for Bidault's whole foreign policy, which led him to adopt an anti-Soviet policy thereafter.[79]

Meanwhile the CFM drew to its close amidst continued disagreement. In mid-April in discussions on the Byrnes Treaty, Bidault repeated the French view that such a pact must be supplemented by other measures, whilst Molotov wanted the Treaty to be altered completely, so as to embrace such principles as four-power control of the Ruhr. Marshall accused the Russians of wanting no agreement on Germany at all.[80] The end, after fruitless discussions about Austria, came on the 24th. One of the few positive points was a decision to meet again, in London, in November.[81]

What made the Moscow CFM doubly important for shifting France towards the Western powers, however, was the fact that, behind the scenes, Bidault had succeeded in reaching a settlement on Ruhr coal supplies with the Anglo-Saxons. Despite Bidault's disappointment with Marshall's attitude at the beginning of the conference,[82] the American and British foreign ministers soon agreed to hold experts' talks on the coal problem with France, on a three-power basis. (Some Americans were so keen to win over France to the Western side in late March that they favoured an independent Ruhr.)[83] Alphand duly met Anglo-American representatives on 15 March and told them that, as Auriol and Teitgen had explained to Marshall in Paris, unless France obtained half-a-million tons per month from Germany in 1947, and a million tons per month in 1948, the Monnet recovery plan would be unworkable and Germany would soon be reviving more rapidly than France. Alphand wanted an agreement to divide German coal between exports and internal use, and he wanted the inter-Allied European Coal Organisation (ECO)[84] to treat Saar mines as part of French output in future – a move which would provide a major boost to French production whilst preserving a large French share in the allocation of coal from other areas of Western Germany. The Anglo-Americans doubted whether other Allied states on the ECO would agree to the last idea,[85] but the French position hardened over the following days. On 20 March, to Bevin's deep annoyance, Bidault made clear to the whole CFM that France would settle nothing at Moscow until coal supplies were resolved.[86] In Paris Teitgen told Caffery that a failure to agree on coal could only help the PCF and obstruct French co-operation with the Bizone, and in London Massigli appealed to Prime Minister Attlee to fulfil the promises made to Blum in January.[87]

There were actually talks about coal in the formal CFM discussions in mid-April, but these made no progress.[88] Instead Franco-Anglo-American talks, beginning in late March, provided Bidault with a breakthrough in the form of a 'sliding scale' agreement, by which German coal exports would grow as a proportion of total production. By 7 April a basic agreement had been reached, and the French Cabinet approved it two days later, Thorez being assured that this did not rule out a later four-power agreement or imply any loss of French independence on other issues in Germany.[89] Letters of agreement on the sliding scale were finally exchanged on 19 April by which, at a daily production level of 280,000 tons in Western Germany, 21 per cent of coal would be exported, and 25 per cent would be exported at an output of 370,000 tons.[90] This was less than

France had hoped for, but Bidault had at least obtained a written commitment on future coal supplies.[91]

The Moscow CFM had ended in disappointment. Bidault, like Marshall and Bevin, left with a painting from Molotov as a present. 'Otherwise', recalled General Catroux, 'all three left with empty hands'.[92] In the French Cabinet Thorez feared that Bidault had become more closely tied to the Anglo-Saxons for little reward, and even criticised French policy on the Saar. Other ministers feared Thorez was preparing for a break with his colleagues on foreign policy.[93] Arriving back in Paris on 29 April Bidault tried to put the best gloss possible on the conference: 'We did our best and we worked hard. We retain our hope and our determination to succeed. But no time must be lost. The interests of France, which are also those of justice, have been respected.' After a moment's hesitation, he added: 'We have also brought back a little coal'.[94]

The Foreign Minister told Auriol that the CFM had at least clarified differences on Germany and agreement might be possible at its next meeting.[95] A lengthy report by the Quai d'Orsay was also optimistic, recalling how long the CFM had taken in 1945–6 to settle the Italian and East European treaties.[96] However the results, or lack of results, of the Moscow conference were obviously of major significance for France's future. There was concern in the Quai that the resolution of the German problem had been set back still further and that the Germans could only profit from the Allied disagreements. In this situation the view that Massigli had pressed for so long, and with which individuals like Henri Teitgen sympathised, could only gain ground: France must work with the Anglo-Americans to resolve the future of *Western* Germany alone, seeking concessions on the Ruhr, Saar and reparations in return for offering trizonal co-operation.[97]

* * *

In the ten weeks following Bidault's return from Moscow, events on the political and economic level united to reinforce the shift towards a pro-Western policy. First, of enormous importance, came the expulsion of the Communists from the Ramadier government. In early 1947 Caffery believed that the 'long hand of the Kremlin' found the PCF and CGT to be its most useful tools in Europe,[98] and a British politician returned from a trip to the Continent convinced that Paris was the control centre of a heavily-armed and ruthless 'secret army' ready to act on orders from Moscow.[99] Some members of the French government shared such fears. On 7 March Ramadier, Coste-Floret and the Interior Minister, Edouard Depreux, shocked Auriol with reports of a heavily-armed, clandestine paramilitary organisation in existence south of the Loire[100] and the danger of armed insurrection led Ramadier to approve secret measures, to prevent military communications systems being disrupted by strike action.[101] During March the Premier feared a general malaise in France caused by rationing, the black market, the slow pace of reconstruction, CGT demands for reform, and the threat of a right-wing party being formed under de Gaulle.[102]

Meanwhile disagreements within the coalition government were growing, particularly over the attempts to pacify Indo-China after the Viet Minh rising of late 1946. On 18 March Billoux, the Defence Minister, caused a furore when he refused to rise with the rest of the Assembly to honour French forces in Indo-China, and on 22 March PCF back-benchers breached tripartite co-operation by refusing to vote in favour of military credits in Indo-China. Thorez, who can have had no wish to destroy the government in the midst of the Moscow CFM, blamed the back-benchers' abstention on 'extremists', and PCF ministers did support the government, but Ramadier warned that he would not tolerate such behaviour in future.[103] In April there were more disagreements on the decision to repress the anti-colonial movement in Madagascar and Caffery doubted whether the Communists could remain in the government.[104] It has been suggested that the Truman Doctrine helped to bring about the disruptive PCF policy on Indo-China in March,[105] and André Philip told an American official that what was happening in Paris was 'primarily a battle between the United States and the Soviet Union'. The minister also talked of throwing 'the Communists out of the Cabinet' once the economy improved.[106]

In early May the Communists and their colleagues fell out again, this time over salary increases, following a strike at Renault car factories. On May Day there were workers' demonstrations all over France, and on 4 May the Communists refused to support the government in a vote of confidence on its economic and social policy. It proved a highly important moment. PCF leaders evidently hoped to remain in office, but Ramadier surprised them by expelling all Communists from his Cabinet. In case of a violent reaction to this, the military were put on alert and General Revers, now the Army Chief of Staff, was ready to recall troops from the ZOF to act in France if necessary. There was, however, no major disorder. Instead the PCF, many of whom hoped to return quickly to government, were quiescent, the Renault strike was settled in mid-May, and military forces stood down.[107] Only in retrospect were the events of May 1947 seen as a major turning point, removing the PCF from government for decades. In many ways, by their policy since March, Thorez's party invited Ramadier's action, and Ramadier told Bogomolov and Caffery that the expulsion had no international significance. There were questions, however, as to American involvement in Ramadier's decision, which, significantly, coincided with the expulsion of the Italian Communists from Alcide de Gasperi's government in Rome. Direct US influence would be difficult to prove but Jefferson Caffery's staff had long wanted the PCF out of office and opposed their return to power, once this was achieved.[108] In early May Caffery had told Ramadier, what was really already obvious, that Franco-American co-operation would be easier without the Communists[109] and the Ambassador now asked the US government to give all possible economic assistance to the French government, beset as it was by continuing coal and food shortages and the dangers of political extremism to Left and Right. He described the significance of France to Washington in terms of what might be described as a 'domino theory': 'if the Communists won, the Soviet penetration of Western Europe, Africa, the Mediterranean and Middle East would be greatly facilitated, and our position in . . . Germany rendered precarious . . .'.[110]

* * *

147

On 9 May, the Cabinet fully discussed the results of the Moscow conference. Bidault did not disguise the disagreements with the Anglo-Saxons, on the Ruhr-Rhineland for example, but he depicted Stalin as someone interested simply in bartering, who would give France nothing without concessions in return, whilst Marshall was honest, liberal and democratic. Bidault warned that the world was dividing and that everyone wished to know which way France would turn. This analysis worried the internationalist Auriol, who favoured an approach to Bogomolov to try to resolve Franco-Soviet differences,[111] and who hoped, along with Ramadier that the expulsion of the PCF need not affect relations with Moscow.[112] Signs that France might continue its 'middle way' between East and West were also seen in the Cabinet on 21 May, when Bidault said that Britain ought to act more independently of the Americans, whilst Ramadier raised the possibility of asking Russia for wheat supplies.[113] In reporting on the Moscow CFM to the Assembly's Foreign Affairs Commission furthermore, Bidault continued to take the line that France had maintained its own case at the conference, denied there was any plan for trizonal fusion and looked forward to the next CFM in November.[114]

Elsewhere, however, Bidault continued to show a preference for links with the West rather than the East. At the end of the Moscow CFM, he had talked to Ernest Bevin about the European scene and was pleased when the Foreign Secretary talked of developing Anglo-French co-operation in order to match the strength of the superpowers.[115] After returning home Bevin seemed ready to fulfil his long-discussed policy of Western European co-operation by exploring the possibility of a treaty with Belgium. Bidault decided to follow suit. During May talks with Belgium did not get beyond preliminary soundings[116] and the Quai d'Orsay was still generally disappointed with the state of Franco-Belgian relations since the war.[117] However, on 8 June Bidault met the Belgian Foreign Minister, Paul-Henri Spaak, secretly in Belgium, told him that the Soviet leaders were narrow-minded and untrustworthy and said that he would now rely on the Anglo-Saxons.[118] A few days later Bidault privately told an American journalist that it would be reassuring to have US atomic-bombers based on the Elbe![119]

Meanwhile progress had stalled on the treaties with Czechoslovakia and Poland which Bidault had promised in February. During March the Poles had submitted a draft treaty to Paris with terms similar to the Franco-Soviet treaty: a twenty-year term, automatic assistance against a German attack, consultation in the event of a German 'policy of aggression', and promises of wider (cultural and economic) co-operation. However French officials were determined that their commitments to Poland and Czechoslovakia should not go beyond their treaty commitments to Russia and Britain,[120] and from the start some were very doubtful about the idea of a treaty. General Teyssier, the military *attaché* in Warsaw, had written to Paris on 1 March arguing that a Polish alliance was not urgent because Germany was not yet a military threat, that Poland was as weak as she had been in 1939, and that the Russians probably hoped to use the treaty proposal to tie France to the East and upset Britain and America. Massigli too remained critical of the proposal,[121] and British doubts about France's East European treaties had become quite evident in late March. Orme Sargent told Massigli that a Czech alliance would dilute the value of the treaty of Dunkirk, that the French should not over-stretch themselves in the East as they had done in the inter-war years, that Czechoslovakia was under virtual Soviet control, and that economic links, rather than political ones, were the best way to wean the East Europeans from Moscow. On another occasion Oliver Harvey told Couve that France should confine its alliances to major powers like Britain and Russia, or neighbouring states like Belgium and Holland. Couve, who did not share Massigli's anglophilia, told Harvey that the policy which the British recommended would cut Europe in two, but the Americans shared British doubts. In May a State Department official declared that French links to Eastern Europe would have an adverse effect on US policy towards Europe.[122]

During April, as the Moscow conference continued, pressure revived from the Czechs for Bidault to visit Prague on his way home. The Czechs followed the Poles in submitting a draft treaty to Paris on 7 April, and Masaryk expressed disappointment at the slow pace of negotiations. Ambassador Maurice Dejean shared his sense of exasperation, but the Quai continued to procrastinate.[123] The Czechs came to suspect that Anglo-American pressure was the real cause of French reticence, and certainly Anglo-American views seem to have had some impact on Bidault. At Moscow, when asked by Bevin about the Czech and Polish treaties, he minimised their significance. The Frenchman then made the odd claim that they had only ever been promised in order to please the PCF and that this was no longer necessary. The British Foreign Office was at a loss to understand what this meant, and even in retrospect it is hard to interpret. It may suggest that the ousting of the Communists by Ramadier had already been planned, it may merely reflect Bidault's desire to be rid of them, or it may confirm that the East European treaty talks were only ever intended to 'buy' PCF approval for the Treaty of Dunkirk. After the CFM Bidault insisted that he still wanted a Czech treaty, but it was not until the end of May that the Quai handed their counter-proposals on a treaty to the Czech Ambassador in Paris.[124]

Since the French still adhered to the principle of making the Czech treaty before that with Poland, the delays in the Czech negotiations also served to delay progress on the Polish front. Late in April Zygmunt Modzelewski expressed the hope that Bidault would deal with a treaty quickly and that, even if the Czech pact was signed first, the terms of both East European treaties could be announced simultaneously. A month later he was even more frustrated, and sent a formal note to Paris complaning about the lack of response to Poland's draft treaty since March. In late June Modzelewski was still being told that progress on a Polish treaty must be secondary to that with Czechoslovakia,[125] and by now all European countries were faced with a far more significant economic question. On 5 June, at Harvard University, the American Secretary of State, George Marshall, had offered to underwrite a European-wide recovery programme and all European attention now focused on the question of the 'Marshall Plan'.

*　*　*

During the first half of 1947 economic necessity continued to point France towards reliance upon the United States. On 14 January the Blum Cabinet, in yet another of its many important decisions, had formally approved the Monnet Plan for recovery and modernisation drawn up during 1946.[126] Originally intended to cover the period 1947–50 but later extended to 1952,[127] the Plan aimed to achieve the production levels of 1938 by the end of 1947, to match the peak levels of 1929 during 1948, and then to expand beyond these. It relied on a united national effort however, and would mean an estimated deficit of nearly $7 billion, a sum which the Blum loan of 1946 came nowhere near to covering. Although trade had recovered somewhat by the end of 1946, and although bilateral agreements with other European countries (under which specific lists of commodities were exchanged) had helped in reviving French exports, the country faced daunting problems of continued inflation, discontent over rations and low wages, continued reliance on 'luxury' exports and, of course, problems with obtaining coal and wheat supplies. France also shared the general European problem of the 'dollar gap'. With America the most powerful economy in the world, the greatest creditor nation, and the source of food, raw material and machinery, it was vital to earn dollars to pay for dollar imports, but this proved extraordinarily difficult. Too often French exports went to non-dollar areas.[128] In January Catroux had approached the Soviet Minister for Trade, Anastase Mikoyan, about increasing Franco-Soviet trade, but Mikoyan felt both economies were too weak to allow this.[129] In February Alphand had explained the dollar gap to Auriol and the President had said that France should organise the European economies to reduce competition between them and help mutual reconstruction. When Alphand responded that such a 'preferential' system might antagonise Washington, Auriol declared that America must be brought round to see the wisdom of European co-operation.[130]

Bidault explained to George Marshall, at the end of the Moscow conference, that French hopes of recovery from the time of the Blum-Byrnes accords had been dissipated. Without further coal supplies, loans and increases in manpower, French production and exports would stagnate, there would be inflation, falling living standards and rising discontent, perhaps even civil war. The Moscow CFM promised an improvement in the coal situation, but it would be some time before Ruhr coal exports recovered even to the levels of early 1946 and the World Bank was currently proving reluctant to grant large credits to France. Marshall was sympathetic. Indeed he showed concern at the extent of suffering across Europe, and talked of finding a long-term problem to the continent's problems.[131] Marshall repeated his fears about Europe in public after returning to Washington, with the dramatic statement, 'The patient is sinking while the doctors deliberate',[132] and instructed the State Department to study ways of tackling the continent's problems.

It can be argued that claims of a major economic crisis in 1947 were exaggerated, not least by European statesmen eager for US aid. The dreadful weather of February only had a short-term impact and across Western Europe the year as a whole saw production levels being maintained. Only in Germany was there real social distress; elsewhere problems were often caused, not by starvation or economic collapse, but by spending on over-ambitious social reforms and modernisation plans, like the Monnet Plan.[133] However in certain key countries there *were* real difficulties and dangers. Britain experienced financial disaster, for example, when it tried to make sterling freely convertible into dollars, as promised under the US loan agreement of 1945,[134] and France and Italy were strategically important states, with strong Communist parties, facing inflation, social discontent and a loss of morale. In France salaries did fall behind prices in 1947, coal imports from America were a major burden, wheat was in short supply and there was an increasing number of strikes by the middle of the year.[135] On 9 May the World Bank finally agreed to give France a loan, as agreed in principle in the Blum-Byrnes accords, but it was only for $250 million, with a willingness to consider a similar amount later in the year.[136] The Americans had also agreed on a supply of 362,000 tons of wheat to France, after talks with the Minister of Agriculture, François Tanguy-Prigent, in February[137] but even this proved inadequate and had to be increased a few months later.[138]

During May Henri Bonnet began to gather information on US preparations for a comprehensive attack on Europe's economic problems. The Ambassador indeed built up a much fuller picture of the nascent 'Marshall Plan' than the British Embassy. On 7 May, in a conversation with Marshall on coal and wheat supplies, Bonnet gathered that the Secretary of State wanted a general solution to Europe's economic problems, and that he would try to convince the American people that this was needed.[139] Later Bonnet reported that Marshall had set up special study of a possible aid plan. The Ambassador at first doubted whether Congress would be prepared to grant large sums in aid, but on 27 May (in a telegram which was circulated to the Cabinet) he reported more detailed thinking in Washington about a recovery programme, which Europeans themselves would draw up and which the US would then finance, a request being put before Congress in 1948. The plan would require a joint European effort, concentrate on improving key areas of production and would include the use of German resources.[140] That this information was all accurate was confirmed in Marshall's Harvard Speech on 5 June.[141] Bonnet had already reported that most influential American opinion saw a reconstruction plan as a means to utilise US resources against the Soviet menace,[142] and after the Harvard Speech he wrote that Marshall's main aim was to revive Western Europe as a 'centre of opposition' to creeping, Kremlin-inspired communism.[143]

Much has been made since of Ernest Bevin's quick response to the Harvard Speech and his subsequent leadership of the West Europeans,[144] but thanks to Bonnet the French seem to have been much better prepared for Marshall's announcement. On 6 June Lewis Douglas, the US Ambassador to London, whose father had been a friend of Clemenceau, warned Massigli that France should act quickly to prevent the British and the Americans from dominating the Marshall Plan.[145] The next day Bidault told Bonnet to tell Marshall that France was studying the speech,[146] and on 10 June the Ambassador was asked to say that France agreed with the need for a comprehensive recovery programme, in which the Europeans would do all possible to help themselves. France was ready to contribute to this programme and believed that action on it should be taken quickly, through a system of committees rather than a grandiose conference.[147] However, the British had already made their own approach to Washington and, on 10 June, suggested Anglo-French talks on the Marshall Plan. To this Bidault readily agreed.[148] He then reported the Harvard Speech and his initial response to it to the Cabinet. The Cabinet meeting also saw an exposé on the economic situation from the Minister of Finance, Robert Schuman, which could only heighten the desires for a swift, coherent response to Marshall's offer. Higher

151

prices, poor exports and recent strikes had harmed French reconstruction, and Schuman recommended new economies and tax increases to deal with the situation.[149] It was against a background of political and social division, and grave economic problems, that France prepared to act on the Marshall Plan. June saw strikes in the coal mines, navigation companies and banks; many Socialist ministers were doubtful about Schuman's economic measures and even wanted to bring the PCF back into government; and Ramadier had to be dissuaded by Auriol from resigning. Only in early July did the political pressures ease, when the government survived a vote of confidence on its policies.[150]

A vital question about the Marshall Plan was what the Soviet response would be to it. Vincent Auriol was concerned in mid-June that, whilst the Harvard speech left it open for Russia to join the Marshall Plan, Bidault and some Americans seemed pessimistic about the chances of Soviet inclusion.[151] The Quai was careful to keep the Russians informed of Bonnet's contacts with Washington, and Bidault told Duff Cooper that he wanted to involve Moscow in the Plan, but the French themselves talked only to the Americans and British at first and the Soviets were suspicious of their exclusion from such Western contacts.[152] A Quai memorandum of 16 June stated that lines should be 'kept open' to Russia, partly because of French reliance on such East European imports as Polish coal. However, it was far from certain that the Soviets would join in, and it was partly because of this that officials ruled out working through UN bodies, like the new 'Economic Commission for Europe', based in Geneva. The UN bodies were also felt to be inappropriate because they would be slow to act. For France speed was of the essence in tackling the 'dollar gap', hence the desire in Paris for an effective system of committees, directed by a central committee (including the Americans) to control the Marshall Plan. Genuine European co-operation, to build up production, was felt essential by Alphand's officials.[153]

On 17–18 June Bevin came to Paris to discuss the Marshall Plan with Bidault. There was some sense of rivalry between the two. Bidault told Caffery that he feared Bevin wished to 'steal the show'. 'The truth . . .', Caffery believed, 'is that Bidault wanted to steal the show and Bevin beat him by a day or two'.[154] However the talks between them went well. The British readily agreed that the UN Commission in Geneva should be avoided and that a number of expert committees should draw up an aid request. They agreed too, to invite the Soviets to discuss the Harvard Speech, on a three-power basis, preferably the following week. Whilst Ramadier genuinely seems to have wanted to involve the Russians at this time, however, both Bidault and Bevin told Caffery that they hoped Moscow would reject Marshall aid, and an article in *Pravda* suggested that this would indeed be the Soviet course.[155] Significantly a Quai memorandum of 19 June noted that, given the interest in Marshall aid from such West European countries as Italy and the Benelux, it should be possible to proceed without Russia.[156]

On 19 June the *chargé* in Moscow, Pierre Charpentier delivered a message to Yacob Malik, the Deputy Foreign Minister, inviting the Soviets to discuss the Marshall Plan with Bidault and Bevin. Malik was frosty[157] and three days later Charpentier had to make another visit to the Soviet Foreign Ministry to try to get a reply. On the second occasion, however, he was seen by Molotov, who seemed in peculiarly good humour and said he would come to Paris on the 27th.[158] Arrangements were quickly made and the Foreign Minister, with a large entourage of 95 experts, duly arrived at Le Bourget Airport, in the middle of a heat wave, on the 26th. The flight was early, Bidault was late to meet his guest, and there was not much trust on either side. Molotov bluntly asked Bidault what he and Bevin had done behind Russia's back. Meanwhile, in the Quai Jacques Dumaine could only wonder 'will [the Soviets] succeed in throwing a spanner into the machinery, or shall we be able to circumvent their delaying tactics?'[159] and Bevin feared that even if Russia did accept Marshall aid this would only take resources from the rest of Europe.[160]

A report by the intelligence service, SDECE, based on sources in the Russian Embassy, suggested that Molotov might not be entirely negative. The Soviet Embassy had been surprised by the size of the Foreign Minister's entourage, having been told to expect only twenty people under the leadership, not of Molotov himself but his *Chef de Cabinet*, Boris Podzerov. Economic experts like Mikoyan, in the Kremlin, were apparently genuinely interested in exploring the Marshall Plan, whilst Stalin and Molotov were said to have their own motives for keeping up talks on the Harvard Speech: the Marshall Plan, coming after the Truman Doctrine and the expulsion of the Communists from government in Paris and Rome, was seen as putting Moscow on the defensive; but if Stalin could delay its progress whilst tightening his grip on Eastern Europe and strengthening the position of the French and Italian Communists (by launching agitation with a view to getting them back into government), a strong negotiating position could be created which would allow Stalin to meet Truman and resolve their differences in a summit meeting.[161] Important elements of this extremely interesting explanation of Soviet tactics, with Mikoyan interested in US aid and Molotov more doubtful, are confirmed in a much later British source.[162]

The meetings with Molotov lasted from 27 June to 2 July, faced immediate disagreement and ended with the Russian walking out. Bidault opened the conversations with the proposal for a number of committees to study Europe's needs and draw up a plan for submission to Washington. Bevin supported the idea of swift action to devise a comprehensive plan but Molotov seemed neither keen to act quickly – he spent much of the conference on the telephone to Stalin – nor to draw up a comprehensive plan. He insisted that Marshall aid must not infringe national sovereignty; rather, individual states should submit their own requests to America who, he felt, should give some idea of the total amount of aid that was available. There was some justification for Molotov's suspicion that Bidault and Bevin had already decided much without him, and it was understandable that Moscow did not want to reveal its economic plans and statistics to the US. However a series of bilateral loans, such as Molotov proposed, was exactly what American planners wished to avoid. Loans such as those granted to Britain in 1945 or France in 1946 had failed to set Europe on its feet after the war. In such a situation 'multilateralism' was unworkable, a thriving world economy was impossible, Europeans could not afford American products and Communists seemed ready to exploit the economic malaise. What was needed was a *comprehensive* plan in which Europe could act together to tackle its economic problems. This indeed was the only specific 'condition' Marshall had made at Harvard. How far it would infringe on national independence was unclear. However the Americans were not ready to discuss amounts of aid available until a viable European plan had been formulated. Another argument raised by Molotov was that the Marshall Plan would lead to the industrial revival of Germany, thus putting an end to reparations and recreating a German menace. This was an important point. Bevin certainly favoured Germany's economic resuscitation to an extent, as a way to help European recovery as a whole. The French, however, still hoped to keep strict limits on their old enemy.

It was Bidault who did most to try to reassure Molotov that there was no Anglo-French 'collusion' against Russia, that the Marshall Plan need not infringe on Soviet sovereignty and that the German economy would not be revived, but both sides continued to talk past each other on all these issues.[163] In any case Bidault's main motive for playing a conciliatory role may only have been to blame the Soviets for the failure of the conference. 'It really must not look as though we are showing them the door', he explained to one of his officials.[164] Jean Monnet took a similar view: if at all possible he asked Bidault to avoid a breakdown with Molotov, because this could divide both Europe and France; but if there had to be a breakdown it should be for clear reasons and after attempts to placate Molotov.[165] Bevin never seemed genuinely interested in involving the Soviets in Marshall aid[166] and even Auriol and Ramadier, who had genuinely wished for the USSR's inclusion, proved willing to proceed without it if necessary. The Cabinet agreed on 2 July in fact to issue an invitation to European states to attend a conference on Marshall aid, even if the Soviets refused.[167] The conference broke up that day in disagreement. Molotov had rejected Bidault's attempts to placate him and, as Bevin put it, 'walked out uttering threats'.[168] Such tactics were a mistake, helping to confirm the impression that Russia had never intended to discuss the Marshall Plan seriously, and helping also to drive the French and British together.

Bevin was very impressed by Bidault's 'statesmanlike' performance at Paris.[169] The Dunkirk Treaty, events at the Moscow CFM and the expulsion of the Communists from the Cabinet had all seemed to point France towards Western co-operation during the early months of 1947, but now France had clearly shown whose 'side' she would choose in the Cold War. This choice reflected the liberal-democratic preferences of its leaders, its geographical position, the desire to influence the future of the Ruhr and the temptation of American money. The decision to break with Molotov at Paris had been taken, however, in the knowledge that it could provoke greater opposition from the Left within France and divide Europe down the middle. Couve and Alphand believed that the continent now stood at the crossroads. The Kremlin was, they supposed, banking on Europe's economic disintegration, which local Communists could then exploit. 'The Soviets, however . . . have forced Europe to band together to save itself', Couve told Jefferson Caffery, 'They . . . have established the European bloc'.[170]

Chapter 8

The Impact of the Marshall Plan.
July – December 1947.

Does one believe that France is a pygmy between two colossi? No. The country which listens to the voice of wisdom and humanity is not a pygmy.
– Vincent Auriol, in his *Journal du Septennat*, 16 December 1947.

In the wake of the Paris conference, encouraged by a message of support from George Marshall, Georges Bidault and Ernest Bevin prepared to hold a conference of European states to discuss the Marshall Plan.[1] The vital question was whether East European states would join in such discussions. If they did not, Europe would be riven in two, for Paul-Henri Spaak said that the Benelux states, like Britain and France, would attend a conference even without the Soviet satellites.[2] Eventually fourteen West European states agreed to join the talks with France and Britain.[3]

From the outset Couve de Murville feared that Moscow would prevent the East Europeans from accepting Marshall aid,[4] but the Quai d'Orsay felt that these states had much to gain from American assistance[5] and the Americans seemed to want them to join.[6] It took several days in fact before the Russians formally circulated a telegram to European capitals, explaining Molotov's motives for leaving the Paris talks, and condemning the Marshall Plan as an attack on national sovereignty.[7] In the meantime, on 4 July, the Czech Foreign Minister, Jan Masaryk, said his country would at least enter negotiations about Marshall aid on a 'preliminary' basis, and the Poles took a similar position. Their interest in the Marshall Plan was evidently fuelled not only by economic self-interest (75 per cent of Czech trade was with the West) but also by the confused indications from the Kremlin about its own response to Marshall aid. But then, on 8 July it was learnt that Masaryk and the Czech Prime Minister, the Communist Klement Gottwald, had been called to discuss the matter with Stalin himself in Moscow. Within a few days the Soviet dictator told them and the Poles to stay out of the Marshall Plan, which was described as an attempt to isolate the USSR from the rest of Europe. The Czechs and Poles then joined the other Soviet satellites in condemning the Plan as an attack on national sovereignty and a bid to revive the German economy.[8]

The visit of Gottwald and Masaryk was doubly important for France because, whilst in Moscow, the Czechs also discussed the future of their alliance negotiations with Paris. During June, after many delays, work had begun in earnest on drafting French treaties with Czechoslovakia and Poland. However one problem in particular had arisen. This was the East European insistence that the signatories should be committed to act not only against Germany, but also against any allies of Germany, the so-called '*états tiers*'. The Czechs wanted such a clause because they feared a repetition of the situation in the 1930s, when Hitler used the Hungarians to put pressure on Prague. In Paris, however, there was grave concern over who, exactly, would be included in the vague phrase '*états tiers*' and the Quai was unready to agree to such a choice of words. The Czech Cabinet then became divided on the problem.

Interestingly, when Gottwald and Masaryk visited Moscow Stalin did *not* rule out the conclusion of a Franco-Czech treaty. Indeed he categorically stated that an alliance could be negotiated. However, by arguing that Prague *should* seek satisfaction on the *états tiers* issue the Soviet leader actually did nothing to resolve the differences in the Czech Cabinet. Perhaps because of this the Quai heard nothing more about a pact until early August, by which time it was the French holiday season and rapid progress was impossible. Meanwhile there were parallel delays in the talks on a Franco-Polish treaty, which had always been treated by Paris as secondary to that with Czechoslovakia. On 10 July the French had put counter-proposals to the Polish draft treaty, submitted to Paris months before, but Deputy Foreign Minister Modzelewski now said that, like the Czechs, he wanted to cover the problem of *états tiers*. Worse than this, he said that he could foresee the US being treated as a German 'ally', under the terms of the treaty if the Americans revived Germany.[9]

From Moscow General Catroux warned that Stalin's decision to restrain Eastern Europe from participation in Marshall aid would have grave consequences for France, which was now seen in the Kremlin as an antagonist, acting as America's stooge in a scheme which threatened the Soviet Union's position in Eastern Europe.[10] Russian diplomats confidently asserted that the Marshall plan was specifically designed to break the Soviet hold on Eastern Europe,[11] though whether the Americans actually intended such an outcome is debatable.[12] The US was mainly concerned, not with Eastern Europe, but with the economic salvation of *Western* Europe, and it was the reconstruction of Western Europe which was also of prime importance to Bidault. The Foreign Minister told President Auriol that by organising themselves properly the West Europeans could advance speedily and unitedly, whilst preserving their national independence, and that by disproving Soviet criticisms of the Harvard Speech they might even draw the East Europeans back into the fold.[13] Already the American Under-Secretary of State, Will Clayton, had visited London, then Paris, to discuss Marshall aid. In London he told René Massigli that there was no Marshall 'Plan' in detail beyond the Harvard speech, but that Washington wanted a European request for assistance in September to give time for congressional action.[14] During talks with Alphand and Monnet in Paris he emphasised that the Europeans should plan to achieve economic stability within four years and should lower the trade barriers between themselves to create a single, thriving market on the US model.[15] This would both undercut support for Communism, based as it was on economic discontent, and make further American expenditure unnecessary. In early July, however, a major blow struck the French, which seemed to justify one of Molotov's main criticisms of the Marshall Plan: the American and British governors in Germany agreed to increase industrial output in the Bizone and to place control of the Ruhr coal mines in German hands.

* * *

In early 1947 French policy towards Germany still aimed to hold down its level of industry whilst using coke from the Ruhr to build up steel production in France. There were continuous worries, however, that the Anglo-Saxons (despite some differences between them) would increase economic output in the Bizone and hand back control of the coal mines to the Germans.[16] After the Moscow CFM, and the failure to resolve Germany's future on a four-power basis, it was perhaps inevitable that action would quicken on the Bizonal level. In late May the French were dismayed by political reforms which created a Bizonal 'Economic Council', in Frankfurt, of representatives from the *Länder,* who could propose political measures to the US and British governors. When the French protested that this amounted to the recreation of a German government, the Anglo-Saxons retorted that the new Council was under Allied control and had limited powers, but Paris continued to see the reforms as portending a centralised and over-powerful Germany.[17] Meanwhile, at the end of the Moscow CFM, Marshall and Bevin had agreed to study an increase in the Bizone's industrial levels; Massigli warned Bidault that in Britain 'it is impossible to distinguish the German problem from the Russian problem'; and the Harvard Speech hardened the desire of the American General Clay to utilise German resources for European recovery, *not* by stripping it of coal and industrial machinery as the French wanted, but by restoring its output, consuming fuel and raw materials *within* Germany, and allowing the country to trade in European markets. This would also have a political impact, by holding out the chance to Germany of rejoining the community of nations as an equal.[18] After Harvard, the Quai d'Orsay also recognised the need to embrace Germany in the Marshall Plan somehow, but there were many problems with such a course. If it was followed on a three-power basis, without Russia, it would effectively mean the end of four-power co-operation in Germany, prejudging the outcome of the next CFM and risking a violent Soviet response. Such a policy would also necessitate France's entry into 'trizonal' arrangements. The development of trizonal links had already been considered in Paris, of course, but the Quai was determined to get concessions in return for such a step, particularly in the form of a decentralised German administration and control of the Ruhr.[19]

Once the Soviets had decided to stay outside the Marshall Plan, Bidault made it plain in conversations with Bevin, Caffery and Duff Cooper that he could accept neither an increase in German industrial output nor any Bizonal decision on the ownership of the Ruhr mines. The French knew by now that the Anglo-Saxons were discussing both these topics. An increased level of industry, Bidault insisted, would invite attacks from the Communists and the political Right within France and was unnecessary, since Germany's output was actually still below that set under the level of industry plan of March 1946. He also insisted that France should be given guarantees on future deliveries of coal and other reparations before German output was changed. Bevin, however, argued that the industrial future of Germany could not remain unsettled forever

157

and that future output there needed to be planned ahead, not least in order to contribute to general European recovery under the Marshall Plan.[20] On 9 July Bidault met America's Will Clayton, and argued that, by tapping the Ruhr's resources, France and the Benelux states could fulfil Europe's industrial needs. Clayton was no more reassuring than Bevin, being eager to cut US occupation costs and to resolve Germany's economic future. Nonetheless both Clayton and Caffery urged Washington to show 'extreme care' towards France on the German problem.[21] In the State Department, in fact, Bidault's delicate position on Germany was appreciated, as were the dangers of economic discontent and Communist strength in France[22] and it was because of the fear of upsetting Bidault that Marshall and Bevin decided to delay any announcement about an increased level of industry at this time, until after the matter was explained to the French.[23]

On 16 July US and British officials met Chauvel, Couve and others, and explained the need to increase German production, so as to end the financial drain on Anglo-American taxpayers and set Germany on a sound economic footing. Chauvel however was not reassured,[24] and when Caffery and another visitor to Paris, Averell Harriman, met Bidault they found him in an 'hysterical condition', complaining once more that an increased level of industry was unnecessary, that French steel output should be expanded in preference to Germany's and that the Anglo-American decision, coming on top of the breach with the Soviets, would place the Ramadier government 'in a tragic situation'.[25] In the Cabinet, Auriol urged that a formal protest should be made to Washington and London. He feared that Soviet attacks on American policy might be justified, and even suggested that a Soviet-American meeting should be held to try to resolve matters.[26] The Quai d'Orsay actually seems to have been less agitated than it appeared over Anglo-American plans. A circular telegram of 16 July to French embassies actually said that Paris would reconsider its position on Germany *if* the next CFM meeting failed. Changes would then be easier to justify in propaganda terms. The point was that the Anglo-Americans must not act before giving the CFM one last chance of agreement. Other documents confirmed that the Quai was not averse to joining trizonal arrangements in west Germany, so long as it received concessions on political decentralisation, reparations, coal supplies and industrial controls, and did not have to share in the large financial deficit of the Bizone.[27] Nonetheless Bidault called Caffery and Duff Cooper to see him on the evening of 17 July, complained about decisions being taken 'behind his back', talked of resigning his post, and bluntly stated the essence of his dilemma: 'I know full well that our zone must join yours but I cannot do it at the mouth of a gun'. He handed each ambassador a formal note and a personal letter to Marshall and Bevin, explaining that having 'burned its bridges' with Russia, France seemed faced by a policy which would 'appear to French public opinion as justifying the position taken by Mr Molotov . . .', and that he would 'protest solemnly and publicly' about any increase in Germany's level of industry. So far as France was concerned the level of industry and the future of the Ruhr were issues to be settled on a *four-power* basis, not by the Bizonal authorities.[28] Bidault told Auriol that if this appeal failed to move the Anglo-Saxons he would fly to Washington to see President Truman face-to-face.[29]

It seemed perfectly clear to Caffery, after Bidault's appeal, that the Foreign Minister was prepared to change France's German policy in the long term, and certainly if the next CFM meeting failed, but that he was terrified about the impact of precipitate action on French opinion,[30] and Ambassador Bonnet put just this point to State Department representatives.[31] The PCF could make great propaganda capital of the German issue, and it seemed more sensible to MRP leaders to delay Germany's economic rehabilitation until this could be dovetailed with a completed Marshall Plan proposal.[32] So Marshall and Bevin took their earlier decision, to delay an increase in the level of industry, one step further. They now said they would defer any action until France had had an opportunity to express its view on their plan.[33] Bidault recognised that this was no more than a respite. In the Cabinet Ramadier supported the Foreign Minister's policy of opposition to the Anglo-Saxons and the Finance Minister, Robert Schuman, expressed the view that the US could not claim to be interested in French security whilst reviving Germany. The domestic dangers of a revived Germany were highlighted during an Assembly debate on foreign affairs on 25–26 July (the first since the Moscow CFM) when there were calls for East–West co-operation and controls on Germany.[34]

Meanwhile the arguments with the Anglo-Saxons provoked renewed debate among French officials about future policy. René Massigli, long an advocate of trizonal co-operation, argued that, since the next CFM was likely to fail anyway, France should avoid pointless protests and concentrate on resolving west Germany's future with Washington and London. Bonnet believed that, with Congress determined to cut the costs of occupation and with Americans eager 'to make Germany a bastion of resistance against the Soviets', France's best course was to integrate Germany into a European-wide reconstruction plan which suited French needs,[35] and a Quai memorandum of 24 July which was sent to Bidault and Auriol argued that, in order to take full advantage of Marshall aid France must resolve both its financial problems internally (its archaic fiscal system, high inflation and budget deficit) and the German problem externally. If the financial situation was tackled, and if Germany contributed to European recovery without being revived ahead of France, then France could gradually re-establish its independence in the world, offer material benefits to its people *and* obtain security vis-à-vis her ancient opponent. The memorandum noted that, although France's position had weaknesses, in that she needed Marshall aid desperately and could not afford to alienate both Russia and America, she also had means of resisting American 'dictatorship' in that the Marshall Plan would be unworkable without her.[36] Just as interesting were the views of French officials in Germany. The Consul-General in Munich, Louis Keller, argued on 30 July that France might be able to achieve a decentralised German government if it worked with federalists *within* Germany. Members of the Bavarian government, for example, were keen federalists. If France joined trizonal arrangements she could work with Germans themselves against the Anglo-Americans, and could offer 'a new road by which Germans could join a European union as equals'. St Hardouin visited Bavaria at this time and agreed with Keller that politicians there might favour France's federalist approach to German government.[37]

159

On 4 August the Anglo-Saxons informed Bidault that they were ready to hear French views on Germany, both on the level of industry question and the control of the Ruhr coal mines. Initially the French were upset, partly because the Anglo-Americans seemed ready to increase Bizonal output whatever France said, but also because they seemed to want merely a written exposé of French views. Caffery, however, assured the angry Bidault that his arguments would receive 'full consideration' and the Anglo-Americans eventually agreed that French views should be heard face-to-face, at a conference in London later in the month.[38] This was despite complaints from General Clay about the delays being caused by France.[39] The preparations which Alphand put under way in the Quai for the three-power talks implicitly accepted that there *could* be changes in German industrial output and were significant for clarifying the concessions France would require before agreeing to co-operate with the Anglo-Americans in Western Germany. These concessions should include a limit on annual German steel production of ten million tons, the maintenance of industrial limits and prohibitions on German industry, the inclusion of Saar coal in French production, international control of the Ruhr, guaranteed coal and steel supplies from Germany to its neighbours, a German obligation to contribute to European recovery, a decentralised government structure, and a US security guarantee on the lines of the Byrnes Treaty.[40] The desire to *separate* the Ruhr-Rhineland from Germany was thus dropped but the Ruhr remained, nonetheless, the centre of French concerns. As President Auriol recognised, the Ruhr was vital for Great Power co-operation because it was essential to everyone's designs on Germany: as the source of reparations to meet Soviet demands, as the powerhouse for European recovery in Anglo-American plans, and as the key to France's security. This was why the French were so anxious to treat the Ruhr as a *four*-power concern, and not as some Bizonal 'possession'. Auriol hoped the area could come under UN-control in a kind of European 'Tennessee Valley Authority', but the Quai was less fanciful, keeping to the argument used at the Moscow CFM, that coal and steel industries in the Ruhr should be placed under a system of international management[41] and insisting, in all talks on the Marshall Plan, that Germany's contribution must be consistent with *four*-power decisions.[42] During informal talks in mid-August with Clayton, Caffery and others, Bidault revealed what was to become a constant French aim over the following months. He wanted to establish a body in the Ruhr, including French, US, British and Benelux representatives, which would allocate the region's coal and steel between domestic and international use.

The Americans listened to these ideas but were clearly resolved to increase Bizonal production in order to show Congress that US financial burdens would be eased, to give hope to the Germans and to generate wider European recovery. The Americans were not yet ready to give Bidault any compensation in the form of special controls on the Ruhr though they did hold out the prospect of future talks on the subject.[43] A short time later, on 22 August, the London three-power talks began and proved little more than cosmetic. Hervé Alphand and René Massigli insisted that French recovery must be kept ahead of Germany's, advocated a long occupation of Germany and international control of the Ruhr, and said that an amended level of industry would be acceptable on certain conditions: it must be without prejudice to decisions by the next

CFM, reparations deliveries to France should be guaranteed, and there should be increased Ruhr coal exports. However the Americans and British simply repeated their motives for raising the level of industry and refused to enter into any real negotiations. The best the Frenchmen could get was a promise of talks in Berlin on increased coal supplies, and much time was spent in wrangling over the wording of the communiqué, issued on 28 August.[44] The following day the Anglo-Americans in Berlin announced their increase in the level of industry to 10.7 million tons of steel production, and were immediately lambasted by the Russian Marshal Sokolovsky.[45]

There was some succour for the French in September when the Anglo-Americans agreed to revise the sliding scale for coal exports in France's favour.[46] This at least eased Monnet's worry that Ruhr coke might soon be used up within Germany, crippling French steel production.[47] However there was another disappointment in mid-September when the Americans and British agreed to establish 'a German Coal Management ... in the hope that German miners will produce more coal if they are working under German direction'.[48] This was despite the French hope that the Ruhr mines would be put under international management, and the French and Benelux governments quickly protested at the measure, the French complaining that the new scheme would form the 'most powerful cartel in Europe . . .'.[49] It took two months before the Anglo-Saxons responded, however, and then it was only to insist that Allied safeguards over the mines were sufficient and that the new plans would not prejudice any future international controls on the Ruhr.[50] Although US representatives in Europe recommended to Washington that talks about the Ruhr should be held with France in the near future,[51] it was far from clear when the Quai d'Orsay would be able to discuss this vital question with the Anglo-Americans.

Despite the problems over Germany and the refusal of the Eastern European states to take part, the conference called by Bidault and Bevin to discuss the Marshall Plan met in Paris on 12 July and proved successful. British and French officials continued to work together closely as leaders of the sixteen-member Committee of European Economic Co-operation (CEEC), which was established. A small steering committee and a number of specialist committees were set up to devise a European recovery plan.[52] It was clear to Monnet and Alphand that, in order to induce the US Congress to provide funds, Europe would have to present a well-documented case, make realistic estimates of its needs, aim at achieving a balanced trading position over the period of US aid, and address deep-seated problems including, at a national level, financial problems, and at an international level, the existence of protectionist trade barriers.[53] However the French soon found themselves differing with other states on how to achieve these aims. The Dutch, for example, were ready to expand German industrial production as part of a general recovery plan, whilst the Belgians and others objected to the French wish to finance the Monnet Plan with Marshall aid. The French argued that long-range modernisation and construction plans would impress the Americans, by showing that a strong, stable Europe could be achieved in a short time but others felt that France, with its ambitious Monnet Plan already in being, would thereby obtain large sums without necessarily contributing to *general* European recovery. The Americans shared this view arguing that Marshall aid must make Europe as a whole self-sustaining within four years, at the lowest cost; it must *not* finance a series of costly national recovery plans.[54] Notwithstanding later claims that the Monnet Plan was somehow the 'model' for Marshall aid,[55] France's nationalistic attitude was seen by Washington as part of a general malaise in the Paris talks by late August, where each European country was concerned not with united European action but with its own recovery – although France's attitude was not as negative about co-operation as were some others. Despite its insistence that the Europeans should draw up a plan without American interference (thus avoiding any impression of 'dictatorship') the State Department decided by late August to give some indication of its desiderata in any plan. The Department wanted to see the maximum possible 'self-help' in Europe.[56] Once again the watchful Bonnet gave some advance warning of American thinking.[57]

On 30 August, American representatives met members of the Paris steering committee and criticised their current estimated need of nearly $30 billion in aid. The Americans wanted to see common action through a joint organisation, and greater efforts to improve intra-European trade and financial stability, with the aim of achieving self-sufficiency within four years. Both Alphand and Britain's Sir Oliver Franks were doubtful about achieving the last aim, however, and other states were reluctant to establish a powerful joint organisation in Europe which was likely to impede their national economic planning. On 1 September, after the Europeans had done little to change their plans, the Americans went further and asked the steering committee to postpone the meeting of CEEC foreign ministers, planned for the 15th, at which the recovery plan was to have been approved. The Europeans were astonished and responded that it was too late to make fundamental changes to their plan.[58] Bidault complained that Washington's behaviour gave credence to Molotov's view that Marshall aid was an infringement of sovereignty, but heavy pressure was put on him and Ramadier by Clayton and Caffery to make amendments to the plan,[59] and the Europeans eventually agreed to defer the foreign ministers' meeting.[60] The US was satisfied over the next few days with amendments committing the Europeans to achieve financial stability, develop intra-European trade and establish a 'continuing organisation'[61] and a final agreement was signed on 22 September for formal presentation to Washington. Amongst the issues which it blurred was the position of Germany, which it was intended should contribute to European recovery without being allowed to grow faster than its neighbours.[62]

Notwithstanding the desire to defend national independence, the CEEC conference also marked an advance, if an undramatic one, for the idea of pooling of European economic strength via customs unions. On 2 August Alphand recommended a customs union with the Benelux states or Italy to Bidault as a way to alter Europe's economic position radically whilst impressing US opinion. The benefits of a Western European customs union to France had of course been discussed during the war, but little had been done since, and it had been feared that America would oppose such 'protectionist' schemes. Now, however, Marshall aid could provide the financial lubrication for progress and there were clear signs, not least from Will Clayton, that a customs union would be seen in Washington as the most effective way to expand and strengthen the European economy. Furthermore, Alphand argued, France could well take the lead in this field since he felt Britain had no interest in customs unions.[63] Bidault took the idea to the Cabinet a few days later and pointed out that links to both Italy *and* Benelux could help France with manpower and markets, and form a powerful trading bloc. A union with Italy alone would be less useful. The Cabinet left it to Bidault how he proceeded with this matter[64] and on 13 August, Alphand made a speech in the Marshall Plan steering committee calling for customs unions as a way to expand European trade.[65] Various problems soon emerged for Alphand's project, however. First, despite his suppositions, the British did prove ready to look at a customs union and agreed with France and other states in early September to establish a Customs Union Study Group in Brussels which, as its title suggested, would explore the ground on the technicalities of a union.[66] The Benelux states refused to go any further than the Study Group as yet, because of their desire to keep in step with Britain.[67] This meant that the only state actually willing to establish a customs union with France was Italy.

Since the signature of the Italian peace treaty in February, the Rome government had approached Paris on several occasions for an improvement in relations and had even suggested a treaty of amity between them. The French remained reticent, partly because of the need to ratify the peace treaty,[68] but during the ratification debate in June Bidault told the National Assembly that he hoped for co-operation with Italy in future.[69] Then, at the CEEC on 12 July the Italian Foreign Minister, Count Carlo Sforza, made a bold call for European states to abandon economic nationalism in favour of multilateral co-operation. Sforza wanted Italians to become the 'heralds' of European co-operation and had a particular interest in working with France. Such a policy would help Italy overcome its sense of inferiority after Mussolini, to regain international status and to tackle its economic problems,[70] and on 2 August the Italian Ambassador told Alphand that Rome was ready to enter a customs union with France.[71] This was the same day that Alphand had written about customs unions to Bidault. Not all officials were enthusiastic about Italian co-operation, however. The French *chargé d'affaires* in Rome, Georges Balay, feared Italy would try to exploit East–West divisions to alter its peace treaty and that the Anglo-Americans might condone breaches in the treaty's military clauses. These fears were shared by Massigli,[72] and though the Italian peace treaty entered into force in September, problems continued thereafter between Paris and Rome in carrying out such clauses as the Alpine border amendments.[73] Neither could Italy be considered a formidable partner in a customs union. She could provide a source of manpower, certain minerals, and a market for French goods, but she was overpopulated, economically backward and competed with France in the production of wine, textiles, and automobiles.[74]

It was partly to impress the Americans that France agreed to establish a commission with Italy to study a customs union.[75] This commission held three meetings in late 1947, made a number of detailed studies and in December produced a lengthy report. The report saw no fundamental reason to rule out a union, which could help economic reconstruction and lead to specialisation in production, but there were clear problems caused by the weak state of Italian industry, France's desire to absorb *skilled* labour from Italy (as opposed to absorbing excess Italian manpower in general) and the fact that the two were competitive, not complementary, in many areas of production. Indeed the best prospects for Franco-Italian co-operation seemed to lie in the field of 'market-sharing' agreements to reduce competition between them. Bidault's officials also warned, in a note to him covering the commission's report, that a customs union might have such far-reaching effects that it could necessitate a full economic union.[76] There were clearly grave problems then for any customs union with Italy.

After the CEEC conference Alphand, Oliver Franks and other European officials journeyed to Washington to explain their plan, before it went before Congress. The Europeans asked America to meet the whole of their requests and emphasised their agreement to carry out such US conditions as the creation of a permanent organisation.[77] Meanwhile, however, the situation in certain European countries, including France, was seen as being so desperate that the Americans gave attention to the idea of 'interim aid', to be provided before the Marshall Plan proper came into effect. A meeting of US representatives in Europe, in early August, agreed that the short-term situation in France, Italy and Britain was serious enough to justify emergency aid, even if this meant calling a special session of Congress. Marshall aid was not likely to be approved by Congress until March 1948, but France was already using its gold reserves to meet basic supplies of food, coal and other raw materials. To make matters worse, the French wheat crop was described as 'the worst since 1815'.[78] On 12 September the Quai informed Caffery, in a memorandum, that France's dollar and gold reserves would dry up during the following month and that $600 million would be needed to maintain necessary imports until Marshall aid began to flow.[79]

The end of the CEEC conference saw a series of Franco-American exchanges on French economic needs and the State Department began to study interim aid in earnest. Despite the personal sympathy of Marshall however, French hopes of covering the whole of their short-term trade deficit down to March 1948 via interim aid proved too ambitious. The State Department baulked at the idea of asking Congress for anything more than 'emergency' supplies to offset cold and hunger. When Congress met there was much concern in Paris about the conditions that might be placed on aid,[80] but an interim aid agreement was finally agreed in Paris on 2 January. It provided $284 million to the end of March. As with previous agreements – lend-lease in 1945 and the Blum loan in 1946 – this was essential for French survival, though less than Paris wanted. It also included various commitments, which were of some embarrassment to Bidault, about French economic policy and US oversight over how the aid was spend.[81]

*   *   *

One important factor which encouraged the US to grant interim aid was the continued deterioration of East–West relations. In early August General Catroux traced a steady growth in Soviet obstructionism, isolation and defensiveness in foreign affairs since the Truman Doctrine, with a refusal to join in Marshall aid, suspicion of Western co-operation in Germany and a tightening grip on Eastern Europe. Catroux saw little prospect of agreement at the next CFM, due in November. Instead his Embassy feared that the Soviets were preparing, psychologically, for war with the United States and that the Kremlin saw France as part of the American 'bloc'.[82] Increasingly after August Catroux felt isolated in his Embassy, as telephone calls to Soviet citizens were met with silence, invitations to dinner were refused, and the Foreign Ministry failed to resolve difficulties over visa applications.[83] On the international scene in September US and Soviet representatives clashed publicly at the UN General Assembly meeting in New York, and Auriol gave thought yet again to an appeal for *détente* between the two sides.[84] Yet at the same time the President was aware of the growing vulnerability of France to *internal* divisions as a result of the *international* rift. Intelligence reports from the Ministry of the Interior suggested the Soviet Embassy was making preparations with the PCF and CGT to disrupt Marshall aid,[85] and the country seemed ripe for large-scale discontent. Prefects' reports for the month ending 10 September depicted a pessimistic nation, lacking faith in its leaders and with many Communist sympathisers, whilst in the Cabinet every new financial restraint and fiscal measure served to intensify existing divisions.[86]

It was against this depressing background that, on 22–27 September, to the surprise of Western foreign ministries, a conference was held in Poland between the Communist parties of Russia, Eastern Europe, France and Italy. Here in the wake of the CEEC conference, the Soviet Politburo member, Andrei Zhdanov, enunciated a new outlook on international affairs. Zhdanov saw a world divided into two opposing blocs, in which the Communist parties must co-operate against US 'imperialism'. The PCF was ordered to abandon all attempts to work with 'bourgeois' elements in France, and the PCF representative, Jacques Duclos, was chastised for 'opportunism' and lack of revolutionary zeal in the past. He was forced to admit the error of his party's ways and promised to mobilise the French people against the USA and the Fourth Republic. The conference established an 'Information Bureau' ('Cominform') in Belgrade which was seen by many in the West as recreating the old Comintern, with its aim of world revolution. All in all the conference seems to have had two aims: first, to unify the Eastern European Communists (some of whom had been tempted by Marshall aid) against America and around Moscow; and secondly, to goad the French and Italian Communists into sabotaging the Marshall Plan, which the Soviets clearly saw as a threat to their security, promising as it did a stronger, more united and pro-American Western Europe.[87] At first on the French side there were doubts about the significance of Cominform.[88] Apparently to avoid any impact on the French municipal elections in October,[89] the new Zhdanov line was not made public until 22 September. Catroux then analysed it as a demonstration that Moscow did have Allies, and as an attack in particular on Western European Socialists, who were seen as dividing the working class. But he felt that the Soviets expected a long struggle with America, rather than war.[90]

The new Zhdanov line, attacking the French governments, the Americans, Marshall aid and the revival of Germany, was seen in the Assembly on 28 October, in a lengthy, much-interrupted speech from Duclos.[91] The speech ended an uncertain period since May during which the PCF had kept open the possibility of a return to office, and moderated its attacks on the government. From now on the Communists would castigate their former government allies as American stooges, whilst being condemned themselves as Soviet puppets. The

SFIO in particular found the new situation distressing. Léon Blum described the Cominform decisions as 'a declaration of war against socialism'[92] but not all SFIO activists were sympathetic to Blum. Activists had been disappointed for some time with the party's declining vote at elections and their leaders' tendency to compromise socialist principles in working with the MRP. Guy Mollet, who had replaced Blum's protegé Daniel Mayer as Secretary-General of the SFIO in 1946, had previously favoured a close alliance with the PCF and was very critical of Ramadier's premiership. The Socialists were vital to the survival of the Fourth Republic after October 1947, but they remained in government only with a great sense of unease both over domestic affairs and over foreign policy. An alliance with capitalist America, the danger of East–West conflict, and the revival of Germany, with its militarist traditions, all provoked doubts in the party. Only a minority went so far as to advocate 'neutralism' but within the general context of Western co-operation and anti-communism many favoured continuing controls on Germany and the development of a 'third force' between the two superpowers, in which France would co-operate with other European nations and work for East–West peace.

The appeal of an international 'third force' was reinforced by the notion of a domestic 'third force' which stood against the extremes of Left and Right. For it was not just the PCF which threatened the existence of the Fourth Republic after September 1947. Since early in the year there had been rumours that General de Gaulle was about to form his own nationalist movement to represent the French people.[93] Even some close to him feared that this could be branded a 'fascist' ambition,[94] but de Gaulle hinted publicly at what was in his mind in a speech at Bruneval on 30 March[95] and eight days later, after a vain personal attempt by Ramadier to win him over to the Fourth Republic,[96] the General made clear his political aims in a speech at Strasbourg.[97] The *Rassemblement du Peuple Français* (RPF) was then formally launched and was seen by many conservatives and Catholics as a real alternative to Communism and the weaknesses of the Fourth Republic. De Gaulle's authoritarian organisation, his charismatic leadership and vision of a strong presidency all suggested a neo-fascist movement but his support grew rapidly and an RPF rally at Vincennes on 5 October attracted half-a-million followers. Ironically many were ex-Vichyites. Shortly afterwards, in the municipal elections, RPF candidates took 38 per cent of votes, compared to 30 per cent for the PCF, 18 per cent for the SFIO and a paltry 9 per cent for the MRP.[98] With no general election necessary for several years the RPF could only win national power by winning deputies from other parties, and it particularly tried to attract them from the MRP. In due course, the General's extremism, his lack of an economic policy and the dangers he held for dividing the country, lost him support as did his belief in the inevitability of another war.[99] However in 1947–48 he was a major menace, threatening the position of the MRP, just as the PCF threatened the Socialists.

Faced by the formation of Cominform and the rise of the RPF, President Auriol could see that East–West divisions beyond France both reinforced, and were reinforced by, divisions within the country. At Marseilles in early October, Auriol finally delivered the speech he had long wanted to make on the need for world peace. The speech was praised by Ambassadors Catroux and Massigli, both of whom were visiting Paris, and both the President and Massigli agreed that joint Anglo-French action *vis-à-vis* the superpowers could form the basis of a move towards a lowering of international tensions.[100] Bidault, however, was pessimistic and seemed himself to favour a pro-Western and anti-Soviet line. He told the Cabinet that the UN was 'dead' and that three years experience had shown the impossibility of working with Russia. The municipal election results added to the air of despondency in government over social discontent, increasing political division and the danger of politically-instigated strikes.[101] Ramadier still hoped that minimum salary increases and other economic measures could stave off both popular unrest and inflation, and Auriol still believed that the Fourth Republic could survive, but on 28 October the government survived a vote of confidence by only twenty votes, with some MRP members joining the opposition.[102]

Meanwhile the US watched French political developments with mounting concern. In June Caffery had hoped the PCF and RPF would 'cancel each other', but Freeman Matthews, head of the Office of European Affairs, suggested that a 'secret fund' should be established to finance anti-communists in France.[103] Over the next few months, as the RPF strengthened, the PCF grew more militant and the municipal elections approached, Caffery feared that a 'showdown' was looming and that Marshall aid might come too late to save the Fourth Republic. He urged the provision of interim aid and a relaxation in the pace of German revival as ways to help Prime Minister Ramadier.[104] By October Caffery argued that Washington should establish contacts with General de Gaulle, who seemed to be emerging as a strong alternative to the PCF, and could be seen as the lesser of two evils. The State Department was very cautious, however, about co-operating with someone who seemed anti-democratic and likely to alienate the whole of the French working-class. (Like Monnet, the US was all too aware that France's economic recovery relied on the support of its workers.[105]) The British Foreign Office, too, feared de Gaulle's authoritarianism and believed he would be hard to deal with if he returned to power.[106] Although Caffery did establish contacts with Gaston Palewski, and other members of the General's entourage, he never met the General himself, partly because of fears of the response if news of such a meeting leaked to the public.[107]

In November 1947 President Auriol's faith in the institutions of the Fourth Republic was tested to the full, as the strike movement which had begun during October rapidly intensified against a background of further price increases. A public service strike began on the 7th, a docks strike on the 14th and by the 27th there was almost a total stoppage.[108] In the midst of the unrest Ramadier's administration collapsed, and a government crisis was added to France's troubles. Fortunately for the Republic, a successor to Ramadier was found quickly, in the shape of the MRP's Robert Schuman.[109] The new Cabinet, and especially the Socialist Minister of the Interior, Jules Moch, was determined to take a tough approach to the issue of internal unrest, if necessary by using armed force, and early in December the discontent began to ease. There were stories of workers resisting attempts to turn the strikes into an overtly political weapon, and it became clear that the Communists had failed to create mass action in favour of a new regime. Instead they had alienated most of the population.[110] (It was a similar story with a series of strikes in Italy, at the same time.) It could of course be argued that the main intention

167

of the Communists was not to overthrow the government, but to undermine the value of Marshall aid,[111] but the end of the strikes brought great relief to the West. A series of government economic measures on 8 December heralded the rapid demise of the stoppages and four days later the country was back at work.[112] Bidault believed that the PCF had turned the working-class against itself[113] and the clearest evidence for this was a split in the CGT, brought about when the moderate followers of Léon Jouhaux decided to form a new organisation, the *Force Ouvrière*. Caffery considered it to be 'the most important event that has occurred in France since the Liberation'.[114] However the events of November–December left many problems. Working-class support was still needed for economic recovery, higher salary increases had been granted which threatened further inflation, and the strikes had succeeded in weakening the French economy, making the need for Marshall aid even greater.

* * *

In September 1947 it had seemed, for a brief time, that the French might be able to forge an international 'third force' with the British, thus answering Socialist desires for an escape from the Cold War. At the end of the Marshall Plan conference Ernest Bevin had visited Ramadier, for what was meant to be a courtesy call. As had happened before, however, Bevin turned a discussion with a French leader into a dramatic proposal for wide-ranging Anglo-French co-operation. He suggested once again that, especially by drawing their colonial empires together, France and Britain could match the might of the superpowers, and recommended to an excited Ramadier that they should study co-operation in the fields of tourism, trade and colonies.[115] In assessing the Bevin–Ramadier interview, Chauvel described Bevin's talk as 'vacuous' but Massigli felt Chauvel was being too dismissive. The Ambassador argued that Bevin did have a genuine fear of US–Soviet dominance, as well as a genuine interest in Anglo-French unity. Co-operation with Bidault in the Marshall Plan had, Massigli felt, shown the British the value of working with France, where previously there had been doubts in London about the reliability of French governments. Furthermore the Foreign Office seemed keen to follow up the Bevin–Ramadier talk, and in early October both Bevin and Oliver Harvey said they were studying economic co-operation with France.[116] Over the following weeks, however, Paris heard little more of Bevin's grandiose schemes, and Chauvel's pessimism seemed the more realistic interpretation of Bevin's talk with Ramadier. Britain's economic ministries were reluctant to give priority to trade with France, felt unable to expand tourism for financial reasons, and believed that a European customs union – which genuinely attracted Bevin – would damage trade with the Commonwealth.[117]

Bevin's proposals for Anglo-French colonial co-operation were perhaps the most interesting aspect of his talk with Ramadier. In fact, French and British officials had already been involved in talks on imperial co-operation especially in sub-Saharan Africa (where nationalist movements were less advanced than in Asia). Not only Anglo-French, but also Belgian, and even Portuguese and South African representatives, had attended conferences since 1944 on such subjects as education, disease and forestry. It was tempting to believe that by building on this technical co-operation, African resources could be tapped to help European recovery, reducing reliance on the almighty dollar. Auriol was interested in the proposal and Alphand raised the idea of a West African customs union. If successful, a union between the two largest colonial empires could indeed provide the basis for the 'third force' for which many Frenchmen hoped. Such notions were actually however as impractical as they were ambitious. The French and British had entirely different colonial philosophies, the former's based on central control and 'assimilation' in the French Union, the latter's on 'benevolent domination' and evolution towards a much looser Commonwealth structure. French administrators were terrified by the pace of British policy towards autonomy, whilst the British Colonial Office could have no interest in creating a centralised union with France. A second and equally daunting problem, especially for proposals of economic reliance on Africa was that the continent south of the Sahara was vast and underdeveloped. It would demand an enormous capital investment over many years to be of real use. Yet in 1947–48 Europe had not even rebuilt its own capital base after the war. Attempts to act were also undermined by the indifference of local administrators, who feared a diminution in their own authority and had insufficient staff to take on new burdens.[118]

A further, major difficulty with any proposals for Anglo-French co-operation after the war, it must also be said, was the aversion on the British side to 'impractical' and 'idealistic' schemes. Ernest Bevin, though grandiose in vision, was intensely pragmatic and practical in carrying plans through. The Foreign Office were also opposed to 'hasty' action in the wake of the Bevin–Ramadier interview and somewhat taken aback when Bidault inspired an article in *l'Aube* raising the idea of a Franco-British Union. Such a Union had been proposed in June 1940 as a way to keep the French Empire in the war against Hitler, but the Foreign Office evidently did not think that times were so desperate again.[119]

* * *

Instead of seeing the formation of a 'third force' the latter months of 1947 were most vital for laying the basis for future French co-operation with Britain and America in the fields of German revival and European defence. Despite the arguments over an increased level of industry and mine ownership, the French in September 1947 were firmly attached to the idea of three-power co-operation if the next CFM failed. There were some, like General Koenig, who disapproved of such a course, but to many in the Quai, and even to officials in Germany like Emile Laffon, trizonal links seemed inevitable if four-power agreement proved impossible. France's dilemma was admirably set out by François Seydoux, the representative of the Commissariat-General for German and Austrian Affairs in Germany, writing on 15 September, who argued that East–West tension was likely to mean the division of Germany regardless of French action. True, a Western German state would not be as powerful as a united Germany, but if the Anglo-Americans insisted on its economic revival, it would still be more powerful than France. Thus, if France did not try to control Western Germany's development, by seeking guarantees from the Anglo-Americans, she would have to watch helplessly as the new state developed against her interests.[120] It was still the Quai's hope that, even if the French policies of 1945–47 needed radical refinement, France should continue to seek such guarantees as a decentralised German administration, limits on German steel output, and an international mechanism to share out the resources of the Ruhr. If she joined in trizonal arrangements she would also want a limited share in financing the trizonal trade deficit, and the maintenance of French commercial advantages built up since 1945 in the ZOF.[121]

The UN General Assembly in New York after 16 September allowed Bidault to explore these issues with Bevin and Marshall. In conversation with the latter on the 18th Bidault said that, in view of the likely failure of the next CFM, he had authority to discuss the whole German problem in secret, and Marshall agreed in principle to hold three-power talks on Germany if the CFM failed.[122] After informal talks between French and US officials, Bidault met Marshall again and put forward a memorandum explaining France's 'sufficient but essential' position on the key problem, the Ruhr. Reserving the question of the actual ownership of industries for the moment, the Frenchman again asked for an 'International Authority' in the Ruhr, to apportion coal and steel between exports and internal use. The Ruhr would be 'integrated into a reorganised European economy being . . . considered a European asset'. Marshall promised to study the memorandum.[123] Meanwhile Bidault had also raised his proposal for three-power talks with Bevin,[124] and Anglo-French conversations took place in London in October, when Chauvel explained the latest French views on the Ruhr, discussed tactics to pursue at the next CFM and defined a kind of agenda for future three-power talks. Chauvel made it clear that France could only promise to co-operate with the Anglo-Saxons in return for firm guarantees, and pointed out to Bevin that, by joining trizonal arrangements, France would increase the risk to her security enormously, by antagonising the Soviets. France therefore favoured military talks with Britain. Bevin was as enthusiastic as he had been with Ramadier a month earlier, talking of the studies that were under way in London on European economic and colonial co-operation, to link together Britain, France, the Benelux states, Italy and Africa. Though he was not yet ready to discuss military policy with France, saying this should remain in the background until after the CFM, he evidently believed that Anglo-French differences in Germany could easily be ironed out.[125]

Bevin's position on military conversations was particularly significant at this time since, after July 1947, the French armed forces had to face up to the danger of another European war. It has already been seen that the EMDN had given thought since 1945 to the dangers of war with Russia,[126] but that French armed forces were unfitted for a major conflict.[127] In May 1947 General Juin had been appointed Commissioner-General in Morocco and replaced, as acting head of the EMDN, by General Jean Humbert. Humbert soon became deeply concerned at the military imbalance in Europe between the motley array of Western forces and the massive strength of the Red Army.[128] After the breakdown of the talks with Molotov in Paris on Marshall aid, Humbert initiated a series of studies on the dangers of war, covering such points as likely lines of Soviet attack, possible defence positions and the chances of maintaining France's neutrality.[129] With reports on the state of the Army in 1947–48 continually revealing a lack of modern equipment, mediocre training and a confusion of command[130] it was always clear that, in any war in which she became involved France would need allies. In the absence of government directives the armed forces had to make plans for war on three possible bases: neutrality, an alliance with America, or an alliance with Russia.[131] Yet it was clearly the Soviets who were the great menace, with predictions that the Red Army could reach the Pyrenees in only twenty days,[132] and by 6 October, the EMDN had prepared a highly-important note, sent to Ramadier, laying out the possible basis for talks with the Americans, who were obviously the only power able to match Russia militarily. This note in surveying potential lines of defence in Europe ruled out a retreat to Britain, the Pyrenees and North Africa as surrendering too much, even if it would be easy to defend. It also criticised an attempt to hold the Rhine and the Alps as marking too great a retreat. Ideally the EMDN preferred a 'forward defence' of the Elbe, which would mean the protection of *all* Western Europe, but it was recognised that this would require a massive build up in US–European resources, a united command, and probably the use of atomic, bacteriological and chemical weapons. Humbert's staff were also adamant that France should have a leading role in preparing such a plan, with a French part in any 'Combined Chiefs of Staff' with America and Britain.[133]

The need for a US alliance was strongly reinforced by the preparations for three-power co-operation in Germany. On 26 September Bidault had asked for studies to be made of the impact of trizonal 'fusion' on the ZOF[134] and on 18 October the EMDN replied that, whilst they could see no significant technical objections in adjusting to bizonal administrative methods, there were important military implications in such a move. Fusion 'would constitute a decisive phase on the road of abandoning neutrality', and if France took this course she must obtain military guarantees about her security from America and Britain.[135] It was in light of such considerations that Chauvel had discussed the matter with Bevin on 21 October. On 27 October an EMDN memorandum was presented to Ramadier, designed to get a government decision to abandon neutrality. Given France's geographical position, her inadequate armed forces and the might of the Red Army this memorandum argued that it was simply impossible to maintain neutrality in war. Even with British and Benelux support it would be impossible to meet a Soviet assault, and a withdrawal to North Africa could no longer provide salvation: African nationalism and a lack of economic and military resources would make it impossible to expel the Russians from France from bases in North Africa, as Hitler had been expelled from Occupied France in 1944. The strategic logic was inescapable. France must ally with all possible European states – even Switzerland and Spain were mentioned – and the US. Only the US could rearm France and, equally important, help to keep military controls on Germany. It was also pointed out that, whilst a US–Europe alliance would take time to build up its defences, its very existence could *deter* war in the first place.[136]

On 4 November the National Defence Committee discussed the subject of neutrality, though without taking a final decision upon it. Here the Army Chief of Staff, Georges Revers explained the need for co-operation with America and Europe and Auriol pointed out the dangers of *internal* subversion in Western Europe by Communists. Ramadier said that political and military leaders must address the problem of neutrality and Revers said that he had already established contacts with other allied military staffs.[137] Revers, the one-time *Chef de Cabinet* of Admiral Darlan,[138] had in fact discussed possible joint French–US–British strategic planning with the US military *attaché* in October, and later contacted both Swiss and Spanish military figures about possible defence co-operation. His contact with a representative of the Franco regime, which he claimed was approved by War Minister Coste-Floret, caused consternation when it was discovered by Auriol, who had not been told even though he was nominally the head of French defence planning.[139] In December, Robert Schuman approved more talks with the British and the Americans about the defence of Europe. These talks were held between General Billotte, France's military representative at the UN, and his British and US opposite numbers, early in the New Year, and Bidault also knew of them. Earlier Billotte had urged on de Gaulle, Bidault and the EMDN the need for a US alliance, but, as it transpired, the New York talks were no more than a preliminary exchange of views.[140]

*　*　*

Although France, America and Britain were ready to co-operate in Germany on a Western group if the next CFM broke down, there were lingering hopes that four-power co-operation could continue and, more important, determination to lay the blame for any breakdown at the door of the Soviets. Chauvel felt the last point was vital from the viewpoint of French domestic politics.[141] Ambassador Catroux visited Molotov in Moscow on 5 November, in a last effort to win him over to French plans on federalism and the Ruhr, but Molotov said that Soviet policy remained unchanged from the last CFM, a position which seemed to promise an impasse in London.[142] The *Direction d'Europe* recognised in early November that even if the CFM survived beyond the next meeting in London, it would be very difficult to maintain even the shadow of a 'middle role' between East and West since both the Anglo-Saxons and Soviets were likely to continue organising their own respective zones in ways detrimental to French interests, and because the Americans would prove reluctant to grant Marshall aid to France without German revival.[143] France might continue to differ with the Anglo-Americans in Germany but, in contrast to the Moscow CFM she must base her German policy on co-operation with Washington and London. The main aim now was to secure France's case – on the Ruhr, a decentralised government with strong *Länder*, and reparations payments – on a three-power basis.[144] Massigli continued to have discussions with the Foreign Office on tactics to pursue at the CFM,[145] and before Marshall left for the London conference Bonnet reminded him of French desiderata in the Ruhr, though the Quai realised that the move from four-power to three-power co-operation would still be a difficult decision.[146]

There were those who disagreed with the need for trizonal fusion, a proposal which had not yet been discussed by the Cabinet. General Koenig feared that fusion would destroy France's independence, leave her a poor relation in Western Germany and increase East–West division. Koenig's links to de Gaulle made him distrusted by many in the government at this time, but Auriol sympathised with these fears about fusion[147] and there were also doubters in the Quai d'Orsay. On 20 November one official, Geoffroy de Courcel argued that trizonal fusion would harm France's trade with the ZOF, force her to share the Bizone's financial deficit, quicken the political-economic resuscitation of Germany and encourage a *riposte* from the Soviets, who might well form a centralised German government in Berlin, thereby tempting Western Germany to their side. This last danger was already well appreciated in the Quai, where one document described a Soviet–German combination as 'the greatest danger which could face us'. René Massigli, however, soon produced a series of counter-arguments to Courcel. The Ambassador agreed that France must win solid concessions before agreeing to fusion but he did not think a trizone need be damaging. France could obtain financial and commercial guarantees in any fusion agreement; the Soviets were likely to take action in their zone regardless of French policy; and – as he had argued since 1946 – fusion would give Paris influence over Anglo-American policies in West Germany.[148]

When the 'conference of the last chance'[149] met in London on 25 November there was no real surprise when it faced one area of deadlock after another.[150] Among other points Molotov continued to refuse to discuss the Saar[151] and insisted that a centralised German government should be created.[152] Bidault's personal antipathy towards the Russian continued unabated,[153] and on 7 December (with the French strikes now under control) Bidault told Marshall and Bevin that the CFM ought to be brought to an end on the first suitable issue.[154] A week later Bidault remained firm in his belief that there should be a clean break with the Soviets[155] and on the 15th, in a plenary meeting, he supported Marshall when the latter condemned the Soviets for blocking all agreement and called for the CFM to adjourn. No date was set for it to meet again.[156] Instead the French, who had repeated their willingness to enter into trizonal co-operation throughout the conference,[157] were anxious to get discussions under way on this subject with Bevin and Marshall before Bidault returned to Paris.[158]

On 17 December Bidault met Bevin and the latter proved as loquacious and domineering as ever. He now favoured military talks with the French and, with what Massigli described as 'a remarkable imprecision in the choice of words' wanted to form a European 'federation', through 'flexible advances', which would be backed by US support. He was confident that once Western Europe was strong the Soviet danger would recede, and even suggested that Germany would be a greater long-term menace. Bidault, irritated by Bevin's long discourse, agreed to send Revers to London for staff talks, gave reassurances that France's domestic situation was secure, and predicted that the Kremlin would soon destroy the last vestiges of democracy in Czechoslovakia.[159] Later Bidault met Lewis Douglas, the US Ambassador to London, and then Marshall himself. The Americans wanted two sets of talks between themselves, Britain and France about the future of Germany. First they proposed to discuss trizonal co-operation (in such fields as monetary policy and communications) and the future of the Saar, in talks in Berlin between the zonal commanders. Secondly, they wanted a three-power conference in London about Germany's political organisation and the future of the Ruhr, beginning sometime in January. Bidault agreed to such talks despite fears of Koenig's reaction, but made clear that France would need real concessions in order to agree to trizonal fusion.[160] (Talks were also held at an Anglo-American level after the conference.[161])

On 19 December, after returning to Paris, Bidault reported the failure of the CFM to the Cabinet. Given France's military weakness he now advocated the abandonment of French neutrality, the pursuit of a joint military effort with Britain, the Benelux and United States, and the development of France's atomic capability. He confessed that differences on Germany were still a barrier to full co-operation with the Anglo-Saxons, but the Cabinet agreed with his general policy. It was a highly significant moment.[162] Neutralism was finally laid to rest and, as had seemed inevitable for many months, France chose an alliance with the West over one with the East. There was some caution in this. Auriol for one still hoped for peace, was fearful of PCF action within France, felt that any West European security preparations should ostensibly be directed against Germany and was determined not to accept trizonal fusion before gaining satisfaction on the Ruhr.[163] However when Bidault told the Assembly's Foreign Affairs Commission on 20 December, that 'Our liberty of action is intact' it was really bluff.[164] A few days later he met Paul-Henri Spaak at a Catholic conference in Brussels and discussed Western European co-operation,[165] and on 23 December Massigli proposed to the British that an approach be made to Belgium for an alliance.[166]

Meanwhile links with the East were being broken one by one. Many saw the strikes of November–December as representing Soviet interference in French internal politics, and on 14 November came direct evidence of Soviet links to paramilitary groups in France, when the police uncovered a cache of arms at a repatriation camp for Soviet prisoners of war, the Camp de Beauregard. The French, well aware of the dangers to their own repatriation work in Russia if they responded to the police find with tough action, decided simply to expel the Soviet officials involved. In reply to this, however, the Russians showed no mercy. They complained about the police search and, on 8 December withdrew their repatriation team from France, simultaneously expelling the French mission from Russia. Bidault feared that the Kremlin might even recall Ambassador Bogomolov from Paris and as a precaution ordered Catroux not to return to Moscow after the London CFM, which he had attended.[167] The Camp de Beauregard incident was accompanied by a violent anti-French press campaign in Moscow, and drew complaints from Soviet representatives for months afterwards.[168] It may well have been related too to a Russian decision, brusquely announced on Radio Moscow on 9 December, to call off talks which had been under way since October on a possible small wheat loan to France.[169] By mid-December Franco-Soviet bilateral relations were in a terrible state[170] and it was a similar story with the rest of Eastern Europe. Although talks had continued on alliances with Czechoslovakia and Poland, in late 1947 they made little progress. The East Europeans adopted the Zhdanov line on international affairs after the founding of Cominform, criticised French relations with the Anglo-Americans in Germany, and joined together in a vitriolic press campaign against the French government during the period of strikes.[171] Thus Europe had indeed been split down the middle. From now on Bidault would have to try to defend French national interests in the context of three-power, not four-power, co-operation.

Chapter 9

Alliance without Security.
January – June 1948.

– France, not just for the sake of reconstruction but simply in order to live, cannot at present rely on its own resources.
Hervé Alphand, writing to Georges Bidault, 3 February 1948 (from the latter's private papers, box 79).

Early in January 1948 Georges Bidault left Paris for a holiday on the Riviera believing that conversations would soon begin with Britain and America, in which France could press its case on the future of Western Germany. Before leaving he approved general instructions for the talks, which were sent to General Koenig. These showed a large degree of continuity with previous French aims on such subjects as industrial and security controls, reparations payments, and international exploitation of the Ruhr. Reassurances in all these areas would be needed before Paris agreed to trizonal fusion. Above all France wanted to avoid the creation of a centralised German government because of the fear that the Germans, if presented with a choice between Frankfurt or Berlin as a capital, would always choose loyalty to Berlin – and thus become tied to Russia. 'A Germany which fell under the domination of the East', declared the instructions, 'would be without doubt the greatest danger which France has ever known'. In joining three-power talks France was most certainly *not* prepared to accept previous Anglo-American decisions regarding Western Germany's future. As in previous talks at four-power level, France had its *own* policy, and was determined to make its view heard. The most interesting section of the document concerned French hopes for Germany's future:

> On the economic plane, but also on the political plane one must . . . propose as an objective to the Allies and to the Germans themselves, the integration of Germany into Europe . . . Europe is the only hope which, other than a new Reich, can be offered to the germanic world, and it is also . . . the only means to give life and consistency to a politically decentralised, but economically prosperous Germany . . .

Thus Germany could co-operate with other states as an 'equal' in future so long as she was weakened internally first by the creation of strong *Länder*, and externally by a process of European integration.[1]

Unfortunately, whilst Bidault was absent from Paris, the Anglo-American commanders in Germany, Clay and Robertson, presented France with a *fait accompli* in Germany that placed the whole of tripartite co-operation at risk.[2] Although Bidault had asked the Americans to avoid any action which might

175

upset Franco-Anglo-American co-operation in Germany,[3] Clay and Robertson were determined, after the London CFM, to allow Germans to administer their own affairs.[4] During meetings with the Minister-Presidents of the bizonal *Länder*, in Frankfurt, the two Generals agreed to expand the size and powers of the 'Economic Council' of German representatives founded in mid-1947,[5] and to create both an upper house and a High Court. The French, who had not expected such far-reaching decisions, were furious with the latest moves towards 'a veritable German government', which had been made despite Marshall's and Bevin's promises to consult the French on German affairs. Chauvel immediately instructed Bonnet and Massigli to complain forcefully about the matter,[6] but both Ambassadors soon discovered that neither the State Department nor the Foreign Office had expected the Clay–Robertson decisions in the form they were issued either.[7] Neither did the US and British Ambassadors in Paris seem *au fait* with the Frankfurt meetings.[8] France was clearly in an embarrassing position. She had abandoned her neutralist stance, desperately needed Marshall aid and could not realistically avoid links with the Bizone. On the other hand she could not meekly accept such cavalier treatment from the Anglo-Saxons, remained genuinely fearful of Germany's resuscitation and was terrified too of a possible Soviet *riposte* to the Frankfurt decisions. The behaviour of Clay and Robertson strengthened the Quai in the view that France must gain firm guarantees about future Anglo-American policy *before* she accepted trizonal fusion.[9]

Massigli hoped that Paris would present her case on the Frankfurt decisions in a constructive manner,[10] but the Americans showed no such moderation in return. General Clay, feigning surprise at the French protests, believed that reforms in Germany had been delayed long enough and that the French should agree to trizonal fusion immediately. The State Department too felt that the French government should tell its people 'the facts of life' and abandon all remnants of its 1945 German policy. The most that was offered to Armand Berard, the *chargé* in Washington when he visited the State Department, was an undertaking to consult France on all *future* decisions in Germany.[11] On 14 January, after returning from holiday, Bidault called in the US and British Ambassadors, and repeated Chauvel's complaint about the actions of Clay and Robertson. The Foreign Minister warned that such behaviour could render his position in the Cabinet 'untenable'. The new British Ambassador, Oliver Harvey, who had just replaced Duff Cooper, fortunately seemed eager to placate Bidault and promised to provide full official details on the Frankfurt agreements.[12]

Bidault told the Cabinet that he would maintain pressure on London and Washington,[13] and a few days later the Anglo-Americans agreed to hear French views about the Frankfurt arrangements, whilst denying any intention to create a German government.[14] The *Direction d'Europe* drew up a memorandum which was presented to the Anglo-Americans on 22 January, criticising the powers which had been given to the Bizonal Economic Council. The paper argued that a German administration should be formed 'from below', with strong *Länder* and the bare minimum of central authority, as France had always advocated.[15] As in August 1947, however, French views did nothing to deflect the Anglo-Americans from their course. Both replied that French fears of a new German 'government' were exaggerated, that the 'provisional' Frankfurt arrangements were necessary to tackle economic problems in the Bizone, and that a more decentralised system would be inefficient.[16] Chauvel remained concerned[17] and on 4 February the French issued another note, saying they were not appeased by the Anglo-American explanations.[18]

The Frankfurt agreements were published on 9 February.[19] When Bidault informed the Cabinet, President Auriol complained that the Anglo-Americans were dividing Germany and would allow Russia to pose as the champion of German reunification. Once again, it was the danger of a Soviet-German combination, such as had occurred in the Rapallo treaty after the Great War, and in the Hitler–Stalin Pact of 1939, which was of concern to many in France. On both earlier occasions the combination had proved disastrous for French diplomacy and security, and now the Paris government seemed caught in a trap. The American and British governments might claim to want co-operation with France, but what they actually meant was that France should fall in with their policies on Germany's future, as a politically and economically strong barrier to Communism. This would exacerbate tensions with Russia and, as Auriol and some in the Quai agreed, could backfire, driving German nationalists into the arms of the Kremlin, who could offer reunification. Yet on the other hand, France had to resolve its relations with the Bizone and, as Bidault told the Cabinet, might have to accept trizonal fusion as the price for obtaining a share in the Ruhr.[20] A full discussion of Western differences in Germany was now arranged for later in the month, in London.

In these circumstances the 'European' solution to the German problem grew in appeal. This was evident in a telegram from St Hardouin on 20 January, who wrote, 'What we offer the Germans is ... a valuable and active role in the reconstruction of a Europe conceived as an organised and harmonious whole'. He believed that such a policy could prove attractive to many Germans, would give them hope for the future and help them to preserve their nascent democracy, and yet that it could also provide the means to limit and control Germany. French policies in Germany should 'not be presented in the form of a sanction', as they had been since 1944, but as 'the aspect of a European experience'. German resources should be tapped to help in European reconstruction, but Germans themselves should have an equal role in the institutions created. St Hardouin had put these views to Koenig, who was sympathetic to them, and on 23 January, the latter was told by Paris that a more liberal and constructive policy should be taken to Germans in the ZOF in future. This policy should show the Germans that they 'can play an honourable role in a Europe ... united and strong'.[21]

* * *

The arguments over Germany during January 1948 did not prevent progress in creating a West European alliance. In early January the French continued to pressure the British to negotiate a treaty with Belgium,[22] but only in mid-January, after informing the Americans, did Ernest Bevin agree to this. Bidault and Chauvel were reminded by Oliver Harvey that Bevin hoped to tie Europe, the Commonwealth and the USA into a democratic system, in answer to the Soviet threat. This system would be bound together by common ideals and would mobilise moral and material force in order to preserve Europe from Communism. Within Europe all Western areas, even Spain, should be associated together. The means of association would vary from state to state and, in the tradition of Britain's 'unwritten' constitution, progress would evolve gradually. However as a first step Bevin wanted to offer an alliance, modelled on the Treaty of Dunkirk, to Belgium, Holland and Luxembourg, and then perhaps to other states. Bidault agreed that a joint Anglo-French *démarche* should be made for such an alliance[23] and on 21 January British and French representatives got a favourable response from the Belgians and the Dutch.[24] The next day, in the House of Commons, Bevin gave a public outline of his vision of 'Western Union',[25] but Massigli warned that the Foreign Secretary would want to preserve links with the British Commonwealth whilst pursuing European co-operation, and would prefer precise agreements to any ambitious hopes of a European federation.[26] Bidault congratulated Bevin on the speech, and the two prepared to discuss a draft treaty with the Benelux states based on the Dunkirk model.[27]

The Benelux ministers decided to meet together, on 29 January, to discuss the Anglo-French proposal for a pact. However, even before they met, it was clear that they did not like the idea of using the Treaty of Dunkirk as a model for the new alliance. Dunkirk was an anti-German pact but the Benelux States, and especially the Dutch, had long shared the Anglo-American desire to revive Germany. Furthermore, it seemed clear that Russia, not Germany, was the menace against which Western Europe must unite. The Benelux states, partly through fear of French domination, also wanted to act *together* in defence of Benelux interests in any new alliance. For all these reasons they therefore came to favour, not the Dunkirk model, but a regional security treaty such as that recently negotiated between members of the pan-American movement, the Rio Pact.[28] The US sympathised with these Benelux arguments.[29] The three foreign ministers also wanted to develop economic co-operation in Western Europe, to be included in talks on the future of Western Germany, and to hold military staff talks with Britain and France.[30]

In Paris there was great reluctance to accept the Benelux views. Bidault was unwilling to antagonise Russia and wanted to keep an alliance on an anti-German basis. He believed that the British supported the Dunkirk model and Oliver Harvey seemed to agree. Harvey said that Bevin had promised Stalin that all West European alliances would be anti-German: anything else could enrage the Soviets.[31] This reassuring analysis was soon overtaken though, as sympathy grew in London for the idea of a 'Rio-style' multilateral pact. The French became very concerned and upset when one of Bevin's junior ministers, Hector McNeil, met Benelux ministers in Brussels. His visit had been arranged some time before but it included discussions of a multilateral alliance and seemed to strengthen British support for this proposal. In mid-February London agreed formally to submit a Dunkirk-style draft treaty to the Benelux states for discussion, but Bevin also suggested a meeting of the five foreign ministers involved in the talks, and Bidault feared that this would turn into an attempt to isolate him on the question of a multilateral, anti-Soviet treaty.[32] By mid-February the situation had become deadlocked. The Benelux states wanted a multilateral treaty, not exclusively directed against Germany,[33] whilst the French argued that such a treaty would enrage Stalin and further divide Europe,[34] at a time when Western Europe had no US security guarantee.[35]

The West Europeans were only saved from their own divisions by Soviet action. For in February, a Communist coup in Prague destroyed the last vestiges of Czech democracy.[36] The French, Americans and British jointly protested at the coup, though this was an empty gesture.[37] In early March came a further blow with the death of Jan Masaryk, probably by suicide, possibly by murder. A stunned President Auriol pointedly sent a letter of condolence to President Benes, but not to Premier Gottwald.[38] For a time the Prague coup struck terror into Europeans and Americans. The analysis by Jacques Dumaine was typical: 'Communism is merely repeating what Nazism did (ten) years previously'.[39] Ambassador Maurice Dejean, and also General Catroux, had a more rational analysis however, explaining that Stalin wished to tighten his control on Eastern Europe whilst avoiding war.[40] Catroux believed that Soviet policy in early 1948 was increasingly motivated by fears of 'encirclement', with France as one of its 'imperialist' opponents.[41] The General favoured a policy of conciliation and patience to break down the walls of suspicion, but wrote on 12 February that Moscow would only really trust France if she became a 'People's Republic'.[42] Meanwhile, in Paris, intelligence reports continued to suggest that the Soviets and PCF would indeed try, by propaganda, strikes and attacks on the government, to turn France into such a 'People's Republic',[43] and on the European plane, all hope of preserving meaningful links to the Soviet satellites via, for example, French treaties with Czechoslovakia and Poland were now lost. The Prague coup made further conversations with the Czechs impossible and, although the Poles agreed to sign a new commercial-financial accord with France, the Warsaw government put an end to their year-old treaty talks with France.[44]

The same events which destroyed links to Eastern Europe gave new life to the West European alliance, however. Couve de Murville remained doubtful about replacing the anti-German Dunkirk treaty,[45] but on 28 February Massigli told the British there was no longer any need to pander to Soviet views; France would accept a multilateral pact.[46] In the light of the Prague coup Bidault was more anxious than ever to win US approval, and American support for a multilateral treaty remained strong.[47] Thus, as Bidault and Bevin exchanged congratulations on the first anniversary of the Treaty of Dunkirk[48] talks began on a much more extensive alliance with the Benelux states. The negotiations were held in the Belgian Foreign Ministry. Chauvel went to London beforehand to ensure a joint Anglo-French approach in the discussions, and this succeeded in controlling the Benelux states somewhat. The French even managed to get anti-German remarks inserted into the treaty. The text, which was negotiated remarkably smoothly, included commitments to general economic, social and cultural co-operation and, in its vital security clauses, was directed against *any* aggressor.[49]

The Brussels Pact was intended by all its members to be much more than a military alliance, and to lead to further European co-operation, but when the French Cabinet approved the pact on 16 March Bidault said, significantly, that it would have no use unless it was backed by American aid.[50] When the treaty was signed the following day, in Brussels, the need for US support was also paramount in everyone's mind. *En route* to the Belgian capital, Bidault travelled with Bevin, who had arrived in Paris a few days earlier. Both men wished to make much of the new Brussels Pact, Bidault eager to establish a regular series of meetings between the pact members, Bevin talking of co-operation in the social and financial fields and joint action against Communist subversion. However both men also wanted a US commitment to European defence and Bevin said that the British would soon be approaching America to discuss an *Atlantic* defence system.[51]

In fact, as early as 4 March Bidault himself had written to George Marshall, referring to the Prague coup and urging US military assistance to Europe. The Secretary of State had written jointly to the French and British Foreign Ministers on the 13th saying that America would consider what action to take after the Brussels Pact was signed, and the next day Bidault had repeated his appeal for assistance. What the Quai d'Orsay wanted at this time was both material aid and the definition of a clear line of defence in Europe over which the Russians could not advance without provoking war. In a letter to Henri Bonnet, Chauvel spoke of the need to avoid the mistakes of the 1930s, when Hitler had picked off his victims in turn while France and others made empty protests. The Quai feared that, as in the Truman Doctrine a year before, the US was willing to antagonise Russia without making effective preparations for war.[52] Since the failure of the London CFM, France, along with Britain and the Benelux States, had proved ready to start building European security co-operation without a US guarantee, but with the implicit understanding that America would back them in some way. Yet now Washington seemed reticent.[53] From Prague, Maurice Dejean had written on 12 March that, whilst Western Europe had concentrated on securing Marshall aid, the Soviets had secured political, economic and military control over half the continent and possessed on overwhelming military force. France, through its geographical position and large Communist majority, was left particularly exposed to Soviet pressure. Dejean wanted to see much more than economic aid and diplomatic talks in the West. To prevent the Red Army marching to the Atlantic a defensive line of 'men and steel', judiciously placed and well-organised was needed. Only behind such a line could Europe feel secure, allowing it to rebuild its material strength, although there *was* a risk, as Dejean realised, of provoking Russia into a 'preventive war' by such preparations.[54]

On 17 March, having signed the Brussels Pact[55] the five foreign ministers of the Pact members met together and agreed that another appeal should be made to Marshall for military assistance.[56] Even this achieved little, however. Although Truman welcomed the Brussels Pact, in a statement to Congress, his promise 'that the US will . . . extend to the free nations the support which the situation requires' was again vague,[57] and in a message to Bidault the following week Marshall was reluctant to set a date for any military talks.[58]

* * *

West European defences in early 1948 were certainly inadequate. After the London CFM, Bevin had agreed that the French army chief General Revers should visit London to begin the staff talks, which had first been discussed by Chauvel and Bevin in October. It was hoped that Revers could establish personal contacts with the British chiefs of staff, discuss the military situation in Europe and lay the basis for future co-operation. Ambassador Massigli was somewhat disappointed with the reticence of the British military about the visit however. Bevin might favour co-operation with Paris but the British chiefs of staff were generally suspicious of the French, partly because of supposed Communist infiltration in Paris, but also because they distrusted Revers, whose right-wing views were well-known. In London the United States was always viewed as a much more impressive military ally than France, for good practical reasons, and the British wished to maintain their 'special relationship' with the US military. The British also feared that their view of the military situation was so pessimistic, that it would frighten Revers even if they did explain it to him. The British planners believed that a Soviet invasion of Europe was actually unlikely, because of Russia's need to recover from the last war. The main vehicle for Soviet expansion in Western Europe was the 'fifth column' of local Communists. If war did occur, however, the British felt Western Europe would be indefensible and planned to concentrate on the defence of the British Isles, the Middle East and sea lanes, not unlike their strategy in the last war. The only military figure in London who *did* show much real interest in Revers's visit was Field-Marshal Montgomery, Chief of the Imperial General Staff. Montgomery was a maverick in London, who did favour an efficient Western military organisation, and hoped that the Europeans could form a defensive line along the Rhine, though he also had some criticisms to make about the state of the French Army when he met Revers on 23 January. Revers returned to Paris, much encouraged by Montgomery's desire for common defences but with no concrete concessions of joint Anglo-French planning. President Auriol sensed the reticence of the British[59] and also remained distrustful of Revers. (In early 1948, indeed, there was talk of replacing the Army Chief, who added to his problems by bickering with the Inspector-General of the Army, Jean de Lattre.[60]

There were some Franco-American military talks in early 1948. It has already been seen that there were contacts between US, French and British military representatives at the UN,[61] and the French representative, General Billotte followed these up with an irregular series of talks, with General Matthew Ridgway, then with General Wedemayer. The visits by 'Mr Ward', as Billotte was known, were kept secret, but were evidently known to Schuman, Marshall Truman, the US chiefs of staff (first Eisenhower, then Omar Bradley) and Bidault. It was Billotte who took the lead in requesting meetings, which were held every two or three months until April 1949. He invariably wanted to involve the US in specific commitments and wished to include France in the Anglo-American 'Combined Chiefs of Staff', which the French believed still handled global strategic planning, but which had actually become practically defunct. Amongst other items he discussed a possible German contribution to Western defence and, on 29 April, delivered a letter for Schuman to Marshall begging for a strategic agreement on the use of forces in a future war.[62]

There were other contacts. On 28 January, for example, in Paris, Bidault and Teitgen met Major-General Harold Bull, Deputy Director of Organisation and Training. The MRP ministers told Bull that the French people had rejected

Communism and that Europe now needed psychological reassurance before it could put up its own defences. A strategy for defence was needed, and Teitgen asked the US to equip forty French divisions to provide this. If, in the event of war, Western forces retreated to the Pyrenees and North Africa it would be impossible to liberate Europe without devastating the continent.[63] Whilst the Americans were willing to listen to such views, however, they were not very forthcoming about what aid they might actually provide. In Washington, as in London, it was felt that an actual Soviet invasion of Western Europe was unlikely. Washington was reluctant to pour millions of dollars into Europe to build up its defences, preferring instead to concentrate on economic recovery through Marshall aid. The Americans were ready to consider some commitment to European defence in due course if the Europeans themselves wanted this, but it took months in 1948 to clarify exactly what form such a US commitment would take.

The British received rather more details about US thinking than did the French. It will be recalled that, on 17 March, Bevin had told Bidault about forthcoming Anglo-American talks on 'Atlantic' security. Bevin had also, on 16 March, forewarned Schuman and Jules Moch of these talks. The Prime Minister did not seem very interested and merely remarked, presumably referring to Billotte's mission, that France had her own representatives in Washington.[64] If Schuman believed that Billotte's talks were as significant as those held on an Anglo-American basis however, he was very much mistaken. Talks between US, British and Canadian officials were held at the Pentagon, from 22 March to 1 April and, although they resulted in no firm decisions, they did include discussions about a possible 'North Atlantic Pact'. The French had been excluded deliberately from the talks by the US, ostensibly because of fears about security leaks. Not only did the existence of Communist supporters in French ministries cause concern, but also it was believed that Moscow had broken French codes. At least one participant felt the exclusion of the French was a mistake, however, since it meant that Paris was left in ignorance about the likely form of a US guarantee. Also, ironically, one of the British officials involved, Donald Maclean, was a Soviet spy.[65]

One point which the Americans did consistently urge was the need for the Europeans themselves to take the initiative in defence preparations. As with the Marshall Plan talks in 1947, this was to avoid the impression of 'dictatorship' and to prove to Congress that Europeans were worthy of support. The US was also reluctant to take on the burden of ensuring Western security for ever more. One leading US official even told the British Ambassador that in due course there should be in Europe 'a third force ... strong enough to say "no" both to the Soviet Union and to the United States',[66] an idea strikingly similar to that favoured by many Frenchmen. On 17 April the five Brussels Pact signatories did develop their co-operation further by establishing a Consultative Council at ministerial level, which would hold regular meetings. A Permanent Commission of Ambassadors was established in London, as was a Military Committee, which was asked to study current needs and resources. These decisions were accompanied by yet another appeal to the US for assistance from Bidault and Bevin. However in Washington the US Under-Secretary, Robert Lovett, told the French and British Ambassadors that

America needed still further reassurances about the Europeans' willingness to defend themselves. Lovett presented them with a series of questions about Brussels Pact defence resources, the possibility of pooling and standardising equipment, and the harmonisation of military organisations.[67] As has been pointed out elsewhere, Western military preparations were facing a 'vicious circle': the Americans were reluctant to render assistance unless the Europeans proved ready to defend themselves; but the Europeans were reluctant to make military preparations without the assurance of US support.[68] When Bidault outlined the new Brussels Pact organisation to the Cabinet on 21 April, Auriol warned that military preparations must not upset Moscow: 'Precipitate nothing; it would be a disaster'.[69] Chauvel's officials, in assessing the military situation at this time, noted two main points: first, that for some years even the US and Brussels powers together could not prevent the Red Army marching to the Pyrenees; and secondly that 'the war potential and secret arms' of the Americans would eventually ensure a Western victory. However the prospect of ultimate victory was unlikely to reassure those who would be victims of an initial Soviet occupation. In the short term it seemed prudent to study the transfer of the government and army to North Africa in the event of war.[70]

In mid-May the Brussels powers told Washington, in reply to Lovett's questions, that they did intend to pool their resources, standardise equipment, and harmonise their military commands, and that they hoped, very ambitiously, 'to fight as far east in Germany as possible.'[71] At this time the French and British resisted Italian pressures for membership of the Brussels Pact because it was felt that they would be a strategic liability, with a large Communist Party and exposure to Yugoslav attack. The French wanted to concentrate on the defence of Germany, and felt that the Mediterranean might be covered by a separate pact with, perhaps, a Scandinavian pact in the north.[72] The urgent question remained how to secure a US commitment to the defence of Germany. Earlier in the year the Quai had studied amendments to the Byrnes Treaty, to turn it into a French-American-British alliance, but the Americans themselves felt the Byrnes Treaty was now redundant.[73]

In sounding out US representatives in April and May Bonnet found that Washington might consider both an alliance with the European powers, and a 'military assistance programme', but it seemed unlikely that a treaty could be made before the presidential election in November, and it was not clear what geographical area it would cover; defences would take years rather than months to build and military aid would only be given if (in addition to Marshall aid) it did not prove too burdensome to the US economy. General Bradley made clear to Bonnet in one conversation that America could not simply accede to the Brussels Pact, because congressional rights under the US Constitution would not allow her to accept an 'automatic' commitment to go to war. Yet France's need for a US commitment grew ever more desperate. Both Couve and Catroux feared that the Soviet Union might soon try to force the West out of the exposed enclave of Berlin, and Chauvel remained convinced that what was needed was the establishment of a 'trip-wire', covering all Western Europe, over which the Red Army could not step without provoking a Third World War.[74]

It is clear that, in the Spring of 1948, France wanted the firmest possible US commitment to European defence, going far beyond a general declaration of support and embracing such elements as military aid, expanded armed forces and a united command. By late April they were ready to accept a US Supreme Commander of Western Forces, they hoped that American assistance would induce the British to commit troops to the Continent and they looked forward to membership of the Anglo-American 'Combined Chiefs of Staff'. Massigli believed that the first step should be a united command, under an American general, in Germany.[75] In May, however, it became clear that the Americans were only prepared in the immediate future to offer a general guarantee of European defence in the form of a regional security pact, although this might be followed by military aid. This, the Americans believed, would give Europeans the psychological reassurance they needed in order to continue with the vital work of economic reconstruction. A resolution was put before the Senate by Arthur Vandenberg to pave the way for such a treaty, and Bonnet told the Quai that any US commitment would have to be based on this resolution. Although Robert Lovett told Bonnet that the US wanted 'practical' security measures in preference to empty guarantees, there was disappointment in Paris at the American procedure. Bonnet believed that neither a treaty, nor military aid, would be forthcoming in less than six months, and meanwhile Washington seemed determined to press on with the revival of Germany, dismissing fears that this could provoke war.[76]

The Vandenberg Resolution was passed on 11 June and a few weeks later the US invited the Brussels powers and Canada to discussions on a regional pact in Washington.[77] In July the Americans also sent General Lyman Lemmitzer to London, to sit as an observer on the Brussels Pact military committee, and President Truman was ready to look at a 'Mutual Defence Assistance Programme' to Europe. These were all dramatic decisions, which laid to rest any lingering chances of an American return to isolationism. Yet a look at the US proposals for future action, revealed many differences with French desires. Where the French wanted a strong alliance, the Americans were (as Bradley had warned) reluctant to make any 'automatic' commitment to go to war. Where the French wished to concentrate on drawing a defence line in Germany, the Americans were already giving thought to a much wider pact, embracing Scandinavia, Italy and Portugal. Where the French urgently wanted military aid, ideally to equip twenty-five French divisions, the Americans wanted to concentrate on rebuilding their own forces first and baulked at the idea of reviving the wartime 'lend-lease' programme.[78] For the moment, the Europeans must build up their own forces and in the event of war could only rely on help from US occupation forces in Europe, and the Strategic Air Command.[79]

* * *

While tentative discussions on a US military guarantee were under way, the Marshall aid programme had been carried into effect. It was partly in order to reap full advantage from American assistance that, in January, the Cabinet had accepted a range of measures (known as the 'Mayer Plan') to tackle inflation and achieve monetary stability in France,[80] including a massive devaluation of the franc. The French upset the British by fixing a different rate of exchange for convertible and non-convertible currencies, in order to maximise the benefits of the devaluation. The British, concerned for the position of sterling, claimed it would create monetary instability across Europe, and for a time there were bitter arguments. However, under pressure from the IMF, France agreed to put a time limit on the dual rate and the British reluctantly accepted this.[81] Alphand was critical of Britain's behaviour, but on 3 February in a review of France's international economic policy, he wrote that Anglo-French co-operation was 'absolutely indispensable for the equilibrium of Europe'. Recognising that France 'cannot, for the present, count on its own resources', Alphand wanted as much as ever to build a 'modern' European economy through customs unions, a policy which he believed was 'inspired by the same spirit as that which animated M. Bevin' in the 'Western Union' concept. Alphand also waxed enthusiastic about American financial assistance over recent years, praising the sacrifices of the US people, and insisting that there was no condition on American aid which could be interpreted as an affront to French dignity.[82] Support for Marshall aid, and for the idea of European economic union, was now strong among the French public too.[83]

In January in order to impress the US Congress with evidence of European co-operation,[84] France and Britain sent a joint mission around CEEC capitals to sound out support for a permanent economic organisation, as had been promised to the Americans in September.[85] The French were ready to see a strong organisation created, to ensure close European co-operation and to please Washington. However the British were much less keen to accept restrictions on their national economic planning and the Anglo-French mission did not find much enthusiasm for a strong organisation in the CEEC states generally.[86] A conference of the sixteen powers was finally held in March and set up a working group to look at a permanent organisation. The Americans hoped that a strong, permanent secretariat would be created to oversee the application of Marshall aid. It should collect information, maintain contacts with Washington and have powers to settle problems which arose.[87] Nevertheless, when the sixteen powers met again a month later, they decided to set up a much weaker Organisation for European Economic Co-operation (OEEC) on lines preferred by Britain, with national representatives in a strong position and the secretariat unable to make policies. The French got one of their officials, Philip Marjolin, appointed as Secretary-General, but their hopes that the US would force Britain to give wide powers to Marjolin proved vain. Another chance to advance towards Alphand's vision of a 'modern' European economy was lost and Anglo-French differences were clear.[88]

Meanwhile on 3 April Congress had finally approved Marshall aid, and a businessman, Paul Hoffmann, was sent to Europe as 'Economic Co-operation Administrator' to represent US interests. Over the first fifteen months, $1,655 million was provided to France, its colonies and the ZOF.[89] A bilateral Franco-American agreement on the supply of aid was finalised on 28 June, on similar lines to agreements with each other OEEC state. There was concern over some of the conditions that the Americans demanded, including certain French budgetary restrictions, access to strategic materials in the French Union, and even 'most favoured nation' treatment for Germany. However the agreement was approved easily by the Assembly, where the ratification debates were poorly-attended.[90]

Jean Monnet told President Auriol in January that SC conditions for aid were nothing to fear, and that what mattered was a united economic effort in France.[91] In March, after a visit to Britain, where he was impressed by the control of inflation and recovery of trade, Monnet had begun to advocate an Anglo-French economic federation as a way to match the two superpowers. He hoped that, if France could achieve political and financial stability, the British would be ready to take up the idea of such a federation, instead of relying on the Commonwealth and the American alliance.[92] The following month, whilst visiting the US, he clarified his ideas further in letters to Bidault and Schuman. Monnet was determined to use Marshall aid, not to make France reliant on the Americans, but to make her independent. He believed that Americans themselves wanted a thriving, independent France as a collaborator in world affairs, not as a puppet. Monnet also argued however that 'the idea that sixteen sovereign countries will co-operate effectively is an illusion. I believe that only the creation of a *Federation* of the West including England [sic], will permit us in a short time to resolve our problems and finally to prevent war'. Unfortunately, Monnet was not clear about exactly how such a federation could be created.[93] Other French officials agreed that US aid must not mean US domination, that France must overcome its current 'inferiority complex' in order to achieve economic stability and that, once US assistance ended, France must rely on her own resources, the French Union and European co-operation to give her strength.[94]

The predominance of national sovereignty in the OEEC was not the only failure for radical economic co-operation in Europe in 1948. The Franco-Italian customs union talks, begun in 1947, also faced difficulties. In early January the Italians were eager to progress with the idea and a study by officials from the Quai and the Ministry of Finance argued that the gains of a customs union would outweigh its costs, especially if the scheme helped to bolster democracy in Italy, where it seemed a popular proposal. There were few signs of popular enthusiasm for the union in France, however, and the officials also said that a customs union embracing France, Italy and the *Benelux* states[95] would make better economic sense.[96] In mid-January, therefore, the French sounded the Benelux states out on the idea of studying a five-power customs union. (The French argued that Britain should be left out of such a study because 'links to the Dominions paralyse her action').[97] That the Italians were upset by this French interest in approaching the Benelux, is apparent from an Italian telegram intercepted later in the month by SDECE,[98] and as it transpired the Benelux states showed no enthusiasm for customs union talks. The Dutch in particular feared French ambitions, wanted to keep close to Britain, and still disagreed with Paris about the economic revival of Germany.[99] It was decided in Paris not to let the Benelux contacts impede progress,[100] the Quai being confident that if the Franco-Italian union proved successful others would eventually join.[101] On 7 February the Cabinet agreed to continue talks with the Italians alone, on the understanding that the union could later be extended to others.[102]

After further talks Bidault travelled to Turin to sign a protocol on a customs union, amidst great publicity, with Count Sforza, the Italian Foreign Minister. The customs union proposal remained popular in Italy and the Turin meeting, on 20 March, was deliberately staged to influence Italy's forthcoming elections in favour of pro-Western parties. It was at Turin too that Bidault announced that France, America and Britain now supported the return of Trieste to Italian control. This came after weeks of Italian pressure for some major Western concession before the elections. On the electoral level the Turin meeting was a success. To the relief of the French the polls on 18 April proved a Christian Democratic triumph. (It had been feared that a Communist victory would harm the Marshall aid programme and encourage trouble from the PCF.) However in itself the customs union protocol of 20 March was unimpressive. It simply set up another Franco-Italian commission to bring a union into effect, in stages.[103] Already there were signs that certain French businessmen, especially agricultural interests were opposed to forming a union with one of their main competitors,[104] and throughout 1948 the opposition of such vested interests grew.[105] The French government remained committed to a union[106] and a customs union treaty was finally agreed on 26 March 1949. However it was quite a modest affair and had, arguably, already been overtaken by OEEC efforts to reduce European trade barriers on an inter-governmental level. French businessmen continued to dislike the union which had still not been put into effect by Spring 1950.[107] (Renewed attempts to develop links on a French-Italian-Benelux basis in 1949–50 also failed[108].) The Franco-Italian customs union had kept the idea of radical economic co-operation alive, and confirmed France's position as *the* leading advocate of economic integration,[109] but it did little to advance Alphand's desire for a 'modern' European economy.

* * *

The first half of 1948 saw vital decisions on the future of Western Germany. On 13 February Bidault had made a major speech to the Assembly, in which he described the breakdown of relations with Russia, spoke in favour of wide-ranging West European co-operation and declared that the solution to the German problem was 'the integration of a pacific Germany in a united Europe . . .'[110] This was the first major public declaration of the policy defined in the Quai at the start of the year and was designed to set the scene for tripartite talks on Germany's political and economic future which were about to begin in London.[111] In preparing for the London talks, Bidault told the Cabinet, on 21 February, that France must obtain security guarantees and the economic integration of Germany into a European whole before agreeing to trizonal fusion. Specifically France must obtain a US security commitment, the maintenance of reparations payments and industrial limits, a decentralised political structure, and an international authority in the Ruhr with control over the management of industry and powers to apportion coal and steel production between internal and international use. The Socialist Jules Moch protested that France seemed by its policy to be dividing Germany into two, but Bidault and Schuman argued there was no alternative to three-power talks. The Foreign Minister pointed out that America and Britain were bound to carry out measures to settle the future of Western Germany anyway. If France wanted to influence the future of this vital area she *must* enter tripartite talks.[112]

The first session of the London conference opened on 23 February, with Massigli leading the French delegation, and it was immediately agreed to allow Benelux representatives into the talks.[113] Before the conference French officials made clear to Washington their desire for a federal government structure, effective control of the Ruhr and the demilitarisation of Germany, and the head of the American delegation, Ambassador Lewis Douglas, seemed ready to reassure Massigli on all these issues.[114] In the second meeting in London Massigli agreed to study trizonal co-operation under the Marshall aid programme only after stating the need for adequate security guarantees, economic limits on Germany and for priority in European reconstruction to be given to Germany's wartime victims.[115] Nonetheless, it is evident that the French faced a difficult conference. Bevin had told the British Cabinet that he was prepared to give France guarantees only so long as she was prepared to build Germany up as a barrier to Communism. General Clay (somewhat ahead of the State Department) wanted to establish a German central government soon[116] and Marshall argued that the 'French preoccupation with Germany as a major threat . . . seems to us outmoded and unrealistic . . .' The Americans and British failed to see that Paris did not so much fear Germany, as a Russo-German combination resulting from Anglo-Saxon policies, which would allow Russia to pose as the champion of reunification. In direct contrast to the French, the Americans believed that, to prevent Western Germany being drawn into the Soviet orbit, the area must be revived politically and economically, as a distinct entity from eastern Germany.

Lewis Douglas was prepared to use American economic strength, through Marshall aid, to drive France into line.[117] This was an important point because the French zone was now moving towards a trade deficit, largely because of the removal of the Saar, with its coal exports, from ZOF trade figures. This meant that the need for Marshall aid to the ZOF was growing and also increased pressures to accept trizonal fusion. So long as the French did not have to accept too large a share in any trizonal deficit, and were able to maintain trade preferences in the ZOF, fusion would help resolve zonal financial problems.[118]

The most important subjects discussed in London were the Ruhr, the political organisation of Germany and security measures. Massigli used every opportunity to underscore the importance of the Ruhr to France, and defended controls on the region as a way to resist Soviet penetration there. He put the case for an International Authority to appoint managers, enforce Allied industrial limits, and distribute resources between German and external uses. The issue of ownership of the Ruhr industries, he argued, should be 'reserved'. None of the other conferees, however, felt that international management of industries was desirable. Britain felt that general international controls on the Ruhr would suffice. Lewis Douglas wanted to establish an international body only after the Allied occupation ended and, to avoid the idea of a 'punitive' measure, argued that an Authority should control heavy industry over a wide area of Western Europe, not simply the Ruhr. The last idea may have seemed compatible with French thinking about German economic integration into a European whole, but actually Paris was not yet ready to 'pool' its resources with the Germans on an equal footing.

A study group on the Ruhr was established,[119] and its work produced mixed results for France. It recommended that the Ruhr's coal and steel resources should be distributed by an International Authority, as France wanted, and that the Authority should be established before a German government came into being. However the Authority would have to rely on the Allied military commanders to enforce its decisions and, so long as the occupation continued, actual administration of the Ruhr industries would be under the present Bizonal control bodies, the so-called 'Essen groups'.[120] Meanwhile, as Bevin made clear to Massigli, France would only gain membership of the Bizonal control bodies if she accepted trizonal fusion.[121] When fusion was discussed by the conference on 2 March, however, Massigli kept to the argument that fusion could only be considered in the general context of agreements on Western Germany's future. For the moment, France was only ready to study the harmonisation of trizonal policies, in such specific areas as trade, communications and monetary reform, short of full fusion, which was to be held 'in reserve' as a final concession to the Anglo-Americans.[122]

During the talks on political organisation Massigli advocated a decentralised structure with most powers residing in the *Länder*. As at the Moscow CFM a year before, France also wanted the central legislature to be made up of *Länder* representatives, and dismissed all idea of popular elections. The Benelux states sympathised with these views, but both the Americans and the British, favoured sufficient centralised power to provide for economic stability in Germany. They were ready to alter *Länder* borders so as to ensure that no *Land* was predominant (in the way Prussia had been), and they would give wide authority to the *Länder* but they wanted a central government with specific powers, and an element of election in forming a legislature. In the near future furthermore they hoped that a democratically-elected Constituent Assembly could meet, to draft a West German constitution. A study group revealed surprisingly wide agreement on the general *form* of a constitution – a two-house parliament, with wide powers to the *Länder*, democratic guarantees, and the approval of the constitution in votes at *Länder* level. Nevertheless, there were wide differences on such details as the election of parliament, the exact division of powers between the centre and the provinces, and whether there should be a head of state. As a result it was agreed to adjourn the conference, to allow the differences to be studied in Berlin, under the auspices of the zonal commanders.[123]

In late 1947, of course, the French General Staff had insisted that if three-power co-operation was pursued in Western Germany it would mark an important step in the abandonment of France's neutralist policy and must be accompanied by adequate security measures. Regarding security issues Lewis Douglas ruled out the idea of a three-power Byrnes Treaty,[124] but suggested the creation of a 'Military Security Board' of Allied representatives to enforce demilitarisation measures within Germany. He also reaffirmed the commitment to keep US troops in Europe until peace was assured, and said that America would work with the Brussels Powers to prevent German aggression. As yet, however, he only spoke on an 'unofficial' basis, which really left the future security situation open.[125]

On 6 March the London talks were adjourned, after the issue of a *communiqué* which revealed that wide-ranging discussions had taken place about west

Germany's future.[126] The French brushed aside Soviet protests about this,[127] but a circular telegram, regarding the London conference sent out by the Quai, noted concern over the creation of a German government, and feared that America's 'hasty and dangerous' policies would backfire upon her: 'The real peril in Germany is the association of Germany and the Soviet Union. That is ... the reason why France wants guarantees ...'.[128] In Cabinet, Bidault, supported by Schuman, recommended approval of the London decisions, insisting that France had gained much in the Ruhr, but neither President Auriol nor Jules Moch were fully convinced that the International Authority could really control German industrialists in future.[129] Notwithstanding such doubts, later in March Koenig met Generals Clay and Robertson in Berlin to put studies under way on the German Constitution, and also on the possible harmonisation of trizonal policies.[130] Instructions to Koenig for these discussions stated, once again, that he should avoid any commitment to accept actual trizonal fusion. France was only willing to accept trizonal agreements on commerce, communications and monetary reform in the short-term in order to ameliorate economic problems. Regarding the German Constitution, Koenig was told that, 'France cannot accept the reconstitution in Germany of a Reichstag, elected by universal suffrage'. A lower chamber of parliament could be elected via the *Länder*, but central powers must be limited and the government should operate through the provincial bureaucracies.[131]

The Berlin discussions only further heightened French worries over the pace at which the US wished to progress towards a strong German government. General Clay still seemed to view talks with France as an unwelcome impediment to Bizonal progress and tried to turn the talks into decisions on principles rather than technicalities. One US official, Edward Litchfield, caused grave concern when he handed François Seydoux a memorandum which advocated the establishment of a 'provisional' German government, and then the calling of a constituent assembly, in September. The French were quite unwilling to set a date for a constituent assembly before knowing the conditions under which it would meet and, at any event, did not foresee its meeting before November.[132] Neither did they see any need to form a 'provisional' German government before the constituent assembly finished its work. It soon transpired that the State Department had no previous knowledge of the Litchfield memorandum: that document actually reflected only Clay's views.[133] However the sense of shock in Paris was none the less for that, and the American commander, supported by the British General Robertson, caused further problems when he insisted to Koenig on 1 April that all discussions were useless unless France immediately accepted the twin principles of the trizonal fusion and the creation of a German government. Koenig was quite exasperated by Clay's tactics. Clay's political adviser, Robert Murphy, still blamed French doubts on an inability to see the Soviet Union as a greater menace than Germany,[134] but Murphy's argument merely reflected the continuing inability of Americans to see the real cause of French concern – the fear of a Soviet-German combination, provoked by the American policy of dividing Germany and creating a strong west German State. As one French official noted, regarding Clay and Robertson, 'The creation of a provisional Government [and] the reunion of a Constituent Assembly ... seem to them the only means to fight against communism'.[135]

Massigli complained about Clay's behaviour to Lewis Douglas in London and repeated that France would only accept a German government in return for 'substantial concessions'.[136] Ideally France had always wanted four-power agreement in Germany, but if a west German entity had to be formed, it must be politically and economically weak.

In the midst of the difficulties in Berlin, on 6 April, Maurice Couve de Murville interrupted a holiday on the Riviera to fly to Germany on General Clay's personal aircraft. Couve had let it be known that he wished to see Clay because of growing tension with the Soviets. Marshall Sokolovsky had just walked out of the Allied Control Council, and Couve was quite pessimistic, fearing war might be possible. He was particularly concerned about the position of Berlin, from which it seemed Stalin might drive the West with ease. In two days of talks Clay, an admirer of Couve's youthful ability (and of his fluent English), treated his guest well. Together they drew up a draft plan for future progress in Germany. It was a compromise proposal in which Clay dropped the idea of a 'provisional' government, and Couve accepted that a constituent assembly could meet no later than 1 September 1948. The assembly, elected on a *Länder* basis, would devise a constitution for approval by the Allies and the people of each *Land*. *Länder* borders would be amended, and when a German government was formed trizonal fusion would also be put into effect.[137] This was an important moment. For although the Berlin discussions between the zonal commanders were unable to settle many of the detailed differences between the three powers on a German Constitution, even Koenig was willing to accept the Couve-Clay memorandum as a 'basis for discussion'. It seemed a fair compromise on general issues and left many details to be settled. Thus two of the keenest supporters of the tough *Gaulliste* approach to Germany – Couve and Koenig – seemed ready to accept a constituent assembly at an early date. In addition, during the talks on trizonal harmonisation, it was agreed to work for currency reform and a common trade policy in Western Germany.[138]

On 14 April Bidault outlined the Couve-Clay memorandum and the results of the Berlin discussions to the Cabinet, which listened in silence to his exposé. Again Auriol and Moch were fearful of the Soviet reaction to such decisions. The Cabinet agreed to proceed with the Couve-Clay plan, but without enthusiasm. They laid down a condition that a '*Vorparlament*' of minister-presidents should meet ahead of the constituent assembly, in order to carry out border changes to the *Länder* and to draw up a document to serve as a basis for the assembly's work.[139] In the Quai d'Orsay Pierre de Leusse, head of the *sous-direction* for central Europe, shared the concern of many ministers that, if universal suffrage was introduced, it would undermine the position of the *Länder* and foster the recreation of strong national, and *nationalist*, political parties. De Leusse also continued to fear that the formation of a Western German government would make the West responsible for Germany's division, lead Russia to form a government in Eastern Germany and even spark off war.[140] In a speech at Poitiers on 18 April, Schuman emphasised the need for political decentralisation in Germany,[141] and instructions to Massigli's delegation for the second round of the London conference, which began on 20 April, stated that the Couve-Clay memorandum was the 'extreme limit' of French concessions. Massigli was to press for a *Vorparlament*, the avoidance of universal suffrage in elections, and the definition of Allied powers in an Occupation Statue.[142] Even these instructions failed to satisfy some ministers. Auriol and Moch were still extremely concerned about the likely Soviet response to Western decisions and the possible formation of a pro-Soviet government in Berlin. Bidault still argued that the Anglo-Americans would take action on a Bizonal basis in any event, but his statements did not reassure Socialist ministers who wrote collectively to Schuman on 22 April to complain about the Foreign Minister's policy.[143]

The second session of the London conference provoked only more concern. On the Ruhr, Alphand believed that France had already retreated far enough, but early in the talks the Americans seemed ready to emasculate the proposed International Authority in the Ruhr (IAR), by removing all references to 'security' from the agreement upon it, changing its name to a 'Commission', and giving it only consultative powers. The Americans also wanted Paul Hoffmann, head of the Economic Co-operation Administration, to have a say in the use of the region's coal and steel. However the French already feared that Hoffmann favoured German economic revival[144] and resisted this American pressure. In the end, in late May, though the IAR basically preserved the form discussed at the first London sessions its powers were further eroded because it had to allocate Ruhr coal and steel 'consistent with the programmes of' the OEEC.[145]

The issue of a German government was, predictably, the most divisive issue in the new talks. It was soon clear, despite Benelux support for France, that more compromises would be necessary to reach agreement. For France the danger of a nationalist German revival, or of sparking a war with Russia, remained intense, yet the Anglo-Americans refused to be deflected from their chosen course, and the US remained unready to offer any security guarantee to Europe.[146] On 5 May Bidault persuaded a reluctant Cabinet to accept an element of universal suffrage in elections to a German assembly. Once again Bidault said that, if there was no compromise, the Anglo-Americans would act anyway and he talked of a new approach to America for a security commitment. However ministers still wanted a *Vorparlament* to meet, wanted a strong element of *Länder* representatives in parliament and, against Bidault's wishes, favoured an appeal to the Soviets to join in the London decisions before they were carried out.[147] After the Cabinet meeting Bidault and Chauvel both told Oliver Harvey about French concern at the Soviet reaction to Western policy and of Socialist doubts in the government.[148] Massigli meanwhile kept up pressures on Lewis Douglas for a US security commitment to Europe.[149]

Douglas at this time believed the London conference could be concluded within a matter of days,[150] but in Paris fears were growing daily more intense. France had compromised on the Ruhr and German government, she would lose control of the ZOF once fusion occurred, and she faced the joint dangers of a revived Germany and a potentially violent Soviet response without any US security guarantees. France was in a weak position vis-à-vis the Anglo-Americans: her aim of a separate Ruhr-Rhineland was long since undermined, her influence in Germany was limited, she needed US financial aid and, if she did refuse trizonal co-operation, the Anglo-Americans (with four-fifths of German heavy industry) would simply proceed without her. Nonetheless officials on 10 May recommended that Bidault should state French doubts plainly to the Anglo-Americans and seek a delay in the recreation of a German government.

It was indicative of the desperation in Paris however that, whereas some advisers were ready to walk out of the London talks, others argued that a policy of Franco-German reconciliation should be adopted, to by-pass the East-West conflict.[151] A memorandum of 7 May argued that, in view of Germany's economic revival, France would well advised to seek the integration of the Ruhr, Lorraine and Dutch-Belgian industry, with the long-term aim of a Franco-German-Benelux customs union. This would have both economic and political benefits, in that it would tie Germany to the West European economy, reducing temptation to join the Soviets. There were clear parallels here with wartime ideas. (Significantly the paper did not see Britain as a likely customs union member, because of her imperial commitments.) Two weeks later there was talk of offering Germany 'a Western federation' as an alternative to reunification and Soviet domination.[152] Officials in the *Sous-Direction* for Central Europe believed that through European unity France could increase its security, control German policy and yet offer Germany equality. The British might be reticent about the idea, but if France put her ideas onto the political agenda they would *have* to be addressed.[153]

The intense reconsideration of French policy in May 1948 was influenced by an exchange of letters between Walter Bedell Smith, the US Ambassador in Moscow, and Vyacheslav Molotov, early in the month. In an attempt to defuse the growing tension with Russia, the Americans tried, by an approach from Smith to Molotov, to show that they did not intend to provoke trouble in Germany. This action could be seen as meeting French worries about US bellicosity. However, Washington acted without consulting its allies, and the Soviets leaked Bedell Smith's letter (and a negative reply by Molotov) in an attempt to sow dissension in the Western ranks.[154] For Bidault the exchange of letters came as an added complication to his troubles and he tried to minimise its importance when reporting it to the Cabinet on 12 May. Bidault said that US policy remained unchanged and, in view of Molotov's negative attitude, that Western policies must proceed. Once again Auriol and Moch were not convinced.[155] In the Quai, the Smith-Molotov exchange served to stimulate thinking in Paris about French tactics in the Cold War, culminating in a note from the Quai to Auriol on 17 May. Though offended by America's unilateral approach to Russia, France needed to co-operate with Washington; superpower tensions seemed likely to continue, leaving France vulnerable to Soviet attack. In this situation France's policy should be to build up her own and Western strength, to pursue bilateral relations with Russia on a 'correct' basis, to associate France and Britain with any American action, and to work in the long term for *détente* with Moscow. Thus France would maximise her own influence, whilst strengthening the West and holding out the promise of peace. The memorandum also underlined an immediate danger in Western policy, however: at the London conference France was making too many concessions, and war with Russia could easily be provoked. In view of this France must ask for a reconsideration of the London decisions.[156]

In London discussions were still under way,[157] when, on 19 May, Massigli warned that France might seek a delay in creating a German government. Lewis

193

Douglas said that such a decision would harm Western German morale and demonstrate weakness in the face of Russia,[158] but on 20 May the French sent two notes to the Anglo-Americans. One stated that the Western powers should develop their security preparations, particularly through US support for the Brussels Pact. The second stated France's support for the gradual political and economic revival of Germany, and expressed a readiness to proceed with such policies as monetary reform, a Western 'trade pool' and revisions to the *Länder* borders, but it also expressed concern at the Soviet reaction to Western policies, questioned whether the Germans themselves wanted a constituent assembly, and suggested that such an assembly should not be created yet.[159] In having the two notes approved, Bidault told ministers that he wanted a US security guarantee to accompany German revival.[160] (He told Caffery that France feared Soviet action against Berlin.[161]) By now the Foreign Minister was very worried about criticisms from his colleagues in the Cabinet, who were not prepared to antagonise Russia without US support. He himself was doubtful about what the two notes might achieve, but he felt it best to be prudent and hoped that French-American-British military co-operation could begin soon in Germany, in case the worst should occur.[162]

The two notes came too late in the day to sway the Anglo-Americans, and served merely to draw accusations of French 'vacillation' and 'weakness'. The Americans had just decided, of course, to provide security guarantees on the lines of the Vandenberg resolution, and were determined to proceed with the London decisions as a whole, if necessary on a Bizonal basis.[163] Bevin, on the other hand, told Massigli that, while Britain did not wish to choose between America and France, it had to consider the importance of US financial support.[164] On 26 May, a formal reply from Marshall in his hand, Bidault informed the Cabinet of the completely negative response to the French notes and saw no alternative to accepting the London decisions: 'If we wish to act alone we will lose everything', he said – a Western German government would be formed anyway and Marshall aid to France could be ended.[165] Even MRP ministers were intensely worried by the situation, however. Teitgen pointed out that the Red Army could reach Bayonne in eight days, and that the Anglo-Americans were risking war at the worst possible time. He and Schuman both wanted a fuller US security commitment, possibly a reinforcement of their troops in Germany. Auriol, thoroughly exasperated by Bidault, vainly suggested that a meeting with Russia should be sought. Bidault himself seemed increasingly isolated. It was decided to put the London decisions before the Assembly for approval.[166]

On 1 June the London conference ended. In addition to the creation of the IAR, France was also pleased with the promise of a Military Security Board to guarantee German demilitarisation, which Douglas formally conceded on 20 May.[167] There were also agreements on certain trizonal measures such as a 'trade pool' and monetary reform. However the most significant decisions related to a German government. Zonal commanders were to call a meeting of minister-presidents by 15 June to examine possible changes to *Länder* borders, as the French had wanted. A constituent assembly would be convened by 1 September with members 'chosen in each of the existing states under such procedure as shall be adopted by the legislative body of each', thus maintaining the separate identity of each *Land* as France wanted.[168] The assembly would draft a democratic, federal constitution, for approval by the military governors and by a referendum in the *Länder*. Allied rights would be defined in an Occupation Statute.[169] The Americans and British warned Massigli that if any part of the agreements was rejected by France the whole would still be carried out in the Bizone. The Anglo-Americans maintained the pressure on France by ratifying the accords quickly themselves and refusing to invite the Soviets to join in the decisions. Massigli made clear however that winning Assembly approval for the package would not be easy.[170]

Massigli himself believed that the alternative to accepting the London accords was too terrible to contemplate. A Western German government would be set up in the Bizone anyway; France would be excluded from the Ruhr and unable to cover the trade deficit of the ZOF; co-operation within the Marshall Plan and Brussels Pact would be undermined; and France would even find herself excluded from any East-West dialogue, since the Kremlin would wish to talk primarily with Washington.[171] Many officials in the Quai agreed with him. Whatever its faults, the London settlement seemed 'the only result possible at the present time' and, perhaps most importantly, it could pave the way for Franco-German co-operation in future:

> To refuse to ratify this accord would be equivalent to France renouncing its role on the continent . . . No Franco-German political co-operation will be possible if American and Soviet propaganda pose simultaneously as the defenders of the German people against the 'maximalism' of a France obsessed.

The 'maximalism' of 1945 should be abandoned, but that did not mean that France would accept US policy; rather, Paris would retain its independent line in a radically altered form, and would make its own unique contribution to the German situation by offering Franco-German reconciliation in a European framework.[172] The *Sous-direction* for Central Europe was now ready to study the idea of extending the international controls in the IAR to Western Europe generally, and on 18 June a meeting was held between Monnet, Alphand and their officials which agreed to study both an economic union in Western Europe and the development of Franco-German trade.[173]

However, the Cabinet remained divided on the London accords, as seen in a special meeting on 2 June. In view of the forthcoming parliamentary debate, Bidault wished to underline that there was no room for compromise on the accords: Bevin supported America's policy of firmness and the London decisions would go forward on a Bizonal basis whatever France did.[174] Washington and London simply did not see the danger of a Soviet riposte to the accords in the way France did. The British Foreign Office had already shown René Massigli an intelligence estimate to prove that Russia was making no preparations for war. Jefferson Caffery told a French official that, if the Red Army did launch an attack 'it would be halted by atomic bombs' (an exaggerated claim, since there were no atomic bombers yet in Europe).[175] Nonetheless, in the Cabinet on 8 and 9 June Socialist ministers yet hoped for amendments to the London accords and Auriol wanted an appeal to be made to the Anglo-Americans to hold talks with Russia. The President did *not* fear an immediate Soviet invasion, but he did fear Soviet pressure on the Western sectors of Berlin, which would face the West with the choice between war or 'a Munich'.[176] French popular and parliamentary opinion had reacted badly to the London decisions which were roundly condemned in a speech by de Gaulle on 9 June.[177] When sounding out parliamentary opinion, Caffery found much ill-feeling against the 'high-handed' Bidault and warned the State Department that the Assembly was likely to demand 'supplementary guarantees' to the London accords, if it passed them at all.[178] The British decided to send a Labour Party delegation to Paris to win over Socialist deputies, but Auriol hoped to turn the tables on the mission, and use it to explain French fears to Britain.[179]

Since his Assembly speech in February, Bidault, incredibly, had made no attempt to prepare popular opinion for the retreat in French policy which the London agreements represented. Despite the clear doubts of Socialists within the Cabinet he had continued with a policy which was bound to disappoint even his own supporters. Vague controls on the Ruhr, the loss of French independence and the recreation of a German government were not the policy which the MRP had stood for since 1945. Bidault was doubtless correct that France had little choice but to accept the London accords. However the actual decision was now in the hands of the Assembly and the omens for its approval were not good. On 9 June the Assembly's Foreign Affairs Commission agreed to recommend the accords to deputies for consideration by only one vote.[180] Also in discussing tactics for the debate, the Cabinet was not even prepared to make the Assembly's decision into a vote of confidence.[181] Whatever occurred in the debate, Jacques Dumaine felt that it would be followed by Bidault's fall from office.[182]

For five days the future of France's relations with the Western allies hung in the balance. Bidault opened the Assembly debate on 11 June, defending the gains he had made in the areas of demilitarisation and control of the Ruhr, and claiming to have restrained Anglo-American plans for the recreation of a German government. He insisted that France must accept the London accords or face isolation, but deputies seemed unimpressed. Roland de Moustier felt Bidault had presented 'the funeral oration to a policy'; on the far left, Billoux and Cot argued that France would do better to co-operate with Russia; and, most disturbing of all, André Philip announced that the Socialists had not decided which way to vote on the accords.[183] On 14 June Chauvel visited London and made a personal appeal to Lewis Douglas and the British for amendments to the London agreements, but he could win no changes,[184] and he returned to Paris where he worked for the passage of the accords behind the scenes. His support for Bidault contrasted with the unease of some officials, like Couve de Murville, who had grave doubts about the Foreign Minister's policy.[185]

Ironically, at the last minute, the government was helped not by its allies abroad, but by its enemies at home. On 15 June violent clashes took place at Clermont-Ferrand between police and Communist-led strikers. This came only two days after violence involving the RPF at Nevers. Then, when debate revived at the Palais Bourbon on 15 and 16 June deputies began to concentrate, not on the simple question of a 'yes' or 'no' vote, but on the more complex issue of amendments and reservations to the London accords. In a speech on 16 June Bidault continued to insist that there was no real alternative to the accords and that by obtaining a permanent presence in the Ruhr, the complete separation of the Saar and a US presence in Europe, France was in a superior position to that of 1919. He also talked of Franco-German reconciliation in a new European environment and said that, since the London conference had left many details unresolved, the government could still try to ameliorate Anglo-American policy. Paul Reynaud, the ex-premier, and Pierre-Olivier Lapie, one of the architects of the Treaty of Dunkirk, then came forward with a resolution embodying certain 'reservations' to the London accords and, in the end, this was passed by the narrow vote of 297 to 289. The reservations were quite predictable: there should be firm controls on the Ruhr; reparations payments, political decentralisation and a long occupation must be guaranteed; four-power co-operation should be sought; and the political and economic organisation of Europe must be developed.[186] The American government treated the reservations as indications of major French concerns rather than as 'conditions' for further progress.[187] The important point was that the London accords could now be fulfilled on a three-power basis.

Chapter 10

The Birth of NATO.
June 1948 – April 1949.

What is grave is that the division of the world is no longer simply a division of interests
... It is fundamentally an ideological division.
– Robert Schuman, speaking to the National Assembly's Foreign Affairs Commission, 9
March 1949 (from the Commission's *procès verbaux*).

Despite the narrow margin by which the Assembly approved them, the London
accords heralded a new agenda for France and the Western alliance. Although
divisions remained in the French government on foreign policy, and although
support for Communism and neutralism remained strong in the country, France
now supported a policy of European co-operation in a wider Atlantic framework,
with controls on a revived Germany as part of this. Within a short time of the
accords' passage however, France faced further differences with its Allies and
the terrifying prospect of war with Russia.

   With the first moves to implement the London decisions, came the long-
feared Soviet attempt to drive the French, Americans and British from Berlin.
On 24 June, a few days after the Western powers introduced a new currency
into west Germany, the Soviets enforced a full blockade on land routes into
the city. Berlin, entirely surrounded by the Russian zone, was an obvious
place to put pressure on the West if, as Molotov told Catroux, the Soviets
wanted to force a new four-power conference on Germany.[1] By April many
diplomats, as well as the intelligence service SDECE, expected growing Soviet
pressure on Berlin.[2] Bidault believed the Western powers must try to stay in
the city, because a retreat under Soviet pressure would ruin Allied prestige
throughout Germany,[3] but his officials feared that, even without threatening
war, the Soviets 'dispose of sufficient means to force us to quit the former
German capital'. It was clear that the Soviets might see the London Accords
as a threat to their security, and in mid-June the French tried to delay currency
reform and maintain personal links with Russia's Marshall Sokolovsky. Bidault
and Schuman believed that, by such moderation, they could at least ensure
that the Russians received the blame for any crisis over Berlin.[4] Any hopes
of avoiding a crisis, however, proved vain. Soon after the blockade began,
the Soviets also refused to take the chair at the four-power *Kommandatura*
(control body) for Berlin, and the East-West breakdown seemed complete.[5]
The Anglo-Americans began to airlift supplies to the city but it was doubtful
how long this could provide a lifeline, and meanwhile Berlin only had supplies to

last a month.[6] The French Air Force was 'unfortunately in no state to participate' in the airlift.[7]

In view of their traditional enmity with Germany, the French could have no desire 'to die for Berlin',[8] and doubts soon arose in Paris about the wisdom of holding the city. Pierre de Leusse told Jefferson Caffery that it had been a mistake to overstress Berlin's importance in the past.[9] Unsurprisingly, one of those most concerned about events was Vincent Auriol, who had long feared provoking Russia into war, and who hoped for a 'third force' to be created by the Brussels powers which could mediate between the superpowers. Auriol told the Cabinet in mid-April that, with America unable to provide real defences in Europe and with Russia in fear of 'encirclement', a war was possible in which France would be overrun. As the representative of French 'permanence' he must do all possible to prevent this and hoped that a four-power Summit could be held to resolve the Cold War.[10] Such talks had not, of course, taken place and now, as the Berlin crisis broke, the President feared a 'new Munich' or war. For Berlin in 1948 seemed as difficult to protect as had Czechoslovakia ten years earlier.[11]

By late June, Bidault seemed to share some of Auriol's pessimism. Although General Clay was taking a bellicose line, the Berlin position seemed untenable. It was partly to restrain the Americans that Bidault requested Franco-Anglo-American talks about Berlin, with a view to approaching the Russians for a settlement.[12] It was soon agreed to hold such talks in London.[13] The fact they were held was seen in Paris as a success for French diplomacy, but the Anglo-Americans continued to dominate the important decisions. On 6 July identical notes were sent to Moscow by the Western powers, but the notes stated a willingness to hold discussions on Berlin only *after* the blockade was lifted.[14] The British seemed determined to carry out the London accords regardless of Soviet pressure and some in Paris wondered whether the US had decided to launch atomic war against Moscow.[15] Neither did the Russians seem ready to back down. On 14 July, after a worrying delay, they replied to the recent Western notes by insisting on Western responsibility for the division of Germany.[16] Bidault remained pessimistic about the situation. It seemed impossible to supply Berlin in the long term by air; an appeal to the UN to bring about talks was unlikely to succeed; and any hope of forcing the Soviets to lift the blockade lay entirely in US hands.[17] As seen in a mid-July conversation between Massigli and Lewis Douglas, the West appeared to face an insoluble dilemma. Douglas asserted that Berlin *must* be held and that this realistically meant that a land route to the city must be opened but, as Massigli said, any attempt to break open a land route could provoke Armageddon.[18] Notwithstanding such analyses, President Truman decided to stay in Berlin, to make more approaches to Russia and rely on the airlift to keep Berlin alive.[19]

* * *

It was at this critical moment that, on 19 July, after a series of disagreements, the Schuman government fell from office after Socialist criticism of the military budget. At first it seemed that the crisis would be quickly overcome. Auriol nominated André Marie, a Radical, as premier on 21 July, but Marie's government soon became divided and itself fell on 27 August. Only on

11 September, after two weeks of uncertainty, was a more secure premier invested. Henri Queuille, another Radical, was modest and colourless but he nonetheless proved adept at holding his ministry together and survived as premier for more than a year.[20] He faced a country which had become cynical over the divisions in government. The long government crisis had done nothing for France's reputation in America[21] or Britain.[22] René Massigli feared that it undermined the value to Britain of French co-operation[23] and Bonnet feared it could make America reluctant to provide more Marshall aid to France.[24]

The major ministerial casualty of the crisis was Georges Bidault. In March he had still seemed a popular Foreign Minister,[25] but the London accords had made him a liability. 'Bidault's departure seemed sad to me because it took place without fuss', wrote Jacques Dumaine.[26] Chauvel, who had always worked with Bidault amicably, felt that the strain of work on the sensitive Foreign Minister had contributed as much as the London accords to his decline.[27] Jean Monnet later commented: 'I liked and admired Bidault's goodwill, intelligence and courage: he performed great services in these post-war years. It was not his fault that France was weaker than her international partners.'[28] Actually, only a few months later, after a long rest, Bidault had 'recovered his sleep, his appetite and his ironic charm' and was working for a return to high office.[29]

The new Foreign Minister was another Christian Democrat, the former premier, Robert Schuman. A thin, stooping figure, with a distinctive hooked nose, Schuman was modest, deferential, austere, a deeply religious man but also a political realist, independently-minded yet with a strong sense of service to the state. At college it was said, Schuman had been asked by a friend if he could copy one of his exercises. Schuman replied 'I shall let you do it, but I would remind you that you are committing a sin'.[30] A Catholic, born in 1886 of Lorraine parents in Luxembourg, when Lorraine was part of the German Empire, Schuman had begun his political life in Wilhelmine Germany. After 1919 he had worked for the reintegration of Alsace-Lorraine into France.[31] Auriol felt him a better minister in Cabinet than Bidault: shorter, sharper and less improvised. Chauvel found that his new minister took to foreign affairs easily.[32] Schuman's character was not such as to impress the British – 'too much of the mystic for my liking', wrote one of Bevin's junior ministers[33] – but he worked well enough with them and the Americans.[34] He was eventually much-praised for his policies of European unity and rapprochement with Germany, though his commitment to these ideas at the outset should not be exaggerated. He had often defended Bidault's position in the Cabinet discussions of early 1948, and his Poitiers speech of 18 April[35] reflected a fear of concessions to Germany. Neither should it be forgotten that the Quai d'Orsay had already, under Bidault, developed many elements of a policy for Franco-German reconciliation.

* * *

The end of the government crisis in September did not see the end of internal problems in France. Prices continued to rise, RPF support did not begin to decline until 1949, and October 1948 saw a new wave of strikes, which seemed blatantly political in intention. The strikes occurred simultaneously with a meeting of the UN General Assembly in Paris. Hundreds of foreign dignitaries and pressmen were thus on hand to witness France's humiliating divisions.[36] The strikes caused special concern in America where there were fears about the effect of French instability on the Marshall plan.[37]

Intense pressure was in fact put on the Paris government to tackle its economic and financial problems by the Americans in 1948. Washington found a new means to influence French policy at this time, in the so-called 'counterpart funds'. These were the amounts of local currency raised in Europe when goods and material provided under Marshall aid were sold. Fear that counterpart funds would add to inflation, if released into the economy, led the US to insist on their being frozen in an account at the Bank of France. Although the French economy seemed to be improving in early 1948, inflation remained a major problem.[38] In April, however, the US did agree to release a large proportion of counterpart funds, built up under the interim aid programme, for certain defined purposes,[39] and Monnet, supported by leading Americans in Europe, including David Bruce, the US Marshall Plan representative in Paris, argued that counterpart funds raised under Marshall aid should be used in financing France's reconstruction and modernisation plan. In 1947, of course, the US had said the Marshall Plan was *not* designed to finance grandiose national recovery plans. However in 1948, after long negotiations the US government agreed to Monnet's wish. Thereby it can be argued that America saved the Monnet Plan. Since the January 1948 economic package (the 'Mayer Plan') with its determined attack on inflation, the Monnet Plan had seemed in danger because spending on it added to inflationary pressures. However American aid amounted to half of public investment in the Monnet Plan in 1949 and so made it much easier to finance. American support for the Monnet Plan in this way was a unique practice under Marshall aid: all the other OEEC states together barely matched the amount of counterpart funds utilised in France.[40]

The US had many good reasons for providing such aid. First it helped European recovery as a whole. Secondly, in summer 1948, with a good harvest and better coal supplies in Europe, US planners began to put the emphasis on expanded production in the OEEC states, rather than emergency measures for day-to-day survival, and saw the Monnet Plan as ensuring that US money was well spent. Finally US assistance helped to strengthen Queuille's new centrist government. However the American government did not provide such help for no reward. It is significant that Queuille saw David Bruce on 11 September – the day of the new premier's investment – and that counterpart funds under Marshall aid were released a fortnight later, only after the government promised various measures on credit, taxation and spending controls. Even then amounts were only released for certain purposes and reviews took place before further amounts were given.[41] On 20 October Schuman warned the Cabinet that Americans wanted a better economic performance from France in 1949–50.[42] US officials maintained their pressure for financial measures from Queuille during November,[43] and early in December, once the latest strike wave had passed, Bruce went to see the Premier again to underline the fact that future aid would require sound French financial policies. In particular, he said, the release of counterpart funds relied on the maintenance of credit controls, reform of the tax system and non-inflationary spending.[44]

French ministers became quite resentful about all this US pressure in early December, and the Quai feared that action to impress the US would not be taken. Chauvel and Alphand saw financial strength as being important not only to impress the US, but also to maintain France's standing in the OEEC and to win the respect of west Germans. Even Schuman was felt not to see the urgency of the problem, and Chauvel appealed over the Foreign Minister's head, to Auriol, to take action. There was a separate problem however of *what* action to take. Monnet feared that officials at the Ministry of Finance might yet seek a balanced budget by cutting back on his recovery plan, and that politicians too would find it easier to cut spending on the Monnet Plan than to increase unpopular taxes. He considered he might even have to resign as head of the Plan. But it soon transpired that a compromise was possible. The government agreed to a range of taxation and spending measures, and the Monnet Plan did not face the swingeing cuts that had been feared.[45]

The events of December 1948 could be seen simply as more evidence of America's shaping French policy through economic levers. Even within the supposedly 'long-term' Marshall Plan, the US could regularly use Congressional reviews and the release of counterpart funds as pressure-points to ensure good French behaviour.[46] The US was able to use Marshall aid to force certain national economic policies on France, as well as to oppose Communism, and (despite French doubts) to obtain the revival of Germany.[47] As with lend-lease or the 1946 Blum loan however, the advantages and pressures were not all one-way. The French could use fears of Communism and economic collapse to manipulate Washington, and US and French interests often combined. Anti-inflation measures, for example, were arguably in the country's own best interest. In the last analysis, without US aid, the financial *attaché* in Washington considered, the French economy would be 'completely asphyxiated'.[48]

Whilst the French struggled through their political and economic problems, the Berlin blockade remained a constant threat to the peace. One by one, attempts to resolve the differences with Russia failed, and SDECE feared that the forthcoming US election and the exposed position of Berlin might yet lead to Western concessions in Germany.[49] Bilateral Franco-Soviet relations meanwhile remained very poor. On 8 April General Catroux had made his last visit to Molotov, before ending his ambassadorship. Catroux did not ask to see Stalin, nor did he send the customary final telegram to Paris, summarising his mission. Measured against his original instructions from de Gaulle to build up the Franco-Soviet alliance, he could only consider his mission a failure.[50] His successor, Yves Chataigneau, a generous and mild-mannered individual, formerly Governor-General of Algeria, made his first visit to Molotov in mid-July. The Frenchman raised the old, distressing problem of soldiers from Alsace-Lorraine who were still unaccounted for in Russia. In reply Molotov simply complained about France's attitude to Soviet repatriation efforts, especially the Camp de Beauregard episode.[51] Soviet policy towards France lost all its subtlety in 1948. At a reception in late June even the wily Bogomolov bluntly reminded a French official that Russia was a powerful state whose 'frontiers are not very far distant from yours',[52] and there was Soviet support in Autumn 1948 for the strikes in France.[53] (President Auriol took the opportunity to complain about such activity in a personal meeting in November with Andrei Vyshinsky, who was attending the UN Assembly.[54]) Chataigneau soon concluded, like many US and British analysts that the Soviets, whilst avoiding war, wished to expand across Europe and towards the Middle East, hence their blockade of Berlin.[55]

On 28 July the first Cabinet of the Marie government approved an American proposal for an approach by the three Western powers for an audience with Stalin himself on Berlin.[56] Chataigneau co-ordinated the approach with the US and British Ambassadors in Moscow[57] and they succeeded in meeting the Soviet dictator on 2 August. Stalin was ready to lift the blockade if the London accords were suspended and a Soviet *deutschmark* was introduced as the currency of all Berlin. The Quai was ready to follow up these ideas, although Chauvel wanted to ensure that the new Soviet currency was under four-power control, that it was introduced simultaneously with the end of the blockade (to avoid any Soviet trickery) and that a four-power discussion on Germany's future was held by the CFM in Paris.[58] Several difficult meetings followed in Moscow with Molotov, but in late August a compromise was reached on the lines mapped out earlier: the blockade would end, a Soviet *mark* would be introduced into Berlin under four-power control, and a meeting on Germany would follow. The four commanders in Berlin were asked to settle the technicalities of the first two issues.[59] The Quai remained concerned in August about the supply situation in Berlin, and were ready to suspend the London accords, if necessary, to resolve the crisis.[60]

In September events turned for the worse. In the Berlin talks it proved impossible to settle the technical details of the compromise sketched out in Moscow. The Soviets, antagonised by the continuing moves towards a Western German government, evidently decided to test Western resolve over the oncoming winter. Under French and British pressure the Americans agreed to another appeal to Moscow, but two meetings with Molotov in mid-September failed to get anywhere. On the 15th, Schuman reported the situation to the new Queuille Cabinet and the Premier asked, plainly, if Berlin could be abandoned. Schuman replied that Berlin was now seen by all the West, and especially west Germans, as a symbol of resistance against Soviet Communism.[61] He assured the Cabinet on 1 October, however, that he would seek all possible compromises with Russia, and hoped that the UN session in Paris could be used to put pressure on Moscow to negotiate.[62] The UN, however, was a poor weapon to use, thanks to the Russian veto: as one US official admitted, the only real weapon the West could use against the Soviets was the threat of war.[63] The Russians refused even to take part in debates on the Berlin problem after it was accepted onto the Security Council agenda. To Schuman's dismay Bevin and Marshall also continued to take a hard line, still refusing to talk to the Soviets before the blockade was lifted and now confident that the airlift would save the beleaguered city.[64] The best Schuman could get from the Anglo-Americans was a willingness to approve efforts by Juan Bramuglia, Acting President of the Security Council, and a group of neutral nations to find a compromise settlement on Berlin.[65]

Those efforts at compromise continued into the New Year and the British at least became more sympathetic to them.[66] The Americans, however, remained uncompromising. The US criticised the neutrals' peace attempts, condemned French vacillation, and pressed ahead with such moves as municipal elections in Berlin in December, which proved a major defeat for the German Communists.[67] In the end American toughness was rewarded. The airlift *did* succeed in keeping Western Berlin alive, west Germans were encouraged by the resolute defence of their former capital, and in January 1949 Stalin showed the first signs of a readiness to compromise in an interview with the US journalist, Kingsbury Smith.[68] Although the French, Americans and British remained united during these months in their determination to hold Berlin and their opposition to Soviet bullying, the differences between Paris and Washington were significant once again for showing their different perspectives on Cold War tensions. The Americans, confident of their own power, were determined never to back down. The French, exposed to Soviet invasion, not at all eager to make Berliners into heroes,[69] and powerless to control events, were always more ready to seek an opening for peace. Schuman was sometimes at a loss to know what the US hoped to achieve by their negative attitude, whilst certain Americans viewed French behaviour as tantamount to treachery.[70]

*   *   *

Franco-American differences were compounded by events in Western Germany. In June 1948 the main French concern was to see the Minister-Presidents of the various *Länder* carry out the London accords to the letter.[71] By the end of the month, however, it was clear that German doubts about Western policy cut much deeper than expected. In contrast to the long-standing beliefs of Generals Clay and Robertson, the Minister-Presidents did not want to draw up a West German constitution at all. They feared that by doing so they would be made responsible for dividing their country in two. This, in a sense, fulfilled many of the French warnings from earlier in the year, and Koenig recommended to Paris that, if the Minister-Presidents adhered to their position, France should accept their views. It would then be possible to form a weak *Länderrat*, draw up an Allied Occupation Statute, and proceed in Germany on a decentralised basis, more akin to France's original wishes.[72] The three Western governors formally explained the London accords to the Minister-Presidents on 1 July and, in a meeting at Coblenz several days later, the latter confirmed their opposition to the Allied decisions. General Clay was bitterly upset, and ready to bludgeon the Germans into line. Importantly, however, the Minister-Presidents did *not* rule out all idea of political change. Instead of a Constituent Assembly drafting a new Constitution, they were ready for a 'parliamentary council', elected by the various *Landtäge*, to draw up a 'basic law', which would serve as a 'provisional' basis for government until Germany could be reunited.[73] Thus the image of a 'divided' Germany would be played down. Although the Coblenz programme emphasised the power of the *Länder* in ways France wanted, Tarbé de St Hardouin warned Paris that the German proposals were not all to be welcomed. The independent behaviour of the Minister-Presidents and their desire for reunification with the East were worrying for France, as was a reluctance they had expressed to alter *Länder* borders.[74]

General Koenig's hope of reasserting a French solution to Germany's Constitution proved largely vain. Bidault instructed the French commander to accept the Coblenz proposals on changes in nomenclature (the 'parliamentary council' and 'basic law'), whilst insisting that other parts of the London accords, such as the redrawing of *Länder* borders, be carried out.[75] Despite Clay's continuing doubts, the Allies then agreed on changes to the vocabulary of the London accords which the Minister-Presidents accepted.[76] To Koenig's satisfaction, after much debate, approval of the 'basic law' was left in the hands of the *Länder* rather than made subject to a popular referendum.[77] Less pleasing was that when the 'Parliamentary Council' met in Bonn on 1 September, representatives from Berlin were allowed to attend as 'observers'.[78] Meanwhile, on 16 August, Koenig, Clay and Robertson had also made other important decisions for the future. They set up working groups to study an Occupation Statute and the future of Allied controls, agreed to start work on a Military Security Board, and decided to introduce freedom of movement between the Western zones.[79]

* * *

In the face of new developments in Germany the Quai d'Orsay's policy of Franco-German reconciliation and European co-operation gathered pace, and won the full support of Schuman.[80] A Quai memorandum of 14 July argued that French opinion must be educated about the need both for German revival and for Franco-German *rapprochement*. France would 'offer to a future German government a third solution between American economic expansionism and Soviet political expansionism'. That solution would be 'a Franco-German economic and political association' within the general context of Western co-operation which would also build up resistance to Communism. To develop such a policy France would take a less exploitative attitude towards its zone and establish personal links with German politicians. In fact such a policy, fostered by Jacques Camille Paris, head of the *Direction d'Europe*, had already begun. In June, for example, a round table discussion had been held between French and German mayors.[81] (Franco-German meetings at a popular level could be traced back well before this.) By September, to the Quai's satisfaction, the German press was showing an interest in the French policy of reconciliation, and in early October Schuman himself visited the ZOF and met various German representatives.[82] There were, however, dangers in this course. Later in October, after discussing the problem with François Seydoux (but not, significantly, Koenig), St Hardouin wrote a sombre letter to Schuman supporting the policy of Franco-German reconciliation but warning that the Anglo-Americans still did not appreciate French security needs, that West Germany was potentially a very powerful state, and that the attraction of many Germans to their old capital, Berlin, remained strong.[83]

By late October in fact there was a series of problems facing France in Germany. In the talks at the Parliamentary Council in Bonn, for example, under the chairmanship of Konrad Adenauer, the Germans had quickly begun to act independently. They let the 'observers' from Berlin play a deliberative role in discussions; members behaved as representatives not of the *Länder*, but of political parties; and they began to discuss issues far beyond the Basic Law.[84] A furious Koenig eventually managed to persuade Clay and Robertson to send a letter to Adenauer, asking that debates be confined to the Basic Law,[85] but even in these debates the French became extremely concerned because of the German tendency to grant wide financial, legal and police powers to a future central government.[86] Meanwhile, in early October, after a series of studies on possible *Länder* boundary changes, the Minister-Presidents proposed only to hold a referendum to see if Baden and Württemberg should be united.[87]

On an inter-Allied level the French were upset by a number of developments. One concerned the US desire to cut back further on reparations removals, to answer congressional criticisms over financial costs in Germany. France had never got much in the way of reparations from Germany anyway, thanks to practical difficulties in designating and dismantling industrial plants, and also because of increases in Bizonal industrial levels.[88] Even so, by August 1948 the German people themselves were very resentful about the removal of reparations, and protest strikes were called in the ZOF on the issue.[89] On 25 August the Quai had to state publicly its commitment to continue with reparations.[90] It was then that the Americans, ostensibly for the good of the Marshall aid programme, asked the French and British to suspend reparations altogether until the situation was studied by a US committee under George Humphrey.[91] Both Schuman and Bevin were upset by this, fearing that reparations would be difficult to recommence once they were stopped, but they eventually agreed to slow the pace of dismantlement.[92] The US insisted that changes were needed if Congress was to grant Marshall aid in future.[93] The French still saw their policy on German industry as consistent with that of 1945, aiming to destroy German war potential, control key industries and secure a peaceful German contribution to European recovery.[94] Alphand told the Humphrey Committee, once it visited Europe, that it was vital to know what industrial limits would be placed on Germany *before* a government was established there, and that controls on the Ruhr were needed *before* a process of German integration into Europe could safely begin. Thinking of Congress's financial concerns, he also insisted that Germany would be self-supporting by 1952 under existing limits and that European steel capacity as a whole was good.[95] The British shared French worries about cuts in reparations[96] and even General Clay felt that Congress was stirring up trouble for no good reason, since Germany was still unable to fulfil current industrial limits.[97] Eventually, in March 1949, the French and British did agree to cut the number of factories for dismantlement as reparations, but only as part of a wider package which defined industrial prohibitions and limitations in Germany.[98]

A second problem in three-power relations was trizonal fusion. In his meeting with Clay and Robertson on 16 August, Koenig pointed out that France accepted monetary reform and freedom of movement in the three zones, and that France was ready to join an external trade pool, and in return he asked for a place on the Bizonal 'Essen group' which controlled the Ruhr coal mines. A share in controlling the mines was, of course, an important prize for Paris in trizonal co-operation and in September Koenig repeated his appeal. In October, however, Clay and Robertson said that France could not join the Essen groups until full trizonal administrative fusion took place.[99] Koenig was predictably distraught, and made his feelings known to Paris. After the London CFM broke down in December 1947, he pointed out, France had decided to use the possession of the ZOF as a precious bargaining counter with which to win valuable concessions. Yet in the London accords it was France who made most concessions and, by implication, accepted trizonal fusion. The ZOF, small and sinking into debt, had proved of little value as a lever for concessions. In effect the creation of a trizonal trade pool, the details of which were settled late in the year,[100] meant that trizonal *economic* fusion had occurred, though full *administrative* fusion would not come until a West German government was established. Koenig, who had little interest in notions of Franco-German *rapprochement* also warned that there might be a revived menace across the Rhine as early as Spring 1949.[101]

An even worse area of difficulty, however, was the Ruhr. After the London accords Paris pressed for detailed talks on an International Authority (IAR), [102] but only on 6 October did Schuman, Marshall and Bevin agree to hold talks on the IAR in London, beginning on 11 November. Just before the London conference opened, however, Clay and Robertson made yet another of their important periodic decisions on German revival. On this occasion, in the preamble to Bizonal Law 75, published on 10 November, the two commanders announced that an elected German government should eventually decide the issue of ownership of the Ruhr coal and steel industries. In defending this action the Anglo-Americans argued, as usual, that it was necessary to reassure Germans about their future. The French had known since August in fact that the ownership issue was under consideration but Law 75 created grave problems for Schuman. The French government had never formally renounced its belief that there should be Allied ownership of the Ruhr industries. One of the main Assembly reservations on the London accords, furthermore, had been that these industries should be closely controlled. Neither could the French see any need to make an announcement about ownership just yet, since it was intended to leave the Ruhr mines in the hands of trustees in the short term.[103] When the conference to establish the IAR began, Alphand complained about the Clay-Robertson decisions[104] and on 19 November Schuman, whilst acknowledging that France was forewarned of Law 75, made a formal complaint to the US and British Foreign Ministers.[105] On 2 December, after two days of debate in which Socialist discontent with Western policy was quite apparent, the Assembly added its voice to the clamour, and demanded the 'Europeanisation' of Ruhr coal and steel as the 'only way to conciliate the needs of European security and the need to allow the German economy to find . . . its equilibrium'.[106]

Ironically, General Clay saw the French protests as an unnecessary fuss designed to win public sympathy for them in the IAR talks.[107] In fact, at every important step in three-power co-operation Clay and Robertson had pre-empted international discussions with unilateral steps. The Marshall Plan was just beginning in July 1947 when they proposed an increased level of industry. The Frankfurt decisions of January 1948 had come just weeks before the London three-power conference. Now a similar crisis had been created with a provocative announcement only one day before the IAR conference.

Coming after recent developments in Germany, Law 75 created a crisis for French policy in Germany. In the *Sous-direction* for Central Europe there was concern at the centralising tendencies of the Parliamentary Council, the reparations cuts, and France's exclusion from trizonal bodies, all of which pointed towards Germany's reconstruction without sufficient controls.

Meanwhile the IAR and Military Security Board, the bodies conceded to France at the London conference, had yet to be established, the policy of European integration, by which France hoped to control Germany, had barely begun, and all the time the west Berliners were becoming heroes in American and British eyes.[108] Already, at the end of October, Schuman had asked Koenig to raise all these problems with Clay and Robertson.[109] The French Governor, however, went beyond his instructions in a meeting of zonal commanders on 4 November, when he also raised the Ruhr problem and told the US and British commanders that he would withhold approval for the West German constitution if their policies did not change. Clay and Robertson took this as a major challenge and Koenig's threat was somehow leaked to the press. Some in the Quai seem to have been pleased with the publicity, but others were dismayed by Koenig's negative behaviour.[110] Jacques Camille Paris, believing that Koenig's attempts to sabotage the London accords would also ruin the hopes of a Franco-German *rapprochement,* wanted to force a showdown with the General at the first opportunity.[111] Schuman too was determined to preserve the policy of *rapprochement* and told Jefferson Caffery that the real problem with Law 75 was not its content, but its *timing,* which seemed to suggest an attempt to cheat France over the IAR conference. Ideally France needed to slow down German revival until the policy of European unity was developed far enough to control Germany, and France itself grew stronger. In conversations with Anglo-American representatives, President Auriol said international control of the Ruhr should continue for twenty or thirty years to allow a policy of European integration.[112]

On the US side in November there was a recognition that the fracas over Law 75 was 'symptomatic of a larger concern' in France, and Lewis Douglas for one felt the Ruhr ownership issue should have been more fully discussed.[113] General Clay and his political adviser, Robert Murphy, remained opposed to the French policy, as they saw it, of inserting ornate guarantees and safeguards into every decision concerning Germany. However even they recognised that certain French worries were genuine and that some security controls on Germany were needed. Marshall himself decided that France ought to be pacified with a major concession: she should be allowed onto the 'Essen groups' before full trizonal fusion took place.[114] On 17 November furthermore, Clay and Robertson agreed that a meeting should be held with Adenauer to remind him of Allied desiderata in the Basic Law, especially the principle of decentralised power.[115] Ideally Schuman would have liked a conference with Marshall and Bevin about Germany at this time, but the Americans and British opposed this claiming (ironically) that it would antagonise Russia,[116] and in fact the IAR talks proved favourable to France. Marshall formally announced on 19 November that France could join the Essen groups and by Christmas the IAR had been defined. The main French concerns in the talks were to ensure supplies of coke to themselves and to give the IAR sufficient powers to prevent industrial cartels, the return of Nazi owners or the use of Ruhr resources for aggressive purposes. These concerns were largely met. It was also confirmed that the ownership of Ruhr industries could eventually be settled in a peace treaty, and that the IAR might inherit Bizonal controls on coal and steel if the occupation ended. Importantly, Alphand resisted a renewed US attempt to extend the IAR's powers over Western Europe in general. Again, despite the apparent compatibility of such a scheme with the French policy of European integration, the French wanted to secure special controls on Germany first, to allow integration time to succeed later. There were still limits to the IAR from the French viewpoint. It relied on the Allied governors to enforce its decisions and had to take account both of OEEC plans and 'the essential needs of Germany'. German leaders too disliked the Ruhr statute, a development which showed that a Franco-German *rapprochement* would not be easy if France insisted on tight controls over Germany as a precondition.[117]

In the aftermath of Law 75 the Quai's desire for Franco-German reconciliation and German revival within a European framework had, if anything, been strengthened. A memorandum of 30 November even said that, 'We have to abandon a part of our sovereignty to a democratic European organisation which would render a new Franco-German conflict economically and politically impossible'. Links between French and German politicians were again advocated, as were mixed Franco-German companies and a Franco-German-Benelux customs union – which would be more formidable than a Franco-Italian union, and which Britain would – it was presumed – not wish to join. Regarding current measures to control Germany the paper suggested that future modifications in Allied powers should be allowed, that France should not insist on ornate veto powers in trizonal agreements, that the IAR powers *could* eventually be extended to other areas of Western Europe, and that Germany should share Allied military costs not as an occupation force, but as a *defence* force.[118] Other memoranda too showed an appreciation that Germany's revival was now unstoppable, that a French policy of protest merely served to alienate the Americans, British and Germans, and that France must try to strengthen herself and build a 'community of interests' with Germany. One possibility was the creation of 'a European steel pool, in which Germans and French would share equally and exercise common control . . .'.[119]

Hopes of a Franco-German *rapprochement* continued nevertheless to be dogged by old fears and suspicions. At the end of 1948 the French were pleased that talks, held in Berlin since September, resulted in the establishment of a Military Security Board, with powers to ensure military, industrial and scientific demilitarisation,[120] but there were worries at the same time over Soviet attempts to found a military force in eastern Germany, and suggestions in the US press about a West German defence force.[121] French fears also continued over centralisation in the Basic Law in early 1949. Certain officials, such as de Leusse's deputy, Pierre Maillart, still argued in mid-February that French and European security was being endangered by Anglo-Saxon support for German revival.[122] The French found succour from an unexpected source in mid-February however when St Hardouin reported that Clay had 'revealed himself as an ardent advocate of federalism' at a meeting with Koenig and Robertson. In fact both Clay and Koenig (but not Robertson) criticised the Parliamentary Council for ignoring the guidelines laid down by the Allies in November. In early March, the three commanders recommended a number of modifications to the Basic Law, including, amongst other points, clarification of central government powers, stronger *Länder* finances and the political separation of Berlin from West Germany.[123]

A more complex problem was that surrounding the drafting of an Occupation Statute, which defined Allied rights in ensuring a democratic Germany, in controlling certain reserved areas of government (such as foreign policy) and in securing the practical needs of the occupation forces. Talks had been under way on such a document since September between the commanders in Germany. The Quai recognised that a Statute should ideally be as simple as possible, defining general Allied rights and not appearing too restrictive to Germans.[124] However all three Allied drafts, including the French text devised in Baden-Baden, were quite detailed and predictable differences soon arose as the French resisted Anglo-American pressure to give wide powers to the Germans.[125] By December there were two major differences. First, the Anglo-Americans wished occupation costs to be paid by the federal German government, whereas the French wanted costs to fall on the *Länder*. Secondly the French objected to having German members on an arbitration court to settle German-Allied disputes.[126] To General Clay's annoyance, the Statute was then referred to an ambassadors' conference in London, which opened in January.[127] However the London talks too failed to make progress on the Statute, the draft of which became a long and complex document, full of intricate reservations and controls. In February Clay was quite frustrated on the issue and eager to use financial levers to force Paris into line, whilst Bevin too complained about French 'obstructionism'.[128] Aware of these strong feelings, Massigli told Chauvel that France must decide once and for all whether she wanted to pursue the policy of Poincaré or Briand, to enforce draconian controls on Germany, (as Koenig seemed to want) or to co-operate with it (as Camille Paris favoured). Massigli supported the latter course, believing that a detailed Occupation Statute would be greeted with derision by the Germans and suggested that a simpler document, a general statement of Allied rights, would be better.[129]

It was largely thanks to Schuman that in February and March the deadlock over the Statute was resolved on the lines suggested by Massigli, and as a part of a wider reconsideration of German policy. Already, in November, Schuman had sent André François-Poncet, a pre-war Ambassador to Berlin, to be Koenig's *chargé de mission*. It was hoped that François-Poncet could provide a more positive and refreshing view than Koenig on events in Germany. Amongst other things, the new appointee soon showed an insightful appreciation of General Clay. Clay was a man of action, eager to progress in Germany and impatient at French doubts, but François-Poncet did not feel he was anti-French. Rather the General did not appreciate the reasons for France's caution.[130] Within a few months François-Poncet was fully sympathetic to the view that France must stop lagging behind the Anglo-Americans and take the lead in tying Germany into a European framework. Auriol and others might continue to fear that a revived Germany would become militarist and expansionist, perhaps even allying with Russia, but there was an alternative view that West Germans had put militarism behind them, with the destruction of the *junkers* and the Nazis, and that they favoured Western co-operation. François-Poncet believed that one step that would improve matters would be the replacement of the Allied occupation authority by civilian controls.[131] Civilian high commissioners should be appointed to act, not as an Allied 'government' but as the defenders of reserved Allied rights, whilst Germans handled their own day-to-day administration. Military forces would remain in Germany, however, to be used as a last resort in backing the high commissioners. Schuman approved both this approach and the idea of a simpler Occupation Statute, setting out the broad lines of reserved Allied powers. Both he and François-Poncet explained these ideas in March to the US official George Kennan, who was on a mission to Germany to see how differences on the problem could be resolved.[132] But the Americans knew that Schuman had formidable opponents to his policy such as Koenig.[133]

The French proposals had an immediate appeal in the State Department, where a Franco-German *rapprochement* and a voluntary German role in the Western alliance were major aims.[134] In mid-March Schuman also put the proposals on a civilian high commission to Bevin, who found them an excellent idea,[135] and on 20 March the French minister had a secret, informal conversation with Clay himself, lasting three and a half hours. Schuman had asked for the meeting, the State Department had approved it, and a sceptical Clay arrived in Paris in civilian dress, intending to complain about French policy. He did not mince his words, accusing France of being as obstructionist at three-power level as Russia had been in four-power conferences, and differences between the two men remained at the end of their conversation. However the meeting saw a minor miracle. Schuman was now ready to keep Allied controls to a minimum, with a simplified occupation statute; Clay said France should take the lead in seeking a *rapprochement* with Germany, and described the discussions as the best he had ever had with a Frenchman. The General was still doubtful as to whether Schuman could push his policy through against the doubters in Paris,[136] but in late March the Americans accepted an idea, originally suggested by the French many weeks before, that the three Western foreign ministers should resolve their differences on Germany in a face-to-face meeting, in Washington.[137]

* * *

By the time the Washington talks were held in April 1949, France had advanced with another important element in its German policy, the development of European co-operation. Although Aristide Briand had led the way in advocating a European federation in 1929–30, and although seventeen groups (some with several thousand members) existed in France to promote European union in early 1948,[138] the Quai was slow to take an interest in European political unification. The federalist groups seemed extremely diverse in approach[139] and the British government was uninterested in grandiose dreams of political union.[140] A much-publicised Congress at the Hague in May 1948, attended by many French and European political leaders, showed the growing support for the European ideal however, and the Quai had already noted German interests in continental unity.[141] In the wake of the London accords, given French interest in controlling Germany within a wider framework, increased official interest in European political unification was probably inevitable. A Quai memorandum of 1 July in fact set out French aims within the Brussels Pact as being to develop European co-operation, partly as a response to the growing public demand for this, and to develop a 'peaceful and lasting' solution to the

211

German problem. It was proposed that, at the next session of the Brussels Pact Council, France should ask for two studies to be established, one by the Brussels power themselves, on a European Assembly (an idea emanating from the Hague Congress) and the other, by the OEEC, on a European economic union.[142]

In mid-July Georges Bidault put the proposal for two studies to the Brussels Pact foreign ministers, defending them as the way to win popular support and build up Europe's economic strength. The British, however, were particularly sceptical about such studies,[143] and Massigli felt that Bidault only suggested them in a last, desperate bid to cling to office.[144] (The Foreign Minister knew that a European Assembly was growing in popularity.[145]) Massigli may have been too harsh. Bidault remained adamant long afterwards that his dramatic proposals of July 1948 were seriously-intended, and an important step towards European unity,[146] and they certainly fitted into other policies being developed in the Quai. In mid-August however it was Robert Schuman who put a new, more modest proposal to the French Cabinet, simply recommending the study of a European Assembly, by the Brussels powers, on the lines desired by the 'International Commission for European Unity', an umbrella organisation for federalists. The Assembly would be designed to foster European co-operation and, importantly, would have only consultative powers. The French still feared British opposition to this quite modest scheme and it was therefore decided to make sure of Belgian support before putting the idea to the Brussels powers.[147]

The road towards a European Assembly did not prove easy. The news of the French Cabinet's support for an Assembly soon leaked to the press and although the Italians,[148] the US[149] and even the Dutch,[150] seemed sympathetic to the idea, Paul-Henri Spaak, perhaps because of British doubts, was slow to respond to the French suggestion that Belgium should co-sponsor a proposal to the Brussels powers. Only on 31 August, in a personal meeting with Schuman, did Spaak finally agree to this.[151] Meanwhile the British seemed displeased at French behaviour[152] and were given plenty of time to draw up a list of possible problems with an Assembly, which they gave to Massigli on 2 September, after the issue was raised in the Brussels Pact Permanent Commission. The British believed a European federation to be quite unrealistic, feared that 'undesirable elements' – like the Communists – would use an Assembly for propaganda purposes, and wanted to know in detail how such a body would be established.[153] The French actually had quite a simple reply to the British: they did not want a European federation as yet, merely a *study* of an Assembly, and the study itself would resolve the practical problems which Britain had raised. As Paul Ramadier (now Minister of Defence) explained to Bevin in late September, an Assembly would provide a 'vision' for common people, mobilising them behind West European co-operation, in whichever way this developed.[154] Bevin remained sceptical about an Assembly, telling Schuman that ministerial meetings were a better, more practical route to take,[155] but Schuman was undaunted, believing that new European institutions must be developed, that this would please the US and that it would help resolve the German problem.[156] One significant point was that Konrad Adenauer had welcomed France's support for a European Assembly.[157] In mid-October Massigli assured the Brussels Permanent Commission that France remained 'ready to examine all suggestions', but the British refused to set up a study group on an Assembly until the Brussels Council discussed the issue late in the month. The Quai, at this time facing so many other problems in their German policy, feared a deep division between the empirically-minded British, with their 'Commonwealth approach' to co-operation, and the legalistically-minded continentals, who wanted an institutional framework for greater unity.[158]

The Brussels Council of 25–26 October provided a breakthrough for the Brussels powers. In a compromise settlement a 'Preparatory Commission' was established at government level to look at both an Assembly and Bevin's idea of a new ministerial-level institution.[159] It met in Paris in late November. The French designated a powerful group of (mainly) pro-European politicians, to represent them, whereas the British delegation was largely made up of former officials.[160] The Quai officials continued to see a major difference between themselves – with their desire for radical advances in economic and political co-operation in Europe in order to control Germany—and the British—who were concerned with other problems such as the Cold War and dollar gap, and content with ministerial co-operation.[161] French officials hoped to draw West Germany into the Council of Europe at an early date, so as to instil the 'European ideal' into the new state, and were ready to surrender an element of national sovereignty to secure this. British attitudes created a difficult dilemma for French planners. It seemed that, in order to forestall German domination of a united Europe, joint Anglo-French action would be a vital necessity. Yet the British were unwilling even to study a popular Assembly, let alone surrender national sovereignty to European bodies.[162]

When the Preparatory Commission, in mid-December, produced an interim report favouring the establishment of both a Ministerial Council and an Assembly,[163] Bevin's doubts about the whole proposal were renewed. In a meeting with Schuman in mid-January Bevin again expressed fears about the embarrassment an 'irresponsible' Assembly could cause to European governments.[164] When the Preparatory Commission reopened, the British even suggested that any Assembly should be no more than a 'conference' of national delegations voting en bloc.[165] Finally, at another Brussels Council meeting late in the month, Bevin conceded the formation of an Assembly, though the delegations to this would be chosen according to the preference of each member state.[166] Technical work then began to organise the 'Council of Europe' as the new body became known, and it finally held its first annual meeting in September, with both a consultative Assembly and a Council of Ministers.[167] Its powers were restricted, it did not initially include Germany and it was therefore something of a disappointment for France. Nonetheless, it proved a first step to further political co-operation and it opened the way for west German membership. It was located in Strasbourg on the Franco-German border – a venue suggested, ironically, by Bevin as a symbol of reconciliation between the old enemies. The pressure to create an Assembly had also helped to make France the leading advocate of European political union. Auriol believed the country had 'regained the high moral leadership of European nations' in the debate over the Council of Europe and Bonnet felt that Americans now saw France as the 'motor' for European unity.[168]

* * *

By April 1949 France had also made important steps towards securing a US guarantee for Europe. Despite the danger of war in 1948–49, Western defences were appallingly weak. Because of equipment deficiencies, the French military in Spring 1948 (under the so-called 'Plan R') did not feel able to mobilise all their forces in the event of war, and expected a rapid retreat to North Africa. In June Schuman, as Premier, had ordered that plans should be readied in case war broke out over Berlin. He hoped that the Rhine might be held, along with a 'redoubt' in the Austrian Alps, but an eventual retreat from France seemed inevitable. One man who opposed the easy acceptance of a new 'Dunkirk' was General de Lattre, the Army's Inspector-General,[169] who organised a meeting in Strasbourg between 29 July and 5 August to discuss the defence of the ZOF. The situation was so desperate that German rearmament was suggested.[170] In mid-June the three Western governors had agreed that a united Western command structure was needed in Germany, and in August three-power staff conversations were held in Wiesbaden on a possible defence of the Rhine.[171] Meanwhile the British favoured the formation of a Brussels Pact command organisation and suggested this idea to General Paul Ely, the French representative on the Brussels Pact Military Committee.[172] The Quai d'Orsay, still dismayed at the lack of British military commitment to Europe, would have preferred membership of a *global* planning body with America and Britain, with a US Supreme Commander and a defence line on the Elbe. However the British proposal would at least provide a much-needed defence structure in Europe,[173] and in late September Brussels Pact defence ministers agreed to establish a 'Western Union Chiefs of Staff' (WUCOS) with a British chairman and British Air Force commander, but with French commanders for the Army and naval forces. It was still hoped to find an American supreme commander in due course, but meanwhile WUCOS would prepare Europe's defences and, if war broke out, take command of Brussels Pact forces.[174]

It was largely thanks to the efforts of de Lattre that in late 1948 the French ruled out the idea of a rapid withdrawal to North Africa in war. Instructions to the French Army in November, laid out its four main tasks as being: to defend the Rhine in co-operation with the Allies, to maintain order within France (a vital point given the Communist 'fifth column') and defend the country in war; to maintain the cohesion of the French Union; and fulfil international treaties.[175] However French armed forces, at about 600,000, numbered little more than they had after the 1946 financial cuts,[176] and the creation of WUCOS, though an important step, brought its own problems. Defence Minister Ramadier, at first asked Alphonse Juin to take the post of WUCOS Army Commander. Juin however, with some justification, saw WUCOS as an empty shell, quite inadequate to defend Europe until greater US forces arrived. He preferred to keep his post as Commissioner-General in Morocco.[177] So Ramadier turned to Jean de Lattre, who readily agreed to accept the post.[178] De Lattre was already committed to the creation of a strong military 'deterrent' in Europe, using US, European and African resources,[179] and in this he seemed to share the general approach of the WUCOS chairman, Britain's Bernard Montgomery. Montgomery, alone among the British chiefs of staff in early 1948 had pressed for the maintenance of British forces on the Continent in the event of war, and the creation of a Brussels Pact defence structure.[180] In October Montgomery told Massigli that a precipitate retreat must be avoided if conflict broke out;[181] in November he told Auriol and Ramadier that the US and Brussels Pact forces must be built up to hold the Rhine, and he even professed to fear German links to Russia.[182] Unfortunately however Montgomery and de Lattre soon developed a strong mutual antipathy. Both were vain and self-confident and Montgomery, a terse, practical and undemonstrative individual, was easily antagonised by the elaborate, sensitive and unpunctual de Lattre. They argued over numerous subjects, from the costs and accommodation of WUCOS to major strategic issues. De Lattre feared that Montgomery's main aim was to ensure the defence of Britain in war. Montgomery was offended that the French treated him not as a genuine 'Supreme Commander' but merely as the chairman of a study committee.[183]

The bickering between de Lattre and Montgomery reflected genuine French impatience with British attitudes to defence in 1948. The EMDN were exasperated at British planners, who combined ambitious schemes for the defence of the Middle East (still an area under London's domination) with insufficient attention to the defence of Europe. The British believed war with Russia was unlikely before the late 1950s, and were reluctant to share defence plans with the French. The French were concerned with the danger of an 'accidental' conflict in the near future and wanted practical steps to build up Western forces, not least by securing a firm US commitment to continental defence. The EMDN resented London's close links with Washington, believed that France could represent 'European' interests far better than could the British, and still hoped for a three-power Combined Chiefs of Staff, with an American Supreme Commander in Europe.[184] In October Ramadier told the Cabinet that the Brussels Pact was of limited use without US forces,[185] a point reinforced by the fact that the Defence Minister ideally wanted to hold the line, not of the Rhine, but of the Elbe.[186] Ramadier always saw Montgomery's appointment as a temporary expedient until an American commander was appointed, and believed Montgomery's main role was to carry out studies of defence needs. By early 1949, many studies *had* been made and the French. The French wanted to move onto practical preparations for defence, with US material aid to build up European forces.[187] The EMDN and Cabinet were still disappointed with London's desire to defend Britain, the Middle East and the high seas, rather than continental Europe.[188]

In June, of course, the US government had invited Canadian and Brussels Pact representatives to discuss a US guarantee but in the first round of secret talks in Washington, from 6 July to 10 September, there were deep divisions between the French and the Americans. The chief American negotiator, Under-Secretary Robert Lovett, made it clear from the start that large-scale military aid to Europe was not on offer in the short term, because of budgetary considerations, and that there would be no unilateral US guarantee. Any treaty had to be based on the Rio Pact, with a mutual guarantee between members, and the Europeans would have to do the utmost to defend themselves. Congressional rights would prevent the US government from making an 'automatic' promise to go to war against an aggressor, yet Lovett wanted the 'North Atlantic Pact' to spread over a wide area to deter a Soviet attack. The French, fearful of an 'accidental' conflict at an early date, were very disappointed with the US position, and Henri Bonnet left Lovett in no doubt about the differences between them. The French did not want to antagonise Russia for the sake of a vaguely-worded paper guarantee, nor did they want to threaten the Soviets with 'encirclement'. The French believed that a geographically extensive pact would merely dissipate resources, and produce liabilities rather than assets, especially if such a large, weak and exposed country as Italy was included. Bonnet argued that the Brussels powers had already taken grave risks in preparing their defences, that Washington must provide an effective guarantee and that the US and Canada should concentrate on reinforcing the Brussels powers alone as a barrier to a Soviet attack where it mattered – in Western Germany.[189]

At the Brussels Pact Council meeting on 19–20 July, everyone agreed on the need to proceed with the Washington talks but Bidault (supported by Spaak) complained about American views on a treaty, and felt he had been misled in the past as to what to expect from them. The French seemed more impressed by the arrival of Lyman Lemnitzer, as America's observer on the Brussels Pact military committee, than they were by the Washington talks.[190] The British, who had close links with the Americans and had done much to shape the idea of a multilateral 'Atlantic Pact', became very concerned about French doubts. Far from representing 'European' interests in their contacts with the US, the British had helped to devise a scheme which did little to reassure the French.[191]

In Washington in early August the French and Americans remained far apart on the Atlantic Pact.[192] The French hoped for support from the other Brussels powers for their case, but only received sympathy from Spaak[193] and Bonnet became more blunt and outspoken in expressing himself. On 17 August he told Marshall that France wanted to join the Combined Chiefs of Staff and that she would only join an Atlantic Pact on three conditions: if plans for the defence of Germany were agreed, if the US rearmed French forces and if more US troops were sent to Europe.[194] A special meeting a few days later failed to resolve the Franco-American differences, and British and Canadian diplomats became extremely concerned that the French were putting a US commitment to Europe at risk through what was seen as a selfish interest in their own defence.[195] Late in the month British, American and Canadian diplomats all put pressure on Schuman to change French tactics. The political crisis in Paris made it difficult to get a swift response, but Schuman decided he would have to change policy.[196] In early September Bonnet continued to ask the Americans both for the rearmament of French forces and a discussion on strategy in the event of war, but he now accepted the idea of a multilateral pact over a wide area, and approved a report recommending that such a treaty be negotiated. The report accepted that a war in Europe was possible, through accident or miscalculation, but another important reason for making a treaty was to provide Europeans with psychological reassurance.[197] The US also agreed at this time to provide the French with enough equipment, from excess stocks in Germany, to arm three divisions.[198]

The Brussels Council accepted the principle of an Atlantic Pact in late October, as did the French Cabinet. However there were still many French doubts about the treaty. Ramadier remained eager to get US forces into a united command structure, and Schuman believed it would be best to form separate Mediterranean and Scandinavian Pacts, rather than to include all countries in a single alliance. The French were desperate to preserve the importance of the Brussels Pact, and to concentrate on building an effective defence of the Rhine, rather than to dissipate resources.[199] Differences between France and the Anglo-Americans continued after 10 December when (following Truman's triumphant re-election as President) the Washington talks reopened with the aim of drafting a North Atlantic Treaty (NAT). The new Secretary of State, Dean Acheson, was an ardent supporter of links to Europe and persuaded Congress that a long-term US guarantee to Europe was a vital necessity.[200] The French were aware of the historical significance of America's commitment but disappointed at the non-automatic nature of the new alliance: each member would respond to an attack on any other member only according to its own constitutional process. This was in order to preserve congressional rights. Schuman told the French Cabinet that it was the best that could be done,[201] but it further underlined the need to get US troops into Europe so that America became involved in war at the outset. It was important, Chauvel told Bonnet, to ensure that the Americans kept at least 'four men and a corporal' in Germany.[202]

The most difficult issue in the talks after December was that of the geographical extent of a pact. The Americans wanted to include Scandinavia in an alliance, a desire reinforced by Soviet diplomatic pressures on Norway at this time. The French doubted whether Scandinavia was ready to enter a wide alliance, however. Armed forces there were small, Sweden wished to maintain its neutrality and a 'Nordic alliance' seemed more appropriate for the area. The French noted that 'we have no interest in seeing the axis of security pass too far towards the north ...', since it was the Rhine which needed to be defended most. Bonnet and Auriol also feared enraging the Soviets with the threat of 'encirclement' if the NAT was widely extended.[203] These arguments over Scandinavia became enmeshed with others about the Mediterranean. Hitherto the French had not welcomed proposals to allow Italy into the Brussels or Atlantic pacts,[204] despite continued pressure from Count Sforza to embrace his country in such arrangements.[205] The British also disliked the idea of including Italy, which was large and vulnerable, and might wish to revise the 1947 peace treaty as the price of joining an alliance. The Americans too seemed reticent on Rome's inclusion.[206] In November, however, the French decided to change policy, in favour of Italian entry. Schuman told Italy's Prime Minister, de Gasperi, of this in a meeting on 23 November and de Gasperi was delighted.[207]

The French had decided that if the Pact was to be extended to countries like Portugal and Iceland, there simply was no good reason to exclude Italy, which was essential to Mediterranean defence – an area of special concern to France. To omit Italy, whilst including other countries, would place her in an exposed position and upset Italian opinion.[208] The French had also decided that, if the Pact was be extended at all, it should provide protection to French-dominated North Africa – Morocco, Tunisia, and Algeria – even though these lay far from the Soviet Union. Algeria was particularly important, Chauvel told Bonnet, because it was constitutionally part of France. There was also a major strategic concern in that, if Scandinavia was included in the alliance but areas south of the Alps were not, 'the axis of the pact would be shifted towards the north, with a tendency for us to assume major responsibilities in the Arctic region'. Thus, in order to keep the Rhine as the central pivot of the alliance and to defend France's Mediterranean interests, North Africa must be used to counter-balance the influence of Scandinavia. Italy's membership would make North Africa's inclusion more acceptable.[209] Bonnet argued for the inclusion of Italy and North Africa to the Washington conferees on 22 December, saying that it was ridiculous to cover Alaska (part of the US) in an Atlantic pact whilst omitting Algeria (part of France). The other countries were extremely reluctant to protect French 'colonial' interests as part of a security pact, however, and the British remained ardently opposed to Italy's inclusion.[210] Schuman was concerned at the deep divisions in Washington though Bonnet favoured a tough line.[211] In the New Year, the French did retreat somewhat, and dropped their demand for Morocco and Tunisia to be protected by the NAT, but they were firm about the inclusion of Algeria and Italy.[212] The Italians themselves added strength to the French case by formally requesting membership of the new pact, and the Americans and Canadians then became more sympathetic to Italy's inclusion in the talks, though not to Algeria's.[213] Bevin remained unenthusiastic about including either Algeria or Italy.[214]

A decision was finally forced on the issue of geographical extent in late February when the Americans wanted to bring Norway into the Washington talks as a response to renewed Soviet diplomatic pressure on Oslo. All the other conferees agreed to the US request except Bonnet, who upset everyone by saying that Norway could only be included in the talks if Italy was too. On 1 March Bonnet even said that, if Norway was brought in whilst Italy was excluded, France herself might not join the new alliance! Acheson was furious and Schuman was soon forced to concede that a Norwegian representative could enter the talks. Schuman insisted however that an immediate decision must be made on Italy's position, and it was soon decided to allow Italy into the alliance. Acheson also said Algeria could be covered under the Pact, and in early March Portugal, Denmark and Iceland were invited to join the final stages of the talks.[215] There were still certain countries, such as Finland and Yugoslavia, which were open to Soviet pressure but lay outside the Atlantic Pact,[216] but an extensive 'trip-wire' had now been drawn, over which the Red Army could not march without provoking war. In the Cabinet Ramadier remained disappointed that Scandinavia had been included in the Pact, but Yvon Delbos, a Radical minister and Foreign Minister in the 1930s, declared 'The peace is one and indivisible. If you leave out a country, they will be attacked and exploited one-by-one'.[217] Delbos even raised the question of whether Greece and Turkey should be included in the Atlantic Pact, but Schuman, the Quai and Auriol all viewed this as extending the alliance too far.[218] The irony was that the main Russian criticisms about the extent of the Pact, when it was publicised in March, were about its extension to Italy and North Africa – the very areas France had wanted to cover.[219]

Throughout the Atlantic Pact talks France had continued to ask for US military aid and a leading role for Paris in global strategic planning. Both Queuille and Schuman pressured Marshall on these points during the UN Assembly meeting in Paris. The EMDN believed that France's important global interests meant that she should share in global planning, they continued to resent

British links to America and wanted their own representatives at the Pentagon. Bonnet proposed to the Americans in early 1949 that a Franco-Anglo-American 'Defence Council' should be formed, and it was suggested that Juin should visit Washington, to establish co-operation with the Pentagon. The US Joint Chiefs of Staff showed little liking for a Defence Council, partly because they wanted to keep American forces under American control, but also because they did not see France as an important global power.[220] In January 1949, however, the US did begin preparations for a Military Aid Programme (MAP) to Europe, to start after the Atlantic alliance was signed.[221] On 1 March the Americans talked to Ernest Bevin about an MAP worth over one billion dollars, mainly in the form of transferred supplies (but also with some direct financial assistance), on condition that Europeans made the maximum possible effort themselves. The effort must not, however, impede economic recovery through the Marshall Plan. Bevin asked that the French be informed of this as soon as possible, and Schuman was duly given a note by Caffery and Harriman two days later. 'It is interesting to note', Caffery told Washington 'that Schuman . . . treated MAP as something which he had long been awaiting . . .'.[222] Given the continuous pressure from France for US military aid since early 1948, Caffery ought not to have been surprised by this. Ironically however, when the US note was discussed by Schuman, Auriol, Queuille, Ramadier and others on 7 March, there were doubts about it. French ministers were not confident that they could bear the costs of a greater defence effort themselves, as the Americans wanted. Auriol was, predictably, worried about offending the Soviets through a rearmament effort, and there were fears over the domestic political scene, where cantonal elections were due in late March and the PCF were pursuing a 'peace offensive' – a new Soviet propaganda line in early 1949 which played on popular fears of war and accused the US of imperialism. As a result Schuman told the Americans that, whilst France wanted MAP, she did not wish to announce it publicly until after the cantonal elections. Preparations did, however, begin amongst the Brussels powers for the presentation of a formal request to Washington for military aid.[223]

In late February Jean Chauvel was succeeded as Secretary-General of the Quai by Alexandre Parodi, a wartime *Gaulliste*, a former Cabinet minister and recently French representative at the UN. (Chauvel had asked for an overseas posting some months before). Parodi discussed the NAT with Auriol on 8 March, and many of the old fears about the alliance were raised in the conversation: US policy was too bellicose; Russia could be provoked into war by fears of encirclement; a narrower, more effective alliance would have been preferable to the far-flung and imprecise Atlantic pact.[224] The Cabinet, meeting on 16 March, agreed to sign the Pact but ministers feared the response to it from Russia and the general public.[225] From Washington, Bonnet believed that Congress would prove reluctant to approve the MAP, that the US would continue to antagonise Moscow – perhaps by reviving Germany's military capability – and that France would continue to face the threat of invasion from Russia in future, in a situation of permanent 'armed peace'[226] When the treaty text was published on 18 March Schuman publicly defended it as a way to re-establish the balance of power. He denied that it infringed French independence and claimed that it offered immediate US assistance in war. Earlier he had told the Assembly's Foreign Affairs Commission that France must stand up to Russia's 'ideological expansion' and promised, 'It is not illusory guarantees which we look for. It is realities'.[227] Jacques Duclos, however, speaking for the PCF, attacked NATO as anti-Soviet, heralding higher defence spending and likely to lead to German rearmament.[228]

* * *

On 30 March, before leaving to sign the NAT in Washington, Schuman assured the Cabinet that he would press Acheson for a policy of 'peace and defence'. The creation of effective defences must be matched by a readiness to talk to the Soviets.[229] Once in Washington Schuman met Acheson and pointed out that, if the Red Army did conquer Western Europe, France would effectively cease to exist. Acheson was not ready to share strategic defence planning with France as Schuman wanted, but he did say that 'the real work' of NATO's military machine could be handled by four powers – America, Canada, Britain and France – and thus promised a leading role of a sort to Paris.[230] On 4 April Schuman, seconded by Bonnet, signed the NAT for France. The NAT would last at least twenty years, it included undertakings to develop economic co-operation and defence capacities and it established a Ministerial Council, with a defence committee, on lines similar to the Brussels Pact. It promised that 'an armed attack against one or more [members] . . . shall be considered an attack against them all', but this promise would only come into effect 'in accordance with . . . constitutional processes'. The NAT did nothing directly to improve military defences on the ground.[231] It was perhaps appropriate that, at the signing ceremony, the band played 'I've got plenty of nothing'.[232] The following day the Brussels powers presented a formal request to the Americans for military assistance, but it was not clear how easily Congressional approval for this would be.[233] Although Bevin told Acheson on the 7th that 'I detect a greater confidence in France as a result of the step we have taken', Caffery was perhaps a better judge believing, 'that in spite of the very great advantages of the pact to France its signature is only half the battle to defeat [the] basic feeling of insecurity in this country'.[234]

The NAT signature was only one aspect of the Washington talks, however. On 1 April Schuman, Acheson and Bevin met for their first tripartite meeting on Germany. There would be many more such meetings over the next few years, meetings which helped create the impression that France had become one of the 'inner three' members of the Western alliance. By now Schuman had the reassurance of knowing that an American security commitment to France was about to be made, and that European co-operation was being developed in the Council of Europe, whilst Acheson seemed eager to co-ordinate Western policies in Germany.[235] As regards Berlin, the Western airlift had proved able to keep the city supplied over the winter and Stalin had decided that the blockade must be ended. Secret talks had been held between the US and Soviet representatives at the UN, and in the 1 April meeting, Schuman and Bevin gave their approval to these. There were doubts about Stalin's good intentions but it was hoped to end the blockade, and to hold a new four-power conference to discuss Germany in the near future.[236] Large parts of the 1948 London accords had now been carried out, including the drafting of agreements on a Ruhr Authority and Security Board, and everyone now agreed with Schuman that a simplified Occupation Statute should be drawn up to define future Allied rights.[237]

Fuller three-power talks on Germany were held on 6–7 April, by which time the Americans had drawn up a short, general Occupation Statute.[238] The Americans hoped to convince France at last that Germany would be safely revived only within a wider European framework, in a recovery programme which would benefit the continent in general.[239] This fitted in with Schuman's vision, although the Cabinet was adamant that there must still be special controls on Germany.[240] Ironically the French desire to resolve points of difference with the Anglo-Americans at this time was strengthened by the prospect of a new four-power CFM. The French had wanted a settlement of the Berlin crisis more than anyone, but Pierre de Leusse pointed out that four-power talks could throw the whole German question back into the melting pot and that the Americans, British and Soviets might even find common ground on a centralised German government and an early end to the occupation. A CFM would also raise problems for the idea of a 'European' framework for German recovery, which Stalin was certain to oppose, and any settlement might bring the Soviets into the control of the Ruhr. The *Direction d'Europe* warned that France must therefore establish firm agreements with the Anglo-Americans on German government, the occupation and the Ruhr *before* entering talks with Russia.[241] These arguments could be read simply as a reflection of French nervousness and fear about Germany, their continuing distrust of Anglo-American policy and their helplessness in the face of US and Soviet power. But they also showed that, whatever France's desire for peace with Moscow, France itself was gaining a vested interest in the *division* of Europe. As the Cold War established itself as the new order in the world, so French aims became moulded to the new reality, and aims in Germany – especially the idea of controls on Germany within a West European framework – relied on *Western* co-operation alone. Agreement with Russia at this point would have meant negotiations on a reunited Germany which could have ruined all hopes of Franco-German integration.

A comprehensive Western position was achieved in agreements signed on 8 April in Washington, which included a short Occupation Statute, a definition of continued tripartite controls on Germany and the restatement of Allied desiderata in the Basic Law. A highly important step was the decision, suggested by Schuman in March, to replace the military governments in Germany with a civilian High Commission. This would put an end to the bickering between Generals Clay and Koenig, it would establish a new principle of German autonomy under the supreme authority of the occupation powers, and would thus help to lay the basis for 'the closest integration ... of the German people under a democratic federal state within the framework of a European association'. After years of division and debate, the Western powers seemed at last to have achieved a common approach to the German problem.[242]

France, the Cold War and the Western alliance, 1944–9

No ordeal changes the nature of man; no crisis that of states.
– Charles de Gaulle, writing in his *War Memoirs* (volume III, 57).

In December 1944 Charles de Gaulle made an anti-German alliance with Josef Stalin to serve as the basis for future French security policy in Europe. Four years and four months later Robert Schuman signed a multilateral pact with the United States and other North Atlantic countries which was principally intended as a defence against Soviet aggression. Strictly speaking the Franco-Soviet Treaty and the North Atlantic Treaty (NAT) were not incompatible, and the former was not denounced by Moscow until 1954 when the Western Allies were committed to the rearmament of Germany. Yet there can be no doubt that, between 1944 and 1949, as a new world was born from the ashes of war, French foreign policy underwent a profound transformation. During the war de Gaulle not only favoured a revival of the pre-1917 Franco-Russian alliance, he had also spoken of a Europe 'from the Atlantic to the Urals', saw France as a potential 'bridge' between Washington and Moscow when tension between them became apparent and, notwithstanding his fundamental belief in French *grandeur*, believed that co-operation with all the Big Three powers was essential to French interests. Russia was vital to European security, the ally which would help France to enforce the new peace settlement against Germany in the way it had been impossible to enforce the Treaty of Versailles. America was essential to global security, the country which would supply France with the means for reconstruction and modernisation and so remove the underlying economic weaknesses that had dogged policy in the 1930s. Britain, though seen by de Gaulle as the author or many French problems in the era of appeasement, was close to France in her imperial interests, liberal-democratic values and security needs in Western Europe, the friend who did most to secure a leading French role in the German occupation, the UN and the Council of Foreign Ministers. De Gaulle hoped, as he explained to Georges Bidault in April 1945, to be treated more as an equal by the Big Three as time went on:

> The intention of the Powers which find themselves in the strongest position at the end of the present war, is to 'realise' their gains as soon as possible. This is the case with Russia and the US, and ... with Britain. It is in France's interest not to precipitate matters; although she is momentarily weak, she is nevertheless recovering a little more power and influence every day.[1]

By 1949 the situation was very different. Hopes of maintaining the wartime Grand Alliance on the basis of a common fear of Germany proved illusory. In contrast to 1918, when many Germans did not even believe that they had been defeated, Hitler's *Reich* had been utterly crushed. The Soviets, after the Red Army's success in destroying the *Wehrmacht*, and the United States, with the advent of the atomic bomb, had little to fear from Germany. Both became chiefly concerned with the menace presented by the other, both were prepared to appeal to Germans for support, and French attempts to act as an arbiter between them were useless. Russia remained the most powerful military force on the Continent but became a potential menace to Western Europe. America remained vital to French economic reconstruction but its influence over French policy became very great, and it was the power which pressed most for Germany's industrial revival. Britain, especially in the Marshall Plan and Brussels Pact, worked closely with France but seldom treated this as an equal partnership and was critical of many aspects of French policy. As for France herself, despite her leading role in important international organisations, she never achieved the political stability, economic strength or military might to match the Big Three. The country seemed powerless in the face of the Cold War, overwhelmed by the might of the superpowers. Even French officials veered between exaggerated stories of Soviet-American tension – as early as September 1944 an intelligence report claimed that certain US authorities 'consider an eventual conflict between the US and USSR to be inevitable. They ask themselves on which side France will be'[2] – and absurd fears of a Soviet-American condominium, as at the time of the Bedell Smith letter to Molotov in May 1948.

In early 1948 the British and Americans, in so far as they pursued a coherent policy, wanted France to accept that Russia was the greatest threat to the peace and that Western Germany must be resuscitated as a barrier to Communism, but France never saw Cold War developments in the same way that the Anglo-Americans did. The French recognised Stalin's brutality, were often victims of Soviet contempt and resented Russian domination of Eastern Europe. Yet the Americans and the British could also seem overbearing and contemptuous in French eyes, desiring, like the Soviets, that France should play a role subservient to *their* wishes, and from the French perspective it often seemed that the Anglo-Americans antagonised the Soviets, as well as the reverse. Certainly Paris saw President Truman as being unnecessarily bellicose in his 'Truman Doctrine' speech of March 1947. By December 1947 a series of developments – the Marshall Plan, the rift with the PCF and the breakdown of the CFM – led the French themselves to demand a closer US military commitment to Europe and it is tempting to interpret this as a response simply to 'a credible Soviet threat . . .'.[3] But the French complaint was actually that, having done much to antagonise Moscow, America was not ready to protect those countries which were most vulnerable to Soviet attack.

Whereas Washington and London wanted to revive Germany and adopt a strong policy towards Russia in 1948, Paris wished to control Germany and adopt a more pacific line towards Russia. It is unjust to explain French policy solely in terms of an outmoded obsession with the German menace. Although the French were still fearful of Germany, they were also concerned with the impact of Western policy on Russia, which might well launch a 'preventative' war in response to German revival. Equally to be feared was a Soviet-German combination, which the French had warned against since 1945, and which might be created if Russia was able to pose as the champion of German reunification. Whereas many Anglo-Americans believed that a politically-centralised and economically-resuscitated Western Germany was the only way to ensure that German people resisted Soviet domination, the French believed that only a decentralised and industrially-weakened Germany would remove the twin dangers of a new German militarism and a Soviet-German combination. Neither were French fears helped by US and British military policies in 1948. Paris was ready to abandon neutralism and to adhere to three-power (as opposed to four-power co-operation) in Germany only on the implicit understanding that an American security guarantee would be provided to her, but in Spring 1948 Americans seemed to believe that a Soviet invasion of Western Europe was unlikely, that US occupation forces in Germany were a sufficient sign of America's commitment to European defence and that the main need was to proceed with the Continent's economic reconstruction through Marshall aid. US reticence about an alliance, as well as fears about German revival, led French ministers to favour a moderate line towards Russia in May 1948.

By July the Americans had acknowledged that an alliance was required to give psychological reassurance to Europe whilst economic reconstruction proceeded, but it cannot be said that the form of guarantee which America proposed was very reassuring for France. The French, already exasperated by British military thinking in the Brussels Pact, wanted a firm military guarantee aimed at defending the Rhine, and with a leading role for Paris in strategic planning. What they got was a loose, geographically-extended alliance, which provided them with only limited reassurances about what would occur if the Russians attacked. Neither was the signature of NAT followed by the resolution of these problems. President Truman requested a Military Aid Programme from Congress in July, which was approved a few months later, but large-scale US rearmament did not begin until the Korean War in mid-1950. Extra US divisions and an American Supreme Commander for NATO only arrived in 1951, and then only after France had agreed to the principle of West German rearmament, the ultimate step in German recovery and one which provoked bitter controversy for years afterwards. France did get a seat, alongside America and Britain, on the NAT 'Standing Group' for military planning, established in September 1949, but this did not bring the longed-for close relationship between the US and French military. The Americans continued to control their own strategic plans and would only join in NATO's 'Regional Planning Groups' for Europe as a 'consulting member'.[4]

* * *

Despite the strength of America and Russia after the war, France was not completely powerless. As the strategic centre of Western Europe, the second largest state on the Continent and the second largest colonial empire in the world, she was an important prize in the struggle between the superpowers. Many of the Americans and British (though not perhaps General Clay) realised that the loss of France from the Western cause could be followed by the loss of the rest of Europe. As early as 1945 the French themselves saw that they could use America's suspicion of Communism and Soviet power to demand financial support from Washington. In these circumstances it has to be asked whether French policy-makers could not have used their assets more wisely to maintain the country's international standing and sense of pride. After all, de Gaulle proved quite adept in 1940–46 in maintaining an image of independence even though he actually relied on the Western allies for his very survival. True, de Gaulle had been able to play off the Anglo-Saxons against the Soviets on occasions, a tactic which became impossible after 1947, but then again, the Americans would have liked to see France, and other West European nations, behave with greater independence and self-confidence in 1948. There were certainly many suggestions of alternative policies to those which Bidault followed. René Massigli advocated a British alliance and membership of the Bizone at an early date; others suggested a 'moral' role for France, the leadership of smaller powers, or, in the case of the Communists, a Soviet alliance. Numerous factors, however, in addition to Cold War tensions, conspired together to prevent a more assertive foreign policy.

Not the least of France's problems was her own internal weakness. In 1945 all Frenchmen agreed on the need for national renewal, for a healthy economy and an effective Constitution which would provide the basis for an active international role. De Gaulle, never one to put faith in alliances and international organisations, believed that, in the last analysis, France must rely on her own resources. In the economic field the nation had not only to recuperate from war and tackle short-term problems, like inflation and food shortages, but also to reverse her long-term industrial stagnation. Alphand, Monnet and other planners always recognised, however, that France could not achieve a radical economic transformation on her own. US financial aid was essential, a customs union with the Benelux states would bring major benefits, and France needed to use German resources – industrial plant, manpower and, most especially, coal. There was an extremely close relationship between France's economic needs and her foreign policy, and it is impossible to understand one without the other. Clearly, France's requirements of coal, cereals and credits from America always – even under de Gaulle – made her likely to turn to the US side in any superpower confrontation, and gave Washington considerable leverage in French affairs.

In retrospect France's acceptance of large scale American aid in the Marshall Plan was a highly significant moment. It brought about joint Anglo-French leadership of the West Europeans, created new opportunities for European customs unions, and offered long-term assistance which, amongst other things, helped to finance the Monnet Plan without fuelling inflation overmuch. Yet acceptance of US aid also had its costs, even in economic terms. By dividing Europe down the middle the Marshall Plan also cut France off from trading partners in the East; by completing the breakdown with the Communists it also meant divisions between French workers and their employers; and by embracing German revival it threatened France's policy of tapping the resources of the Ruhr. In 1949, thanks to Marshall aid, a good 1948 harvest and lower public spending, France's economic situation was improving. Inflation was lower, industrial output was increasing, and major shortages had ended. The

Monnet Plan's ambitious aims were still far from realisation, however: Germany was reviving much faster than France wished, European economic integration had not progressed far, and France remained unable to afford substantial armed forces.

The political scene in post-war France was similarly depressing. Despite hopes of a new unity born of the Resistance, politics had become fragmented and the Constitution of the Fourth Republic proved little better than that of the Third in ensuring decisive government. In 1946–47 the Communists, with over a quarter of the popular vote, were vital in preventing an early move towards Western co-operation such as Massigli favoured, and even after their expulsion from government their popularity, propaganda attacks and ability to threaten widespread disturbances weakened government policy. The emergence of de Gaulle's *Rassemblement* added further complications and the coalition administrations of the centre often proved divided among themselves. After the resignation of de Gaulle, with his very personal style of diplomacy, the Quai d'Orsay was able to assert its primacy in foreign affairs, and to develop reasonably consistent policies under the two MRP ministers, Bidault and Schuman. But other institutions – the EMDN, the Ministry of Finance, the occupation authorities in Germany, or the National Assembly – could challenge the Quai's authority at times, the Quai itself was often divided in its view of policy (especially on Germany), and there were clear differences between MRP and Socialist ministers in the Cabinet. Often MRP ministers kept important information on foreign and defence policy from their Socialist colleagues. The worst confusion came in the summer of 1948 when, at a highly significant moment in international affairs, with the Berlin blockade, Atlantic Pact talks and beginning of work on a German Basic Law, France found herself with a lengthy government crisis, a change of foreign ministers and then a new wave of strikes.

In a situation where French independence was restricted by Cold War developments and internal weakness, one obvious possibility was that the country should join together with other states in a similar position, in order to assert themselves together on the international stage. In Europe there were a number of states with whom the French attempted co-operation, but with all of them there were difficult problems. The Poles and Czechs were inter-war allies, co-operation with whom might help to limit Soviet power in the East. But the Munich crisis had already demonstrated France's inability to project its power into Eastern Europe, and the Soviets easily excluded French influence from crossing the Elbe. The Italians hoped to work closely with Paris and were the first country to join her in customs union talks. But the French insisted on punishing Italy for its behaviour during the war and there were practical difficulties facing economic co-operation between the two. The French would always have preferred a customs union to include the Benelux states, but they wished to build their own customs union first, were fearful of French domination, milder than France in their attitudes towards Germany and reluctant to join in any organisation without the support of the strongest West European nation, Great Britain.

The question why Franco-British co-operation was not developed further is clearly an extremely important one. The two had entered the Second World

War together in 1939, union had been proposed between them in the dark days of June 1940 and there was some success for their partnership after 1947, in the Treaty of Dunkirk, the Marshall Plan and the Brussels Pact. Britain, with its stronger, more industrialised economy, could have made a European customs union viable, helped France to control Germany, and perhaps even have made a 'third force' possible in world affairs. Research has shown that Ernest Bevin himself took a genuine interest in ideas for colonial, military and economic co-operation which might make a Western European union the equal of the superpowers.[5] There was, however, a host of factors operating against an Anglo-French combination because of their differing national perceptions and interests. In the economic field, whereas France concentrated on modernising her post-war economy and accepted (at least until 1948) an element of inflation to do this, the British concentrated on holding down inflation and lacked a comprehensive reconstruction plan. When, in 1946, Alphand suggested a joint Anglo-French economic plan to Bevin, the latter (who disliked the French official) snapped, 'We don't do things like that in our country'.[6] In the commercial field French luxury goods were not wanted in Britain in the early post-war years and later, as French modernisation proceeded, her goods became competitive with those of Britain.[7] Imperial co-operation was undermined by differences in colonial philosophy and a lack of capital with which to develop colonial resources. Military co-operation suffered from the weakness of the French, British distrust of French security and differences in strategic outlook, with the British desiring to defend the Middle East whilst the French defence axis ran from Metropolitan France to North Africa.

The war had left Britain far more powerful than France, closer to the United States and, so far as French officials could see, likely to choose co-operation with the Empire-Commonwealth over that with Europe. The French wanted to be treated as an equal by London, but the disparity in resources between them made a genuine 'partnership' difficult. The French sometimes found the British to be quite overbearing, especially in the case of the garrulous and domineering Bevin, whom Bidault never forgave for having dubbed him 'the dear little man'.[8] Although co-operation between them seemed to be possible in January 1948, with Bevin's vision of 'Western Union', the French rapidly became disaffected with Britain's policies in the Brussels Pact. As Maurice Vaïsse has shown, Paris turned in defence issues to reliance upon the US, and in European questions to the idea of a European Assembly.[9] As early as May in fact, Quai officials were prepared to consider a Franco-German-Benelux combination, led (of course) by France, from which Britain was expected to exclude itself. Bevin for his part was dismayed when France, rather than play the role of Britain's loyal lieutenant in Europe, adopted 'premature' and 'unrealistic' schemes for continental union. He was contemptuous of her political instability and unable to see that the proposals for European institutions could be a logical reflection of French national interests (which could not be catered for in a purely 'Atlantic' framework) and a sign of France's continuing desire to control events, as well as a response to fear and failure. In 1949 Britain did indeed turn to the US alliance and the Commonwealth in preference to Western Europe. And yet, the incomprehension was not all one-sided. Massigli believed that one important factor in Anglo-French estrangement was France's inability to explain her proposals in terms which the pragmatic and practical British could comprehend. In February 1949, for example, the ambassador wrote to Alphand that a note on long-term economic co-operation, which had been sent to Britain, was simply too abstract, failing to demonstrate Britain's interest in continental co-operation or to answer, in concrete terms, London's worries about Commonwealth trade.[10] The final reason for the estrangement of the two countries, however, was their very different approach to the German problem, where Britain could never be expected to share French concern to the extent of accepting a loss of sovereignty in order to control Germany.

*　*　*

The fate of Germany impinged on all areas of post-war French foreign policy and was fundamentally important in shaping France's response to the Cold War and European unity. Before the war ended French planners had developed quite a comprehensive policy on Germany, based on the bitter experience of three invasions from across the Rhine in one lifetime and having much in common with plans devised after the First World War. It is easy in retrospect to argue that France's deep-seated fear of Germany was outmoded in the post-1945 context, that she overestimated her ability to carry her policy through, and that she ought to have seen that a mutual fear of Germany was unlikely to unite the Big Three for long. It is also difficult, however, to see how the French, following four years of Nazi occupation and given their traditional role as a Great Power, could have thought in radically different terms. It also needs to be understood that the country's German policy was designed to provide France herself with the economic resources to build a thriving, modern economy. The fact that France's policy was essential to both her international security aims *and* her post-war economic recovery made it extremely difficult to alter at a later date, especially when it proved so popular with the French people.

French planners saw their intentions of controlling Germany and tapping its resources for general European recovery as logical and sensible in view of past experience. The fact that they proved impossible to fulfil was not simply because of French weakness, but also because of East–West competition in Germany. Even in 1945 Britain's reluctance to let the Soviets share in the control of the Ruhr presented problems for French ambitions. The Ruhr was central to French concerns, but the British treated it in effect as their 'own' possession. In 1946 the Soviets and the Americans both proved willing to bid for German support and the French seemed isolated in German affairs, possessing only a small zone which, except for the Saar, was weak in resources. Although the French hoped, as late as March 1947, to preserve an independent policy, and were ready to contemplate co-operation with Russia, it was always most likely that they would turn to work with the Anglo-Americans, if only because the latter controlled the Ruhr. Nevertheless, when France adopted a policy of tripartite Western co-operation she did so cautiously and retained many of her previous aims. The Moscow CFM saw her end her insistence on the political separation of the Ruhr-Rhineland, but she still hoped, ambitiously, to bargain for industrial controls, security guarantees and political decentralisation in Germany. The difference was that she would do this in a three-power, rather than a four-power context. She did not plan meekly to accept an Anglo-Saxon vision of Germany's future.

The essential difficulty for French policy in Germany after 1945 was how to secure a German economic contribution to European recovery without recreating a new military menace. France never desired to 'pastoralise' Germany, as the US did in the Morghenthau Plan of 1943, but rather to use its resources safely, whilst granting German people a tolerable living standard. From the first, furthermore, French plans foresaw the return of Germany to the comity of nations, so long as this was on a basis of pacific co-operation, not domination. This explains why on several occasions the supposedly 'anti-German' de Gaulle spoke about the Rhine as an 'artery' for co-operation rather than a war frontier. To allow for such co-operation, however, certain conditions must first be met which would guarantee Germany's good behaviour. In 1945–47 it was planned to achieve this by separating the Ruhr-Rhineland and decentralising the rest of Germany. The Ruhr's resources would be utilised safely after being removed from German hands; Germany would turn to light industrial production and France and the Benelux states would supply Europe's heavy industrial needs. This policy has already been admirably explained by the British historian, Frances Lynch. But in early 1946 even French officials in Germany conceded that French policy risked economic ruin in Germany.[11] In 1947–49 France sought, in three-power talks, a strong control authority in the Ruhr and a decentralised west German government, and began to put great accent on European integration as a way to control Germany, though it was vital to secure controls within Germany *first*, before proceeding with European integration. But the Ruhr authority alienated German opinion, political decentralisation was largely a failure, and European integration did not progress far. The British and the Americans consistently argued that a German contribution to European recovery required the use of resources *within* Germany and the creation of an effective German government.

In 1949 France faced the danger of a run-away German revival, with a centralised government and heavy industrial base, and with the Anglo-Americans prepared to make only limited concessions to French fears. True, there were signs that the Germans themselves had undergone a fundamental transformation and abandoned militarism forever. In March 1947 in fact, Konrad Adenauer, who became Germany's first post-war Chancellor two years later, told a French official that the division of Germany must be accepted and that Western Germany's future lay with the West, in the defence of Romano-Christian culture.[12] The Quai noted too, in June 1947, that a meeting of German Minister-Presidents seemed more interested in creating a liberal-democracy in Western Germany than in reunification with the East.[13] Yet the French could be forgiven for remaining distrustful of the Germans and debate continued to rage in Paris between those, like Koenig and Couve de Murville, who put the accent on a policy of control in Germany, and those like François-Poncet and Camille Paris, who were more ready to pursue a policy of *rapprochement*. After the Washington talks in April 1949 there were still those in the Quai who remained critical of the German Basic Law[14] and France continued to favour Germany's inclusion 'in the European community' only alongside firm guarantees of the country's democratisation, denazification and demilitarisation.[15] President Auriol was still concerned about a possible nationalist revival in Germany and of a Russo-German combination, although Schuman himself felt that the last possibility was now extremely remote. The Foreign Minister did not believe that Germans would ever wish to become a People's Republic, nor did it appear that the Russians would accept Germany's reunification as a liberal-democratic state.[16] Europe and Germany, by implication, were likely to remain divided for years to come.

In October 1949, exasperated by the failure to get France and Germany to work together in the framework of Atlantic co-operation, and accepting that Britain would not join a European union, Dean Acheson told Schuman, 'Now is the time for French initiative to integrate the German Federal Republic promptly and decisively into Western Europe.[17] Only in May 1950, however, did the French decisively move to seize the initiative in German – and European – affairs, with the Schuman Plan. Based on ideas which had actually been circulating in Paris for two years or more, the Plan proposed to create a supranational authority through which to control the coal and steel industries of France, West Germany and any other country which wished to join. From a French point of view such a body would limit Germany's industrial independence, guarantee coal supplies from the Ruhr without alienating German opinion, make a Franco-German conflict impossible, and create a framework for wider *rapprochement* with Germany. To Adenauer it offered equality of treatment, a chance to tie the new Germany to other liberal-democracies, and an opportunity to change the policies of France, the occupation power which had hitherto opposed German revival. From a European perspective the Plan answered the Dutch (and, to a lesser extent, the Belgian and Italian) point that German economic revival was desirable; it provided an industrial economy (West Germany) which could balance the agricultural economies of France, the Benelux states and Italy; and, importantly, it allowed for progress without British membership.

The Schuman Plan's significance should not be exaggerated. It did not create a 'third force' able to match the superpowers, it embraced only two industries in six states, and its supranational element proved to be limited. To a large extent it represented a French retreat, in that Paris had to accept Germany, not as a weakened and subsidiary partner in European co-operation, as had been intended in 1948, but as an equal. It seems preposterous indeed to claim that the Plan 'controlled' Germany: it only worked because the German government proved ready to embrace West European integration in preference to a revived nationalist policy. Neither can the Schuman Plan be said to have brought a rapid change in French popular fears of Germany, for in the 1950s the French continued to seek ornate controls on their old enemy with the complex scheme to raise German armed forces only within a European Army. Nonetheless French planners like Jean Monnet deserve praise for their imagination and boldness. In May 1948 France had seemed to be staring at an abyss in foreign affairs, an abyss almost as dark as that which had faced them a decade before. In May 1950 however, it was seen that France was capable of having an impact on its external environment through independent action. French opposition to German recovery in 1945–49 had helped to damage European and Western co-operation in many spheres, but in 1950 the very fact that French fears drove them to accept the need for pooled sovereignty with Germany, opened up new vistas for them in the leadership of the movement towards European unification. France's fear of Germany may have appeared exaggerated later. But was it not the fear of a return to militarism and authoritarianism in Germany that also led Adenauer and other German liberal politicians to accept the radical course of European integration?

* * *

There were many reasons why France joined the Atlantic alliance in April 1949. The country's geographical position, liberal-democracy, capitalist economy, Western culture and imperial interests all pointed her towards this. The threat presented by the Red Army and the need for US financial assistance made such an arrangement seem vital. France joined the alliance for reasons which were different to those which exactly inspired America or Britain, however, and her hopes and fears for the future were also different to theirs. They never shared her apprehension about German revival to the same extent, they had not fallen from Great Power status to defeat and occupation during the war, they were not as vulnerable to Soviet invasion, nor did they have a large Communist minority that appeared capable of plunging them into civil war. The French frequently felt that the Anglo-Americans showed no understanding of their concerns: the unilateral actions of Generals Clay and Robertson in Germany, often made without proper reference to their governments, were particularly unsettling. In response the Americans and British could draw up a long list of, what seemed to them, legitimate complaints about French attitudes. Did the French really expect the US to provide large-scale military aid to Europe in 1948 in addition to Marshall aid? How could France expect a US military guarantee, yet deny this to other threatened countries such as Norway? Why did France not abandon its demand for the political separation of the Ruhr at an earlier date? Why did Bidault not explain to the French public in Spring 1948 that a major change in France's German policy was inevitable?

Differing perspectives between states are inevitable and the divisions between France, Britain and America (for there were always important differences between Britain and America too) in 1949 should not be exaggerated. The three did share common values, France was deeply grateful for US economic support, Paris did come to accept the division of Europe and indeed (not least in the pursuit of Franco-*West* German reconciliation in the context of West European integration) moulded her policies to suit this. Nevertheless, in tracing France's move from a Franco-Soviet alliance in 1944 to the Atlantic Pact in 1949 one also traces, inevitably, the roots of later disagreements within the Western alliance. Given the differences between France and Britain over Germany, the Brussels Pact and European Assembly in 1948, their inability to agree on the Schuman Plan in 1950 is not surprising. And in the debates over the Atlantic treaty may be found some reasons for de Gaulle's decision to take French forces out of NATO in the 1960s, after he returned to power and insisted once more that her independence be respected.

Notes

(Unless otherwise stated, place of publication is London)

Introduction

1. G. Elgey, *La République des Illusions, 1945–51* (Paris, 1965), 40.
2. C. de Gaulle, *War Memoirs, Vol. I, The Call to Honour* (1955), 9.
3. See especially C. de Gaulle, *L'Armée de Métier* (Paris 1934).
4. I owe this story to Dr C. M. Andrew of Corpus Christi College, Cambridge. On the de Gaulle–Churchill relationship see F. Kersaudy, *Churchill and de Gaulle* (1983).
5. For a short, general discussion of Anglo-French relations during the war see E. Barker, *Churchill and Eden at War* (1978), 31–122.
6. The Levant problem has received close attention from historians, but see especially Sir L. Woodward, *British Foreign Policy in the Second World War, Vol. I* (1970), 564–70 and *IV* (1975), 268–329 on the crises of 1941 and 1943.
7. Again, there are a large number of books on Franco-American relations in wartime, but notably: M. Viorst, *Hostile Allies: FDR and Charles de Gaulle* (1965); M. Ferro, *De Gaulle et l'Amérique* (Paris, 1973), part 1; and J. G. Hurstfield, *America and the French Nation, 1939–45* (Chapel Hill, North Carolina, 1986).
8. In general see M. Vigneras, *Rearming the French* (Washington, 1957); J. J. Dougherty, *The Politics of Wartime Aid: American Economic Assistance to France and French North-West Africa, 1940–6* (1979). According to Dougherty military lend-lease totalled $2,294 million to France, civilian lend-lease added $548 million and in return France provided $868 million in 'reciprocal aid'. Slightly different figures are given in G. Bossuat, 'L'aide américaine à la France après la seconde guerre mondiale', *Vingtième Siècle*, 9 (1986), 33.
9. See W. L. Langer, *Our Vichy Gamble* (New York, 1947).
10. E. Roosevelt, *As He Saw It* (New York, 1946), 115. And on Roosevelt's contempt for de Gaulle see, for example, E. Roosevelt, *The Roosevelt Letters* (1952), 456–7; O. Bullitt, ed., *For the President, Personal & Secret* (1973), 568; W. D. Hassett, *Off the Record with FDR* (1960), 152–3.
11. The full Resistance story is told by N. Noguères et al., *Histoire de la Résistance en France* (Paris, 5 vols., 1967–81) but a shorter introduction is H. R. Kedward, *Resistance in Vichy France* (1978). On the French Communists see R. Tiersky, *French Communism, 1920–72* (Columbia University Press, 1974), chapter 5; S. Courtois, *Le PCF dans la Guerre: de Gaulle, la Résistance, Staline . . .* (Paris, 1980); and for a strong defence of the PCF by one of de Gaulle's PCF ministers, F. Billoux, *Quand nous étions ministres* (Paris, 1972).
12. On the events in Algiers see especially: A. Kaspi, *La Mission de Jean Monnet à Alger* (Paris, 1971); A. L. Funk, *The Politics of Torch* (Kansas University Press, 1974); G. de Charbonnières, *Le Dual Giraud – de Gaulle* (Paris, 1984).
13. On Bogomolov see R. Murphy, *Diplomat among Warriors* (1964), 256–8; H. Macmillan, *War Diaries: the Mediterranean, 1943–5* (1984), entries of 13 Oct. and 1 Nov. 1943; R. Massigli, *Une Comédie des Erreurs* (Paris, 1978), 49–50.
14. Franco-Soviet wartime relations are discussed in: A. J. Rieber, *Stalin and the French Communist party, 1941–7* (1962), 7–50; C. de Grunwald, *Les Alliances Franco-Russes* (Paris, 1965); M. Mourin, *Les Relations Franco-Soviétiques, 1917–67* (Paris, 1967). There is a review of relations by the Quai in Ministère des Affaires Etrangères (MAE), Z/URSS/51 (25 Oct. 1944), and on de Gaulle's dissatisfaction with Russia in 1944 see MAE, Guerre/Alger/1264 (8 May).

15. For a fuller discussion see: J. B. Duroselle, 'Une création *ex nihilo*: le ministère des affaires etrangères du Général de Gaulle, 1940–2', *Relations Internationales*, 31 (1982), 313–22; also G. Dethan, 'France', in Z. Steiner, ed., *The Times Survey of the Foreign Ministeries of the World* (1982), 213–4.
16. Guerre/Alger/1487 (10 Oct. 1942).
17. ibid. (17 Jan. 1944).
18. France's inter-war policies are best reviewed in J. Néré, *The Foreign Policy of France, 1914–45* (1975).
19. Guerre/Alger/715 and 717, *passim*.
20. Guerre/Alger/718 and 1535, *passim*, and 1487 (10 Feb. 1944). And on the 12 August decisions: Service Historique, Armée de Terre, Vincennes, 4Q 10, dossier 5 (14 Dec.); P. Lassalle, 'Note sur la délimitation de la zone d'occupation', L'Institut d'Histoire de Temps Présent et l'Institut Charles de Gaulle, *De Gaulle et la Nation face aux Problèmes de Défense* (Paris, 1983) 227.
21. See R. Baillet, *De Gaulle et l'Europe* (Lyons, 1979), 33, 83–7.
22. Guerre/Alger/718 and 728 (17 and 30 Sept.); Massigli, *Comédie*, 37–8; R. Poidevin, 'René Mayer et la Politique Extérieure de la France', *Revue d'Histoire de la Deuxième Guerre Mondiale*, 134 (1984), 73–4. And, on French views of 'multilateralism', see: Guerre/Alger/686 (1 May, 1944); F. Bloch–Lainé & J. Bouvier, *La France Restaurée, 1944–54: dialogue sur le choix d'une modernisation* (Paris, 1986), 89–95. Mayer's paper is reproduced in *Institut Pierre Renouvin: travaux et recherches*, 2 (1988), 58–62.
23. J. Monnet, *Memoirs* (1978), 208–9 and 221–3. For ideas on European co-operation in 1944 from an official close to Monnet see: R. Marjolin, *Le Travail d'une Vie* (Paris, 1986), 128–31.
24. Guerre/Alger/718 (25 Oct.), 728 (Oct.), 729 (30, 31 Oct.); Massigli, *Comédie*, 38–42; *Institut Pierre Renouvin*, 62–6.
25. Guerre/Alger/718 (23 Oct.)
26. Massigli, *Comédie*, 29.
27. Guerre/Alger/728 (21 Aug.)
28. Guerre/Alger/718 (11, 28 Dec.).
29. Archives Nationales, Bidault Papers, box 82 (3 Dec., attached to note of 22 Nov. 1944).
30. Guerre/Alger/729 (2 Jan. 1944); Massigli, *Comédie*, 46. At this time all post-war studies were put under the control of André Philip.
31. According to a note by Blum–Picard of 27 March. See MAE, Z/Belgique/47 (2 Oct. 1944).
32. Guerre/Alger/718 (24 Feb.); C. de Gaulle, *War Memoirs, Vol. II, Unity, Documents* (1959), 618; Massigli, *Comédie*, 46; and M. and S. Bromberger, *Les Coulisses de L'Europe* (Paris, 1968), 90.
33. Guerre/Alger/718 (15, 17 March); Massigli, *Comédie*, 47–8.
34. Guerre/Alger/729 (18 March).
35. C. de Gaulle, *Discours et Messages, 1940–6* (Paris, 1970), 380–90.
36. Guerre/Alger/718 (20 March); Massigli, *Comédie*, 49–50.
37. Guerre/Alger/718 (20, 21 March).
38. ibid. (19 April).
39. ibid. (April–July); and on Dutch–Belgian views see J. W. Brouwer, 'Répondre à la Politique Européenne Française', in M. Dumoulin, ed., *La Belgique et les Débuts de la Construction Européenne* (Brussels, 1987), 60–8.
40. Guerre/Alger/729 (16 June).
41. Massigli, *Comédie*, 54–5; Macmillan, *War Diaries*, 10 July 1944.
42. See Woodward, *Second World War, V* (1976), 181–97.
43. Bidault papers, reference 779 (unindexed when consulted); and see Guerre/Alger/

1264 (23 July). Cot gave a similarly positive report about Russia to the Consultative Assembly's Foreign Affairs Commission later in the year: Assemblée Nationale, procès verbaux de la Commission des Affaires Etrangères (29 Nov., 6 Dec.).
44. Z/URSS/51 (3 Sept.).

Chapter 1

1. In general see R. Aron, *Histoire de la Libération de la France* (Paris, 1959); and on the French Army see J. S. Ambler, *The French Army in Politics* (Ohio State University, 1966), 70–81.
2. See especially, J. P. Rioux, *The Fourth Republic, 1944–58* (1987), chapter 2.
3. See for example Ministère des Affaires Etrangères (MAE), Z/Grande Bretagne/35 (10 and 11 Jan. 1945).
4. *Foreign Relations of the United States (FRUS), 1945, IV,* 661–5.
5. C. de Gaulle, *War Memoirs, Vol. III, Salvation, 1944–6* (1960), 8–9.
6. Teitgen, cited in J. Lacouture, *De Gaulle, Vol. II, La Politique, 1944–59* (Paris, 1985), 43–4.
7. De Gaulle, *Salvation,* 14, 45.
8. Debré and Claude Mauriac, cited in Lacouture, *La Politique,* 28, 209.
9. F. Seydoux, *Mémoires d'Outre-Rhin* (Paris, 1975), 82–5.
10. On Bidault see B. Ott, *Georges Bidault: L'indomptable* (Annonay, 1978) and G. Elgey, *La République des Illusions, 1945–51* (Paris, 1965), 126–30.
11. C. Mauriac, *The Other de Gaulle: diaries, 1944–54* (1973), 201.
12. L. Joxe, *Victoires sur la Nuit: mémoires 1940–6* (Paris, 1981), 243–4; and see G. Bidault, *Resistance* (1967), 59–60.
13. Mauriac, *The Other de Gaulle,* 53.
14. Bidault, *Resistance,* 60–1, 63.
15. See, for example, *Journal Officiel, Débats, Assemblée,* 17 Jan. 1946, 92–5, 102–4, 107.
16. By an *ordonnance* of 13 April and decree of 17 July. The following account of the organisation and major appointments in the Quai is based on: G. Dethan, 'France', in Z. Steiner, ed., *The Times Survey of the Foreign Ministries of the World* (1982), 214–20; Histoire de l'Administration Française, *Les Affaires Etrangères et le Corps Diplomatique Français, vol. II, 1870–1980* (Paris, 1984), 621–4, 650–3; J. Baillou and P. Pelletier, *Les Affaires Etrangères* (Paris, 1962); the *Annuaire Diplomatique et Consultaire de la République Française* (Paris, annual for 1947–49), which includes brief bibliographical details of all Quai staff.
17. G. Pedroncini, 'Journal de René Mayer', *Revue d'Histoire de la Deuxième Guerre Mondiale,* 129 (1983), 89.
18. Bidault, *Resistance,* 63; J. Chauvel, *D'Alger à Berne, 1944–52* (Paris, 1972), 77.
19. C. de Gaulle, *Discours et Messages, 1940–6* (Paris, 1970), 439–40; *FRUS, 1944, III,* 729–31, and see *1944, I,* 86–8.
20. Archives Nationales (AN), Bidault papers, box 78 (14 Sept., meeting with Cooper); MAE, B/Etats-Unis/107 (13 Sept., report of press service), 119 (29 Sept., re Caffery); *FRUS, 1944, I,* 1207 and *III* 731–6; Sir L. Woodward, *British Foreign Policy in the Second World War, vol. III* (1971), 73–9; and on Caffery see S. P. Sapp, *The US, France and the Cold War* (Ph.D. thesis, Kent State University, 1978), 9–12.
21. Evidence of Henry Stimson's diary, cited in G. Kolko, *The Politics of War* (1973), 93; *FRUS, 1944, III,* 737–9; and see J. G. Hurstfield, *America and the French Nation, 1939–45* (Chapel Hill, North Carolina, 1986), 220–1.
22. MAE, Z/Grande Bretagne/35 (29, 30 Sept., 16; 17 Oct.), and B/Etats-Unis/119

(13, 16 Oct.); W. S. Churchill, *The Second World War*, vol. *VI* (1954), 214–5; Woodward, *Second World War*, *III*, 79; R. Rhodes James, *Anthony Eden* (1986), 284. Churchill's speech laid down a difficult condition for recognition in the form of an elected French Assembly.

23. *FRUS, 1944, III*, 739–41; Churchill, ibid., 215–6; Woodward, ibid., 80–1; W. F. Kimball, ed., *Churchill and Roosevelt, the complete correspondence, vol. III: Alliance declining* (Princeton, N.J., 1984) 355–6.

24. Recognition of France could also pave the way for the recognition of the Italian government, and so win Italian–American votes: see H. G. Nicholas, ed., *Washington Despatches* (1981), 443.

25. W. D. Leahy, *I Was There* (1950), 321–2.

26. *FRUS, 1944, III*, 742–3.

27. ibid., 743–4; Churchill, *Second World War*, *VI*, 211, 217; Woodward, *Second World War*, *III*, 82–4; Kimball, *Alliance declining*, 367–8.

28. Bidault papers, box 82 (23, 24 Oct.); de Gaulle, *Salvation*, 48; C. de Gaulle, *War Memoirs*, vol. *III, Salvation, Documents* (1960), 54–66; de Gaulle, *Discours et Messages*, 456–69; Mauriac, *The Other de Gaulle*, 52–3; *FRUS, 1944, III*, 744–8; Woodward, ibid., 84–5.

29. MAE, Guerre/Alger/1264 (7 Aug.); Récherches Internationales à la Lumière du Marxisme, *Les Entretiens de Gaulle–Staline* (Paris 1959), 26–8.

30 *FRUS, 1944, I*, 85–6 and *III*, 729–30.

31. *FRUS, 1944, I*, 86–7; *Entretiens de Gaulle–Staline*, 29–30.

32 Public Record Office (PRO), London, FO 371/42060/5118, 8818; A. Berard, *Un Ambassadeur se Souvient, vol. I, Au temps du Danger Allemand* (Paris, 1976), 528–33.

33. *FRUS, 1944, I*, 88.

34. De Gaulle, *Salvation, Documents*, 27–8; *Entretiens de Gaulle–Staline*, 34–5.

35. De Gaulle, *Discours et Messages*, 443–51.

36. Mauriac, *The Other de Gaulle*, 21–3, 44.

37. De Gaulle, *Salvation, Documents*, 31.

38. *FRUS, 1944, I*, 90–3.

39. De Gaulle, *Salvation, Documents*, 30–1.

40. MAE, Z/URSS/51 (25, 27, 31 Oct.; 6 Nov.); and on the change in attitude see W. A. Harriman, *Special Envoy to Churchill and Stalin* (1976), 375.

41. *Entretiens de Gaulle–Staline*, 36–40; *FRUS, 1944, I*, 79–80, 92–6; Woodward, *Second World War, vol. V* (1976), 259.

42. *FRUS, 1944, I*, 96–7.

43. ibid., 97–8; *Woodward, Second World War, III*, 85.

44. Bidault papers, box 82 (11 Nov.); de Gaulle, *Salvation, Documents*, 81–3; *FRUS, 1944, I*, 98–100.

45. The decision was published on 9 October. V. Y. Ghebali, *La France en Guerre et les Organisations Internationales, 1939–45* (Paris, 1969) 199–200; *FRUS, 1944, I*, 737–43, 764–5; T. M. Campbell and G. C. Herring, eds., *The Diaries of Edward R. Stettinius Jr, 1943–6*, (New York, 1975), 111–2, 118.

46. De Gaulle, *Salvation*, 48–9; Chauvel, *D'Alger à Berne*, 96–7. And on Roncalli as Ambassador see: A. G. Roncalli (Pope John XXIII), *Mission to France, 1944–53* (1966); E. Fouilloux, 'Extraordinaire ambassadeur? Mgr. Roncalli à Paris', *Revue Historique*, 279, (1988), 101–28.

47. T. Sharp, *The Wartime Alliance & the Zonal Division of Germany* (Oxford, 1975), 77; F. R. Willis, *The French in Germany* (Stanford, Cal., 1962), 14.

48. See Sharp, ibid., 76–9.

49. De Gaulle, *Salvation, Documents*, 37; A. D. Chandler, *The Papers of Dwight D. Eisenhower, The War Years, vol. IV* (Baltimore, 1970), 2233.

50. De Gaulle, *Salvation*, 49–51, and see *Documents* 54–5 regarding 25 October.
51. MAE, Y/278 (21 Aug.); Guerre/Alger/1487 (21 Aug.); Bidault papers, box 60 (21 Aug.).
52. Y/369 (25 Sept.).
53. Y/362 (8, 9 Nov.); Y/394 (9, 20 Nov.); Bidault papers, boxes 60 (9, 20 Nov., and see Dec.) and 63 (8, 19 Nov.).
54. B/Etats Unis/107 (15 Jan.) and 119 (20, 23 Nov.); Y/7 (4–6 Nov.); Z/Grande Bretagne/35 (24, 31 Oct; 1, 3 Nov.); Bidault papers, box 80 (3, 21 Nov.); de Gaulle, *Salvation*, 52–3 and *Documents*, 67; Woodward, *Second World War, VI*, 85–6.
55. Massigli papers, vol. 53 (3 Nov.); Chauvel, *D'Alger à Berne*, 82–3.
56. On the visit in general see: Z/Grande Bretagne/35 (10–21 Nov.); C. de Gaulle, *Lettres, Notes et Carnets, 1943–5* (Paris, 1983), 352–3, *Salvation: Documents*, 79–81, and *Discours et Messages*, 475–6; Chauvel, ibid., 82–7; Churchill, *The Second World War*, 217–22; G. Pawle, *The War and Colonel Warden* (1963), 327–30; M. Gilbert, *Road to Victory: Winston S. Churchill, 1941–5* (1986), 1057–62; James, *Anthony Eden*, 286; *The Times* (14 Nov.).
57. Z/Grande Bretagne/35 (4, 7, 8 Nov.); Bidault papers, box 78 (4 Nov.).
58. Z/Grande Bretagne/35 (17 Nov.); Z/Généralités/4 (18, 24 Nov.); Massigli papers, vol. 53 (11 Nov., verbatim record); de Gaulle, *Salvation*, 53–5; Woodward, ibid., 86–90.
59. De Gaulle, ibid., 55–8. Churchill, *Second World War*, 218–9 says only that he and de Gaulle 'found plenty to talk about' on the 13th.
60. AN, Edouard Depreux papers, box 4 (17 Nov.).
61. *FRUS, The Conferences of Malta and Yalta* (Washington, 1955), 16–17, 283–8; Churchill, *Second World War III*, 219–22; Woodward, *Second World War, III*, 90–91; Ministry of Foreign Affairs of the USSR, *Stalin's Correspondence . . . during the Great Patriotic War of 1941–5*, (Moscow, 1957), part 1, 270–2; Kimball, ed., *Alliance declining*, 390–4.
62. Z/URSS/51 (14, 16 Nov); Bidault papers, box 82 (14 Nov.); de Gaulle, *Salvation*, 58; and see A. Werth, *De Gaulle* (1965), 182–3.
63. Bidault papers, box 83 (n.d.).
64. De Gaulle, *Salvation, Documents*, 56; and see Z/URSS/51 (25 Oct.) on Quai hopes for improved relations with Moscow.
65. *Sunday Times* (11 Nov.); Bidault, *Résistance*, 65; G. Catroux, *J'ai vu tomber le Rideau de Fer* (Paris, 1952), 12–13; A. de Porte, *De Gaulle's Foreign Policy, 1944–6* (Harvard University Press, 1969), 65–6, 71–4.
66. *Journal Officiel, Débats Assemblée*, 21 Nov. 1944, 309; 22 Nov., 330–2; de Gaulle, *Discours et Messages*, 480–5; and see also Assemblée Nationale, procès verbaux de la Commission des Affaires Etrangères (20 Nov.), for a speech by Bidault.
67. Z/URSS/51 (16–24 Nov.); Bidault papers, box 82 (20–23 Nov.); Massigli papers, vol. 93 (13 Dec.); Chauvel, *D'Alger à Berne*, 88.
68. Z/URSS/51 (27 Nov. – Dec.); de Gaulle, *Salvation*, 61–3; A. Juin, *Mémoires, vol. II, 1944–58* (Paris, 1960), 60–5; and J. Laloy, 'A Moscou: entre Staline et de Gaulle', *Revue des Etudes Slaves*, 1982, LIV, 137–41.
69. De Gaulle, ibid., 63; Lacouture, *La Politique,*, 87 (citing interview with Garreau).
70. De Gaulle, ibid., 64–5. Bidault and Dejean held separate political talks with Molotov, and Juin had talks with the Soviet military.
71. For example; Bidault, *Resistance*, 66; Laloy, 'A Moscou', 143.
72. There are great differences between the French and Soviet versions of this first meeting: de Gaulle, *Salvation*, 65–6, and *Documents*, 83–6; *Entretiens de Gaulle–Staline*, 43–50. See also Chauvel, *d'Alger à Berne*, 89; Laloy, ibid., 144; and, on the draft treaty text, Massigli papers, vol. 78 (22 Dec., enclosing 3 Dec.).
73. De Gaulle, *Salvation*, 68; and *Documents*, 87; Laloy, ibid., 143.

74. De Gaulle, *Salvation*, 66–7, and *Lettres, Notes et Carnets*, 348–9; Juin, *Mémoires, 1944–58*, 66; and G. Elgey, *La République des Illusions, 1945–51* (Paris, 1965), 15.

75. V. Mastny, *Russia's Road to the Cold War* (New York, 1979), 228–9.

76. General Sikorski Institute, *Documents on Polish–Soviet Relations, 1939–45, vol. II* (1965), 795; and see Bidault papers, box 89 (5 Dec.).

77. Bidault, ibid. (14 Nov.); Harriman, *Special Envoy*, 375–6.

78. De Gaulle, *Salvation*, 68–71; and *Documents*, 87–96; *Entretiens de Gaulle–Staline*, 51–60; Harriman, ibid., 376–7. After the meeting Molotov gave Bidault the Soviet counter-proposal to the French draft treaty: Massigli papers, vol. 78 (22 Dec., enclosing 6 Dec.).

79. *Documents on Polish–Soviet Relations*, 489.

80. Roosevelt did not like the idea of a Franco-Soviet–British pact, because it could undermine the value of the United Nations for world security. *FRUS, Malta and Yalta*, 288–91; *Stalin's Correspondence, I*, 277–82 and *II*, 170–2; Churchill, *Second World War*, 222–6; Woodward, *Second World War*, 91–4; Kimball, ed., *Alliance declining*, 440–1, 444–5.

81. De Gaulle, *Salvation*, 71 and *Documents*, 96–7; Lacouture, *Le Souverain*, 91 (citing Palewski interview); Laloy, 'A Moscou', 146; Churchill, ibid., 226–7; Woodward, ibid., 93–5.

82. De Gaulle, *Salvation*, 71–3, and *Documents*, 97–101, *Entretiens de Gaulle–Staline*, 61–9; Laloy, ibid., 146–7.

83. De Gaulle, *Salvation*, 73, 75, and *Documents*, 101–3.

84. Z/URSS/51 (10, 17 Dec.); Z/Pologne/54 (9 Dec.) Bidault papers, box 89 (9 Dec.); de Gaulle, *Salvation*, 75–82; *Documents*, 103–5; Bidault, *Resistance*, 68–9; Harriman, *Special Envoy*, 377–8; Juin, *Mémoires*, 70–2; Laloy, 'A Moscou', 147–52; B. Ledwidge, *De Gaulle* (1982), 191.

85. Chauvel, *d'Alger à Berne*, 89–90; and see Massigli papers, vol. 93 (11, 13 Dec.; 2, 4, 11 Jan.).

86. H. Alphand, *L'étonnement d'Etre* (Paris, 1977), 181.

87. See G. H. Gallup. ed., *The Gallup International Public Opinion Polls, France, 1939, 1944–75, vol. I*, (New York, 1976), poll of March 1945 showing 83 per cent support for the Soviet alliance.

88. Y/7 (22 Dec.).

89. See Mastny, *Russia's Road to Cold War*, 229–30.

90. Z/Pologne/54 (23–30 June, 1945); Bidault papers, box 89 (June–July, 1945).

91. *Journal Officiel, Débats, Assemblée*, 22 Dec., 579–81, 590–2, 595–6; de Gaulle, *Salvation, Documents*, 105–10; and *Discours et Messages*, 486–9; Elgey, *République des Illusions*, 39. Bidault and de Gaulle had reported on the treaty to the Cabinet on 17 December: Pedroncini, 'Journal de René Mayer', 94.

92. De Gaulle, *Salvation*, 58, 83; Bidault, *Resistance*, 67, 69–70.

93. Bidault papers, box 82 (25 Dec.).

94. Z/Pologne/54 (28 Dec.); E. Raczynski, *In Allied London* (1962), 252.

95. Z/Pologne/54 (31 Jan.).

96. R. Massigli, *Une Comédie des Erreurs* (Paris, 1978), 68–71; Massigli papers, vol. 93 (11, 30 Dec.).

97. Churchill, *Second World War*, 227–8; Woodward, *Second World War, III*, 95–6.

98. Churchill College, Cambridge, Duff Cooper papers, DUFC/4/5 (31 Dec.).

99. See Z/Allemagne/82 (Feb. 1945).

100. Bidault, *Resistance*, 63.

Chapter 2

1. C. de Gaulle, *War Memoirs, Vol III, Salvation* (1959), 139–47 and *Documents*, 203–10; de Gaulle, *Lettres, Notes et Carnets, 1943–5* (Paris, 1983), 368; J. de Lattre, *Ne Pas Subir: Ecrits 1914–52* (Paris, 1984), 309–11; A. D. Chandler, ed, *The Papers of Dwight D. Eisenhower, The War Years, Vol IV*, (Baltimore, 1970), 2392; and see also A. Juin, *Mémoires, Vol II, 1944–58* (Paris, 1960), 75–88.
2. De Gaulle, *Salvation*, 147–51 and *Documents*, 210–11; de Lattre, ibid, 317–9; Chandler, ibid, 2396 and 2399–401; D. Eisenhower, *Crusade in Europe* (1948), 395–6.
3. See above, 26.
4. Ministère des Affaires Etrangères (MAE), Y/7 (20 Dec. and see 15 Dec.).
5. ibid., (1 Jan.).
6. De Gaulle, *Lettres, Notes et Carnets*, 366; *Foreign Relations of the United States (FRUS), The Conferences of Malta and Yalta* (Washington, 1955), 292–3, 299.
7. G. Bidault, *Resistance* (1967), 85.
8. Archives Nationales (AN), Georges Bidault papers, box 80 (24 March).
9. MAE, Z/URSS/51 (27 March, 1 April).
10. MAE, B/Etats Unis/245 (15 Sept.); AN, F60/920, *passim*; J. Monnet, *Memoirs*, (1978), 224–5.
11. J. J. Dougherty, *The Politics of Wartime Aid* (1978), 163–9.
12. B/Etats Unis/245 (Jan.–Feb.); Archives Economiques et Financières (AEF), B. 33001; and see MAE, René Massigli papers, vol 91 (4 Jan., Alphand letter).
13. B/Etats Unis/119 (2 Feb.).
14. B/Etats Unis/245 (Feb.); F60/898 (19 Feb.) and 920 (15, 28 Feb. and n. d.); Bidault papers, box 80 (15, 16 Feb. and see 20 Nov.); Centre Jean Monnet, Lausanne, Monnet Papers, AMF/3/1/1,2, 4 and 6–10; Monnet, *Memoirs*, 225–6; P. Mioche, *Le Plan Monnet: genèse et elaboration, 1941–7* (Paris, 1986), 78–81.
15. In general see Dougherty, *Wartime Aid*, 173–83 and 189–201.
16. See for example J. Lacouture, *De Gaulle, Vol II, Le Politique 1944–59* (Paris, 1985), 113–14, 187.
17. AEF, Pleven papers, box 7 (4, 17 April, including quote); de Gaulle, *Salvation*, 118–23; P. Mendès-France, *Oeuvres Complètes, Vol II, Une Politique de l'Economie, 1943–54* (Paris, 1985), 55–126, 147–52.
18. For example in *Combat* on 22 May 1945.
19. See S. Bernstein, 'French power as seen by the Political Parties after World War II', in J. Becker and F. Knipping, eds, *Power in Europe?* (New York, 1986), 163–82.
20. See P. Buton, 'Le PCF et l'Armée', in L'Institut d'Histoire de Temps Present et l'Institut Charles de Gaulle, *De Gaulle et la Nation face aux Problèmes de Défense, 1945–6* (Paris, 1983), 155–8.
21. R. Tiersky, *French Communism, 1920–72* (Columbia University Press, 1974), 123–36.
22. See above, 22–3.
23. See above, 24; and on the tactics of French representatives see H. Footitt and J. Simmonds, *France 1943–5* (Leicester, 1988), 176–7.
24. S. P. Sapp, *The US, France and the Cold War: Jefferson Caffery and American–French relations* (PhD, Kent State University, 1978), 19–22; ibid., 180–81; and on the State Department see note 28.
25. Bidault papers, box 61 (Nov., 27 Dec.); *FRUS, 1944, I*, 427.
26. Lord Strang, *Home and Abroad (1956)* (1956), 220.
27. *FRUS, 1945, III*, 161–2.
28. *FRUS, Malta and Yalta*, 293–4; *FRUS, 1945, III*, 162–4.

29. *FRUS, Malta and Yalta*, 295, 729; *FRUS, 1945, III*, 177–81.
30. MAE, Y/121 (13–19 Jan.); B/Etats Unis/107 (15 Jan.); de Gaulle, *Salvation*, 83 and *Documents*, 110–11; *FRUS, Malta and Yalta*, 296–7.
31. Y/121 (20 Jan.); Public Record Office (PRO), London, FO 371/49066/1176.
32. M. Gilbert, *Road to Victory: Winston S Churchill, 1941–5* (1986), 1154–5, citing Churchill papers.
33. De Gaulle, *Salvation*, 83–4.
34. Stettinius put the French memorandum of 15 Jan. to Roosevelt without comment: *FRUS, Malta and Yalta*, 295–8.
35. C. de Gaulle, *Discours et Messages, 1940–6* (Paris, 1970), 502–14.
36. R. Sherwood, *The White House Papers of Harry Hopkins, vol II, 1942–5* (1949), 838; Bidault papers, box 80 (22 Jan.).
37. Y/7 (27, 28 Jan.) and 121 (8 Feb.); Bidault papers, box 80 (27–29 Jan.); *FRUS, 1945, IV*, 665–9 (including quotes from Caffery and Bidault); de Gaulle, *Salvation*, 84–7, 90 (including quote) and *Documents*, 11–16; Sherwood, *White House Papers*, 839–40; C. Bohlen, *Witness to History* (1973), 170; G. Pedroncini, 'Journal de René Mayer', *Revue d'Histoire de la Deuxième Guerre Mondiale*, 129 (1983), 96–7.
38. T. M. Campbell and G. C. Herring, eds, *The Diaries of Edward R Stettinius Jr 1943–61* (New York, 1975) 210–12.
39. See Sapp, *US, France and the Cold War*, 28–33, for a full account.
40. *FRUS, Malta and Yalta*, 570–3; Sherwood, *White House Papers*, 843; V. Beriejkov, *J'étais Interprète de Staline* (Paris, 1985), 314.
41. Sherwood, ibid, 849.
42. *FRUS, Malta and Yalta*, 498–9, 611–34, 699–711, 718–9, 885–6; 897–901; Sherwood, ibid., 849–50; Sir L. Woodward, *British Foreign Policy in the Second War, vol V* (1976), 275–82, 291–3, 297–8; W. S. Churchill, *The Second World War, vol VI* (1954), 307–9; W. A. Harriman, *Special Envoy to Churchill and Stalin* (1976), 402; Campbell and Herring, eds, *Diary of Stettinius*, 236–8. The Soviet Foreign Ministry's documents, *The Tehran, Yalta and Potsdam Conferences* (Moscow, 1969) have been doctored and only refer to the French zone on 126. As early as 25 October Vladimir Dekasonov told Roger Garreau that a French zone could be taken from areas designated to America and Britain: see Y/448 (25 Oct.).
43. Y/121 (12 Feb.) and 123 (14 Feb.); *FRUS, Malta and Yalta*, 948, and see 968–83; *FRUS, 1945, I*, 67–9; de Gaulle, *Salvation*, 87–9 and *Documents*, 118–21.
44. De Gaulle, *Salvation*, 87 and *Discours et Messages*, 515–19.
45. Bohlen, *Witness to History*, 204–5; W. D. Leahy, *I Was There* (1950), 383.
46. B/Etats Unis/107 (1 March), 119 (24 Feb., 1 March); Y/121 (14 Feb.); de Gaulle, *Salvation*, 89–92 and *Documents*, 121–3; *FRUS, 1945, IV*, 672–7; C. Mauriac, *The Other de Gaulle: Diaries 1944–54* (1973), 93–5.
47. Y/121 (13 Feb.–3 March).
48. Y/121 (13 and 16 Feb.); Y/675 (16 Feb.); Bidault papers, box 61 (16 Feb.); *FRUS, 1945, IV*, 669–71.
49. Y/121 (16–24 Feb.), 123 (25 Feb.) and 675 (20–25 Feb.); de Gaulle, *Salvation Documents*, 123–5 and *Lettres, Notes et Carnets*, 393–5; *FRUS, 1945, I*, 74, 76, 80, 83, and *IV*, 671–2.
50. MAE, Z/Grande Bretagne/35 (20–23 Feb.); Y/123 (25, 28 Feb.); FO 371/49066 /2359–3116; J. Chauvel, *D'Alger à Berne 1944–52* (Paris, 1972), 92–5; Woodward, *The Second World War, III* (1971), 97–9. France adhered to the Declaration on Liberated Europe in April: Y/121 (6, 14, 21 April).
51. Y/107 (28 March), 123 (4–9 March) and 675 (27 Feb.–7 March); *FRUS, 1945, I*, 90–3, 95–112; De Gaulle, *Salvation*, 197; Campbell and Herring, eds, *Diary of*

Stettinius, 269–72, 278–82; V. Y. Ghebali, *La France en Guerre et les Organisations Internationales, 1939–45* (Paris, 1969), 200–3.

52. See Y/40 (16 Jan.) on the Quai's view of 'small' nations. The Paul Boncour commission, which drew up the amendments, had been set up in December, following France's adhesion to the UN Declaration of 1942. Y/123 (Dec–March) and 124 (3 April); *FRUS, 1945, I* 201–3 and *IV*, 677–80; Campbell and Herring, ibid, 302; Ghebali, *ibid*, 200, 203; A. W. de Porte, *De Gaulle's Foreign Policy, 1944–6* (Harvard, 1968), 104–14. And see *Journal Officiel, Débats, Assemblée*, 27 March, 772–86; Bidault papers, box 80 (Nov.–Dec. 1944).

53. Britain's rating had risen slightly from 14 per cent to 18 per cent. In March 56 per cent expressed dissatisfaction with US attitudes towards France. G. H. Gallup, ed, *The Gallup International Public Opinion Polls, France, 1939, 1944–67* (1976). See also Footitt and Simmonds, *France 1943–5*, 211–14.

54. Y/362 (1 May – 25 June) and 690 (1 March – 1 May); Bidault papers, box 82 (30 March); *FRUS, 1945, III*, 1175–9, 1184–6, 1190–1209, 1220–1, 1230–6; *FRUS, The Conference of Berlin (Potsdam)* (Washington, 1960), 36–7, 512, 535–6; M. Mourin, *Les Relations Franco-Sovietiques* (Paris, 1967), 282.

55. G. A. J. Catroux, *J'ai vu tomber le Rideau de Fer* (Paris 1952), 9–13, 23–7, 31–7, 62–70; and see Bidault papers, box 82 (20, 30 March) for Catroux's pessimism regarding San Francisco.

56. For example, Massigli's papers, vol. 93, *passim*.

57. Woodward, *Second World War, III*, 95–6; Churchill, *Second World War, VI*, 227–8.

58. Z/Grande Bretagne/35 (9 Jan.); Massigli papers, vol 53 (30 Dec.; 9, 11, 25 Jan.; 7 Feb.); Bidault papers, box 78 (30 Dec.) R. Massigli, *Une Comédie des Erreurs* (Paris, 1978), 71.

59. Z/Grande Bretagne/35 (24–29 Jan.); Massigli papers, vol 53 (23 Jan.).

60. Y/40 (16 Feb.); Bidault papers, box 78 (1 Feb.).

61. De Gaulle, *Discours et Messages*, 515–9; Woodward, *Second World War, III*, 96–7.

62. The text was shown to the British. Z/Grande Bretagne/35; FO 371/49066/2788 and 49067/3587. The treaty was very different to a draft treaty drawn up during the war which aimed at a general *entente* in the fields of security, economics and Imperial interests: Bidault Papers, box 78 (nd).

63. FO 371/49066/2029.

64. ibid. (13 March); Massigli papers, vol 91 (13 March); Massigli, *Comédie*, 72–3.

65. The story of events in April can only really be constructed from British sources: FO 371/49067/4331 – 5274; PREM 8/173: Woodward, *Second World War, III*, 99–102. But see Massigli, ibid. 73; de Gaulle, *Lettres, Notes et Carnets*, 408 (letter to Bidault of 11 April).

66. De Gaulle, *Salvation: Documents*, 237–9; FO 371/49067/5427.

67. Gallup, ed, *Opinion Polls*, April 1945, shows 79 per cent support for the treaty idea.

68. The treaty was not discussed at San Francisco by Bidault and Eden: FO 371/49068/6595.

69. Z/Allemagne/30 (12 Feb.); Y/679 (12 Feb.) and 689 (Feb.–April); Bidault papers, box 60 (7 and 12 Feb.); and see M. T. Bitsch, 'Un rêve Francais: le désarmement économique de l'Allemagne', *Relations Internationales*, 51 (1987), 313–20.

70. Bidault papers, box 60 (22 Jan.).

71. Chauvel, *d'Alger à Berne*, 110–11.

72. Bidault, *Resistance*, 85–6.

73. Y/369 (30 March); Bidault papers, boxes 60 (30, and see 9 March), 63 (30 March).

74. See for example: Y/369 (1 May) and 689 (17 April); Massigli papers, vol 63 (17 April).

75. Chauvel, d'Alger à Berne, 109–10; Assemblée Nationale procès verbaux de la Commission des Affaires Etrangères (Feb.–June, *passim*.)
76. R. Murphy, *Diplomat among Warriors* (1964), 292–3.
77. A Berard, *Un Ambassadeur se Souvient, vol II, 1945–55* (Paris, 1978), 22.
78. Y/448 (17 April) and 692 (29 Dec., and see 17 Jan.); *FRUS, 1945, III*, 161–2.
79. The French originally favoured a joint occupation of Austria, but requested Tyrolia (which they eventually received) as their portion in the event of an occupation by zones.
80. Y/448 (17 April) and 692 (29 Jan.–9 Feb., including information on the Soviet Zone); Bidault papers, box 61 (2 Feb., 17 April); *FRUS, Malta and Yalta*, 297–8; *FRUS, 1945, III*, 182–3; P. Lassalle, 'Securité Française face à l'Est dans l'immédiat après-guerre', in *De Gaulle et la Nation face aux Problèmes de Défense*, 109–11. And see Service Historique, Armée de Terre (SHAT), Vincennes, 4Q 10, dossier 5 (22 Nov.–14 Dec.) on French reaction to the Soviet Zonal boundary.
81. Y/448 (17 April); Bidault papers, box 61 (9, 23 March); T. Sharp, *The Wartime Alliance and the Zonal Division of Germany* (Oxford, 1975), 165–71. The Russians did warn the French about British doubts: Z/URSS/51 (2 March).
82. See for example: Y/448 (16,23,24 May) and 692 (28 March, 24–28 April, 4 and 16 May); Bidault papers, box 61 (24 April; 23,24 May); de Gaulle, *Lettres, Notes et Carnets*, (Paris, 1984), 18 (including quote), 23–4; Sharp, ibid., 173–6, 181–4.
83. On US–French contacts see: Y/448 (2–20 April) and 692 (9 March–17 April); *FRUS, Malta and Yalta*, 297–8; *FRUS, 1945, III*, 182–3, 215, 222–3. And on de Gaulle's continuing hopes for a large zone in mid-April: C. de Gaulle, *Mémoires de Guerre: Le Salut, 1944–6* (Paris, 1959), 503–4. As late as 1 May Molotov expressed the hope to Bidault that the French and Soviet zones *would* touch: Bidault papers, box 82 (1 May).
84. *FRUS, 1945, III*, 242; Chandler, *Papers of Eisenhower, Vol IV*, 2640–1.
85. *FRUS, 1945, III*, 246–54; Chandler, ibid., 2623–4; Sharp, *Wartime Alliance*, 172–3, 176–8.
86. On the crisis see: de Gaulle, *Salvation* 167–70, *Documents* 220–6, and *Lettres, Notes et Carnets, 1943–5*, 404–7, 426; *FRUS, 1945, III*, 288 and *IV*, 680–7; Chandler, ibid., 2657–8 and 2670; Sharp, ibid., 137–41. The American memoirs which exaggerate the 'defeat' suffered by France include Eisenhower, *Crusade in Europe*, 412–3 and H. S. Truman, *Year of Decisions*, 156–7.
87. *FRUS, 1945, IV*, 686–7.
88. Sapp, *The US, France and the Cold War*, 70.
89. Y/448 (14,16,23,29 May; 5–11 June) and 692 (28 April – 4 June); Bidault papers, box 61 (23,24 May); *FRUS, 1945, III*, 255–6, 260–2, 275–6, 278, 297, 306–10, 320–2, 332, 339, 342–4. On negotiations for a zone see also: Y/692 (*passim*); SHAT, 4Q 10, dossier 5 (16 May – 11 June).
90. De Gaulle, *Salvation, Documents*, 272–3; the original is in Y/692, dated 11 June.
91. On Berlin see: Y/448 (26 June–21 July) and 692 (March – July); *FRUS, Conference of Berlin, I*, 597–64; Sharp, *The Wartime Alliance*, 186–98.
92. The additional agreements also included US transit rights across the French zone and French access to the Baden provincial archives. *FRUS, Conference of Berlin, II*, 1001–5; Sharp, ibid., 198–203.
93. Y/448 (*passim*, 1945–6).
94. De Gaulle, *Salvation*, 202–3; Chauvel, *d'Alger à Berne*, 108.
95. M. Hillel, *L'Occupation Française en Allemagne, 1945–9* (Paris, 1983), 142.
96. De Gaulle, *Salvation*, 203–4; Gallup, *Public Opinion Polls, France*, May 1945.
97. *Journal Officiel, Débats, Assemblée* 15 May 1945, 1051–3. On de Gaulle's declarations at the end of the war: de Gaulle, ibid., 175–6, *Documents*, 227, 231–2, *Discours et Messages, 1940–6*, 545–52, and *Lettres, Notes et Carnets*, 440–3.

98. De Gaulle, *Salvation*, 91, and *Documents*, 125–6.
99. Y/7 (14,16 April).
100. Y/8 (23 April, 1946).
101. Truman, *Year of Decisions*, 15; J. Bishop, *FDR's Last Year* (1974), 640.
102. B/Etats Unis/119 (20 April); Truman, ibid., 68–9.
103. De Gaulle, *Lettres, Notes et Carnets 1943–5*, 417–25; Paul-Emile Naggiar papers, MAE, vol. 12 (4, 17 April).
104. Paul Boncour papers, MAE, vol. 253 (note by Schlumberger).
105. De Gaulle, *Salvation: Documents*, 236–7.
106. De Gaulle, *Salvation*, 196–9; and in general see Ghebali, *La France en Guerre*, (Paris) 203–10.
107. On this point, see Bidault papers, box 80 (12 March).
108. Y/124, 125 (*passim*.); de Gaulle, *Salvation: Documents*, 245–6; *FRUS, 1945, I*, 574–5, 581–2, 588, 628–31; de Porte, *De Gaulle's Foreign Policy*, 114–25; M.-C. Smouts, *La France à l'ONU: premier rôle et second rang* (Paris, 1979), 48–69.
109. Truman, *Year of Decisions*, 83–5.
110. Y/124 (30 April).
111. Bidault papers, box 82 (1 May).
112. De Gaulle, *Salvation, documents*, 245–6.
113. B/Etats Unis/119 (10 May); Y/124 (10 May); MAE, Asie, 1944–55, Dossiers Généraux, vol. 47 (10 May).
114. *FRUS, Conference of Berlin*, 16–17; Bidault papers, box 81 (9 Aug.).
115. *Ibid* 17–18; *FRUS, 1945, IV*, 687–91; Truman, *Year of Decisions*, 158–9.
116. Y/124 (18–22 May); *FRUS, 1945, IV*, 691–700; Berard, *Un Ambassadeur*, 26. Grew was not alone in his ideas. In March 1946 the British minister Hugh Dalton felt that the Saar population should be replaced by 'Poles and others who can readily be assimilated into the French population': Hugh Dalton Diary, British Library of Political and Economic Science, London, entry of 22 March 1946.
117. Z/Italie/92 (10, 20 Sept.; and 1945 in general on the separatist movements); and see Bidault papers, box 92 (21 March) on studies of Alpine border changes.
118. Z/Italie/92 (15 Jan.).
119. De Gaulle, *Lettres, Notes et Carnets, 1943–5*, 437; P. Guillen, 'Les Relations Franco-Italiennes de 1943 à 1949', *Revue d'histoire Diplomatique*, (1976), 129–34.
120. Z/Italie/92 (3 April); *FRUS, 1945, IV*, 725–8; de Gaulle, *Salvation*, 160–2, 179–80, *Documents*, 222, *Lettres, Notes et Carnets, 1943–5*, 416–7.
121. Bidault papers, box 92 (16, 18 May); de Gaulle, *Salvation: Documents*, 246–7, *Lettres, Notes et Carnets, 1945–51*, 17, 21–2; *FRUS, 1945, IV*, 695–700, 728–32; and see A. Tarchiani, *Dieci Anni Tra Roma e Washington* (Milan, 1955), 66–7.
122. But, at the time, de Gaulle did approve a tough line by Doyen. De Gaulle, *Salvation*, 180–1; Sapp, *The US, France and the Cold War*, 63–4; and see Z/Italie/92 (30 May).
123. On the exchanges of letters see: de Gaulle, *Salvation*, 181–2, *Salvation*, 265–6, 269–72, *Lettres, Notes et Carnets, 1945–51*, 32; *FRUS, 1945, IV*, 732–5. On the consideration in Washington: Truman, *Year of Decisions*, 160; Sherwood, *White House Papers, II*, 904–5; Leahy, *I Was There*, 436; G. Kolko, *The Politics of War* (1969), 93 (citing Stimson diary); Churchill, *Second World War, VI*, 493–4.
124. *FRUS, 1945, IV*, 736–7; Berard, *Un Ambassadeur*, 28. And on Massigli: Massigli papers, vol 91 (2 June); Bidault papers, box 92 (7 June).
125. *FRUS, 1945, IV*, 737–40.
126. ibid., 740–1; FO 371/49075/7205; Sapp, *The US, France and the Cold War*, 63–4; and see Bidault, *Resistance*, 76–8.
127. There was also a 15-mile 'demilitarisation zone' on the Franco-Italian border, and the Italian government agreed to respect Valdotian rights. The French were upset

later in the year when the military government was brought to an end. Bidault papers, box 92 (31 July, 23 Nov.); de Gaulle, *Lettres, Notes et Carnets, 1945–51*, 55–6, 135; *FRUS, 1945, IV*, 741–57.

128. Massigli papers, vol. 93 (12 June); and see Truman's condemnation of de Gaulle in *Year of Decisions*, 155.
129. De Gaulle, *Salvation*, 180–3.
130. De Gaulle, *Lettres, Notes et Carnets, 1943–5*, 423–4.
131. For example, Hansard, House of Commons debates, vol. 408, col. 1290.
132. For two very different French accounts of the mounting crisis see: de Gaulle, *Salvation*, 183–8; Chauvel, *d'Alger à Berne*, 104–7; and see Woodward, *Second World War, IV* (1975), 324–33 on Britain's concern.
133. For an excellent critique of de Gaulle's account of the Levant crisis in *Salvation* see F. Kersaudy, 'Le Levant', in *De Gaulle et La Nation face aux Problèmes de Défense*, 249–61. Of the numerous accounts of the crisis see: de Gaulle, *Salvation*, 188–92; Churchill, *Second World War, VI*, 490–3; de Porte, *De Gaulle's Foreign Policy*, 135–51; G. Kirk, *The Middle East in the War* (1952), 292–305; H. M. Sachar, *Europe leaves the Middle East* (New York, 1972), 135–51.
134. De Gaulle, *Salvation*, 192.
135. FO 371/49068/7531.
136. De Gaulle, *Salvation: documents*, 253–64.
137. See 2/URSS/51 (2 March), 52, (3 June); Woodward, *Second World War, IV* 338–43.
138. Sapp, *The US, France and the Cold War*, 58–63. And on US attitudes in general: de Gaulle, *Salvation, Documents*, 249–50; *FRUS, Conference of Berlin, I*, 959–61; Truman, *Year of Decisions*, 161; Woodward, ibid., 337–8.
139. De Gaulle, *Salvation*, 193; J. Vendroux, *Cette Chance que j'ai eue... 1920–57* (Paris, 1974), 124.
140. *Journal Officiel, Debats*, 16 June, 1114–30, and 19 June, 1134–50; de Gaulle, *Salvation*, 194–5 (including quote), and *Discours et Messages*, 573–80. For a deputy's view see also: A. Pierre-Viénot, 'The Levant Dispute: The French case', *London Quarterly of World Affairs, IX*, 3 (Oct. 1945), 219–28. Gallup, *International Public Opinion Polls, France*, July 1945 shows the French people also felt Britain was most to blame for the crisis.
141. See J. W. Young, The Foreign Office and the Departure of General de Gaulle, 1945–6' *Historical Journal, XXV*, (1982), 209–16.

Chapter 3

1. Ministère des Affaires Etrangères (MAE), Y/281 (30 June).
2. Y/692 (30 July); *Foreign Relations of the United States (FRUS), 1945, vol. III*, 820–3.
3. A *Mission Militaire pour les Affaires Allemandes* was created on 18 Nov. 1944 under General Louis-Marie Koeltz to deal with the Allies on French interests in Germany until the occupation began. Under this body was an *Administration Militaire* which recruited staff and prepared directives for the occupation forces. The directives relied heavily on similar work by Eisenhower's staff at Supreme Headquarters. See J. Vaillant, 'L'Occupation Française en Allemagne', in l'Institut d'Histoire de Temps Présents et l'Institut Charles de Gaulle, *De Gaulle et la Nation face aux Problèmes de Défense* (Paris, 1983), 221.
4. See directives issued by the *Secrétariat-Général aux Affaires Allemandes et Autrichiennes*: Y/282 (16, 30 July); Y/650 (19 July); Archives Nationales (AN), Bidault Papers, box 61 (19 July).

5. Y/363 (7 July); AN, F60/900 (7, 13 July).
6. Y/281 (2 June).
7. Bidault papers, box 61 (20 June).
8. See R Butler, ed., *Documents on British Policy Overseas (DBPO), Series 1, Vol 1* (London, 1984), 71.
9. Y/282 (15 July)
10. On these points see Vaillant, 'L'occupation Française en Allemagne', 222–3.
11. Established by a decree of 7 July 1945, the *Comité Interministériel pour les Affaires Allemandes et Autrichiennes* (Interministerial Committee for German and Austrian Affairs) included de Gaulle, Bidault, René Mayer, the zonal commanders from Austria and Germany, and representatives from the defence ministry, economic ministries and EMDN. See Y/650, 651. There was also a *Sous-commission Economique* of officials, under Alphand.
12. The *Commissariat-Général* was created by a decree of 26 Dec. 1945, which also established an interministerial *Commission des Territoires Occupés* which discussed such day-to-day occupation matters as food and fuel supplies personnel and transport. Y/651 (for meetings of the commission); Y/653 (26 Dec., 31 Jan.).
13. For discussions of French occupation policy: F. R. Willis, *The French in Germany* (Stanford, Cal., 1962); C. Scharf & H. J. Schröder, *Die Deutschlandpolitik Frankreichs und die Französische Zone, 1945–9* (Wiesbaden, 1983); and a 'popular' account, M. Hillel, *L'Occupation Française en Allemagne* (Paris, 1983).
14. M. F. Ludmann-Obier, 'Un aspect de la chasse aux cerveaux', *Relations Internationales*, 46 (1986), 195–208, especially 208.
15. The meeting had been rumoured for some time: Y/126 (18 June).
16. C. de Gaulle, *War Memoirs, Vol. III, Salvation* (1959), 199–201; and see A. Fontaine, 'Potsdam: a French view', *International Affairs*, 46 (1970), 466–74.
17. Y/7 and 362 (25 June); *FRUS, The Conference of Berlin (Potsdam)*, (1960) 128–9, 512, 938, 961–2. At this time Bonnet also feared that a visit by Harry Hopkins to Stalin could lead to a US-Soviet *entente* which could damage French interests: MAE, B/Etats Unis/107 (25 June).
18. Y/121 and 126 (5 July); *FRUS, Conference of Berlin*, 147–8, but see 219.
19. Y/126 (7 July); MAE, René Massigli papers, vol. 60 (7 July).
20. *FRUS, Conference of Berlin*, 251–3.
21. ibid., 592–6.
22. B/Etats Unis/107 (24 Jan.); Y/448 (29 June). Actually, in January, there were fears in Washington that French policy in the Rhineland could result in eventual 'annexation': *FRUS, The Conferences of Malta and Yalta* (Washington, 1955), 297–8.
23. *FRUS, Conference of Berlin*, 496–7, see also 183, 989–1103.
24. At the same time the EAC was run down. Y/126 (31 July–2 Aug.); Y/134 (31 July); Bidault papers, box 6 (31 July); and for the Potsdam protocol see: ibid., 1543–7; *DBPO, vol. I*, 1263–77.
25. On the Anglo-Saxon explanations see: Y/126 (4–14 Aug., 9 Dec.); B/Etats Unis/107 (Aug.); Bidault papers, box 6 (4 Aug.). On Molotov see: Bidault papers, box 6 (25 Aug.), G. Catroux, *J'ai vu tomber le Rideau de Fer* (Paris, 1952), 106–8.
26. Y/126 (4 Aug.); Bidault papers, box 6 (7 Aug.).
27. Y/126 (2 Aug.); C. de Gaulle, *Lettres, Notes et Carnets, 1945–51* (Paris, 1984), 52–3.
28. Y/126 (4 Aug.); *FRUS, Conference of Berlin*, 1548–9. St Hardouin had raised exactly the same points with Murphy in mid-July, when 'central agecies' were already rumoured: Y/282 (15 July).
29. Y/126 and 134 (4–8 Aug.); Bidault papers, box 6 (7 Aug.); de Gaulle, *Lettres, Notes et Carnets*, 54–5; *Documents Français relatifs à l'Allemagne, Août 1945 –*

Fevrier 1947 (government publication, Paris, 1947), 7–11; *FRUS, Conference of Berlin*, 1549–55.

30. Y/126 (9 Aug.).
31. Y/126 (17 Aug.); *FRUS, Conference of Berlin*, 1556–7.
32. This decision was kept secret to prevent Germans 'scuttling' the ships, as they had after the first World War. B/Etats Unis/107 (27 Sept.); F60/922 (13 Sept.); *FRUS, Conference of Berlin*, 1557, 1564–6.
33. De Gaulle, *Lettres, Notes et Carnets*, 20.
34. ibid., 37–8; MAE, Asie 1945–55, Dossiers Généraux, vol. 47 (28 May – 25 June); *FRUS, Conference of Berlin*, 938–40, 1341–9, 1548.
35. Y/19 (20 Aug.); de Gaulle, *Salvation: Documents*, 283; H. S. Truman, *Year of Decisions* (1955), 389.
36. For discussions of Indochina during the war see especially: W. Lafeber, 'Roosevelt, Churchill and Indochina, 1942–5' *American Historical Review*, 80 (1975), 1277–95; C. Thorne, 'Indochina and Anglo-American relations, 1942–5', *Pacific Historical Review*, XLV (1976), 73–96; W. R. Louis, *Imperialism at Bay* (1977), 27–47, 283–5, 436–7, 551–2; J. Valette, 'Le Gouvernement des Etats-Unis et l'Indochine', *Revue d'Histoire de la Deuxième Guerre Mondiale*, 138 (1985), 43–62; G. C. Herring, 'The Truman Administration and the Restoration of French Sovereignty in Indochina', *Diplomatic History*, 1 (1977), 97–117.
37. *FRUS, 1945, VI*, 295, 300.
38. But especially the British. On de Gaulle's views sees: de Gaulle, *Salvation: Documents*, 281–2, and *Lettres, Notes et Carnets*, 57–9, 69–72, 78, 82–4 88–9; MAE, René Mayer papers, vol. 2 (16 Sept.).
39. P. M. Dunn, *The First Vietnam War* (1985) gives a full account of Gracey's mission.
40. On the return of French rule in Indochina in 1945–6 see especially: P. Isoart & C. Hesse d'Alzon, 'Les charges de l'heure: l'Indochine', *De Gaulle et la Nation face aux problèmes de Défense*, 264–82; and the introduction to G. Bodinier, *Le Retour de la France en Indochine, 1945–6: textes et documents* (Vincennes, 1987).
41. De Gaulle, *Lettres, Notes et Carnets*, 105.
42. P. Isoart, 'Les charges de l'heure', 268–70.
43. De Gaulle agreed to a meeting in principle on 29 May, in either France or America, but did not want to hold it at the time of a Big Three meeting. Dates were finally set in July. B/Etats Unis/119 (3 July); Y/19 (29 May, 3–12 Aug.); de Gaulle, *Salvation*; 205–6, and *Documents*, 247–8, 275; A. Berard, *Un Ambassadeur se souvient, Vol. I, Au temps du Danger Allemand* (Paris, 1976), 27; *FRUS, 1945, IV*, 700–2.
44. Y/7 (20 July, 3 August).
45. ibid. (16 Aug.); B/Etats Unis/119 (23 July), the views of Armand Berard.
46. *FRUS, 1945, IV*, 703 and see 703–7 in general on Caffery's view of French policy.
47. B/Etats Unis/245 (especially 20 Aug.); F60/921 (17–20 Aug.).
48. See, for example, Bidault papers, box 80 (17 Aug.).
49. On the briefs for the visit see: Y/19 (13 Aug.); Bidault papers, boxes 60 (Aug. 1945), 63 (11 Aug.), 80 (11–21 Aug.), and 81 (7 Aug.).
50. Bidault papers box 80 (21 Aug.). On the Trieste problem in 1945 as a forerunner of containment see R. Rabel, 'Prologue to Containment' *Diplomatic History*, 10 (1986), 141–60.
51. B/Etats Unis/107 (21 Aug.).
52. Y/681 (16 Aug.); Bidault papers, box 81 (16 Aug.).
53. See Y/19 (7 Sept.); de Gaulle, *Salvation: Documents*, 289–91 (including first quote); and H. G. Nicholas, *Washington Despatches* (1981), 609–10, 613 (including

second quote). On the visit in general see: de Gaulle, *Lettres, Notes et Carnets*, 62–6, and *Discours et Messages, 1940–6* (Paris, 1970), 602–9; Berard, *Un Ambassadeur*, 29–30; H. Alphand, *L'Etonnement d'Etre* (Paris, 1977), 187.

54. S. Bidault, *Souvenirs* (Paris, 1987), 34–41.

55. De Gaulle, *Salvation*, 206–13; J. L. Gormly, *The Collapse of the Grand Alliance, 1945–8* (Baton Rouge, Louisiana, 1987), 16 (on Bidault); and see Berard, *Un Ambassadeur*, 30–1 on US power.

56. *FRUS, 1945, IV*, 725.

57. Y/19 (22 Aug.); Bidault papers, box 80 (22 Aug.); de Gaulle, *Salvation: Documents*, 283–7; *FRUS, 1945, IV*, 707–11.

58. Bidault and Byrnes had a further meeting on the 24th. Y/19 (23, and see 24, Aug.); Bidault papers, boxes 6 and 80 (23, 24 Aug.); *FRUS, 1945, IV*, 711–24; *FRUS, Conference of Berlin*, 1557–64.

59. F60/900 (26 June). Bidault had raised this problem with Caffery after Potsdam: Y/126 (4 Aug.).

60. Y/19 (24 Aug.); Bidault, box 80 (24 Aug. and see 31 Aug. for conclusions about the visit); de Gaulle, *Salvation: Documents*, 287–9.

61. B/Etats Unis/245 (especially 26 Aug.); Bidault, box 80 (26 Aug.); F60/921 (31 Aug., 1 Sept.).

62. Centre Jean Monnet, Lausanne, Monnet Papers, AMF 3/2/1–19, 3/3/2–30, and see 4/3/5, 6, 10 on coal; J. Monnet, *Memoirs* (1978), 226, 228; F. Lynch, *The Political and Economic Reconstruction of France* (Ph.D., Manchester University, 1981), 300–2; P. Mioche, *Le Plan Monnet: Genèse et Elaboration, 1941–7* (Paris, 1987), 81–4; and see de Gaulle, *Lettres, Notes et Carnets*, 103 on the October loan agreement.

63. For French accounts of the London CFM: Berard, *Un Ambassadeur*, 33–59; Catroux, *Rideau de Fer*, ch. 10. And on French preparations: Y/134 (15 Aug. – 10 Sept.) 676 (31 July – 5 Sept.), 679, 680 and 681; Bidault papers, box 6 (15, 18 Aug., 5 Sept.).

64. *FRUS, 1945, II*, 109.

65. On Labour views see: T. D. Burridge, *British Labour and Hitler's War* (1976), 142–4, 159–60. On Foreign Office thinking see *DBPO, vol. I*, 234–51, 868–80.

66. MAE, Z/Grande Bretagne/35 (9 Aug.); Bidault papers, box 78 (9 Aug.); Massigli papers, vol. 53 (9 Aug.).

67. Public Record Office (PRO), London, FO 371/49069/9595; Alexander Cadogan diary, Churchill College, Cambridge, ref. 1/15 (13 Aug.); Oliver Harvey diary, British Library, London, manuscript 56400; D. Cooper, *Old Men Forget* (1954), 361.

68 Bidault papers, box 78 (16 August); FO/371/49069/9525, and 45581/6094; R. Massigli, *Une Comédie des Erreurs* (Paris, 1978), 61, 69–70, 74–6.

69. FO 371/49069/9525; Cooper, *Old Men Forget*, 362.

70. De Gaulle, *Salvation: Documents*, 279–80.

71. FO 371/45582/6321.

72. De Gaulle, *Salvation: Documents*, 291–2, and (the full version) *Lettres, Notes et Carnets*, 75–7.

73. *The Times*, 10 Sept.; Z/Généralités/4 (10, 12 Sept.); MAE, René Mayer papers, vol. 2 (11 Sept.); de Gaulle, *Salvation: Documents*, 292–7, and *Discours et Messages*, 614–19; Berard, *Un Ambassadeur*, 33–4; Massigli, *Comédie*, 76–8.

74. Z/Grande Bretagne/35 (11 Sept.); Bidault papers, box 78 (10 Sept.); Massigli papers, vol. 53 (11, 13 Sept.); Mayer papers, vol. 2 (13 Sept.).

75. Mayer papers, vol. 2. (11, 13 Sept.).

76. He made this apparent *before* the conference: Y/676 (4 Sept.); Bidault papers, box 78 (10 Sept.).

77. On the Chequers meeting see: Z/Grande Bretagne/35 (15 Sept.); ibid. (13, 15 Sept.); Massigli papers, vol. 53 (15 Sept.); FO 371/45582/6840, 6960; R. Bullen, ed., *DBPO, Series 1, Volume 2* (1985), 190–2; Cooper, *Old Men Forget*, 263–4; and see J. Chauvel, *D'Alger à Berne, 1944–52* (Paris, 1972), 63–4.

78. Bidault papers, box 6 (19 Sept.).

79. J. W. Young, *Britain, France and the Unity of Europe, 1945–51* (Leicester, 1984), 19–21.

80. See, for example, Berard, *Un Ambassadeur*, (Paris) 50–1.

81. On the first meeting see: MAE, *Conseil des Ministères des Affaires Etrangères (CMAE), vol. I, Londres* (Paris, 1946), 1st meeting; *FRUS, 1945, II* 112–23; *DBPO, vol. II*, 100–10. Copies of the French records on all London meetings are in: Y/135, 136; Bidault papers, box 6; and shelved, as reference AFA, at the *salle de lecture*, MAE.

82. Y/134 (18 Aug.; 5, 11 Sept.) and 676 (18 Aug., 5 Sept.); Bidault papers, box 6 (18 Aug; 5, 12 Sept.); and see *DBPO, vol. II*, 85–7, 136–41.

83. For copies of the memorandum see: Y/134 (dated 13 Sept.); Bidault papers, box 6 (14 Sept.); *Documents Français relatifs à l'Allemagne*, 13–15; *CMAE, Documents relatifs à l'Allemagne, 1945–7* (Paris, 1948), 4–6; *FRUS, 1945, II*, 177–9 and *III*, 869–71; *DBPO, vol. II*, 148–50; B. Ruhm von Oppen, ed., *Documents on Germany under Occupation, 1945–54* (1955), 66–8. See also Y/369 (6 Sept.) 679 (8 Sept.) and 689 (8 Sept.) on French views on the Germany border.

84. Mayer papers, vol. 2 (16 Sept.); de Gaulle, *Lettres, Notes et Carnets*, 81–2.

85. The memorandum was accepted onto the agenda on 17 Sept.: *CMAE, vol. I*, 6th meeting; *FRUS, 1945, II*, 203; *DBPO, vol. II*, 196.

86. *CMAE, vol. I*, 23rd mtg.; Bidault papers, vol. 6 (27 Sept.); *FRUS, 1945, II*, 399–410; *DBPO, vol. II*, 382–8; Berard, *Un Ambassadeur*, 57–8.

87. Bidault papers, box 6 (27, 28 Sept.); *CMAE, vol. I*, 25th mtg.; *FRUS, 1945, II*, 428–34; *DBPO, vol. II*, 410–13; Berard, ibid., 58. Until early October Bidault hoped it might be possible to discuss the Ruhr with British *and* US officials immediately after the CFM closed: Y/394 (8–12 Oct.); Bidault papers, box 61 (8 Oct.).

88. Y/134 (29 Sept.); Bidault papers, box 6 (30 Sept.); de Gaulle, *Lettres, Notes et Carnets*, 89.

89. On the development of French reparations policy see, e.g., Y/363 and 369 (20 July); Bidault papers, box 80 (11 Aug.); F60/900 (9 April; 28, 31 May); AN, Raoul Dautry papers, box 165 (especially 14 June, 20 July).

90. The French delegation to the Reparations Commission was established by de Gaulle on 3 August, with representatives from the Quai, the Chiefs of Staff and various economic ministries. See Y/362 (3 Aug. – 6 Sept.) and 690 (28 July – 18 Aug.); F60/922 (13 Aug. – 5 Sept.); Bidault papers, box 63 (10, 18 Aug.); Dautry papers, ibid. (Aug.–Sept.) *FRUS, 1945, III*, 1254–5, 1262–6, 1278–87.

91. For the French memorandum: *CMAE, documents relatifs à l'Allemagne*, 6–7; *FRUS, 1945, II*, 285–7.

92. See above, note 24, on the Potsdam agreements.

93. Y/362 (3 Oct.).

94. Discussions on the issue occured on 25 and 27 Sept.: *CMAE, vol. I*, 21st, 24th and 29th mtgs.; *FRUS, 1945, II*, 370–8, 421–5, 475–8, and *III*, 1293–8, 1306, 1309–10, 1321, 1324–9; *DBPO, vol. II*, 361–5, 399–404, 430–4; Berard, *Un Ambassadeur*, 57–8; and see Y/134 (26 Sept.); Y/362 (14, 22 Sept.).

95. See above.

96. Y/134 (16 Sept.) and see 680 (*passim*); Bidault papers, box 92 (9 Aug.–24 Sept.; Jan. 1946); Mayer papers, vol. 2 (16–18 Sept.); de Gaulle, *Lettres, Notes et Carnets*, 81, 180–1. The French also wanted a 'demilitarised zone' on the Italian side of

the Alps: *CMAE, vol. I*, 6th mtg.. And Bidault demanded the restitution of goods removed by Italy from France: 7th mtg.

97. *CMAE, vol. I*, 3rd and 4th mtgs.; Bidault papers, box 6 (14 Sept.); Mayer papers, vol. 2 (14 Sept.); *FRUS, 1945, II*, 158–63; Berard, *Un Ambassadeur*, 37–9; *DBPO, vol. II*, 152–67.

98. *CMAE, vol. I*, 8th–11th mtgs.; Mayer papers, vol. 2 (19 Sept.).

99. C. Mauriac, *The Other de Gaulle: diaries 1944–54* (1973), 133.

100. Y/134 (15 Sept.); Bidault papers, box 6 (14, 15 Sept.) and box 92 (14 Sept.); Mayer papers, vol. 2 (14 Sept.); *CMAE, vol. I*, 3rd–4th mtgs.; *FRUS, 1945, II*, 166–75; Berard, *Un Ambassadeur*, 39–41; *DBPO, vol. II*, 152–67.

101. De Gaulle, *Lettres, Notes et Carnets*, 81.

102. Mayer papers, vol. 2 (15 Sept.); *CMAE, vol. I*, 5th Mtg.; *FRUS, 1945, II*, 186–94; Berard, *Un Ambassadeur*, 42; *DBPO, vol. II*, 172–80.

103. Mayer papers, vol. 2 (25 Sept.); de Gaulle, *Salvation: Documents*, 302–3; P. Nenni, *Tempo di Guerra Fredda: Diari, 1943–56* (Milan, 1981) 148. See also Bidault papers, box 91 (10 Oct., talk with Saragat).

104. See Y/134 (21 Sept.) for a review of the CFM at this point.

105. On the growing Soviet-Western differences: Berard, *Un Ambassadeur*, 35, 41–4, 51–5.

106. Z/Généralités/45 (19 Sept.).

107. *FRUS, 1945, II* 313–5; *DBPO*, 292–4, 298–300. On the exclusion of China and France see Gormly, *Collapse of the Grand Alliance*, 75–84. And on Soviet policy: J. Knight, 'Russia's Search for Peace: the London CFM, 1945', *Journal of Contemporary History*, 13 (1978), 137–63. On Britain: A. Bullock, *Ernest Bevin: Foreign Secretary* (1983), 129–37. And on the US: J. F. Byrnes, *Speaking Frankly* (1947), ch.5.

108. Truman and Attlee appealed separately to Stalin for a change of heart. *FRUS, 1945, II*, 328–33, 378–9; *DBPO, vol. II*, 312, 323–5, 347–8; H. S. Truman, *Year of Decisions* (1955), 453–6; *Stalin's Correspondence. . . . during the Great Patriotic War*, (Moscow, 1957) part I 375–8 and part II, 271–3.

109. On the meeting with Byrnes see: Y/134 (26 Sept.); Bidault papers, box 6 (22 Sept.); Mayer papers, vol. 2 (23 Sept.); *FRUS, 1945, II*, 330–1.

110. On Bevin see: Y/134 (26 Sept.); Bidault papers, box 6 (23 Sept.); *DBPO, vol. II*, 297.

111. Bidault papers, box 6 (23 and 25 Sept.); Massigli papers, vol. 60 (24 Sept.).

112. Y/134 (24 Sept.).

113. Ibid. (25 Sept.); Bidault papers, box 6 (25 Sept.).

114. H. Nicolson, *Diaries and Letters, 1945–62* (1971), entry for 25 Sept..

115. Mayer papers, vol. 2 (28 Sept.).

116. Berard, *Un Ambassadeur*, 59. See also: Y/134 (26 Sept.); Bidault papers, box 6 (28 Sept.).

117. *CMAE, vol. I*, 27th – 31st mtgs.; *FRUS, 1945, II*, 381–4, 410–18, 425–8, 435–9, 444–56, 475–508, 517–29; *DBPO, Vol. II*, 388–92, 397–9, 405–8, 416–30, 437–45, 449–61.

118. Y/134 (29 Sept.); Bidault papers, box 6 (30 Sept.); de Gaulle, *Salvation: Documents*, 304, *Lettres, Notes et Carnets*, 89–90, and, for a public statement of 12 October on France's role in the eastern treaties, *Discours et Messages*, 634–5.

119. *CMAE, vol. I*, 32nd and 33rd mtgs.; *FRUS, 1945, II*, 529–57; *DBPO, vol. II*, 461–71. For a French review of the CFM see Y/134 (19 Oct.).

120. J. Dumaine, *Quai d'Orsay, 1945–51* (1958), 8–9.

121. *FRUS, 1945, II*, 559.

122. See for example Bevin's talk to Bidault of 3 Oct.: Bidault papers, box 6; *DBPO, vol. II*, 484–5. Or, for various US explanations: Y/134 (31 Oct.); B/Etats Unis/107 (10 Oct.); Berard, *Un Ambassadeur*, 64–6.

123. Y/8 (17 October).
124. R. Dennett and R. K. Turner, eds, *Documents on American Foreign Relations, vol. VIII* (New York, 1948): 2–6. For French reaction: B/Etats Unis/107 (5 Nov.); Y/8 (29 Oct. – 2 Nov.); Bidault papers, box 81 (27 Oct.).
125. Cited in Knight, 'Russia's Search for Peace', 155.
126. Z/URSS/51 (29 April; 4, 12 May) and 52 (25, 26 June); Catroux, *Rideau de Fer*, chs. VIII and IX.
127. Catroux, ibid., 117–18; Z/Généralités/4 (20–30 Sept.).
128. Z/URSS/52 (15 Oct.).

Chapter 4

1. For the speeches see C. de Gaulle, *Lettres, Notes et Carnets 1945–51* (Paris, 1984) 91–8. And on the visit see: C. de Gaulle, *War Memoirs, vol. III Salvation* (1959), 215–7; H. Navarre, *Le Temps des Verités* (Paris, 1979), 207; J. Dumaine, *Quai d'Orsay, 1945–51* (1958), 7–8.
2. C. de Gaulle, *Discours et Messages* (1940–46) (Paris, 1970), 622–3.
3. ibid., 624–6.
4. ibid., 627–41. See Ministère des Affaires Etrangères (MAE), Z/Généralités/4 (13, 15 Oct.) on Belgian press coverage.
5. De Gaulle, *Salvation*, 218–19.
6. For example, Z/Belgique/34 (25 Aug., 30 Oct.).
7. Z/Généralités/4 (12 Dec. 1944; 22 May; 13, 18 Sept. 1945).
8. Z/Belgique/47 (2 Oct.).
9. P. H. Spaak, *The Continuing Battle* (1971), 80.
10. Z/Belgique/34 (9 Nov.); Archives Nationales (AN), Georges Bidault papers, box 102 (9 Nov.).
11. Z/Belgique/34 (3, 14, 22, 24 Nov.; 19 Dec.); Z/Généralités (24 Nov.); Bidault papers, box 102 (22 Nov.).
12. Z/Belgique/37 (2–20 Jan.); AN, F60/898 (29 Dec.; 2, 15 Jan.).
13. See above, 42.
14. Z/Belgique/34 (2–26 Feb.) and 37 (1–19 Feb.); Bidault papers, box 102 (21 Feb.).
15. Bidault papers, box 102 (17–18 March).
16. ibid. (31 March). For discussions see: J. W. Brouwer, 'Répondre à la politique européenne française,' in M. Dumoulin, ed., *La Belgique et les Débuts de la Construction Européenne* (Brussels, 1987), 68–74; R. T. Griffiths and F. M. B. Lynch, 'L'échec de la Petite Europe: le conseil tripartite, 1944–8', *Guerres Mondiales*, 152 (1988), 40–5.
17. Public Record Office (PRO), London, FO 371/49066/2029 (20 Feb.); FO 371/49067/8820 (22 July); R. Butler, ed., *Documents on British Policy Overseas (DBPO), Series I, vol. I* (1984), 1214–15.
18. FO 371/49067/4381 (de Gaulle – Hore Belisha Conversation, April).
19. Z/Belgique/34 (1 Oct.) and 37 (records of all 1945 sessions); F60/923 (records of sessions); Bidault papers, box 102 (10 Aug.); Griffiths and Lynch, 'L'échec de la Petite Europe', 45–9.
20. Z/Belgique/34 (1 Oct.).
21. See for example V. Auriol, *Journal du Septennat, vol. I, 1947* (Paris, 1970), 124; Brouwer, 'Répondre a la politique Française', 71–4.
22. J. Dumaine, *Quai d'Orsay*, 7–8.
23. Z/URSS/52 (16 Oct.).
24. ibid. (Oct.); Z/Généralités/4 (12, 21 Oct.).

25. Z/URSS/52 (28 Oct.); Bidault papers, box 82 (28 Oct.).

26. Z/Généralités/4 (27 Nov.).

27. FO 371/59952/2411; R. Bullen, ed., *DBPO, Series I, vol. II* (1985), 314–6.

28. Bidault papers, box 78 (23 Sept.); *DBPO, vol. II*, 316–23.

29. Spaak, *Continuing Battle*, 85–6; F. van Langenhove, *La Securité de la Belgique* (Brussels, 1971), 174–82.

30. Z/Généralités/4 (1 Dec. 1944). And on Lie's wartime ideas see: O. Riste, 'Norway's "Atlantic Policy", 1940–5', *NATO Review*, 29, 2 (April, 1981), 22–8.

31. Z/Généralités/40 (26 Dec.; 5 Jan.).

32. De Gaulle, *Discours et Messages*, 639–41; J. Moch, *Une si longue Vie* (Paris, 1976), 204–5.

33. Assemblée Nationale, Procès Verbaux de la Commission des Affaires Etrangères, 5, 19 & 26 Dec. 1945; 27 Feb. and 15 March 1946.

34. For general discussions see: P. Brundu, 'L'Espagne Franquiste et la politique etrangère de la France', *Relations Internationales*, 50 (1987), 165–81; A. Dulphy, 'La Politique de la France à l'Egard de l'Espagne Franquiste, 1945–9', *Revue d'Histoire Moderne et Contemporaine*, XXXV (1988), 123–40.

35. See P. Guillen 'Les Relations Franco-Italiennes de 1943 a 1949', *Revue d'Histoire Diplomatique* (1976), 135.

36. See above, 29.

37. On the two-sided nature of French policy after 1943 see: R. Massigli, *Une Comédie des Erreurs* (Paris, 1978), 36. For general analyses of Franco-Italian relations in 1944–5 see: Z/Italie/84 (Oct. 1944), 85 (1 May, 1 Oct. 1945); Bidault papers, box 91 (dated 14 Oct. 1945, but clearly 1944), 92 (12 Oct.).

   General discussions include: P. Guillen, 'Les Relations Franco-Italiennes', 112–60 (but especially 112–29) and 'La réinsertion internationale de l'Italie après la chute du fascisme, 1943–7', *Relations Internationales*, 31 (1982), 333–49.

38. Couve had previously been France's representative on the Allied Consultative Council in Italy. Z/Italie/84 (Nov.–Feb.); de Gaulle, *Salvation: Documents*, 122.

39. De Gaulle, ibid., 116–18; Bidault papers box 91 (3 Feb.).

40. Above, 54–5.

41. Bidault papers, box 92 (16 July); and see de Gaulle, *Lettres, Notes et Carnets*, 54.

42. For example: de Gaulle, *Salvation: Documents*, 276–7, 297–9; P. Nenni, *Tempo di Guerra Fredda: Diari, 1943–56* (Milan, 1981), 137–9.

43. See especially the French preparations for talks on the Italian treaty: Bidault papers, box 92 (9–20 Aug., 15 Sept., n.d.).

44. On wartime relations with eastern Europe: H. Batowski, 'La France Libre et l'Est Européen', *Revue d'Histoire de la Deuxième Guerre Mondiale*, 115 (July, 1979), 79–88; A. Marès, 'La France Libre et l'Europe centrale et orientale', *Revue des Etudes Slaves*, LIV (1982), 305–36.

45. Z/Pologne/54 (4, 22 Aug.; 29 Oct.); Bidault papers, box 82 (12 Jan.).

46. Z/Pologne/66; Z/Tchécoslovaquie/62, 63.

47. Z/Tchécoslovaquie/56 and 60 (Aug. 1944 – Jan. 1946); Bidault papers, box 76 (May 1945 – Feb. 1946); E. Benes, *The Memoirs of Dr. Eduard Benes* (1954), 179–80, 184, 231–7.

48. For a full discussion of French doubts see: Y. Lacaze, 'Edouard Benes et la France Libre a la lumière des documents diplomatiques Français', *Revue d'Histoire Diplomatique*, 97 (1983), 279–321.

49. Z/Pologne/54 (Aug. 1945-Jan. 1946); Bidault papers, box 89 (12 Jan.); de Gaulle, *Discours et Messages*, 632–3, 638–9; and on Benes views see Z/Généralités/4 (25 Oct.).

50. MAE, Y/282 (11 Oct.); MAE, *Documents Français Relatifs à l'Allemagne, 1945–7*

(Paris 1947), 16; *Foreign Relations of the United States (FRUS), 1945, vol. III*, 841–5, 871–7, 883.

51. *FRUS, 1945, III*, 846–52, 884–5, 887–8.
52. J. W. Young, 'The Foreign Office, the French and the post-war division of Germany, 1945–6' *Review of International Studies*, 12 (1986), 223–8.
53. Y/134 (2, 3 Oct.), 282 (2 Oct.); Bidault papers, box 6 (28 Sept.; 2, 3 Oct.); MAE, René Mayer papers, vol. 2 (28 Sept.).
54. For example, *FRUS, 1945, III*, 878.
55. Young, 'The Foreign Office, the French and the post-war division of Germany', 228. See also Montgomery of Alamein, *Memoirs* (1958), 366–7.
56. Z/URSS/52 (15 Oct.).
57. Y/283 (15 Dec.); *FRUS, 1945, III*, 911.
58. Y/282 (15 Oct.).
59. Bidault papers, box 6 (28 Oct.).
60. FO 371/46989/7657, 7659.
61. De Gaulle, *Discours et Messages*, 627–41.
62. De Gaulle, *Lettres, Notes et Carnets*, 106–8.
63. Navarre, *Le Temps des Verités* 208–11.
64. Young, 'The Foreign Office, the French and the post-war division of Germany' 228–9. On Massigli's approach see also: Y/282 (16 Oct.); Bidault papers, box 61 (26 Oct.); MAE, René Massigli papers, vol. 63 (16 Oct.) and 91 (26 Oct.). And on the Quai's position: Y/134 (28 Oct.), 282 (18, 24, 26 Oct.), 283 (6, 10 Nov.), 394 (24 Oct.), 395 (28 Oct.) 650 (15 Oct., meeting of the interministerial committee); Bidault papers, box 6 (28 Oct.). And on de Gaulle: *FRUS, 1945, III*, 890–1.
65. Young, ibid., 229–30. In late October the British warned Massigli that French policy could lead to a 'Big Three' system in Germany, but in early November denied that they were about to carry out such a policy: Y/282 (30 Oct.), 283 (5 Nov.); Massigli papers, box 63 (30 Oct.). On the toughening US line in November see: Y/282 (8, 13 Nov., 5 Dec.); Bidault papers, box 61 (28 Jan.).
66. Y/284 (12 Jan.) for a general review. The compromise was suggested in the Interministerial Committee on Germany.
67. Bidault papers, box 61 (1 Dec.).
68. Ibid., box 60 (4 Dec.); Y/283 (4 Dec.).
69. J. Moch, *Rencontres avec de Gaulle* (Paris, 1971), 116–18.
70. Y/283 (18 Dec.); Bidault papers, box 61 (19 Dec.); but see R. Murphy, *Diplomat among Warriors* (1964), 352. At the same time Eisenhower pressed Bonnet to agree to central agencies: Y/283 (21 Dec.); A. Berard, *Un Ambassadeur se Souvient*, 63.
71. On the debate over France's role see, for example, J. Gimbel, *The American Occupation of Germany* (Stanford, 1968), 17–33; J.H. Backer, *The Decision to Divide Germany* (Durham, N.C., 1978), 133–9; H. Schmitt, ed., *US Occupation in Europe after World War II* (Kansas, 1978), 67–72, 89–91.
72. Bidault papers, box 60 (5 Sept.)
73. Y/394 (8 Oct.); de Gaulle, *Lettres, Notes et Carnets*, 101–2.
74. Y/394 (8–26 Oct.), 395 (26 Oct.); Bidault papers, box 60 (20 Oct.), 61 (19–26 Oct.); PRO, CAB 129/9 CP (46) 156.
75. Z/Grande Bretagne/35 (23 Oct.).
76. See S. Greenwood, 'Bevin, the Ruhr and the Division of Germany', *Historical Journal*, 29 (1986), 203–12.
77. Massigli papers, vols. 53 and 63 (10 Nov.).
78. Y/394 (26 Oct.), 395 (13–20 Nov.); Bidault papers, box 61 (13–20 Nov.); Berard, *Un Ambassadeur*, 63; *FRUS, 1945, III*, 895–908, 910–13.
79. Y/395 (1, 6 Dec.); Bidault papers, box 61 (1 Dec.); G. Catroux, *J'ai vu tomber le Rideau de Fer* (Paris, 1952), 138–9.

80. Y/395 (12 Dec.); Bidault papers, box 61 (12, 22 Dec.); Catroux, ibid., 139–44; H. Alphand, *L'Etonnement d'Etre* (Paris, 1977), 188–91; *FRUS, 1945, III*, 920–2.
81. Bidault papers, box 61 (3 Dec.); *FRUS, 1945, III*, 915–6.
82. Bidault papers, box 61 (12, 28 Jan.).
83. Y/389 (14, 15 Jan.); ibid., box 60 (8 Jan., for statistics on Ruhr trade) 61 (11–16 Jan.); FO 371/55399/621 and 55400/1901, 1963.
84. G. H. Gallup, ed., *The Gallup International Public Opinion Polls, France, vol. I* (1976).
85. On 27 Dec. de Gaulle issued instructions that levels of industrial production in Germany should be set without prejudice to the future of the Rhur: *Lettres, Notes et Carnets*, 153.
86. Mayer papers, vol. 6 (15 Jan.); discussed in R. Poidevin, 'René Mayer et la Politique Extérieure de la France, 1945–53', *Revue d'Histoire de la Deuxième Guerre Mondiale*, 134 (April, 1984), 75–7.
87. Y/362 (24 Oct.); *FRUS, 1945, III*, 1353–6.
88. Y/363 (30 Oct. – 16 Dec.); Bidault papers, box 61 (29 Oct.; 2, 11 Nov.); *FRUS, 1945, III*, 1345, 1364, 1367–8, 1373–4, 1422–3, 1426–7, 1440–1, 1462–3. Bidault told the Assembly's Foreign Affairs Commission that restitution had priority over reparations: Assemblée Nationale, Procès verbaux de la Commission des Affaires Etrangères, 12 Dec. 1945.
89. Y/364 and 651 (18 Jan.); *FRUS, 1946, V*, 481–9.
90. Y/363 (13, 21 Dec.); B.U. Ratchford and W. D. Ross, *Berlin Reparations Assignment* (Chapel Hill, NC, 1947), appendix F.
91. See, for example, AN, F60/918 (27 Sept. 1944). And see above 18.
92. On the use of coal by the Allies see: Archives Economiques et Financières, René Pleven papers, box 5A9 (5 July).
93. Bidault papers, box 71 (17 April).
94. F. M. B. Lynch, *The Political and Economic Reconstruction of France, 1944–47* (Ph.D, Manchester University, 1981), 5, and see 113–31 on the Franco-German coal problem.
95. Bidault papers, box 64.
96. *FRUS, The Conference of Berlin (Potsdam)* (Washington, 1960), 608–10, 612–21, 626–30; F. S. V. Donnison, *Civil Affairs and Military Government in North West Europe* (1961), 395–9, 404–5, 414.
97. F60/922 (June–July); de Gaulle, *Salvation: Documents*, 273–4.
98. Bidault papers, box 61 (11 Aug.); de Gaulle, ibid., 278; *FRUS, Conference of Berlin*, 622, 624–6, 636–7; Donnison, *Civil Affairs*, 414–15.
99. On the coal situation in general see: Y/89; F60/922; Lynch, *Reconstruction of France*, 133–7. On the ECO see Donnison, ibid., ch. 22. And on French policy: R. Poidevin, 'La France et le charbon allemand', *Relations Internationales*, 44 (1985), 366–8.
100. See above 66.
101. Y/89 (8 Nov. 21 Dec.); F60/922; de Gaulle, *Lettres, Notes et Carnets*, 111–12, 129–30; *FRUS, 1945, III*, 1536–46.
102. J. P. Rioux, *The Fourth Republic, 1944–58* (1987), 59.
103. On the crisis see: G. Elgey, *La République des Illusions, 1945–57* (Paris 1965), 60–73; de Gaulle, *Salvation*, 267–71.
104. S. P. Sapp, *The US, France and the Cold War* (Ph.D, Kent State University, 1978), 71–2, 97–9; FO 371/49078/12778–12922 and 49079/13850.
105. Y/134 (31 Oct., 6 Nov.); Catroux, *Rideau de Fer*, 127.
106. On the calling of the conference: *FRUS, 1945, II*, 578–87, 596–601; *DBPO, vol. II*, 635–41, 644–9, 654–6.
107. Y/127 (7, 8 Dec.); Bidault papers, box 6 (8 Dec.); *FRUS, 1945, II*, 601–2.

108. Y/127 (7, 8 Dec.); Bidault papers, box 6, (7, 8 Dec.); Massigli papers, vol. 60 (8 Dec.); *DBPO, vol. II*, 660–2.
109. De Gaulle, *Salvation*, 275–6.
110. MAE, B/Etats Unis/107 (25 Dec.); Y/127 (18 Dec. – 2 Jan.); Bidault papers, box 6 (22–30 Dec.); Catroux, *Rideau de Fer*, ch. XI; *FRUS, 1945, II*, 706–7, 741–3, 760, 815–7; *DBPO, vol. II*, 905–13.
111. *FRUS, 1945, II*, 761.
112. The account of the Cabinet meeting is from; Moch, *Rencontres avec de Gaulle*, 97–104 and Moch, *Une si longue vie*, 203–4. On the wedding see S. Bidault, *Souvenirs* (Paris, 1987), 43–5. And on US pressure on France to agree to the decisions: B/Etats Unis/107 (31 Dec.); Y/127 (31 Dec.); *FRUS, 1945, II*, 824–6 and *1946, II*, 1–3; S. Kertesz, *The Last European Peace Conference: Paris 1946* (New York, 1985), 71–2, reproducing Quai note of 31 Dec..
113. In a meeting of 2 Jan.: Moch, *Rencontres*, 104–6.
114. B/Etats Unis/107 (10–14 Jan.); Y/127 (3, 14, 17 Jan.); Bidault papers, box 6 (3, 8, 14 Jan.); *FRUS, 1946, II*, 3–6, 8; Moch ibid., 106–7; C. Mauriac, *The Other de Gaulle: Diaries 1944–54* (1973), 145–6; Kertesz, *Last European Peace Conference*, 75–6. The French also accepted a place on a new Far Eastern Commission, though they were disappointed to be excluded from Allied control machinery in Japan: Y/127 (29 Dec., 4 Jan.). And France agreed to join the Big Three in seeking the control of atomic energy via the UN: Bidault papers, box 6 (27 Dec., 5 Jan.).
115. Z/URSS/52 (30 Nov. – 19 Dec.); Catroux, *Rideau de Fer*, 139.
116. Massigli papers, vol. 91 (20 Nov.).
117. Z/Grande Bretagne/35 (31 Dec.).
118. J. W. Young, *Britain, France and the Unity of Europe, 1945–51* (Leicester, 1984), 21–3. See also de Gaulle, *Salvation: Documents*, 375–9, 381–2, and *Lettres, Notes et Carnets*, 140–2, 172–3; Elgey, *République des Illusions*, 85–6.
119. Moch, *Rencontres*, 108–11 and *Une si longue vie*, 206–7.
120. *Journal Officiel, Débats*, 15 Jan., especially 3–5 (Mayer), 8–14 (Bonte), 78–83 (Bidault).
121. De Gaulle, *Salvation*, 271–8, sees the defence cuts issue as most vital in the decision to resign.
122. Moch, *Rencontres*, 119–34, and *Une si longue vie*, 207–11.
123. De Gaulle, *Salvation*, 279–80; L. Joxe, *Victoires sur la Nuit* (Paris, 1981) 277–80; Elgey, *République des Illusions*, 88–93.
124. Mauriac, *The Other de Gaulle*, 111–3, 117; J. W. Young, 'The Foreign Office and the Departure of General de Gaulle', *Historical Journal*, 25 (1982), 209–16.
125. *FRUS, 1946, V*, 400–1; PRO, Ernest Bevin papers, FO 800/464/46/1–4; A. D. Cooper, *Old Men Forget* (1954), 364–5; J. Chauvel, *D'Alger à Berne, 1944–52* (Paris, 1972), 133.
126. *Journal Officiel, Débats*, 22 Jan. 1945, 138–9; de Gaulle, *Salvation: Documents*, 382–3. On this reasoning see also: Mauriac, *The Other de Gaulle*, 150–1; British Library, Oliver Harvey papers, manuscript 56402 (20 March 1945, where Gaston Palewski told Harvey that de Gaulle would establish a strong France, then retire); Churchill College, Cambridge, Duff Cooper papers, DUFC/4/5 (31 Dec., an even earlier, similar story from Palewski).
127. Mauriac, ibid., 147–9.
128. ibid., 146.
129. J. Lacouture, *De Gaulle, vol. II, La Politique* (Paris, 198), 209, citing interview with Mauriac.
130. The accounts are fragmentary and contradictory but Gay seems to have been fore-warned of the resignation by de Gaulle and been sworn to secrecy; embarrassed, Gay decided to warn Chauvel, and it was Chauvel who warned Bidault discreetly;

Bidault thus learnt of the resignation before it occurred and along with another minister, Vincent Auriol, tried to return to Paris by aeroplane; the aircraft took off with other passengers but in view of the fog the pilot refused to carry two VIPs. G. Bidault, *Resistance* (1967), 102–3; S. Bidault, *Souvenirs* (1987), 46–8; Chauvel, *D'Alger à Berne*, 130–1; Elgey, *République des Illusions*, 86–8, 90; and on the remarks to Duff Cooper see the latter's papers, DUFC/4/6 (27 Jan.).

131. On the crisis and Billotte's activities see Elgey, *République des Illusions*, 99–113, 118. On Billotte's contact with Duff Cooper see FO 371/59957/754 and 59958/1671.

132. Cited in Lacouture, *Le Souverain*, 249.

133. Mauriac, *The Other de Gaulle*, 164–5, 194–6.

134. The phrase was used in his radio address of 10 December: *Discours et Messages*, 656–9.

135. Mauriac, *The other de Gaulle*, 152.

136. Dumaine, *Quai d'Orsay*, 43.

Chapter 5

1. Archives Nationales (AN), Georges Bidault papers, box 82 (25 Dec. 1944; 9 Jan., 6 July 1945).

2. ibid. (15 Nov. – 2 Jan.).

3. G.A.J., Catroux, *J'ai vu tomber le Rideau de Fer* (Paris, 1952), 144–54.

4. *Négociations Franco-Américaines relatives à la politique économique internationale* (government publication, Paris, 1946) includes the main commitments. See also: Ministère des Affaires Etrangères (MAE), B/Etats Unis/245 (Aug. – Dec. 1945); Bidault papers, box 80 (Dec.).

5. 'Sur les aspects économiques de la politique extérieure française, 1943–7', *Institut Pierre Renouvin: travaux et recherches*, 2 (1988), 50–7, especially 57 (reproducing minutes of the 27th meeting of the *Commission des Approvisionnements*, 24 Oct. 1945).

6. AN, F60 Ter/386 (31 Oct.).

7. AN, 80 AJ/1 (6 Dec. – including quote – 13 Dec., 10 January, 16–19 March); AN, F60/902 (14, 21 Feb.); Fondation Jean Monnet, Lausanne, Monnet Papers, AMF/1/1/3–5, 45, 47; J. Monnet, *Memoirs* (1978), 226–9, 232–49.
   And for discussions of the Monnet Plan see: P. Mioche, *Le Plan Monnet: Genèse et Elaboration* (Paris, 1986), especially 114–21, 125–6; P. Mioche, 'Aux Origines du Plan Monnet', *Revue Historique*, 215 (1981), 405–38, and 'Le Démarrage du Plan Monnet', *Revue d'Histoire Moderne et Contemporaine*, 31 (1984), 398–416; F.M.B. Lynch, 'Resolving the Paradox of the Monnet Plan', *Economic History Review* (May, 1984), 229–43.

8. Monnet papers, AMF 3/5/15–16 and 4/0/2–3 (9 and 10 Oct.; and see 'Sur les aspects économiques . . .', *Institut Pierre Renouvin*, 2, 55–6.

9. Above, 38.

10. E.F. Penrose, *Economic Planning for the Peace* (Princeton, NJ, 1953), 322.

11. Archives Economiques et Financières (AEF), René Pleven papers, 5A9 (8 Dec.).

12. ibid. (21 Nov.).

13. Mioche, *Le Plan Monnet*, 126–8.

14. Monnet papers, AMF, 4/0/2–3 (9 Oct.), and in general on the Keynes talks see AMF 4/0/1, 4–9, 14, 18–20.

15. B/Etats Unis/119 (31 Jan., 4 Feb.).

16. *Foreign Relations of the United States (FRUS), 1946, Vol. V.* 405–6, 408; J. Dumaine, *Quai d'Orsay*, 1945–51 (1958), 39.

17. B/Etats Unis/119 (21 Feb.); MAE, Y/8 (23 Feb.).

18. Monnet had earlier hoped to begin talks in Washington in December, with a high-powered delegation led by Bidault: Mioche, *Le Plan Monnet*, 89, 128.
19. *FRUS, 1946, V,* 399–400.
20. Blum forewarned Caffery of the loan mission several days before its announcement and evidently did not think the talks need last long – an optimism similar to Monnet's. ibid., 409.
21. At the same time a separate group held talks on fiscal matters. B/Etats Unis/246 (16 Feb. – 16 March); Bidault papers, box 80 (20 Feb., nd); ibid., 412, 414–15, 417–18.
22. *Wall Street Journal* (4 Feb.), article by R. Moley.
23. B/Etats Unis/246 (16, 18, 21 Feb. and see 9 April); Bidault papers, box 80 (1 Feb., n.d.); Monnet, *Memoirs*, 249–50.
24. B/Etats Unis/246 (22, 23 Feb.).
25. Bidault papers, box 80 (20 Feb.).
26. ibid. (20 Feb.); B/Etats Unis/246 (20 Feb.).
27. Monnet papers, AMF 4/1/4 (15 Feb.).
28. Mioche, *Le Plan Monnet*, 130–1.
29. Monnet papers, AMF 4/2/9 (27 March, Vergeot memorandum).
30. *FRUS, 1946, V,* 409–17; Bidault papers, box 80 (22 Feb.).
31. On preparations for the talks: F60/923; Monnet papers, AMF 4/1/1–25; Bidault papers, box 80 (23 Feb., 18 March, and see 20 Feb.).
32. G. Elgey, *La République des Illusions, 1945–51* (Paris, 1965), 118–19; Churchill College, Cambridge, Duff Cooper papers, DUFC/4/6 (20 March).
33. Dumaine, *Quai d'Orsay*, 48, 52.
34. Bidault papers, box 61 (28 Feb.).
35. ibid., box 82 (2, 9–11 March).
36. J.M. Blum, ed., *The Price of Vision: the diary of Henry A. Wallace, 1942–6* (Boston, 1973), 562–3.
37. *FRUS, 1946, V,* 412–13.
38. Monnet, *Memoirs*, 249–50. On the statistics see 80 AJ 4 (March).
39. Lynch, 'Resolving the Paradox', 238.
40. On the talks in general see: *FRUS, 1946, V,* 425–30; Monnet, *Memoirs*, 249–53 (quote from 250); Mioche, *Le Plan Monnet*, 130–34; F.M.B. Lynch, *The Political and Economic Reconstruction of France* (PhD, Manchester University, 1981), 310–25. On Blum's speeches see, for example, B/Etats Unis/246 (11 April).
41. B/Etats Unis/246 (4 April).
42. Monnet papers, AMF 4/1/26.
43. On coal see ibid., AMF 4/3/98–131, especially 104 and 110 (including quotes); B/Etats Unis/246 (18 April, 3 May).
44. B/Etats Unis/246 (22 April).
45. Monnet, *Memoirs*, 250–52.
46. L. Blum, *L'Oeuvre de Léon Blum* (Paris, 7 vols., 1955–63), *1945–47* (1958), 188–96; B/Etats Unis/246 (25, 29 March).
47. Elgey, *République des Illusions*, 140–1; and see *FRUS, 1946, V,* 430–1.
   The Quai had hoped, in early March, that an agreement could be concluded before the French elections for the practical reason that elections would delay the process of ratification: Bidault papers, box 80 (9 March).
48. *FRUS, 1946, V,* 421–2, 425.
49. ibid., 431–4.
50. ibid., 440–6, 450.
51. On 22 and 23 May, respectively: B/Etats Unis/246 (22 May): ibid., 451–2.
52. *FRUS, 1946, V,* 453–64.
53. B/Etats Unis/247 (19 July).

54. B/Etats Unis/246 (28 May, 5 June); F60/923 (28 May, nd); Bidault papers, box 80 (27–28 May); Monnet papers, AMF 4/4/4–8, 4/5/1; Blum, *L'Oeuvre, 1945–47*, 201–3; Mioche, *Le Plan Monnet*, 133–4.

55. On this point see: Monnet papers, AMF 4/5/2–3.

56. Monnet, *Memoirs*, 253–6.

57. Mioche, *Le Plan Monnet*, 294–9, reproducing Billoux memorandum.

58. For a full recent statement sympathetic to the Communist case see A. Lacroix–Riz, 'Négociation et Signature des accords Blum–Byrnes', *Revue d'Histoire Moderne et Contemporaine*, 31 (1984), 417–47. This has won a response from I.M. Wall, 'Les Accords Blum–Byrnes', *Vingtième Siècle*, 13 (1987), 45–62. Blum gave a balanced report on the loan to the Assembly's *Commission des Affaires Etrangères* on 25 July: *Bulletin des Commissions, Assemblée Nationale Constituante* (government publication, Paris, 1947), 71–2.

59. *FRUS, 1946, V*, 464.

60. Y/284 (12, 17, 19, 24, 31 Jan., 22 Feb.) and 651 (18 Jan., minute 7); Bidault papers, box 61 (22 Feb.).

61. Bidault papers, box 61 (2 Feb.); and on wheat supplies see MAE, Z/Allemagne/85 (Jan.–Feb.). Clay *did* recommend to Washington that wheat supplies be used as a pressure-point against France: J.E. Smith, ed., *The Papers of Lucius D. Clay, Vol. I, 1945–47* (Bloomington, Indiana, 1974), 151–2 (26 January).

62. Y/284 (12 Feb., 5 March); Bidault papers, box 60 (21 Feb., 4 March), 61 (12 Feb.); *Documents Français Relatifs à l'Allemagne, 1945–47* (Paris, 1947), 17–19; *FRUS, 1946, V*, 507–8.

63. Y/284 (5 Feb.); Bidault papers, box 61 (5, 14 Feb.); *FRUS, 1946, V*, 496–8; and see A. Berard, *Un Ambassadeur se Souvient, 1945–55* (Paris, 1978), 76.

64. Bidault papers, box 80 (6 Feb.).

65. For example: Y/397 (1 and 9 March); ibid., boxes 61 (17, 25 Feb.), 80 (5 March).

66. *FRUS, 1946, V*, 505–7, 516–20, 524–5, 527–8; Smith ed., *Clay Papers*, 165–6.

67. *FRUS, 1946, V*, 509–11. On Blum's views see: Blum, *L'Oeuvre, 1945–47, passim*,; M. Newman, 'Léon Blum, French Socialism and European Unity, 1945–50, *Historical Journal*, 24 (1981) 189–200.

68. S.P. Sapp, *The US, France and the Cold War* (PhD, Kent State University, 1978), 117.

69. Z/Grande Bretagne/36 (18 February); MAE; René Massigli papers, Vol. 53 (1, 18 Feb.), and see Vol. 653 (28, 29 Dec.; 3, 16 Jan.) on British views; Public Record Office (PRO), London, FO 371/55399/1407 and 55400/2188, 2311.

70. Y/284 (1, 3, 8 March) and Y/397 (1 March); *Documents Relatifs à l'Allemagne*, 20–3; Berard, *Un Ambassadeur*, 76; *FRUS, 1946, V*, 512–5; B. Ruhm von Oppen, *Documents on Germany under Occupation, 1945–54* (1955), 110–13.

71. Y/377 (14 March) and 397 (5–19 March); Bidault papers, box 61 (23 March); Massigli papers, Vol. 63 (19 March); FO 371/55401/3650, 3652, 4225; *FRUS, 1946, II*, 27–8, 36, 81–2.

72. Byrnes took this approach on the advice of Robert Murphy: *FRUS, 1946, V*, 528–9.

73. Clay *was* sympathetic however to the Saar's attachment to France. Smith, ed., *Clay Papers*, 189–90. 192–201; *FRUS, 1946, V*, 540; and see L.D. Clay, *Decision in Germany* (1950), 73–8.

74. Y/370 (7 Jan., 28 Feb.). On the use of German labour see: Y/650 (meeting of the Interministerial Committee on Germany of 25 Sept. and 27 Nov. 1945).

75. Y/364 (27 March); *FRUS, 1946, V*, 533–4; Ruhm von Oppen, *Documents on Germany*, 113–18; and see the discussion in M.-T. Bitsch, 'Un rêve français:

le désarmement économique de l'Allemagne', *Relations Internationales*, 51 (1987), 322–4.

76. Y/364 (8, 9 March); *FRUS, 1946, V*, 520–4.
77. Y/370 (13 April).
78. See Smith, ed., *Clay Papers*, 186–7.
79. On Clay's decision see: ibid., 203–4, 212–23; *FRUS, 1946, V*, 545–56; FO 371/55424/4662. On the case that Clay directed himself at France see especially: J. Gimbel, *The American Occupation of Germany* (Stamford, 1968), 52–61.
    On France's reaction to Clay's decision see: Y/370 (1 May, early June), 377 (nd), 398 (5 July, for Clay–St Hardouin conversation; 4 Sept.). And on the French contacts with Russia: Y/286 (25 June), 370 (15, 20 June), 377 (20 June), 398 (20 June); Bidault papers, box 61 (15 and 20 June).
80. G. Kirk, *The Middle East, 1945–50* (1954), 107–15; J.W. Young, *Britain, France and the Unity of Europe, 1945–51* (Leicester, 1984), 24–5.
81. House of Lords debates, Vol. 139, cols. 1294–5.
82. Y/390 (March) and 397 (24 March); Z/Grande Bretagne/36 (24 and 31 March)
83. A Gallup poll showed 68 per cent of French people in favour of a British treaty. G.H. Gallup, *The Gallup International Public Opinion Polls, France, Vol. I* (1976), April 1946. In general see Young, *Britain, France and the Unity of Europe*, 29–30, 36–7.
84. Z/Grande Bretagne/36 (1, 16 Jan.; 12 March); Bidault papers, box 78 (1 Feb., regarding Bevin's dislike of the PCF); Massigli papers, Vol. 53 (1 Feb.), and 93 (22 Feb., 5 March); R. Massigli, *Une Comédie des Erreurs* (Paris, 1978), 80–1.
85. Churchill College, Cambridge, Duff Cooper papers DUFC/4/6 (28 March, and see 13, 20 March on the PCF danger).
86. Y/295 (1 April), 390 (1, 3 April) and 397 (1–3 April); Z/Grande Bretagne/36 (3–5 April); Bidault papers, box 60 (1 April); J. Dumaine, *Quai d'Orsay*, 52–3.
87. Y/285 (4 April), 390 (4–6 April) and 397 (5 April); Z/Grande Bretagne/36 (6–24 April); Bidault papers, boxes 60 (4 April) and 78 (3, 4 April); British Library, Oliver Harvey papers, manuscript 56402 (6 April); Massigli, *Comédie*, 82; J. Chauvel, *D'Alger à Berne, 1944–52* (Paris, 1972), 164–5; A.D. Cooper, *Old Men Forget* (1954), 367; *The Times*, 5, 6, 8, 10 April.
88. *FRUS, 1946, V*, 422–5.
89. Y/391 (20 April, 2 May), 397 (24 April – 9 May); Bidault papers (28, 29 April, 9 May, and see the rather odd piece of evidence dated 29 March regarding Bevin's 'embarrassment' at British policy); Massigli's papers, Vol. 63 (26, 30 April); Harvey papers, manuscript 56400 (diary for 25, 26, 28 April). On the British decisions see especially: PRO, CAB. 128/5, CM, (46) 36; CAB. 129/8, CP (46), 139 and 156; S. Greenwood, 'Bevin, the Ruhr and the Division of Germany', *Historical Journal*, 29 (1986), 205–9.
90. The latest information was that they continued to do so: Y/397 (17 April). On US views: *FRUS, 1946, II*, 486–8, and *V*, 541–2; Smith, ed., *Clay Papers*, 192–201.
91. ibid., (23, 24 April).
92. Massigli papers, box 93 (20, 23, 28 May).
93. *Conseil des Ministres des Affaires Etrangères (CMAE), Vol. II, Paris, 25 avril – 16 mai* (Paris, 1946), 1st meeting; *FRUS 1946, II* (1970), 94–5; and on the CFM in general see Catroux, *Rideau de fer*, 182–7. Copies of the *CMAE* volume can be found in: box AFA. C-3 (shelved at MAE); Y/141; and Bidault papers, box 6.
94. Bidault papers, box 6 (29 April); and on Eastern Europe see Y/140 (19, 20, 23 April).
95. Z/Grande Bretagne/32 (27, 28 May).

96. ibid. (24 July).
97. ibid. (16 Oct., and see 3 Nov., 13 Dec. and 31 Jan. regarding Bevin's dissatisfaction with the 'appeasement' attitudes in *The Times*.
98. For French observations on these see especially Z/URSS/40 (5, 15 April, 24 Oct.).
99. Z/Grande Bretagne/32 (22 Feb.).
100. B/Etats Unis/202 (11–14 Feb.; 1–4, 13 and 29 March – including quote on Iran from last); Z/URSS/40 (13, 16 Feb.; 11, 13, 18 March) and 41 (29 March). On Byrnes's speech of 28 Feb. see: R.L. Messer, *The End of an Alliance* (Chapel Hill, N.C., 1982), 188–90.
101. Dumaine, *Quai d'Orsay*, 31.
102. *CMAE, Vol. II*, 1st, 2nd, and 4th meetings; *FRUS, 1946, II*, 79–80, 94–106, 121–2, 165–5, 165–75; ibid., 55–6; A.H. Vandenberg, ed., *The Private Papers of Senator Vandenberg* (1953), 267–8.
103. See above, note 93, on 1st meeting (quote from FRUS); Harvey papers, manuscript 56400 (diary for 25 April). China remained excluded from the European peace treaties.
104. Y/285 (25 April); Z/URSS/52 (17 Feb., 9 March, 29 April).
105. Dumaine. *Quai d'Orsay*, 58; and see Bidault papers, box 6 (1 May).
106. *FRUS, 1946, II*, 203–6 (1 May). Vandenberg, ed., *Private Papers*, 269–70, gives the impression that the idea for private meetings was Byrnes's.
107. *CMAE, Vol. II*, 7th meeting and 1st informal; *FRUS, 1946, II*, 212–22; Vandenberg, ibid., 272–3.
108. *CMAE, Vol. II*, 13th–15th, 17th, and 18th meetings and 5th informal; *FRUS, 1946, II*, 301–32, 348–52, 387–93, 404–16, 419–22; Vandenberg, ibid., 280–1.
109. Bidault papers, box 92 (Jan., 12 Feb., 30 March, 23 April); *FRUS, 1946, II*, 10–11, 23–4, 28.
110. *FRUS, 1946, II*, 37–8.
111. *CMAE, Vol. II*, 3rd and 4th meetings; ibid., 134–40, 153, 175–6; Vandenberg, ed., *Private Papers*, 265–6.
112. *CMAE, Vol. II*, 16th meeting; *FRUS, 1946, II*, 353–7, 368–72, 381.
113. *CMAE, Vol. II*, 3rd, 25th, 29th and 30th meetings; *FRUS, 1946, II*, 128–34, 139, 603–6, 678–9, 688–9.
114. There were major differences on this issue, however: *CMAE, Vol. II*, 2nd, 13th and 18th meetings, 3rd and 4th informal; *FRUS, 1946, II*, 112–22, 126–7, 286–96, 298–300, 339–45, 402–4, 420, 422–3.
115. *CMAE, Vol. II*, 4th meeting; *FRUS, 1946, II*, 106–7, 155–63, 174–5, 194, 205; Vandenberg, ed., *Private Papers*, 267.
116. *CMAE, Vol. II*, 3rd and 6th informal, 17th meetings; *FRUS, 1946, II*, 333–8, 361–4, 423–4, 384–7.
117. *CMAE, Vol. II*, 5th, 8th–10th and 17th meetings, 2nd informal; *FRUS, 1946, II*, 140–6, 148–52 (and map), 177–84, 190, 222–46, 249–56, 387.
118. Y/287 and 397 (25 April); *Documents Relatifs à l'Allemagne*, 24–7; Ruhm von Oppen, *Documents on Germany*, 125–8; *FRUS, 1946, II*, 109–12.
119. See above, 70.
120. See above, 109.
121. Y.356 (16 May) and 397 (15, 16 May); *CMAE, Vol. II*, 7th–9th informal meetings; *FRUS, 1946, II*, 393–402, 426–36; Vandenberg, ed., *Private Papers*, 281–4.
122. See above, 66.
   Byrnes had also put the idea to Stalin in December 1945, who seemed favourable: J.F. Byrnes, *All in One Lifetime* (1958), 337.
123. Y/356 (25 Feb.); Bidault papers, box 61 (25 Feb.); *FRUS, 1946, II*, 190–3 (version of 30 April, slightly amended from original).

124. Y/356 (23 April), 390 (11 April); Bidault papers, box 60 (11 April), 61 (13 April); Chauvel, *d'Alger à Berne*, 184–5.

125. Neither Bevin nor Molotov gave a response to the Byrnes Treaty before the CFM. Y/356 (27 March; 4, 13 April); Bidault papers, box 61 (13 April); *FRUS, 1946, II*, 56–8.

126. Y/356 (30 April); Z/URSS/52 (29 April); *CMAE, Vol. II*, 4th meeting; *FRUS, 1946, II*, 166–75, 190–3, and see 146–7, 367–8; Vandenberg, ed., *Private papers*, 267–8.

127. Z/Grande Bretagne/32 (3 May).

128. B/Etats Unis/108 (20, 21 May); Z/URSS/41 (14, 20, 21 May).

129. Y/140 (7 May); Z/URSS/41 (5 June); Catroux, *Rideau de Fer*, 187.

130. De Gaulle for the moment kept his silence on the new constitution.

131. McNarney had now replaced Eisenhower. General Clay remained as Deputy Governor and bore most of the burden of discussions with other occupying powers.

132. *FRUS, 1946, V*, 434–40.

133. Dumaine, *Quai d'Orsay*, 59–60.

134. *FRUS, 1946, V*, 441, 446–50, 459; FO 371/59961/4391, 4554.

135. C. Mauriac, *The Other de Gaulle: Diaries 1944–54* (1973), 198–203, 206–10, 232–3.

136. J.-P. Rioux, *The Fourth Republic, 1944–58* (1987), 102.

137. Dumaine, *Quai d'Orsay*, 62–3.

138. For a time it was feared that the French election would delay the start of the CFM's second session: Y/147 (12 June).

Chapter 6

1. *Conseil des Ministres des Affaires Etrangères (CMAE), Vol. III, Paris, 14 juin – 12 juillet* (Paris, 1946) 19th mtg.; *Foreign Relations of the United States (FRUS), 1946, vol. II*, 493–506. On the CFM in general see: Ministères des Affaires Etrangères (MAE), Y/149 (records of full meetings) and 151 (records of informal meetings); and G. Catroux, *J'ai vu tomber le Rideau de Fer* (Paris, 1952), 187–209.

2. *CMAE, vol. III*, 30th, 33rd – 38th mtgs., 14th and 15th informal; *FRUS, 1946, II*, 691–5, 742–54, 769–74, 781–839, 850–4.

3. See, for example, Y/140 (12, 13 June); Archives Nationales (AN), Georges Bidault papers, box 78 (14 June).

4. MAE, B/Etats Unis/202 (23 June); MAE, Z/URSS/41 (23 June).

5. Y/147 (12, 26 June); *FRUS, 1946, II*, 508–9, 582–3.

6. *FRUS, 1946, V*, 566–7.

7. *CMAE, vol. III*, 23rd, 24th and 28th mtgs.; *FRUS, 1946, II*, 483–6, 547–9, 556, 558–98, 601–3, 658–9, 664–8.

8. *CMAE, vol. III*, 21st, 22nd, 30th, 34th and 38th mtgs.; *FRUS, 1946, II*, 539–41, 546, 686–8, 755–70, 839–40, 850–1, 854–5.

9. Their fate would be decided by the UN if the CFM could not resolve the question within one year of an Italian peace treaty. Ultimately the issue did go to the UN and, to French dismay, Libya was made independent in 1951. *CMAE, vol. III*, 29th, 33rd and 41st mtgs., and 10th informal; *FRUS, 1946, II*, 557–63, 675–8, 713–4, 738–40, 751–2, 899–900, 907–8.

10. *FRUS, 1946, II*, 582–3 (22 June).

11. Bidault had first had suggested a temporary international regime for Trieste on 21 June. *CMAE, vol. III*, 30th–33rd mtgs., 11th and 13th informals; ibid., 570–4,

641–6, 689–91, 703–12, 714–22, 730–8, 751–3; A. H. Vandenberg, ed., *The Private Papers of Senator Vandenberg* (1953), 293–5; and see Y/147 (29 June) on earlier Soviet press criticism of French policy on Trieste.

12. P. Nenni, *Tempo di Guerra Fredda: Diari 1943–56* (Milan, 1981), 236, 250–2, and for a review of Italian policy see A. Varsori, 'De Gasperi, Nenni, Sforza and their role in post-war Italian foreign policy', in J. Berker and F. Knipping, eds, *Power in Europe?* (New York, 1986), 89–114.

13. On French policy see especially: P. Guillen, 'Les Relations Franco-Italiennes de 1943 à 1949, *Revue d'Histoire Diplomatique*, (1976), 136–45 and 'La France et la Question du Haut-Adige, 1945–6', *Revue d'Histoire Diplomatique*, 100 (1986), 293–306. On Italian complaints to the US: *FRUS, 1946, II*, 646–7.

14. G. Bidault, 'Agreement on Germany: key to world peace', *Foreign Affairs*, 24 (1946), 571–8.

15. Y/286 (3 July).

16. *CMAE, vol. III*, 38th mtgs.; *FRUS, 1946, II*, 842–50.

17. *CMAE, vol. III*, 39th mtg.; MAE, *Documents Français Relatifs à l'Allemagne, 1945–7* (Paris, 1947) 28–32; B. Ruhm von Oppen, ed., *Documents on Germany under Occupation, 1945–54* (1955), 144–8; *FRUS, 1946, II*, 860–79.

18. *CMAE, Vol. III*, 40th–42nd mtgs.; *Documents Rélatifs à l'Allemagne*, 33–4 (Bidault's 12 July speech); *FRUS, 1946, II*, 881–99, 901–2, 907–13, 935–9.

19. Byrnes, however, was keen to minimise differences with the French about central agencies. *FRUS, 1946, V*, 577–80.

20. Bidault papers, box 6 (10 July).

21. *FRUS, 1946, V*, 576–7.

22. Y/286 (22 July); and see ibid. 465–6.

23. Y/287 (2 Sept.); Z/URSS/52 (2 Sept.). The speech was indeed consistent with an analysis of Soviet policy written by Charpentier on 8 April: Y/285.

24. Y/286 (26, 27 July); MAE, René Massigli papers, vol. 63 (27 July).

25. Bidault papers, box 60 (18 July, and see 15 June); Massigli papers, vol. 63 (18 July).

26. Y/287 (4 Aug. and on the general situation, see 30 Aug.), 377 (21, 29 July and see 2 Aug. for Koenig's concerns); Bidault papers, box 61 (21, 29 July, 4 Aug.); *FRUS, 1946, V*, 580–1.

27. But he undertook to establish links with the Anglo-Americans: Massigli papers, vol. 93 (24 July); and see *FRUS, 1946, V*, 596.

28. Y/286 (31 July), 377 (30, 31 July; 3 Aug.; n.d.); Bidault papers box 60 (30 July) and 61 (29 July; 5, 6 Aug.). The French put their plan for 'Allied offices' to the ACC in August, but with no success: Y/377; *FRUS, 1946, V*, 587–96; *Documents Relatifs à l'Allemagne*, 35–9.

29. *The Times*, 29 July 1946, 4.

30. *Recueil des Documents de la Conférence de Paris, vol. I* (Paris, 1946), 1st plenary; *FRUS, 1946, III*, 26–9; copies of mtgs. in Y/243–6. See box AFA. C-1 (shelved at the Quai d'Orsay) for the four-volume *Recueil des Documents*.

31. J. Dumaine, *Quai d'Orsay, 1944–51*, (1958) 67–8.

32. *FRUS, 1946, III*, 131–62.

33. Dumaine, *Quai d'Orsay*, 82.

34. On these see: Y/241, 242; F. Seydoux, *Mémoires d'Outre-Rhin* (1975), 90–2.

35. S. Kertesz (an Hungarian delegate), *The Last European Peace Conference; Paris, 1946* (New York, 1985), 20.

36. Dumaine, *Quai d'Orsay*, 71–4.

37. Bidault papers, box 92 (30 July); and see Bidault's speech to the 19th and 32nd plenaries in *Recueil des Documents, vol. I*.

38. See *FRUS, 1946, III*, 16–19, 294–6, 332–3 and *IV*, 119–23, 306–7, 426–8.

39. *Recueil des Documents, vol. I*, 48th plenary; *FRUS, 1946, III*, 859–61; Dumaine, *Quai d'Orsay*, 84.

40. It was not certain, however, whether the political situation in France would allow Bidault to attend: Y/167 (15 Oct.); *FRUS, 1946, III*, 856–9.

41. For the text of the speech: See Bidault papers, box 61 (6 Sept.); Ruhm von Oppen, *Documents on Germany*, 152–60.

42. B/Etats Unis/173 (6–11 Sept.); Y/287 (5–10 Sept.) and 288 (11–21 Sept.); Bidault papers, box 61 (20 Sept.).

43. Y/287 (7 Sept., St Hardouin's view; 9 Sept., *Direction d'Europe* note); Massigli papers, vol. 93 (9 Sept.); and see Chauvel, *D'Alger à Berne*, 185.

44. *FRUS, 1946, V*, 603–5.

45. Y/288 (26 Sept.).

46. ibid. (3 Oct.); Y/9 (4 Oct.); and see Bidault papers, box 61 (17 Sept.).

47. Y/288 (5, 18 Oct.).

48. B/Etats Unis/202 (7, 26 Sept., on US popular opinion); Y/9 (on Wallace, 13–26 Sept.); G. H. Gallup, ed., *The Gallup International Public Opinion Polls, France, vol. I* (1972), March and Sept. 1946, Feb. 1947.

49. Massigli papers, vol. 93 (24, 25 July); J. W. Young, *Britain, France and the Unity of Europe, 1945–51* (Leicester, 1984), 32–3.

50. MAE, Z/Grande Bretagne/36 (17 July); R. Massigli, *Une Comédie des Erreurs* (Paris, 1978), 84.

51. Z/Grande Bretagne/36 (2 Aug.); Bidault papers, box 78 (2 Aug.); Massigli papers, vol. 53 (2 Aug.); Massigli, ibid., 84–5.

52. He discussed this idea with Duff Cooper's deputy, Ashley Clarke in late July: Public Record Office (PRO), London, FO 371/59978/7069.

53. R. S. Churchill, ed., *The Sinews of Peace* (1948), 198–202; and on its general effect see W. Lipgens, *A History of European Integration, vol. I, 1945–7* (Oxford, 1982), ch. II.

54. Bidault papers, box 78 (14 June).

55. The French upset Bevin by appealing over his head to Premier Attlee for an improvement in economic relations. Bevin, who was preparing for economic talks in any case, was critical of Alphand for this action. But the Quai believed that the appeal to Attlee broke the deadlock. For a full discussion see Young, *Britain, France and the Unity of Europe*, 37–42. And on the Quai's view of the talks, see especially: Z/Grande Bretagne/37 (15 Feb.); ibid (5 Sept.).

56. Y/287 (3, 4 Sept.), 398 (4 Sept.), and see Y/288 (for another official's talk on Germany, 25 Oct.).

57. Y/288 (22 and 24 Oct.); Massigli papers, vol. 93 (25 Oct.); J. Chauvel, *d'Alger à Berne, 1944–52* (Paris, 1972), 185–6.

58. H. Dalton, *High Tide and After* (1962), 157.

59. Massigli papers, vol. 93 (16 Sept. and 5 Oct.); see also Y/288 (8 Oct.).

60. ibid. (9 Oct.); Chauvel, *d'Alger à Berne*, 165.

61. FO 371/59955/8989, 8895; Churchill College, Cambridge, Duff Cooper papers, DUFC/4/5 (11 Oct.).

62. Y/288 (16 Sept.; 8, 11, 18 Oct.); Y/289 (1 and 23 Nov.).

63. Z/Pologne/54 (March–May); Bidault papers, box 89 (11 March; 3, 20, 27 April; 3 May).

64. Z/Pologne/54, 55 (June–July).

65. Z/Tchécoslovaquie/60 (24 April–8 May); Bidault papers, box 76 (27 April).

66. Z/Tchécoslovaquie/60 (July–Aug.; 16 Oct.). The document quoted literally talks of 'a bullet which we aimed at our feet'.

67. Z/Pologne/55 (27 June, 16–27 July, 14 Nov.). On Garreau's view see: V. Auriol, *Journal du Septenat, vol. I, 1947* (Paris, 1970), 60–1.

68. On this argument: P. Buffutot, 'La politique militaire du Parti Socialiste aux lendemains de la Libération', *Revue d'Histoire de la Deuxième Guerre Mondiale*, 110 (1978), 87–102; R. Frank, 'The French dilemma: modernisation with dependence, or independence and decline' in J. Becker and F. Knipping, eds., *Power in Europe?* (New York, 1986), 266–7. And in general see J.-P. Rioux, 'Les forces politiques et l'Armée', and the two essays by R. Frank and L. Philip on 'Les crédits militaires: contraintes budgétaires et choix politiques', in l'Institut d'Histoire de Temps Present et l'Institut Charles de Gaulle, *De Gaulle et la Nation face aux Problèmes de Défense, 1945–6* (Paris, 1983), 59–69, 173–96.

69. *Journal Officiel, Assemblée, Débats*, 3 April. On military planning and the budget in 1946–7 see Service Historique, Armée de Terre (SHAT), Vincennes, 4Q 2, dossier 2 (*passim*).

70. Discussions on the Army in 1945–6 can be found in: J. Vernet, 'L'armée de Terre en 1945–6' and J. Delmas, 'De Gaulle, la défense nationale et les forces armées, 1944–6', both in *Revue d'Histoire de la Deuxième Guerre Mondiale*, 110 (1978), 7–24 and 45–78; J. Delmas, 'Reflections on the notion of military power through the French example', in Becker and Knipping, eds., *Power in Europe?*, 339–46; and the essays by Vernet, Delmas, C. Lévy and P. Lassalle in *De Gaulle et la Nation*.

71. P. Masson, 'La Marine Française en 1946', available in both ibid., *Revue d'Histoire*, 79–86 and ibid., *De Gaulle et la Nation*, 47–53.

72. J.-P. Dournel, 'L'Armée de l'Air en 1946' in ibid., *Revue d'Histoire*, 25–44; P. Facon, 'L'Armée de l'Air', in ibid., *De Gaulle et la Nation*, 205–12.

73. Y/8 (31 Oct. 1945; 17 Jan., 13 and 20 March, 5 Sept. and 27 Dec. 1946).

74. R. A. Pollard, *Economic Security and the Origins of the Cold War, 1945–50* (New York, 1985), table I.A.

75. J. Lewis, *Changing Direction* (1988), 250–1.

76. T. G. Patterson, *On Every Front* (1979), 155–6.

77. P. Lassalle, 'Securité Française face à l'Est dans l'immédiat après-guerre', in *De Gaulle et la Nation*, 118.

78. G. Soutou, 'La France et le problème du réarmement allemand, 1945–55', paper presented to the Nuneham Park conference, 'Problems of West European Security', 9–11 Nov. 1988, 4.

79. M. Gowing, *Britain and Atomic Energy, 1939–45* (1964), 49–52, 289–96, 342–6; and, on Roosevelt, M. J. Sherwin, *A World Destroyed: the Atomic Bomb and the Grand Alliance* (New York, 1975), 132–3, 135–6, 289–91.

80. C. de Gaulle, *War Memoirs, vol. II, Unity, 1942–44* (1959), 245; B. Goldschmidt, introduction to L'Institut Charles de Gaulle, *L'Adventure de la Bombe: de Gaulle et la dissuasion nucléaire* (Paris, 1985), 25.

81. See A. Coutrot, 'La Création du CEA', in *De Gaulle et la Nation face aux problèmes de défense*, 127–33.

82. M. Gowing, *Independence and Deterrence: Britain and Atomic Energy, 1944–52, vol. I* (1988), 153–8, 339–41; Goldschmidt, *L'Aventure*, 26–7.

83. J. J. Dougherty, *The Politics of Wartime Aid* (1978), 163–4.

84. Cited in Delmas, 'Reflections on the notion of Military Power', 342.

85. Of the numerous works on French colonial policy see especially: D. B. Smith. *The French Colonial Myth and Constitution-Making in the Fourth Republic* (New Haven, Conn., 1973); H. Grimal, *Decolonisation* (1978); R. F. Holland, *European Decolonisation* (1985).

86. On the origins of the Indochina war: G. Bodinier, *Le Retour de la France en Indochine, 1945–6: textes et documents* (Vincennes, 1987); S. Tonneson, *1947* (Paris, 1987). And on the April 1947 decisions: SHAT, 4Q 2, dossier 2 (15 March – 3 April).

87. J.-P. Rioux, *The Fourth Republic, 1944–58* (1987), 106.

88. ibid., 110.
89. *FRUS, 1946, V*, 468–79; Paterson, *On Every Front*, 57, citing White House Daily Summary.
90. On the crisis: G. Elgey, *La République des Illusions, 1945–51* (1965), 230–4.
91. Y/289 (1, 6, 25 Nov.); Bidault papers, box 61 (16 Nov.); *FRUS, 1946, II*, 1143–4. French concern was provoked by contacts between Clay and Sokolovsky about a compromise settlement of economic problems, on which see: J.H. Backer, *The Winds of History* (1983), 149.
92. Y/167 (28, 30 Nov.).
93. ibid (3–6 Dec.).
94. Y/167 (7–10 Dec.) and 290 (Dec.); *CMAE, Vol. IV, New York* (Paris, 1947), 18th, 19th, 22nd and 23rd mtgs.; *FRUS, 1946, II*, 1464–6, 1469–76, 1481–91, 1521–32, 1555–8. Copies of the *CMAE* volume can be found in: box AFA. C-3 (shelved at the MAE); Bidault papers, box 6. Records of meetings are also in Y/168.
95. Z/Sarre/15 (9–18 Dec.); *CMAE*, ibid., 19th mtg.; *Documents relatifs à l'Allemagne*, 40–1; *FRUS, 1946, II*, 1481–91.
96. For example: Z/Sarre/15 (22 June, 25 July); Y/651 (9 March, interministerial committee); Bidault papers, boxes 60 (21 Feb., 4 March and see 6 Nov. 1946 – wrongly attributed to 1945 – for Koenig's views) and 61 (10 Oct.).
97. *FRUS, 1946, V*, 607–10, 621; FO 371/55801/11541, 11690, 12362.
98. The Cabinet discussed the issue on 20 November: Z/Sarre/15 (10 Jan. 1947).
99. ibid. (9 Nov.–7 Dec.); Y/290 (4 Dec.); Bidault papers, box 61 (9, 16 Nov.).
100. Z/Sarre/15 (29 Dec.; 3, 4, 13, 15 Jan.); Z/URSS/52 (13, 15 Jan.); Bidault papers, box 61 (15 Jan.); Catroux, *Rideau de Fer*, 212–3.
101. Z/Sarre/15 (23–29 Dec.); *FRUS, 1946, V*, 655–8; L. D. Clay, *Decision in Germany* (1950), 132–3.
102. Auriol, *Journal, 1947*, 47.
103. Y/289 (15 Nov.).
104. Y/290 and 356 (6 Dec.).
105. Blum's government had resigned the day before.
106. Y/288 (22, 25, 26 and 30 Oct.), 289 (4, 6, 19, 22 and 30 Nov.), 290 (including a recommendation from Koenig's office that Germany should be divided into three confederations – a western one looking to France and the Benelux for economic succour, a northen one looking to Russia, and a southern one with economic ties to Austria), and 291 (8, 17–23 Jan.).
107. Y/291 (15 Jan.); Z/Allemagne/82 (15 Jan.); Bidault papers, box 7 (15 Jan.).
108. Y/398 (16 Jan – 6 Feb.); Bidault papers, box 60 (16, 17 Jan., 1 Feb.); *Documents Français relatifs à l'Allemagne*, 42–64; and see P. O. Lapie, *De Léon Blum à de Gaulle* (Paris, 1971), 30–1.
109. Lapie, ibid., 34; E. Depreux, *Souvenirs d'un Militant* (Paris, 1972), 229–30.
110. Young, *Britain, France and the Unity of Europe*, 39–40.
111. On the economic approach: Z/Grande Bretagne/36 (23 Dec.), 37 (4 Jan.); Bidault papers, box 78 (23 Jan.); Massigli papers, vols. 53 (23 Dec.) and 93 (24, 26 Dec.); Massigli, *Comédie*, 87; Lapie, *Blum à de Gaulle*, 60–1.
112. Z/Grande Bretagne/36 (27 Dec.); Massigli papers, vol. 53 (1 Jan.); Earl of Bessborough, *Return to the Forest* (1962), 129; A. D. Cooper, *Old Men Forget* (1953), 369–70; Chauvel, *d'Alger à Berne*, 191–2; Lapie, ibid., 53–7; Massigli, ibid., 87–9.
113. Y/89 (21, 22 March); *FRUS, 1946, V*, 768–9; and see MAE, René Mayer Papers, vol. 6 (23, 28 Feb.) on coal needs.
114. Y/89 (12, 16, 17, 23 April); Bidault papers, box 64 (12–14 April); Mayer Papers, vols. 3, 4; Centre Jean Monnet, Lausanne, Monnet papers, AMF 4/3/8 (15

April); R. Poidevin, 'La France et le charbon allemand', *Relations Internationales*, 44 (1985), 369.

115. The Ruhr still provided only 15 per cent: A. S. Milward, *The Reconstruction of Western Europe, 1945–51* (1984), 133.

116. See above, 102.
   The figure of 20 million tons over 20 years had been decided by the Planning Council on 16 March.

117. Y/89 (May–Sept.); *FRUS, 1946, V*, 770–1, 779–87. For discussions see: F. M. B. Lynch, *The Political and Economic Reconstruction of France* (PhD, Manchester University, 1981), 163–5; Milward, *Reconstruction*, 136–7; Poidevin, 'France et Charbon Allemand', 369–70.

118. 300,000 tons as against 700,000. Milward, ibid., 133.

119. Y/90 (5, 11, 26 Oct.).

120. Y/90 (10–14 Oct.); Bidault papers, boxes 64 (10 Oct.) and 80 (5 Oct., letter from Min of Production).

121. Y/90 (8, 14 Nov., and see Dec., For talks on the issue in New York), 398 (13 Nov.).

122. Domestic production, at 4.1 million tons in September was above the 1938 average of 4 million; Saar monthly production stood at 132,000 tons compared to 134,000 in 1938: Y/90 (18 Nov.).

123. Z/Grande Bretagne/37 (4, 9 Jan.); Bidault papers, box 78 (1–9 Jan., last including quote from Cooper); Fondation Nationale des Sciences Politiques, Paris, Leon Blum papers, 4 BL 3/Dr. 2/Sdrc (1–9 Jan.); Massigli papers, vol. 53 (3, 4, 6 Jan.), and see 93 (9 Jan.) on Chauvel's doubts about the visit; Lapie, *Blum à de Gaulle*, 54–5; Massigli, *Comédie*, 89–90.

124. Blum papers, ibid. (9 Jan.), Massigli papers, vol. 53 (9 Jan.).

125. Z/Grande Bretagne/37 (13–20 Jan.); Bidault papers, box 78 (10, 14, 21 Jan.); British Library of Political and Economic Science, Hugh Dalton diary, 17 Jan. 1947; Massigli papers, vols. 53 (18 Jan.) and 93 (16, 20 Jan.); Cooper, *Old Men Forget*, 371–2; Lapie, *Blum à de Gaulle*, 66–70; Massigli, *Comédie*, 90; and see Y/90 (15 Jan., re. coal).

126. C. L. Sulzberger, *A Long Row of Candles* (Toronto, 1969), 336–7.

Chapter 7

1. J. Chauvel, *D'Alger à Berne, 1944–52* (Paris, 1972), 154.

2. V. Auriol, *Journal du Septennat, Vol I, 1947* (Paris, 1970), 17–18, 21–3.

3. ibid., 27–9.

4. Bidault continued to criticise the British alliance long after: *Resistance* (1967), 140–2.

5. G. Elgey, *La République des Illusions, 1945–51* (Paris, 1965), 242–4, and see 248–9.

6. Auriol, *Journal, 1947*, 94–5 (meeting of 21 Feb.).

7. ibid., 40, 130.

8. *Foreign Relations of the United States (FRUS), 1947, III*, 689.

9. After his recent encouragements to Blum the French wanted to exclude Duff Cooper from a role in the treaty talks. On these points: Ministère des Affaires Etrangères (MAE), René Massigli papers, Vol. 93 (24 Jan.).

10. On the negotiations: MAE, Z/Grande Bretagne/37 (23 January – 19 March); Archives Nationales (AN), Georges Bidault papers, box 78 (28 January – 3 March); ibid., Vol. 55 (28 January – 18 March); Auriol, *Journal, 1947*, 56–7, 80–1, 87, 100–1, 105–6, 118–9 (including Cabinet discussion); Bidault, *Resistance*, 140–3; Chauvel, *D'Alger à Berne*, 192–3; A.D. Cooper, *Old Men Forget*

(1953), 372–3; R. Massigli, *Une Comédie des Erreurs* (Paris, 1978), 91–5. On the parliamentarians: Assemblée Nationale, Procès Verbaux de la Commission des Affaires Etrangères (5, 12, 19, February); *Journal Officiel, Débats*, 28 February, 538; and on the popularity of a treaty: G.H. Gallup, ed., *The Gallup International Public Opinion Polls, France, Vol. I* (1976), May 1947. For discussions of the significance of the treaty to British policy see: J. Baylis, 'Britain and the Treaty of Dunkirk'; *Journal of Strategic Studies*, 5 (1982), 236–47; S. Greenwood, 'Return to Dunkirk', *Journal of Strategic Studies*, 6 (1983), 49–65; B. Zeeman, 'Britain and the Cold War', *European History Quarterly*, 16 (1986), 343–67.

11. Auriol, ibid., 17–18, 56–7; H. Alphand, *L'Etonnement d'Etre* (Paris, 1977), 197.
12. Massigli papers, Vol. 55 (18 March).
13. C. Mauriac, *The Other de Gaulle: Diaries 1944–54* (1973), 228–9, 231, 246; J. Vendroux, *Cette chance que j'ai eu . . .* (Paris, 1974), 205.
14. Y/292 (24 Feb., and see 1 Feb.), 293 (17 Feb.); Bidault papers, box 61 (24 Feb.); Massigli papers, Vol. 63 (17, 19 Feb.); see also: Y/91 (15, 31 Jan. – 3 Feb. – British assurances on German production); Y/378 (1 Feb., Massigli–Sargent meeting).
15. Bidault papers box 62 (Feb., especially 11 Feb.); Auriol, *Journal, 1947*, 78; and see Y/399 (27 March).
16. Massigli papers, Vol. 55 (25 Feb.).
17. ibid., Vol. 91 (6 Feb.); and see Y/371 (29 Jan.).
18. In December, after agreement on forming the Bizone had been reached, the British Chancellor of the Exchequer, Hugh Dalton, had suggested to Massigli that France should join it in order to help Britain control the Americans. But Massigli feared that France's German policy was too different to that of the Anglo-Americans and that such a move would commit Paris to an anti-Soviet system. Y/378 (8, 11 Dec.).
19. Auriol, *Journal, 1947*, 115.
20. Z/Belgique/34 (10 March); Bidault papers, box 102 (10 March). On the Dutch: Z/Grande Bretagne/37 (23 Jan., and see 4 April on later Luxembourg interest in a treaty).
21. J.W. Young, *Britain, France and the Unity of Europe, 1945–51* (Leicester, 1984), 55–6, 59.
22. Z/Tchécoslovaquie/60 (15 Jan. – 27 Feb.); Bidault papers, box 76 (14, 19 Feb.; 18 April); Auriol, *Journal, 1947*, 80–1 (on the Cabinet); Assemblée Nationale, procès verbaux de la Commission des Affaires Etrangères, 19 Feb. 1947.
Bidault also told the Commission that they had considered treaties with Rumania and Yugoslavia but that these would be difficult to negotiate, the Rumanian because of political instability in Bucharest, the Yugoslav because of Tito's emnity with America and Britain. On the Rumanian treaty idea see also: Z/Roumanie/26 (3–28 Feb.).
23. Z/Pologne/55 (13 Jan. – 20 Feb.); Bidault papers, box 89 (13, 18 Feb.); Auriol, ibid., 78.
24. Y/391 (13 Jan.); Z/URSS/52 (13, 15 Jan.); Bidault papers, box 82 (13, 15 Jan.), and see box 61 (15 Jan. and n.d., note on reparations, including consideration of Franco-Soviet co-operation); G. Catroux, *J'ai vu Tomber le Rideau de Fer* (Paris, 1952), 212–14.
25. Y/291 (8, 16 Jan.).
26. Z/URSS/52 (21, 25 Jan. – 10 Feb.); Bidault papers, box 61 (21 Jan.).
27. Y/291 (27 Jan.), 292 (2 Feb.); Bidault papers, box 61 (27 January, 2 Feb.); Catroux, *Rideau de Fer*, 214.
28. Y/292 (20 Feb.); Bidault papers, box 61 (20 Feb., and see 13 Feb. on Catroux's delivery of France's Ruhr memorandum to the Soviet Foreign Ministry); Auriol, *Journal, 1947*, 89; Catroux, ibid., 217–18.

29. Z/URSS/52 (11 Feb.).
30. Massigli papers, Vols. 55 (13 Feb.) and 93 (10, 13 Feb.).
31. Bidault, *Resistance*, 142.
32. Z/URSS/52 (n.d.); Bidault papers, box 82 (5 March).
33. Bogomolov told Auriol that Russia was interested in the idea of a tripartite Franco-Soviet-British pact. French intelligence sources believed this reflected a desire to forestall a 'Western bloc'. Auriol, *Journal, 1947*, 113–5, 123–4, 133–4.
34. *FRUS, 1947, II*, 154–5, and *III*, 689.
35. B/Etats Unis/120 (12, 13 Feb.); Y/9 (13 Feb.), and 291 (27, 30 Jan.); Bidault papers, box 80 (12 Feb.); *FRUS, 1947, II*, 156–8.
36. Bidault papers, box 61 (6 Feb.).
37. ibid., boxes 61 (19, 26 Feb.; 4 March) and 80 (19 Feb.).
38. Y/9 (21 Feb.); C.L. Sulzberger, *A Long Row of Candles* (Toronto, 1969), 340.
39. On this point see: Y/185 (1 March); J. Dumaine, *Quai d'Orsay* (1958), 108.
40. Bidault papers, boxes 62 and 66 (22 Feb.).
41. Y/371 (7 Feb.); Bidault papers, box 7 (22 Feb.).
42. Auriol, *Journal, 1947*, 167–8.
43. Y/371 (29 Jan.).
44. Bidault papers, box 7 (14, 15 Feb.; 1 March) and see box 60 for a memorandum (30 Dec. 1946) by Commandant Gossault of the Ministry of National Defence calling for the 'Europeanisation' of the Ruhr.
45. On 25 February the Russian Marshall Sokolovsky bitterly attacked the creation of the Bizone. See Y/378 (4 March, 1 April).
46. Bidault papers, box 7 (4 March); and on Koenig's views see Auriol, *Journal, 1947*, 109.
47. *Journal Officiel, Débats*, 27 Feb., 499–501 (Reynaud speech) and 501–4 (Bonte), 28 Feb., (Bidault); Assemblée Nationale, procès verbaux de la Commission des Affaires Etrangères, 29 Jan., and see 19 Feb.; Bidault papers, box 7 (which show that, in preparing his speech, Bidault drew on documents from 1919–20); and see Auriol, ibid., 100–1.
48. In general see: Y/198, 291, 292; Bidault papers, box 7; *FRUS, 1947 II*, 1–138. And on Belgian views: G. Kurgan–van Hentenryk, 'La Belgique et le relèvement économique de l'Allemagne', *Relations Internationales*, 51 (1987), 350–2.
49. Auriol, *Journal, 1947*, 88–9.
50. Bidault papers boxes 60 (25 Feb.) and 7 (8 March).
51. Y/185 (8, 14 March), 378 (8 March), 379 (8 March); Bidault papers, boxes 7 (8 March), 60 (n.d.) and 61 (11 March).
52. AN, F60/903 (5 March).
53. Y/90 (18, 21 Feb.), 91 (1, 4, 7 March); *FRUS, 1947, II*, 187–9.
54. B/Etats Unis/119 (6 March); Y/9, 91 and 399 (6 March); Bidault papers, boxes 64 (8 March) and 80 (11, 13 March); Auriol, *Journal, 1947*, 131, 136, 673–6; *FRUS, 1946, II*, 190–5 (including quote).
55. *FRUS, 1947, III*, 690–5; P. Sapp, *The US, France and the Cold War* (Kent State University, Ph.D., 1978), 135, including quotes.
56. Bidault, *Resistance*, 143; S. Bidault, *Souvenirs* (Paris, 1987), 71–2 (including Bidault's joke); F. Seydoux, *Mémoires d'Outre-Rhin* (Paris, 1975), 106 (according to which Bidault was outwardly confident about co-operation with Russia).
57. Catroux, *Rideau de Fer*, 221–2, and in general see Ch. XVI.
58. Y/91 (11 March); Bidault papers, boxes 7 (10, 11 March), 61 (10 March); Auriol, *Journal, 1947*, 138–9; *FRUS, 1947, II*, 241–2. Bidault also pressed Bevin on coal in a meeting of 10 March: Y/91 (10 March); Public Record Office (PRO), FO 800/465/France/47/10 (Bevin papers) (15 March).
59. Bidault papers, box 81 (6 March, and see 10 March – 4 April). For the text of

the speech: M. Carlyle, ed., *Documents on International Affairs, 1947–8* (1952), 2–7.

60. Y/9 (10 March).
61. Catroux, *Rideau de Fer*, 223–6; Z/URSS/43 (March).
62. Auriol, *Journal, 1947*, 143–4, 148–9.
63. For records of the meetings see: *Conseil des Ministres des Affaires Etrangères (CMAE), Vol. V, Moscou* (Paris, 1947), available shelved, box AFA.C-3, at MAE; *CMAE, documents relatifs à l'Allemagne, 1945–7* (Paris, 1948), 28–334; Bidault papers, box 7 (not exhaustive), the records in Y/149–151, 185, 186, 293 and 294, and *FRUS, 1947, II* (1972). Bidault's major statements are in: *Déclarations de M. Georges Bidault . . . au CMAE: Moscou, Mars–Avril 1947* (Paris, 1947).
64. They met on 13 March: Y/185; Bidault papers, boxes 7 (14 March) and 80 (13 March); *FRUS, 1947, II*, 246–9.
65. Y/293 (17 March); Z/URSS/52 (17 March); Bidault papers, box 7 (18 March); Auriol, *Journal, 1947*, 236–7; Bidault, *Resistance*, 146–7; Seydoux, *Mémoires*, 108.
66. *FRUS, 1946, II*, 396–7, 400–1; and see Bidault papers, box 7 (21 March).
67. Bidault papers, box 7 (19 March); Auriol, *Journal, 1947*, 149. In fact Bidault also told the CFM on 1 April that the issues of coal supplies *and* the Saar must be resolved before all others: *CMAE, Vol. V*, 18th meeting; *FRUS, 1947, II*, 299–301.
68. *CMAE, Vol. V*, 8th–10th meetings, and see 18th, 23rd meetings on economic issues: *FRUS, 1947, II*, 258, 262–66.
69. *CMAE, Vol. V*, 11th, 12th and see 19th meeting; *FRUS, 1947, II*, 271–2, 276–8.
70. Public Record Office, London, FO 800/272 (Sargent papers), (20, 26 March).
71. W. Bedell Smith, *Moscow Mission, 1946–49* (1950), 207–8.
72. Bidault papers, box 7 (31 March).
73. Auriol, *Journal, 1947*, 179–80.
74. *CMAE, Vol. V*, 21st, 26th and 27th meetings; *FRUS, 1947, II*, 311–3, 327–8, 330.
75. *CMAE Vol. V*, 24th–26th meetings; Y/399 (10–11 April); *FRUS, 1947, II*, 320–8; Auriol, *Journal, 1947*, 186 and 757 note 18.
76. Smith, *Moscow Mission*, 209.
77. C. Bohlen, *Witness to History* (1973), 262.
78. Catroux, *Rideau de Fer*, 236–7.
79. Seydoux, *Mémoires*, 108–10.
80. *CMAE, Vol. V*, 28th, 29th meetings; *FRUS, 1947, II*, 332–6; and on the views of the Quai and EMDN see Y/356 (Nov.–Dec.; 20, 25 Feb.; 14, 15 April).
81. *CMAE, Vol. V*, 42nd, 43rd meetings; *FRUS, 1947, II*, 381–90.
82. See above, 142.
83. *FRUS, 1947, II*, 249; J.H. Backer, *Winds of History* (New York, 1983), 176–7 (which discuss John Foster Dulles's support for an independent Ruhr and the very different views of Lucius Clay).
84. On the ECO see above, 89.
85. Bidault papers, box 7 (15 March).
86. *CMAE, Vol. V*, 10th meeting; *FRUS, 1947, II*, 265–6, 274.
87. Y/91 (12, 24, 31 March), 399 (18, 24 March); Bidault papers box 64 (31 March); Massigli papers, Vol. 60 (24, 28 March); *FRUS, 1947, II*, 400–1 (Teigen–Caffery meeting).
88. *CMAE, Vol. V*, 29th, 30th meetings; Y/91 (17 April); *FRUS, 1947, II*, 336, 345–7.
89. Y/91 (27 March), 186 (5 April); Bidault papers, boxes 7 (27, 31 March; 1, 5, 7, 9 April) and 64 (21 March); Auriol, *Journal, 1947, II*, 184–6 (Cabinet meeting); and on the US tactics see *FRUS, 1947, II*, 476–8.
90. Y/91 (19, 21 April); Bidault papers, boxes 7 (9, 10 April) and 64 (9, 19, 21 April); *FRUS, 1947, II*, 485–8.

91. The German coal export situation eased over the following months: Y/91 (*passim*).
92. Catroux, *Rideau de Fer*, 242.
93. Elgey, *République des Illusions*, 276, and see 283 for an exchange between Bidault and Thorez in Cabinet.
94. *The Times*, 30 April; ibid., 276; and see Bidault, *Resistance*, 148–9.
95. B/Etats Unis/107 (29 April); Y/186 (29 April); Bidault papers, boxes 7 (10 May) and 81 (29 April); and see the document reproduced in *Institut Pierre Renouvin: travaux et recherches*, 2 (1988), 67–8.
96. Y/185 (n.d.).
97. Bidault papers, box 7 (n.d. and 16 April).
98. *FRUS, 1947, III*, 690–2.
99. Bodleian Library, Oxford, Lord Woolton papers, box 77 (2 April, 1947); copied in Massigli papers, Vol. 78 (given to Massigli by Lord Kemsley).
100. Auriol, *Journal, 1947*, 132.
101. The British learnt of these military preparations. Elgey, *République des Illusions*; 261–3, PRO, FO 371/67680/3210.
102. Auriol, *Journal, 1947*, 150.
103. ibid., 153, 156–60 and 163–6 on the Cabinet discussions.
104. *FRUS, 1947, III*, 699–703.
105. Elgey, *République des Illusions*, 259–60, and see 282–3.
106. This on 3 April: *FRUS, 1946, III*, 696.
107. On the expulsion see especially: Auriol, *Journal, 1947*, 204–18; Elgey, *République des Illusions*, 285–91.
108. E. Rice-Maximin, 'The US and the French Left, 1945–9', *Journal of Contemporary History*, 19 (1984), 735–7; and see M.P. Leffler, 'The US and the Strategic dimensions of the Marshall Plan', *Diplomatic History*, 12 (1988), 281. On Ramadier's statement to Bogomolov: Elgey, ibid., 292.
109. Elgey, ibid. 278–9.
110. *FRUS, 1947, III*, 709–13.
111. Auriol, *Journal, 1947*, 219–24.
112. ibid., 236–7, 243.
113. ibid., 233.
114. Assemblée Nationale, procès verbaux de la commission des affaires etrangères, 14, 21 and 23 May.
115. Bidault papers, box 80 (30 April).
116. There is no evidence upon them from the French side, but see: Young, *Britain, France and the Unity of Europe*, 60–1.
117. Z/Belgique/34 (17 April, 2 June).
118. Spaak quickly informed the British. Again I have found no evidence from the French side, but see: PRO, FO 371/67724/5529; Churchill College, Cambridge, diary of Hughe Knatchbull–Hugessen, 11 June; and especially P.H. Spaak, *The Continuing Battle*, (1971), 90.
119. Sulzberger. *Long Row of Candles* 361.
120. Z/Pologne/55 (12–30 March); Bidault papers, box 89 (30 March, 2 April).
121. Z/Pologne/55 (1 March); Auriol, *Journal, 1947*, 114–15.
122. The British were also upset that Spaak seemed to be considering Eastern Europe treaties, but Spaak's exact intentions seem unclear. Z/Tchécoslovaquie/60 (31 March, 24 May); Bidault papers, box 76 (29 March, 14 May) and see box 102 (7, 8 March on Spaak); FO 371/67663/2363, 3323.
123. Z/Tchécoslovaquie/60 (17 April, 6 May); Bidault papers, box 76 (18 April, 6 May).
124. Z/Tchécoslovaquie/60 (26, 3 May), 61 (2, 9 June); Bidault papers, box 76 (6, 9, 12, May, 4 June); and on Bidault's conversation with Bevin, FO 371/67663/3744.

125. Z/Pologne/55 (23 April – 24 June); Bidault papers, box 89 (18 April – 24 June).
126. AN, 80 AJ 1 (27 Nov., 7 Jan.) and 2 (texts of plan); J. Monnet, *Memoirs* (1978), 260–1; in general see P. Mioche, *Le Plan Monnet: Genèse et Elaboration 1941–7* (Paris, 1987), Chapter VII, and see 184–93 for party attitudes.
127. To coincide with the Marshall Aid programme.
128. On French problems see: F.M.B. Lynch, *The Political and Economic Reconstruction of France* (Manchester University, PhD, 1981), 55–82, 107–10.
129. Z/URSS/52 (11 Jan.).
130. Auriol, *Journal, 1947*, 78.
131. Y/186 (20 April); Bidault papers, box 7 (20 April); *FRUS, 1947, II*, 367–70; Seydoux, *Mémoires*, 110.
132. B. Ruhm von Oppen, *Documents on Germany under Occupation, 1945–54* (1955), 227.
133. A.S. Milward, *The Reconstruction of Western Europe, 1945–51* (1984), Chapter 1.
134. See above, 99.
135. Milward, *Reconstruction*, 15–16, 35.
136. *FRUS, 1947, III*, 696–7, 708–9.
137. B/Etats Unis/247 (18 Feb.); Bidault papers, box 80 (27 Jan., 12 Feb.). Shortages also continued in the ZOF: Z/Allemagne/86.
138. B/Etats Unis 247 (23 April – 15 May); Bidault papers, box 80 (29 April – 4 June); Auriol, *Journal, 1947*, 137–8, 224–5, 248; *FRUS, 1947, III*, 701–8, 715, and see 716–7.
139. Bidault papers, box 81 (7 May).
140. ibid. (22, 27 May).
141. For the text of the speech: Bidault papers, box 20 (6 June); Carlyle, ed., *Documents on International Affairs, 1947–8*, 23–6.
142. Y/2 (28 May), and see Z/URSS/43 (29 May).
143. ibid. (9 June); Bidault papers, box 81 (9, 18 June).
144. A. Bullock, *Ernest Bevin: Foreign Secretary* (1983), 404–6.
145. Massigli, *Comédie*, 99–100.
146. Y/228 (7 June); *Documents de la Conférence des Ministres des Affaires Etrangères . . . 27 juin au 3 juillet 1947* (government publication, Paris, 1947), 9.
147. Bonnet put Bidault's views to the US in an aide-memoire of 13 June. Y/228 (10 and 13 June); Bidault papers, box 20 (10, 13 June); *Documents de la Conférence . . .*, 10–12; *FRUS, 1947, III*, 251–3.
148. Bidault papers, box 20 (12, 14 June); Massigli, *Comédie*, 100; and see *FRUS, 1947, III*, 253–5.
149. Auriol, *Journal, 1947*, 266–9.
150. ibid., 278–82, 284, 287–9, 294, 329.
151. ibid., 274–5, 277–8.
152. Y/228 (14, 17 June); Bidault papers, box 20 (14, 17 June).
153. Bidault papers, box 20 (16 June); Y/228 (14 June); Auriol, *Journal, 1947*, 266–7.
154. *FRUS, 1947, III*, 255–6.
155. Bidault papers, box 82 (17, 20 June); *Documents de la Conférence . . .*, 15–16; Auriol, *Journal, 1947*, 284–5, 292; ibid., 255–63; and see Dumaine, *Quai d'Orsay*, 127–8.
156. Bidault papers, box 82 (19 June).
157. Y/128 (19–23 June); Y/228 (16, 18, 21 June); Bidault papers, box 20 (16, 18 June).
158. Y/128 (23 June); Bidault papers, box 82 (22 June); *Documents de la Conférence . . .*, 17; and see *Journal Officiel, Débats, Assemblée Nationale*, 23 June, 2325, for a hopeful announcement of the forthcoming Paris conference by Bidault.
159. Y/128 (25–27 June); Dumaine, *Quai D'Orsay*, 128–9; *FRUS, 1947, III*, 296.
160. Y/128 (24 June)

161. Bidault papers, box 20 (2 July).
162. FO 371/105963/4 (5 March 1953). I am grateful to Dr. John Kent, of the London School of Economics, for pointing this source out to me.
163. For records of the talks see: Y/128 (27 June – 3 July); Bidault papers, box 82 (27 June – 3 July); *Documents de la Conférence . . .* , 21–61.
164. Dumaine, *Quai d'Orsay*, 130.
165. Bidault papers, box 84 (1 July, and Charpentier telegram of same date, on Soviet tactics).
166. For example, Dumaine, *Quai d'Orsay*, 130–1.
167. Auriol, *Journal, 1947*, 311–3, 319–22, and see 303, 322–5.
168. E. Roll, *Crowded Hours* (1982), 52.
169. Bevin spoke well of Bidault to Massigli, American representatives and the British Cabinet: Bidault papers, box 78 (4 July); Massigli papers, box 91 (4 July); PRO, CAB. 128/10, CM (47) 60; *FRUS, 1947 III*, 302–3, 307, 310–11; Massigli, *Comédie*, 101.
170. *FRUS, 1947, III*, 308–9.

Chapter 8

1. Marshall, like Bevin, was pleased with Bidault's performance at Paris: *Foreign Relations of the United States (FRUS), 1947, Vol. III*, 308, 312–3.
2. Ministère des Affaires Etrangères (MAE), Y/128 (2, 3 July).
3. Y/129 and 228 (July); Archives Nationales (AN), Georges Bidault papers, box 20 (July).
4. *FRUS, 1947, III*, 303–4.
5. Y/128 (4 July).
6. Y/129 (3 July), 228 (1, 2 July); Bidault papers, box 20 (23 June; 1, 3 July).
7. Y/128 (9 July).
8. Y/129 (4–10 July), 130 (6 Aug., 5 Sept.) and 228 (7 July); Bidault papers, boxes 20 (7–15 July), 76 (8, 16 July) and 90 (9, 10 July); V. Auriol, *Journal du Septennant, Vol. I, 1947* (Paris, 1974), 331, 336, 338–41.
9. MAE, Z/Tchécoslovaquie/61 (6 June – 2 Aug.); Z/Pologne/55 (10–21 July); Bidault papers, boxes 76 (6 June – 23 July) and 89 (3–21 July); Auriol, *Journal, 1947*, 338–41, 350–2.
10. Bidault papers, box 20 (16 July); Auriol, ibid., 356–7.
11. For example, Bidault papers, box 84 (28 July).
12. It was a point evidently considered by George Kennan, but even for him was a secondary motive for launching the Marshall Plan. See J. Gaddis, *The Long Peace* (1987), 155–7.
13. Auriol, *Journal, 1947*, 349–53.
14. Y/129 (27, 28 June).
15. *FRUS, 1947, III*, 315–8.
16. See above, 136.
17. Y/378 (20, 23 May) and 379 (June); Bidault papers, boxes 61 (22 May) and 62 (June); *FRUS, 1947, Vol. III*, 923–4.
18. On the Marshall–Bevin talks see: *FRUS, 1947, II*, 356–8, 472–6, 479–85, 490–1. On Clay see especially: J.E. Smith, ed., *The Papers of Lucius D. Clay, Vol. I, 1945–7* Bloomington, Indiana, 1974), 377–82; *FRUS, 1947, III*, 263–4. Massigli's quote is from MAE, Z/URSS/43 (23 May).
19. Y/128 (18 June).
20. Z/Grande Bretagne/38 (15 July); Bidault papers, box 62 (1–3, 8, 15 July, including talks with Bevin); *FRUS, 1947, III*, 312–3 (Caffery–Bidault talk 4 July); Public

Record Office, London FO 371/62407/5572 (Duff Cooper talk, 7 July); and, on Bonnet's reports see Auriol, *Journal, 1947*, 348.

21. Y/129 (9 July); Bidault papers, box 62 (9, 11 July); Auriol, ibid., 337; *FRUS, 1947, II*, and 983–6 and *III*, 328–30.

22. *FRUS, 1947, III*, 717–22.

23. *FRUS, 1947, II*, 986–90.

24. Y/399 (16 July); Bidault papers, boxes 62 (16, 19 July), 63 (18 July); *FRUS, 1947, II*, 993–6.

25. Bidault papers, boxes 61 and 80 (16 July); *FRUS, 1947, II*, 997–9.

26. Auriol, *Journal, 1947*, 354–6.

27. Y/379 (16, 17 July), 375 (21 July); Bidault papers, box 61 (16 July).

28. Y/295 (17 July); Y/376 (18 July); Bidault papers, box 62 (17–19 July); *FRUS, 1947, II*, 991–3.

29. Auriol, *Journal, 1947*, 359–60.

30. *FRUS, 1947, II*, 996.

31. Auriol, *Journal, 1947*, 358–9; ibid., 1000–3.

32. *FRUS, 1947, III*, 722–4.

33. Y/375 (17, 22 July); Bidault papers, box 62 (21 July); *FRUS, 1947, II*, 997, 999–1000, 1003–11, 1013–14; R. Massigli, *Une Comédie des Erreurs* (Paris, 1978), 103.

34. Bidault had, however, made a statement on 20 June saying that he had defended France's case in full at the Moscow CFM. Auriol, *Journal, 1947*, 362–3, 365–6; *Journal Officiel, Débats, Assemblée*, 20 June, 2289–92, 25 July, 2542–70, and 26 July, 3585–3612.

35. On 28 July Massigli suggested a 'sliding scale' for German steel output, which would increase in proportion to French production. Y/379 (14 July); Bidault papers, boxes 60 (28 July) and 61 (14 July); MAE, René Massigli papers, Vol. 91 (28 July). On Bonnet see: Auriol, *Journal, 1947*, 788, note 23.

36. Bidault papers, box 63 (24 July); ibid., 375, 381–4, 388–9, 695–9. It was evidently on the basis of this memorandum that Monnet talked to Clayton on 29 July: *FRUS, 1947, II*, 1011–12.

37. Y/295 (30 July; 2 Aug.).

38. The French were upset that the USA Secretary of War had publicly said there was no agreement to consult France on the level of industry. Y/375 (4, 9 Aug.); Bidault papers, box 62 (4 Aug.); Auriol, ibid., 381, 386, 389, 391, and 787, note 18; *FRUS, 1947, II*, 1014–17, and *III*, 349–50, 353; S.P. Sapp, *The US, France and the Cold War* (Kent State University, PhD, 1978), 213–14.

39. *FRUS, 1947, II*, 1008–11, 1026–7; J.H. Backer, *Winds of History*, (New York, 1983), 193–4; Smith, *Clay Papers*, 383–92, 394–7, 399, 401–6.

40. Y/295 (10 Aug.); Bidault papers, boxes 20 (2 Aug.), 60 (11 Aug.), 62 (Aug.) and 63 (memoranda of 5 Aug.); Massigli papers, Vol. 63 (5 Aug.).

41. Y/399 (5 Aug.); Bidault papers, box 60 (7 Aug., Auriol memorandum); Auriol, *Journal, 1947*, 389. The EMDN also favoured controls on Germany in a European framework: Service Historique, Armée de Terre (SHAT), Vincennes, 4Q 10, dossier 6 (29 July).

42. For example, FO 371/62579/6970.

43. Auriol, *Journal, 1947*, 402; *FRUS, 1947, II*, 1029–42, 1046–7.

44. Y/376 (22–28 Aug.), 399 (14, 23 Aug.); Bidault papers, box 62 (22–28 Aug.); Masssigli papers, Vol. 64 (*passim*); Auriol, ibid., 408–9, 414; *FRUS, 1947, II*, 1047–9, 1055–66. The communiqué may be read in: *L'année Politique, 1947* (Paris, annual), 355–6; B. Ruhm von Oppen, *Documents on Germany under Occupation, 1945–54* (1955), 238–45; and M. Carlyle, ed., *Documents on International Affairs, 1947–8* (1952), 625–6.

45. Y/375 (27 Aug.); Auriol, ibid., 425, *FRUS, 1947, II*, 1066–8; Ruhm von Oppen, ibid., 239–45; Carlyle, ed., ibid., 623–4, 626–32.
46. Bidault papers, box 64 (Sept.); *FRUS, 1947, II*, 1089–98; Smith, ed., *Clay papers*, 417–19, 422–3, 426, 438–40.
47. J. Monnet, *Memoirs* (1978), 274.
48. Talks on mine ownership were held by America and Britain between 12 Aug. and 10 Sept. Bidault had been forewarned of this on 11 July: Bidault papers, box 62 (11 July); *FRUS, 1947, II*, 938–68 (quote from 965).
49. Y/375, 376 (13 Sept.).
50. *FRUS, 1947, II*, 971–7.
51. ibid., 1068–72.
52. Z/Grande Bretagne/38 (15 July); Bidault papers, boxes 20 (11–15 July) and 78 (15, 16 July).
53. Bidault papers, box 20 (18 July, Monnet paper; and 2 Aug., Alphand paper).
54. *FRUS, 1947, III*, 333–5, 338–9, 347, 368; A.S. Milward, *The Reconstruction of Western Europe, 1945–51* (1984), 66–7, 71–3, 75–7.
55. P. Melandri and M. Vaisse, 'France: from Powerlessness to the Search for Influence', in J. Becker and F. Knipping, eds., *Power in Europe?* (New York, 1986), 462.
56. *FRUS, 1947, III*, 343–4, 348–9, 350–60, 364–91 (quote from 372).
57. Auriol, *Journal, 1947*, 414.
58. Bidault papers, box 20 (10 Sept.); *FRUS, 1947, III*, 405–8, 412–17, 420–3.
59. Bidault papers, box 20 (10 Sept.); Aveyron departmental archives, Rodez, Paul Ramadier papers, 52 J 67 (11 Sept.).
60. Bidault papers, box 20 (11, 12 Sept.); *FRUS, 1947, III*, 423–30.
61. *FRUS, 1947, III*, 431–7.
62. Y/130 (22 Sept.); Bidault papers, box 20 (22 Sept.).
63. Bidault papers, box 20 (2 Aug.).
64. Auriol, *Journal, 1947*, 391.
65. Z/Généralités/5 (14 Aug.).
66. ibid. (6–15 Sept.); Auriol, *Journal, 1947*, 429; and on British policy see J.W. Young, *Britain, France and the Unity of Europe, 1945–51* (Leicester, 1984), 67–9.
67. Y/130 (9 Oct.).
68. Z/Italie/87 (27 Feb. – July), including French draft treaty of amity); Bidault papers, box 91 (10 March; 3, 17 May).
69. *Journal Officiel, Débats, Assemblée*, 13 June, 2111–12.
70. Z/Italie/90 (15 July); C. Sforza, *Cinque Anni a Palazzo Chigi* (Rome, 1952), 50–2; P. Guillen, 'Le projet d'Union Economique entre la France, L'Italie et le Benélux', in R. Poidevin, ed., *Histoire des Débuts de la Construction Européenne, 1948–50* (Brussels, 1986), 143–5. On Sforza's policies see A. Varsori, 'De Gasperi, Nenni and Sforza', in Becker and Knipping, eds., *Power in Europe?* (London, New York and Munich) 99–104.
71. Z/Italie/90 (2 Aug.).
72. Z/Italie/87 (1, 26 Aug.).
73. ibid. (Aug. 1947 – Feb. 1948).
74. Bidault papers, box 91 (11 Aug.).
75. Z/Italie/90 (5 Sept.); Guillen, 'Le projet d'Union Economique', 143–4.
76. Z/Italie/90 (13–30 Sept.; 8, and see 22 Nov. on labour; 22 Dec.), and 91 (6 Jan.); Bidault papers, box 91 (Sept., 22 Dec.); Guillen, ibid., 145.
77. Y/130 (Oct.–Nov.) and 228 (Nov.); Bidault papers, box 20 (Oct.–Dec.); *FRUS, 1947, III*, 446–70.
78. *FRUS, 1947, III*, 303, 311, 344–6, 360–3, 726–9 (quote from 362–3). Ramadier had told Clayton that the wheat crop was the worst since the wars of Napoleon: Ramadier papers, 52 J 67 (11, 16 Sept.).

79. *FRUS, 1947, III*, 744–7.
80. Y/228 (19, 29–30 Nov.) and 229 (Dec.); Bidault papers, box 80 (Sept.–Dec.); ibid., 470–84, 756–9, 775–86, 801–3, 807–9, 815–17.
81. MAE, B/Etats Unis/ 248 (Dec.–Feb.); Y/131 (5 Feb. 1948); Archives Economiques et Financières, B.18220, Bidault papers, boxes 20 (Dec.–2 Jan.) and 80 (Dec.); *FRUS, 1947, III*, 820–5; Auriol *Journal, 1947*, 651; and see Bidault's account to the Assemblée Nationale's Commission des Affaires Etrangères, procès verbaux of 5 Jan. 1948.
82. Bidault papers, box 83 (8, 19, 27 Aug.), and see 84 (19 Nov., regarding Soviet psychological and propaganda preparations for War); Auriol, ibid., 398.
83. G. Catroux, *J'ai vu Tomber le Rideau de Fer* (Paris, 1952), 261–6.
84. Auriol, *Journal, 1947*, 445–6, and see 438–9, 457–8.
85. ibid., 419–21, and see 428–9.
86. ibid., 426–37, 440–2, 455, 464–5.
87. On the debate over what exactly happened to Duclos at the Cominform meeting see: E. Reale, *Avec Jacques Duclos au Banc des Accusés* (Paris, 1958); J. Duclos, *Mémoires, Vol. IV, 1945–52* (Paris, 1971), 217–20.
88. Auriol, *Journal, 1947*, 467.
89. R. Tiersky, *French Communism*, (Columbia University Press, 1974), 166.
90. Z/Généralités/32 (6–29 Oct.); Bidault papers, box 83 (7, 29 Oct.).
91. *Journal Officiel, Débats, Assemblée*, 28 Oct., 4915–26; and see *FRUS, 1947, III*, 795–6.
92. Quoted in L. Marcou, *Le Kominform* (Paris, 1977), 69 and see 64–70 in general on the SFIO.
93. See, for example, Auriol, *Journal, 1947*, 75 (11 Feb.).
94. C. Mauriac, *The Other de Gaulle: diaries 1944–54* (1973), 234–44.
95. C. de Gaulle, *Discours et Messages, 1946–58* (Paris, 1970), 41–6.
96. In a secret meeting: J. Tournoux, *Le Feu et la Cendre* (Paris, 1979), 26–8.
97. De Gaulle, *Discours et Messages*, 48–55.
98. A. Werth, *France, 1940–55* (1957), 374.
99. On de Gaulle's fear of war since resigning office, see for example: Mauriac, *The Other de Gaulle*, 154, 164, 176, 181–2, 200–1; Tournoux, *Le Feu*, 13–16, 25, 35–7, 40, and *l'Histoire Secrète* (Paris, 1962), 249–50.
100. Auriol, *Journal, 1947*, 462–3, 467–9.
101. ibid., 474–5, 482–6.
102. ibid., 495–57, 503, 505–7.
103. There is no evidence that such a fund was created: Sapp, *The US, France and the Cold War*, 224–8.
104. *FRUS, 1947, III*, 730–2, 736–8, 748–9, 750–1, 761–5.
105. ibid., 766–73, 790–2.
106. FO 371/67681/3753, 6622; 67682/8619, 8893, 9972.
107. De Gaulle did, however, meet John Foster Dulles in December. *FRUS, 1947, III*, 792–5, 622–5, 629–31; and see *1948, III*, 630–3 for reconsideration of the question of a Caffery–de Gaulle meeting.
108. F.M.B. Lynch, *The Political and Economic Reconstruction of France* (PhD, Manchester University, 1981), 79, gives a table of working days lost every month in 1947.
109. On the political crisis see Auriol, *Journal, 1947*, 523–4, 541–6, 554–84; G. Elgey, *La République des Illusions, 1945–51* (Paris, 1965), 339–47, 356–8.
110. Auriol, ibid., 588–9, 591–5, 607–8, 612.
111. On the question of PCF motivations see: ibid., 617–8; *FRUS, 1947, III*, 797–8, 803–6, 813–14 and, on Marshall's view, B/Etats Units/107 (7 Dec.).
112. Auriol, ibid., 609–11, 614–15, 619–23, 627.
113. H. Nicolson, *Diaries and Letters, 1945–62* (1971), entry of 3 Dec.

114. *FRUS, 1947, III*, 819–20, 823–4.
115. Z/Grande Bretagne/38 (22 Sept.); Bidault papers, box 78 (22 Sept.); Auriol, *Journal, 1947*, 468–9.
116. Z/Grande Bretagne/38 (29 Sept.–3 Oct.); Bidault, boxes 62 (1 Oct.), 78 (24 Sept., 1, 3 Oct.); Massigli papers, Vols. 53 (1 Oct.), 91 (24 Sept.), 93 (26, 30 Sept., 3 Oct.); Massigli, *Comédie*, 104.
117. Young, *Unity of Europe*, 70–3.
118. On colonial co-operation see: J. Kent, 'Anglo-French colonial co-operation 1939–49', *Journal of Imperial and Commonwealth History*, 17 (1988), 55–82; M. Michel, 'La coopération intercoloniale en Afrique noire, 1942–50', *Relations Internationales*, 34 (1984), 155–71; and on administrative differences, K. Robinson, 'Colonialism French-style, 1945–55', *Journal of Imperial and Commonwealth History*, 11 (1982), 24–30.
119. Young, *Unity of Europe*, 71.
120. On the Laffon–Koenig debate see: Auriol, *Journal, 1947*, 458. And for Seydoux: Y/296 (15 Sept.).
121. For example: Y/379 (1 Oct.) and 399 (9 Sept.); Bidault papers, box 80 (17 Sept., n.d.).
122. Bidault papers, box 80 (18 Sept., and see 12 and 23 Sept.); Auriol, *Journal, 1947*, 444–5; *FRUS, 1947, II*, 680–2.
123. Y/296 (10 Oct.), Y/399 (23, 29 Sept., 8 Oct.); Bidault papers, box 62 (8 Oct.); *FRUS, 1947, II*, 682–5.
124. Bidault papers, box 62 (18 Sept.).
125. Chauvel was in London 19–22 Oct. and held his main discussion with Bevin on the 20th: Y/201 (20 Oct., and see 27, 28 Oct. on the French position on trizonal co-operation at this time; and see 4 Nov. on information about Anglo-US talks on Germany); Z/Grande Bretagne/38 (20 Oct; and see n.d. on Anglo-US talks); Massigli papers, Vols. 65 (21 Oct.) and 93 (24 Oct.); PRO, FO 800/465/France/47/26 (Bevin papers); *FRUS, 1947, II*, 695 and see 687–99 on Anglo-US talks.
126. See above, 126.
127. See above 125–7; and on the general aims of the armed forces in 1947 see Auriol, *Journal, 1945–7*, 145–7.
128. J. Delmas, 'Reflections on the Notion of Military Power through the French example', in Becker and Knipping, eds., *Power in Europe?*
129. Ramadier papers, 52 J 74 (especially 29 July); SHAT, 4Q 2, dossier 2 (29 July).
130. Fondation Nationale des Sciences Politiques, Edouard Daladier papers, 5 DA 12, Dr. 1 (especially Revers report of 1 Jan. 1948).
131. Ramadier papers, 52 J 74 (1 Oct.).
132. Auriol, *Journal du Septennat, Vol. II, 1948* (Paris, 1974), 99.
133. Ramadier papers, 52 J 74 (6 Oct.).
134. Y/379 (26 Sept.).
135. Possibly as a 'scare' tactic the EMDN suggested that, if France wished to preserve her neutrality, she should hand the ZOF (which was soon likely to become a financial liability) over to the Anglo-Saxons. Y/380 (18 Oct.); Ramadier papers, 52 J 68 (18 Oct).
136. Ramadier papers, 52 J 74 (27 Oct.).
137. Auriol, *Journal, 1947*, 512–13, 524 and, on the 'international brigades' see 485–6, 521–3.
138. In 1940–42.
139. It was Coste-Floret who had brought Revers in as Army Chief, replacing General de Lattre: Auriol, *Journal, 1947*, 649–50 and *1948*, 15, 26, 41; and on the talks

with the US attaché, R.A. Best, *Cooperation with Like-minded Peoples: British Influences on American Security Planning 1945–49* (1986), 172.

140. M. and S. Bromberger, *Les Coulisses de l'Europe* (Paris, 1968), 78–81; General Billotte, *Le Passé au Futur* (Paris, 1979), 50, 52, 58–9, and see 33–45, 60–66 on Billotte's views; Elgey. *République des Illusions*, 380; M. Vaisse, 'L'échec d'une Europe Franco-britannique', in *Histoire des Débuts de la Construction*, edited by R. Poidevin (Brussels 1986), 382.

141. Y/201 (6, 10 Nov.); and on Chauvel, see both Massigli papers, Vol. 93 (12 Nov.) and *FRUS, 1947, II*, 702–3.

142. Y/201 (6 Nov.); Bidault papers, box 84 (5 Nov., but see 22, 28 Oct. on rumours that the Soviets would be more positive); *FRUS, 1947, II*, 712–13.

143. Y/380 (7, 10 Nov., and see 10 Dec. report by the Finance Ministry on the likely impact of Anglo-American financial policies in Germany).

144. Y/201 (4 Nov.), 296 (14 Nov.), 380 (13 Nov.); Bidault papers, box 62 (14 Nov.); Massigli papers, Vol. 65 (4 Nov., instructions to delegation).

145. He held talks with Oliver Harvey: Y/201 (11–12 Nov.) and 380 (21 Nov.).

146. Y/296 and 399 (18 Nov.); *FRUS, 1947, II*, 720–2; Massigli papers, Vol. 65 (6 Nov).

147. Auriol, *Journal, 1947*, 519–20, 523, 541–2.

148. Y/201 (20, 24 Nov.), 296 (14 Nov., regarding fusion as a 'final' concession), 380 (20, 22 Nov.); Massigli papers, Vol. 65 (4 Nov., including quote, and 22 Nov.).

149. M. Debré, *Trois Républiques pour une France: mémoires, 1946–58* (Paris, 1988), 62. Elgey, *République des Illusions*, 327 uses the same phrase to describe the Paris meetings with Molotov on Marshall aid.

150. The Deputies meeting, 6–22 Nov., could make no agreed report to the CFM: Y/201 (10, 13, 18 Nov.); *FRUS, 1947, II*, 703–12.

151. *Conseil des Ministres des Affaires Etrangères, (CMAE), Vol. VI, Londres* (Paris, 1947), 3rd and 4th meetings, *FRUS, 1947, II*, 734–7. Copies of the meetings can be found in Y/187–9, 201 and 202, and shelved at the MAE in box AFA C-3. For a resumé of the conference see Y/202 and 300 (5 Jan.) and in general see Catroux, *Rideau de Fer* Ch. XVIII.

152. *CMAE, Vol. VI*, 5th and 6th meetings.

153. See for example his comments about Molotov in Nicolson, *Diaries and Letters*, entry of 3 Dec.

154. *FRUS, 1947, II*, 754–5.

155. ibid., 769–70.

156. *CMAE, Vol. VI*, 17th mtg., ibid., 770–2.

157. Y/201 (29 Nov.); *FRUS, 1947, II*, 737–9, 756.

158. Massigli papers, Vol. 93 (8 Dec., the view of Chauvel). See Y/201 (17 Dec.) for fears of unilateral action in the Bizone.

159. Z/Grande Bretagne/38 (17, 29 Dec.); Y/229 (17 Dec.) and 297 (17 Dec.); Massigli papers, Vol. 65 (17 Dec.); Massigli, *Comédie*, 105–6; A. Varsori, *Il Patto di Bruxelles, 1948* (Rome, 1988) 36–8.

160. Y/201, 229 (17 Dec.) and 297 (17, 22 Dec.); *FRUS, 1947, II*, 811–15, and see 829–30 for France's formal acceptance of the two sets of talks, given by Bonnet on 22 December.

161. The French were given an expurgated version of a Bevin–Marshall talk of 17 Dec., Y/297 (27 and 29 Dec.); Z/Grande Bretagne/34 (17 Dec.); *FRUS, 1947, II*, 815–29, and *III*, 818–19, and *1948, III*, 1–2; Varsori, *Patto di Bruxelles*, 38–9.

162. Auriol, *Journal, 1947*, 637–9.

163. ibid., 629, 649–50 and see 631.

164. Y/201 (20 Dec.).

165. Spaak was interested in Franco-Anglo-Benelux economic co-operation: Z/Belgique/34 (26 Dec.); Bidault papers, box 102 (26 Dec.).

166. Massigli papers, Vol. 93 (26 Dec); FO 371/73045/321, 322; Massigli, *Comédie*, 106. Bidault had raised the idea of a French-British-Belgian treaty with the Brussels embassy in September as a way to control Germany: see Z/Belgique/34 (30 Sept.).

167. A repatriation accord with Russia had been signed in June 1945. Auriol *Journal, 1947*, 587, 623–4; Catroux, *Rideau de Fer*, 292–3.

168. Z/URSS/53 (9, 10, 18 Dec.; 12 Feb.); Bidault papers, box 82 (16 Dec.); Catroux, ibid, 293–7.

169. The French originally asked in August for 1.5 million tons of wheat, but in November the Russians offered only 200,000 tons. Bidault papers, box 82 (Oct.–Dec.); *FRUS, 1947, III*, 736, 749–54, 759–61, 766, 773–4.

170. Z/URSS/53 (18 Dec.).

171. The British remained wary of French talks with the East Europeans. Z/Pologne/56 (Sept.–Dec.; see 18, 25 Nov. on the British); Z/Tchécoslovaquie/61 (Sept.–2 Jan.; see 25, 17 Nov. and 3 Dec. on Britain);' Bidault boxes 76 (Oct.–Dec.) and 89 (Dec.); Massigli papers, Vol. 78 (25 Nov., on British views). Auriol, *Journal, 1947*, 473, 584–5.

Chapter 9

1. Koenig was given more detailed instructions for talks he was to hold in Berlin on the harmonisation of trizonal policies and the integration of the Saar into the French economy. Ministère des Affaires Etrangères (MAE), Y/298 (4 Jan.); and see V. Auriol, *Journal du Septennat, Vol. II, 1948* (Paris, 1974), 22.

2. The French had had rumours of the forthcoming action since mid-December: Y/382 (Dec.–Jan.)

3. Archives Nationales (AN), Georges Bidault papers, box 80 (27 Dec.).

4. See especially, J.E. Smith, ed., *The Papers of General Lucius D. Clay, Vol. II, 1948–9* (Bloomington, Indiana, 1975), 475–8, 501–2, 513–18.

5. See above, 157.

6. Y/382 (9 Jan.). The Cabinet was informed on 10 Jan.: Auriol, *Journal, 1948*, 26.

7. Y/382 (9–11 Jan.); Y/380 (11 Jan., re. US), MAE, René Massigli papers, Vol. 65 (8, 9 Jan.); *Foreign Relations of the United States (FRUS), 1948, Vol. II*, 21–2, 34n; A. Berard, *Un Ambassadeur se Souvient 1945–55* (Paris, 1977), 136.

8. Y/382 (12–13 Jan.); MAE, Henri Bonnet papers, Vol. I (12 Jan.); *FRUS*, ibid., 20–1.

9. Y/382 (12, 15 Jan.); on Soviet propaganda see Y/294 (7 May).

10. Massigli papers, Vol. 93 (12 Jan.).

11. Y/382 (15, 16, 17, 21 Jan.); *FRUS, 1948, II*, 22–3, 26–8 (including quote); Smith, ed., *Clay Papers, Vol. II*, 534–9, 543–6; L.D. Clay, *Decision in Germany* (1950), 178–81; J.H. Backer, *Winds of History* (New York, 1983), 209–10, simply follows Clay's account.

12. Y/380 (17 Jan., Harvey mtg.); *FRUS, 1948, II*, 21n. On contacts with the British see also: MAE, Z/Grande Bretagne/38 (17 Jan.); Massigli papers, Vol. 65 (13 Jan.).

13. Auriol, *Journal, 1947*, 34–5 and see 39.

14. Y/380 (19 Jan.) and 382 (16, 19 Jan.); and see *FRUS, 1947, II*, 28–31, 34–5, 37–9.

15. Y/300 (22 Jan.), 380 (22, 24 Jan.), 381 (22 Jan.) and 382 (17, 21, 22 Jan.).

16. Y/300 (30, 31 Jan.) and 383 (29 Jan., 1 Feb.); Massigli papers, Vol. 65 (29 Jan.); *FRUS, 1948, II*, 43, 45–8, 53–4.
17. Z/Généralités/20 (31 Jan.); Massigli papers, Vol. 54 (31 Jan.).
18. Y/300 (4, 5 Feb.) and 383 (4 Feb.); Massigli papers, Vol. 93 (2 Feb.).
19. B. Ruhm von Oppen, *Documents on Germany under Occupation, 1945–54* (1955), 268–79.
20. Auriol, *Journal, 1947*, 66–8, 73–4; and on Quai views, Y/298 (24 Jan.).
21. Y/298 (20, 23 Jan.); Z/Allemagne/82 (20 Jan.).
22. Public Record Office, London, FO 371/72979/212; Auriol, *Journal, 1948*, 28.
23. These were the same meetings at which the Frankfurt agreements were discussed: Z/Généralités/20 (17 Jan.) and Grande Bretagne/38 (17 Jan.); Y/380 (17 Jan.); and on Anglo–US talks, *FRUS, 1948, Vol. III*, 3–6, 8–9.
24. An approach to Luxembourg followed on 23 January. Z/Généralités/20 (19–27 Jan.); Auriol, *Journal, 1948*, 43.
25. Hansard, House of Commons debates, Vol. 446, cols. 387–409; and for an analysis see A. Varsori, *Il Patto di Bruxelles, 1948* (Rome, 1988), 39–49.
26. Z/Généralités/20 (5 Feb.); R. Massigli, *Une Comédie des Erreurs* (Paris, 1978), 107–9.
27. Z/Généralités/20 (22–24 Jan., and see 7 Jan. for Bidault's desire to keep to the Dunkirk model, partly to avoid complications in the continuing treaty talks with Czechoslovakia and Poland).
28. ibid. (24, 28 Jan.); Auriol, *Journal, 1948*, 51. On Belgian and Dutch policy see: A. Manning, 'Les Pays-Bas face à l'Europe', and J. Stengers, 'Paul-Henri-Spaak et le traité de Bruxelles', in R. Poidevin, etc., *Histoire des Débuts de la Construction Européenne, 1948–50* (Brussels, 1986), 26–33, 119–44.
29. *FRUS, 1948, III*, 3, 6–10; Varsori, *Patto di Bruxelles*, 50–4.
30. Z/Généralités/20 (31 Jan.; 2, 7 Feb.); Auriol, *Journal, 1947*, 69–70; Massigli, *Comédie*, 109–10; Varsori, ibid., 59–60.
31. Z/Généralités/20 (4 Feb.); Massigli papers, Vol. 54 (31 Jan.); and see Auriol, ibid., 72–3.
32. Z/Généralités/20 (4–28 Feb.); Auriol, ibid, 70–1, 77–8, 85, 107; Varsori, *Patto di Bruxelles*, 69–79; Massigli, *Comédie*, 110–11.
33. Z/Généralités/21 (16–19 Feb.); *FRUS, 1948, III*, 26–9.
34. Z/Généralités/21 (17 and see 28 Feb.).
35. *FRUS, 1948, III*, 29–30.
36. Action had continued to be expected against Czechoslovakia: Auriol, *Journal, 1948*, 73. And for French coverage of the coup see especially Bidault papers, box 76.
37. Z/Tchécoslovaquie/61 (26 Feb.); Bidault papers, box 76 (25 Feb.); Auriol, ibid., 110–11, 114.
38. Auriol, ibid., 138, 146–7, 150; J. Dumaine, *Quai d'Orsay, 1945–51* (1958), 159–60.
39. Dumaine, ibid., 158.
40. Auriol, *Journal, 1948*, 119.
41. G. Catroux, *J'ai vu Tomber le Rideau de Fer* (Paris, 1952), 291, 297.
42. Z/URSS/53 (12 Feb., and see 27 Feb., 24 March); Bidault papers, box 84 (7, 12 Feb.).
43. See Auriol, *Journal, 1948*, 61, 63–4, 74–7, 104–6, 120–1; 124–5, 130, 133, 141–3, 153, 167–9, 184–5, 217.
44. Z/Pologne/56 (Jan.–Feb.); Bidault papers, box 89 (file on financial accords).
45. M. Vaisse, 'L'Echec d'une Europe franco–britannique', in Poidevin, *Débuts de la Construction Européenne*, 372, citing Roland de Margerie.
46. Z/Généralités/21 (28 Feb.); and see *FRUS, 1948, III*, 34–5.

47. Z/Généralités/21 (7 March).
48. ibid. (2, 3 March).
49. ibid. (27 Feb. – 13 March) and 22 (15–17 March); *FRUS, 1948, III*, 35–9, 42; Auriol, *Journal, 1947*, 123, 137–8. For accounts of the talks: J. Chauvel, *D'Alger à Berne, 1944–52* (Paris, 1972), 195–8, a somewhat confused account; G. Rendel *The Sword and the Olive* (1957), 278–80; Varsori, *Patto di Bruxelles*, 85–92.
50. Auriol, ibid., 150.
51. Z/Grande Bretagne/38 (17 March); FO 371/73053/2340 and 73055/2559.
52. Bonnet papers, Vol. I (18 March, enclosing 4, 13, 14 March); *FRUS, 1948, III*, 38, 49–50 and see 52–3; Massigli, *Comédie*, 134.
53. On this point see: Stengers, 'Spaak et le traité de Bruxelles', 140.
54. Bonnet papers, Vol. I (17 March, enclosing 12 March).
55. For the Brussels Pact text: R. Vaughan, *Post-war Integration in Europe* (1976), 24–7.
56. It was sent by Bevin and Bidault: Z/Grande Bretagne/38 (17 March); *FRUS, 1948, III*, 55–6; Varsori, *Patto di Bruxelles*, 100–3.
57. *FRUS*, ibid, 54–5; H. Truman, *Years of Trial and Hope* (1956), 255–7.
58. MAE, B/Etats Unis/114 (25 March); *FRUS*, ibid., 68.
59. At this time Paul Stehlin, the air *attaché* on Massigli's staff, began discreet talks with the British on air defence. Service Historique, Armée de Terre, Vincennes (SHAT), 4Q 37, dossier 2 (25 Jan.); Massigli papers, Vol. 93 (1, 2, 4, 26 Dec.; 7, 12, 26, 28 Jan. and see 30 Jan. on Stehlin); Auriol, *Journal, 1948*, 57, 64–5; Massigli, *Comédie*, 117; Montgomery of Alamein, *Memoirs* (1958), 456; P. Stehlin, *Témoignage pour l'Historie* (Paris, 1964), 342–3; Varsori, *Patto di Bruxelles*, 54–9; J.W. Young, *Britain, France and the Unity of Europe, 1945–51* (Leicester, 1984), 74–5, 80–1. On British defence planning see especially Lewis: *Changing Direction* (1987); M. Dockrill, 'British attitudes towards France as a Military Ally', Unpublished paper, King's College, London, 18–25.
60. Auriol, ibid., 29–30, 234–7.
61. See above, 172.
62. *FRUS, 1948, III*, 110–11, and *1949, IV*, 294–5; G. Elgey, *La République des Illusions, 1945–51* (Paris, 1965), 381; and on the Combined Chiefs see: R.A. Best *'Cooperation with Like-minded Peoples': British influences on American security policy, 1945–9* (1986), 27–40.
63. Bull had been sent to Europe by Eisenhower: *FRUS, 1948, III*, 617–22.
64. FO 371/72979/2560.
65. C. Wiebes and B. Zeeman, 'The Pentagon negotiations, March 1948', *International Affairs*, 59 (Summer, 1983), 356; E. Reid, *Time of Fear and Hope* (Toronto, 1977), 45–6, 53–5, 72; *FRUS, 1948, III*, 69–75.
66. According to the US record: *FRUS*, ibid., 11, but see also 7–12. And see J. Gaddis, *The Long Peace* (1987). 57–61.
67. Z/Généralités/22 (19 March – 21 April); Bonnet papers, Vol. I (22 April); *FRUS*, ibid., 91, 123–4; Massigli, *Comédie*, 114–17; Auriol, *Journal, 1948*, 192, 195–6.
68. M. Folly, 'Breaking the Vicious Circle', *Diplomatic History*, 12 (1988), 59–77. On British and European pressures to get a US guarantee see also: N. Petersen, 'Who Pulled Whom and How Much', *Millennium*, 11 (1982), and 'Negotiating the Atlantic Treaty', *Review of International Studies*, 12 (1986), 187–203.
69. Auriol, *Journal, 1948*, 192–3.
70. Massigli papers, Vol. 79 (20 April, note by the *Secrétariat de Conférences*).
71. Paul Ely papers, SHAT, box 26, dossier 1 (fiches on response to US questionnaire; and see 15 April and 8 May on the need for US support); *FRUS, 1948, III*, 123–6.
72. It was also feared that the Italians would try to change the 1947 peace treaty. Z/Généralités/23 (8–14 May); Massigli papers, Vol. 94 (1 May); ibid., 114–16.

73. Y/356 (10 Feb.); *FRUS, 1948, II*, 60–65.
74. Z/Généralités/22 (9, 11, 15, 19, 22 April); Bonnet papers, Vol. I (15, 17, 21, 30 April); 3 May); Auriol, *Journal, 1948*, 169–71.
75. Z/Généralités/20 (30 April); Massigli papers, Vol. 94 (3 May); and on the idea of a single command in Germany, Bonnet papers, Vol. I (19 May).
76. B/Etats Unis/114 (13–26 May); Bonnet papers, Vol. I (24 May).
77. *FRUS, 1948, III*, 139.
78. Truman, *Years of Trial and Hope*, 259–61.
79. K.W. Condit, *The History of the Joint Chiefs of Staff, Vol. II, 1947–9* (Wilmington, Delaware, 1979), 366–8.
80. On the 'Mayer Plan' see: Auriol, *Journal, 1948*, 8–9, 11–17; R. Frank, 'The French Dilemma', in J., Becker and F. Knipping, eds., *Power in Europe?* (New York, 1986), 268–9; G. Bossuat, 'Le poids de l'aide américaine sur la politique économique et financière de la France en 1948', *Relations Internationales*, 37 (1984), 22–3.
81. Bidault papers, box 79 (18 Jan. – 3 Feb.); AN, René Mayer papers, box 7 (Dec. – Jan.); *FRUS, 1948, III*, 592, 597–616, 623; D. Mayer, ed., *René Mayer* (Paris, 1983), 141–4; R. Poidevin, *Robert Schuman* (Paris, 1986), 166–70.
82. Bidault papers, box 79 (3 Feb.).
83. G.H. Gallup, ed., *The Gallup International Public Opinion Polls, France, Vol. I* (1976), Sept. and Dec. 1947; March 1948.
84. At first the French and British proposed to hold a new CEEC conference, but the Americans felt this could prove embarrassing rather than helpful. Bidault papers, box 21 (7, 8 Jan.); *FRUS, 1948, III*, 352–6.
85. Y/131 (14–16 Jan.); Bidault papers, box 21 (14 Jan); *FRUS*, ibid; 356–7, 359–61, 365–6; Auriol, *Journal, 1948*, 35.
86. Y/131 (Jan.–Feb.); Bidault papers, box 20 (Jan.).
87. Y/131 (March); Bidault papers, box 20 (Feb.–March); *FRUS, 1948, III*, 381–6, 391–408, 412.
88. Y/131 (April); Bidault papers, box 20 (March–April); M.J. Hogan, *The Marshall Plan* (1987), 123–7; A. Milward, *The Reconstruction of Western Europe, 1945–51* (1984), 172–9.
89. $1,400 million to France, $163 million to the French Union, $81 million to the ZOF and $11 million to the Saar. B/Etats Unis/248 (7 April). On Hoffmann see Bidault papers, box 21 (6 April).
90. Bidault papers, box 22 (June–July); Mayer papers, box 6; *FRUS, 1948, III*, 432–3, 445–7, 454–5; Auriol, *Journal, 1948*, 260, 281, 285–7; *L'Année Politique, 1948* (Paris, annual), 403–9; Bossuat 'Poids de l'aide américaine', 17–26.
91. Auriol, ibid., 44.
92. ibid., 144–5.
93. Bidault papers, box 21 (18 April); Centre Jean Monnet, Lausanne Monnet papers, AMF 22/1/1–8; J. Monnet, *Memoirs* (1978), 271–4; *Jean Monnet – Robert Schuman Correspondence* (Lausanne, 1986), 35–8.
94. Bidault papers, box 22 (28 June; 3 July).
95. In November France, Italy and the Benelux states had established a joint trade payments system, later extended to other states. Archives Economiques et Financières, Paris, B.33853.
96. Z/Italie/91 (6, 7, 10 Jan.); Bidault papers; box 91 (10 Jan.); and see P. Guillen, 'Le Projet d'Union Economique entre la France, l'Italie et le Benélux' in Poidevin, ed., *Origins of European Integration*, (Paris) 151–64.
97. Bidault papers, box 91 (8, 12, 14 Jan.). But Chauvel informed Oliver Harvey that France hoped to hold talks with the Benelux states: Z/Généralités/20 (17 Jan.); and see Massigli papers, Vol. 54 (31 Jan.).

98. Bidault papers, box 91 (31 Jan.).
99. ibid. (16–31 Jan.); Z/Généralités 5 (11 Feb.) and 20 (26 Jan.; 3 Feb.).
100. Z/Italie/91 (18 Jan.).
101. Bidault papers, box 91 (27 Jan.)
102. Z/Italie/91 (10, 13 Feb.); Auriol, *Journal, 1948*, 51, 72.
103. It had originally been planned to sign the protocol in Paris. Z/Italie/87 (24 Feb.–26 March) and 91 (17, 21 Feb.; 20 March); Bidault papers, box 91 (20–29 Feb.). On the Italian elections see: R. Bouthillon, 'Les élections Italiennes de 1948', *Revue d'Histoire Diplomatique*, 99 (1985), 257–301; J.E. Miller, 'Talking off the gloves: the US and the Italian elections', *Diplomatic History*, 7 (1983), 35–55; and A. Varsori, 'La Gran Bretagne e le elizioni politiche italiane', *Storia Contemporanea*, 13 (1982), 5–70.
104. For example, Z/Italie/91 (31 Jan.).
105. ibid. (1, 22 Oct.); and see Milward, *Reconstruction of Western Europe*, 253–4.
106. Bidault's successor, Robert Schuman, remained deeply committed to working with Italy: Z/Généralités/23 (23 Nov.); C. Sforza, *Cinque anni a Palazzo Chigi* (Rome, 1952), 69–81, 91–108.
107. There were protocols on trade, payments and manpower: Z/Italie/91 (26–29 March and 12 May, 1949); Bidault papers, box 91 (Jan.–March, 1949; 7 March and 6 April, 1950).
108. R.T. Griffiths and F.M.B. Lynch, 'L'Echec de la "Petite Europe" and les négociations Fritalux/Finebel', *Revue Historique*, 274 (1984), 159–89.
109. See E. Serra, 'Dall' unione dognale italo–francese alla CECA', in K. Schwabe, ed., *Die Anfänge des Schuman Plans* (Baden-Baden, 1988), 174–82.
110. *Journal Officiel, Débats*, 13 Feb., 741–7; and on the debate as a whole see: 13 Feb., 732–47; 27 Feb., 1198–1215; 4 March, 1329–43; 5 March, 1392–1409; 11 March, 1653–69.
111. Conversations in Berlin in early 1948, about trizonal administrative co-operation, had got no further than an agreement to treat Saar coal and trade as entirely separate from the rest of Germany. Reparation payments to France were adjusted accordingly and General Clay still saw the agreement as a major concession to France: *FRUS, 1948, II*, 29–33, 41–5, 55–9, 73.
112. Z/Grande Bretagne/38 (n.d., instructions to Massigli); Auriol, *Journal, 1948*, 106–7, and see 98–9; and see Y/304 (17 April, instructions to delegation). For insights into French policy on Germany at this time see: P. Mendès-France, *Oeuvres Complètes, Vol. II: Une Politique de l'Economie, 1943–54* (Paris, 1985), 226–9 (speech to Unesco, 19 Feb.); A. Philip, 'France and the Economic Recovery of Europe', *Foreign Affairs*, 26, 2 (Jan. 1948), 325–34.
113. Y/300 (23 Feb.); Massigli papers, Vol. 65 (23 Feb.); *FRUS, 1948, II*, 82–3.
114. *FRUS, 1948, II*, 63–5, 70; Massigli papers, Vol. 65 (20 Feb.).
115. Y/300 (24–25 Feb.); *FRUS, 1948, II*, 84–5, 87–9.
116. PRO, CAB. 128/12, CM (48) 2 and CAB. 129/25, CP (48) 5; Smith, ed., *Clay Papers, Vol. II*, 548–9, 555–60.
117. *FRUS, 1948, II*, 70–3. 107, 113, and on Anglo–US talks before the London conference see 24–6, 35–6, 40–3, 49–51, 68–9, 75–81.
118. Y/381 (28 Feb., 5 March).
119. Y/300 (26–27 Feb., 2 March), 399 (27 Feb.); Massigli papers, Vol. 65 (27 Feb., 2 March); *FRUS, 1948, II*, 91–4, 97–100; and see Auriol, *Journal, 1948*, 119, 126.
120. Y/300 (4–5 March); Y/399 (6, 8 March); Massigli papers, Vol. 65 (5 March); *FRUS, 1948, II*, 124–8, 130–1, 134–7, 140–1.
121. Massigli papers, Vol. 65 (2 March).
122. Y/300 (2, 3 March), 381 (2 March); ibid. (2 March); *FRUS, 1948, II*, 114–17.

123. Y/300 (28 Feb., 1–3, 5 March); Massigli papers, Vol. 65 (28 Feb., 1–2 March); *FRUS*, ibid., 107–10, 131–4.

124. Y/300 (28 Feb.); Massigli papers, Vol. 65 (28 Feb.); *FRUS*, ibid., 104–7.

125. Y/300 (2, 5 March), 357 (5 March) and 399 (2 March); Massigli papers, Vol. 65 (5 March); *FRUS*, ibid., 94–5, 101–2, 110–11, 122–3, 138–9.

126. But the Bizone and ZOF were to be treated as separate entities for Marshall aid. Y/300 (6 March); Massigli papers, Vol. 65 (communiqué); *FRUS*, ibid., 134–5, 140–3; and on the US reaction, see B/Etats Unis/114 (8 March).

127. Y/300 (6 March), 302 (20 March, 5 April), and 304 (14 April)

128. Y/301 (7 March).

129. Auriol, *Journal, 1948*, 122–3, 135–7.

130. Y/302 (20, 23 March); *FRUS, 1948, II*, 148–54; Smith, ed., *Clay Papers, Vol. II*, 587–8, and see 569–74 on Clay's reaction to the London conference decisions on the Ruhr.

131. Y/301 (12, 13 March and see 15 March for criticisms of the instructions by Michel Debré). A special commission was established in the Quai to study France's precise desiderata regarding Germany's political future: Y/654 (9 March); Y/301 (12 March).

132. Y/301 (19, 20 March), 302 (23, 24 March).

133. Y/302 (26 March–9 April); Massigli papers, Vol. 93 (27 March); *FRUS, 1948, II*, 151–2, 154–6, 163–6.

134. Y/302 (1 April); *FRUS*, ibid., 156–63; Smith, ed., *Clay Papers, Vol. II*, 608–11; and on fusion see also Y/381 (2, 3 April).

135. Y/381 (3 April).

136. Y/302 (9 April); Massigli Papers, Vol. 65 (9 April).

137. Bonnet papers, Vol. I (15 April); Massigli papers, Vol. 65 (8, 14 April); *FRUS, 1948, II*, 169–70, 175–6; Chauvel, *d'Alger à Berne*, 199; Clay, *Decision in Germany*, 397–400.

138. Y/302 (12 April) and see 304 (14, 16, 19 April); Massigli papers, Vol. 65 (14, 15 April); *FRUS*, ibid., 166–8, 170–87.

139. The Cabinet recommendation on a Varparlament came too late to be included in the recommendations of the zonal commanders at the end of the Berlin talks however. Auriol, *Journal, 1948*, 174–80.

140. Massigli papers, box 67 (19 April).

141. *L'Année Politique, 1948*, 329–31.

142. Y/304 (17, 21, 23 April); Massigli papers, Vol. 66 (21, 23 April), 67 (22, 24 April).

143. Auriol, *Journal, 1948*, 190–2.

144. See Bidault papers, box 21 (6 April).

145. Y/399 (21, 22 April; 6 May); Massigli papers, Vol. 66 (22, 23 April; 15 May), 67 (6 May); *FRUS, 1948, II*, 197–9, 200–7, 285–8, 290–1, Milward, *Reconstruction of Western Europe*, 154–5.

146. Y/304 (24, 28 April), 305 (1, 3 May); Massigli papers, Vol. 67 (1, 3 May); *FRUS*, ibid., 237–9, 262–5.

147. According to Auriol, Bidault did not carry out Cabinet instructions exactly on the last point: Auriol felt the intention was to *discuss* the London decisions with Moscow, but Bidault wanted the Russians to be asked to *accept* them. Y/305, 399 (5 May); Auriol, *Journal, 1948*, 212–14, 218.

148. Y/305 (10 May).

149. Massigli papers, Vol. 66 (5 May); *FRUS, 1948, II*, 232 and see 233–4, 248 on US thinking about security.

150. *FRUS, 1948, II*, 230–1.

151. Y/305 (10, 15, 19 May); Z/Allemagne/82 (8 May).

152. Z/Allemagne/82 (7, 21 May).
153. Y/301 (21 May, including quote), 306 (21 May).
154. For the letters: M. Carlyle, ed., *Documents on International Affairs, 1947–8* (1952), 153–9; and see B/Etats Unis/204 for the general response.
155. Auriol, *Journal, 1948*, 223–7; and see Y/305 (11 May), on Bidault's thinking.
156. Z/URSS/53 (17 May), but for earlier, similar ideas: Bonnet papers, Vol. I (7 May); Auriol, ibid., 219.
157. On, for example, demilitarisation: Y/357 (20 May); *FRUS, 1948, II*, 256–8.
158. *FRUS*, ibid., 255–6, 258.
159. Y/306 (20 May); Z/Généralités/23 (20 May).
160. Auriol, *Journal, 1948*, 231–2.
161. *FRUS, 1948, II*, 266n.
162. Massigli papers, Vol. 94 (21 May).
163. Y/305 (21 May), 306 (21 May); Massigli papers, Vols. 67 (20, 21 May) and 94 (22 May); *FRUS, 1948, II*, 266–72 275–7 and *III*, 635–7; Smith, ed., *Clay Papers*, 656–8.
164. Massigli papers, Vol. 67 (25, 26 May); and see Y/305 (26 May); Auriol, *Journal, 1948*, 242–3.
165. In early May Lewis Douglas had threatened Massigli that if France did not join a trizonal 'trade pool' Marshall aid to the ZOF might be terminated. Bidault related this warning to the Cabinet: Bidault papers, box 22 (1 and see 21, 22 May); Massigli papers, Vol. 67 (1 May); *FRUS, 1948, II*, 216–18; Auriol, ibid., 232.
166. Auriol, ibid. 238–42; and see *FRUS*, ibid., 273–4 on Bidault.
167. A long occupation was also promised. Y/357 (20 May); Massigli papers, Vol. 67 (20 May); *FRUS, 1948, II*, 291–4.
168. The French were satisfied with this. See especially Massigli papers, Vol. 67 (31 May).
169. Y/305 (communiqué), 306 (1 June, Report); *FRUS, 1948, II*, 309–17.
170. Y/306 (passim); *FRUS*, ibid., 298–9, 301–3, 308–9, 318–20.
171. Y/306 (3 June); Massigli papers, Vol. 67 (3 June).
172. Y/306 (3, 4 June).
173. Y/399 (12 June); Z/Allemagne/83 (23 June).
174. Auriol, *Journal, 1948*, 243, 255.
175. Massigli papers, Vol. 94 (31 May) and see Vol. 67 (8 June); B/Etats Unis/114 (8 June); and see ibid., 256.
176. Auriol, ibid., 258–61.
177. *L'Année Politique, 1948*, 334–5.
178. *FRUS, 1948, II*, 317–18, 320–4.
179. Auriol, *Journal, 1948*, 262–3, and see 263–4, 266 on Assembly opinion.
180. Two sessions were held: *Bulletin des Commissions, Assemblée Nationale, Vol. III* (government publication, Paris, 1951), 1548. I found only the second session in: Assemblee Nationale, procès-verbaux de la Commission des Affaires Etrangères, 9 June.
181. Auriol, *Journal, 1948*, 265–6.
182. J. Dumaine, *Quai d'Orsay* (1958), 171–2.
183. *Journal Officiel, Débats, Assemblée*, 11 June, 3454–78, 12 June, 3484–97. There was a break in the debate on 13–14 June.
184. Y/307 (15 June) Massigli papers, Vol. 67 (14–15 June, records of talks); Chauvel, *d'Alger à Berne*, 200–1; and see Auriol, *Journal, 1948*, 269–70.
185. G. Bidault, *Resistance* (1967), 161–2; Chauvel, ibid., 201–2; G. Elgey, *La République des Illusions* (Paris, 1965), 385.
186. *Journal Officiel, Débats, Assemblée*, 15 June, 3522–49, 16 June, 3560–99.
187. Y/307 (18, 19 June); *FRUS, 1948, II*, 335–7; Auriol, *Journal, 1948*, 275–6.

Chapter 10

1. Ministère des Affaires Etrangères (MAE), Z/URSS/53 (8 April).
2. MAE, Henri Bonnet papers, Vol. 1 (15 April); V. Auriol, *Journal du Septennat, Vol. II, 1948*, (Paris, 1974), 205–6, 182–3.
3. MAE, René Massigli papers, Vol. 67 (22 April).
4. MAE, Y/341 (11, 12, 22 May; 9 June; and see 9–26 June on the blockade's beginning).
5. Y/334 (1 July).
6. Y/341 (26 June).
7. Y/343 (10 Aug., page 5).
8. In covering the blockade in general I have relied heavily on A. Shlaim, *The US and the Berlin Blockade* (Berkeley, Cal., 1983). French evidence has already been discussed in R. Fritsch – Bournazel, 'Mourir pour Berlin: die Wandlungen der Französischer Ost – und Deutschlandpolitik während der Blockade,' *Vierteljahrshette für Zeitgeschichte*, 35 (1987), 171–92.
9. *Foreign Relations of the United States (FRUS), 1948, Vol. II*, 916–17.
10. See for example, Auriol, *Journal, 1948*, 66–8, 78–80, 161, 164, 171–4, 177–80, 185–8, 205–6, 209–10, 233–4, 244.
11. ibid., 248–9, 282–3, 285.
12. Y/307 (24, 27–28 June), 341 (28, 29 June); ibid., 292–3. For a very different image of Bidault's policy: F. Seydoux, *Mémoires d'Outre-Rhin*, (Paris: 1975), 115.
13. Y/307 (28 June); Y/341 (29–30 June; 3 July); Massigli papers, Vol. 94 (3 July).
14. Y/341 (1–8 July); *FRUS, 1948, II*, 933–53.
15. Auriol, *Journal*, 307–8, 312–13; J. Dumaine, *Quai d'Orsay* (1958), 173.
16. Y/341 (10, 13, 14 July) and see 342 (15–22 July on continuing talks in London).
17. Auriol, *Journal*, 316–17.
18. Massigli papers, Vol. 94 (17 July); Y/342 (17 July).
19. Shlaim, *Berlin Blockade*, 305–10.
20. On the crisis: Auriol, *Journal*, 318–38, 388–438. On Queuille: Actes de Colloque de Paris, Oct. 1984, *Henri Queuille et la République* (Limoges, 1987).
21. On the US reaction: B/Etats Unis/120 (26 July); Z/Généralités/23 (27 Sept.); *FRUS, 1948, Vol. III*, 637–42, 646–59.
22. On Britain: Z/Grande Bretagne/39 (20, 26 July); Public Record Office (PRO), London, FO 371/72949–51 (*passim*).
23. Z/Grande Bretagne/39 (15 Sept.); Y/314 (30 Oct.) See also: Massigli papers, Vols 54 (3 Sept., 30 Oct.), 67 (20 July); R. Massigli, *Une Comédie des Erreurs* (Paris, 1978), 121–2.
24. Archives Nationales (AN), F60 Ter./379 (27 Aug.).
25. G.H. Gallup, *The Gallup International Public Opinion Polls, France, Vol. I* (1976), March 1948.
26. Dumaine, *Quai d'Orsay*, 175.
27. J. Chauvel, *d'Alger à Berne, 1944–52* (Paris 1972), 202–3.
28. J. Monnet, *Memoirs* (1978), 274–5.
29. Dumaine, *Quai d'Orsay*, 181.
30. ibid., 190.
31. On Schuman's early life see especially C. Pennera, *Robert Schuman, 1886–1924* (Paris, 1985), but also: R. Rochefort, *Robert Schuman* (Paris, 1968); R. Hostiou, *Robert Schuman et l'Europe* (Paris, 1969). Fullest and most stimulating on his career as foreign minister is R. Poidevin, *Robert Schuman, homme d'état* (Paris, 1986). Schuman's own *Pour l'Europe* (Paris, 1964) is short and generalised.

32. Auriol, *Journal*, 338; Chauvel, *d'Alger à Berne*, 203, 206–7.
33. Kenneth Younger, diary, 14 May 1950. By kind permission of Lady Younger. My thanks to Professor Geoffrey Warner for providing me with access to the diary.
34. Especially the Secretary of State, 1949–53, Dean Acheson: see his *Present at the Creation* (1970), 271.
35. See above, 191.
36. See especially Auriol, *Journal*, 453–4, 456–9, 461–21, 466–72, 475–6, 493–5, 503, 511–13, 517–18, 526–7, 541.
37. *FRUS, 1948, III*, 662–4, 666–74, 677–82.
38. F60 Ter/378 (Report on first quarter for 1948).
39. Archives Economiques et Financières, Paris, B.18220 (Jan.–April); G. Bossaut, 'Le poids de l'aide américaine sur la politique économique et financière de la France et 1948', *Relations Internationales*, 37 (1984), 23.
40. Figures on the exact value of Marshall aid differ. F. Bloch–Laine and J. Bouvier, *La France Restaurée, 1944–54* (Paris, 1986), 153–4; A. Milward, *The Reconstruction of Western Europe, 1945–51* (1984), 107–12; Monnet, *Memoirs*, 269–70; M. Hogan, *The Marshall Plan* (1987),152–5. In mid-1948 the OEEC, under US pressure, drew up a long-term programme for investment, production and trade. The US hoped this would force genuine integration in Europe but, as in 1947, the Europeans divided on national lines. The French again tried to safeguard the Monnet Plan, arguing that OEEC states should be able to point out developments which gave them self-sufficiency: Y/131 (Aug.); Aveyron departmental archives, Rodez, Paul Ramadier papers, 52 J 119 (3 July–1 Aug.), 120 (7 Aug.); Hogan, *Marshall Plan*, 161–5; Milward, *Reconstruction*, 180–91.
41. AEF, B.18220 (Sept.); Bloch–Laine and Bouvier, ibid., 160–1; Bossuat, 'Poids de l'Aide americaine', 26–8; *FRUS, 1948, III*, 649–51, 659–60, 666–72; and on French policy, see A. Pinay, *Un Français comme les Autres* (Paris, 1984), 39–44.
42. Auriol, *Journal*, 490.
43. F60 Ter/378 (16, 24, 30 Nov. and see 2 Dec.). The series F60 Ter, includes the papers of the Secretariat of the Interministerial Committee on European Economic Co-operation, created in June 1948 to handle relations with the US Economic Co-operation Administration and to prepare documents for France's OEEC delegation. The Secretariat was attached to the premier's office and headed by a Finance Ministry official, Pierre-Paul Schweitzer.
44. ibid. (3 Dec.); reproduced in Bloch–Laine and Bouvier, *La France Restaurée*, 303–5.
45. MAE, Henri Bonnet papers, Vol. I (7, 18 Dec.); Auriol, *Journal*, 559–60; 566–9, 573–4; Bossuat 'Poids de l'aide américaine', 29–31, 33–4; Dumaine, *Quai d'Orsay*, 193–4.
46. They continued to do so in 1949: *FRUS, 1949, Vol. IV*, 637–9, 640–1.
47. See the general thesis of Hogan, *Marshall Plan*; Milward, *Reconstruction*, 113–25. But, on US policy, see especially *FRUS, 1948, III*, 300–10.
48. F60 Ter/378 (16 Dec.) and 379 (17, 23 Dec.); and see R.A. Pollard, *Economic Security and the Origins of the Cold War* (New York, 1985), 158–9.
49. But the Soviets were weakened by the break-away of Tito's Yogoslavia in mid-1948: Y/2 (15 Aug.).
50. AN, Georges Bidault papers, box 84 (8 April, and see 18, 22 Feb.); G.A.J. Catroux, *J'ai vu Tomber le Rideau de Fer* (Paris, 1952), 299–300.
51. MAE, Z/URSS/53 (15 July); Bidault papers, box 84 (15 July); Auriol, *Journal*, 306, and see 63, 138 on Chataigneau.
52. Bidault papers, box 84 (29 June).
53. In the Soviet press: Z/URSS/53 (Nov.–Dec.).
54. Auriol, *Journal*, 545–7.

55. Bidault papers, box 84 (12 July.)
56. Auriol, *Journal*, 338–9; and on US decision, *FRUS, 1948, III*, 971–3, 977–82, 986–95.
57. Y/342 (28 July–1 Aug.); *FRUS*, ibid., 995–8.
58. Y/342 (3, 4 Aug.); *FRUS*, ibid., 999–1007; Auriol, *Journal*, 348; Seydoux, *Mémoires*, 116–17.
59. Y/342 (6, 7 Aug.,); 343 (8–20 Aug.), 344 (21–31 Aug.); *FRUS*, ibid., 1018–21, 1024–7, 1035–8, 1042–7, 1058–60, 1065–8, 1085–99; Auriol, ibid., 360–1, 368; Seydoux, ibid., 117–18.
60. Y/343 (10 Aug.); Massigli papers, Vol. 97 (Camille Paris to Massigli, 19 Aug.).
61. Y/345, 346 (*passim*); *FRUS, 1948, III*, 1147–9, 1152–73; Auriol, *Journal*, 439; Seydoux, *Mémoires*, 118.
62. Auriol, ibid., 455.
63. Y/347 (25 Sept., and see 24–29 Sept. on the use of the UN).
64. Z/Grande Bretagne/39 (2, 5 Oct.); Auriol, *Journal*, 473, 489; *FRUS, 1948, II*, 1214–16, 1225–6.
65. Y/347 (*passim*); Auriol, ibid., 500–1; *FRUS* ibid., 1238–9.
66. See especially Y/348 (*passim*); Auriol, ibid, 510, 525–6, 531, and *Journal, 1949* (Paris, 1977), 53, 69–70.
67. On French concern at the elections: Y/348 (25, 29 Nov.); Auriol, *Journal*, 539–40, 560–2.
68. Auriol, *Journal, 1949*, 73–4, 77–9, 83–5, 91–3, 100.
69. The French were concerned at the efforts of the new Mayor of West Berlin to tie the city closer to western Germany: ibid., 97, 105, 123–4.
70. On Schuman see ibid., 64–6 for example. In January General Clay wanted to force France and Britain into line on Berlin by refusing to cover their trade deficits in Germany: J.E. Smith, ed., *The Papers of General Lucius D. Clay, Vol. II* (Bloomington, Indiana, 1974), 986–7.
71. Y/307 (22 June).
72. ibid., (28 June); Auriol, *Journal, 1948*, 276, 280–1.
73. Y/310 (1–12 July); *FRUS, 1948, II* 378–81, 385–92.
74. Y/310 (10 July); and see Auriol, *Journal, 1948*, 308–9.
75. Y/310 (12 July); Auriol, ibid., 316–17.
76. Y/310 (15, 18, 19 July), 311 (20–26 July); Auriol, ibid., 313, 339–40; *FRUS, 1948, II*, 403–13; Smith, ed., *Clay Papers*, 746.
77. Y/311 (27–30 July, 2 Aug.).
78. On this issue see: Y/311 (3–31 Aug.), 312 (1, 3 Sept.); *FRUS, 1948, II*, 415–18; Auriol, *Journal, 1948*, 360, 368; Smith, ibid., 787, 790.
79. Y/311 (17 Aug.).
80. In addition to his biography of Schuman, see R. Poidevin, 'Le Facteur Europe dans la politique allemande de Robert Schuman', in R. Poidevin, ed., *Histoire des Débuts de la Construction Européenne* (Brussels, 1986), 311–26.
81. Z/Allemagne/83 (9–14 June, 14 July, 31 Aug.).
82. ibid. (9–10 Oct.); Auriol, *Journal, 1948*, 474; Poidevin, *Schuman*, 208–9, and on Schuman's policy see 220–3.
83. Y/314 (21 Oct.); Z/Allemagne/83 (21 Oct.); discussed in Poidevin, 'Le Facteur Europe', 312–13.
84. Y/312 (10 Sept.).
85. Y/313 (15–17, 29–30 Sept.); *FRUS, 1948, II*, 421–6.
86. For example, Y/313 (9, 12 Oct.); but see Y/314 (27 Oct.), for more reassuring signs on federalism, and Y/317 (9 Dec.) for more balanced judgements later in the year.
87. Y/313 (3, 6 Oct.); *FRUS, 1948, II*, 427–30, 432–4.

88. By the end of 1949, 110 factories had been dismantled in the ZOF; of which France received 22, and 6 of these only partially. France received less in reparations from Germany than America and Britain (insofar as French removals were accounted for).
89. The *Land* governments of Baden and Wurttenberg resigned in August in protest over reparations. See Y/372 (Aug.); Auriol, *Journal, 1948*, 360, 368.
90. *L'Année Politique, 1948* (annual, Paris), 411.
91. Y/372 (Aug.–Sept.); *FRUS, 1948, II*, 790–2, 796–8, 802–14.
92. Y/372 (5 Oct.); Z/Grande Bretagne/39 (2 Oct.); *FRUS*, ibid., 816–24, 826–31.
93. For example Y/372 (21 Sept.).
94. ibid. (8 Oct.).
95. Y/373 (7 Dec.).
96. As seen when Anglo-French representatives met the Humphrey Committee in December: Y/373 (Dec.); *FRUS, 1948, II*, 843–52.
97. Smith, ed., *Clay Papers*, 787–9, 799–800; *FRUS*, ibid., 798–800.
98. Y/373, 374; *FRUS* ibid., 550–92; B. Ruhm von Oppen, *Documents on Germany under Occupation* (1955), 386–9.
99. Y/311 (17 Aug.), 312 (10 Sept.), 314 (16, 17, 26 Oct.).
100. An agreement for France to join the Bizonal Joint Export-Import Agency was made in October, later than hoped. A trizonal commercial accord was only approved by the Cabinet in December: Y/381 (July–Dec.); *FRUS, 1948, II*, 677–81; Auriol, *Journal 1948*, 563; and see Smith, ed., *Clay Papers*, 886–7.
101. Y/381 (10 Nov.).
102. For example, Auriol, *Journal, 1948*, 360.
103. Y/399 .(Oct.–Nov.), 400 (4 and 16 Nov.); *FRUS, 1948, II*, 456–61; Auriol, ibid., 489–90, 531; Smith, ed., *Clay Papers*, 880–1. For text of Law 75: Ruhm von Oppen, *Documents on Germany*, 335–43. And for a defence of it: L.D. Clay, *Decision in Germany* (1950), 329–33.
104. Y/373 (Nov.), 399 (10, 11 Nov.); *FRUS*, ibid., 472; Auriol, ibid., 521, 524–5.
105. Y/400 (19 Nov.); and see Auriol, ibid., 542–3, 545.
106. *Journal Officiel, Débats, Assemblée*, 30 Nov., 7302–16, and 2 Dec., 7326–36, 7343–55, 7360–70; Auriol, ibid., 552.
107. Smith, ed., *Clay Papers*, 923–4.
108. Y/313 (n.d.), 314 (21 Oct.), and see 318 (17 Dec.) for continuing concern on these points.
109. Y/314 (29 Oct.).
110. Y/315 (4–6, 8, 13 Nov.); Z/Allemagne/83 (15, 16 Nov.); *FRUS, 1948, II*, 434–40; Smith, ed., *Clay Papers*, 413–16 (Clay guessed there were differences between Koenig and Schuman).
111. Massigli papers, Vol. 97 (10, 13 Nov.).
112. *FRUS, 1948, II*, 479; Auriol, *Journal 1948*, 554–5, 559–60, 574–5.
113. *FRUS*, ibid., 492–4 (including quote), 515–16.
114. Y/315 (24 Nov.) and 316 (27 Nov.); ibid., 517–28, 1338–40; and see 492–502, 542–3; Smith, ed., *Clay Papers*, 934–6.
115. On this and subsequent action see Y/315 (24 Nov.), 316 (27 Nov.), 317 (4–7 Dec.), 318 (16, 17 Dec.), *FRUS*, ibid., 440–3; Ruhm von Oppen, *Documents on Germany*, 343–5; and on British views see Y/400 (29 Nov.).
116. Z/Grande Bretagne/39 (14 Dec.).
117. Y/316 (15, 16 Nov.), 317 (30 Nov., 2 Dec.), 318 (18, 23 Nov.), 400 and 401 (*passim*); *FRUS, 1948, II*, 472–597; Auriol, *Journal, 1948*, 582–3, 586; Milward, *Reconstruction of Europe*, 160–2; and, for the agreement, *L'Année Politique, 1948*, 418–24. See also Schuman's optimistic report in the Assemblée Nationale, Commission des Affaires Etrangeres, proces verbaux, 29 Dec.

118. Z/Allemagne/83 (30 Nov.).
119. Y/318 (13 Dec., two memoranda).
120. The Cabinet approved it on 29 December and its creation was formally announced on 17 January. Y/357 (*passim*, especially 16 July and 18 Aug. on French desiderata), 358 (Dec.–Jan.); Auriol, *Journal, 1948*, 583.
121. Z/Allemagne/21 (2, 24 Oct.; 6, 11, 16 Dec.); but see *Le Monde*, 27 Nov., an article by Maurice Duverger on possibilities for a Franco-German army.
122. Y/321 (14, 15 Feb.); and see Auriol, *Journal, 1949*, 128.
123. Y/321 (16–19, 23–28 Feb.); Y/322 (1–3, 5 March and *passim*); Auriol, ibid., 118, 136.
124. Y/312 (14 Sept. and n.d.).
125. ibid, (9, 11 Sept.); *FRUS, 1948, II*, 598–606.
126. See especially: Y/313 (24 Sept.), 316 (30 Nov.), 317 (1, 2, 4, 6 Dec.); *FRUS*, ibid., 606–27, 630–7; Auriol, *Journal, 1948*, 562–3.
127. Y/318 (15–30 Dec.); *FRUS*, ibid., 640–1, 650–62; Smith, ed., *Clay Papers*, 947–58.
128. The State Department took a much more moderate line than Clay. See especially: Y/319 (5, 11, 17–30 Jan.), 320 (1–12 Feb.), 321 (22 Feb.); *FRUS, 1949, III*, 1–42 and see 82–113; Smith, ibid., 990–9, 1001–4, 1013–15, 1029–30, 1047–54.
129. Massigli papers, Vol. 94 (5, 14 Feb.).
130. Y/317 (1 Dec.); and see Z/Allemagne/79 (1, 21 Feb.) on French hopes that the new Secretary of State, Dean Acheson, would control Clay.
131. Auriol, *Journal, 1949*, 103–6, but see 114–15 on Auriol's fears.
132. Y/322 (2 March); *FRUS, 1949, III*, 113–14.
133. *FRUS, 1948, II*, 434, note 1.
134. *FRUS, 1949, III*, 118–55, especially 121, 137–42.
135. Z/Grande Bretagne/39 (13–14 March); PRO, FO 800/465/FRANCE/50/6 (Bevin papers).
136. *FRUS, 1949, III*, 115–17; Smith, ed., *Clay Papers*, 1056–8, but see 1063, 1066–8; Clay, *Decision in Germany*, 425–8. And on the occupation statute see Y/322 (24 March); *FRUS*, 62–73.
137. Y/321 (9 March) and 322 (9, 16, 25 March); *FRUS, 1949, III*, 89–90, 105.
138. A. Greilsammer, *Les Mouvements Fédéralistes en France* (Paris 1975), 33–45.
139. Z/Généralités/6 (17 July, 1947).
140. Winston Churchill was more sympathetic. Z/Généralités/4 (23 Jan., 17 Feb., 4 Dec. 1947; 28 Feb., 19 March, 1948) and 6 (31 Aug. 1947; 16 Feb. 1948).
141. For example, Y/305 (March 1948, Palatinate memorandum); Z/Généralités/6 (11 March 1947; 20 March, 1948).
142. Z/Généralités/23 (1 July).
143. Z/Généralités/10 (19 July); Massigli papers, vol. 73 (19 July); Chauvel *d'Alger à Berne*, 198; and see M.–T. Bitsch, 'La Rôle de la France dans la naissance du Conseil de L'Europe, in Poidevin, ed., *Débuts de la Construction Européenne*, 165–98.
144. Massigli, *Comédie*, 145, 156.
145. In for example the Assembly's Foreign Affairs Commission: *Bulletin des Commissions, Assemblée Nationale, Vol. IV* (Paris, 1951), 1730.
146. G. Bidault, *Resistance* (1967), 164–5; and see Chauvel, *d'Alger à Berne*, 212.
147. Z/Généralités/10 (18, 19 Aug.); Auriol, *Journal, 1948*, 368; Chauvel, ibid., 210.
148. Z/Généralités/10 (24, 30 Aug.; 1 Sept.), 11 (2 Nov., Schuman's rather tardy reply to Sforza).
149. *FRUS, 1948, III*, 222–3.

150. Z/Généralités/10 (20, but see 25, 28 Aug.).

151. ibid. (21, 25 Aug.–3 Sept.); Auriol, *Journal, 1948*, 371. On Spaak's somewhat duplicitous behaviour, see: *FRUS, 1948, III*, 647.

152. Z/Généralités/10 (21, 24–26, 28, 30 Aug.).

153. ibid. (2, 7, 8 Sept); Massigli, *Comédie*, 158–9; J.W. Young, *Britain, France and the Unity of Europe, 1945–51* (Leicester 1984), 109–12.

154. Z/Généralités/10 (28 Sept.–1 Oct.) and 24 (30 Sept.).

155. Z/Grande Bretagne/39 (2 Oct.).

156. Z/Généralités/10 (7 Oct.) and see Massigli, *Comédie*, 160 on Schuman's wider vision.

157. ibid. (28 Aug.).

158. Z/Généralités/10 (14 Oct., including quote), 11 (15, 20–23 Oct.).

159. Z/Généralités/11 (25, 26 Oct.) and see 23 (27 Oct.) on US support; Auriol, *Journal 1948*, 502; Massigli, *Comédie*, 160–1.

160. Z/Généralités/11 (5–26 Nov.).

161. A third possible course was the development of the OEEC. ibid (8, 12, 18, 30 Nov.).

162. Z/Généralités/12 (29 Dec.; 4, 5 Jan.).

163. On the work see: Z/Généralités/11 (26 Nov.–4 Dec.). 12 (26 Nov.–17 Dec.); Bitsch, 'La naissance du Conseil de l'Europe', 179–88.

164. These talks, in London, were arranged mainly to discuss the German problem, but included other issues. See especially: Y/399 (14 Dec., proposal for talks); Z/Grande Bretagne/39 (29 Dec.; 6, 11, 13, 14 Jan.); Z/Généralités/12 (1–7 Jan.); Auriol, *Journal, 1949*, 31–2; Massigli, *Comédie*, 162–3; and see H. Beyer, *Robert Schuman: l'Europe par la Reconciliation Franco-allemande* (Lausanne, 1986), 72–7 (reproducing Bevin letter to Schuman of 29 Dec.).

165. Z/Généralités/12 (18–20 Jan.).

166. ibid. (27–28 Jan.); Massigli, *Comédie*, 164.

167. In general see Bitsch, 'La naissance du conseil de l'Europe', 192–6.

168. Auriol, *Journal, 1949*, 72; Z/Généralités/12 (9 Feb.).

169. Auriol, the nominal head of defence planning, was upset not to be informed of military plans. Auriol, ibid., 261–2; J. Delmas, 'Reflections on the notion of Military Power through the French example', in J. Becker and F. Knipping, eds., *Power in Europe?* (New York, 1986).

170. E. Béthouart, *La Bataille pour l'Autriche* (Paris, 1966), 162, and see 160–3 generally; see also *FRUS, 1948, III*, 676 on Bethouart's advocacy of German rearmament. French planners wanted an estimate of German military capacity in order to ascertain how this might affect the military balance in Europe, be it on the Western or Eastern side: Service Historique, Armée de Terre, 4Q 10, dossier 6 (26 Jan. 1948) and see 4Q 2, dossier 2 (30 Sept. 1948); which calls for the use of Germans in defence of the ZOF and for the use of Franco's Spain in the defence of Europe.

171. K.W. Condit, *The History of the Joint Chiefs of Staff, Vol. II, 1947–49* (Wilmington, Del., 1979), 368–72; Smith, ed., *Clay Papers*, 679–80, 772–3, 828–9.

172. G. Mallaby, *From my Level* (1965), 156–7.

173. Massigli papers, Vol. 79 (12 July).

174. Auriol *Journal, 1948*, 446–7, 459–61; Massigli, *Comédie*, 124–5.

175. Ramadier papers, 52 J 69 (27 Oct.); P. Guillen 'La France et la Question de la Défense de l'Europe Occidentale, 1948–50', *Revue d'Histoire de la Deuxième Guerre Mondiale*, 144 (1986), 80–1.

176. In August 1948 there were a total of 599, 208 in the armed forces, including 405, 869 in the army, 76,010 in the air force (whose numbers had revived), 57,680 in the navy, 55,251 gendarmerie and 4,218 in ancillary services: *Journal Officiel, Débats*,

Assemblée,, 31 Aug. But to these should be added about 159,000 in colonial forces: see Ramadier, ibid., 52 J 69 (Aug.).

177. Auriol, *Journal, 1948*, 460, 495; A. Juin *Mémoires, Vol. II, 1944–58,* (Paris, 1960), 165–71.

178. Auriol, ibid., 483–4; J. de Lattre, *Ne pas Subir: Ecrits, 1914–52* (Paris, 1984), 393; S. de Lattre, *Jean de Lattre, Mon Mari, Vol. II, 1945–52* (Paris 1972), 142–3.

179. In addition to the evidence above see also: J. de Lattre, ibid., 387–9 (memorandum of 20 June).

180. He could not, however, convince the British chiefs of staff actually to *reinforce* forces on the continent. PRO, DEFE 4/10 (6, 27 Jan.; 2, 4 Feb.), 111 (9, 19 March), 12 (8 April), 13 (10 May, 6 June), 15 (3 Aug.); Montgomery of Alamein, *Memoirs* (1958), 456–66.

181. Massigli papers, Vol. 94 (13, 19, 26 Oct.); Ramadier papers, 52 J 86 (19 Oct.); Massigli, *Comédie*, 125–7.

182. Auriol, *Journal, 1948*, 533–5. But see Montgomery, *Memoirs*, 46–7 on his support for German rearmament.

183. See especially Auriol, *Journal, 1949*, 42, 58–60, 71–2; S. de Lattre, *Jean de Lattre*, 144–7; Mallaby, *From My Level*, 174–5.

184. AN, René Mayer papers, box 10 (5 Aug. and n.d.).

185. Auriol, *Journal, 1948*, 474–5 and see 483–4.

186. Partly to stop the Ruhr falling easily into Soviet hands: ibid., 562.

187. See for example, Auriol, *Journal, 1949*, 11–12, 53, 83; and on planning at this time see de Lattre, *Ne Pas Subir*, 394–405, 429–33.

188. Auriol, *Journal, 1949*, 53, 171, 185–6; Poidevin, *Schuman*, 299–300.

189. Z/Généralités/10 (29 July and 21 Aug., studies of Rio Pact); Massigli papers, Vol. 79 (17 July, note by *Secrétariat Général*); *FRUS, 1948, III*, 142–3 (Bonnet's instructions), 148–60, 163–90; Auriol, *Journal, 1948*, 297–8, 318. It should be noted that most French papers on the Atlantic Pact talks, as in the Brussels Treaty talks, are in the archives of the Secretary-General's office, as yet unreleased.

190. Massigli papers, Vol. 79 (19–20 July); Massigli, *Comédie*, 135–6; and see above.

191. FO 371/73060/5784; 73074/6123, 6142. At a dinner with Massigli, Bevin had the audacity to state that he too feared the danger of war with Soviet Russia and wanted the US to direct military aid at the Brussels powers: Massigli papers, Vol. 54 (30 July). See also E. Reid, *Time of Rear and Hope* (Toronto, 1977), 117–18.

192. *FRUS, 1948, III*, 206–13.

193. FO 371/73075/6632; Canada, Department of External Affairs, box 289242 (hereinafter DEA), NATO negotiations 1948–9 (28 Aug.); Reid *Fear and Hope*, 115–16.

194. *FRUS, 1948, III*, 643–4.

195. ibid. 214–21; FO 371/73074/6278, 73075/6630; DEA (10, 20, 21 Aug.); Reid, *Fear and Hope*, 114–15, 118–19.

196. *FRUS*, ibid., 645; FO 371/73075/6947–8; DEA (24–28 Aug.); Reid, ibid., 119–22.

197. *FRUS*, ibid., 228–32, 237–50; DEA (4 Sept.).

198. *FRUS*, ibid., 253, 648–9, 664–6.

199. Auriol, *Journal, 1949*, 501–2, 536; Massigli, *Comédie*, 136–7; and see Ramadier papers, 52 J 86 (Sept., memorandum on Atlantic alliance).

200. In general see Z/Généralités/25 (21 Feb.; 9, 19 March).

201. Auriol, *Journal, 1949*, 127; and see Massigli, *Comédie*, 139–41.

202. Chauvel, *d'Alger à Berne*, 209.

203. Z/Généralités/25 (4, 25, 26 Nov.; 18 Feb.) and 26 (19 March); Moselle departmental archives, Metz, Robert Schuman papers, 34 J 14 (11 Feb.); MAE, Henri Bonnet papers, Vol. 1 (8 Dec.); Auriol, *Journal, 1949*, 77, 93, 113–14, 116,

118–19; Massigli, *Comédie*, 136. In general see: G. Lundestad, *America, Scandinavia and the Cold War, 1945–9* (New York, 1980); N. Petersen, 'Britain, Scandinavia and the North Atlantic Treaty', *Review of International Studies*, 8 (1982), 251–68.

204. See above, 183.

205. Z/Généralités/23 (1, 8 Oct.); C. Sforza, *Cinque anni a Pallazo Chigi* (Rome, 1952), Chapter 9; E. Ortona, 'Italy's entry into the Atlantic alliance' (two parts), *NATO Review*, 29, 4 (1981), 19–23 and 5 (1981), 29–33; B. Vigezzi 'Sforza, la diplomazia italiana fra patto di Bruxelles e patto atlantica', *Storia Contemporarea*, (1987), XVIII, 5–43.

206. Z/Généralités/25 (13, 25 Nov.; 23 Dec.); Bonnet papers, Vol. 1 (13, 29 Nov.); Ramadier papers, 52 J 86 (23, 29 Oct.); Reid, *Fear and Hope*, 200–3. In general see: M.H. Folly 'Britain and the issue of Italian membership of NATO'. *Review of International Studies*, 13 (1987), E. Smith, 'The US and the inclusion of Italy in the Atlantic treaty', *Diplomatic History*, 7 (1982).

207. Z/Généralités/25 (23 Nov.); Z/Italie/91 (23 Nov.); Dumaine, *Quai d'Orsay*, 191.

208. Bonnet papers, Vol. 1 (29 Nov.); Ramadier papers, 52 J 86 (23, 29 Oct.).

209. Z/Généralités/25 (23 Dec.); Bonnet papers, Vol. 1 (5 Jan., including quotes); Chauvel, *d'Alger à Berne*, 208–9; Massigli, *Comédie*, 138.

210. Schuman papers, 34 J 14 (22 Dec.); *FRUS, 1948, III*, 324–42; DEA (22, 24, 27 Dec.); Reid, *Fear and Hope*, 214–15.

211. Bonnet papers, Vol. 1 (Dec.).

212. *FRUS, 1949, IV*, 5; Auriol, *Journal, 1949*, 9–11. Reid, ibid., 216–17.

213. Z/Généralités/25 (13, 14 Jan.); *FRUS*, ibid., 7–9, 18–24, 27–34, 45–6, 76–7, 107–8; DEA (8 Jan.–7 Feb.); Auriol, ibid., 17, 82, 127; Reid, ibid., 202–6.

214. Z/Grande Bretagne/39 (11–14 Jan.).

215. Schuman papers, 34 J 14 (8, 9, 14 Feb.); *FRUS*, ibid., 122–35, 141–5, 151–6, 173–7; Auriol;, ibid., 135–6; Reid, ibid, 206–8, 217–18.

216. On their position see Z/Généralités/26 (10, 18 March).

217. Auriol, *Journal, 1949*, 150–1.

218. Z/Généralités/40 (25 Jan., 26 Feb., 12, 19 March, and 7 April); ibid., 82–3. The French even feared the Soviet reaction to a widely extended Council of Europe: Z/Généralités/13 (30 March – 1 April).

219. The French believed this was because of Soviet concern about the Yugoslavian situation. Z/Généralités/25 (7 March). But Soviet complaints continued: MAE, Europe 1949–55/Généralités/17 (28 July, 2 Aug., 23 Sept.).

220. Z/Généralités/23 (4 Oct., and see 23 Sept.); Schuman papers, 34 J 14 (31 Jan., 11 Feb.); *FRUS, 1948, III*, 677–82, and *1949, IV*, 3–5, 107–8, 120–1.

221. Bonnet papers, Vol. 1 (11 Jan., 21 Feb.); *FRUS, 1949, IV*, 54–9, 110–13, 626–30; Auriol, *Journal, 1949*, 124; K.W. Condit, *The History of the Joint Chiefs of Staff, Vol. II, 1947–9* (Wilmington, Delaware, 1979), 410–23.

222. *FRUS*, ibid., 136–9, 146–50; and on the French military's interest in improved defences see: Z/Généralités/25 (5 March).

223. Auriol, *Journal, 1947*, 144–7 and see 155; *FRUS*, ibid., 229–32, 634–5.

224. Auriol, ibid., 148–9.

225. ibid., 158–60.

226. Z/Généralités/26 (19 March).

227. R. Poidevin, *Robert Schuman* (Paris: 1986), 301–2; Assemblée Nationale, procès verbaux de la Commission des Affaires Etrangères, 9 March and see 16, 23 Feb.

228. *Journal Officiel, Débats, Assemblée*, 22 March, 1703–5.

229. Auriol, *Journal, 1949*, 174.

230. *FRUS, 1949, IV*, 255–7, 265–6, 291; and see ibid., 207.

231. For the text see: *FRUS*, ibid., 281–5; M. Carlyle, ed., *Documents on International Affairs, 1948–9*, (1953), 257–60.
232. D. Stikker, *Men of Responsibility* (1966), 286–7.
233. *FRUS, 1949, IV*, 285–8; Z/Généralités/27 (8 April).
234. Churchill College, Cambridge, Ernest Bevin papers, BEVN II/6/7 (7 April); *FRUS*, ibid., 288–9.
235. On these points see: Y/322 (31 March); Auriol, *Journal, 1949*, 143–4, 178.
236. On Berlin see: Y/349 (21 March, 2 April); *FRUS, 1949, III*, 700–1, 709–12; R. Acheson, *Present at the Creation* (1970), 269–70, 272; Auriol, ibid., 181–3.
237. *FRUS, 1949, III*, 158–61.
238. Y/323 (4, 6, 7 April); ibid., 162–75; Smith, ed., *Clay Papers*, 1073–81; and see Acheson, *Present*, 286–9.
239. Smith, ibid., 1068–72.
240. Y/324 (7 April).
241. Y/322 (9 March), 349 (2 April).
242. Y/324 (April); *FRUS, 1949, III*, 229–37; Ruhm von Oppen, *Documents on Germany*, 374–85; Acheson, *Present*, 289–90; Auriol, *Journal, 1949*, 188.

Conclusion.

1. C. de Gaulle, *War Memoirs, Vol. III, Salvation, Documents*, (1959), 236–7.
2. Ministère des Affaires Etrangères (MAE), Z/URSS/40 (30 Sept., and see 27 June for another absurd tale).
3. J. Gaddis, *The Long Peace* (1987), 46.
4. On France and NATO in 1949–50 see: P. Guillen, 'La France et la Question de la défense de l'Europe occidentale', *Revue d'Histoire de la Deuxième Guerre Mondiale*, 144 (1986), 83–98.
5. See especially: J. W. Young, *Britain, France and the Unity of Europe, 1945–51* (Leicester, 1984); G. Warner's essay in R. Ovendale, ed., *The Foreign Policy of the British Labour Governments* (Leicester, 1984); J. Kent, 'Bevin's Imperialism and the idea of Euro-Africa', in M. Dockrill and J. W. Young, eds., *British Foreign Policy, 1945–56* (1989), ch. 3.
6. British Library of Political and Economic Science, Hugh Dalton diary, 10 Sept. 1946.
7. See R. Frank, 'France – Grande Bretagne: la mésentente commerciale, 1945–58', *Relations Internationales*, 55 (1988), 323–39.
8. G. Bidault, *Resistance* (1967), 128–9.
9. See M. Vaisse, 'L'échec d'une Europe Franco-Britannique', in R. Poidevin, ed., *Histoire des Débuts de la Construction Européenne* (Brussels, 1986), 369–89.
10. MAE, René Massigli papers, vol. 91 (4 Feb. 1949).
11. The only way to shift heavy industrial production from Germany whilst maintaining a reasonable standard of living there seemed to be to transfer population to countries like France, where there was a skilled manpower shortage. But such a policy proved too draconian and the French themselves never proposed it to the CFM.
    POWs were employed in France after the war but had to be released, under international agreements, by the end of 1948. The French continued to hope that many would remain voluntarily and that displaced people might move to France from Germany and Austria, but there were problems in accommodating them and in getting machines for them to work on: Archives Nationales, F60 Ter/ 384 (23 Sept. 1948).
    On economic issues in general I have, of course, been much influenced by

F.B.M. Lynch, *The Political and Economic Reconstruction of France* (Ph.D., Manchester, 1981).

12. MAE, Y/293 (25 March 1947).
13. Y/295 (15 July 1947).
14. Z/Allemagne/84 (23 April 1949).
15. MAE, EU/Europe 1949–55/Allemagne/254 (nd).
16. V. Auriol, *Journal du Septennat, vol. III, 1949* (Paris, 1977), 193–200, 205–9.
17. Acheson to Schuman, 30 Oct. 1949, reproduced in H. Beyer, ed., *Robert Schuman* (Lausanne, 1986).

Select Bibliography

Official Sources

French Government

Archives Economiques et Financières (AEF), Rue de Rivoli, Paris.
- Series B: Documents of the central administration, Ministry of Finance (formerly series F30).

Archives Nationales (AN), Paris.
- Series 80 AJ: Archives of the Planning Commission (*Commissariat au Plan*) including the Monnet Plan.
- Series F60: Archives of the *Présidence du Conseil* (premier's office), including the Interministerial Economic Committee (*Comité Economique Interministériel*).
- Series F60 Ter.: Archives of the secretariat-general of the interministerial committee on European economic co-operation (*Comité Interministériel pour les Questions de Coopération Economique Européenne*).

Assemblée Nationale, Paris.
- *Journal Officiel Débats, 1944–49*, (including the Consultative and Constituent Assemblies, 1944–46). (Consulted at the University Library, Cambridge.)
- Procès verbaux de la Commission des Affaires Etrangères, 1944–49. (Consulted at the Assembly's archives.)
- *Bulletin des Commissions, Assemblée, 1944–49*. (Consulted at the Assembly's archives.)

Ministère des Affaires Etrangères (MAE), Quai d'Orsay, Paris.
- Series Asie 1944–55 (subdivided by topic or country, and then by volume number)
- B: Series B, *Amerique*, 1944–52 (North and South America, subdivided by country, then by volume number.)
- EU: Series EU, *Europe*, 1949–55 (subdivided by country, then volume.)
- Series Guerre, 1939–45 (volumes from the Free French foreign ministry in *Alger*, that is Algiers).
- Y: Series Y, *Internationale*, 1944–49 (various international issues including Germany, Marshall aid, international conferences, etc., subdivided by volume number only.)
- Z: Series Z, *Europe*, 1944–49 (subdivided by country or topic, then by volume number. Thus Z/URSS/43 represents series Z, sub-series USSR, volume 43.)

Also available, shelved, at the Quai d'Orsay are:
- Boxes, reference AFA, which include French records of the Council

293

of Foreign Ministers (CMAE) meetings, 1945–49, and the 1946 Paris Peace Conference as well as a selection of *Documentation Française, Notes et Etudes*.
- The annual publication *Annuaire Diplomatique et Consulaire de la France.*

Service Historique, Armée de Terre (SHAT), Vincennes.
- Series 4Q: papers of the EMDN (certain volumes only.)

Government Publications.

- *Négociations Franco-Americaines relatives à la politique économique internationale* (1946).
- *Documents Français Relatifs à l'Allemagne, 1945–7* (1947).
- *Declarations de M. Georges Bidault . . . au Conseil des Ministres des Affaires Etrangères, mars–avril 1947* (1947).
- *Documents de la Conférence des Ministres des Affaires Etrangères . . . 27 juin au 3 juillet 1947* (1947).
- *Conseil des Ministres des Affaires Etrangères, documents relatifs à l'Allemagne, 1945–7* (1948).

American Government

Foreign Relations of the United States (volumes regularly published by the US Government Printing Office), including *The Conferences of Malta and Yalta* (1955) and *The Conference of Berlin (Potsdam)* (1960).

British Government

Hansard, debates of the Houses of Commons and Lords.
Public Record Office, Kew:
- CAB. 65, 66:   War Cabinet minutes and memoranda.
- CAB. 128, 129:   Cabinet minutes and memoranda, post-war.
- DEFE 4:   Chiefs of Staff papers.
- FO 371:   Foreign Office correspondence.
- FO 800:   Foreign Office private paper collections.
- *Documents on British Policy Overseas, Series 1* (1984–), edited by R. Butler, and subsequently R. Bullen (volumes regularly published by Her Majesty's Stationery Office).

Canadian Government

Department of External Affairs (DEA), box 289242, 'North Atlantic Security Pact', 1947–9 (microfiche 2268/1–69, Leeds University Library).

Soviet Government

- *Les Entretiens de Gaulle – Staline* (Paris, 1959, under the auspices of Récherches Internationales à la lumière du Marxisme).
- *Stalin's Correspondence during the Great Patriotic War of 1941–45* (Ministry of Foreign Affairs, 1957).
- *The Tehran, Yalta and Potsdam Conferences: Documents* (Progress Publishers, Moscow, 1969).

* * *

Private Papers

Bevin, E., Churchill College, Cambridge and Public Record Office, Kew (Series FO 800).
Bidault, G., Archives Nationales, Paris (Series 457 AP).
Blum, L., Fondation Nationale des Sciences Politiques, Paris.
Bonnet, H., Quai d'Orsay, Paris.
Daladier, E., Fondation Nationale des Sciences Politiques.
Dautry, R., Archives Nationales (Series 307 AP).
Dejean, M., Quai d'Orsay, Paris (Dossiers as Political Director, Series Y.)
Depreux, E., Archives Nationales (Series 456 AP).
Duff Cooper, A., Churchill College, Cambridge.
Ely, P., Service Historique, Armée de Terre, Vincennes.
Harvey, O., British Library, London.
Koenig, P., Service Historique, Armée de Terre, Vincennes.
Marie, A., Archives Nationales (Series 445 AP).
Massigli, R., Quai d'Orsay (Reference: Papiers d'Agents, 217).
Mayer, R., Archives Nationales (Series 563 AP) and Quai d'Orsay (Papiers d'Agents, 251).
Monnet, J., Centre Jean Monnet, Lausanne, Switzerland. (Consulted, on microfiche, at the Section Contemporaine, Archives Nationales.)
Naggiar, P.-E., Quai d'Orsay (Papiers d'Agents, 199).
Paul–Boncour, J., Quai d'Orsay (Papiers d'Agents, 253).
Pleven, R., Archives Economiques et Financières, Paris (Series 5A).
Ramadier, P., Archives Départementales de l'Aveyron, Rodez (Series 52J).
Reynaud, P., Archives Nationales (Series 74AP).
Schuman, R., Quai d'Orsay and Archives Départementales de la Moselle, Metz (Series 34J).

* * *

Published memoirs, diaries and private papers

Acheson, D., *Present at the Creation: My years at the State Department* (London, 1970).

— *Sketches from Life of Men I have Known* (1961).

Adenauer, K., *Memoirs, 1945–53* (1966).

Alphand, H., *L'étonnement d'Etre* (Paris, 1977).

Auriol, V., *Mon Septennat* (Paris, 1970).

— *Journal du Septennat* (7 vols., Paris, 1970–).

Bedell Smith, W., *Moscow Mission* (1950).

Benes, E., *The Memoirs of Dr Eduard Benes* (1954).

Berard, A., *Un Ambassadeur se Souvient, Vols. I and II* (Paris, 1976 and 1978).

General Bethouart: *La Bataille pour l'Autriche* (Paris, 1966).

Bidault, G., *Resistance* (1967).

Billotte, General, *Le Passé au Futur* (Paris, 1979).

Billoux, F., *Quand nous étions ministres* (Paris, 1972).

Blum, L., *L'oeuvre de Léon Blum* (several vols., Paris, 1955–).

Bohlen, C.E., *The Transformation of American Foreign Policy* (New York, 1969).

— *Witness to History, 1929–69* (New York, 1973).

Byrnes, J.F., *Speaking Frankly* (1947).

— *All in one Lifetime* (1958).

Campbell, T. M., and G. C. Herring, eds., *The Diaries of Edward R. Stettinius, Jr., 1943–6* (New York, 1975).

Catroux, G., *J'ai vu Tomber le Rideau de Fer* (Paris 1950).

Chandler, A. D., *The papers of Dwight D. Eisenhower: the War Years, Vol. IV* (Baltimore, 1970).

Chauvel J., *Commentaire, Vol. II: d'Alger à Berne* (Paris, 1972).

Churchill, W.S., *The Second World War, Vol. VI, Triumph and Tragedy* (1954).

Clay, L.D., *Decision in Germany* (1950).

Cooper, A.D., *Old Men Forget* (1953).

Dalton, H., *High Tide and After: Memoirs 1945–60* (1962).

Debré, M., *Trois Républiques pour une France: mémoires, 1946–58* (Paris, 1988).

Depreux, E., *Souvenirs d'un Militant* (Paris, 1972).

Duclos, J., *Mémoires, Vol. IV, 1945–52* (Paris, 1971).

Dumaine, J., *Quai d'Orsay* (1958).

Eden, A., *The Reckoning* (1965).

Eisenhower, D., *Crusade in Europe* (1948).

Forrestal, J.V., *The Forrestal Diaries* (New York, 1951).

de Gaulle, C., *L'Armée de Metier* (Paris, 1934).

— *War Memoirs* (3 vols., and 3 documents vols., 1955–60.)

— *Discours et Messages, 1940–6* (Paris, 1970).

— *Lettres, Notes et Carnets, 1943–5* (Paris, 1983) and *1945–51* (Paris, 1984)

Harriman, W.A. *Special Envoy to Churchill and Stalin* (1976).

Joxe, L., *Victoires sur la Nuit: mémoires 1940–6* (Paris, 1981).

Juin, Maréchal *Mémoires, 1944–58* (Paris, 1960).

Kennan, G.F., *Memoirs, 1925–50* (Boston, 1967).

Kimball, W.F., ed., *Churchill and Roosevelt, the complete correspondence, Vol. III, Alliance declining* (Princeton, NJ, 1984).

Langenhove, F. van, *La Securité de la Belgique* (Brussels, 1971).

Lapie, P.O., *De Léon Blum à de Gaulle* (Paris, 1971).

de Lattre, J., *Ne Pas Subir: Ecrits, 1914–52* (Paris, 1984).

Leahy, W.D., *I Was There* (New York, 1950).

Macmillan, H., *War Diaries: the Meditarranean, 1943–5* (1984).

Marjolin, R., *Le Travail d'une Vie* (Paris, 1986).

Massigli, R., *Une Comédie des Erreurs* (Paris, 1978).

Mauriac, C., *The Other de Gaulle: Diaries, 1944–54* (1973).

Mendes–France, P., *Oeuvres Complètes, Vol. II, Une Politique de L'Economie, 1943–54* (Paris, 1985).

Moch, J., *Rencontres avec de Gaulle* (Paris 1971).

— *Une si Longue Vie* (Paris, 1978).

Monnet, J., *Memoirs* (1978).

— *Jean Monnet – Robert Schuman Correspondence* (Lausanne, 1986).

Montgomery of Alamein, *Memoirs* (1958).

Murphy, R., *Diplomat among Warriors* (1964).

Navarre, H., *Le Temps des Verités* (Paris, 1979).

Nenni, P., *Tempo di Guerra Fredda: Diari 1943–56* (Milan, 1981).

Nicolson, H., *Diaries and Letters, 1945–62* (1971).

Pinay, A., *Un Français comme les Autres* (Paris, 1984).

Reale, E., *Avec Jacques Duclos au Banc des Accusés* (Paris, 1958).

Peltier, Rear Admiral, *Soviet Encounter* (1955).

Reid E., *Time of Fear and Hope: The Making of the North Atlantic Treaty* (Toronto, 1977).

Seydoux, F., *Mémoires d'Outre-Rhin* (Paris, 1975).

Sforza, C., *Cinque Anni a Pallazo Chigi* (Rome, 1952).

Sherwood, R., *The White House Papers of Harry Hopkins, Vol. II, 1942–5* (1949).

Smith, J.E., ed, *The Papers of General Lucius D. Clay, 1945–9* (2 vols., Bloomington, Indiana, 1974).

Spaak, P.H., *The Continuing Battle* (1971).

Stehlin, P., *Témoignage pour l'Histoire* (Paris, 1964).

Sulzberger, C., *A Long Row of Candles* (Toronto, 1969).

Truman, H.S., *Year of Decision, 1945* (1955).

— *Years of Trial and Hope* (1956).

Vandenberg, A.H., *The Private Papers of Senator Vandenberg* (Boston, 1952).

Vendroux, J., *Cette Chance que j'ai eue . . .* (Paris, 1974).

* * *

Other Published Books

Backer, J.H. *Winds of History: the German Years of Lucius DuBignon Clay* (New York, 1983).

Becker, J. and F. Knipping, eds., *Power in Europe?* (New York, 1986).

Best, R.A., *'Cooperation with Like-minded Peoples': British Influences on American Security Policy, 1945–9* (New York, 1986).

Beugel, E. van der, *From Marshall Aid to Atlantic Partnership* (New York, 1966).

Bjol, E., *La France devant l'Europe* (Copenhagen, 1966).

Bloch-Lainé, F. and J. Bouvier, *La France Restaurée, 1944–54: dialogue sur les choix d'une modernisation* (Paris, 1986).

Bromberger, M. and S., *Les Coulisses de l'Europe* (Paris, 1968).

Bullock, A., *Ernest Bevin: Foreign Secretary, 1945–51* (London, 1983).

Calvocoressi, P., *Survey of International Affairs, 1947–51* (3 vols., 1952–4).

Carlyle, M., ed., *Documents on International Affairs, 1947–8* (1952) and *1949–50* (1953).

Carmoy, G. de, *The Foreign Policies of France* (1970).

Charbonnières, G. de, *Le Dual Giraud – de Gaulle* (Paris, 1984).

Condit, K.W., *The History of the Joint Chiefs of Staff, Vol. 2, 1947–9* (Wilmington, Delaware, 1979).

Courtois, S., *Le PCF dans la Guerre: de Gaulle, la Résistance, Staline . . .* (Paris, 1980).

Dockrill, M. and J.W. Young, eds., *British Foreign Policy, 1945–56* (1989).

Doise J. and M. Vaisse, *Diplomatie et Outil Militaire* (Paris, 1987).

Donnison, F.S.V., *Civil Affairs and Military Government in North-West Europe 1944–6*, (1961).

Dougherty, J.J., *The Politics of Wartime Aid, 1940–46* (1979).

Dumoulin, M. ed., *La Belgique et les Débuts de la Construction Européenne* (Brussels, 1987).

Duroselle, J.B., *L'Abime, 1939–45* (Paris, 1982).

Elgey, G., *La République des Illusions, 1945–51* (Paris, 1965).

Footitt, H. and J. Simmonds, *France 1943–5* (Leicester, 1988).

Gaddis, J.L., *The Long Peace* (1986).

Ghebali, V.Y., *La France en Guerre et les Organisations Internationales, 1939–45* (Paris, 1969).

Gilbert, M., *Road to Victory: Winston S. Churchill, 1941–5* (1986).

Gimbel, J., *The Origins of the Marshall Plan* (Stanford, Cal., 1976).

Gorce, P.M. de la, *L'Après-Guerre, 1944–52* (Paris, 1978).

Graham, B., *French Socialists and Tripartisme, 1945–7* (1965).

Grosser, A., *La Quatrième République et sa Politique Extérieure* (Paris, 1961).

— *Affaires Extérieures: la politique de la France, 1944–84* (Paris, 1984).

Grunwald, C. de, *Les Alliance Franco-Russes* (Paris, 1965).

Herbst, L., ed., *Westdeutschland, 1945–55: Unterwerfung, Kontrolle, Integration* (Munich, 1986).

Hillel, M., *L'Occupation Française en Allemagne, 1945–49* (Paris, 1983).

Histoire de l'Administration Francaise, *Les Affaires Etrangères et la Corps Diplomatique Française, 1870–1980* (Paris, 1984).

Hurstfield, J.G., *America and the French Nation, 1939–45* (Chapel Hill, NC, 1986).

L'institut Charles de Gaulle and L'Institut d'Histoire de Temps Présents, *De Gaulle et la Nation face aux Problèmes de Défense* (Paris, 1983).

L'institut Charles de Gaulle, *L'Aventure de la Bombe: de Gaulle et la dissuasion nucléaire* (Paris, 1985).

Institut Pierre Renouvin, *Travaux et Recherches, vols. 1 and 2* (Paris, 1988).

Ireland, T.P., *Creating the Entangling Alliance: the Origins of NATO* (Westport, Conn., 1981).

Kersaudy, F. *Churchill and de Gaulle* (1983).

Kertesz, S., *The Last European Peace Conference: Paris 1946* (New York, 1985).

Lacouture, J. *De Gaulle: Le Politique, 1944–59* (Paris, 1985).

Lacroix-Riz, A., *Le Choix de Marianne* (Paris, 1985).

de Lattre, S., *Jean de Lattre* (2 vols., Paris, 1972).

Lipgens, W., *A History of European Integration Vol. 1, 1945–7* (Oxford, 1982).

Marcou, L., *Le Kominform* (Paris, 1971).

Mastny, V., *Russia's Road to the Cold War* (New York, 1979).

Mayer, D., ed., *René Mayer* (Paris, 1983).

Messer, Robert L., *The End of an Alliance: Byrnes, Roosevelt, Truman and the Origins of the Cold War* (Chapel Hill, NC, 1982).

Milward, A.S., *The Reconstruction of Western Europe, 1945–51* (1984). – *The New Order and the French Economy* (Oxford, 1970).

Mioche, P., *Le Plan Monnet: genèse et elaboration, 1941–47* (Paris, 1986).

Mourin, M., *Les Relations Franco-Soviétiques, 1917–67* (Paris, 1967).

Ott, B., *Georges Bidault* (Annonay, 1978).

Poidevin, R., ed., *Histoire des Débuts de la Construction Européenne, 1948–50* (Brussels, 1986).

Pollard, R.A., *Economic Security and the Origins of the Cold War, 1945–50* (New York, 1985).

Porte, A. de, *De Gaulle's Foreign Policy, 1944–46* (Cambridge, Mass., 1968).

Quilliot, R., *La SF10 et l'exercice du Pouvoir* (Paris, 1972).

Rioux, J.P., *The Fourth Republic* (1987).

Rothwell, V., *Britain and the Cold War, 1941–7* (1982).

Ruhm von Oppen, B., *Documents on Germany under Occupation, 1945–54* (1955).

Scharf, and H.J. Schroder, C. *Die Deutschland politik Frankreichs und die Französische Zone, 1945–9* (Wiesbaden, 1983).

Schwabe, K., ed., *Die Anfänge des Schuman Plans* (Baden-Baden, 1988).

Sharp, T., *The Wartime Alliance and the Zonal Division of Germany* (Oxford, 1975).

Sherwin, M.J., *A World Destroyed: the Atomic Bomb and the Grand Alliance* (1975).

Shlaim, A., *The US and the Berlin Blockade* (Berkeley, Cal., 1983).

Smouts, M.C., *La France a l'ONU: premier rôle et second rang* (Paris, 1979).

Tint, H., *French Foreign Policy since the Second World War* (1972).

Tournoux, J., *Le Feu et la Cendre* (Paris, 1979).

Varsori, A., *Il Patto di Bruxelles, 1948* (Rome, 1988).

Vigneras, M., *Rearming the French* (Washington, 1957).

Werth, A., *France 1940–55* (1956).

— *De Gaulle* (1965).

Willis, F., *France, Germany and the New Europe* (1968).

— *The French in Germany* (Stanford, Cal., 1962).

Woodward, L., *British Foreign Policy in the Second World War* (5 vols., 1970–6).

* * *

Articles

Ardia, D., 'Londra, Parigi 1947: l'Europa tra Mosca e Washington', *Storia delle Relazioni Internazionali*, III (1987).

Batowski, H., 'La France Libre et l'Est Européen', *Revue d'Histoire de la Deuxième Guerre Mondiale*, 115 (1979).

Baylis, J., 'Britain and the Dunkirk Treaty', *Journal of Strategic Studies*, 5 (June 1982) 236–47.

— 'Britain, the Brussels Pact and the Continental Commitment', *International Affairs*, 60 (Autumn, 1984).

Bitsch, M.T., 'Une rêve Francais: le désarmement economique de l'Allemagne', *Relations Internationales*, 51 (1987).

Borne D., and J. BOUILLON, 'Réflexions de Paul Ramadier, Décembre, 1947', *Revue d'Histoire Moderne et Contemporaine*, XXXV (1988).

Borrodziej, W., 'Polen und Frankreich, 1945–47', *Vierteljahrshefte für Zeitgeschichte*, 36 (1988).

Bossaut, G., 'Le poids de l'aide américaine sur la politique économique et financière de la France en 1948', *Relations Internationales*, 37 (1984).

— 'L'aide américaine a la France après la seconde guerre mondiale', *Vingtième Siècle*, 9 (1986).

— 'La France et les constructions européennes, 1943–57', *Historiens–Géographes*, 319 (1988).

Bouthillon, R., 'Les elections Italiennes de 1948', *Revue d'Histoire Diplomatique*, 99 (1985).

Brundu, P., 'L'Espagne Franquiste et la politique étrangère de la France', *Relations Internationales*, 50 (1987).

Buffotot, P., 'La Politique Militaire du Parti Socialiste aux lendemains de la Libération', *Revue d'Histoire de la Deuxième Guerre Mondiale*, 110 (1978).

Delmas, J., 'De Gaulle, la Défense Nationale et les forces Armées projets et réalités, 1944–46', *Revue d'Histoire de la Deuxième Guerre Mondiale*, 110 (1978).

Dulphy, A., 'La Politique de la France à l'Egard de l'Espagne Franquiste, 1945–49'. *Revue d'Histoire Moderne et Contemporaine*, XXXV (1988).

Duroselle, J.B., 'Une création *ex nihilo*: le ministère des affaires etrangères du Général de Gaulle, 1940–42', *Relations Internationales*, 31 (1982).

Frank, R., 'France–Grande Bretagne: la mésentente commerciale, 1945–48', *Relations Internationales*, 55 (1988).

Gillingham, J., 'Die französicschen Ruhr politik und die Ursprünge des Schuman-Plans', *Vierteljahrshefte fur Zeitgeschichte* 35 (1987).

Greenwood, S., 'Return to Dunkirk: the Anglo-French Treaty of March 1947', *Journal of Strategic Studies*, 6 (Dec. 1983), 49–65.

— 'Bevin the Ruhr and the division of Germany', *Historical Journal*, 29 (1986).

Griffiths R.T., and F.M.B. LYNCH, 'L'Echec de la "Petite Europe" et les négociations Fritalux/Finebel', *Revue Historique*, 274 (1984).

Guillen, P., 'Les Rélations Franco-italiennes, 1943–48', *Revue d'Histoire Diplomatique* (1976).

— 'Le Réinsertion internationale de l'Italie après la chute de fascisme, 1943–47', *Relations Internationales*, 31 (1982), 333–49.

— 'La France et la Question du Haut-Adige, 1945–46', *Revue d'Histoire Diplomatique*', 100 (1986).

— 'La France et la Question de la Défense de l'Europe Occidentale, 1948–50', *Revue d'Histoire de la Deuxième Guerre Mondiale*, 144 (1986).

Henke, K.-D., 'Politik de Widersprüche: zur charakteristik der französischen Militarregierung in Deutschland', *Vierteljahrshefte fur Zeitgeschichte*, 30 (1982).

Herring, G.C., 'The Truman Administration and the Restoration of French Sovereignty in Indochina', *Diplomatic History*, 1 (1977).

Kent, J., 'Anglo-French colonial cooperation, 1939–49', *Journal of Imperial and Commonwealth History*, 17 (1988).

Lacaze, Y., 'Edouard Benes et la France Libre', *Revue d'Histoire Diplomatique*, 97 (1983).

Lacroix-Riz, A., 'Négociation et Signature des Accords Blum–Byrnes', *Revue d'Histoire Moderne et Contemporaine*, 31 (1984).

— 'Securité française et menace militaire allemande, 1945–7', *Relations Internationales*, 51 (1987), 289–312.

Laloy, J., 'A Moscou: entre Staline et de Gaulle', *Revue des Etudes Slaves*, LIV (1982).

Ludmann-Obier, M.F., 'Un aspect de la chasse aux cerveaux: les transferts de techniciens allemands en France, 1945–49', *Relations Internationales*, 46 (1986).

Lynch, F.M.B., 'Resolving the Paradox of the Monnet Plan,' *Economic History Review* (May, 1984).

Marès, A., 'La France Libre et l'Europe centrale et orientale', *Revue des Etudes Slaves*, LIV (1982).

Michel, M., 'La Co-opération intercoloniale en Afrique noire, 1942–50', *Relations Internationales*, 34 (1984).

Mioche, P., 'Aux origines du Plan Monnet', *Revue Historique*, 215 (1981).

— 'Le Démarrage du Plan Monnet', *Revue d'Histoire Moderne et Contemporaine*, 31 (1984).

Newman, M., 'Léon Blum, French Socialism and European Unity, 1945–50', *Historical Journal*, 24 (1981).

Nouailhat, Y.-H., 'Aspects de la politique culturelle des Etats-Unis à l'égard de la France, 1945–50', *Relations Internationales*, 25 (1981).

Pedroncini, G., 'Journal de René Mayer', *Revue d'Histoire de la Deuxième Guerre Mondiale*, 129 (1982).

Poidevin, P., 'René Mayer et la politique extérieure de la France', *Revue d'Histoire de la Deuxième Guerre Mondiale*, 134 (1984).

— 'La France et le Charbon allemand', *Relations Internationales*, 44 (1985).

— 'Frankreich und die Ruhrfrage, 1945–51', *Historische Zeitschrift*, 228 (1979).

Revue d'Histoire de la Deuxième Guerre Mondiale, 110 (1978) – special edition on French armed forces.

Rice-Maximin, E., 'The US and the French Left, 1945–49, *Journal of Contemporary History*, 19 (1984).

Valette, J., 'Le Gouvernement des Etats-Unis et l'Indochine', *Revue d'Histoire de la Deuxième Guerre Mondiale*, 138 (1985).

Wall, I.M., 'Les Accords Blum–Byrnes', *Vingtième Siècle*, 13 (1987).

Wiebes, C. and B. ZEEMAN, 'The Pentagon negotiations March 1948: the launching of the North Atlantic Treaty', *International Affairs*, 59, 3 (Summer 1983).

Young, J.W., 'The Foreign Office and the Departure of General de Gaulle, 1945–46', *Historical Journal*, 25 (1982).

— 'The Foreign Office, the French and the post-war Division of Germany, 1945–46', *Review of International Studies*, 12 (1986).

* * *

Unpublished Works

Deighton-Philips, A., *Britain, the German problem and the Council of Foreign Ministers, 1945–47* (PhD, Reading University, 1987.)

Dockrill, M., 'British perceptions of France as a Military Ally, 1945–50', Seminar Paper, King's College, London, 1989.

Lynch, F.M.B., *The Political and Economic Reconstruction of France*, (PhD, Manchester University, 1981).

Sapp, S.P., *The US, France, and the Cold War*, (PhD, Kent State University, 1978).

INDEX

203, 220–1; and see individual
conferences
Counterpart funds 201–2
de Courcel, G 173
Couve de Murville, M 21, 49, 55, 79,
84, 86–7, 92, 128–9, 140, 143, 149,
154–5, 158, 179, 191–2, 196, 229
Customs union 9–15, 77, 121, 131,
162–4, 168–9, 186–7, 193, 209,
225–7, 230–1
Czechoslovadia 8, 34, 74, 80–2, 122–4,
137, 148–9, 155–6, 173–4, 179, 199,
226

Dalton, H 121
Darlan, F 4, 6, 172
Debré, M 19
Defence Committee 9, 49, 127, 135,
171–2
Dejean, M 12, 21, 30, 81, 124–5, 149,
179–80
Dekasanov, V 13–14, 24, 107
Delbos, Y 218
Denmark 218
Dennery, E 100
Depreux, E 146
Devers, J 36, 50–1
Djibouti 41
Douglas, L 151, 173, 188–9, 191–4, 196,
199, 208
Doyen, General 54–5
Draper, W 141
Duclos, J 81, 165, 220
Dulles, J 143
Dumaine, J 96, 114, 119, 153, 179, 196,
200
Dumbarton Oaks conference 25, 42–3,
53
Dunkirk Treaty, see Anglo-French treaty

Economic Committee;
Anglo-French 121–2, 131;
Interministerial 38, 77, 141
Economy, French 18–19, 30, 37–9, 53–4,
66, 97–104, 112, 125, 127, 141–2, 147,
150–4, 159, 167–8, 184–6, 201–2,
222–3, 225–7
Eden, A 4, 22, 24, 27–8, 40, 43, 45–6,
50, 55–6, 68
Egypt 55, 72
Eisenhower, D 15, 17, 22–5, 36, 39,
50–1, 181
Elections, French 76, 84–5, 90, 101–3,
108–9, 114, 127–9, 132, 165, 219
Ely, P 214

Empire, French 2–4, 6, 12, 21, 28,
41, 43, 52–3, 57, 63–4, 67, 95, 127,
168–9, 185, 214, 224
Essen Groups 189, 206–8
Etat-Major Général de Défense National
71–2, 112–13, 126, 130, 139–40,
170–2, 189, 215, 218–9, 226
Europe, Eastern 6–8, 11–14, 26, 28–9,
31, 34, 38, 42, 46, 52, 60–3, 69, 73–4,
80–2, 90, 97, 109–11, 119–20, 122–5,
128, 137, 146, 148–9, 152, 155–6, 161,
164–5, 174, 179, 223, 226
Europe, Western (co-operation
proposals) 8–15, 26, 29–31, 45, 76–8,
82, 95, 130, 140, 148, 150, 159, 175,
177–8, 187, 193, 195–7, 205, 207–9,
211–13, 220–1, 226–31; see also
Brussels Pact, Council of Europe,
customs unions, Marshall Plan
European Advisory Commission 22–5,
27–9, 39–40, 49–50
European Coal Organization 89, 145
EXIMBANK 67, 97, 99–100, 102–3

Falaize, P 20
Finance ministry 38, 125, 186, 202, 226
Finland 218
Foreign Affairs Commission 49, 78,
136–7, 140, 148, 174, 196, 198, 220
Foreign ministry, French 7, 20–1, 26,
29, 34, 37, 40, 42–6, 48–9, 52, 54–9,
62, 64–5, 71–2, 74, 76–8, 80, 82,
84–6, 88, 91–2, 101, 104, 107–9,
111–12, 119–20, 122–4, 128, 130–1,
136–7, 140–2, 146, 149, 152, 155–9,
161, 169–70, 172–3, 176–7, 180, 183,
186–7, 190, 192–3, 195, 200, 202–3,
205–6, 208–14, 218, 226
Foreign Office, British 3–4, 14, 22–3, 45,
67, 84, 109, 114, 122, 132, 135–6, 149,
167–9, 172, 176, 195
Fouchet, C 31, 33
Franco, General 73, 78
François-Poncet, A 210–11, 229
Frankfurt agreements 175–7, 207
Franks, O 162, 164
Free French 1, 3–4, 6–7, 17–18, 80
Fulton speech 110, 115

Garreau, R 14, 23–4, 33, 44, 80, 82
de Gasperi, A 72, 79, 116, 147, 217
de Gaulle, C 1–9, 11, 13–46, 49–57,
59–60, 62–73, 76–82, 84–96,
98–9, 108–9, 111, 114, 122–3,
125–7, 136, 142, 146, 166–7,